W9-BQL-644

Reading as Communication

CARRIE RICH MEMORIAL LIBRARY
CAMPBELL UNIVERSITY
BUIES CREEK, NC 27506

CAPT. J. RICH MEMORIAL LIBRARY
UNIVERSITY
07508

Reading as Communication

An Integrated Approach to the Teaching of Reading

Frank B. May
Portland State University

Charles E. Merrill Publishing Company
A Bell & Howell Company
Columbus Toronto London Sydney

Published by Charles E. Merrill Publishing Co.
A Bell & Howell Company
Columbus, Ohio 43216

This book was set in Antique Olive and Baskerville

Text Designer: Amato Prudente
Production Coordination: Joan Niewaroski Jaschke
Cover Photograph: Strix Pix
Photo credits
Jean Claude Lejeune: pages 2, 10, and 244; Strix Pix: pages 4, 184, 204, 225, 386, 436, and 478; Columbus Public Schools: page 30; Paul Conklin: pages 34, 75, 131, 246, 274, 310, 327, 358, 388, and 455; © C. Quinlan: pages 64 and 368; Cynda Williams: page 94; Irma McNelia: pages 110 and 338; Irving W. Brueck: page 120; Greg Miller: page 156; Constance Brown: pages 162 and 416; Rohn Engh: pages 220 and 502; Anne Schullstrom: pages 251 and 341; Dan Unkefer: page 394; Peace Corps: page 450; Robert Maust: page 455.

The illustration on page 290 is by James Needham. Copyright © 1980, Economy Company.

Copyright © 1982 by Bell & Howell Company. All rights reserved.
No part of this book may be reproduced in any form, electronic or mechanical, including photocopy, recording, or any information storage and retrieval system, without permission in writing from the publisher.

Library of Congress Catalog Card Number: 82-80076
International Standard Book Number: 0–675–09828–9

Printed in the United States of America
2 3 4 5 6 7 8 9 10—87 86 85 84 83

In memory of my daughter,
Shauna Catherine May. . .

Suddenly the sun discovered
a small hole in the cloud
and poured its golden radiance
down onto a small patch. . . .

174281

Contents

Development • Reasons for Developing Children's
Sight Vocabulary • Sight Words that Are Truly
Basic • Methods of Increasing Children's Sight
Vocabulary • A Sample Lesson on Sight
Vocabulary • Some Essential Ingredients of a
Semantic Vocabulary • Using Dale's Cone of
Experience • Using the Dictionary • Learning Words
through Reading • Learning Words through Context
Clues • Using the Cloze Technique to Improve
Vocabulary • Learning Words through Semantic
Mapping • Learning Words through Affix
Meanings • Summary • Application Experiences for
the Teacher-Education Class • Field Experiences in
the Elementary-School Classroom

The Nature of Phonic Analysis • Reasons for
Teaching Phonic Analysis • Phonic Analysis versus
Communication • Phonics Terminology • The
Analytic Phonics Method • Linguistic Approach A:
The Substitution Method • Linguistic Approach B:
The Phonogram Method • The Synthetic Phonics
Method • The Spelling-Pattern Method • Sample
Lesson Using an Eclectic Approach • Questions and
Answers about Phonics • Summary • Application
Exercises for the Teacher-Education Class • Field
Experiences in the Elementary-School Classroom

The Case for Syllabic and Morphemic Analysis •
When to Introduce Syllabic and Morphemic
Analysis • The What, How, and When of Teaching
Syllabic Analysis • Differences between Syllabic and
Morphemic Analysis • Teaching Morphemic
Analysis • The Elements of Morphemic Analysis •

The Importance of Contextual Analysis to
Communication • Providing Direct Instruction in
Contextual Analysis • Decoding Words with a
Dictionary • Summary • Application Experiences for
the Teacher-Education Class • Field Experiences in
the Elementary-School Classroom

Chapter 5 Increasing Comprehension at the Literal Level 120

Comprehension and Communication • Reading
Comprehension as a Cognitive-Affective Language
Process • A Sample of a Directed-Reading-Thinking
Activity (D-R-T-A) • Reading Comprehension as a
Set of Subskills • Reading Comprehension as an
Interaction of Subskills • Teaching Children to
Recognize Common Sentence Alterations and
Expansions • Teaching Children to Recognize
Expression Clues • Helping Children to Learn to
Develop Images or Associations • Helping Children
Learn to Follow Sequence • Helping Children to
Recollect Significant Details • Coordinating the
Literal Comprehension Skills (Using Questioning
Strategies) • Summary • Application Experiences for
the Teacher-Education Class • Field Experiences in
the Elementary-School Classroom • Appendix 5.1

Chapter 6 Increasing Higher-Level Thinking Skills 156

The Nature of Inferential Thinking • Inferring
Information from What the Author Says •
Determining Main Ideas • Recognizing Details that
Support Main Ideas • Making Predictions •
Understanding Cause-and-Effect Relationships •
The Nature of Critical Thinking • Distinguishing
between Factual and Nonfactual Information •
Evaluating According to Criteria • Evaluating
According to Logic • The Nature of Creative
Thinking • Using the Thinking Skills Holistically •
Summary • Application Experiences for the
Teacher-Education Class • Field Experiences in the
Elementary-School Classroom

Political and Emotional Matters Related to Reading Levels • Whether to Count Self-Corrections • Practice in Using the Informal Reading Inventory • Using the Cloze Technique for Determining Reading Levels • Summary • Application Experiences for the Teacher-Education Class • Field Experiences in the Elementary-School Classroom

Special Concerns Related to Reading Instruction

with Differences • Provide Abundant Readiness Experiences • Help Them Improve Their Self-Concepts • Use a Multimedia Approach • Summary • Application Experiences for the Teacher-Education Class • Field Experiences in the Elementary-School Classroom

Preface

Reading as Communication, An Integrated Approach to the Teaching of Reading, is a basic text divided into three parts: "Fundamental Strategies of Reading Instruction," "Individualizing and Managing Your Reading Instruction," and "Special Concerns Related to Reading Instruction." This comprehensive sequence provides instructors the option of using the text either for a one-term undergraduate course or a more intensive two-term undergraduate course. The text is also suitable for a graduate class in which fundamentals are reviewed and "reconceived" as *means toward the goal of communication* and in which special concerns, such as "miscue analysis" or "individualizing instruction," are handled in more depth.

Some of the themes and sub-themes of *Reading as Communication* are as follows:

1. *A balanced approach toward reading instruction is necessary.* The "great debate" over "meaning-emphasis" instruction vs. "code-emphasis" instruction should be removed from the classroom and relegated to books on the history of education. The "new great debate" over psycholinguistic vs. subskill instruction may need to be examined but certainly not glorified.

2. *Much of our fruitless debate over the nature of reading is similar to the story of several blind men trying to describe an elephant by looking at different parts of its anatomy.* When one looks at reading at its beginning stage, there *is* and *must be* more emphasis given to specific decoding and comprehension subskills than there needs to be given at later stages. It does not follow, however, that teachers should concentrate only on subskills at first and then *later* concentrate on holistic reading and on communication with an author. Subskill instruction, holistic reading, and communication all need to be emphasized from the very beginning.

3. *A child who learns to read for the purpose of communicating with an author normally becomes a good reader.* The teacher who attempts to help children read in this manner normally becomes a good teacher of reading.

4. *A child who has learned all of the subskills involved in reading has not necessarily learned to read.* Reading is a holistic process; that is, it is equal to much more than merely the sum of its parts. Both children and teachers of children need to be shown how to put the parts back together again so that the subskills interact and direct the reader toward the major goal of reading: communication.

5. The nature of reading cannot be captured with a catchy phrase, such as a "psycholinguistic guessing game," a "visual-perceptual act," an "information-processing mode," a "language experience," or a form of "socialized operant conditioning." Reading is all these things and much more. It is educators, learners, experiences, and materials interacting in thousands of different ways under thousands of different conditions. Although this textbook suggests teaching procedures and attitudes that can make a difference in the elementary school classroom, *in the long run, it is the intelligence, concern, and adaptability of the teacher that will make the real difference.*

This book was originally conceived as the third edition of *To Help Children Read,* a modular, competency-based text. However, books, like authors, can be growing, changing, evolving entities. Thus, in response to the author's growth and to the needs of preservice and inservice teachers, the revision has evolved into what is essentially a new book. The format, theme, and content of *Reading as Communication* are, in most respects, quite different from *To Help Children Read.* However, for those instructors who wish to use a competency-based format, behavioral objectives have been incorporated in the *Professional Supplement.* These objectives can be duplicated for the student. In addition, the *Professional Supplement* contains ten multiple-choice questions for each of the chapters. These questions can be used either as pool of items for the instructor's own tests; as a set of chapter-end tests; or as a set of chapter pretests.

Application experiences for the teacher-education class and field experiences for the elementary-school classroom follow each chapter. In addition to several diagnostic inventories that may be copied from this book, many of the chapters and appendices include descriptions of games, sample lesson plans, and learning activities suitable for reading instruction in the elementary classroom. The *Professional Supplement* contains an entire section of miscue analysis transcripts.

Because many education professors feel that their students have not developed adequate study techniques, a well known study approach, the PQ3R, has been incorporated in the text. Students are encouraged and guided toward previewing each chapter before reading it, changing subheadings into questions, reading to answer specific questions, self-recitation, and reviewing. At the end of each chapter, they are asked to check both their literal and inferential comprehension by responding in an open-ended manner to a series of controversial statements pertaining to information in the chapter. The PQ3R method is introduced here by Bogglestar, who also introduces each chapter.

I would like to thank Gil Imholz and Julie Estadt for their excellent editorial guidance in the development of this book. I would also like to thank the reviewers, Eunice Askov, Carol Hodges, and John Savage, for their many helpful suggestions.

Using the PQ3R Method in Reading This Book

Do you have trouble remembering what you read? If you've never used the PQ3R method, you may find it worth trying. This method is described in detail in Chapter 15, but here's the gist of it. All you have to do is to follow these steps:

1. *Preview:* Read the first paragraph in the chapter, the subheadings, and the last paragraph. This only takes a minute or so and it gets your mind *ready* for the chapter.

2. *Question:* Just before you read each section, change the heading into a question. For example, if the heading is "Reading as Communication," you might change it to "Why should reading be considered as communication?" This gives you a specific reason for reading that section.

3. *Read:* Read the section, thoughtfully trying to answer the question you've asked.

4. *Recite:* It only takes another few seconds to ask yourself the question again and to answer it in your own words. It may be a good idea to put your answer in writing.

5. *Review:* At the end of the chapter, before the ideas "slip through the mind like water through a sieve," go back to each subheading, ask your question again, and see if you can recite your answer *without* looking at your notes. If not, check your notes or scan the section until you can.

Simple, isn't it? And it works. To give you a head start, most of the PQ3R work has been done for you in Chapter 1. Starting with Chapter 2 perhaps you'll want to try it on your own.

Reading as
Communication

PART ONE

Fundamental Strategies of Reading Instruction

Chapters

CHAPTER 1

"Grownups just look at those funny little marks, and then they know what to say."

Basing Instructional Practice on the Nature of Reading

Chapter Outline

The Great Debate over the Nature of Reading
The Sam Trap (a Primer in Applebet)
Reading as a Set of Subskills
Learning the Subskills versus Learning to Read
What Children Need to Learn about Authors
Reading and Holism
Some Choices Teachers Must Make before Reading
    Instruction Begins
Reading as a Social Process
Questions and Answers
Summary
Application Experiences for the Teacher-Education Class
Field Experiences in the Elementary-School Classroom
Appendix 1.1

Chapter Preview

This chapter will be about the nature of reading, how children need to learn to communicate with authors, the subskills involved in the act of reading, why reading is a social and holistic process, and the types of choices a teacher has to make before reading instruction can actually begin.

Human beings are creatures who argue about everything: what true love is; what life is; even what a "preppie" is.

The Great Debate over the Nature of Reading

Question: *Just what is the nature of reading?*

Four philosophers from the planet Zania were given permission by Mrs. Kelley, the elementary-school principal, to visit a third-grade classroom in order to determine what Earthlings were talking about when they used the word *reading*. The four philosophers stumbled down the corridor to room 18, Miss Jerinski's room. Neither their eyes nor their ears had become adjusted to the Earth's heavy atmosphere and pollution; consequently, they could see and hear very poorly. Yet, they were determined to examine the phenomenon of reading that seemed to concern so many Earthlings.

Philosopher Alpha studied a child who was being taught by Mr. Blair, an aide to Miss Jerinski. Mr. Blair was showing Cindy that the words *dog, dig,* and *dive* all start with the same letter and that this letter represents the same sound in each word. "Aha," said Philosopher Alpha. "Reading is a decoding or deciphering process. When a child learns to read, she is learning to translate written symbols into spoken ones. Reading is nothing more than decoding."

Philosopher Beta examined a child who was being taught by Miss Jerinski. Miss Jerinski was asking Brad some questions before and after he silently stared at each page of a book. "Eureka," said

Philosopher Beta. "Reading is a process of gathering meaning from written symbols. Reading is nothing more than comprehension."

Philosopher Omega scrutinized a "scope and sequence chart" that had been presented to him by Miss Jerinski. On this chart were phrases such as these:

- Decoding initial consonant letters
- Decoding final consonant digraphs and clusters
- Comprehending main ideas
- Determining differences between facts and opinions

The phrases went on and on. There were handtoes and handtoes of them. (The term *handtoe,* on the planet Zania, refers to a set of twenty.) There were so many different phrases that Philosopher Omega was at first quite confused as to the nature of reading. But suddenly it came to him. "I know exactly what reading is!" he exclaimed. "Reading is one gigantic skill that's made up of many, many tiny subskills. Put all those subskills together and what have you got? Reading!"

Meanwhile, Philosopher Theta was staring at a girl who was, in turn, staring at a book. Every now and then the girl let out a laugh or shook her head, as if disagreeing with someone. Once she even said out loud, "That's a bunch of malarkey!" Several times she wrote down some words that seemed to be similar to, but not the same as, the ones in the book. Philosopher Theta continued to watch in amazement. The girl was totally wrapped up in what she was doing. The book seemed to be entertaining her, sometimes annoying her, and perhaps informing her of something, since she often wrote things down. Theta decided to interrupt the girl and talk to her.

"What is it that you're doing?" he asked.

"I'm reading this book," she said.

Theta scratched his head. "Could you tell me who made that book?"

The girl shrugged her shoulders. "I don't know who made it, but a man named Butterworth wrote it."

Theta squinted at the girl. "Wrote it?"

"Yes," she said. "You know. He made up the story. It's called *The Enormous Egg.*"

Theta nodded his head and stroked his beard. "I see. And when you're reading this story that Mr. Butterworth made up, are you talking with him?"

The girl giggled. "Well, not really," she said. "But in a way I guess I am. It's just as if Mr. Butterworth were telling the story to me."

Theta nodded. "Amazing!" he said. "Truly amazing. Can you read the book in such a way that I might hear what Mr. Butterworth is saying?"

The girl gave Theta a strange look and shrugged her shoulders. "Sure," she said. "I'll read you a little bit of it."

She proceeded to read a short part in which a scientist was explaining how a normal chicken could lay a dinosaur egg. The philosopher gasped and interrupted the girl again. "Are you reading exactly what Mr. Butterworth is saying to you?"

"Sure," she said.

"But how do you know?"

The girl shrugged her shoulders again. "It's right there," she said, pointing to the words on the page. "See those little words here? Mr. Butterworth wrote them down and I'm reading them just the way he wrote them."

Theta smiled. "That's really wonderful, isn't it?"

The girl smiled back. "Ya want me to read some more?"

Theta said, "Yes, please. But first tell me something. Before you read me more, do you have any idea what the words are going to say next?"

"Oh, sure," she said, and proceeded to predict quite closely what the author then said. After listening to her read more and asking her more questions, Philosopher Theta walked out into the corridor to join his three companions. "Reading is a code-emphasis process!" one of them was shouting. "It's a meaning-emphasis process!" another one said. The third one replied mysteriously, his arms spread outward, as if holding a large globe. "Reading is huge," he said. "It's a gargantuan set of decoding and comprehension subskills!"

"Gentlemen," Theta said softly. "I know exactly what reading is." The others waited, staring at him hostilely. "Reading," Theta said, "is a game!"

"A game!" the others cried.

"A game," he said, with a twinkle in his eyes. "A kind of guessing game. In fact, Earthlings have developed a highly sophisticated set of linguistic rules for this game."

"Rules?"

"Yes," Theta replied, chuckling to himself. "Rules about how to think when you want to communicate with someone else. Rules on what sounds you have to make or what symbols you have to write or what order the word-noises have to be in. Rules for what the word-noises will mean."

"Are you saying. . .," Alpha started to ask.

"I'm saying," said Theta, "that reading is a game of communicating with an author. It's a psycholinguistic guessing game."

"A psycholinguistic guessing game!" the other three shouted.

"Exactly," said Theta. "When Earthlings read, they are intelligently guessing what the author is going to say and then confirming their guesses by looking for clues."

"Impossible," said Omega. "Reading is just a vast set of tiny subskills. I can show you right here on this chart. . . ."

"It's nothing more than cracking a code!" said Alpha. . . .

Let's leave the four philosophers from Zania to their argument in the corridor. Their argument, on the surface, seems somewhat silly. Yet, you, the reader of this book, may be profoundly influenced in how you teach reading by the way you resolve that argument for yourself. If you accept Omega's definition of reading, for example, your instructional procedures could be very much different from those of a teacher who accepts Theta's definition.

Educators have argued for decades over whether reading instruction should emphasize decoding more (Alpha's argument) or comprehension more (Beta's argument). Publishers who produced textbooks for reading instruction switched back and forth through the years between a "code-emphasis" approach and a "meaning-emphasis" approach. When the "First Grade Studies" (2, 4) and Chall's book, *The Great Debate* (3), were published in the sixties, the argument seemed to come to a screeching halt. The evidence appeared clearly to favor a decoding emphasis from the very beginning, rather than waiting too long for phonics and other decoding skills to be taught.

But, no sooner had the publishers printed up their new "code-emphasis" textbooks than the debate heated up again, this time led by Goodman (5) and others, whose studies demonstrated that the argument was much more than "code vs. meaning." The argument was really one of whether to teach reading as a set of subskills or to teach reading as a communication process—a "psycholinguistic* guessing game."

What will be stressed in this chapter, and in the entire book, is that reading is NOT an either-or proposition. Both decoding and comprehension are involved. Both the learning of subskills and the learning of how to communicate with an author through psycholinguistic guessing are involved. In other words, all four of our philosophers from Zania were correct in their definitions. But none of them was seeing the whole picture. They were like the fabled blind men trying to describe an elephant, with each of them feeling a different part of its anatomy.

As mentioned in the preface:

1. For children who are first learning how to read there has to be more emphasis given to specific decoding and comprehension *subskills* than there needs to be given for children who have already jumped over the first hurdles.
2. At the same time, teachers who neglect to help children perceive "reading as communication" from the very first stage of reading instruction will probably give them the wrong perception of reading and thereby risk slowing up their progress in becoming good readers.
3. A child who learns to read for the purpose of communicating with an author normally becomes a good reader. The teacher

---

Psycholinguistic refers to the interactions that take place between the thinking processes of individuals and the particular language that they have to learn in order to communicate.

who attempts to help children read in this manner normally becomes a good teacher of reading.

4. A child who has learned all of the subskills involved in reading has not necessarily learned to read.

Research (5,6,7,8,9) personal experiences, and a multitide of shared experiences from practicing elementary-school teachers have convinced me that those four statements are valid. But first let me admit to something. The notion that reading is a form of communication is either from an *experienced* reader's point of view or from the point of view of a child who has been engaged in some form of "language-experience approach" (see Chapter 12). A beginning reader often doesn't perceive reading that way at all. For many beginning readers, reading is like deciphering a secret code. According to Karen, a six-year-old, "Grownups just look at those funny little marks, and then they know what to say."

Reading is not an either-or proposition. Both decoding and comprehension are involved. Both the learning of subskills and the learning of how to communicate with an author through psycholinguistic guessing are involved.

What Karen seems to be telling us is this: before she can communicate very well with an author, she has to learn the grownups' secret code. Once she has deciphered the code, or part of it, at least, she can begin to understand an author's message. Reading, then, from the viewpoint of many children, is decoding as well as communicating (even though decoding is simply a component of communicating).

Perhaps the best way to demonstrate what you and I have been discussing is to put you in the place of a beginning reader like Karen for a few moments. Actually, we can't really put you in Karen's place. You have too big a head start. I'm going to ask you to read something in a strange alphabet, but since you already know one alphabet, all you'll have to do is make a translation from the new alphabet into your own alphabet. This is not what beginning readers have to do, of course. They have to start from scratch with NO alphabet.

As you know, the word *alphabet* derives its name from the first and second letters of the Greek alphabet, *alpha* and *beta*. The alphabet you are about to use is called *applebet*, because the first letter is called *apple*.

You're now invited to read on pages 12 and 13 the first half of a "first-grade" book called *The Sam Trap*, a book that was first written (in English) for a group of children who were having trouble decoding words with the short *a* sound in them. Although this book would be a snap for you to read in our regular alphabet, it will not be so easy in "applebet." The first half will be fairly simple, since many of the words have already been translated for you. At the end of the chapter you may wish to try the second half, which may be much more difficult for you. In any case, please accept your frustration as a learning experience—one that will help you understand a little better how a young child like Karen feels about learning to read.

> ***Answer to question at beginning of section:*** *Reading is both a communication process and a decoding process. A mature reader perceives reading as communication. A beginning reader may perceive it primarily as decoding.*

Reading as a Set of Subskills

Question: *What subskills are involved in the skill called "reading"?*

Now that you've attempted to read *The Sam Trap*, we can talk more about the nature of reading. We've already discussed how reading, to a mature reader, is a process of communicating with an author, whereas a beginning reader may perceive it as a process of

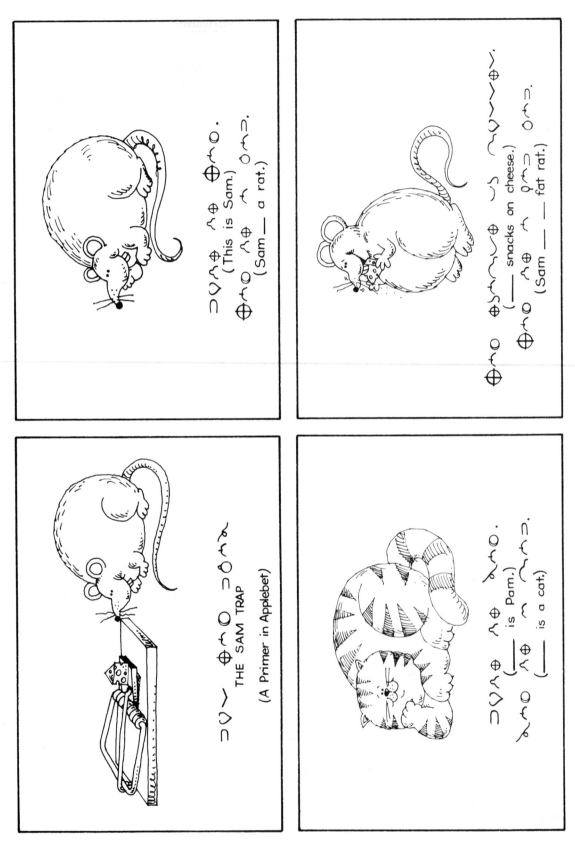

(This is Sam.)
(Sam ___ a rat.)

(___ snacks on cheese.)
(Sam ___ ___ fat rat.)

THE SAM TRAP
(A Primer in Applebet)

(___ is Pam.)
(___ is a cat.)

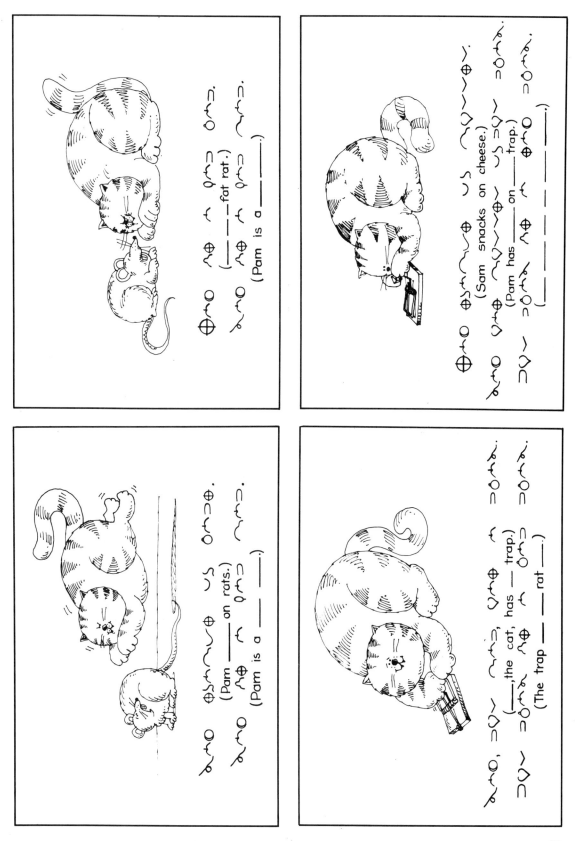

____ fat rat.
(____ the fat rat.)
(Pam is a ____.)

(Sam snacks on cheese.)
(Pam has ____ on ____ trap.)

(Pam ____ on rats.)
(Pam is a ____.)

(____, the cat, has ____ trap.)
(The trap ____ rat ____.)

decoding. When you attempted to read *The Sam Trap,* you were both a mature reader and a beginning reader. Did you find yourself doing a lot of decoding? I'm sure you did. But didn't you also find yourself trying to communicate with the author? That is, didn't you find yourself asking the author questions like these: "Is Pam going to go after Sam?" "Is Sam going to get caught in the trap?" "How is Sam going to get away from Pam?"

As a mature reader, you concentrated on decoding the strange alphabet so that you could find out what the author had to say to you. But, as a beginning reader, you probably found yourself bogged down at times with the decoding process.

This is often the beginning reader's predicament. In the ultimate sense, reading is a form of communication, and a child like Karen is lucky if she realizes this intuitively from the very beginning. But in the instructional sense, reading is also a set of subskills that have to be learned in order to do a better job of communicating with authors. Those subskills are usually divided into two categories: decoding subskills and comprehension subskills. Such a division enables us to talk about the subskills more easily, but it's a false division. In reality, the subskills work together; they interact while a person is reading. We'll talk about this interaction a little later. Right now, let's just look at what the subskills are. The following list is highly abbreviated but will give you the general idea:

Decoding Subskills
(Subskills like these enable a reader to translate printed letters into speech sounds.)
1. Decoding by means of phonic clues (using phonics)
2. Decoding by means of syllable division (breaking words up into syllables before using phonics)
3. Decoding by means of morpheme division (noticing prefixes, suffixes, roots)
4. Decoding by means of context clues (word order and meaning)
5. Decoding by means of visual memory (sight vocabulary)

Comprehension Subskills
(Subskills like these enable a reader to recognize the meanings of words and sentences and to think about what the author is saying.)
1. Determining the appropriate meaning of a word
2. Recognizing punctuation clues that signal intonation and pauses
3. Developing images and associations related to each sentence
4. Following a sequence of events, ideas, or directions
5. Recognizing the main ideas
6. Understanding cause and effect
7. Detecting author bias
8. Predicting what is to follow

Answer to question at beginning of section: *The skill called "read-ing" involves various decoding subskills that enable a reader to translate printed letters into speech sounds; it also involves various comprehension subskills that enable a reader to recognize the mean-ings of words and sentences and to think about what the author is saying.*

Learning the Subskills versus Learning to Read

Question: *When a child learns the subskills, does he now know how to read?*

Teaching children the subskills of reading is not the same as teaching them to read. As an analogy, you could teach me all the different movements I need to make in order to swim, but that wouldn't be the same as teaching me to swim. If you're going to teach me to swim, you may want to give me separate lessons on breathing, kick-ing, and stroking; but you'll also have to give me lessons on putting all the subskills together. When it comes to reading, you can teach a child how to recognize phonic clues; you can give her lessons on using context clues, you can help her learn how to follow a sequence. But until you help her learn how to put several subskills together, you're really not teaching her how to read.

Many teachers have observed children who can pass a test on each separate subskill and still not be able to read very well. Why is this? For one thing, even young children can become "test-wise" after taking a large number of objective-type tests. The answers begin to stand out like gold in a miner's sieve. But the main reason is that these children have not learned to put the subskills together: they haven't learned to coordinate them as they read.

Often teachers (including myself) have spent so much time working with a child on separate subskills, they don't have enough time to encourage the abilities and enthusiasm needed for "real read-ing"—particularly the reading of whole books. The phonics work-sheets and the "questions at the end of the story" have used up the time (and enthusiasm for reading), so it's "time for math" or "time for p.e." We'll be talking much more about this in later chapters. For now, let's just say it's a problem: how do you teach subskills without ignoring "real reading" or without giving children the mistaken notion that "reading is filling out worksheets and things like that"?

Answer to question at beginning of section: *When a child learns all of the subskills of reading, she may still not know how to read. The teacher also needs to show her how to coordinate the subskills during the reading act.*

What Children Need to Learn about Authors

Question: What do children need to learn about authors, and what does this have to do with teaching reading?

I mentioned earlier that a child like Karen is lucky if she learns to perceive reading, from the very beginning, as a way of communicating with authors. If her teachers and parents get this idea across to her, two things will probably happen: 1) she'll stay motivated toward learning to read and 2) she'll develop the type of mental set that will cause her to read for meaning rather than merely for "sounding out the words" or for "getting the diggynabbed assignment done."

On the other hand, if Karen begins to perceive reading as nothing more than sounding out words, filling in blanks, and handing in assignments, you may have a "reluctant reader" on your hands—or at best one who thinks of "school reading" as entirely different from "real reading." From the very beginning of her school days, even while she is in the process of learning all those subskills, Karen needs to be helped to perceive reading as an enjoyable process of communicating with authors.

But let's talk about authors for a moment. You've seen many of them, no doubt, on television talk shows or in person. Perhaps you're an author yourself, or you know one personally. At any rate, you would probably agree that authors have very little in common as far as personality or physical characteristics go. But they do have one need in common. They all need to communicate. More specifically, they all need to entertain or inform.

Let me give you a particular example from a "newspaper report" that I wrote several years ago:

Zoologist Says Dog Yaps Make Sense

LONDON (EPI)—A zoologist from Oxherd University claims to have deciphered the yelps, snarls, and bays of canines. Dr. Feline, who has been studying dog "speech" for years, says that dogs communicate with each other by means of a very elaborate set of noises, which he has dubbed "fanguage."

After travelling through various parts of the world, Dr. Feline has come to the conclusion that there are at least 3,000 different fanguages. Furthermore, he states, most dogs understand only one or two fanguages, resulting in a great deal of confusion, misunderstanding, and dog fights.

Not only are there a great variety of fanguages, but each fanguage has a number of "dogalects" (variations within a fanguage). A hound in one part of a large city, says Dr. Feline, may woof a dogalect which differs in many respects from the dogalect woofed in another part of the city. Dogs from these two parts of the city can usually intercommunicate to some extent, but they find it either irritating or amusing. Dr. Feline has observed, moreover, that each canine acts as though his dogalect were superior to all other dogalects.

Dogalects differ not only among geographical regions, says Dr. Feline, but also between canine classes within a region. The upper-class dogs (consisting of pedigreed animals and those who strive to be like them) woof a different dogalect from the lower-class dogs (consisting of mutts, mongrels, and tramps). For example, the upper-class dogs in London will woof, "Grrr rowlf *urr* yelp," whereas the lower-class dogs will woof, "Grrr rowlf *orr* yelp." According to Dr. Feline, this slight difference is enough to cause frothing of the mouth by upper-class and lower-class dogs alike.

As you can see from examining this allegorical account, I was trying both to entertain and to inform my readers—as if I were a personal friend, telling them something I knew about language in as interesting a way as I could. And this is the way most authors seem to look at their writing—as a means of communicating with people by sharing ideas and feelings. This is true whether the author is trying to write a best-selling novel, a cookbook, or a "Dick-and-Jane" story designed to help first graders learn to read. (Even with a "Dick-and-Jane"-type story, created as a teaching device, the author does try to communicate some type of message.) Once teachers thoroughly grasp this point, some interesting things begin to happen: 1) they notice that they are more inclined to have children read in order to understand the author's message rather than to merely pronounce the words; 2) they find themselves asking children "What does the *author* say?" rather than, "What does the *book* say?"; and 3) they find themselves asking children fewer questions about the extraneous details in a reading passage and more questions about the important ideas or feelings that an author wishes to share.

What I'd really like to persuade you to believe (and to pass on to children) is that authors and readers do communicate. You and I are having a form of conversation right now. It's true that we're missing an important ingredient in any good conversation—your ability to influence what I have to say directly. This is unfortunate. If you *could* influence me, I would then modify what I have to say in order to respond to your ideas and questions—and even your facial expressions. But we ARE having a conversation. You're doing with me just what you do when you chat with other people. You're "listening" to my words; you're predicting what I'm going to say next; you're agreeing or disagreeing with me; and you're even having thoughts about me as a person—"he's nice," "he's obnoxious," "he's interesting," "he's weird," and so on.

As a mature reader, you normally read as if some type of communication were actually taking place. Sometimes this may take the form of imagining yourself listening to the author speaking to you. Other times it may take the form of actually becoming the author—entertaining or informing someone else. This last form is particularly true when you're reading the fast-paced, exciting parts of a novel, and you're devouring the words like popcorn. In either case, whether you're "listening" to the author or pretending to be the author, you're engaged in communication.

> *Answer to question at beginning of section: Children need to learn that authors really want to entertain or inform them and that it's fun to be entertained and informed through the process of reading. Having learned this, they are more likely to stay motivated toward learning to read and more likely to read for meaning rather than mere pronunciation of words or getting assignments done.*

Reading and Holism

> *Question: What is holism and what does it have to do with reading?*

Once beginning readers grasp the principle that reading is a communication process rather than a mere "sounding-out-the-words" process, they will have the desire (but not the ability) to read just the way many skillful readers read. That is, they will want to read with fluency and understanding, as if they, themselves, had written the story, poem, or informational passage. Picture, if you will, a skillful young reader reading a story to the rest of the class. She is reading the story as if she were telling it—as if the story were actually hers. She is *communicating* the story and not just mouthing words that she has translated from print to speech.

Once children develop a mental set of reading for communication and once they've learned some of the subskills of reading, they're ready to read *holistically.* The word *holism* refers to the idea that the whole is greater than the sum of the parts. Applied to the reading act, it means that reading is more than the sum of the subskills of reading. We don't read by adding the subskills together. We read by letting the subskills interact in such a way that we communicate with the author and grasp the author's message. We read by noticing all of the relevant clues that enable us to predict what the author is saying and to confirm those predictions. To put it another way, we make intelligent guesses and continually check enough phonic clues, punctuation clues, word-order clues, and meaning clues to see if we guessed correctly. We put the parts together, but in the process of doing this we create something greater than the sum of the parts: we create (or re-create) the *author's message* (or we reconstruct the message according to our own past experiences).

Perhaps the best way of illustrating this is to show you how an actual third-grade child, who was not a skillful reader, tried to read a sentence from a first-grade book.

Author: Roy saw a little boat pull a big boat.
Tommy: Roy was a little boat pulled by a big boat.

Tommy was indeed trying to re-create the author's message in a holistic way. He read the name *Roy* just the way the author intended it to be read. But when it came to the next word, *saw,* Tommy predicted that the author was going to say *was* (perhaps because Tommy confuses these two words or because he actually thought it was the word the author was going to use next).

So far, so good, as far as Tommy is concerned. "Roy was"—that makes sense. Roy was what? Roy was a little *boat?* "Well, okay," says Tommy to himself. If someone wants to call a little boat *Roy,* that's fine with him. He then comes to the word *pull.* Now, if you had already said, "Roy was a little boat," you wouldn't say "pull" next, would you? That wouldn't sound right. So Tommy says "pulled." You see, he "sees" the word *pulled* instead of *pull* because he's trying to get the author's message, and not just "sound out the words." Now Tommy sees "a big boat." Or does he? No, he sees something that works better. He sees "by a big boat." It all makes sense, doesn't it? This little boat named Roy was pulled by a big boat. (Probably all Tommy misses right now is the name of the big boat.)

Unfortunately, Tommy has completely reversed the author's message. The author was trying to get Tommy to picture a little boat pulling a big boat. But Tommy was more "rational" about the whole thing and had a big boat pulling a little one; which only goes to show you, "the kid's no dummy." As a matter of fact, Tommy's a bright little boy.

Is he a poor reader? Not at all. Not at this stage of his development anyway. Tommy has the most important idea about reading clearly in his mind: reading is a communication process—an interaction between author and reader. We read in order to grasp a message. However, in Tommy's case, he's lacking certain reading subskills that will enable him to detect the author's message more accurately and clearly.

Let me show you what I mean. As Tommy continued reading the story, he had to correct himself on several words. He read *when* for *then, soon* for *some, he* for *his, there* for *here,* and *have* for *gave.* This shows us that he lacks skill in recognizing basic sight words and that he ignores small but significant phonic clues.

Tommy is well on his way toward reading holistically, however. He has the concept of reading as communication, but he's lacking some of the subskills that will enable him to get an author's message. To read holistically he must have both: the concept of reading as a process of communicating with an author, and the decoding and comprehension subskills that will enable him to search for and discover an author's message.

The same thing would be true if Tommy were learning to swim instead of learning to read. To "swim holistically" Tommy must have two things: 1) he must have a concept of what swimming really is (and why one should be moving his body in such a strange way) and 2) he must have learned the separate subskills and how to coordinate them in such a way that he can actualize his concept of what swimming is. As he puts all of the subskills (the parts) together, he gets something greater than the sum of the parts. He gets the sensation of actually swimming, he gets the thrill of accomplishment, he acquires the concept of swimming intuitively rather than just intellectually.

> ***Answer to question at beginning of section:*** Holism *is the theory that the whole is greater than the sum of its parts. Reading is more than the sum of the subskills. Holistic reading requires the concept of reading as communication; it also requires the coordination of numerous subskills with the intention of acquiring the author's message.*

Some Choices Teachers Must Make before Reading Instruction Begins

Question: _____? (Please create your own.)

During the weeks before school begins in the fall, and also during the first few weeks of school, teachers have to make many decisions related to their program of reading instruction. In addition to deciding which definition of reading will influence their instructional practices most, they have many here-and-now types of decisions to make. Mrs. Blanchard, for instance, teaches in a first-grade, self-contained classroom. This is her second year of teaching and she is trying to decide whether to continue using a basal-reader program or to begin the year with a language-experience approach. With the basal-reader program, as described in Chapter 10, she is provided with several basal readers, at various levels of reading difficulty, which are full of fictional stories, poems, informational articles, and plays. She has teacher guides and workbooks to go with each basal reader. And she has tests and other materials that correlate with each of the basal readers.

On the other hand, she's wondering if she might like to try the language-experience approach, at least as a modification of the basal-reader program. With this approach, as described in Chapter 12, children create much of their own reading material by dictating stories and ideas to the teacher or teaching aide. With this approach, children can more readily perceive reading as a communication process, rather than a mere "sound-it-out" process.

A second decision Mrs. Blanchard has to make is how to group her students for instruction. She knows that the experience of reading should be success-filled; therefore, she doesn't want to instruct her students with materials that are too difficult. She decides to group her children primarily on the basis of an informal reading inventory. With this technique, described fully in Chapter 9, each child reads a small portion from several of the basal readers. After listening to a child read, the teacher decides which reader is at the appropriate level of difficulty for him and into which group he should be placed.

A third decision for Mrs. Blanchard, and one that she must continue to make throughout the year, is what specific help each child needs on each of a variety of reading subskills. This she decides through the administration of diagnostic tests (described in Chapter 14), through observation during lessons, through examination of worksheet and workbook results, through individual conferences (described in Chapter 13), and possibly through the use of a skills-management system (described in Chapter 11).

A fourth decision that Mrs. Blanchard is faced with is that of readiness. How ready are the children for reading instruction? Do they all have good auditory- and visual-discrimination skills? That is, can they tell the differences between letter shapes and sounds? Have they learned good listening skills? Can they follow directions? These questions she'll have to answer through examining the results of reading-readiness tests (as described in Chapter 7), through observations during lessons, and through generally getting to know each child personally.

Mr. Nicholson and Miss Porter, a fifth-grade teaching team, have no fewer choices to make than Mrs. Blanchard. Their biggest decision so far has been whether to use an individualized approach, in which children read library books (described in Chapter 13), a basal-reader approach, or a combination of the two approaches. With any of these methods, they need to have a good idea of each child's instructional level. Therefore, like Mrs. Blanchard, they decide to combine the informal reading inventory with a technique called *miscue analysis* (described in Chapter 14). And, like Mrs. Blanchard, they, too, are concerned about readiness. They realize that readiness (as discussed in Chapter 7) is important in all of the grades and not just in kindergarten and first grade.

Answer to question at beginning of section: _____ .

Reading as a Social Process

Question: _____ ?

Perhaps by now it goes without saying that reading is a social process. That is, it involves the willingness on the part of readers and authors to communicate with each other. The authors have to want to communicate their ideas so badly that they stay up late at night writing, revising, polishing, until the information or entertainment they want (need) to provide seems clear or amusing or beautiful or exciting (or, perhaps, in the case of textbooks, not overly burdensome). The readers, on the other hand, have to want to communicate with the author so badly that they stay up late at night reading, studying, pondering (or, in the case of a good novel, gulping) until the information or entertainment they want (need) also seems clear or amusing or beautiful or exciting (or not overly burdensome).

However, while the process of reading is a social act, the process of learning to read is even more so. Children may grasp the idea that reading is communication. They may realize intuitively that the goal of reading instruction is to enable them to approach reading in a holistic way. They may even accept the notion that there are "handtoes" of subskills they must learn before they can "read like big people." And they may eventually understand that you want them to get their decoding and comprehension skills to interact. But underlying all this intellectual understanding and skill development is a social phenomenon—a teacher working with a child.

Research (2,3,4,8) shows us again and again that the teacher is the most important variable in how well a child learns to read. The teacher's self-confidence (which comes partly through his or her knowledge of how to teach reading) seems to be an important factor. The teacher's enthusiasm is another. The teacher's organizational ability is a third. And the teacher's communication of warmth or caring is another.

In most cases, but not all, the teacher's ability to communicate with a child seems to be more important than the child's intelligence quotient, the state of his home life, or any other genetic or environmental factor. This presents a tremendous challenge to teachers—particularly in those situations in which they do not get as much parental, societal, and administrative support and assistance as they need. But it appears to be a fact of life.

It's teachers who make the difference. It's their enthusiasm for reading good books to themselves and to their students. It's their awareness of strategies—those that encourage children to look for ideas and feelings that authors wish to share and not just those that bind children to filling blanks with correct answers (as useful as this sometimes can be). It's their ability to organize the instructional time and materials in such a way that steady growth in reading ability can take place. It's their concern for children and their future. It's all these things and much more that cause teachers to make the difference. And teachers do make the difference.

Answer to question at beginning of section: _____ .

Questions and Answers

Question: But what is reading, really?

Answer: This depends upon what part of the anatomy of reading you're looking at. Reading may be considered a process involving four major abilities. These four major abilities are overlapping and interrelated.

1. *Comprehending*—understanding the meaning of the individual words, the phrases, the sentences, and the author's message.
2. *Decoding*—translating printed words into spoken words (or sub-vocal thought) without necessarily comprehending their meaning; for example, the nonsense word *fridaddle* can be decoded in isolation but not comprehended.
3. *Anticipating*—making intelligent guesses about what the author is going to say next or what the author means by a particular word.
4. *Orchestrating*—using various subskills related to comprehending, decoding, and predicting in a holistic manner in order to grasp an author's message.

Question: What is psycholinguistic guessing?

Answer: It's simply one way that human beings use their intelligence—in this case, making use of language to communicate with authors. Rather than speaking directly with authors about their thoughts, we have to infer their speech and thoughts from the written symbols they use.

Question: When children learn how to engage in psycholinguistic guessing, what are they actually doing?

Answer: A great many things. This book will talk about most of those things. But for now, let's look just at the process of guessing intelligently what words are going to come next as children read.

1. Their intuitive knowledge of the grammatical rules for ordering and ending words allows them to predict whether a noun, verb, or other part of speech is coming next; they also know intuitively how a word should end—with an *s*, an *ed*, an *ing*, etc. For example: "She throws the _____ ." (The reader would predict a noun like *ball, knife,* or *dish.* The reader would also predict the *s* at the end of the word *throw.*)
2. Their awareness of the meaning of the words in the sentence permits them to predict the logical part of speech, rather than just any noun or other part of speech. For example: "He swam across the swift-flowing _____ ." (The reader would predict *river, stream,* or *creek.*)
3. Their own past experiences allow them to bring meaning to the printed page. For example, their experiences with rivers, streams,

or creeks make it possible for them to make use of the language in the sentence in order to predict the final word in the sentence.

4. Their knowledge of phonics (graphophonics) permits them to predict the precise noun or other part of speech that follows. For example: "He swam across the swift-flowing r_ _er." (The reader would predict *river,* rather than *stream* or *creek.* This prediction is made by noticing only minimal phonic clues, rather than by sounding out the entire word.)

5. Their awareness that the author is trying to communicate with the reader enables them to pay attention to the author's message, rather than just the words. For example, in the sentence "Help! I am _____ in this vat of liquid _____," the reader can get the general message, even though he can't get all of the words.

Question: Which is more important for children to learn—psycholinguistic guessing or the various subskills of comprehending and decoding?

Answer: They're equally important, and this book will try to show you why. The subskills of comprehending and decoding should be learned in order to make the process of psycholinguistic guessing a more intelligent one.

Summary

This book, then, is the result of the author's attempt to help you meet the difficult but rewarding challenge of teaching children to read. In Chapter 1, we talked about the importance of teaching in such a way that children perceive reading as a process of communicating with friends called *authors.* We also discussed the various decoding and comprehension subskills involved in the act of reading and the importance of teaching children how to coordinate them. In addition, you were given examples of reading as a holistic process—a process in which the whole is greater than the sum of the parts. You were shown some of the decisions that teachers must make before instruction in reading can begin. And finally, you were reminded that both reading and reading instruction are social interactions, during which the teacher is the major catalyst. It is the teacher's challenge to get children to perceive both reading and the process of learning to read as worthwhile and delightful adventures.

References and Suggested Readings

1. Athey, I. *Essential Skills and Skill Hierarchies in Reading.* Washington, D.C.: National Institute of Education, 1975.

2. Bond, Guy L., and Dykstra, Robert. "The Cooperative Research Program in First-Grade Reading Instruction." *Reading Research Quarterly* 2 (Summer 1967): 5–142.

3. Chall, Jean S. *Learning to Read: the Great Debate.* New York: McGraw-Hill, 1967.

4. Dykstra, Robert. "Summary of the Second-Grade Phase of the Cooperative Research Program in Primary Instruction." *Reading Research Quarterly* 1 (Fall 1968): 49–70.

5. Goodman, Kenneth S. *Miscue Analysis: Application to Reading Instruction,* Urbana, Illinois: National Council of Teachers of English, 1973.

6. Samuels, S. Jay. "Hierarchical Subskills in the Reading Acquisition Process." In *Aspects of Reading Acquisition,* edited by J. Guthrie. Baltimore: Johns Hopkins University Press, 1976.

7. Smith, F. *Understanding Reading.* New York: Holt, Rinehart, and Winston, 1971.

8. Weaver, P. *Research within Reach, a Research-Guided Response to Concerns of Reading Educators.* Washington, D.C.: National Institute of Education, 1978.

9. Williams, J. "Learning to Read: a Review of Theories and Models." *Reading Research Quarterly* 8 (1972–1973): 121–46.

Application Experiences for the Teacher-Education Class

1. With a small group of students in your class, discuss why you agree or disagree with the following statements. Then compare your decisions with other groups. Note: One or more statements may be purposely ambiguous in order to stimulate your thinking abilities. Understanding is the goal in this experience rather than correct answers.

Statements about Chapter 1

LITERAL LEVEL: Did the author actually say these things?

a. A good reader communicates with an author.

b. Most authors have no real need to entertain or inform.

c. Teachers who teach reading as communication usually find that their students begin to concentrate more on pronouncing words correctly.

d. A child who reads holistically makes intelligent guesses and continually checks enough phonic clues, punctuation clues, grammatical clues, and meaning clues to see if he is right.

e. Decoding by means of phonic signals is one type of subskill involved in the reading act.

INFERENTIAL LEVEL: Did the author *imply* these things? Defend your answers.

a. A child can have all the subskills involved in reading and not be a good reader.

    b.   Teachers need to provide plenty of time for children to read whole books.

    c.   Reading is simply the sum of decoding (word recognition) and comprehension (understanding the meaning).

    d.   The intelligence quotient is not a very important factor in determining how well a child learns to read.

    e.   The teacher's ability to communicate with children is the major factor in determining whether a child learns to read.

2.   After looking at the "applebet" (Appendix 1.1) at the end of the chapter, work with a small group or with the entire class to decipher *The Sam Trap*, on pages 12–13 and pages 27–29. Then make a list of those decoding and comprehension skills you used in order to get the author's message. Use the lists of decoding skills and comprehension skills on page 14 to help you with this.

3.   Discuss the frustrations you had in learning to read *The Sam Trap*. How were they similar to, or different from, the frustrations that children might encounter in learning to read with our regular alphabet? Was some of your reading merely translation? What kind of translation do children do when they read? (They translate from what to what?) How is reading our regular alphabet much more difficult for children to learn than it was for you to learn to read the applebet?

4.   Compare the author's message with the way Jennifer reads it. What can you tell about Jennifer's perception of reading? Does she seem to perceive reading as communication? What kind of special help do you think she needs? What do you need to know about the teaching of reading before you can better answer this last question?

Author	Jennifer
"I didn't hear you!" Walter said.	"I don't hear you!" Walter said.
"I called and called," his mother said.	"I cannot call," his mother said.
"I had the radio on," Walter said. "I couldn't hear you."	"I have a radio on," Walter said. "I cannot hear you."
"Well, you can now," his mother said.	"Will you come now?" his mother said.
"I want you to go to the store."	"I want you to go to the store."

Field Experiences in the Elementary-School Classroom

1.   Interview three or four children to determine what their perception of reading is. Ask them questions such as: "What do you think reading is?" "Did you think differently about reading when you were younger?" "Do you think reading is mainly pronouncing the words or understanding the words?" "Do you think that reading is like talking to someone?"

After your interviews have been completed, examine your results and try to arrive at some conclusion about children's perceptions. Then compare your conclusions with others in your teacher education class.

2. Have a child—one who seems to have some difficulty learning to read—read to you. If possible, tape record the reading or take notes on the errors that the child makes. What can you tell about his perception of reading? Does he seem to think that reading is mainly getting the meaning? Does he read as if he's telling you something or as if he is just trying to get through? Why do you think he perceives reading the way he does?

3. Try some of *The Sam Trap* with a good reader. Listen carefully to what she says as she attempts to understand it. If she says very little, ask her questions such as "What are you doing now to help you read it?" while she works on it. What does this tell you about her perception of reading?

Appendix 1.1

The Applebet (and Part 2 of *The Sam Trap*)

	apple				nose		
	bed				ox		
	car				pig		
	door				queen		
	envelope				ring		
	fan				sun		
	gun				toe		
	heart				up		
	ink				vat		
	jam				wand		
	kick				x-ray		
	lip				yam		
	money				zipper		

174281

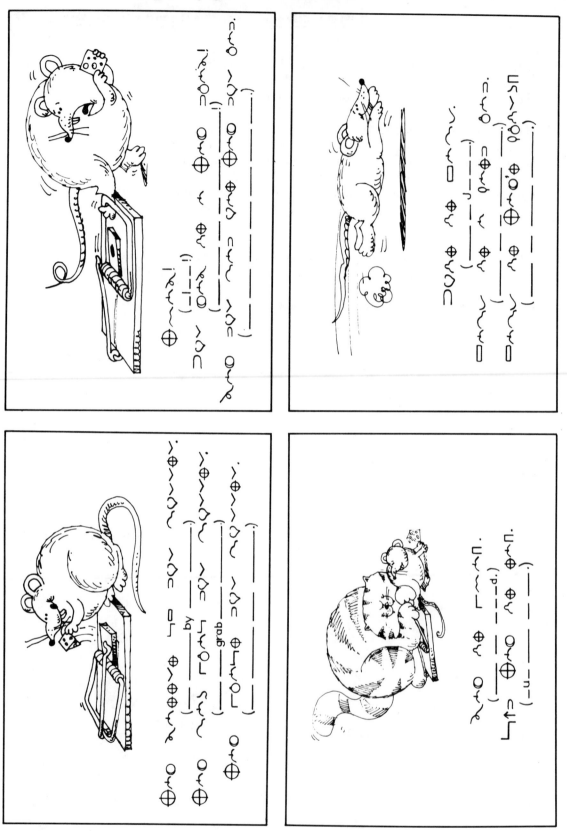

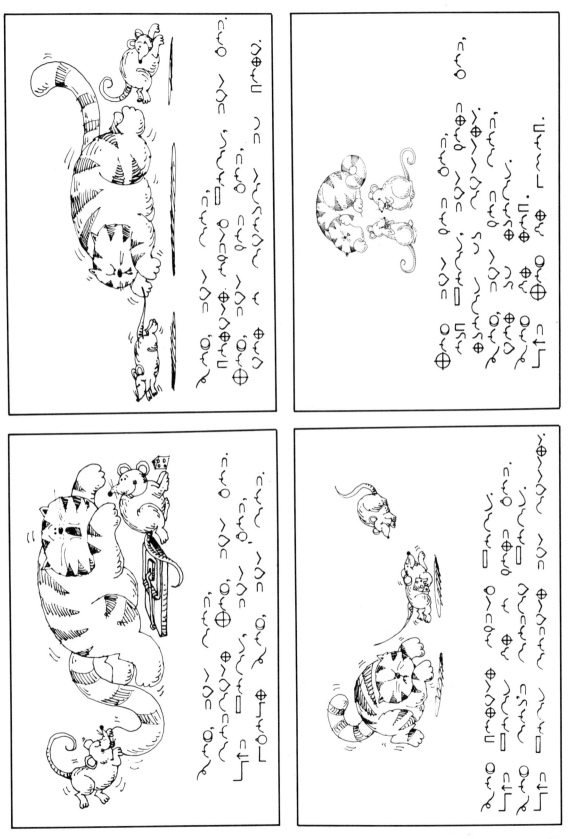

29

CHAPTER 2

*The development of vocabulary should be a holistic
experience enhanced by the contributions of all four
language arts: reading, writing, listening, and speaking.*

Developing Children's Vocabularies

Chapter Preview

Now that we've talked about three fundamental and interrelated concepts related to successful reading instruction—holism, communication, and subskills—we're ready to discuss some techniques of reading instruction: how to develop children's vocabularies, how to teach phonics, how to increase comprehension skills, and so on. In this chapter we'll concentrate on vocabulary—on several vocabularies to be precise. We'll talk first about the importance of oral vocabulary and the integration of reading into the total language-arts program. Then we'll talk about the difference between sight vocabulary and semantic vocabulary, since methods of teaching these two types of vocabulary differ.

> Humans are best known for putting the cart before the horse.

Those of us who teach reading to children sometimes fall into a trap, which, for lack of a better term, I'll call a "language-in-reverse trap." We concentrate so hard on helping children learn to read printed language, we lose sight of the fact (mentioned by so many psycholinguists) that printed language is simply a rough representation of oral language. And this can get us into trouble when we're trying to teach children to read.

Linguists (12, 13, 25) who have studied our own language and other world languages often remind us that oral language is the primary language: in any culture, oral language develops first and written language later—if ever. Researchers (11, 12) who have studied the language growth of children in our culture and other cultures also remind us of the primacy of oral language. Children learn first to speak and listen, and only later to write and read. They remind us, furthermore, that speaking and listening are the crucial foundation stones for the development of writing and reading skills. Without a firm beginning in speaking and listening to words and sentences, children may have difficulty learning to handle the representations of speaking and listening called "writing" and "reading."

Let's look at an example of this: "Over the hill and into the wooded valley he rode, his silver steed flashing in the columns of sunshine that stood, side-by-side, with the giant oaks." How many children would you expect to read or write a sentence similar to that one? If you guessed "no more than one in a hundred," you're probably correct. But why so few? Probably because very few children have the opportunity to listen to such language. Furthermore, very few would ever obtain practice in speaking that way. And without such listening and speaking experiences, the act of writing or reading a similar sentence would seem very unnatural. The children might be able to pronounce or decode every word in the sentence, but the sentence would have little meaning; it would not be understood.

Oral Language is the primary language.

Let's look into this a bit deeper. What happens when Danny tries to read the word *steed* in that sentence we've just seen? He has to translate the printed word into an oral one—either out loud or in his mind. Can he do it? It depends on a lot of things, but largely on his previous oral-language experiences. Even if he uses phonics and pronounces the word correctly, he won't understand the meaning of the word unless it's part of his listening or speaking vocabulary. Even if he looks for context clues in the rest of the sentence (such as the word *rode*), he still won't know whether the word *steed* refers to a car, a bicycle, a horse, or something else. Without an adequate oral vocabulary, reading can be quite a chore. (Without an adequate oral vocabulary, "reading as a psycholinguistic guessing game" can't be an intelligent one.)

Now let's go back to the "language-in-reverse trap" that was mentioned earlier. It works like this. A teacher, Mrs. Merrill, realizes that Danny is having trouble reading certain words or sentence patterns. Her thinking about this problem may run something like this: "Danny is having trouble reading; therefore, I need to provide him with more practice and training in reading."

In some instances this type of thinking will have good results. But in many instances, the teacher has fallen into the "language-in-reverse trap." Many times when children have trouble with reading, it's because they need more help with *oral* language. Rather than provide Danny with a phonics lesson on decoding *steed,* for instance, Mrs. Merrill may need to provide him with some listening and speaking experiences with the word *steed.* Reading a poem or several sentences about steeds to him or having him say the word *steed* every time he hears the word *horse* in a sentence would contribute more toward his reading abilities than several lessons on the *st* sound, the double *e* sound, and so on.

Reading as a Component of the Language Arts

The primacy of oral language should remind all of us who teach reading that reading is merely one component of language. Language has four major components: speaking, listening, writing, and reading—and these four modes of language, as psycholinguists remind us, often interact when human beings think or communicate. This is why it's so important that reading be taught not only as an isolated subject (which is sometimes necessary) but also as part of the total language arts program. This is why it's so important that children be exposed many times during their elementary school years to various forms of "language experience approaches." With a language experience approach children have opportunities to dictate, discuss, and write their own ideas; to see their own ideas in print;

and to read the ideas that they, themselves, have composed. (See Chapter 12 for a thorough description of this approach.) In this way they can see, and be reminded, that "reading" is not an assignment to be completed but a form of *communication.*

In Chapter 5 we'll be discussing some of the procedures that can be used to combine the four language arts in order to help children read and understand various sentence patterns and the way we alter and expand them. In this chapter we'll be looking at ways of expanding children's speaking, listening, writing, and reading *vocabularies.* As children speak and listen to various words, they're preparing themselves for reading and writing them. As children learn to spell words in written form, they're increasing their visual memory necessary for reading these words "by sight." As children read the same words again and again, they are increasing their abilities to spell them, speak them, and listen to them with understanding. The four language arts work together a little like four wheels on a car. By putting the same amount of pressure in each tire you can help the car run smoothly. If one of the tires is short on air, though, you won't get the same smooth ride.

The Difference between Semantic and Sight Vocabularies

Many children who arrive at school for the first time are already equipped with a small *sight vocabulary* (words that can be recognized and pronounced instantly). They've been taught by parents and others to recognize several printed words—words such as *milk, ice cream, Coke, Pepsi, Sesame Street,* and their own names. They see a word such as *milk,* and without using phonic analysis or another word-analysis skill, they can immediately tell you what it is. Or, to put it another way, they can instantaneously pronounce the word through the use of visual memory alone.

Do they also understand the words? That is, are words such as *milk, ice cream, Coke,* and *Sesame Street* part of their *semantic* (meaning) vocabulary as well? Yes, usually they are. But there are some words that children see over and over in their daily lives and learn to pronounce without really understanding their meaning. Sally, for instance, can decode the title of her brother's piano book, *Basic Piano Lessons, Book One.* Her brother has taught her how to "read" the title. He's a born teacher and enjoys pointing to the five words in different orders—*Piano, Book, Basic, One, Lessons*—and having her read each one. Since she is now able to read each word in isolation, we can say that those five words are becoming part of her sight vocabulary. However, only four of those words are part of her semantic vocabulary. She knows what a piano is. She has a pretty good idea of what lessons are ("Those are what teachers teach you"). She knows what a book is, and she even knows that the word *one* can stand for either a quantity or a position. But she has no idea what *basic* means, and furthermore she hasn't cared enough to ask anyone up to this point. So, the word *basic* is part of her sight vocabulary but not part of her semantic vocabulary.

Measuring Children's Vocabularies

A child's sight vocabulary is fairly easy to measure. If you flash a printed word in front of a child for a duration of only one second (assuming she has no vision problem), and she can instantly pronounce the word, that word is part of her sight vocabulary. Your only problem is deciding which words are essential for her to have in her sight vocabulary and determining which of those she already knows through visual memory. (In a later section we'll discuss some solutions to this problem.)

Measuring a child's semantic vocabulary, on the other hand, is not so easy. How do you know that Sally understands a word? Well, we might say she understands the word *piano* because she can point to it. When we say *piano* to her, she doesn't point to her big sister's trumpet, or to the refrigerator, or to the piano bench. In addition to pointing to a piano, she can tell you something about it ("My brother plays it. You can play tunes on it, like 'Mary Had a Little Lamb.' If you hit it up here, it makes a high sound. If you hit it down here it makes a low sound.")

But supposing you ask her to "name a large musical instrument with eighty-eight keys." She may draw a blank if she doesn't know what *keys* are, or what *musical instrument* means, or even what the number *eighty-eight* means. In short she doesn't understand the word *piano* THAT well. You can see, then, that whether a child understands a word or not depends partly on what the measurer means by "understands." Unless teachers keep the concepts of holism and communication in mind, it is possible for them to get confused on this matter and to reinforce learning that does not lead to better reading. Let's talk about this in the next section.

Holism and Communication Applied to Vocabulary Development

From the teacher's standpoint, all that should matter is that the children comprehend a word well enough to help them comprehend the author's message. The word *piano,* like so many words in the English language, has many shades of meaning, depending on how technical or detailed one wishes to be. But one can communicate about a piano without knowing all the intricacies of the strings and soundboard. Generally speaking, it is both inefficient and unwise for the reading teacher to dwell very long on the meanings of words *in isolation.* Remember, from a holistic standpoint, the author's message is the important focus, rather than the author's words.

The notion that a large vocabulary demonstrates one's superior intelligence still lingers on in our society. We are still apt to be impressed by those who use "big words," rather than by people who communicate simply, clearly, and thoughtfully. Such a notion about intelligence easily creeps into our thinking as we work with children. Our goal sometimes becomes one of increasing their vocabulary rather than increasing their ability to communicate. Unfortunately, our tendency to set the goal of a large vocabulary is encouraged by the fact that vocabulary growth is so much easier to measure than communication growth.

This is not to say that teachers shouldn't spend a considerable amount of time strengthening children's vocabularies. This is merely to urge teachers to use the concepts of holism and communication as guides in determining how much time is spent on learning the meanings of particular words. As you recall, holism is the idea that the whole is greater than the sum of the parts. Vocabulary is only part of the whole. One can understand every word in a message in the greatest detail and still not understand the message.

Just take the first sentence of the "report" in Chapter 1 about Dr. Feline: "A zoologist from Oxherd University claims to have deciphered the yelps, snarls, and bays of canines." A child can know such "big words" as *zoologist* and *deciphered* very well and completely miss the author's message, which goes something like this: "I'm going to tell you something about human languages by imagining that dogs communicate the way we do."

Reasons for Developing Children's Sight Vocabulary

Since reading includes decoding and comprehension (and more), you won't be able to actually read the sentence below. But you will be able to decode it. Notice how much more fluently you can decode the second line than the first, even though the second line is longer.

The indefeasible and repathic customs of insabulation

have been highly resistant to innumerable endeavors to modify them.

What made the difference in the two lines? Look back at the two lines for a moment and see if you can tell why you were able to decode the second line more rapidly than the first.

Did your visual memory of sight words help you very much in the first line? Not very likely, since *indefeasible* is a word that isn't commonly used, and both *repathic* and *insabulation* are nonsense words. In the second line, though, your sight vocabulary most likely helped you a great deal.

The point is this: to become a skillful reader, a person has to acquire a large reservoir of sight words. Any other means of decoding words, whether through phonic analysis or any other form of word analysis, is slow and even annoying by comparison. Whenever a person has to slacken the pace to analyze a word according to its letters, suffixes, or other parts, both fluency and comprehension tend to suffer.

What all this means to the reading teacher is simply this: children need to be assisted in developing their visual memory—particularly of high-frequency words that are not spelled the way they sound (words such as *any, right,* and *two*). After all, we mature readers rely on word analysis skills only when visual memory fails. Visual memory is what we want children eventually to rely upon more than any other skill when they are decoding.

This does not mean that phonic analysis and other forms of word analysis are not important for children to learn. On the contrary, they are very important forms of decoding. In fact, they're the means through which many new words are learned and added to a person's sight vocabulary.

Nor does this mean that a large sight vocabulary should be developed before phonic analysis and other forms of word analysis are taught. Research (3) has shown that it's seldom advisable to postpone the teaching of phonic analysis. Whenever this happens, children tend to develop the habit of too much guessing and too little noticing of phonic clues.

But how is a sight vocabulary acquired? Basically by frequent exposure, although there are important factors such as meaningfulness and the quality of visual memory which influence the amount of exposure that is necessary. And this leads to two further questions: 1) what words should teachers concentrate on in developing children's sight vocabularies and 2) what techniques can the teacher use to encourage frequent exposure, meaningfulness, and high-quality visual memory?

Sight Words That Are Truly Basic

The words which seem worthy of special, concentrated attention are those that are most common to children's speaking vocabulary; those which are most frequently encountered in printed materials; those that are generally most difficult to learn; and those which particular children cannot remember.

First, why should we be concerned with a child's speaking vocabulary? Simply because decoding, at the initial stage of learning to read, involves the translation of print to speech (vocal or subvocal). If a word is already of frequent occurrence in a child's speaking vocabulary, the decoding process will lead instantly to comprehension and to an increase in fluency. This greater fluency will in turn lead to quicker comprehension of sentences and longer passages.

For example, read the following sentence: I want to give you this ring for your birthday. All of the words in that sentence are generally quite common to a school child's speaking vocabulary. Suppose we leave out the two most difficult words and assume that the rest are sight words.

I want to give you this _____ for your _____ .

We can see that a large proportion of the meaning of the sentence has already been established and that the tough job of decoding and comprehending has been reduced to only two words, both of which can be partially decoded by using the context clues which the sight words provide.

As for the second criterion—frequency of the word in printed materials—its significance in the selection of those words that should have special attention is probably obvious. But what may not be obvious is how the classroom teacher can take on the Herculean task of determining those words which are most frequently encountered in print, in addition to determining the most common words in children's speaking vocabularies. Fortunately, both of these jobs have already been done for you. Back in the 1930s Dolch (10) compiled a list of 220 "basic sight words," mainly by selecting "tool words" (words other than nouns) that were common to three very comprehensive lists developed in the 1920s. Along with the list of basic sight words, Dolch prepared a list of "ninety-five common nouns" which were common to all three lists. The 220 basic sight words, he then discovered, comprised anywhere from 52 percent to 70 percent of all the words children generally encountered in their assigned reading materials. Thus, by learning these 220 words, the children would have more than half the battle won.

For many years these 220 basic sight words—and to a lesser extent, the 95 common nouns—have been important ingredients in reading programs for children. More recently, however, numerous specialists in the field of reading have developed more up-to-date basic lists of words for children to learn. Table 2.1 provides a summary of eight of those lists.

As is to be expected, these word lists do not agree with each other (although there is remarkable consistency if one looks at only the first 100 high-frequency words in each list). On the one hand, I'm inclined to agree with Johnson that the popular list of basic sight words developed by Dolch "has perhaps outlived its usefulness" (19,

Table 2.1 Lists of High-Frequency Basic Sight Words

Compilers	Sources
Barnard and DeGracie (2)	Kindergarten and first grade basal readers from eight different series (found 103 words common to all eight series).
Dolch (10)	The "basic sight words" based on compilations done in the 1920s.
Hillerich (15)	School texts in grades three through nine, creative writing of children in grades one through eight, adult printed material, primary grade library books, the Dolch lists.
Johns (17)	School texts in grades three through nine, primary grade library books, adult printed material, speech of kindergarten and first grade children.
Johns (18)	The forty-six nouns common to the high frequency words in three out of four of the compilations examined in Johns' 1974 study.
Johnson (20)	Adult printed material and the speech of kindergarten and first grade children.
Moe and Hopkins (22)	Speech of kindergarten, first, and second grade children living in middle-class neighborhoods.
Sherk (26)	Speech of four-, five-, and six-year-old children living in lower-class neighborhoods.

Source: Frank B. May, *To Help Children Communicate* (Columbus, OH, Charles E. Merrill Publishing Co., 1980), p. 175.

p. 30). On the other hand, those who have been using Dolch's basic list should rest assured that a large proportion of the words on his list have not gone out of style. In fact, none of them has gone out of style; it's just that many of them can no longer be considered to be words of high frequency.

About 75 percent of Dolch's 220 basic sight words can be found on the Johnson list, for example. Words such as *the, go,* and *of* are on both lists and are entitled to be called "basic" sight words. Words such as *clean, wash,* and *shall* appear only on Dolch's list and probably should be retired as basic sight words—as should most of Dolch's "ninety-five common nouns." Only about 30 percent of his nouns can be found on the Johnson list. Some of the words that were on Dolch's list of nouns, such as *cow, chicken, corn, duck, farm, farmer,* and *stock* are not to be found on the Johnson list. Instead you will find nouns like *people, world, city,* and *group.*

So, which list should a teacher use? If Dolch's list is out-of-date, is Johnson's list a better one to use? Is Johns' "Word List for the 1970's" the answer? How about Fry's or Mitzel's? One could become slightly neurotic trying to choose from among all the excellent lists that have been compiled.

It seems probable that the nature of today's reading instruction makes all of the lists obsolete for some purposes. Dolch's list was popular at a time when the majority of teachers were using the "look-say method" of teaching reading. Words were presented over and again until children knew the words "by sight." Consequently, visual memory was called upon more than phonics. Only after children had learned a large body of words by sight was phonics introduced. And often phonics was introduced in an incidental fashion, rather than as a systematic form of instruction.

Today, judging from examination of the most popular reading programs and from observations in classrooms, phonics is in vogue. In most programs today, children are receiving phonics instruction either from the beginning of instruction or following a brief exposure to the language-experience approach, in which children first learn to read what they have dictated.

Newer and newer lists are being created to replace the Dolch list, without first examining the question "what kind of list do we need?" Obviously we want children to be able to read words on sight. This is the most efficient means of reading. But the question then becomes "how do we get them to that point?"

Since about three-fourths of the words in "high-frequency" word lists have regular (phonetic) spelling—words such as *hit* and *lunch*—those words can be learned by children through phonics lessons or other word-analysis lessons. For instance, even though the word *hit* is a high-frequency word, it needn't be learned primarily through visual-memory techniques. The word *hit* is highly regular in spelling and can easily be picked up as part of one or more phonics lessons.

This approach will allow you to concentrate your teaching via visual-memory techniques on that portion of high-frequency words that is irregular (nonphonetic) in spelling—words such as *one* and *any.*

In Table 2.2, then, you have a list of ninety-six high-frequency words that should be taught through visual-memory techniques. These ninety-six words were chosen not only because they were irregular in spelling, but also because they were found on at least two of the eight lists described in Table 2.1. Thus, as a list, the words represent oral vocabularies as well as written vocabularies, adults as well as children, lower-income neighborhoods as well as middle-income neighborhoods, and various geographic areas. I'd like to recommend that you use this list both for testing children's sight vocabulary and for selecting words for instruction.

*Table 2.2 Basic Sight Vocabulary—Irregular Words Only**

	A	B	C	D	E	F
1.	anything	give	great	Mrs.	says	very
2.	a	could	group	night	should	want
3.	because	do	have	nothing	some	water
4.	again	does	head	of	something	was
5.	almost	done	knew	brother	the	were
6.	another	door	heard	on	sometimes	wanted
7.	always	buy	know	off	their	what
8.	any	enough	light	one	they	where
9.	are	four	only	long	who	thought
10.	been	from	dog	other	there	father
11.	both	friend	many	own	through	goes
12.	brought	full	might	people	to	work
13.	house	don't	money	put	together	you
14.	city	live	mother	right	today	would
15.	come	gone	Mr.	said	two	your
16.	year	they're	school	our	there's	once

*A guide to the selection of words to test and teach through visual memory.

Methods of Increasing Children's Sight Vocabulary

So now we've come to the problem of how to help children develop a sight vocabulary. That is, what techniques can the teacher use? In a very practical sense, one of the techniques is simply that of having children read (with guidance) the stories and articles in basal readers and other reading materials. In basal readers, for example, the authors have purposely provided frequent exposure to common words. In the primer of one series, the word *see* is introduced in the first story on the first page. It is repeated five times in that story and thirty-two times in the rest of the book, and this includes neither the times it is repeated in the workbook nor the times it will be repeated by the teacher.

A second way of developing sight vocabularies is through the use of Ashton-Warner's technique called "key words" (1). This approach is one of the forms of language-experiences approaches described in Chapter 12. Each day children decide on one or more new words that they want to learn. These words are different for each child in the classroom and have special meaning to them—words such as *mother, father, kiss, fight, love,* and so on. Because these words have personal meaningfulness and some degree of emotional over-tones, they tend to be learned rapidly—more rapidly than "simple" words like *this, then,* and *about.*

A third method of increasing sight vocabularies is through the development of visual memory. *Visual memory,* as this term is applied to reading instruction, is the ability to recognize, recall, and produce letters and letter sequences. Visual memory calls on the child's ability not only to tell the differences between letters and to know their names, but also to remember sequences of letters that represent actual words. (In a very practical sense, visual memory also calls on the child's ability to write the letters from memory—both in isolation and in correct sequence.) Since the development of visual memory is discussed under the topic of readiness in Chapter 7, we won't go into further details on this now. Notice, however, that visual memory is called upon constantly in the sample lesson that will soon follow.

A fourth way of increasing sight vocabularies is through highly structured lessons on specific words that particular children are having trouble learning. The experience of many teachers shows that these lessons need to incorporate spelling. As research (3) has shown, the actual spelling of a word in writing seems to help considerably in developing children's visual memories of the word. Simply having children look at a word as a whole is not enough. Nor does it help most children to notice "configuration clues." Some teachers try to help clarify the visual image of a word by having the children notice the shapes of the words. This approach, though, may create more confusion than clarity in the long run. Configuration clues may clarify the contrast between and and that , but this type of clue is not applicable to he and to or to was and saw .

A Sample Lesson on Sight Vocabulary

The following is an example of a type of lesson that may be used to help particular children who are having trouble remembering how to decode particular words as they read. There are many other ways of having children learn sight words; the following is only *one* way that has proven successful:

Step 1:   *Introduce the words in context.* About two to five words is enough. If you introduce more, it will be difficult for the children to master them. (Normally you will be working with a small group of children, rather than the entire class. It is assumed that they have already learned how to write each letter of the alphabet.)

   A.   Write sentences containing the words on the chalkboard, using manuscript printing. Underline the particular words you will be emphasizing. (Notice in the example below that the underlined words were selected from the list of ninety-six irregular basic sight words in Table 2.2.)

> "Who put my ball there?" he asked.
> "I want my ball back."

    B.   Read the sentences to your small group of children.

    C.   Have the children say the sentences with you.

    D.   Point to one of the underlined words, pronounce it, and ask a child to make up another sentence using the same word. Have a different child do the same with each underlined word.

    E.   Point to one of the underlined words, pronounce it, and ask a child to spell it out loud. Have her pronounce it after she has spelled it. Have a different child do the same with each underlined word.

Step 2:   *Have the children enhance their visual memory and auditory memory of the word.*

    A.   Have them look at one of the words and spell it to themselves. (By having them spell the word out loud and to themselves, you are helping them to enhance their auditory memory as well as their visual memory of the letters in the word.)

    B.   Have them close their eyes and imagine themselves writing it on their paper.

    C.   Ask them to open their eyes to see if they have it correct.

Step 3:   *Ask them to write the same word from memory.*

    A.   Have them look at the word again and spell it to themselves.

    B.   Cover the word and ask them to write the word on their papers.

    C.   Uncover the word and ask them to check to see if they have it correct.

    D.   Check each child's paper to make sure she has the word correct.

Step 4:   *Repeat Steps 2 and 3 for each of the underlined words.* Although writing the word provides excellent *spelling* practice, the main idea is to augment the visual and auditory experience with a kinesthetic experience. In other words, eyes, ears, and arm muscles are all involved in perceiving the word. Regardless of whether such muscle involvement, in itself, makes a difference, or whether the writing simply causes the child to visualize a word more accurately, research, as mentioned earlier, indicates that writing words "helps the child to commit them to his sight vocabulary" (2, p. 124).

Step 5:   *Have them practice recognizing the words in isolation.*
     A.   With the words written on flash cards, expose each one for about one second to the group and ask them to say it out loud.
     B.   Expose each one again to one child at a time.

Step 6:   *Repeat Steps 2 through 5 with the first letter of each word capitalized (Who, There, Want).*

Step 7:   *To ensure that positive transfer takes place, arrange for them to practice the words in context.*
     A.   Go back to the sentences you put on the board at the beginning of the lesson and ask the children to read them without your help.
     B.   Have them search for the words in their basal reader or other reading material.

Step 8:   *Distribute the practice with games and activities over several days and weeks.* There are a variety of ways of making the practice sessions different each time. Here are a few examples of some "practice" sessions:
     A.   Play the number-line game.
        1.   Draw a number line from zero to ten for each child who will play the game.

Betty   0 1 2 3 4 5 6 7 8 9 10

John   0 1 2 3 4 5 6 7 8 9 10

Sam   0 1 2 3 4 5 6 7 8 9 10

        2.   Prepare a stack of about fifteen three-by-five cards, some with →1, some with →2, and some with →3 on them. Place them face down.
        3.   Flash a word card for one second to each child in turn, who must read the card to be permitted to draw a number off the top of the number stack. (She misses her chance if she cannot say it within three seconds after you've flashed the card.)
        4.   The child must then place an X above the correct number on the number line.
        5.   The first one to get to the 10 wins.
     B.   Before children get to go somewhere—lunch, recess, home—they have to tell you the "password," which is simply a word on one of the flash cards.

C. Have the children use one of the self-instructional feedback machines. On one such machine,* for example, the child looks at a flash card, attempts to decode the word printed on it, and then runs the card through a type of tape recorder to hear what the word is. Earphones may be used with the machine, so that other children in the room are not disturbed.

In summary, the steps recommended for a lesson on sight vocabulary are the following:

1. Introduce the words in context.
2. Have the children enhance their visual and auditory memory of the word through spelling.
3. Ask them to write the same word from memory.
4. Repeat Steps 2 and 3 for each of the words.
5. Have them practice decoding the words in isolation.
6. Repeat Steps 2 through 5 with the first letter of each word capitalized.
7. Arrange for them to practice the words in context.
8. Distribute the practice with games and activities over several days and weeks.

For the children who are slow or disabled learners, these steps may be insufficient. Chapter 17 provides information and guidance on working with these children. For most children, however, the steps provide a good way of learning particular words.

In the list of suggested readings at the end of this chapter, you will find books by Anderson, Burie, Mallet, and Russell that contain games designed to strengthen children's sight vocabulary. In addition to those games, I'd like to recommend three that are favorites of the children with whom I've worked. These can be found in Appendix A. They're called "Word Chase," "Word Toss," and "Steal the Words." In Appendix A you'll also find other games that you may wish to order from various companies.

Some Essential Ingredients of a Semantic Vocabulary

We've been talking about increasing children's sight vocabulary. Now let's spend some time talking about developing their semantic vocabulary. *Semantic vocabulary* consists of those words that a person under-

---

*The Language Master (Bell & Howell) or the TTC Magnetic Card Reader (Teaching Technology Corporation) or the efi Audio Flashcard System (Educational Futures, Inc.).

stands well enough to use appropriately in speech and writing or to receive with comprehension in a listening or reading situation. As with the development of a sight vocabulary, the development of a semantic vocabulary can be a holistic experience and is enhanced by the contributions of all four language arts. As one gains understanding of a word through a listening experience, this same word becomes more understandable in a reading situation—and vice versa. As one learns to use a word with understanding in speech, this same word becomes more useful to a person in writing—and vice versa.

The language-in-reverse trap that we discussed earlier should be mentioned again. When children are having trouble reading words with understanding, the solution is not always one of providing more reading practice. The solution is, more often than not, one of providing more practice in speaking and listening to those words.

When we talk about developing children's semantic vocabularies, we run into that difficult measurement problem again. When we say that a child understands a word, what does this really mean? Enough to understand an author's message? Well enough to use the word appropriately in a sentence? It depends, of course, on what one means by "understanding" a word. Does the average adult or child always comprehend a simple word like *run* when it occurs all by itself in print? Probably not, since the word *run* has dozens of meanings. In fact, most large dictionaries have between 100 and 200 entries for this word—ranging from "to move with haste" to "the distance that a golf ball moves along the ground after landing from a stroke."

So when we speak of Frank's "semantic vocabulary," we have to have a rather loose definition in mind—something like "those words that make sense to him in context." That is, he understands their meaning in a particular context.

But perhaps we can get at this term *semantic vocabulary* from a negative standpoint. We do know, for instance, that some children can decode words without understanding their meaning. Such behavior has been labeled "word calling" and is often the result of teaching that emphasizes decoding without enough attention to meaning—not enough concern for "What does that mean to you, Judie? Can you tell me what's happening in your own words?"

Anyone who has tried to learn a foreign language by way of print rather than conversation has probably experienced the phenomenon of word calling. If one learns the phonic principles of Spanish, for instance, it is rather easy to decode the following sentence without comprehending it:

¿Como está usted, señor?

That is, a person can make the right noises, but not know what he is saying.

What is needed, then, for understanding to occur? What is needed for a semantic vocabulary to develop? Essentially, two basic ingredients are necessary: nonverbal experience and verbal experience. Let's take this sentence for example:

> We're going to make a snowman.

Whether Jim understands the word *snowman* in this sentence will depend on his verbal and nonverbal experiences with the word and what it represents. To understand it very deeply, he needs to have had some experiences with real snow. He needs to have experienced the fun and the technical complications involved in building a snowman. It may make the comprehension even deeper if he's had the experience of waiting impatiently for snow of the right stickiness.

But what else does he need besides the experience itself? He needs to have communicated about it—to have listened to others talk about it, and preferably to have talked about it himself. Remember that reading, for young readers, usually involves vocalizing or subvocalizing. It should be somewhat easier, then, for Jim to recognize a printed word that he has often already vocalized himself than one that he has only heard someone else vocalize.

On the other hand, Wyman lives in the deep South and has never experienced the building of a snowman. Is comprehension of the word *snowman* an impossibility for him? In the deepest sense of the word *comprehension,* the answer is yes. But vicarious experiences such as viewing a picture will make it possible for him to "read" the word well enough to comprehend an entire sentence or story about a snowman with fairly deep understanding.

Using Dale's Cone of Experience

Edgar Dale (8) has developed a useful model for teachers to use when planning ways to help children improve their vocabularies (and thus to improve their ability to make good psycholinguistic guesses while reading). This model is called the *Cone of Experience* and is shown in Figure 2.1. To simplify Dale's theory, children learn at the deepest and most intense level through direct, purposeful experiences, the base of Dale's cone. They learn at the shallowest and least intense level through sheer verbal experiences, the tip of the cone. In between the base and the tip of the cone are vicarious (indirect) experiences, which provide different depths and intensities of learning. Next to a direct experience of driving a car, for instance, the deepest and most intense experience would be that of a contrived experience with a mock-up car, one that simulates a road, other cars, a crash, and so on.

In theory at least, the information we receive at the verbal level (including new words) often goes in one ear and out the other,

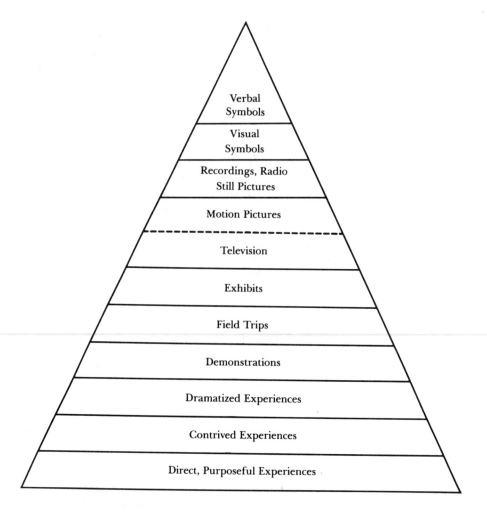

Figure 2.1. *Dale's Cone of Experience. From* AUDIOVISUAL
METHODS IN TEACHING, *Third Edition by Edgar Dale. Copyright 1946, 1954, © 1969 by Holt, Rinehart and Winston. Reprinted by permission of Holt, Rinehart and Winston.*

sticking inside just long enough to use it for passing a test. Information we receive at the direct level of experience (such as the word *hot* the moment we touch a hot stove) tends to stay with us longer and to become a part of our readily available source of words or concepts.

Let's take the words *rozaga hunt* as an example. The best way to teach David about a rozaga hunt would be to take him on one. Let him get up with you in the middle of the night, carry one of the four-celled flashlights in one hand and the sharpened spear in the other, and stumble through the woods toward the swamp. Let him listen to the hurrumping of the bull frogs, the hooting of the owls, and that eerie low whistle of the rozaga. Let him shiver with fright as he unexpectedly comes face to face with one, its fangs and yellow eyes highlighting the swanlike neck covered with dark leathery scales, its snakelike tongue darting in and out of its mouth only three feet away from David's right arm. Let him hear your shout of warning and feel his tight-muscled arm jab the spear through the vital spot, right through the neck. Do you have any doubt that David will forget the word *rozaga?* (The reader should be assured that there are no rozagas lurking about. The rozaga is a creature of the author's imagination.)

Assuming for a moment that the rozaga is a real animal, let us suppose you are teaching a social-studies unit on the rozaga hunters of North Borneo. You are trying to show how these people have adapted to their environment, and since rozaga hunting is their chief means of survival, it is important that your students understand the words *rozaga hunt.* Since you plan to discuss these people on and off for the next few weeks, you want your students to make the words *rozaga hunt* part of their vocabulary. What should you do?

Obviously, you can't provide them with the direct experience of rozaga hunting. So, looking at Dale's Cone of Experience, what would be your next best learning experience? A contrived experience would probably be out because of the time and expense. (Although taking apart and putting together a plaster model of a rozaga would be one type of contrived experience.)

What about a dramatized experience of a rozaga hunt? This would be excellent after they have developed some simpler ideas of what a rozaga is and how a rozaga hunt is carried out. In fact, telling the students that they will eventually get to enact a rozaga hunt will spur most of them on to finding out more about a rozaga hunt.

The next layers of the Cone of Experience suggest the use of demonstrations, field trips, and exhibits. Having someone (such as the teacher) who has seen a movie of a rozaga hunt provide a demonstration of the hunt would help the children get a deeper understanding of the concept. A field trip, in this case, would be impractical, unless you were able to take them to a museum showing exhibits related to the rozaga hunt. At an exhibit, they would be able to see the weapon and perhaps a stuffed rozaga close at hand.

A movie or a televised documentary, although not providing the close-at-hand experience of the exhibit, would provide the emotional impact that has so far been missing in your attempts to get them to understand a rozaga hunt. But if nothing else is available, perhaps you'll at least have some still pictures showing the rozaga and the hunters and perhaps a recording of someone describing an actual rozaga hunt.

As you can see, we've reached the top of the Cone of Experience with nothing left but visual symbols (such as diagrams or maps) and verbal symbols (words and definitions). You could simply write the word *rozaga* on the board and say, "A rozaga is an amphibian with dark leathery scales and a swanlike neck living in the swamps of North Borneo." That would take a lot less time than all the vicarious experiences we've been discussing. And there are plenty of times when that's all a word deserves. But if you truly want the children to make a word part of their vocabularies, you've got to back up the verbal experience with one or more nonverbal ones.

Using the Dictionary

Must all words for a semantic vocabulary be developed through direct or vicarious experiences? What about the "good old dictionary," or just picking up new words in context as the child begins to read for recreation and information? An important point: to learn all words through direct or nearly direct experiences would require the nine lives of a cat. Many words must be added to a person's reading vocabulary just through reading and discussion, looking up words in a dictionary, and through wide, thoughtful reading. And yet, an understanding of explanations that are presented through discussions, dictionaries, and context clues is dependent upon prior experiences—direct, vicarious, and verbal.

For instance, if you look up the word *excursion* in a dictionary you may find this as one meaning, "a short journey or trip." Now, having the children look up this word in a dictionary is a much quicker and more sensible way of getting them to discover its meaning than packing them up and taking them for an excursion—providing you're sure of two things: 1) the children have all experienced a journey or trip and 2) they have all heard (and preferably spoken) the word *trip* or *journey* in this context. (If Bobbie has only heard the word *trip* used in connection with drugs, she may be somewhat puzzled.)

Having children learn a new word through a dictionary, then, is not a bad idea—as long as you've checked the definition to see if it contains only those words that probably do relate to their previous experiences. Just telling them to "look it up," though, may be like inviting them to partake of stone soup (the definition may be as indigestible as a stone).

If you do decide to have children learn a new word through a dictionary, there are other precautions you may want to consider. For one thing, looking up a word in a dictionary is not a single skill. When you get to Chapter 4, you'll see that there are at least ten separate skills that a child must have in order to look up just the pronunciation of a word (see page 110). After making use of those ten skills to find out how to pronounce the word, the child then has to employ another set of skills to find out what it means.

Let's take the word *record* as an illustration of this. Suppose Bobbie, a fifth grader, is asked to read this sentence:

He had an unbroken record of lying to adults.

Naturally her first-image is of a nice uncracked disk that can be placed on a spindle to produce music magically. After all, she can only take meaning from the printed page by first bringing meaning to it. And the meaning she brings to it is based on previous experiences.

Unfortunately the image of an uncracked disk doesn't seem to relate to the author's message. Thus the teacher has her look up the word *record* in the dictionary. After completing the ten steps necessary for determining the word's pronunciation, she discovers that it has two pronunciations.

Then Bobbie looks underneath the definitions and reads the synonyms: *note, phonograph record, catalogue, inventory.* None of these makes any sense when applied to the sentence, so she next starts reading through the various definitions and finds to her dismay that there are an awful lot of them—including some for *record* as a noun and some for *record* as a verb.

"Is it a noun or a verb?" she asks in desperation.

"It's a noun in this sentence," the teacher mercifully replies.

"Does that mean I can skip all these down here?" she asks hopefully.

"Yes," she says. "Just read the ones under *noun.*"

Bobbie reads the first definition: "a written account of events." Bobbie looks at the teacher. "What's an account?" she asks.

"A description."

"A description of events?"

"That's right," the teacher says.

"What does that mean?"

"Well," the teacher says, "it means you had some things that happened and you wrote them down."

Bobbie nods with understanding and looks back at the sentence about the unbroken record of lying to adults. "He has an unbroken written account of lying to adults," she says. "That doesn't make sense."

The teacher smiles. "No, that doesn't make sense. Try the next definition and see if that one makes sense."

Bobbie tries three more and on the third one finds one that seems to fit the meaning of the sentence: "the past performance of a person." Bobbie smiles. "I get it. If he had an unbroken record of lying, it means he's always lied to adults. Is that what it means?"

The teacher agrees and smiles with satisfaction: things don't always work out that easily when a child tries to garner meaning through a dictionary.

In list form, in order for Bobbie to comprehend the meaning of a word that she's looking up in a dictionary, she has to be able to do these things:

1. Determine whether one of the most common synonyms fits the context of a particular sentence
2. Determine the part of speech of the unknown word (not absolutely essential but helpful)

3. Read each definition (preferably under the correct grammatical class) and see whether it matches the context of the particular sentence
4. Rephrase the meaning of the sentence in her own words

Perhaps it is clear, then, that before we ask children to look it up, we'd be wise to teach them all of the subskills involved—the ten listed in Chapter 4 and the four listed above. Each one of the fourteen subskills should probably be used as a focus for a single lesson with the dictionary. Practice exercises to supplement actual dictionary use can be found in most basal-series programs—either in the teachers' guides or in the students' workbooks. Many publishers of school dictionaries will provide teachers with pamphlets on how to provide interesting lessons on dictionary skills. In Chapter 4 are several sample lessons that will serve as guides for developing your own lessons.

Learning Words through Reading

A large number of new words that children add to their semantic vocabulary is acquired through actual reading—of their basal readers, their library books, and their textbooks in the content areas. Before children read a selection in their basal reader or social-studies textbook, for instance, the teacher usually clarifies the meaning of key words in the selection. This tends to increase their understanding not only of the key words themselves but of the entire story or article.

Sometimes teachers discuss far too many words prior to having the children read. Frequently this is due to the fact that teachers' editions of the basal reader or content-area textbook list too many for the teacher to discuss. But whatever the reason, it is usually impossible to do justice to more than three or four words in the time available. Many of the words that the teachers explain to the children can be comprehended through context clues; to clarify these words ahead of time is to deprive the children of the opportunity to practice this valuable skill. Therefore, when selecting key words for prereading discussion, try to choose those that meet more than one of these criteria:

1. Those words which cannot be easily comprehended through the context clues provided in the selection
2. Those words that are crucial to providing the necessary experiential background for the selection (An article about telephone repairs, for instance, might require an explanation of the word "splicing.")
3. Those words which are obviously not part of the sight vocabulary of most students involved

4. Those words that may be difficult to decode as well as comprehend

In addition to learning new words through assigned reading, children may learn numerous words through their informal reading of library books. Most of these words are picked up through context clues and through repetition. The more children read on their own like this, the more their semantic vocabulary generally grows.

Some teachers like to ensure that children pick up additional vocabulary by having them keep cards or a notebook in which they write new words, their definitions, and the sentence that contained each word. The cards or notebooks are periodically used by pairs of children to test each other on how many words they know.*

Learning Words through Context Clues

Context analysis is probably the major tool for building a semantic vocabulary. Unless a child is skillful in using context analysis, no psycholinguistic guessing can take place and little intelligent reading will occur. Yet, unless you demonstrate how to use context clues, many children skip over "hard words" like foot soldiers dodging land mines. A few dutifully plow through a dictionary at the slightest difficulty, thus slowing themselves down far more than necessary.

During regular reading instruction, there are many opportunities to show children how to make an intelligent guess of a word's meaning. Perhaps the best way to motivate children to learn from your demonstration, though, is first to list the words on the board before they begin their reading of a selection. Then, for the first word, tell them only the page number and challenge them to "see who can discover what it means by reading the words around it." If a child gets the meaning correct, have him explain his "secret method" of finding out what it means. Then do the same for each of the other words.

On those occasions when children can't discover a secret method, you will actually need to teach them a method (or refer them to a dictionary). Here are some of the methods you may wish to teach them:

1. "Double-comma" clues: children usually enjoy searching for these. They're straightforward and easy to spot—even by the reluctant reader.

   The *gully,* a deep ditch, was full of water.

   The *galloon,* or braid, was made of silver thread.

---

*See Chapter 13 for more ideas.

2. Definition clues: these are usually easy and need very little demonstration by the teacher.

> "The kind of *poke* I'm talkin' about is a small bag."

> An *ophthalmologist* is a doctor who treats eye diseases.

3. Mood clues: these are much more difficult to use and may require several demonstrations by the teacher.

> The house was dark. The wind was howling through the cracks like ghosts. I was *terrified*.

> First he'd lost his best friend. Then he'd lost his bus fare. He was totally *depressed*.

4. "Building-block" clues: these are simply derivatives—words built by adding suffixes and other word parts to an original word.

> She *unwillingly* walked to school. *(willing)* + *(un)* + *(ly)*

> He was *unfastening* his seat belt.

5. "Interpreter" clues: these are clues derived from the reader's interpretations or inferences and are the most difficult to demonstrate.

> His *opponent* for the boxing match looked much stronger and bigger.

> He was so angry his face was *florid*.

Using the Cloze Technique to Improve Vocabulary

To understand this particular use of the "cloze technique,"* try completing the following passage:

> The racers started their engines and _____ to the starting line. The starting signal was given and the drivers _____ on their accelerators. The roar of the engines was _____ . Thirty seconds later the lead car _____ into the concrete barrier on the north turn and burst into _____ flames.

What skills were required for you to complete the blanks? Not only were you asked to comprehend the author's message, you also

---

*Other uses of the cloze technique will be described in later chapters.

were required to call to mind those verbs and adjectives that would help the author describe the scene accurately and colorfully.

When using this type of device to improve children's vocabulary, it's a good idea to fill in the blanks as a group enterprise. In this way, children can learn words from each other. Billy may fill in the first blank with *drove,* but Ken may think of *coasted,* and Brenda could come up with *taxied.* By writing all three on the chalkboard, the teacher can reinforce their visual image of the words. Then the teacher can help them visualize the subtle differences in the three words, using questions such as these:

1. What picture do you get in your mind when you use the word *coasted? (taxied? drove?)*
2. What are some other times when you might see the word *coasted? (taxied? drove?)*
3. In what way do all three words have the same meaning?
4. In what ways do the three words have different meanings?

Learning Words through Semantic Mapping

Perhaps the best way for you to understand or review the concept of semantic mapping is to complete the semantic map shown in Figure 2.2. (Please see Figure 2.2, p. 58, before continuing).

Now that you've completed Figure 2.2, you can see that semantic mapping is a procedure for extending the meaning of a word by showing the categories of words that relate to it. Semantic mapping is based on the premise that everything we learn must be related to something else that we already understand. If I want to teach the meaning of the fictitious word *rozaga,* for instance, I may relate it to words such as *fangs, swan, leather, snake, hunting, spear, swamp,* and so on.

The advantage of the semantic-mapping process is that it enables a child not only to visualize the relationships, but to categorize them as well. Such categorization reinforces both the understanding of the word in question and the child's ability to perceive similarities and differences in the environment.

The steps that one might use for semantic mapping with children are these:

1. Select a word that you want them to understand in more depth.
2. Provide direct and vicarious experiences related to the word.
3. Have each child write down as many words that she thinks have some relationship to the word as she can.
4. Map and categorize the words together on the chalkboard.
5. Have them create a title for each category. (For Figure 2.2, the categories may be building materials, rooms, and what else?)

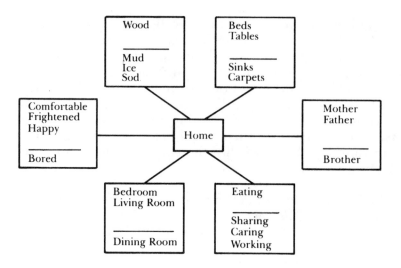

Figure 2.2. *A Semantic Map for the Word* **Home**

Learning Words through Affix Meanings

A large percentage of words are derivatives. The words *unhappy* and *happiness,* for example, are derivatives of the word *happy.* In order for children to understand such derivatives when they see them in print, they need to understand the meanings of *affixes* (prefixes and suffixes) such as *un* and *ness.* They also need to develop a visual memory of such common affixes; ways of developing this visual memory are described in Chapter 5. For now, let me simply remind you of familiar affixes that have a reasonably consistent meaning from one derivative to another.

Affix	*Approximate Meaning*	*Example*
un	the reverse or opposite of	unhappy
anti	against	antigravity
pre	before	preview
re	again	repaint
sub	under	subway
dis	the reverse or opposite of	disappear
ful	full of	colorful
less	without	sleeveless
ness	the quality of being	politeness
proof	able to withstand	waterproof

Summary

In this chapter we've discussed various ways of assisting children in the development of sight and semantic vocabularies. The basic difference between these two types of vocabularies is that a sight vocabulary relies on visual memory and a semantic vocabulary relies on experiential background. Numerous ways of strengthening children's visual memory of particular words have been suggested, along with means of enriching the associations that children have between experiences and words. The development of oral vocabulary and of the language arts in general has been shown to be vital to the development of both sight and semantic vocabularies.

References and Suggested Reading

1. Ashton-Warner, Sylvia. *Teacher*. New York: Simon and Schuster, 1963.
2. Barnard, Douglas P., and DeGracie, James. "Vocabulary Analysis of New Primary Reading Series." *Reading Teacher* 30 (November 1976): 177–80.
3. Bond, Guy L., and Dykstra, Robert. "The Cooperative Program in First Grade Reading Instruction." *Reading Research Quarterly* 2 (1967): 5–142.
4. Burie, Audrey Ann, and Heltshe, Mary Ann. *Reading with a Smile: 90 Reading Games that Work*. Washington, D.C.: Acropolis Books, 1975.
5. Center for Applied Research in Education. *Games, Puzzles, Spirit Masters, Books, and Other Materials Related to Vocabulary Development*. P.O. Box 130, West Nyack, New York 10095.
6. Chomsky, Carol. "Language and Reading." In *Applied Linguistics and Reading*, edited by Robert E. Shafer. Newark, DE: International Reading Association, 1979.
7. Dale, Edgar. "Vocabulary Measurement: Techniques and Major Findings." *Elementary English* 42 (1965): 895–901, 948.
8. Dale, Edgar. *Audio Visual Methods in Teaching*. New York: Holt, Rinehart, and Winston, 1969.
9. Deighton, Lee C. *Vocabulary Development in the Classroom*. New York: Columbia University, Teachers College Press, 1959.
10. Dolch, Edward W. "A Basic Sight Vocabulary." *Elementary School Journal* 36 (February 1936): 456–60.
11. Forester, Ann D., and Norma I. Mickelson. "Language Acquisition and Learning to Read." In *Applied Linguistics and Reading*, edited by Robert E. Shafer. Newark, DE: International Reading Association, 1978.
12. Fromkin, Victoria, and Rodman, Robert. *An Introduction to Language*. New York: Holt, Rinehart, and Winston, 1978.

13. Goodman, Kenneth S. "A Linguistic Study of Cues and Miscues in Reading." *Elementary English* (October 1965): 639–43.

14. Hanf, M. B. "Mapping: a Technique for Translating Reading into Thinking." *Journal of Reading* 14 (1971): 225, 230, 270.

15. Hillerich, Robert L. "Word Lists—Getting it All Together." *Reading Teacher* 27 (January 1974): 353–60.

16. Hunter, Diana Lee. "Spoken and Written Word Lists: a Comparison." *Reading Teacher* 29 (December 1975): 250–53.

17. Johns, Jerry L. "Updating the Dolch Basic Sight Vocabulary for the Schools of the 1970's." Paper presented at the annual convention of the International Reading Association. New Orleans: May 1974.

18. Johns, Jerry L. "Dolch List of Common Nouns—a Comparison." *Reading Teacher* 28 (March 1974): 538–40.

19. Johnson, Dale D. "The Dolch List Reexamined." *Reading Teacher* 24 (February 1971): 449–57.

20. Johnson, Dale D. "A Basic Vocabulary for Beginning Reading." *Elementary School Journal* 72 (October 1971): 29–34.

21. Mallet, Jerry J. *101 Make-and-Play Reading Games for the Intermediate Grades.* Englewood Cliffs, NJ: Center for Applied Research in Education, 1977.

22. Moe, Alden J., and Hopkins, Carol J. "The Speaking Vocabularies of Kindergarten, First-Grade, and Second-Grade Children." *Research in Education* (March 1975) ERIC Report ED 105465.

23. Petty, Walter, et al. The State of Knowledge about the Teaching of Vocabulary. Cooperative Research Project 3128. Urbana, IL: National Council of Teachers of English, 1968.

24. Russell, David H. et al. *Reading Aids through the Grades: a Guide to Materials and 440 Activities for Individualizing Reading Activities.* New York: Columbia University, Teachers College Press, 1975.

25. Shafer, Robert E., ed. *Applied Linguistics and Reading.* Newark, DE: International Reading Association, 1978.

26. Sherk, Jr., John K. *A Word Count of Spoken English of Culturally Disadvantaged Preschool and Elementary Pupils.* Columbia, MO: University of Missouri, 1973.

27. Smith, Frank. *Understanding Reading.* New York: Holt, Rinehart, and Winston, 1971.

28. Smith, James A. *Creative Teaching of the Language Arts in the Elementary School.* Boston: Allyn and Bacon, 1976.

Application Experiences for the Teacher-Education Class

1. Each person in the class can be given one of the following statements to defend or deny. After a few minutes of preparation, all those who have statement *a* should first explain in their own words why it is either

true or false and then read one or two sentences from the book that will demonstrate the author's position on the statement. (The same procedure can be followed for the rest of the statements.)

Statements about Chapter 2

NOTE: Literal-level and inferential-level statements are mixed together for this chapter.

a.   The word *ice cream* is part of the sight vocabulary and semantic vocabulary for many children entering school for the first time.

b.   Sight words are recognized through phonic analysis.

c.   A child's sight vocabulary cannot actually be measured.

d.   Whether a child understands a word or not depends partly on what the measurer means by *understands*.

e.   A child can have a large semantic vocabulary and still not be a good reader.

f.   A sight vocabulary is acquired mainly through frequent exposure; but a word like *mother* or *ice cream* will generally need less exposure than a word like *there* or *any*.

g.   The words that teachers should help children learn through visual-memory techniques are those that are regular (phonetic) in spelling.

h.   Sight vocabulary influences comprehension.

i.   The Dolch lists consist of those words that all children should have in their sight vocabulary.

j.   Lessons on sight vocabularies are similar to lessons on spelling.

k.   To teach all of the words from the "basic vocabulary of ninety-six irregular words" through the use of the game called "Steal the Words," you would need to make six decks of cards with sixty-four cards in each deck. See Appendix. A.

l.   Two basic ingredients are needed for the development of a semantic vocabulary: nonverbal experience and verbal experience.

m.   The word *ocean* is one that would be part of most children's semantic vocabulary.

n.   Learning the meaning of a word through the use of a dictionary is easier than many other ways.

o.   Before children are asked to read a selection, the teacher should explain all words in the selection that may be difficult.

p.   "Double-comma clues" are easier to learn to use than "mood clues."

2.   Prepare a semantic map of the world *tools*. You may wish to do this in small groups and then compare your maps. See pages 57–58.

3.   Construct a "Word Chase" game and try it out with others in the class (see Appendix A).

4.   Carry on a "sight-word-game hunt." Find ideas from books and teachers for games that will help children learn high-frequency words by sight. Each person can explain one to the rest of the class.

5. In groups of two to four people, each person can teach the rest of the small group two "sight words," using the steps suggested on pages 44–47. To make it more interesting and challenging, use irregular and nonsensical words that you make up, such as *phightonni* (/fī′ tə nē).

6. Tell how you would use Dale's Cone of Experience to develop deep meaning for the word *growth* in this story title: *The Growth of a City.*

7. Complete the "cloze" passage together on page 56. See how many different words you can list for each blank.

Field Experiences in the Elementary-School Classroom

1. Develop a semantic map with a small group or with the entire class. You might use a word such as *tools* or *teacher* or *food;* with older children you might use a more difficult word from their social-studies, science, or mathematics textbook.

2. Teach a child to play "Word Chase," "Steal the Words," or some other sight-word-development game (see Appendix A). If possible, include some words in the game that you have determined to be slightly difficult for him.

3. Develop a "cloze" passage similar in format to the one on page 56. Make sure that most of the context words (the words other than those which go into the blanks) are sight words. (If the passage is too difficult, this exercise will not work very well.) Help a group of children complete the passage, using the techniques on page 57.

4. Develop and teach a lesson on learning words through context clues, using the suggestions on pages 55–56. Try to incorporate in your lesson some ways for children to teach you how to use context clues. Teach them the "double-comma clue" and other clues only when you see that they can't discover such clues themselves.

5. Select a word from a selection the children are assigned to read; help the children develop deep meaning for it; use Dale's Cone of Experience to think of nonverbal and verbal experiences for them to have.

6. Teach a child two or three sight words, using the steps suggested in Chapter 2 on pages 44–47. The words you select should be those that the child is having some difficulty remembering.

7. Select one or more children and see how many words in the "basic vocabulary of ninety-six irregular sight words" they recognize in a one-second exposure. You will need to develop flash cards; or, if you use a list, you will need to conceal each word after it's been exposed for one second. (Otherwise they will have time to use phonic-analysis techniques.)

CHAPTER 3

Children need to be taught the various ways of deciphering words without help from others.

Using Phonic and Linguistic Methods of Instruction

Chapter Outline

The Nature of Phonic Analysis
Reasons for Teaching Phonic Analysis
Phonic Analysis versus Communication
Phonics Terminology
The Analytic Phonics Method
Linguistic Approach A: The Substitution Method
Linguistic Approach B: The Phonogram Method
The Synthetic Phonics Method
The Spelling-Pattern Method
Sample Lesson Using an Eclectic Approach
Questions and Answers about Phonics
Summary
Application Experiences for the Teacher-Education Class
Field Experiences in the Elementary-School Classroom

Chapter Preview

It is almost impossible for children to become independent readers unless they gain a reasonable ability to translate printed words into spoken words without relying entirely on visual memory of whole words. If Brenda has to rely on her memory of every word she

---

encounters in print, she's going to do a lot of inaccurate guessing—and a lot of asking others what the word is. Obviously, Brenda needs to be taught some way of figuring out a word by herself. Fortunately, there are several ways that we can teach Brenda to do this. One way is through phonic methods, with an emphasis on hearing the differences between speech sounds. Another way is through linguistic methods, with an emphasis on seeing the differences between letter patterns. In this chapter we'll look at both approaches—phonic and linguistic—and how they can be used together to help children "crack the code." In Chapter 4 we'll look at other ways of "figuring out a word" that can be used alongside of phonic analysis. These other ways are contextual, morphemic, syllabic, and dictionary analysis.

> With Inglish speekene peepel, fonnicks iz much mor than soundene out wirdz.

The Nature of Phonic Analysis

But what is phonic analysis? It is often thought of as merely "sounding out words." This definition, however, is much too simple. Successful phonic analysis requires more sophistication than just "sounding out the letters." For example, how would you "sound out" the nonsense word *cibby*? Should it be pronounced (sĭb′ bē) or (kĭb′ bē)? If you remember (or intuitively use) the phonic generalization that "c before i, y, or e usually has the soft sound," you'll pronounce it (sĭb′ bē). Or will you? Perhaps it should be (sī′ be), using a long *i* sound instead of a short *i* sound. No, not if you noticed the consonant pair in the middle of the word—a phonic signal which warns you that the preceding vowel should probably be short. Or perhaps you recognized that the first syllable contained *ib*, a VC pattern (vowel-consonant letters), which signals a probable short vowel sound. At any rate you can see that phonic analysis is more than merely sounding out the letters. (Think what a mess you'd have if you merely sounded out the word *knight*.)

To be more precise, then, phonic analysis requires these four interrelated steps: 1) the recognition of letters, such as *c, b,* and *y,* and the sounds they represent; 2) the recognition of letter *patterns,* such as *c* before *i* (which signals an *s* sound rather than a *k* sound), *ib* (a vowel-consonant letter pattern signalling a short *i* sound), *y* at the end of a two-syllable word (signalling more of a long *e* sound rather than long *i*; 3) the translation of these letters and letter patterns into sounds (or subvocal speech); and 4) the blending of the phonemes aloud or silently into a single syllable or word. To get a better grasp of this definition, test it out on the nonsense word *dis-sabulate*. See if you can detect the four interconnecting steps. (You'll want to divide the word into syllables first.)

One more thing about the definition of phonic analysis: does phonic analysis simply mean pronunciation? No, it does not. In fact, the purpose of instruction in phonic analysis is not really to teach children to pronounce words. Most children first learning to read should already know how to pronounce the words they meet in print—that is, these words should first be made part of their speaking vocabulary. What the process of phonic analysis allows them to do is to *translate* the printed words into familiar spoken words. In fact, since both auditory and visual skills are involved in this process, it is often referred to as *graphophonic analysis,* a more accurate term.

Reasons for Teaching Phonic Analysis

Why should phonics be taught? By now, perhaps, the answer is obvious. *Phonics* (phonic analysis) is almost the essence of reading during the early stages of learning to read. I say "almost" for two reasons. One could learn to read by merely memorizing sight words—sight words that are introduced by having someone always around to say, "That word is *fantastic* or this word is *rescue*." But it would be extremely difficult to become an independent reader without some way of learning the relationships between letters and letter sounds. The other reason I say "almost" is to remind you again that phonics is only one tool and not the only tool of the independent reader. In fact the more mature that readers become, the less they rely on phonics, and the more they rely on visual memory and context.

Nevertheless, research (2, 5, 10, 16) demonstrates that teaching children phonic-analysis skills helps them learn to read—and to keep on learning through independent word attack. Phonic analysis continues to be important throughout a child's later education. According to Cordts' study of children's vocabulary (7), as children move up in the grades, the number of words that are subject to phonic analysis increases. In their science education, for example, they meet terms like *atomic energy, microscopic matter,* and *astronauts*; and in social studies they are confronted with terms such as *population explosion, Antarctic expeditions,* and *transcontinental railways*—all of which are "phonetic" enough in their spelling to be partially decoded through the use of phonic analysis.

But is our system of spelling consistent enough to warrant the teaching of phonics? After all, what about the inconsistency of words like *bone, done,* and *gone*? True enough, but don't forget words like *bone, cone, drone, hone, phone, shone, stone, tone,* and *zone.* And if you want an even better example of "teachable consistency," think of words that follow a spelling pattern similar to *bill* or similar to *can.* (Here are some for *bill: chill, dill, fill, frill, grill, hill, ill, Jill, kill, mill, pill, quill, rill, sill, spill, still, till, trill,* and *will.*) As another example of "teachable consistency," nearly three-fourths of Dolch's "Basic Sight Words" have a regular spelling pattern.

It is the surprising amount of consistency in our spelling system that has been the chief reason for the increasing popularity of the "linguistic approach" in initial reading instruction. This approach has been responsible for increasing the number of regular words like *can* and *ran* and decreasing the number of irregular words like *come* and *one* in early-reading materials for children. Suffice it to say at this point that a great many teachers are now using reading programs based on the assumption that our spelling system is indeed consistent enough to justify some type of systematic approach that teaches children to predict the speech sounds that should be associated with letters and letter patterns.

Phonic Analysis versus Communication

The fact that our spelling system is consistent enough to justify time spent on phonics in the classroom should not lead a teacher either to overemphasize it or to go to the other extreme and get all upset over the exceptions to phonics "rules" that are frequently encountered. Phonic analysis is merely one tool to use in making an intelligent guess as to the oral equivalent of a printed word. In nearly every case it is best to temper phonic analysis with contextual analysis. In other words, the child learning to read needs to be taught to ask these two questions after decoding a word through phonic analysis: 1) "Does this word make sense in this sentence?" 2) "What is the author saying?"

Take this sentence as an example: Tom went to live with Grandmother. The child who uses phonic analysis and only phonic analysis on the word *live* is in for trouble. Phonic analysis will be quite helpful on the letters *l* and *v,* but it doesn't work on the letter *i.* This is because the VCE pattern (vowel-consonant-final *e* letters) usually indicates a long vowel sound. Thus, total reliance on phonic analysis would produce /līv/ instead of /lĭv/. Only contextual analysis can get the reader back on the track: /līv/ does not make sense, but /lĭv/ does.

Phonics is a probability game, really. A child should be taught to use phonics in the spirit of a detective playing hunches on the basis of the available evidence. A detective who finds mud on the carpet leading from a window to the dead body may rightfully guess that the mud is a straightforward clue to the murderer. The odds are in favor of the guess until the detective looks further and finds that the mud on the carpet matches the mud on his own shoes.

This is not to argue, however, for the belief that "the phonic approach is the best way to teach reading." This type of belief represents an innocent case of naiveté. In the first place, there is no best way to teach every child how to read. Individual children vary too much in their background and learning styles. In the second place, there is no such thing as *the* phonics approach. There are many ways of introducing children to this decoding process. (Most of these will be described in this chapter.) In the third place, overemphasis on any one decoding skill—whether it be phonic analysis, visual memory of sight words, or contextual analysis—will often lead in the long run to students who stumble and mumble, or wildly guess their way through anything harder than "Run, Dick, run." Fourth, a phonics approach introduces consistency where there often is no justification for it. We will always be stuck with inconsistencies like *low* rhyming with *hoe* instead of *how,* and like *done* rhyming with *bun* instead of *bone.*

As a final warning, it is important to realize that not all children can learn to decode through the use of a strictly phonic approach. Some children have very poor auditory discrimination and auditory-memory abilities—abilities that are prerequisites to many phonics methods. Borrowing from the "linguistic approach," which emphasizes visual discrimination rather than auditory discrimination, is generally the best way to help those children. This type of approach is also quite useful for those children whose home language is not English, such as those who speak Spanish, a language whose phonic elements differ considerably from English. (This phonic-linguistic approach will be explained fully in a later section.)

Phonics Terminology

When teachers share ideas for teaching phonic-analysis skills, they use certain terms—the "jargon of the trade," you might say. These same terms are used by authors of teaching manuals, by remedial-reading consultants, and by other people in the profession. Some of the terms will also be useful to you directly in your teaching as you communicate with children. As you study the terms, you will be given an opportunity to test yourself on their meanings.

1. *Word recognition*—The process of translating a printed word into its vocal or subvocal equivalent by any means available, including visual memory of sight words, sentence context, related

pictures, phonic elements and patterns, syllabication patterns, prefixes, suffixes, and the diacritical marks and respellings in dictionaries.

Some authors use the term *word recognition* to mean both pronouncing a word and understanding the concept it represents. Its use in this book, however, will only be in reference to transforming the printed symbol into a speech symbol (whether the speech symbol is understood or not).

The term *decoding* has become more popular in the profession and seems to be superceding the term *word recognition.* However, it should be pointed out that *decoding* to some people means both the translation of words into their vocal or subvocal equivalents and also the comprehension of the words. In this book *decoding* and *word recognition* refer only to the idea of print-to-sound translation.

2. *Word analysis*—Many educators use this term as a synonym for word recognition. Many use it to refer to all of the decoding skills except visual memory of sight words, since instant visual memory seems to require no actual analysis of the words. This is probably a false distinction; the analysis may be simply much more rapid with sight words. In essence, it is probably safe to say that all of the following terms have roughly the same meaning to reading educators: the translation of printed matter into speech or subvocal speech:

- decoding
- word recognition
- word analysis
- word attack
- word identification
- word perception

For further discussion of these terms, see *The Dictionary of Reading Terms,* edited by Theodore L. Harris and Richard E. Hodges (17).

3. *Phonic analysis*—This is one of the subskills under word recognition. It is one of several ways of translating printed symbols into vocal or subvocal symbols. It should not be used as a synonym for "decoding," as it is only one type of decoding skill. Another term for phonic analysis often used by teachers is *phonics* (although this is somewhat of a misnomer). A new term that has been creeping into the jargon of reading educators is *graphophonic analysis. Graphophonology* is the study of the relationships between the written and spoken symbols in a language. When educators use the term *graphophonic analysis,* they are generally referring to phonic analysis—the process a reader uses to recognize the speech sounds that letters or letter patterns represent. The term *graphophonic analysis* has the advantage over *phonic analysis* of recognizing both the visual and auditory skills that are involved in this type of decoding.

4. *Phoneme*—A distinctive speech sound that can contrast one word with another (12). Over forty phonemes in Standard English have been classified, although nonstandard dialects have more or fewer. Linguists discover the various phonemes in a language by determining what changes in speech sounds indicate changes in meaning. For example, the first phoneme in the spoken word *bet* is the *b* sound represented as /b/. If the first phoneme is changed to /p/, we have a change in meaning, from *bet* to *pet*. In Table 3.1, you will see a list of symbols representing most of the phonemes in Standard English. Notice that phonemes are indicated by slash marks, e.g., /k/.

5. *Grapheme*—A written symbol used to represent a phoneme. Table 3.1 contains a list of most of the graphemes used in Standard English. You will notice that sometimes two letters are used as one grapheme to represent a single phoneme, as in the word *chin*, which contains only three graphemes—*ch, i,* and *n*—but four letters. Occasionally more than two letters are used, as in the word *right*, which uses *igh* as a single grapheme to represent the /i/ sound. (This type of generosity, of course, causes all kinds of difficulty for those learning to read.)

How many graphemes are used to write the word *this?* How many letters? How many phonemes are used to say the word? (Answers: three, four, and three.)

How many graphemes are used to write the word *salt?* How many letters? How many phonemes are used to say the word? (Four, four, four.) How about the word *back?* (Three, four, three.) Have you noticed that for every phoneme in a word there is a corresponding grapheme? If there are three phonemes in a word, there are almost always three graphemes. The major exception to this is when we have the letter *x* at the end of the word. In the word *box*, for example, we have four phonemes—/b/ + /o/ + /k/ + /s/—and only three graphemes: *b, o,* and *x*.

Sometimes people mix up the words *grapheme* and *phoneme*. This might be avoided by remembering that *grapheme* comes from the Greek root *graph*, meaning "drawn" or "written." The word *phoneme* has the Greek root *phono,* meaning "sound" or "voice."

6. *Consonant*—Some people consider a consonant to be a letter, although from a linguistic standpoint this is not correct (12). Strictly speaking, a consonant is a speech sound formed by impeding a stream of breath with the lips, tongue, teeth, palate, or alveolar ridge (the part of the jaw in which the teeth are set). Try making the /t/ sound, for instance. What parts of the mouth were used to impede your breath? (Teeth, tongue, alveolar ridge, palate.)

A consonant sound is usually represented by either a single consonant letter or by two letters called a *consonant digraph.* In the word *thin,* for instance, we can hear two consonants—the phoneme /Θ/ and the phoneme /n/. The first consonant is represented by the

Table 3.1 Some Phonemes and Graphemes Used in Standard English

Written Representations of Phonemes	Common Graphemes	Sample Words*
/a/	a	fat
/ā/	ai, a-e, ay	laid, name, pay
/â/	ai(r), a(r)e	hair, fare
/ä/	a(l), a(r)	calm, car
/b/	b, bb	bus, rubber
/ch/	ch, tch	peach, witch
/d/	d, dd	dish, ladder
/e/	e	net
/ē/	e, ea, ee	equal, beat, feet
/ê/	ea(r), ee(r)	hear, cheer
/f/	f, ff, ph	fish, puff, phone
/g/	g, gg	gun, beggar
/h/	h	hack
/hw/	wh	what
/i/	i	in
/ī/	i	lice
/j/	j, dg	jar, fudge
/k/	k, ck	kiss, tack
/l/	l, ll	left, bellow
/m/	m, mm	mat, summer
/n/	n, nn	net, winner
/n̂g/	ng	thing
/o/	o	box
/ō/	o, oa	hope, coat
/ô/	a(ll), aw	ball, awful
/o͞o/	oo	food
/o͝o/	oo	look
/p/	p, pp	pin, shopper
/r/	r, rr	red, furry
/s/	s, ss	sit, mess
/sh/	sh, t(i)	shut, nation
/t/	t, tt	tub, butter
/θ/	th	bath
/th/	th	smooth
/u/	u, o	supper, love
/û/	u(r), i(r)	burn, girl
/v/	v	vat, liver
/w/	w	win
/y/	y	yet
/z/	z, s	zip, hose
/ž/	s(i), g(e)	decision, mirage
/ə/	a, e, i, o, u	about, system, pencil, scallop, circus

*The decoding of the graphemes in these words will vary according to regional and ethnic dialects. Other phonemes not listed include different degrees of stress and pitch and different types of pauses. Such phonemes are just as important as letter sounds, but are too complicated to deal with here; see Chapter 5 for further discussion.

consonant digraph *th* and the second consonant is represented by the consonant letter *n*.

It may help to remember that *consonant* comes from the Latin *sonare,* meaning "to sound." The word *digraph,* pronounced (di' graf), was borrowed from the Greek *di* meaning "two" and *graph* meaning "written." How many consonant sounds are there in the word *thick?* How many consonant digraphs? The answer in both cases is two. See if you can identify the number of consonants, consonant letters, and consonant digraphs in these words: *rich, sing, dash, bath, sock.* Hint: you should get the same three answers for each word. (Try figuring it out before I tell you.) The answers are two, three, and one—two consonants, three consonant letters, and one consonant digraph.

For the dialect called Standard English there are twenty-five consonants (or consonant sounds). However, two of the consonants, the /y/ heard in *yellow* and the /w/ heard in *wet,* are also referred to by linguists as *glides.* This is because they are produced, for one thing, with little or no obstruction of the breath. Also, when these two sounds are in a word, they are always directly preceded or followed by a vowel. To form these sounds, one must glide the tongue either toward or away from a vowel sound. (An understanding of the term *glide* will be necessary for understanding a later term, *diphthong.*)

Two other consonants have a special name. The /l/ and /r/ sounds are called *liquids.* Although the breath is slightly impeded when you make these sounds, no actual friction occurs. Although you will seldom use the words *liquid* and *glide,* it is helpful to understand them and their effects on vowel sounds. It is also helpful to understand them when communicating with a speech therapist. It is quite common for the speech therapist and teacher of reading to work together when a child is having either reading or speaking difficulties.

7. *Consonant blend*—Two or three consonants (consonant sounds) slurred together. A consonant blend is not a single phoneme, but a combination of two or more phonemes. Such a combination is represented by two or more graphemes and therefore by two or more letters (with the exception of the grapheme *x*). What letters represent the consonant blend in *flop?* Notice that the *f* sound and the *l* sound are both heard in the /fl/ blend. What letters represent the consonant blend in *spring?* What three phonemes are slurred together? Do the first two letters in *skill* represent a consonant blend or are they a consonant digraph? Since you can hear the *s* sound /s/ and *k* sound /k/ as separate but slurred phonemes, the *sk* represents a blend. Do the first two letters in *shell* represent a consonant blend or are they a consonant digraph? In the word *shell* the /s/ and /h/ sounds are not being blended together. The separate sounds of /s/ and /h/ are lost when you produce the sound /sh/. Therefore the *sh* is a digraph.

Some authors find the term *consonant blend* to be one that confuses people, since some use it to refer to sounds and others use it to refer to letters. To avoid this confusion, they use the term *con-sonant cluster* to refer to the letters that represent the consonant blend. What consonant cluster do you see in the word *brag*? What consonant blend do you hear? (You see *br*. You hear /b/ + /r/.)

8. *Vowel*—Some people consider a vowel to be a letter, although from a linguistic standpoint this is not correct (12). Strictly speaking, a *vowel* is a speech sound formed by controlling the size and shape of the mouth cavity with the tongue and lips, and by not impeding the breath. To see for yourself how vowels (vowel sounds) are produced, place an index finger in your mouth up to the second knuckle; now rest your teeth gently on your knuckle and say some of the vowels slowly.

There are thirteen vowels in Standard English (although linguists differ on the exact number). You can hear twelve distinctly different vowels in these words: *beat, bit, bite, bawl, bait, bet, band, boot,*

Many children need to see the difference as well as hear the difference.

butcher, but, boat, box. There is also a weak neutral vowel that occurs in the unaccented syllable of many words with two or more syllables, such as *alone, circus, pencil, scallops,* and *happen.*

A vowel is a speech sound that is usually represented by either a single vowel letter or by two letters called a *vowel digraph.* In the word *pan,* for instance, we can hear the short vowel /a/ represented by the letter *a.* In the word *pain* we can hear the long vowel /ā/ represented by the digraph *ai.*

9. *Diphthong*—A speech sound produced by the blending of a vowel followed immediately by a glide (12). The most important diphthongs for reading instruction are the sounds /ow/ and /oy/, as in *out, boy, now,* and *boil.* In *out* and *now* you can hear the short vowel /o/ slurring into the glide /w/. In *boy* and *boil* you can hear the long vowel /ō/ slurring into the glide /y/. The /ow/ diphthong is usually represented by either *ou* or *ow;* the /oy/ diphthong is usually represented by either *oy* or *oi.* (The first syllable in *diphthong,* by the way, is pronounced either /dif/ or /dip/.)

10. *Phonogram*—For teaching purposes, a cluster at the end of a single-syllable rhyming word. It includes at least one vowel letter and one consonant letter. One example of a phonogram is *at,* since it is the ending of so many "rhyming" words: *bat, cat, sat, that,* etc. Other commonly used phonograms that teachers attempt to have children master eventually through visual memory include *an, am, ight, ape, eep, eat,* and others. Phonograms are sometimes called *graphonemes.*

The Analytic Phonics Method

One of the most widely used phonic methods is one called "the analytic method," sometimes referred to as the "whole-word-phonics method." With this method, a teacher helps children break down a set of whole words into their common phonemes and graphemes. Perhaps the best way of illustrating this method is to give you a sample lesson plan in which this method is used.

Suppose you have several students who are having trouble decoding the digraph *sh,* as in *shell* or *dash.* You have already used the lessons in the basal series on *sh,* so you decide to create a brief lesson on *sh* for those students. Your first planning step would be to list several words with *sh* as a beginning and ending digraph. Those ending with the *ash* phonogram would give you a good start: *ash, bash, cash, crash, dash,* and so on. Those ending with the phonogram *ish* might also be listed—*dish, fish, wish*—as well as some beginning with *sh: shell, shut, should,* and *ship.* If possible most of the words

A Self-Quiz on Phonics Terminology

Directions: In this matching quiz, you are encouraged to use an answer more than once if appropriate. You are encouraged to use more than one answer whenever appropriate. Check your answers at the end.

_____ 1. speech sounds (use five answers)
_____ 2. any single distinct speech sound (three)
_____ 3. two letters representing one phoneme (three)
_____ 4. a vowel blended with a glide (one)
_____ 5. combination of letters, such as *ap, at, ape, ash, ill* (two)
_____ 6. one or more letters representing a single phoneme (five)
_____ 7. two letters representing one vowel (two)
_____ 8. two letters representing one consonant (two)
_____ 9. consonants slurred together; two or more phonemes (one)
_____ 10. a speech sound made with no impeding of breath (two)
_____ 11. translating printed symbols into vocal or subvocal symbols through any means (three)
_____ 12. recognizing the relationships between letter patterns and the sounds they represent (two)
_____ 13. two or three letters that can represent a consonant blend (one)
_____ 14. the letters *ch* in *much* (one)
_____ 15. the letters *fr* in *fry* (one)

a. grapheme
b. phoneme
c. consonant
d. consonant letter
e. consonant digraph
f. consonant blend
g. vowel
h. vowel letter
i. vowel digraph
j. graphophonic analysis
k. diphthong
l. word identification
m. phonogram
n. consonant cluster
o. phonic analysis
p. word recognition
q. decoding
r. graphoneme

Answers:
1. b, c, f, g, k   2. b, c, g   3. a, e, i   4. k   5. m, r   6. a, d, e, h, i   7. a, i
8. a, e   9. f   10. b, g   11. l, p, q   12. j, o   13. n   14. e   15. n

should be those that are included in the teacher's guide of a basal reader or other book the children are using for instruction.

Your next planning step would be to create a very brief story using words that end with the digraph *sh*. For example, you might create a story like this:

> *Shelly* likes to eat *fish hash*.
> "I like it," *she* says.
> "*Fish hash* is my favorite *dish*."

After you've put your story on butcher paper or on the chalkboard—and underlined the *sh* words—you are ready to teach your lesson, using the analytic phonics method. Here are some teaching steps you might follow:

1. Read the story out loud to the children in a smooth informal way, as if you were telling the story.
2. Have the children tell it with you while you underline each word with your hand.
3. Now isolate the underlined words by having them say each word right after you say it. Also have them use each word in a sentence.
4. Ask them what letters are the same in each of the underlined words.
*5. Ask them what sound is the same in each of the underlined words. Have them make the sound with you.
*6. Have them close their eyes and raise their hands whenever they hear a word that has the /sh/ sound in it. Read several words to them, with about half of them containing the /sh/ phoneme.
*7. Ask them what sound they should think of when they see the letters *sh* together.
8. (Optional) Use the substitution method and/or the phonogram method as a means of reinforcing what they've learned (described later under Linguistic Approaches).
9. Return to your original story and have each child read part of it—with your help, if necessary.
10. Use a practice activity, such as a game, worksheet, or oral activity; this may be done either the same day or at a later date for review. (See Appendix B for phonics games and activities.)

As you can see from looking at the sample lesson plan, the analytic method requires children to analyze several words to determine the common grapheme and the corresponding phoneme. In other words, they learn a grapheme-phoneme correspondence through discovery rather than through being told ahead of time.

Linguistic Approach A: The Substitution Method

I mentioned earlier that by using only a phonics method you would be making it difficult for those children whose auditory memory and auditory-discrimination abilities are weak. Phonics is primarily an auditory approach. If the children have trouble hearing and remembering the differences in phonemes, then phonic analysis will need to be supplemented with those approaches that emphasize visual differences rather than auditory differences. There are many children, for example, who really cannot distinguish between the short

---

*Some teachers and programs avoid having children pronounce letter sounds in isolation. Instead, children are asked to notice that the words all have the same sound in them and then asked to think of other words that include that sound.

a sound and the short *e* sound or between the short *e* sound and the short *i* sound. You can spend an enormous amount of time trying to make them hear the differences and remember the differences—but it is often in vain. These children need to concentrate on *seeing* differences.

Two approaches which encourage children to see differences are the substitution method and the phonogram (or graphoneme) method—methods that are borrowed from the linguistic approach toward teaching reading. Let's use both of these methods as an extension of the lesson we were discussing in the section on the analytic method.

We've taught the children through the analytic method to think of the /sh/ sound whenever they see the *sh* digraph. For those children who seem unsure of this grapheme-phoneme correspondence, it's time to reinforce it with a more visual approach. To carry on the substitution method, you will need to list several pairs of *regular* words. Each pair shows a *minimal contrast* between the two words; each pair will contain one word with the grapheme you're trying to teach them to decode. For instance:

me	she
Kelly	Shelly
sell	shell
cut	shut
skip	ship

Do you see how the *sh* grapheme is contrasted with another grapheme or cluster in each pair? In the first pair the *sh* grapheme is contrasted with the *m* grapheme. In the last pair the *sh* grapheme is contrasted with the *sk* cluster.

Since the list so far concentrates on the *sh* grapheme only in a *beginning* position, you should extend your list to include words that have the *sh* grapheme at the end. For example:

fib	fish
hat	hash
track	trash
smack	smash
rat	rash
dig	dish
win	wish
mud	mush

Notice how all of the *sh* words from the story were used, along with several others. Now you're ready to use the substitution method by saying something like this:

Step 1: "This first word is *me,* but in this second word you see the letters *sh* instead of the letter *m.*"

Step 2: "So, if this word is *me,* then what is the second word?"

Step 3:   "That's right. This word is *me* and this word is *she*."
Step 4:   "How are the letters different in the next two words?"
Step 5:   "All right. If this word is *Kelly* and the second word starts with *sh* instead of *k*, how would you say the second word?"
Step 6:   Do the same as Steps 4 and 5 for the rest of the pairs.

Just to make sure you understand the substitution method, let me ask you a question. If you wanted to teach the *st* cluster with the substitution method, which of the following pairs of words would show the *minimal contrast* in letters that you need to show.

mist .... mast
stick .... stack
fast .... fan
mash .... mast

Which pair did you choose?

The first pair would be useful for teaching the short *a* since that's what you're contrasting with the short *i*. Do you see what I mean? The second pair would be useful for teaching the short *a* again. The third pair would be good for teaching the decoding of *n*, although if the pair had been reversed, it could have been used to teach *st*. Only the last pair is appropriate for teaching children to decode the *st* grapheme. ("If this word is *mash*, and the second word ends with *st* instead of *sh*, then what is this second word?")

Linguistic Approach B: The Phonogram Method

We've extended our lesson about Shelly and her fish hash by using the substitution method. Now let's extend it one more time by using the phonogram method. (All of these methods would not necessarily be used with the children on the same day; you may need two sessions to complete the lesson. Nor would you need to use all three methods with all of the children.)

To carry on the phonogram method, all you need is two good rhyming words that end with the grapheme you're teaching the children to decode. In our lesson on *sh*, two good words would be *ash* and *dash*. There are many words that rhyme with these words. All you have to do is to write the two words on the board and ask the students to think of other words that end in exactly the same way—with the letters *-ash*.

Notice that we're not asking the children to think of words that rhyme with ash and dash. That would emphasize auditory rather than visual abilities. It's true that many children with good auditory abilities will perceive the words as rhyming words, and that's fine. It's the children that can't perceive rhyming words that we're concerned about—and there are many children who do have this trouble.

What exactly are we emphasizing when we make a list of rhyming words with children? Let's examine such a list:

ash
dash
trash
mash
rash
flash
gash
hash
lash
smash

You can see at a glance that we're reinforcing the correct decoding of the *sh* digraph. We are also introducing or reinforcing the decoding of initial graphemes and clusters such as *d* (as in *dash*), *tr* (as in *trash*), and so on. We are introducing or reinforcing the short *a* sound indicated by this particular spelling pattern (a one-syllable word ending with a vowel letter followed by a consonant digraph). And, perhaps most important of all for those whose auditory-discrimination and auditory-memory skills are weak, we are teaching them through visual memory to decode a very common phonogram, namely *ash*. By helping them memorize this phonogram visually, we will make it easier for them to decode many words such as *cash, cashed; cashing, crash,* and *crashing.*

The Synthetic Phonics Method

Whereas the analytic phonics method has children break words down into grapheme-phoneme units, the approach referred to as "the synthetic method" has them build words up from grapheme-phoneme units. Basically, with the synthetic method the children learn to decode letters in isolation first and then learn how to put them together to make words. (One program using this approach is the Distar program.) As I did with the analytic approach, I'll give you one type of sample lesson plan in which the synthetic phonics method is used. (There are many other types.)

Let's again suppose that you have several students who are having trouble decoding the digraph *sh*. Let's also imagine that some of them are also having trouble with the short *a*. Assume also that you've already used the lessons in a basal reader on these two graphemes.) This time, in planning a lesson for these children, you would make a list for yourself of those regular words of one syllable that include the two graphemes *a* and *sh,* e.g., *shack, ash, bash, cash,* etc. Now you're ready to begin your lesson, using the synthetic phonics approach. Here are some teaching steps you might follow:

1. Write *sh* and *a* on the board. Point to each one and tell them what sound they are to make when they see each one. (Refer to them as the "short *a* sound" and the "*sh* sound.")

2. Have them make the *sh* sound /sh/ and the short *a* sound /a/ whenever you point to them. Make sure each person in the small group can say them.

3. Review the sounds of the graphemes *b, h, m,* and *ck* in the same way—using steps 1 and 2.

4. Have each child write the *sh* and *a*—first on the board and then on their paper. Have them point to what they've written on the board and say the sounds (not the letters).

5. Remind them how to blend sounds together by using a word they already know, such as *mess.* Write it on the board and have them say it slowly: "mmmeeesss." Then have them say it fast: "mess."

6. Point to the isolated graphemes that you've put on the board (*sh, a, b, h, m, ck*). Tell them they "are now going to blend these sounds together to make some words. Whenever I point to one of them, you make the right sound."

7. Point to three graphemes that will produce a word, such as *b, a,* and *sh,* and have them make the appropriate sounds as you point to them /b/ + /a/ + /sh/. Point to the sequence of three graphemes several times, each time faster than the previous time. Finally tell them to "say it fast."

8. Write the word you've just produced, in this case, *bash.* Have each child "say it slowly" then "say it fast."

9. Do the same thing with other possible words: *hash, mash, shack.*

10. Finish the lesson by using some of the words in context with them, e.g., "Do you like to eat *hash?*"

Now that you've seen a sample lesson plan, perhaps you have noticed some advantages and disadvantages of the synthetic phonics method. Would you agree that these are some of the advantages? 1) The child is told what sound is associated with what letter and doesn't have to discover it through analysis of whole words. 2) Children who have trouble learning to decode through analytic phonics often are able to learn to decode through synthetic phonics (2, 10, 24).

Would you agree that these are some probable disadvantages of the synthetic phonics method? 1) By learning to decode graphemes in isolation a child is not learning to recognize phonic patterns, such as the VC pattern in *cap* and the VCE pattern in *cape.* Thus the child is learning, for example, that *a* represents an isolated sound—when in reality the sound of *a* depends on the pattern of letters around it. If the child sees an *a* in a VC pattern, as in the word *cap,* the child should predict that it has a short *a* sound. In a VCE pattern, as in *cape,* the child should predict the long *a* sound. 2) By learning to decode graphemes in isolation, the child may be learning to ignore meaning and to concentrate too much on making the correct sound. 3) Concentration on sounds in isolation may increase a child's difficulty in blending sounds. For example, if *b, a,* and *sh* are first presented as a whole word, the child learns the proper blending of sounds from the very beginning. If these same graphemes are sounded out separately, however, the child is actually trying to blend four phonemes, rather than three: /b/ + /u/ + /a/ + /sh/. The reason for this is that it is nearly impossible to produce most consonant sounds without an accompanying vowel sound.

Nonetheless, despite the disadvantages of the synthetic phonics method, research shows that it works reasonably well for some children (2). Many teachers recommend it for children who are having trouble learning the analytic method. It is advisable that all reading teachers become familiar with this method, so that they can use it with any child who simply is not getting it any other way. After all, it's terribly important that each child learn to read—by whatever method works.

The Spelling-Pattern Method

The pattern or rule method is an auxiliary method used to strengthen children's ability to decode vowel graphemes. Children who have trouble learning to decode graphemes usually have more trouble with vowel letters than with consonant letters. This is because vowel sounds are not spelled with the same consistency as consonant sounds. The long *e* sound, for instance, can be spelled in at least sixteen different ways: *Caesar, equal, team, see, e'en, deceive, receipt, people, demesne, key, machine, field, debris, amoeba, quay, pity.*

Thus, many attempts have been made to help children learn to recognize the most common patterns of spelling that will enable them to predict with some accuracy the correct decoding of vowel digraphs. Sometimes this has unfortunate consequences. One of the common rules that children are taught is this one: "When two vowels go walking, the first one does the talking." This is a catchy rule and easy to remember but it only works in very particular situations. If *o* "walks" with *a,* as in *boat* and *soap,* the rule works pretty well, providing we're only talking about one-syllable words. And it works about two-thirds of the time when *e* walks with *e,* as in *beet* and *beef;* and when *a* walks with *i,* as in *rain* and *wait.* However, don't expect it to work as often when *o* walks with *i* as in *boil,* when *e* walks with *i* as in *weight,* or when *i* walks with *e,* as in *chief.*

If you're going to supplement your phonics lessons with rules, you may have more luck getting children to remember spelling patterns, rather than verbal rules; and it. may be better to limit the number of patterns to six or seven. There is a tendency for some teachers and commercial programs to overburden children with such patterns or rules, thus making them like the plumber who had so many tools in his overalls he couldn't decide which one to use. (By the time he chose his tool, he forgot why he wanted it.)

Several studies have been made on the usefulness or consistency of the many phonic generalizations or patterns which have been taught (1, 4, 6, 11). These studies have made it clear that only a few of the generalizations are consistent enough or relate to enough words to make them worth watching. The following seven are probably worth the effort:

1.   The "c rule": When *c* comes just before *a, o,* or *u,* it usually has the hard sound heard in *cat, cot,* and *cut.* Otherwise, it usually has the soft sound heard in *cent, city,* and *bicycle.*

2.   The "g rule": (similar to the "c rule") When *g* comes at the end of words or just before *a, o,* or *u,* it usually has the hard sound heard in *tag, game, go,* and *gush.* Otherwise, it usually has the soft sound heard in *gem, giant,* and *gym.* (Some important exceptions are *get, give, begin,* and *girl.*)

3.   The VC pattern: This pattern is seen in words such as *an, can, candy,* and *dinner.* As a verbal generalization, it might be stated as follows: in either a word or an accented syllable, a single vowel letter followed by a consonant letter usually represents a short vowel sound. (Most teachers find it easier for children to remember the pattern rather than the rule.)

4.   The VV (vowel digraph) pattern: This pattern is seen in words such as *roach, throat, see, feed, bait,* and *raid.* As a verbal generalization, it may be stated like this: in a word or syllable containing a vowel digraph, the first letter in the digraph usually represents the long vowel sound and the second letter is usually silent. According to Clymer (6), this generalization is quite reliable for *oa* and *ai* but is not reliable for other vowel digraphs such as *ei, ie,* or *oo.* And, of course, it is not valid for diphthongs represented by *oi,* and *ou.*

5.   The VCE (final e) pattern: This pattern is seen in one-syllable words such as *ice, nice, ate, plate, cone, flute, vote,* and *shade.* As a generalization, it might be stated this way: in one-syllable words containing two vowel letters, one of which is a final e, the first vowel letter usually represents a long vowel sound, and the final e is silent.

6.   The CV pattern: This pattern is seen in words or syllables such as *he, she, go, my, cry, hotel, going,* and *being.* As a generalization, it could be stated like this: when there is only one vowel letter in a word or first syllable and it comes at the end of the word or first syllable, it usually represents the long vowel sound.

7.   The "r rule": This rule applies to words like *far, fare, fair, girl, fur, her,* and *here.* As a generalization, it might be stated as follows: the letter *r* usually modifies the short or long sound of the preceding vowel letter. For instance, the word *car* does not illustrate the VC pattern seen in the word *cat;* nor does *fir* represent the VC pattern seen in *fit.* The word *care* usually doesn't illustrate the VCE pattern seen in the word *cape* (although in some dialects it does). Likewise, the word *fair* usually doesn't illustrate the VV pattern in *wait.*

As an application exercise for these seven rules, see if you can decode the following nonsense words: *cag, nait, flin, flinter, plash, gope, cy, genter, sproat, vair, zere, nird, lar.*

Sample Lesson Using an Eclectic Approach

You've now examined a number of phonic and linguistic methods. Let's see how a lesson that combines several methods might look. The lesson I'm about to show you is one that would normally be used for helping children who "didn't get it" when they were taught through their regular instructional materials. Context analysis is somewhat slighted in the early part of this lesson because we're presently concentrating on phonics. But notice how context clues are emphasized at the end.

Imagine, if you will, that some of the children in your class need some special help in decoding the letter *a* in a VCE pattern, as in the words *cake, came,* and *tape.* Here are some steps you can try (although you may not want to do all of these in one sitting):

Step 1:   Put this story on the chalkboard or a paper chart, underlining those words that demonstrate a long /ā/ in a VCE pattern. Read the story to the children, have them read it with you, and then read the underlined words to them, having them say each word right after you say it.

> Dave swam in a lake.
> Then he sat in the sun near some big rocks.
> He saw a snake in a rocky place.
> He put the snake in a jar to keep it safe.
> When he got home he put it in a cage.

Step 2:   Ask them what letters are the same in each of the underlined words.

Step 3:   Ask them what sound is the same in each of the underlined words. Have them make the sound with you. (Call it a long *a* sound.)

Step 4: Have them close their eyes and raise their hands whenever they hear a word that has a long *a* sound in it. Some words that might be used are *snake, snack, hate, hat, rope, paste, past, man, mane, men, cage, lake, not, pin, save, pan.*

Step 5: Make a separate list of the underlined words from the story. Ask the children to listen as you read them to see if they can hear the long *a* sound in each of the words. Ask them if they can actually hear the *e* sound in any of the words. Tell them that the final *e* in those words is called a "silent letter," and draw slash marks through the final *e* in the first two words. Have a child find the silent *e* in each of the other words and draw a slash mark through it. Then show him a way to indicate the long *a* sound by drawing a macron over each *a* in the words, e.g., *snāke̸.* Add words to your list and have other children mark them in the same way.

Step 6: Discuss the VCE pattern seen in these words: *snake, cage, place, safe, hate, rake.* Write VCE over the last three letters in *snake* (snake) and *cage* (cage) and remind them that the VCE stands for vowel letter, consonant letter, and silent *e*. Have children take turns writing VCE over the other words in the proper place. Add these other words to the list and ask them which words they wish to write VCE over: *made, mad, hat, rack, lake, tape, pan, make.*

Step 7: Put word pairs like these on the board or chart: *lice* and *lace, line* and *lane, coke* and *cake, spice* and *space, not* and *note.* For each pair, tell them what the first word is and ask a child what the second one is, e.g., "This word is *lice.* But in the second word, you see the letter *a* instead of *i.* What is the second word?"

Step 8: Ask children to think of words that end like *cake* and *lake.* Write them on the board as they say them, placing them in a vertical column so that the VCE pattern is emphasized. When a word has a homophone, such as *brake* and *break;* put both spellings on the board, but put the one that doesn't fit the pattern in a separate column.

Step 9: Return to the original story and have each child read one sentence—with your help if necessary. After he reads the sentence, ask him a context-analysis question. For example, after he reads the first sentence (*Dave* swam in a *lake.*), ask him:

> How do you know that the last word is *lake* and not *lamp*?
> How do you know that the first word is *Dave* and not *Desk*?

Make sure he explains his answer in terms of context clues and not just phonic clues.

Step 10:   Put a few sentences such as the following on the board (or better yet, put them on a chart ahead of the lesson):

> She <u>gave</u> me her (hate) (hat) to wear.
>
> I did not <u>save</u> my cake. I (at) (ate) it.
>
> I <u>have</u> a (rat) (rate) in a cage.

After reading the underlined words with them, ask them if all the underlined words have a long *a* sound in them. Point out that the VCE pattern usually indicates a long *a* sound but not always, e.g., *have:* "You have to check to see if the way you say the word makes sense in the sentence." Then for each sentence have a child go up to the board and circle the word in parentheses that "makes sense in the sentence" and then read the complete sentence out loud— with your help, if necessary.

Step 11:   Explain the worksheet which you give them for independent work. For the students, of course, the worksheet will provide additional practice; to strengthen the impact of the practice, be sure the worksheet requires some writing and not just checking or circling. For the teacher, the worksheet will provide information on which students need additional help.

Questions and Answers about Phonics

Question: How important is it for me to follow a commercial phonics program exactly as the teacher's guides suggest?

Answer: A quotation from Parker should help answer this question.

> There is little doubt that the majority of these materials have been marketed not to *aid* the teacher, but rather to serve as the primary teaching agent. Their mythical foolproof nature has done nothing but inhibit teachers from exploring their own creative selves and has often eliminated the transference of creative enthusiasm from teacher to student . . . (22, p. 176).

> One of Dykstra's major conclusions (10) after examining the results of the Cooperative Research Program in Primary Reading Instruction, was that the teacher was the major variable in whether children learned to read well or not. It is the teacher's enthusiasm, instructional skills, and knowledge that seem to make the big difference. A good teacher uses a commercial program as one important tool. A good teacher is not a slave to it.

174281

A Sample Worksheet for the Lesson on Long *a* in the VCE Pattern

Note: All directions should be explained to the group before they begin to work individually on the worksheet.

1. The word *came* ends with the letters *ame*. Write four words that end the same way as *came*. Some words have been partly done for you.

   came   bl__m__   s__m__   g__ __ __   _____

2. For each word that has a VCE spelling pattern write VCE above it. One of them already has been done for you. See if you can say the words that you mark:

       VCE
place	lace	rack	rake	lamb	lame
mat	mate	bald	bale	trace	chase

3. For any word that has a VCE pattern put a line over the *a* and a slash mark through the silent *e*. One has been done for you. See if you can say the words that you mark.

rāké	made	mad	scrap	scrape	male
ball	grass	grace	can	cane	cake

4. Circle the words which probably have a long *a* sound in them. One of them is already circled for you. See if you can say the words that you circle.

(face)	fast	gate	chase	chair	grade
cave	snap	take	fat	last	fate

5. Circle the word that makes sense in each sentence. One has been done for you. (Teacher reads these before children begin worksheet.)

   He wore my (hat) (hate).

   My horse is (lamb) (lame).

   I (hat) (hate) that bad man.

   I went to a candy (salt) (sale).

   That is a very (fat) (fate) cat.

Question: How can I get an honest opinion on commercial phonics materials that I may want to use in my classroom? The advertisements for these materials make them sound like a panacea for all reading ills.

Answer: Read the "Clip Sheet" and "Critically Speaking" columns that are in each month's edition of *The Reading Teacher*. To find a review of a particular set of materials (such as a phonics workbook), look in the index of the May issues under "Reviews."

Question: I'm afraid of using phonics. I'm afraid if I use phonics I'll be guilty of the type of instruction that ". . . misleads the beginner into believing that reading is decoding one set of meaningless visual symbols (letters) into another set of meaningless auditory symbols (phonemes) . . ." (8, p. 144). I want my students to see that reading is a form of communication. If I use phonics, they'll get the wrong idea, don't you think?

Answer: Yes, there is a danger of misleading them and creating future problems if you overemphasize phonics. Phonics should nearly always be used in conjunction with an emphasis on meaning. Show children that we use phonics to help us get at the meaning, not just to "sound out a word" and get a nod of approval from the teacher. Keep checking to see if the meaning is clear, And to be doubly sure that they perceive reading as an act of communication, use the language-experience approach along with your phonics or linguistics program.

Question: I feel inadequate in phonics. How can I improve my understanding of it?

Answer: See the Suggested Reading section, especially Heilman and Hull (18, 19).

Summary

Although graphophonic analysis is a form of decoding that experienced readers use in only a cursory way, it is a type of analysis that is crucial for most beginning readers to learn. Without the ability to recognize the correspondence between graphemes and phonemes, it is difficult for the child to become a truly independent reader. In this chapter we have discussed the common terms that reading teachers use and the common phonic and linguistic approaches. These approaches include the analytic, synthetic, substitution, spelling-pattern, and phonogram methods. Several warnings were given in this chapter about the overuse of phonics. The main warning was that phonics instruction should, as much as possible, take place in conjunction with context analysis, so that children are continually encouraged to read for meaning rather than for the correct sounds. In this way phonics can be taught as only one tool in the holistic process of reading.

References and Suggested Reading

1.   Bailey, Mildred H. "The Utility of Phonic Generalizations in Grade One through Six." *Reading Teacher* 20 (1967): 413–18.

2. Bond, Guy L., and Dykstra, Robert. "The Cooperative Research Program in First-Grade Reading Instruction." *Reading Research Quarterly* 2 (Summer 1967): 5–142.

3. Burie, Audrey Ann, and Heltshe, Mary Ann. *Reading with a Smile: 90 Reading Games that Work.* Washington, DC: Acropolis Books, 1975.

4. Burmeister, Lou E. "Usefulness of Phonic Generalizations." *Reading Teacher* 21 (1968): 349–56.

5. Chall, Jeanne S. *Learning to Read: the Great Debate.* New York: McGraw-Hill, 1967.

6. Clymer, Theodore L. "The Utility of Phonic Generalizations in the Primary Grades." *Reading Teacher* 26 (1963): 252–8.

7. Cordts, Anna D. *Phonics for the Reading Teacher.* New York: Holt, Rinehart, and Winston, 1965.

8. Downing, John. "What is Decoding?" *Reading Teacher* 29 (1975): 142–4.

9. Durkin, Dolores. *Strategies for Identifying Words.* Boston: Allyn & Bacon, 1979.

10. Dykstra, Robert. "Summary of the Second-Grade Phase of the Cooperative Research Program in Primary Reading Instruction." *Reading Research Quarterly* 1 (Fall 1968): 49–70.

11. Emans, Robert. "The Usefulness of Phonic Generalizations above the Primary Grades." *Reading Teacher* 20 (1967): 419–25.

12. Fromkin, Victoria, and Rodman, Robert. *An Introduction to Language.* New York: Holt, Rinehart, and Winston, 1978.

13. Fry, Edward. "A Diacritical Marking System to Aid Beginning Reading Instruction." *Elementary English* 31 (May 1964): 526–9.

14. Fry, Edward. *Comparison of Three Methods of Reading Instruction.* Washington, DC: USOE Cooperative Research Project No. 3050, 1967.

15. Greif, Ivo P. "A Study of the Pronunciation of Words Ending in a Vowel-Consonant-Final E Pattern." *Reading Teacher* 34 (December 1980): 290–2.

16. Harris, Theodore L. "Reading." *Encyclopedia of Education Research.* 4th ed. New York: Macmillan, 1969, pp. 1069–1104.

17. Harris, Theodore L., and Hodges, Richard E. (Editors). *The Dictionary of Reading Terms.* Newark, DE: International Reading Association, 1981.

18. Heilman, Arthur W. *Phonics in Proper Perspective.* Columbus, OH: Charles E. Merril, 1976.

19. Hull, Marion A. *Phonics for the Teacher of Reading.* Columbus, OH: Charles E. Merrill, 1976.

20. Lamb, Pose. *Linguistics in Proper Perspective.* Columbus, OH: Charles E. Merrill, 1977.

21. Mallett, Jerry J. *101 Make-and-Play Reading Games for the Intermediate Grades.* West Nyack, NY: Center for Applied Research in Education, 1977.

22. Parker, Robert A. "Crossfire." *Reading Teacher* 29 (1975): 176.

23. Russell, David H., et al. *Reading Aids through the Grades.* New York: Columbia University Teachers College, 1981.

24. Weaver, Phyllis. *Research within Reach.* Newark, DE: International Reading Association, 1978.

Application Experiences for the Teacher-Education Class

1. Each person in the class can be given one of the following statements to defend or deny. After a few minutes of preparation, all those who have statement #1 should first explain in their own words why it is either true or false and then read one or two sentences from the book that will demonstrate the author's position on the statement. (The same procedure can be followed for the rest of the statements.)

Statements about Chapter 3

Note: Literal level and inferential level statements are mixed together for this chapter.

    a. Phonic analysis is the last resort.

    b. Research studies support the teaching of phonics.

    c. Phonic analysis of the nonsense word *ganny* requires four interrelated steps.

    d. There is very little need for phonic analysis in the later grades.

    e. Our spelling system is reasonably consistent.

    f. Phonic analysis needs to be tempered with contextual analysis (as in "They *read* the book, but it was a long time ago.")

    g. "The phonics approach is definitely the way to teach reading, by golly."

    h. The words *word recognition, word identification, word analysis, word perception, word attack,* and *decoding* all mean the same thing.

    i. The words *once* and *though* are irregular words, but *win* and *lotion* are regular words.

    j. A phonogram is a grapheme combined with a phoneme.

    k. The word *crash,* in spoken form, contains a consonant blend, a vowel, and a consonant. In written form it contains a consonant cluster, a vowel letter, and a consonant digraph.

    l. A *diphthong* is any two speech sounds blended together.

    m. There's a good reason for calling the analytic phonics method "the whole-word phonics method."

    n. If you use the substitution method to help a child learn to decode *tr,* these pairs of words would be useful: *rap . . . trap, flee . . . tree, truck . . . stuck, rain . . . train, trail . . . train.*

    o. The phonogram method is nothing more than rhyming words.

    p. With the analytic phonics method, "the children tell the teacher"; with the synthetic phonics method, "the teacher tells the children."

    q. One of the best rules to teach children is that "when two vowels go walking, the first one does the talking."

    r. The game called the "e-boat adventure" is a good one for helping children notice the difference between VC and VCE patterns. (See Appendix B.)

2. You will need three or four separate chalkboards or paper charts for this one. Divide into three or four groups and practice teaching the Sample Lesson Using an Eclectic Approach shown on pages 85–87.

Each person can take one or two of the steps and teach them to the rest of the small group. After each step has been taught, make any suggestions necessary to the person who just played the role of teacher. (You won't need to be creative teachers for this experience; you will have a chance to be quite creative in Experience #3.)

3. Each group used in Experience #2 can now be divided into two subgroups. Subgroup A can develop a brief lesson on decoding the *st* cluster using the analytic phonics method (see pages 76–78). Subgroup B can develop a brief lesson on decoding the *st* cluster using both the substitution method and the phonogram method (see pages 78–81). Subgroup B should assume that Subgroup A's lesson will be taught first. When your lessons are developed, try them out on the other subgroup.

4. Discuss your answers to "A Self Quiz on Phonics Terminology" on page 77.

5. Divide into small groups and prepare a phonics "test" for other people in the class to take. To prepare this test, you will need to create ten nonsense words that illustrate the seven phonic rules and patterns described on pages 84–85. In creating your "words," have at least two rules or patterns illustrated in each word. (The word *cade*, for instance, illustrates #1 and #5.) When one of the other groups takes your test, they will have to decide on the correct pronunciation for each word and which rules or patterns are used in pronouncing it.

Field Experiences in the Elementary-School Classroom

1. Teach a phonics lesson to one or more children. If possible, use at least two different methods—or at least six of the steps shown in the "eclectic approach."

2. Teach a child to play "the e-boat adventure, "Wild Things," or some other phonics game. (See Appendix B.)

3. Try out the "phonics test" that you created in Experience #5 in class by asking a child informally to read the ten nonsense words. As she reads each word, see if she can tell you why it should be "pronounced that way." (Make a game out of this, rather than a test.) See what you can learn about her phonic analysis abilities.

CHAPTER 4

Morphemic analysis requires that the readers recognize common roots, prefixes, and suffixes.

Teaching Syllabic, Morphemic, Contextual, and Dictionary Analysis

Chapter Outline

Chapter Preview

In the last chapter we talked about graphophonic analysis (also termed "phonic analysis" or "phonics"). In this chapter we need to look at some other types of decoding skills that a child needs to learn in order to determine an author's message more efficiently. The mature reader is striving, in a holistic way, to integrate all of the decoding and comprehension skills she can muster, in order to acquire the information or entertainment she desires from an author. Although graphophonic analysis was a highly necessary skill when she was first learning to read, it has decreased in its importance as she has developed her reading power. Along the way toward achieving such power, she has picked up other important decoding skills (as well as comprehension skills). These decoding skills include syllabic analysis, morphemic analysis, contextual analysis, and dictionary analysis.

> Human language is made up of phonemes, morphemes, and syllables just as ours is.

The Case for Syllabic and Morphemic Analysis

Graphophonic analysis, as important as it is, is generally a slow method of decoding. The worst form of graphophonic analysis, and one that should seldom be encouraged, is the "sounding-out" method, in which one letter at a time is translated into a letter sound. For instance, with the "sounding-out" method one would translate *unselected* into ten separate phonemes:

$$/u/ + /n/ + /s/ + /e/ + /l/ + /e/ + /c/ + /t/ + /e/ + /d/$$

Therefore, at the same time that a teacher is giving students a firm foundation in phonics, he should begin to wean them away from an overreliance on phonic signals.

One way of doing this is to gradually introduce them to the concept that a printed word represents larger segments of sound and meaning than mere phonemes. For example, what would be some larger segments of sound and meaning represented by the word *unselected?* In print, this word represents four distinct "beats." These four beats, called syllables, are represented by *un, se, lec,* and *ted,* with *lec* being the loudest one.

The word *unselected* also represents three meaningful units called morphemes: *un, select,* and *ed.* A morpheme is the smallest *meaningful* unit of speech (4). Each morpheme is meaningful in that taking it away could *change* the meaning of the total word. The difference between *select* and *selected,* for example, is the difference between present and past. The difference between *selected* and *unselected* is the difference between positive and negative.

So what we have, then, is a printed word that represents not only phonemes but morphemes and syllables as well. The task of the teacher is to help the child learn how to translate the printed word into all three types of units, but gradually putting more reliance on morphemes and syllables—since this usually reduces the time spent in decoding a word.

When to Introduce Syllabic and Morphemic Analysis

Teaching children to recognize morphemes and syllables can begin very early in reading instruction. It is possible to introduce the word *cats,* for example, shortly after the word *cat* has been thoroughly learned. After several experiences of decoding singular and plural nouns, the child will learn to recognize the ending *s* and to realize intuitively that the word *cats* represents two separate morphemes— /cat/ and /s/; and that the addition or subtraction of the morpheme /s/ changes the meaning of the word.

The same type of understanding can be gained about verb changes such as *jump* and *jumping* or *want* and *wanted;* and also about the effects of adding other types of morphemes called prefixes and suffixes, as in *happy* and *unhappy, hope* and *hopeful.* Gradually the child can be taught to recognize familiar suffixes, prefixes, and other morphemes shown in Table 4.1 on page 105.

In addition to an introduction to morphemic analysis, children can also be introduced rather early to syllabic analysis. Words such as *rabbit* and *cotton,* for example, lend themselves to simple clapping or stamping exercises which illustrate the two distinct syllables or "beats" represented by each word. This type of primitive analysis would eventually lead to a more sophisticated analysis of those particular grapheme patterns that indicate a separation of syllables. In the word *basket,* for instance, the reader can see two vowel letters separated by a pair of consonant letters. This pattern, the VCCV pattern, indicates that two syllables should be uttered and that the break in the word is usually between the two consonant letters. Having broken the word into subdivisions, the child is then able to look for familiar phonic patterns in each one. In the case of the word *bas/ket,* for instance, it is easy to recognize the VC spelling pattern in each subdivision, and this would signal a short vowel sound (or a schwa sound in the unaccented syllable).

It should be clear, then, that without some knowledge of syllabic analysis, the reader's ability to use phonic knowledge is limited to one-syllable words. Thus, making children aware of syllables provides them with two benefits: 1) it allows them to gradually escape from an overreliance on phonics by teaching them to perceive larger units than mere phonemes, and 2) it allows them to expand the use of graphophonic analysis to words of more than one syllable.

The What, How, and When of Teaching Syllabic Analysis

Now that we have discussed the purposes of teaching morphemic and syllabic analysis, let's move on to these three questions: 1) What elements of syllabic analysis and morphemic analysis are worth teaching? 2) What elements are not worth teaching? and 3) What procedures are helpful in teaching the useful elements?

With respect to syllabic analysis, children need to learn how to divide words *mentally* into syllables and what effects the word division will have upon phonic analysis. The process of dividing words into syllables—called either *syllabic analysis, syllabication,* or *syllabification*—is subject to the same type of limitation that phonic analysis has: there are few syllabication rules one can really rely on to help you in pronouncing a word. It's true there are many rules a secretary can use for hyphenating a word that is divided at the end of a typewritten line; but that's not what we're talking about here. We're talking about dividing words mentally in order to decode them better.

You see, a secretary or printer divides words according to *printing* conventions and not according to what's helpful to the reader. For example, a printer would divide the word *hoping* this way: hop-ing. A reader who divides it mentally that way would come up with *hopping;* and, through contextual analysis he'd know that he'd divided it the wrong way. If he then switches to ho-ping, he'll come up with the right pronunciation and the right meaning.

Syllabication, then, becomes a tool for the reader who is searching for meaning—searching for the message that the author is presenting. Syllabication should not be a "busywork" exercise of merely drawing lines between syllables.

You probably recall that in a dictionary you are presented with two ways of dividing each word, first according to printing convention and then according to the need of the reader, e.g., risk/y (ris'/kē) and drift/er (drif'/tər). It would be helpful for the reading teacher to look at word division in this same way—as two separate conventions. As a reading teacher, of course, you're only concerned with the decoding convention and not the printing convention. With this distinction in mind, let's now look at some syllabication rules which are usually helpful when it comes to decoding a multisyllabic word that is not recognized through visual memory.

1. You can *hear* either a vowel sound or a diphthong sound in each syllable (pen/cəl). (Without this understanding children won't

know what word division is all about.) Note: A diphthong is equivalent to a vowel in this rule, e.g., *boiling* has only two syllables.

2. When you see a VCCV pattern in a word you can't "read," (rabbit, basket, rather, bathing) try dividing the word mentally—first between the two consonant letters and then either after or before the two consonant letters. (Why don't we try this rule and see how it works: With rab/bit and bas/ket our first division will work well enough for *decoding* purposes; we now have four examples of the VC letter pattern—*rab, bit, bas, ket,* and the sounds of these syllables can be easily approximated through phonic analysis. With rat/her, however, we have a nonsensical word; but with rath/er we again have letter patterns which can be decoded through graphophonic analysis. With bath/ing we have another nonsensical word; but with bā/thing we have spelling patterns which signal the correct pronunciation.)

3. When you see a VCV pattern in a word you can't "read," (hotel, robin, return, robot) try dividing the word mentally—first before the consonant letter and then after the consonant letter. (With ho/tel, re/turn, and ro/bot our first division leaves us with patterns that can be recognized through graphophonic analysis; in each case the first syllable is a CV long vowel pattern. If we divide them *after* the consonant letter, we get the VC short vowel pattern: hot/el, ret/urn, rob/ot and would pronounce them (hot/tel), (ret/turn), and (rob/bot). Again, contextual analysis or meaning will help us know which division is correct. In the case of ro/bin our first division wouldn't produce a meaningful word; but our second division, rob/in, would.)

4. If you see the CLE pattern at the end of a word you can't "read," (cat/tle, peo/ple, ta/ble), try pronouncing that pattern as a separate syllable with the /l/ sound at the end. (Even though words with double consonants (e.g., fiddle) have a slightly different ending sound, this rule will provide a good approximation of the syllable's sound.)

5. Prefixes and suffixes usually represent separate syllables.

Although some teachers (and reading programs) cover many more rules for syllabication, these five pretty well "cover the waterfront." They are fairly easy for children near the end of grade two to learn but tend to be difficult for younger children. They are probably learned best in a gradual way through a multitude of examples and discovery-type lessons. The most difficult rule to learn seems to be #3. An illustration of one type of lesson on Rule #3 follows:

Sample Lesson on Syllabic Analysis (Rule 3: Words that Include a VCV Pattern)

Step 1:   Introduce sample words in context. Put these two sentences on the board:

The *robin* pulled the worm out of the ground.
Ron made a *robot* that looks like a man.

Read them out loud with the students. Ask how many syllables there are in *robin?* How many in *robot?* Clap the syllables if necessary.

Step 2:   Show them how to divide and decode some sample words. Put words like these on the board in a vertical list: *robin, robot, cabin, babies, shaving, hotel, final, never, music.* Lead them to discover that all of the words in the list have something in common, i.e., they include a VCV pattern. Show how to divide the first two: rob/in, ro/bot. Ask them how the first syllable of *robin* differs from the first syllable of *robot.* Lead them to realize that the first syllable in rob/in has a VC pattern and a short vowel sound, whereas the first syllable in ro/bot has a CV pattern and a long vowel sound. Ask them how *robin* would sound if it were divided like this: ro/bin. Ask them which pronunciation fits the sentence. Ask them how *robot* would sound if it were divided like this: rob/ot. Ask them which pronunciation fits the sentence. (Note: In this lesson, avoid using words with VCE roots that maintain their final *e,* such as hope/ful or rude/ly.)

Step 3:   Let them try decoding some sample words on their own. For each of the remaining words in your list, have children come up to the board and divide the word both ways— before the middle consonant letter and after it. Each time they divide it, they should pronounce it out loud, e.g., ca/bin /kā′ bən/ and cab/in /kab′ ən/. Then they should tell "which pronunciation makes more sense."

Step 4:   Have them develop a generalization or rule. Ask them a question something like this: "What rule can you make up about dividing a word that includes a VCV pattern?" Accept anything similar in meaning to this: "It can be divided either before or after the consonant letter." (For exception to rule, see note in Step 2.) Then ask them: "If it's divided before the consonant letter, will the vowel letter be long or short?" (long). "If it's divided after the consonant letter, will the vowel letter be long or short?" (short). Have them test their rule on some other words; ask them to divide and decode words like the following, both before and after the middle consonant letter: *miner, closet, famous, tulip, Robert, cedar, China, paper, begin.*

In summary, the steps recommended for one way of teaching syllabic analysis are these:

1.   Introduce sample words in context—visually and orally.
2.   Show the students how to divide and decode some sample words.

3. Let them try decoding some sample words on their own.
4. Have them develop a generalization and test it on some other words.

Differences between Syllabic and Morphemic Analysis

Syllabic analysis, as you know, involves the translation of graphemes into units of sound. *Morphemic analysis* involves the translation of graphemes into units of sound and meaning. Take the word *revisited,* for example. Syllabic analysis (in preparation for phonic analysis) would lead to (re-vis-it-ed). Morphemic analysis, on the other hand, would lead to re-visit-ed.

Morphemic analysis is a quicker, more mature, form of analysis. Why is this so? With syllabic analysis, the reader must try different ways of dividing the word while at the same time using phonic analysis to check on her guesses. With morphemic analysis, a reader relies primarily on the visual memory of root words and affixes (such as the root word *visit* and the affixes *re-* and *-ed.*

To make this difference between syllabic and morphemic analysis more distinct, let's look at another example. Syllabic analysis of the word *unhappiness* would yield un/hap/pi/ness and lead to phonic analysis of the syllables. Morphemic analysis, on the other hand, would yield un-happ(y)-ness, because the reader would recognize the meaningful units through visual memory. It's true that the reader may not recognize all the meaningful units; e.g., she may just recognize the prefix and suffix through visual memory and have to decode the root through phonic analysis. Nevertheless, the goal in teaching morphemic analysis is to help the child develop a sight vocabulary of common roots and common affixes (prefixes and suffixes)—in other words, a sight vocabulary of common morphemes.

For a final example, take the word *unhurriedly.* Without reading any further, see if you can decode it, first by syllabic analysis and then by morphemic analysis.

Syllabic analysis of *unhurriedly:* (_____)

Morphemic analysis of *unhurriedly:* (_____)

With syllabic analysis, you should have come up with this: (un/hur/ried/ly). But with morphemic analysis, you would get un-hurr(y)-ed-ly. Do you see the difference? Syllabic analysis requires decoding according to units of sound and is accompanied by phonic analysis. Morphemic analysis requires decoding according to meaningful units and is accompanied by visual memory. Syllabic analysis requires mainly the assistance of phonic analysis. Morphemic analysis requires mainly the assistance of visual memory. (Both require the assistance of contextual analysis, but we'll get to that a little later.)

Teaching Morphemic Analysis

There are two basic ways of teaching morphemic analysis, both of which should probably be used. One way is the derivative approach and the other is the morpheme-recognition approach. (A *derivative* is a word usually formed by adding affixes to a root word.) With the derivative approach, you help children extend root words by adding affixes (prefixes and suffixes). With the morpheme-recognition approach, you help children separate a word into its root words and affixes.

As an example of the derivative approach, let's take the root word *paint*. The teacher would begin listing words such as paint, paints, and painted. Then he might say, "Can anyone add to my list?" Gradually the students and teacher would add more derivatives of *paint*, such as *painter, painting, repaint, repainted, repainting, unpainted, painters*.

As an example of the morpheme-recognition approach, let's look at one type of sample lesson:

Step 1:   Introduce sample words in context. Put these sentences on the board, and read them with the children:

    a.   Fred went walking.

    b.   He walked three miles.

    c.   Sandy was planting seeds.

    d.   She planted them in a neat row.

    e.   Betty was mailing letters.

    f.   She mailed them to her friends.

Step 2:   Help them discover and decode the root words. Ask them what two words in sentences 1 and 2 are almost the same *(walking, walked)*. Then ask them what part of each word is exactly the same *(walk)*. Remind them that this part is called the *root word,* if they have forgotten the term. Have someone underline and read out loud the root word in *walking* and *walked.* Have other children do the same for *planting* and *planted,* and for *mailing* and *mailed* in sentences 3 through 6.

Step 3:   Help them discover and decode the affixes. Ask them how *walked, planted,* and *mailed* are the same (an *-ed* ending). Remind them that *ed* is called a *suffix,* if they have forgotten the term. Have the children circle the suffixes in *walked, planted,* and *mailed* and read the words out loud. Ask them how the suffix differs for the three words—does it always stand for the same sound?

Step 4:   Have them develop a generalization by asking them what three sounds the *ed* suffix represents. Have them test their generalization on some other words, such as *jumped, wanted, farmed,* and any others that they can think of.

Step 5:   Provide them with a worksheet that includes a list of words, most of them having *ed* or *ing* suffixes. Be sure not to use words that necessitate root changes before adding a suffix, e.g., words such as *rub(b)ing* mak(e)ing. Have them circle the suffixes, underline the root words, and later read the words out loud to a partner (a very important way to assure that decoding skills are developed, and not just spelling skills). Have the other partner make up a sentence for each word.

In summary:

1.   Introduce sample words in context—visually and orally.
2.   Help them discover and decode the root words.
3.   Help them discover and decode the affixes.
4.   Have them develop and test a generalization (if one is warranted).
5.   Provide additional practice.

The Elements of Morphemic Analysis

Morphemic analysis requires that the readers recognize common roots, prefixes, and suffixes. It also requires them to recognize compound words, contractions, and Greek and Latin morphemes. For specific examples of these elements of morphemic analysis refer to Table 4.1.

As shown in Table 4.1, there are two major types of suffixes. One type creates a new meaning through inflection. The other type creates a new meaning by producing a derivative. Let's look at the second type first. By adding the suffix *-ful* to the word *help* we can produce the derivative *helpful*. By adding other suffixes, we can form other derivatives: *helper, helpfully, helpless, helplessly.* As we change from the root word *help* to one of the derivatives, we've created a new meaning through the addition of one or more suffixes.

The second major type of suffix is an inflectional ending. An *inflectional ending* (or simply *inflection*) is a suffix that helps communicate the relationship between words in a sentence or longer passage. For instance, we can change from "The book of the minister is here" to "The minister's book is here." We can do this by changing the word order and by adding an inflectional ending to *minister*— from *minister* to *minister's.* The inflectional ending, *'s* thus shows the

Table 4.1   *Some Important Elements of Morphemic Analysis*

Elements	Examples
1. Prefixes	*unlock, repaint, disappear, impossible, incorrect, derail, preview, become, alike*
2. Compound words	*playground, birthday, anything*
3. Contractions	*didn't, let's, it's, she'll, they're, you've, he'd*
4. Greek and Latin morphemes	*tele, graph, phono, photo, port, bi*
5. Derivative-forming suffixes with no root changes	*helper, helpful, helpfully, helpless, quickly, sticky, dangerous, agreement*

6. Suffixes added to modified roots
  a. Final consonant doubled
  b. Final *y* changed to *i*
  c. Final *e* dropped
	
	rubbed, sipping, sitter
	happily, hurries, happier, happiest
	maker, moved, hoping

7. Inflectional suffixes with no root changes	*girls, jumps, jumped, boy's, higher, highest*

relationship between *minister* and *book*. As another example, we can change from "The boy hits the ball" to "The boys hit the ball." By using the inflectional ending, *s,* we can show the relationship between the word pairs: *boy* and *hits, boys* and *hit.*

Some languages rely heavily on inflections to communicate meaning. Modern English relies on word arrangements and inter-relationships (syntax) instead. The inflections that have survived in the English language include *s* for the regular way of indicating plural (boys), *s* for third person indicative verbs (hits), *er* and *est* for the comparative and superlative form of many adjectives and adverbs (faster, fastest), *ed* for the past tense and past participle of regular verbs (buried, potted), and *ing* for the present participle (seeing). (Having *potted* the plant and *seeing* that it was ready, he *buried* it in the ground.)

The Importance of Contextual Analysis to Communication

As well as being a decoding method in its own right, contextual analysis might be called the "psycholinguistic supervisor" of visual memory, phonic analysis, and structural analysis. Visual memory alone, for example, may lead José to decode *raid* as *rail* in this sentence: "The Vikings came in their ships to raid the coast of England." But contextual analysis would warn him that *rail* doesn't make sense—i.e., his psycholinguistic guess was not the correct one.

Let's take another example. For the sentence "Nancy was hoping she could go," suppose Francis syllabicates *hoping* this way: (hop'/ing). Then phonic analysis would tell her that the accented syllable has a short *o*, and she would read, "Nancy was hopping she could go." Contextual analysis, however, would get her back on the track, since she would realize that (hop'/ing) doesn't make sense, but (hō'/ping) does.

To take one more example, suppose Tommy is trying to decode this sentence: "As soon as Bobby shot the ball, the referee blew his whistle." If he tries to use morphemic analysis on *referee*, he'll end up with re-feree, which would sound something like (rē/fuŕ/ē). Contextual analysis would indicate to him that he needs to try some other way of decoding the word. Suppose he next tries to syllabicate the word and comes up with this: (ref'/ər/ē). Again, contextual analysis would indicate that he's off the mark—but only slightly. Now the word sounds vaguely familiar and probably in less than a second he makes sense out of the word by changing it to (ref/ə/re').

We can see, then, that contextual analysis is crucial to the process of decoding words in print (and also to the process of making good psycholinguistic guesses). And we can see more clearly now, how the various means of decoding words work together. In fact, even contextual analysis must often have help from one of the other decoding methods. Take this sentence, for instance:

This poison ivy rash is driving me _____ .

Contextual analysis, alone, may lead Wyman to expect a word like *crazy* or *mad*. But suppose he also uses the minimal phonic clue offered by the first letter. That is, suppose he sees the sentence this way:

This poison ivy rash is driving me w _____ .

Now the words *crazy* and *mad* probably don't even occur to him. Instead, he will be guided by the combination of phonics and context to come up with a word like *wild*, or perhaps *wacky*. And, if he sees the sentence *this* way:

This poison ivy rash is driving me w _____ d.

there would probably be no question in his mind as he reads it; the word is *wild*—it makes sense and it fits the minimal phonic signals that he has noticed.

Perhaps it is also more clearly seen how decoding and comprehension work together to enable a person to "read." We have been treating the process of decoding as it it were separate from comprehension. But as we saw in the sentences just used as examples, children must decode properly in order to comprehend, and they must comprehend the sentence or entire passage properly in order to decode through contextual analysis and to provide the proper check on other means of decoding.

Providing Direct Instruction in Contextual Analysis

It is probably already clear that contextual analysis is a skill that should be developed alongside those of visual memory, morphemic analysis, syllabic analysis, and phonic analysis. Every time the teacher asks a child whether a particular word makes sense in a sentence, he is teaching contextual analysis. However, to strengthen and clarify this skill, specific lessons need to be provided—particularly if you have found through diagnostic testing or observation that certain children are deficient in this form of analysis. These lessons should be designed to help the children see that a particular word "makes sense" in a sentence when it meets three criteria: 1) the word fits syntactically with the rest of the sentence; 2) it fits semantically with the rest of the sentence; and 3) it fits the phonic clues presented by the word itself.

The concept of syntactic sense is a simple one to adults who are familiar with the English language. However, to those children who have developed a habit of "word calling," rather than thoughtful reading, it is an important concept indeed. To help you review this concept yourself, let's look at the following sentence:

Roger is a very good _____ .

Which of these words will fit in the blank: *dog, runs, singer, happy, house, luckily, boy?* Beginning with *dog*, every other one will fit in the blank—even *house*, although *Roger* is not a very likely name for a house. Perhaps a better question would be: which of the words will not fit in the blank? It would be difficult to think of Roger as being a very good *runs* or *happy* or *luckily*. These words simply don't belong in the slot; they are syntactically out of tune. In short, they don't sound right.

This concept of syntactic context can be gained intuitively by children without necessarily using formal terminology such as *nouns, verbs, adverbs,* and *adjectives.* Generally all they need are four types of decoding experiences—one for each of the four major parts of speech. For nouns, for example, they would need sentences such as this one to work with:

The _____ is here. *(paper, swims, quickly, clown, sleepy)*

The teacher can ask the children to select from a set of words those words that can or cannot fit in the blank. He can also have the children think of other words that can and cannot fit in the blank.

For adjectives, the teacher should make use of sentences like this one:

That thing is very _____ . *(funny, boy, slowly, ripe, heavy, eat, cats)*

For verbs, sentences like these would be suitable:

I _____ here. *(am, dog, happily, eat, sad, sleep, sit)*

He _____ it. *(boy, hid, ate, quickly, found, happy)*

And for adverbs, you may use a sentence similar to this one:

They do it _____ . *(fast, come, quickly, heavy, girl, lucky, noisily)*

As mentioned earlier, a particular word makes sense in a sentence when it meets three criteria. The first criterion is syntactic sense. The second one is semantic sense. For helping children discover this criterion, you need to use sample sentences that are not so open-ended. For instance, the sentence below would not be very useful because too many words would have meaning (make semantic sense).

I _____ here. *(live, swim, man, lucky, jump, yellow)*

The following sentence, though, would offer enough semantic context to limit the choice to one word.

John looked at his house and said, "I _____ here." *(sail, man, live, lucky, jump, yellow)*

To help children discover the third criterion—phonic clues— you need to use sample sentences and word choices that allow for ambiguity until phonic clues are noticed. A sentence similar to the following may be useful for this purpose:

I like to _____ in the ocean. *(fish, run, swim, eat, dive, silly)*

After the children realize that either *fish, swim,* or *dive* would fit, you can add a phonic clue to the sentence this way:

I like to d _____ in the ocean. *(fish, run, swim, eat, dive, silly)*

Now the correct word becomes obvious, and through a brief discussion and other examples, you can get them to see the advantage of using both the initial letter and the context as clues for proper decoding.

In summary, three concepts related to contextual analysis should be taught:

1. The word should make sense syntactically (it should sound right).
2. The word should fit the meaning (semantic context) of the sentence (it should make sense).
3. The word should be suited to the minimal phonic clue (it should at least start with the right letter).

Decoding Words with a Dictionary

Try decoding the following "story":

"This cold medicine is wonderful!" said Jane.
"Yes, of course," Dick replied. "It has pseudoephedrine in it."
"And what, pray tell, is pseudoephedrine?" asked Jane.
"You mean you don't know!" said Dick in astonishment.
"I can't quite remember," Jane said coyly.
"Well!" Dick said with a sneer. "I thought everyone knew that pseudoephedrine is a nasal decongestant."
"Oh yes, of course," Jane said sweetly, hiding her irritation. "Now I remember."

Probably you had no difficulty with this story, except perhaps for one of the words. Your visual memory—developed long before you began to read this book on the teaching of reading—undoubtedly stood you in good stead. However, what about the word *pseudoephedrine?* Did you dash for the dictionary as soon as you encountered it? Most people wouldn't. And yet, unless you recognized the Greek morpheme *pseudo,* the dictionary would be your best hope for decoding the word. The general meaning of the word is clear from the context of the story, but its pronunciation is probably not immediately obvious to most of us.

There are two morals to this story. *Moral 1*—a dictionary is necessary in order for children to decode highly irregular words that are not already part of their sight vocabulary—words such as *psychiatrist, pterodactyl, pneumonia, gnome, aisle,* and *fatigue. Moral 2*—most people avoid the dictionary like the plague.

The truth of the second moral may be due to two factors. For one thing, using a dictionary is the slowest method of decoding a word that there is. If the word pops up in the middle of an exciting story, hardly anyone will want to take the time to look it up. In some cases though, when one is trying to gather information rather than read an exciting story, the dictionary can be the quickest route to knowledge. But still it is avoided like the plague. And this leads to the second factor—lack of skill in using a dictionary. Such lack of skill results in a trial-and-error approach for most people—a laborious, painful process that provides punishment rather than reward. So what can be done about it? The next section will offer a few suggestions.

The Nature of "Looking Up a Word"

In Chapter 2 using a dictionary to expand the meaning of a word was discussed. In this chapter we'll talk about decoding a word with a dictionary. That is, we'll talk about determining the pronunciation of a word by using a dictionary.

Using a dictionary needn't be painful.

One secret to success in teaching children to use a dictionary is to avoid assigning dictionary tasks that are too difficult. Too often children are asked to use dictionaries before they are ready to use them. And this leads to plenty of frustration for children and teachers alike.

Let's take the word *fatigue,* for instance. Suppose you ask Henry to look up this word and tell the class how to pronounce it. What skills does he need in order to do this quickly and correctly? Assuming he knows where to find the dictionary (an assumption that could easily be erroneous), he should know first of all that since the word starts with *f,* he will need to open the dictionary somewhere in the first part of the book. If he opens it to words beginning with *g,* he must know that he should now go toward the front of the book rather than toward the back. As soon as he finds the "*f* pages," he shouldn't look randomly for the word *fatigue;* he should head toward the first f pages, since the second letter in *fatigue* is *a.* To put it another way, he should know alphabetical order perfectly. As Henry continues his search, his eyes should only be scanning the top of each page rather than the whole page, for at the top he will find two guide words, which indicate the first and last entry for the page.

Now that he's finally found the word, he should study the respelling in parentheses. In this case it's (fə/tēg′), rather than (fat′/ig/yū), which is what he thought it was going to be. Suppose he's thrown by the pronunciation of (fə), the first syllable. Then he should glance immediately to the bottom of the page at the "Concise Pronunciation Key" to find that (ə) is equal to *a,* as in *alone.* Now, by paying attention to the diacritical mark over the *e,* by noticing the syllabication and the accent mark, and by employing his phonic knowledge of how to translate graphemes into phonemes, he is now ready to tell the class how to pronounce it.

You can see, then, what you've really asked Henry to do! In list form, to be able to decode a word "simply" through the use of a dictionary, he must be able to do these things:

1. Locate the appropriate section of the pages
2. Determine whether the first letter of the word is before or after the page he is reading
3. Determine whether the second letter of the word is before or after the page he is reading
4. Determine whether the third or possibly the fourth letter of the word is before or after the page he is reading
5. Locate the guide words (entry words) that "enclose" the word he's seeking
6. Locate and use the Concise Pronunciation Key, if necessary, to determine the pronunciation of each syllable
7. Use the diacritical marks to determine the pronunciation of certain graphemes
8. Interpret syllabic division correctly

   9. Interpret accent marks correctly
   10. Employ his knowledge of grapheme-phoneme relationships (phonics)

   Perhaps it's clear, then, that before we expect children to use the dictionary—even if it's only for decoding a word and not even to comprehend it better—we had better first teach them the ten skills listed.

Teaching Specific Dictionary Skills

Now let's talk about teaching those ten skills that were listed in the last section. The first skill Henry had to have when he looked up *fatigue* was that of selecting the correct part of the dictionary to look in—the front, middle, or back. Here's an experience you can provide for your students to help them gain this skill. Provide the children with a *school* dictionary designated for their grade level. Then do the following:

A Sample Lesson on the Front, Middle, and Back of a Dictionary

   1.   Print the letters of the alphabet near the top of the chalkboard, with a wide space between the *e* and *f* and the *p* and *q*. Write the words *front, middle,* and *back* above these three divisions.

front part	*middle part*	*back part*
a b c d e	f g h i j k l m n o p	q r s t u v w x y z

   2.   Write these words on the chalkboard under the label *front part,* and ask the children what letters they begin with: *apple, boy, car, dog, elephant.* Tell them that these words can be found in the *front part* of the dictionary. Prove this to them by telling them on what page of their school dictionary to find each word. After they have found each word, ask them whether the word was found in the front part of the dictionary, the middle part, or the back part. (If they don't understand this, review the terms *front part, middle part,* and *back part,* as these apply to things like the *top* of their desks or a *row* of desks.)

   3.   Write *fox, girl,* and *hat* on the board under *middle part* and tell them that these words can be found in the middle part of the dictionary. Point to the letters on the chalkboard and ask them how you knew that. Then ask them to think of other words that they could find in the middle part of the dictionary (words like *ink, jump, king, log, mop, nap, off,* and *pan*). Write them on the board as they dictate them under the label *middle part.*

4. Prove it with two or three of the words by telling them on what page to find them.

5. Write *queen* under the label *back part* and tell them that *queen* can be found in the back part of the dictionary. Point to the letters on the chalkboard and ask them how you knew that. Then ask them to think of other words that they would find in the back part of the dictionary (words like *rabbit, sun, tiger, umbrella, visit, wish, X-ray, yard,* and *zebra*). Write them on the board as they dictate them under the label *back part.*

6. Prove it with two or three of the words by telling them on what page to find them.

7. Write several words on the board and ask them in what part of the dictionary they would expect to find each one—the front part, the middle part, or the back part.

8. Give them a worksheet that contains a list of words with a blank after each one. Have them write *front, middle,* or *back* in each blank. Before they complete their worksheet, review the three parts with them by presenting this verse:

> The front is *a* to *e.*
> The middle is *f* to *p.*
> And so, as you can see,
> The back is *q* to *z.*

Ideas on Teaching Alphabetical Order

The second, third, and fourth skills Henry needed in looking up *fatigue* each require a good grasp of alphabetical order. Let's suppose that he decides that *fatigue* is in the middle part of the dictionary and he happens to turn to page 203. Well, on page 203 he finds words that begin with the letter *h.* Now what does he do? He has to realize that *h* is too far and that he needs to move toward the front of the dictionary until he gets to the *f*s. Once he gets to the *f*s, though, he needs to look for words that begin with *fa.* And once he gets there, he needs to look for words that begin with *fat,* and so on.

Practice exercises on alphabetical order can be found in most reading workbooks. Or you can create your own. It's easy. Just select some words from the teacher's guides to basal readers or from school dictionaries. For the first type of exercise, select words that begin with different first letters. For the second type of exercise, select words that all begin with the same letter but with different second letters. For the third and fourth types of exercise, of course, the third and fourth letters would differ. Once you've taught them how to alphabetize these types of lists, you're ready to teach them how to use "guide words" in a dictionary.

A Sample Lesson on Guide Words

1.   Say something like this to your students: "Now that you've learned how to alphabetize, you're ready to learn how to use guide words. Let's look at some guide words in your dictionary. At the top of page 216 are the words *fast* and *fatten.* Can you find them? These are the guide words for page 216. These two words tell you that all the words on this page begin with the letters *f-a.* Can you tell me why I know that's true? Can you prove it to me?"

2.   "These two guide words tell you that some of the words on this page start with *f-a-s* and some of them start with *f-a-t.* Can you prove this to me?"

3.   "These two guide words tell you that none of the words on this page starts with *f-a-s-s.* How do I know that? Can you prove this to me?"

4.   "These two guide words tell you that none of the words on this page starts with *f-a-t-u.* How do I know that? Can you prove this to me?"

5.   Write *father, fatal, fashion,* and *favor* on the board. Then ask. "Would you expect to find the word *father* on this page? Why? Prove it. Would you expect to find the word *fatal?* Why? Prove it. Would you expect to find the word *fashion?* Why not? Can you prove it? Would you expect to find the word *favor?* Why not? Can you prove it?"

6.   "What guide words do you find on page 285? What things do these two guide words tell you? Do you see the word I've just written on the chalkboard? Would you expect to find this word on this page? Prove it. What guide words do you find on page 95? What things do these two guide words tell you? Without looking at the page, tell me one word that you think will be there. Tell me one word you're sure will not be there."

7.   "On this worksheet is a list of words. After each word, I'd like you to write the two guide words that you found in the dictionary. Let's do the first one together."

Ideas on Teaching the Use of a Pronunciation Key

Now that Henry has learned how to look in the right part of the dictionary and to use guide words, he's ready to learn how to use the pronunciation key that is found at the bottom of every page (or every other page). This key is used in conjunction with the "respelling" that is found in parentheses right after a word. Take the word *feign,* for example. Right after the word *feign,* he is likely to find (fān). Henry would now know that this is a word that rhymes either with *pan* or with *pain.* If he already knows his diacritical marks, he will know it rhymes with *pain.* But if he doesn't know his diacritical marks, he should look down at the bottom of the page he's on (or on the adjacent page) at the "Pronunciation Key" or the "Concise Pronunciation Key." This key is nothing but a list of words that serve as examples. Since Henry is not sure how to pronounce the middle sound in (fān), he should look for a word in the key that also has a macron over the *a,* such as *āce.* Now, assuming he knows how to pronounce *ace,* he would know that (fān) rhymes with pain.

A major technique that can be used to teach Henry and others to use the Concise Pronunciation Key is to use the key with them on a few words each day until they understand it. A few children may need extra drill provided through workbook exercises. However, unless the workbook exercises are followed up with actual use of the dictionary, it is doubtful that such exercises are very useful. This same procedure is appropriate for the other skills on "Henry's list." The only exception may be Skill #10, the use of phonic analysis to decode the graphemes in the word. This skill, of course, should be developed through the regular program of reading instruction.

Summary

Although graphophonic analysis is an important skill for children to learn, there are other equally important word-analysis skills. These include syllabic analysis, morphemic analysis, contextual analysis, and dictionary analysis. Contextual analysis, because of its close relationship to comprehension and to the author's message, should be the overseer or supervisor of the other forms of analysis. When we ask children to look up a word in a dictionary, we are asking them to make use of a long list of specific skills. These specific skills should be taught before we expect children to use the dictionary with confidence.

References and Suggested Reading

1. Burie, Audrey Ann, and Heltshe, Mary Ann. *Reading with a Smile: 90 Reading Games that Work.* Washington, DC: Acropolis Books, 1975.
2. Durkin, Dolores. *Strategies for Identifying Words.* Boston: Allyn and Bacon, 1976.

3. Ehri, Linnea C., Barron, Roberick W., and Feldman, Jeffrey M. *The Recognition of Words*. Newark, DE: International Reading Association, 1978. Describes ways of helping children use morpological, syntactic, and phonological clues in recognizing words.

4. Fromkin, Victoria, and Rodman, Robert. *An Introduction to Language*. New York: Holt, Rinehart, and Winston, 1978.

5. Glass, Gerald G., and Burton, Elizabeth H. "How Do They Decode? Verbalizations and Observed Behavior of Successful Decoders." *Education* 94 (1973): 58–64.

6. Hull, Marion A. *Phonics for the Teacher of Reading*. Columbus, OH: Charles E. Merrill, 1976. See Chapter on "Syllabication and Accent."

7. Russell, David H. et al. *Reading Aids through the Grades: A Guide to Materials and 440 Activities for Individualizing Reading Activities*. New York: Columbia University Teachers College Press, 1981.

8. Wallen, Carl J. *Word Attack Skills in Reading*. Columbus, OH: Charles E. Merrill, 1969. See illustrative lessons on morphemic, syllabic, and contextual analysis.

9. Weaver, Phyllis. *Research within Reach*. Newark, DE: International Reading Association, 1978. See particularly the section on "Integration and Sequence of Subskills in Reading."

Application Experiences for the Teacher-Education Class

1. Working with a partner, modify the following statements in order to make them agree with what the author said or implied. Change the words in any way you wish.

Statements about Chapter 4

   a. Children should learn to decode words through phonic analysis alone.

   b. The purpose of syllabic analysis is to divide words into syllables.

   c. Context analysis includes syllabic analysis and phonic analysis.

   d. The word *antidisestablishmentarianism* has eleven syllables and three morphemes.

   e. As a reading teacher, you should be equally concerned about the printing convention and the decoding convention for dividing words.

   f. Syllabic analysis involves the translation of phonemes into units of sound and meaning; morphemic analysis involves the translation of graphemes into units of sound.

   g. Syllabic analysis requires the assistance of visual memory; morphemic analysis requires the assistance of phonic analysis.

   h. With the derivative approach toward teaching syllabic analysis, you help children separate a word into its root words and affixes.

   i. The word *undecidedly* is a derivative of *side*.

j.   Visual memory is the supervisor or overseer for phonic analysis, morphemic analysis, and contextual analysis.

k.   Morphemic analysis requires the reader to recognize common roots, prefixes, contractions, Greek and Latin morphemes, vowel patterns, and syllable patterns.

l.   Modern English relies heavily on inflectional endings to communicate meaning.

m.   In helping children learn to use contextual analysis, it is important to help them realize that a word should make sense syntactically; it should fit the meaning of the sentence; and it should correspond to all of the phonic clues.

n.   It is a good idea to have children try to look up several words in the dictionary before teaching them specific dictionary skills.

o.   The first specific skill to teach children about a dictionary is how to use guide words.

2.   To see how well you understand the five syllabication rules discussed on pages 99–100, try analyzing these nonsense words with a partner. First draw a vertical line between the syllables according to the way that makes the word sound right to you. Then underline the syllable that you think may receive the strongest accent. Next decide whether the accented syllable has a VC, CV, VCE, or VV vowel pattern and write the pattern in the first blank next to the word. Finally, decide whether the vowel sound in the accented syllable has a long sound or a short sound. Write *S* for short and *L* for long in the second blank next to each word. When you're all finished, compare your results with others in the class.

Example: hit/ting VC   S
   1. prebatting ____ ____
   2. tathering ____ ____
   3. chodin ____ ____
   4. inlaskin ____ ____
   5. reflubbering ____ ____
   6. rilling ____ ____
   7. domble ____ ____
   8. unstode ____ ____
   9. boaving ____ ____
   10. bockerm ____ ____

3.   With your partner create seven or more nonsense words that illustrate the syllable rules on pages 99–100. Give your words to two other people as a test and ask them to do two things with them: a) pronounce them for you, and b) tell you what rule they used in pronouncing them.

4.   Divide into small groups of four to eight people. One or two people in each of the small groups can "teach" the others the syllabic-analysis lesson on pages 100–102; one or two, the morphemic-analysis lesson on pages 103 and 104; one or two, the contextual-analysis lesson on pages 107–109; and one or two the dictionary lesson on pages 112 and 113. (For the dictionary lesson you will need two or three school dictionaries for each group. If these are not available, you may wish to omit this lesson.)

Field Experiences in the Elementary-School Classroom

1. Try out the syllabication test that you created in Application Experience #3 by asking a child informally to read the list of nonsense words. As she reads each word, see if she can tell you why it should be "pronounced that way." What "rules" for syllabication does she seem to be using? What rules does she need to learn? Does she perceive syllabication as mere word division or as a prelude to phonic analysis?

2. Teach a child how to use a "morphemic spy code." With this code each prefix, suffix, or root word stands for a letter. For example, here's a message in MSC (morphemic spy code) that you can present to her:

   IN—ABLE/MENT—ABLE/TION—HEAT/OPEN/MENT/ED.

   Tell her that *In* stands for the letter *I* and *ABLE/MENT* stands for the word *am*. Ask if she can figure out what two-letter word *ABLE/TION* stands for. If she doesn't get it right away, say that it stands for *at*. Now ask what four-letter word *HEAT/OPEN/MENT/ED* stands for . . . *(home)*. Ask her what the decoded message is? (I am at home.)

   Help the student make up some spy-code messages to give to someone else. Use the following morphemic spy code after reading it with her (including the words in parentheses):

a = able (as in *comfortable*)	n = ness (as in *politeness*)
b = bi (as in *bicycle*)	o = over (as in *overcharge*)
c = con (as in *concentrate*)	p = pre (as in *precook*)
d = dis (as in *discover*)	q = quit
e = ed (as in *wasted*)	r = re (as in *repaint*)
f = ful (as in *hopeful*)	s = sub (as in *subway*)
g = glue	t = tion (as in *connection*)
h = heat	u = un (as in *unlock*)
i = in (as in *incomplete*)	v = visit
j = join	w = wax
k = kiss	x = x-ray
l = less (as in *helpless*)	y = yawn
m = ment (as in *excitement*)	z = zip

   Before you leave, present the student with a copy of the code and another message to decode. Ask her to read it first in code and then the decoded way:

   TION/HEAT/ABLE/NESS/KISS—YAWN/OVER/UN!!

3. Teach a lesson on syllabic analysis similar to the one on pages 100 to 102.

4. Teach a lesson on morphemic analysis similar to the one on pages 103 and 104.

5. Teach a lesson on contextual analysis similar to the one on pages 107–109.

6. Teach a lesson on the dictionary similar to the one on pages 112 and 113.

CHAPTER 5

When reading a story aloud to children, occasionally have them close their eyes and picture what you're reading.

Increasing Comprehension at the Literal Level

Chapter Outline

Please read Bogglestar's message before you go on to the first section:

> I like people, both the human kind and our kind. Furthermore, I really like people who like people. Since I like people, I guess that means I like myself. And, by rights, I should hate people who hate people. But then . . . by hating people I'd have to hate myself. And that's no fun at all!

Comprehension and Communication

Now there's a message that you probably comprehended on the first reading! There's not much doubt of what this passage says, is there? But why is it so easy to comprehend? Is it because you can decode each word at sight? Is it because each word is part of your semantic vocabulary? Is it because of your intuitive grasp of syntactic rules? Or is it because you're a mature reader who has learned to "get it all together" and to search for the author's message?

Allow me to demonstrate this point. This will be mildly frustrating to you, but try to carry out my request (to the bitter end). In a moment you'll be asked to read the next paragraph. But I'm going to ask you to read each . . . word . . . separately, allowing a full three seconds for each word. This will take you about 150 seconds, or two and one-half minutes, but I think you'll find that it's worth it. I want you to see how difficult it is to get an author's message when you read only words. For each word that you read, count to three slowly, while at the same time thinking about that word. Are you ready? Begin.

122

Because . . . comprehension . . . depends . . . a . . . great . . . deal . . .
on . . . rapid, . . . as . . . well . . . as . . . accurate, . . . word . . . recognition, . . . one . . . possible . . . way . . . to . . . improve . . . reading
. . . comprehension . . . is . . . to . . . be . . . sure . . . that . . . word . . .
- . . . recognition . . . skills . . . are . . . developed . . . to . . . the . . . point
. . . where . . . they . . . are . . . automatic . . . — . . . accurate, . . . rapid,
. . . and . . . done . . . without . . . conscious . . . attention . . . (19, p.
88).

What have you learned from this experience? That one can
miss the forest for the trees? That one can miss the message for the
words? Did you sense that "reading comprehension" involves more
than stringing decoded words together? What differences did you
notice between your comprehension of the first passage by Bogglestar
and the second passage about word recognition? Was it easier to
comprehend the first one only because the words and sentences were
shorter? Or did part of the difference occur because you were searching for the message in the first passage and were merely reading
words in the second?

Perhaps by now I've more than made my point. Reading comprehension is not a passive form of understanding. It is an active,
searching type of behavior. By rights the phrase *reading comprehension*
ought to be thought of as a verb phrase, rather than a noun phrase.
It's too bad that our language allows us to use it as a subject rather
than a predicate, thus lulling us into believing that it's a quantity or
quality rather than a moving, vibrating, bustling interaction.

Reading Comprehension as a Cognitive-Affective Language Process

Most reading specialists seem to agree with Stauffer ". . . that reading
is largely a thinking process . . . a dynamic, action-filled way of
responding to printed symbols, and not a product or a school subject
. . ." (17, p. 3). Dr. Stauffer, along with many other educators, has
devoted a large proportion of his professional energy helping teachers and instructional-material developers understand and implement
this basic and significant idea about reading. An important addition
to this idea, however, is the one suggested by many psycholinguists—
that reading is not only a thought process, but a language process as
well. As Palmer (11, p. 10) explains it, reading is "an activity done to
reduce uncertainty in print." To reduce this uncertainty, the reader
relies on both nonvisual information, such as previous information
gained about a topic, and visual information, such as sight words,
familiar suffixes, and punctuation.

To reduce uncertainty and obtain meaning, readers do not need to make use of all the information available to them. Instead, they use the most direct route and as few cues as necessary to reach their goal—comprehension. . . . To comprehend during reading, then, students predict as they read, selecting only the most productive cues and sampling the graphic language as they test their predictions. When predictions are not confirmed, readers then engage in greater visual analysis. . . . Instead of becoming passive identifiers of letters and words, students become active searchers for meaning during reading . . . (11, p. 10).

Teachers who once grasp these ideas about reading as a combination of thought and language processes tend to find themselves changing their teaching behavior in the following ways:

1. They maintain comprehension rather than "decoding" as their major desired outcome for their students.
2. They search through teacher's guides for ideas but do not use them during lessons like a recipe book. They are free from the "tyranny of following the guide."
3. They refrain from correcting every mistake a child makes, but allow him instead to search for meaning, to use minimal language clues, to correct most of his own mistakes as a result of unclear meaning, and they even allow substitutions that do not alter the grammar or meaning of the author's message.
4. They recognize that each child differs in thinking abilities and modes and emotional attachment toward a particular reading selection. "Children differ not only in motivation, attitude, and purpose but in the ability to grasp, assimilate, retain, and use information as well . . ." (17, p. 3). Because of such differences, these teachers do not expect to receive the same answer from each child to one of their questions. Furthermore, they do not ask the same questions of each child. Their interaction with children becomes a dynamic one, rather than a static one based on the expected answers listed in a teacher's guide.
5. They ask fewer factual-type questions at the literal level and require more inferential, critical, and creative thinking (17).
6. Their reading lessons become not "round-robin" sessions of listening to each child read in turn, nor round-robin sessions of asking set questions and expecting set answers. Instead their reading lessons become what Stauffer refers to as "Directed Reading-Thinking Activities" (D-R-T-A). With the D-R-T-A approach, children are cognitively (thoughtfully) and affectively (emotionally) involved in three basic steps:
   a. Predicting what the author is going to say and thus 1) establishing their own individual purposes for reading—in order to determine how good their predictions were and 2) necessitating the search for visual and nonvisual clues that conform or negate their predictions

b. Reading silently and reflectively in order to discover what the author actually does say

c. Proving by reading orally to the teacher and peers that all or some of their predictions were correct

7. The role of these teachers during reading lessons becomes one of "intellectual agitator" (17, p. 45) frequently asking, in various forms, these three questions:

a. What do you think?
b. Why do you think so?
c. Can you prove it?

A variety of studies (17) have shown that this type of flexible approach, based on the recognition of individual differences in student cognitive-affective styles, results in higher levels of comprehension.

A Sample of a Directed-Reading-Thinking Activity (D-R-T-A)

Mrs. Stineberg was carrying on a D-R-T-A with a small group of first graders who were getting ready to read for the first time a story called "Magic Doors." The story they were about to read went like this:

*Magic Doors**

Johnny's mother asked him to go to the big new store at the corner.

His little brother Howie said, "I want to go too! I want to go too! I'll be good."

So Johnny took his little brother to the big new store.

There were two big doors.

One door had the word IN on it. The other door had the word OUT. Johnny and Howie went to the IN door. Whish! The door opened all by itself!

Howie said, "Look at that. It's magic!"

"You are silly!" said Johnny. "It isn't magic. The new doors work by electricity."

MRS. S: Look at the title of this story and tell us what you think the story is going to be about.

JACKIE: Maybe about some doors that open by magic when you say

---

*Bank Street College of Education, *Uptown, Downtown,* rev. ed. (New York: Macmillan, 1965). Reprinted by permission of the publisher.

"Open Sesame," and inside the doors you find gold and jewelry and things like that.

MRS. S: That's an interesting idea, Jackie. What makes you say that?

JACKIE: Well, I remember this story my Daddy read to me once, and that's what happened.

MRS. S: All right. Who has another idea?

BONNIE: I think it's going to be about some doors in a closet that lead into another land with witches and elves and things.

MRS. S: Well, that sounds possible. Why do you think your idea is right?

BONNIE: Umm, well . . . I heard a story like that once.

MRS. S: I'll bet you did. There's a story like that called "The Lion, the Witch, and the Wardrobe."

RONNIE: Yeah, maybe that's the one.

MRS. S: Turn the page and look at the picture on the next page. Maybe that will give you another idea of what this story is going to be about."

DAVID: Oooh, I know.

MRS. S: David?

DAVID: It's a picture of a supermarket. I'll bet the magic doors are those doors that open all by themselves.

MRS. S: Do you see anything else in the picture that makes you think that David is right?

SANDRA: There's a lady walking through one of the doors and she's not pushing on it or anything.

MRS. S: Yes, you did some very careful looking, Sandra.

RONNIE: Maybe she already pushed the door and it's just staying open for a while.

MRS. S: Yes, that's quite possible, Ronnie. Well, why don't you read the story now to see if you can find out why the author called the story "Magic Doors."

All right, now that you've finished the story, can anyone prove that his or her idea about the magic doors was right?

JACKIE: Well, there wasn't any gold or jewelry inside the doors. (Laughing) But there was something even better!

MRS. S: (intrigued) What, Jackie?

JACKIE: Ice cream!

MRS. S: (laughing) How do you know, Jackie?

JACKIE: Because the magic doors led inside a supermarket, and that's where we always buy our ice cream.

MRS. S: I see. . . . Well, what were the magic doors, really?

DAVID: They're just what I said. They're doors that open all by themselves.

MRS. S: You were right, David. But what really makes the doors open?

RONNIE: An electric motor or something.

MRS. S: Can you find a sentence that proves what you just said, Ronnie?

RONNIE: Sure. The last sentence says, "The new doors work by electricity."

In this illustration you can see how the teacher allowed each child to come up with her own hypothesis, thus providing each one with a specific purpose for reading the selection. Each child was then allowed time to read the selection at her own pace. And finally each child was encouraged to demonstrate the validity of her hypothesis. Thus the children were engaged in a true thinking process that involved both their intellect and emotions.

Reading Comprehension as a Set of Subskills

The skill called "reading comprehension" is often thought of as a quantity of separate but slightly connected subskills. This might be referred to as the "bunch of bananas" theory. The student merely has to eat each banana (learn each subskill) and he has therefore consumed (learned) the entire bunch. This theory would be similar to the notion that one can understand how a watch works by studying each of its parts separately.

This is not to say that reading comprehension can't be broken up into various subskills. It can be. Just as playing tennis can be. And . . . the subskills can be practiced in isolation—both for reading comprehension and playing tennis. Not a bad idea at all. But . . . it's hard to imagine a tennis instructor's insisting that she has produced a tennis player by merely teaching him the subskills of playing tennis— holding the racket properly, turning the wrist, and so on. The tennis instructor would make sure her student learned how to put all the subskills together. In the same way, the reading instructor needs to help children learn how to put the subskills together in order to understand what is being read.

When the reader is attempting to comprehend what an author is saying, a great deal of thinking may take place. Some of this thinking may be at the literal (or memory) level; some, at the inferential (or interpretive) level; some, at the critical (or judgmental) level; and some, at the creative (or inventive) level. All four of these levels interact with each other, thus producing an understanding that should be close to what the author was trying to say to the reader. And, at each level of thinking, there are subskills that interact with each other. At the literal level, for example, a reader may be doing all of these things at roughly the same time:

1. Recognizing that context signals provide clues on the meaning of a particular word that is puzzling to him
2. Noticing syntactic clues to meaning
3. Recognizing common sentence patterns (or the way they've been changed or expanded)
4. Noticing punctuation clues and how these affect expression and meaning

5. Developing mental images or associations with past experiences
6. Following a sequence of events or ideas
7. Recollecting significant details that the author has already presented

In the next section let's look at how complex this process of reading comprehension really is.

Reading Comprehension as an Interaction of Subskills

The whole is greater than the sum of its parts. I apologize for reminding you of this again, but it is a crucial idea in understanding how to teach reading comprehension. Let me demonstrate it for you this way:

> When the great white shark goes hunting, it does not bother to circle its prey and wait for the right moment to attack. This twenty-foot monster isn't afraid of anything. It attacks without worrying about enemies. It attacks without any warning!

In order for Kathie to comprehend this selection, she has to make her comprehension subskills interact. The subskills must work together to give her the complete message. Let's take just the first sentence, for example: When the great white shark goes hunting, it does not bother to circle its prey and wait for the right moment to attack. In this sentence what is the appropriate meaning for the word *right*? Does it refer to direction—right vs. left? Does it refer to moral behavior—right vs. wrong? Or does it refer to accuracy—the right instance vs. the instance that is too soon or late? By "recognizing that context signals influence the meaning of the word" (the first subskill in our previous list), Kathie can quickly determine that the word *right* refers to accuracy. What context clues, you ask? Well, she knows we're talking about a hunting *shark* and not a praying monk—so she's pretty sure that the word *right* does not refer to moral behavior. She also notices that we're talking about "the right *moment* to attack" rather than "the right *direction* for attack"—so she's certain we're talking about a precise time.

As she reads the first sentence, Kathie must also realize that the word *right* is in the syntactic position to describe the word *moment*. If the word *right* had been in a different syntactic position, its meaning would have been quite different. For instance, if the phrase were "wait for the right to attack" rather than "wait for the right moment to attack," the meaning of the word *right* would be quite different. (It would be in the syntactic position of a noun rather than an adjective.)

At the same time that Kathie is determining word meanings, she must also recognize intuitively the many alterations and expansions that the sentence has undergone. The basic sentence pattern in the first sentence is this: It circles its prey. This basic pattern has been altered and expanded many times. It's been altered by changing it from positive to negative: It does not circle its prey. It's been expanded by adding the verb phrase "bother to," as in "it does not bother to circle its prey." And it's been expanded by adding a qualifying clause—"When the great white shark goes hunting"—as well as a second predicate—"and wait for the right moment to attack." In order for understanding to take place, these types of alterations and expansions must have been part of Kathie's previous listening and speaking experiences. Otherwise, she will have a great deal of difficulty comprehending the first sentence in the selection (even if she can read each of the words in that sentence).

Notice that the first sentence has a significant pause, represented by a comma, after the word *hunting*. "When the great white shark goes hunting, it does not bother to. . . ." What should this comma mean to Kathie? It should mean, for one thing, that the word *hunting* should be stressed rather than *goes*. (Try pausing after the word *goes* and you'll see what I mean.) It also should mean that the shark is just "hunting" rather than "hunting it." (Try pausing after the word *it* to see what I mean.)

Nowhere in the first sentence of the selection does it say that the shark heads straight for its prey when it attacks. However, Kathie should be able to *infer* this information from what has been implied. (It does say that the great white shark does not bother to circle its prey, which implies that it heads straight for its prey.) Having inferred this, Kathie can now develop the image in her mind of a shark charging straight for a helpless victim.

Perhaps this is enough to show you how the subskills of reading comprehension must work together to produce understanding when a person reads. If Kathie is a skillful reader, she uses her comprehension subskills and their interactions instantaneously. The inexperienced reader, however, often needs specific training and practice. Let's look, then, at how you can teach or reinforce some of the separate subskills, and then how you can help children learn to put them together. At the end of this chapter we'll look at how one teacher used particular questioning strategies in order to help her students not only to read holistically, but also engage in creating predictions, individual purposes, and "proof" in order to understand an author's message.

Teaching Children to Recognize Common Sentence Alterations and Expansions

Although a sizable reading vocabulary is an essential ingredient in reading comprehension, a mature reader relies on more than his vocabulary to understand a passage. Like the musician who reads musical phrases, as well as notes and measures, the good reader reads not only letters and words, but sentences as well. José may know all the words in a sentence and still not be able to read it with comprehension. Why is this? Simply because the pattern of the words doesn't make sense to him, i.e., he is not used to that particular order or arrangement of words.

Ted, for example, was quite capable of reading "He found his ball there." However, when he was later confronted with the sentence "There he found his ball," he said it didn't make sense. He could read each word all right, but the sentence had no meaning for him. Not having spoken this pattern alteration before, his vocalization of the printed sentence provided him with no memory clues. It was "a silly sentence" as far as he was concerned. Research indicates that this boy's problem is not an isolated instance: reading comprehension and sentence-structure understanding are significantly related.

Studies by Pavlak (11), Reid (12), and Ruddell (13) all demonstrate that reading comprehension is dependent to a great extent on the similarity between the sentence patterns in the reading material and the sentence patterns normally used by children in their oral language. For example, if Tommy is not used to using the passive voice in his speech, his comprehension will suffer when he is faced with a sentence like this one: The hamburger was gobbled up by the hungry dog. Since Tommy is used to using the active voice, he would have less trouble if the sentence were written: The hungry dog gobbled up the hamburger. Other studies by Gibbons (7), MacKinnon (9), and Strickland (17) also show the strong relationship between sentence structure and reading comprehension.

The fact that reading comprehension is more than "mere vocabulary" makes it imperative for reading teachers to understand certain aspects of the structure of our language. Linguists have discovered, for example, that nearly all English sentences can be "generated" (created) by using or transforming a small number of basic sentence patterns. Six patterns that are common in materials written for elementary-school children can be found in the following "story." Can you detect the difference in the patterns?

> The coyote was in the barn. The man came quickly. The man looked angry. The coyote was his enemy. The man shot the coyote. The man gave his wife the tail.

The six patterns are these:

1. (Determiner) + Noun + Be verb + Prepositional phrase   The coyote was in the barn.

2. (D) + Noun + Intransitive verb + (Adverb)   The man came quickly.

3. (D) + Noun + Linking verb + Adjective   The man looked angry.

4. (D) + Noun + Linking   The coyote was his enemy.
   verb + (D) + Noun

5. (D) + Noun + Transitive   The man shot the coyote.
   verb + (D) + Noun

6. (D) + Noun + Transitive   The man gave his wife the
   verb + (D) + Noun + (D) +   tail.
   Noun

Most children have listened to these patterns so often, they arrive at school already able to recognize them reasonably well. However, these patterns can be altered and expanded in countless ways, and this is where children may have trouble. If they are not used to hearing particular alterations or expansions, many sentences may not make any sense to them in print.

Just hearing the pattern alterations or expansions on TV often doesn't seem to be enough. To make them part of their speaking and reading tools, children need to hear themselves utter the alterations and expansions and need to be reinforced or assisted by others. In a home in which verbal fluency is considered highly desirable, this type of assistance takes place quite often. The infant says, for exam-

In a home in which verbal fluency is valued, children learn sentence patterns, alterations, and expansions easily.

ple, "Daddy shoes," and the mother spontaneously replies, "Do you see daddy's shoes? I see his shoes, too." Thus the child learns in a natural way to refine and alter a basic sentence pattern. In a home in which verbal fluency is not considered highly desirable, of course, such reinforcement and teaching seldom takes place.

For many children, then, the teacher must provide oral-language experiences that complement and supplement those received at home. Before we go on to how you can help children expand their repertoire of sentence alterations and expansions, we need to do three things: 1) review a few terms that are necessary for an understanding of this subject, 2) see how well you understand the six basic sentence patterns, and 3) introduce some of the common alterations and expansions.

Terminology Needed for the Teacher's Understanding

Determiner: In the following two sentences the determiners are in italics:

> *The* house is mine.
>
> *This* green house is mine.

A *determiner* is a type of adjective used to signal a noun or a descriptive adjective followed by a noun. The determiner class includes *a, an, the, my, their, this, that, these, those, his, her,* and *your.*

Direct object: In the following two sentences, the direct objects are in italics:

> The lady beat the *rug.*
>
> The boy kissed the *girl.*

A *direct object* is the noun or pronoun "receiving" the action.

Indirect object: In the following two sentences, the indirect objects are in italics:

> The police officer gave my *father* a ticket.
>
> The lady gave the *door* a kick.

In the first sentence, the direct object is *ticket* and the indirect object is *father.* In the second sentence, the direct object is *kick* and the indirect object is *door.* As you can see, the *indirect object* represents the noun or pronoun "receiving" the direct object.

Transitive verb: In the following sentence, the transitive verb is in italics:

> The boy *ate* the pie.

The direct object of ate is *pie.* A *transitive verb* is a verb that is accompanied by a direct object (and can be changed to a passive form: The pie was eaten by the boy).

Intransitive verb: In the following two sentences, the intransitive verbs are in italics:

> The mail *came.*

> He *jumped* off the chair.

Neither *came* nor *jumped* has a direct object in these sentences. (The word *came* is almost always an intransitive verb, but *jumped* could be either a transitive or intransitive verb, depending on the sentence. If it has a direct object, as in "the horse jumped the creek," then it is a transitive verb.) An *intransitive verb,* then, is one that is not accompanied by a direct object (and cannot be changed to a passive form).

Linking verb: In the following sentences, the linking verbs are in italics:

> The child *is* happy.

> The child *seems* happy.

> The child *is* a boy.

> A boy *becomes* a man.

In slightly oversimplified terms, a *linking verb* is a special type of intransitive verb that serves as a connection between the subject (*child* or *boy*) and a word that describes or complements the subject (*happy, boy, man*). A "Be Verb" (*is, was,* etc.) is often a linking verb, but not always; e.g., in "he was killing time," *was* is not a linking verb. But in the sentence "he was a killer," the word *was* is a linking verb.

Understanding the Basic Sentence Patterns

In order for you to help children recognize common sentence patterns, you need to make sure you understand them yourself. If you find the patterns puzzling there are many more examples of each one in Appendix 5.1 of the end of the chapter.

Now, for a quick test on what you have just reviewed (or learned for the first time). Answers follow the test.

1. Underline the determiner: Your "quick tests" are killing me.
2. Underline the direct object: I hate tests of all kinds.
3. Underline the indirect object: He threw the batter a curve.
4. Underline the transitive verb: He ran and tossed the ball.
5. Underline the intransitive verb: The car stopped but hit the tree.
6. Underline the linking verb: The garbage smelled bad and overpowered him.
7. Write *a* if the word in italics is a transitive verb; *b* if it is an intransitive verb; *c*, linking verb; *d*, direct object; *e*, indirect object; and *f*, determiner. Use each letter only once.

_____ I *love* tests.
_____ I hate your *tests*.
_____ *This* medicine smarts.
_____ You *look* puzzled.
_____ Let's give *'em* the business, Mack.
_____ The plumber *came* yesterday.

Answers:
1. Your   2. tests   3. batter   4. tossed   5. stopped   6. smelled   7. a, d, f, c, e, b

---

Now see if you can match the basic sentence patterns with the sample sentences that illustrate those patterns.

_____ 1. The man drank my milk.
_____ 2. A horse was in the park.
_____ 3. The man gave the woman his word.
_____ 4. The girl smiled kindly.
_____ 5. The boy was a teenager.
_____ 6. This thing smells awful

a. (D) + Noun + Be verb + Prepositional phrase
b. (D) + Noun + Intransitive verb + (Adverb)
c. (D) + Noun + Linking verb + Adjective
d. (D) + Noun + Linking verb + (D) + Noun
e. (D) + Noun + Transitive verb + (D) + Noun
f. (D) + Noun + Transitive verb + (D) + Noun + (D) + Noun

Answers:
1. e   2. a   3. f   4. b   5. d   6. c

Understanding the Pattern Alterations and Expansions

Now that you have a better understanding of the basic sentence patterns children are confronted with in reading, we can move on briefly to some of the common pattern alterations and expansions they also face. First study Table 5.1. Then you may wish to check your understanding by altering and expanding the sentence following the table.

Now that you've examined Table 5.1, try altering and expanding the following sentence to see if you understand the table: My brother lost my money.

The present-tense alteration would be: My brother loses my money. The adjective expansion might be: My crazy brother lost my money. By using Table 5.1, you should be able to create several other alterations and expansions.

Teaching Procedures

Much of the teaching related to the comprehension of sentence patterns, alterations, and expansions can be integrated with regular instruction in reading or with the learning experiences that the teacher instigates in her language-arts program. Suppose, for example, that the teacher and children were reading a story from a first-grade basal reader and came to this passage:

> Soon Mr. Green came.
> He went into the street,
> and he made the car stop.
> Then hop, hop went the rabbit
> out of the street.
> And hop, hop it went
> off into the trees.*

By asking the children to think of other ways to say each sentence, the teacher can help them become more aware of various patterns, alterations, and expansions. The first sentence, for instance, could be modified to read "Mr. Green came soon" or "Mr. Green came very soon." The third sentence might be modified to read "Then the rabbit went hop, hop out of the street," or "Then the rabbit hopped out of the street," or "The little frightened rabbit then hopped right out of the street and into the bushes," and so on. Once children get used to this procedure, such "incidental" learning need take no more than an additional minute or two in an occasional reading lesson. This same procedure, of course, can be used with upper-grade children, many of whom delight in creating interesting alterations and expansions.

---

*From page 72 of "Green Feet," *Keys to Reading*. (Oklahoma City, OH: Economy Company, 1972).

Table 5.1 Some Common Pattern Alterations and Expansions of the Sentence: The man shot the coyote.

	Alterations
1. present	The man shoots the coyote.
2. future	The man will shoot the coyote.
3. present perfect	The man has shot the coyote.
4. past perfect	The man had shot the coyote.
5. future perfect	The man will have shot the coyote.
6. progressive	The man is shooting the coyote.
7. infinitive	The man had to shoot the coyote.
8. affirmative	The man did shoot the coyote.
9. plural subject	A man shoots. Men shoot.
10. passive	The coyote was shot by the man.
11. pronoun	He shot him.
12. Did?	Did the man shoot the coyote?
13. negative	The man did not shoot the coyote.
14. What?	What did the man shoot?
15. When?	When did the man shoot the coyote?
16. There	A coyote is here. There is a coyote here.
17. sequence	The man came quickly. Quickly the man came.
	Expansions
1. adjective	The angry man shot the coyote.
2. prepositional phrase	The man with the gun shot the coyote in the head.
3. adverb	The man shot the coyote quickly.
4. compound subject	The man and the boy shot the coyote.
5. compound predicate	The man shot and killed the coyote.
6. relative clause	The man who had a gun shot the coyote.
7. compound sentence	The coyote was here and the man came quickly.
8. dependent clause	Because the coyote was his enemy, the man shot the coyote.

More direct teaching may be utilized in a teacher's language-arts program. Odegaard and May (15), for example, in a study of children's creative composition, found that third-grade children gained significantly from direct instruction in sentence patterns and pattern modifications. At the end of a series of brief lessons, the children were found to be using a greater number of patterns and alterations in their writing, and their written stories were considered by independent judges to be more creative than those of a control group.

Direct instruction should be oral at first, with reading and writing coming later. Experience indicates that informal lessons of about five to ten minutes work best. It's best not to analyze the sentences with the children by talking about nouns, verbs, and so on. Sentence alterations and expansions are something they must gain intuitively through a great deal of listening and speaking. When you try analyzing the sentences with them, their interest in learning sentence alterations and expansions seems to diminish.

The procedures for direct instruction can be similar to the following. (These procedures seem to be suitable for any grade level, including kindergarten—providing the teacher relies on oral language, rather than written.)

Step 1: Introduce the children (preferably a small group) to a set of model sentences. Do this first orally by reading the model sentences to them. (Later, in the same lesson, you can present them in writing providing they are reading at the second grade level or above.) You might start with Pattern 5, since that seems to be the one with which most children are quite familiar:

The boy ate his apple.
The girl threw the ball.
That horse bit his rider.
The man drove his car.
A dog drank the water.
My mother spanked my sister.

Step 2: Have them "make up sentences which sound like these." This should be done orally at this point. One or two written sentences might be required from the children at the end of the lesson, if you wish to evaluate how well each child comprehends the pattern (but go easy on this or you'll kill their interest). If a child states a sentence that doesn't fit the pattern, simply say something like this: "You're close, Jerry. You're almost in the Pattern Club, but not quite. Listen some more and then try again in a few minutes." *Note:* if you find this exercise too difficult for your students, break it into smaller steps by making all of the determiners and the direct objects the same:

The boy ate the apple.
The girl threw the apple.
The horse bit the apple.
The man smashed the apple.

In this way, all they have to think of at first are a simple subject and verb. Then you can have them modify the sentences they have created—first by changing the determiners to words like *this, that, your, my, his, her,* and *a;* then by changing the direct objects to words like *ball, rider, car,* and so on. (That horse bit his rider.)

Step 3: After they are all "in the Pattern Club," show them the model sentences in writing or read them to the children one at a time again. After each one, have them "listen to how I change it." For example:

The boy ate his apple. . . . The boy eats his apple.
The girl threw the ball. . . . The girl throws the ball.

After you've read two or three of these pairs of sentences, read them another one and challenge them to "change it in the same way." Like this:

TEACHER: The horse bit his rider.
CHILD: The horse bites his rider.

This part of the exercise, then, becomes an opportunity for children to get into a "New Pattern Club."

Step 4: After they are in the New Pattern Club, challenge them to get into one more pattern club. This time expand your pattern rather than alter it. Like this:

TEACHER: The boy ate his apple. . . . The hungry boy ate his apple.
TEACHER: The girl threw the ball. . . . The happy girl threw the ball.
TEACHER: The horse bit his rider.
CHILD: The angry horse bit his rider.
TEACHER: Good. You're in the club.

In summary, the four steps recommended for direct instruction on sentence patterns, alterations, and expansions are as follows:

1. Introduce them to a set of model sentences (all illustrating the pattern you wish them to recognize)
2. Have them create sentences like the model ones
3. Introduce them to an alteration of some of the model sentences and let them alter the rest in the same way
4. Introduce them to an expansion of some of the model sentences and let them expand the rest in the same way

Teaching Children to Recognize Expression Clues

Suppose someone asks you this question in a letter: "Are you going there?" Which one of these is probably meant by the question?

    a. Are *you* going rather than someone else?
    b. Are you *going* there or have you already been there?
    c. Are you going *there* instead of somewhere else?
    d. *Are* you going there, or are you just bluffing?

It depends, of course, on which word the letter writer meant to stress. And your comprehension of the intent depends on which word you do stress. If the writer meant for you to accent *there,* and you accented *you,* a serious misunderstanding could ensue. ("What does she mean, am *I* going? Doesn't she think I'm good enough to go?")

We've talked about a person's reading comprehension's being influenced by understanding of words and sentences. Now we need to look at another component of the comprehension process—the component often referred to as "expression." The word *expression* is a general term that covers three specific signals—stress, pitch, and pause. Without the proper use of these three signals, it can be quite difficult for one person to comprehend another person's speech or writing. You've seen one example of this difficulty already. Now look at this one. A scribbled note from your friend says, "Come join us at the park buy some ice cream sandwiches and pop." Which of these did your friend probably mean?

    a. You're to join them at the park but first buy some ice cream, sandwiches, and pop.

    b. Join them at the park but first buy some ice, cream, sandwiches, and pop.

    c. Join them at the park but first buy some ice-cream sandwiches and some pop.

You decide that your friend meant the third alternative; you buy the stuff and drive to the park in your hot car. By the time you get there, the ice-cream sandwiches look like burnt toast floating in a puddle of milk. Your friend laughs hysterically and says, "I didn't want you to bring us anything. I just meant you could buy some ice cream, sandwiches, and pop for yourself—here—at the park!"

Quite likely you can think of other incidents when confusion arose over misplaced stress or pauses. During a conversation you have with another person, that person's intonation, gestures, and so on will usually provide the clues that are necessary for comprehension to occur. But when a person is reading what another has to say, he has to provide his own interpretation of what the stress, pitch, and pause patterns should be. And sometimes the reader makes the wrong interpretation, as in the case of the melted ice-cream sandwiches.

Teachers will sometimes say to children, "Read it with more expression, Susan!" or "Read it as if you were just talking to us, Ronny." In most cases this probably demonstrates the teacher's understanding of how important pitch, stress, and pauses are to good reading comprehension. But just telling children to "put more expression into it" is often not enough. Instead, they need to be shown why expression is important, what it sometimes "looks like" in print, and how one can determine the proper pitch, stress, and pauses that are necessary for reading with comprehension.

First task: Showing them why expression is important.   This can be handled in a manner similar to the way I tried to show you why it is important. For instance, suppose you and the pupils come across this passage in a story from a basal reader:

> Bill watched Jim throw the ball.
> Bill called, "Hey! Show me how to throw, Jim."

By reading the second sentence out loud to the children in a variety of ways, you can help them see the relationship between expression and comprehension. Some of the ways this sentence can be read as follows:

    a. Bill called, "Hey! Show me how to *throw,* Jim."
    b. Bill called, "Hey! Show *me* how to throw, Jim."
    c. "Bill!" called Hey. "Show me how to throw *Jim.*"
    d. Bill called, "Hey! Show me how to throw Jim?"
    e. Bill called, "Hey! Show me how to throw *Jim!*"
    f. Bill called, "Hey! Show me how to throw *Jim.*"

Just by reading this sentence in a variety of ways—and letting them try their hand at it—you can help them discover intuitively why pauses, pitch changes, and stress variations are important.

Second and third tasks: Showing them what symbols are used in print to indicate expression. Showing them how to determine the proper pitch, stress and pauses.   The need for printed symbols for stress, pitch, and pauses becomes evident to children during an experience like the one just described. The importance of commas seems obvious to them when they realize that without them *Jim* is thrown instead of the ball and *Bill* is called by *Hey* instead of calling "Hey!" himself. Likewise, they can see that a period, a question mark, and an exclamation point are not just simple stops like commas, but indicators of pitch changes as well.

With the uses of a language-experience approach (described in Chapter 12), the teacher can casually show the children how to use punctuation and underlining as he takes dictation of their stories. Suppose one of the children dictates this, for instance:

Bob said, "Did you take my hat?"

The teacher can show in a natural way how to separate the speaker's message from the actual speaker, and how to use capital letters, commas, quotation marks, and question marks. As the children read what they have dictated, the teacher helps them notice the graphic expression marks in order to read the message in the way that they, the original authors, intended the message to be read. This type of experience demonstrates vividly to children the importance of expression to reading comprehension. Sometimes, of course, stress is indicated by letters in italics or uppercase, e.g., "I want *you* to eat it. I've had ENOUGH!" But often a reader is expected to provide her own italics, as in the case of the following passage:

Bill watched Jim teaching Harry how to throw.
Bill called, "Hey! Show me how to throw, Jim."

In a case such as this, the child must learn to rely on context for a clue as to which word to stress. Since Bill has been watching Jim teach Harry how to throw, it is likely (but not certain) that Bill would say, "Hey! Show *me* how to throw, Jim."

In addition to the types of experiences with stress, pauses, and pitch that have already been described, the teacher can provide the children with dittoed stories that are completely lacking in punctuation. The children are then asked to insert capital letters, periods, commas, question marks, and exclamation marks and to underline the word in each sentence that should be given the most stress. A brief example follows. You may want to try it yourself.

I'll do it Roy shouted Terry you run back to town and get some copper wire clippers and some electricity tape tell them Roy sent you and tell them we'll be needing more copper wire soon.

Excellent practice in reading with expression can be gained by having the children read plays to each other—or stories that have a lot of dialogue. Whatever practice materials are used, however, positive reinforcement should be given for meaningful expression and not just for interesting variations in pitch or stress. Some children can appear to be reading with magnificent expression, yet show through their answers to questions that they had very little idea of what they were reading.

Helping Children to Learn to Develop Images or Associations

It is not unusual to find this skill underdeveloped with children who are having trouble comprehending what they read. Jimmy, a fifth grader whose reading comprehension was poor, was asked to read a passage similar to this one:

> The bright sails flapped fully in the wind, and the boat shot forward. Jack hung on to the tiller for dear life and desperately steered for shore.

Jimmy "read" it reasonably well, decoding each word correctly and using proper expression. Then, however, he was asked, "What picture in your mind did this give you?" And his answer was, "I don't know."

Well, what picture did you get in your mind? Presumably something like this: a sailboat, perhaps some water that is wavy from the wind, sails bulging and flapping, a boy holding tight to a horizontal handle in the rear of the boat, his face tense with anxiety and his eyes searching for the shore. Perhaps you even had fleeting memories of your own sailing experiences—or, lacking such experiences, your own experiences on another type of boat, combined with motion pictures you've seen of sailing boats. In other words, as you read the passage, you developed images and associations, and these helped you to comprehend the passage fully.

Here are some types of experiences you can use with children to help them develop this skill:

1. When reading a story aloud to children, occasionally have them close their eyes and picture what you're reading. Once in a while you may wish to pause to discuss their "pictures" or to write a descriptive word or phrase on the board.
2. Have them first read a passage silently and then draw a picture of what they see "in their heads."
3. Ask the children first to read a passage silently and then tell what they "saw."
4. Have them first read a passage silently and then tell what personal experiences it made them remember.
5. Arrange for them first to read a passage silently and then pantomine what they "saw."
6. Have one child read a passage aloud while other children pantomime the picture they "see."

Helping Children Learn to Follow a Sequence

This is one of the basic comprehension skills, for without this ability, a child cannot follow a narrative, an explanation, many descriptive passages, or a set of directions. Narrative writing requires the reader to remember the major events in a story that have already happened.

Expository writing requires her to connect the first part of an explanation to the second part, the second part to the third part, and so on. With descriptive writing, people or settings are often described in a particular order that doesn't make complete sense until the last part of the description is presented. For example, "He was cold; his fur was matted; his snout had ice crystals forming on it; even his feeble bark showed his weak condition. He was a seal in trouble."

Here are some types of experiences you can use with children to help them develop the skill of following a sequence:

1. Have the children work in pairs. Each member of the pair should read silently the same set of directions. Then one person should attempt to follow the directions while the other person judges whether he followed the directions correctly.
2. Provide children with directions for making things—paper airplanes, paper costumes for dolls, cookies, et cetera. Have them work in pairs so they can check each other's comprehension of the directions.
3. Have them read a story; then decide in what order to place pictures depicting events in the story.
4. Ask them to read a story, then tell it or act it out to some other children.
5. Provide a child with a set of directions for a game; then have her explain the game in sequence to some other children.
6. Ask the children to read informative passages on sequential occurrences, such as the water cycle or the cycle of life for a butterfly; then explain the cycle to some other children; or depict the cycle in a sequential drawing.

Helping Children to Recollect Significant Details

Research (8) indicates that many teachers spend more time developing this comprehension skill than any other. Such research does not tell us, however, whether this is because teachers feel it is the most important skill or because it is the easiest one to develop. In either case, unfortunately, it is easier for teachers to create detail-oriented questions than thought-provoking ones. For example, it's easier to come up with "What did the third little pig use to make his home?" than something like "What might have happened if he had made his house out of blocks of ice?" To encourage teachers to reduce the proportion of detail-oriented questions, an increasing number of teachers' guides to basal readers now include a variety of suggested thought-provoking questions to use along with detail-oriented ones.

In one way, though, this ability to recollect significant details is interwoven with the ability to determine main ideas (which will be discussed in the next chapter). For when one is looking for main ideas in a passage, one is unconsciously selecting those details that indicate that an idea is a main idea. And when one is consciously searching for significant details, it is often for the purpose of supporting a main idea gained from the passage. Sometimes, of course, you are looking for particular details simply because that's all you're interested in at the moment. For example, you may just be curious about when New York's underground city began, or who was the first person to climb Mt. Everest, in which case you would usually only have to scan a selection to find out. In short, one looks for details to satisfy a particular purpose or to support a main idea. The following are some ideas for helping children develop this skill:

1. Help the children change a story into a brief newspaper report. Help them write it as a reporter does, telling who, what, where, and when. The same can be done for an historical event described in a social-studies book.
2. Help the children to change a story into a telegram of twenty-five words or less. Show them how to include only the most important details. The same can be done for an historical event described in a social-studies book.
3. After they have decided on the main idea for a passage, have them find or remember details that support their decision.
4. Ask them to scan a reading selection from a basal reader, social-studies book, or science text to find highly factual information. This is best done orally in small groups, with the first child to find it reading the answer.
5. Develop their appreciation for literary devices by having them read aloud those sentences, phrases, or words that "help paint a picture for the reader."

Coordinating the Literal Comprehension Skills (Using Questioning Strategies)

As mentioned earlier, learning the separate subskills involved in reading comprehension won't do children much good unless they also learn to put them all together when they read. Such coordination depends partly on the child's motivation and intelligence, of course. But it also depends on the questioning strategies of the teacher.

Studies (6) show, for instance, that giving children a number of detail-oriented questions before they read a selection causes them to read for specific answers rather than main ideas or appreciation of the author's message. Post-reading questions, on the other hand, particularly when used at short intervals, such as after each page or paragraph, tend to encourage greater depth of comprehension (5).

You can see, then, that if a teacher wants his students to learn to coordinate the various comprehension skills, it is not advisable to have them read just to answer detail-oriented questions. This can have only one result: children who perceive reading as "finding answers that the teacher wants," rather than children who read in order to get ideas and enjoyment from another human being. If you want children to read for ideas and enjoyment, then you will need to start them off with more open-ended questions or with the type of "intellectual agitation" discussed on page 125 ("What do you think? Why do you think that? Can you prove what you're saying is correct?"). Here's an example of an "open-ended" beginning, which gradually leads toward the teacher's playing the role of intellectual agitator.

TEACHER: Do you know what kinds of things you can find underneath the streets here in New York City?

BARBARA: Oh, I know. Subways!

TEACHER: That's right. Can anyone think of something else you might find underneath the streets?

DONALD: There are all kinds of pipes under the streets. I know, because my dad told me. And they're full of water.

JANET: I know what's under there. Monsters!

TEACHER: Well, I hope that's not true.

BILL: Aren't there wires and things like that under there?

TEACHER: Yes, there are over four million miles of wire under our streets. That's enough wire to go around the world over 160 times! Do you know why that wire is there?

KEN: It's for sending messages.

BILL: Naw. It's for telephones.

TEACHER: Well, I'll tell you what. I'd like you to find out why that wire was put down there in the first place. Read the first page of the story to yourself and then let's stop and talk about it for a minute.

Here's the page the teacher asked them to read:

In 1888 a terrible snowstorm hit New York City. Tall poles snapped, and electric wires fell into the street. People were killed by electric shock. Some were killed by the falling poles. And nearly a thousand died in the fires that broke out.

The mayor saw that he must do something to make his city a safe place to live. He asked electricians to put electric wires safely underground. Then the mayor sent men out to take down the wooden poles.

These electric wires were the beginning of America's amazing underground city in New York. Today the narrow streets and the sidewalks hide more than four million miles of wire. In some places there are so many wires and pipes that two fingers cannot be pushed between them. . . .*

After the children had read the page silently, the teacher carried on a discussion with them in such a way that several comprehension subskills needed to be used in a coordinated fashion:

TEACHER: Well, now you know why they put the wire under the streets. What do you think it looks like under the streets? Can you get a picture in your mind?

BILL: I think it looks like spaghetti.

TEACHER: (joins in laughter) You may be right, Bill. What do you think it looks like, Barbara?

BARBARA: I don't know, but I know it doesn't look like spaghetti.

TEACHER: Who can find a sentence on this page that tells what it looks like? . . .

KEN: Oh, I know. It's the last sentence. It says, "In some places there are so many wires and pipes that two fingers cannot be pushed between them. . . ."

TEACHER: Yes, and maybe that's why Bill said it must look like spaghetti down there.

BILL: Yeah, like a whole bunch of spaghetti all squished together.

TEACHER: Would it be like uncooked spaghetti that comes out of the box all straight, or would it be like cooked spaghetti that's all piled up on your plate?

JANET: Oh, I know. It would be like uncooked spaghetti when it comes out of the box.

TEACHER: (nodding approval) Why do you think so, Janet?

JANET: Because that's what they do with wires and pipes.

TEACHER: They lay them out straight?

JANET: Yes.

TEACHER: Have you seen people do it that way?

JANET: Yes. That's the way they do it. They don't bunch it all up like cooked spaghetti.

TEACHER: (laughing) I'm sure you're right. Has anyone else watched people put in wires and pipes anywhere?

BILL: Yeah, I have. My uncle does that kind of thing for a living. He puts wires in buildings.

TEACHER: He's an electrician?

BILL: Yeah.

TEACHER: All right. Now let me ask you something else about the page you just read. Did they take down the wooden poles before or after they put the wires under the street?

---

*From page 250 of "Air Pudding and Wind Sauce," *Keys to Reading* (Oklahoma City, OK: Economy Company, 1972), adapted from "Amazing Underground City," by Edward Hymoff (*Boy's Life*, August 1963).

DONALD: I know. They took them down afterwards.

TEACHER: Can you find two sentences on this page that prove you're right?

DONALD: Yes. Here it is: "He asked electricians to put electric wires safely underground. Then the mayor sent men out to take down the wooden poles."

TEACHER: Good. Those are the two sentences I had in mind. Now let's try one more thing before we go on to the next page. Which do you remember happening first—the mayor's deciding to make his city safe, the electric wires falling into the street, or the terrible snowstorm?

JANET: The snowstorm happened first, because that's what caused the other two things.

TEACHER: I see. The snowstorm caused the wires to fall down. . . .

JANET: Yes, and then the mayor decided to make the city safer.

TEACHER: All right. And how did he decide to make the city safer, Ken?

KEN: By putting the wires under the streets.

TEACHER: Fine. Now before you read the next two pages, let me ask you another question. . . .

As you can see, the teacher led the discussion in such a way that the children had practice using three comprehension subskills. She got them to create images and associations by asking them to picture what it looks like under the streets, by clarifying the analogy between wires and spaghetti, and by asking if anyone had already watched someone laying wires or pipes. She had them recollect significant details by asking them to find specific sentences in the passage that would justify their statements. And she strengthened their ability to follow a sequence by asking them to place events from the story in the proper order. Thus she encouraged the children to coordinate all three subskills in an effort to understand the author's total message on a particular page.* At the same time she helped the children to make predictions, thus allowing for individual purposes; she also encouraged them to prove the validity of their predications.

Summary

The message in this chapter is this: reading is much more than the understanding of each separate word in a passage; "reading comprehension" is not only dependent upon vocabulary, but upon the coordinated use of other recognition and thinking skills. At the literal

---

*Note: As will be discussed in Chapter 13, it is important that children also have many experiences of reading without being interrupted for discussion.

level of comprehension, these skills include the recognition of semantic and syntactic "context clues," the recognition of common sentence-pattern alterations and expansions, the recognition of expressions clues, the development of associations or images, the following of a sequence, and the recollection of significant details. The teacher's questioning strategies pertaining to a reading selection determine to a large extent the breadth and depth of a child's comprehension of that selection, and also help the child develop his own purposes for reading.

References and Suggested Reading

1. Carin, A., and Sund, R. *Developing Questioning Techniques.* Columbus, OH: Charles E. Merrill, 1971.
2. Carroll, J. "The Nature of the Reading Process." In *Theoretical Models and Processes of Reading,* edited by H. Singer and R. Ruddell. International Reading Association, 1976.
3. Davidson, Roscoe. "Teacher Influence and Children's Levels of Thinking." *Reading Teacher* 22 (May 1969): 702–4.
4. Davis, Frederick B. "Research in Comprehension in Reading." *Reading Research Quarterly* 3 (Summer 1968): 499–545.
5. Frase, Lawrence T. "Learning from Prose Material: Length of Passage, Knowledge of Results and Position of Questions." *Journal of Educational Psychology* 58 (October 1967): 266–72.
6. Frase, Lawrence T. "Boundary Conditions for Mathemagenic Behaviors." *Review of Educational Research* 40 (June 1970): 337–48.
7. Gibbons, Helen D. "Reading and Sentence Elements." *Elementary English Review* 18 (1941): 42–6.
8. Guzak, Frank J. "Teacher Questioning and Reading." *Reading Teacher* 21 (December 1967): 227–34.
9. MacKinnon, A. R. *How Do Children Learn to Read.* Copp Clark, 1959.
10. Odegaard, Joanne M. and May, Frank B. "The Effects of Instruction in Creative Grammar on the Creativity of Third-Graders' Stories." *Elementary School Journal* 73 (December 1972): 156–61.
11. Pavlak, Stephen A. "Reading Comprehension—A Critical Analysis of Selected Factors Affecting Comprehension." Ph.D. dissertation, University of Pittsburgh, 1973.
12. Reid, J. "Sentence Structure in Reading." *Research in Education* 3 (May 1970): 23–7.
13. Ruddell, Robert B. "The Effect of Oral and Written Patterns of Language Structure on Reading Comprehension." *Reading Teacher* 18 (January 1965): 270–5.
14. Sanders, Norris M. *Classroom Questions: What Kinds?* New York: Harper and Row, 1966.
15. Schwartz, Elaine, and Sheff, Alice. "Student Involvement in Questioning for Comprehension." *Reading Teacher* 29 (November 1975): 150–4.
16. Singer, H. "Active Comprehension: from Answering to Asking Questions." *Reading Teacher* 31 (8) (1978): 901–8.

17. Stauffer, Russell G. *Directing the Reading-Thinking Process.* New York: Harper and Row, 1975.

18. Strickland, Ruth G. "Implications of Research in Linguistics for Elementary Teach." *Elementary English* 40 (1963): 168–71.

19. Swenson, I., and Kulhavey, R. "Adjunct Questions and Comprehension of Prose by Children." *Journal of Educational Psychology* 66 (2) (1974): 212–5.

20. Weaver, Phyllis. *Research within Reach, A Research-Guided Response to Concerns of Reading Educations.* Newark, DE: International Reading Association, 1979.

21. Wiesendanger, K. D., and Wollenberg, J. P. "Prequestioning Inhibits Third Graders' Reading Comprehension." *Reading Teacher* 31 (8) (1978): 892–5.

Application Experiences for the Teacher-Education Class

1. Working with a partner, modify the following statements in order to make them agree with what the author said or implied. Change the words in any way you wish.

Statements about Chapter 5

a. It is quite possible for a reader to miss the author's individual words by concentrating so much on the author's message.

b. Reading comprehension should be thought of as a quality rather than a quantity.

c. Reading comprehension should be broken up into subskills that are then practiced in isolation; it is confusing to children to have to practice them in a coordinated way.

d. One comprehension skill that children need to develop is that of recognizing that phonic signals influence the meaning of a word.

e. As a person reads this sentence—When the great white shark goes hunting, it does not bother to circle its prey and wait for the right moment to attack—she can determine the appropriate meaning for the word *right* by paying most attention to the word *great.*

f. Tommy can read "The hungry dog gobbled up the hamburger" but has trouble reading "The hamburger was gobbled up by the hungry dog." This is probably because Tommy does not know the words *was* and *by* very well.

g. In the sentence "The police officer gave my father a ticket," the word *father* is the direct object.

h. "This girl played in the park" is an example of Pattern #1.

i. "The man has shot the coyote" is the past perfect alteration of "The man shot the coyote."

j. The direct teaching of sentence alterations and expansions should be carried on as a substitute for regular instruction in reading.

k.   When teaching children sentence alterations and expansions be sure to make it primarily a written experience and analyze each sentence according to parts of speech.

l.   Children should learn to recognize graphic signals of stress, pitch, and pause (expression clues) in order to do a better job of reading out loud to others.

m.   A child who develops images and associations as she reads is really daydreaming rather than reading.

n.   The skill of following a sequence is important for comprehension of narrative prose, explanations, and directions, but not for descriptive passages.

o.   Research indicates that teachers spend too little time developing children's abilities to recollect significant details.

p.   Studies show that giving children a number of detail-oriented questions before they read a selection causes them to read for the author's message.

q.   The teacher's questioning strategies have very little to do with the breadth and depth of a child's comprehension of a reading selection.

2.   After everyone has read the following story, "The Road Home," divide the class into four groups. Each group can develop a set of questions for one of the four pages in the story. The questions should be designed to improve children's reading comprehension and should include both prereading and postreading questions. The prereading questions should stimulate children to read for their own individual purposes and for the purpose of understanding and appreciating the author's message. The postreading questions should encourage the interaction of three literal-thinking skills: developing associations or images, following a sequence, and recollecting significant details; they should also provide opportunities for children to "prove" their predictions (see pages 144–145 and 146–147 for illustrations of this). After the small groups complete their questions they can exchange them.

"The Road Home"
by
FRANK B. MAY

Page 1

On the day it happened, the girl and her new horse, Sparlight, seemed to fit perfectly into the peaceful autumn day. The slow-moving horse and rider, the quiet country road, the bright colored leaves, the billowy clouds—all locked together to make a picture worth painting.

Shauna was taller than most girls her age, and her long yellow braids, bouncing against her sleeveless blouse, accented her height. In spite of her lankiness, she could appear quite graceful at times, particularly on top of a horse. She was riding bareback, because Sparlight had proved to be a reasonably safe horse and was responding well to the girl's gentle manner of training him. Besides, the saddle was heavy and a real bother to put on.

Although the horse only ambled along, Shauna didn't mind the slow pace; she wanted to savor the beautiful colors and the sweet odors of fall. She stopped to chat with a neighbor woman who lived about a mile from her house. As they passed the time of day, Shauna noticed that Sparlight was getting quite restless.

Page 2

"I must have frightened him," said the neighbor.

"Oh, I don't think so," Shauna said, to comfort her companion. "He probably just wants to get going. I guess I'd better get home before they begin to wonder about me."

Shortly after she turned the horse toward home, he seemed to get over his nervousness and started to walk as peacefully as he had before. Shauna forgot about the horse and noticed the beauty around her again. A huge cloud slid in front of the sun, and all of the colors immediately became deeper. Suddenly the sun discovered a small hole in the cloud and poured its golden radiance down onto a small patch in front of the girl. She was enchanted and wondered what the world would look like when she got inside that golden patch.

It was at this point that the horse bolted, and Shauna felt herself sliding off. She knew she was too far off the horse to prevent the fall, so she resigned herself to it and hung onto the reins. She landed with her full weight on her right hand. Feeling only a brief twinge of pain, she looked up to see Sparlight standing near and looking down at her. Shauna's left hand was still clutching the reins. Her right arm felt very strange, which caused her to look at it as she got up. When she saw her arm, panic rushed into her brain, causing her to scream with fright: "Help! Mommy! Daddy!"

Her right arm was just a dangling piece of flesh. It was bent the wrong way at the elbow and twisted all out of shape. Shauna felt sick and weak. Dropping the reins, she grabbed her right wrist with her left hand, trying to hold up the lifeless arm and make it seem all right again.

Page 3

Now the badly frightened girl wondered what to do next. Her first impulse was to grab the horse's reins and lead him home. Then she realized how difficult that would be and how much easier it would be to walk home without him. No, that would be wrong, thought Shauna, as her conscience began to hurt too. He might run away . . . might get lost . . . might eat too much and founder . . . I've got to get him home.

Shauna tried to hold the reins in her right hand and still hold her right wrist with her left hand. But the fingers on her right hand wouldn't work; they had no feeling in them at all. She wanted to scream for help again, but she knew no one would hear. Using just her left thumb and index finger to hold up her right arm, she tried slipping the other three fingers around the reins. Finally she managed to wedge the reins between the three fingers and her right wrist. Tugging gently at the reins she urged Sparlight to come with her. The horse was totally unaware of his rider's agony and refused to leave the lush grass he had

174281

discovered. With renewed desperation Shauna pulled vigorously at the reins. At last the horse began to move.

Page 4

With agonizing slowness the girl struggled toward her house by the same route that had seemed so beautiful only a short while before. Each time she looked up at her house in the distance she began to sob. It was still so far away! Forcing herself to look down at the road and not up at the house, she plodded on numbly. All she could think about was getting to that house; no thoughts came to her about how the arm was to be fixed, how she would be sure to use a saddle next time, how she would try to stay more alert. Those thoughts all came later. Now her only goal in life was to get to her house.

After an eternity of watching her feet move slowly in front of her, Shauna dared to look up. There was her home, only a short distance away. A sob welled up and she found herself screaming in a piteous voice: "Help! Mommy! Daddy!" Her shouts frightened the horse, and she had to make a desperate effort to keep him from running away, after all her hard work. When she looked up again, her father was running toward her. Sobbing with relief, she handed the reins to him and wailed her story of torture in four brief words: "I broke my arm!"

When they reached the house together, her mother ran out to comfort her, and Shauna told her the same story with tears running down her cheeks: "Mommy, it's broken! It's broken!"

But she was home.

3. With a partner, complete the following exercise on sentence patterns and expansions. Then compare your results with the rest of the class.
   a. (1) The monkey climbed the ladder. (pattern)
      (2) The monkey had to climb the ladder. (alteration)
      (3) Because the monkey was curious, he had to climb the ladder. (expansion)
   b. (1) My father drove my car.
      (2) My father had to drive my car.
      (3) Because my father was broke, he had to drive my car.
   c. (1) The train jumped the track.
      (2) _____.
      (3) Because the train was broken, it jumped the track.
   d. (1) Your sister took my book.
      (2) _____.
      (3) _____.
   e. (1) Her flebonk zagged his delbur.
      (2) _____.
      (3) _____.
   f. (1) _____.
      (2) His delbur had to zag a flurtop.
      (3) _____.
   g. (1) _____.
      (2) _____.
      (3) _____.

4. With a small group, take turns being a "leader" of a pattern club. Everyone should turn to Appendix 5.1 at the end of Chapter 5. If you were the leader of Pattern One, you would simply read out loud the sentences under Pattern One and then ask the others to "try to get into the club by making up a sentence that fits the pattern." After all persons in the small group get into the club, the leader should ask them to write a nonsense sentence such as "The flebonk was in the malps." Then share the nonsense sentences before going on to Pattern Two. If you have time, see if you can alter and expand some of the patterns, using Table 5.1 on page 136 as your guide.

Field Experiences in the Elementary-School Classroom

1. Try the pattern-club idea (described on pages 137–138) with a small group of children. Be ready to make the adaptation in Step 2 if the experience seems too difficult for the children. (Be sure to do this orally—at least during the first part of the lesson.)

2. Plan a reading-comprehension lesson related to an assigned story or article. Teach the lesson to one or more children. Prepare prereading and postreading questions for each page in the story or article. The prereading questions should stimulate the children to read for the purpose of understanding and appreciating the author's message. The postreading questions should encourage the interaction of at least three literal-thinking skills: developing associations or images, following a sequence, and recollecting significant details. (See pages 144–147 for an illustration of this.)

3. Select a child who seems to have at least average word-recognition skills but demonstrates poor comprehension. Have him read aloud to you from selections that are slightly below his frustration level. Try to determine, by listening to his reading and by asking questions, whether he is deficient in any of the comprehension skills listed from 1 to 7 on pages 127–128. Then think of ways that these skills may be improved, using what you've learned in Chapter 5. (You may wish to use a tape recorder for this experience.)

Appendix 5.1

Examples of Six Common Sentence Patterns

Here are some examples of Pattern 1 (read them out loud if possible):

(D) + Noun + Be verb + Prepositional phrase.
The girl was inside the house.
My friend was outside the car.

The bear was in the zoo.
Bob was behind the door.
The doctor was in the hospital.
His doctor was under the table.
A nurse was near the bed.
The flebonk was in the malps.

Now you make up two or three. Check them later with one of your colleagues.

_____

_____

_____

Here are more examples of Pattern 2 (read them out loud, if possible):

(D) + Noun + Intransitive verb + (Adverb)*
The boy walked slowly.
The boy walked.
Susan walked.
That girl played under the house.
This girl played in the park.
My mother worked in the morning.
The giant spoke grumpily.
That flebonk lived in the malps.

Now it's your turn again. Make one of them nonsensible if you can.

_____

_____

The following are more examples of Pattern 3:

(D) + Noun + Linking verb + Adjective
The candy seemed sweet.
That candy was sweet.
His shirt looked dirty.
Your dress was pretty.
The monkey seemed clever.
That child was cruel.
Alice appeared snobbish.
The flebonk was masty.
That flebonk smelled yucky.
My flebonk tasted delicious.

Notes: An adverb is not always needed. Also, a prepositional phrase may be used instead of an adverb.

Here are more examples of Pattern 4:

(D) + Noun + Linking verb + (D) + Noun
The dog was his friend.
The dog became his friend.
The dog remained his friend.
Bob was a snob.
That girl became my sweetheart.
Her brother remained a fink.
Your costume was a scream.
My flebonk became a skiddle.
His skiddle remained a nurgle.

The following are more examples of Pattern 5:

(D) + Noun + Transitive verb + (D) + Noun
The monkey climbed the ladder.
My father drove a car.
This motor ran the pulley.
Jim owned this place.
The train jumped the track.
Your sister liked my brother.
Her flebonk zagged his delbur.
His delbur zagged a flurtop.

Here are more examples of Pattern 6:

(D) + Noun + Transitive verb + (D) + Noun + (D) + Noun
The woman gave her dog a bone.
The woman fed her son a steak.
My father spared the beggar a dime.
The king granted Columbus an audience.
The club awarded Felix a prize.
Mr. Jones offered Mother a hand.
My uncle left my sister a fortune.

CHAPTER 6

A good way to increase children's ability to make predictions is to have them read part of a story and then draw what they think will happen next.

Increasing Higher-Level Thinking Skills

Chapter Preview

In the last chapter we considered reading comprehension both as an interaction of various subskills and as a purposeful, searching type of cognitive-affective language behavior. However, we looked at only one level of comprehension, namely the literal level. In this chapter we'll consider other levels of comprehension, often referred to as the inferential, critical, and creative levels. In talking about these levels, though, we'll need to keep in mind that such a division among the thought processes is both arbitrary and artificial and used only to help us communicate about them. In reality, these levels of thinking often overlap and interact with each other and with the literal level; such overlap and interaction occur particularly when teachers use questioning strategies that encourage children to read for their own individual purposes.

Furthermore, we can't really help children improve these levels of reading comprehension merely by teaching each thought process in isolation. Children must also be taught how to use them in a coordinated fashion as they attempt to communicate with an author. In other words, we can't assume that by teaching children each separate process of higher-level thinking, they will automatically use those processes when they are reading independently. (It will be assumed, however, that some teaching of the thought processes in isolation will increase children's understanding of them.)

Let's look, first, at some ways of providing children practice with the higher level thought processes in isolation. Following this, we'll talk about how we can help children learn to use them in a holistic purposeful fashion.

Humans have to think when they write or read, but
seldom when they speak or listen.

The Nature of Inferential Thinking

Inferential thinking, as it applies to reading, requires such thought
processes as inferring information from what has been implied by
the author, determining what the author's main ideas are, recognizing those details that support the author's main ideas, making predictions about what the author is going to say next, and understanding the cause-and-effect relationships that the author is suggesting.

To clarify the difference between literal thinking and inferential thinking, let me use an illustration: Billy looked out of the
window and saw that his mother's car was wet. "Mom, your car's wet,"
he said. Ben, on the other hand, looked out of the window and
noticed that not only was the car wet but the sidewalk, the street, the
lawn, and the trees as well. "Mom," Ben said, "It's been raining." Billy
was using literal thinking and Ben was using inferential thinking.
Billy reported exactly what he saw. Ben inferred some things about
what he saw and reported his inference rather than his observations.

When some people read, they stick pretty much to what the author says. Others, when they read, communicate more with the author. "Oh, you mean this?" they almost say. Or "wait a minute; I'll bet I know what you're going to say next." No one really knows, at this point, whether the difference between literal-minded readers and inferential-minded readers can be explained as a difference between intelligence, personality characteristics, or training. The general opinion is that all three factors play a part and that some children will need much more training than others. (Furthermore, there may be some children who will never get very good at inferential thinking.) But in any case, it does seem to be advisable to begin children's training in inferential thinking at the earliest grade level—not only during reading instruction, but also during other types of instruction and experiences.

Inferring Information from What the Author Says

This thinking process can be practiced on even simple reading passages such as the following:

One hot day Roy went on a boat ride.
He went with his teacher and his school friends.

To give children practice at *literal thinking,* the teacher might simply ask, "What kind of a day was it when Roy went on a boat ride?" But to give children practice at *inferential thinking,* the teacher could ask, "What season of the year do you think it is—winter, summer, spring, or fall?" To answer the latter question, they would have to make inferences based on the words *hot, teacher,* and *school.* Robert may say "summer" because of the word *hot.* Jill may say, "No, it can't be summer because Roy is going with his teacher and school friends." Frank may then say, "I'll bet it's either spring or fall." All three children will be engaged in inferential thinking. The teacher has helped them to communicate with the author rather than merely absorbing the author's words.

Determining Main Ideas

The significance of this ability is probably self-evident. Both inside and outside of school, people are frequently faced with the necessity or desire of capturing the gist, essence, theme, or most important point in a printed message, whether this be a report, a poem, a newspaper editorial, or something else. To test your ability to determine main ideas, try reading the same selection you read in Chapter 5 and then choosing the best title for it:

> In 1888 a terrible snowstorm hit New York City. Tall poles snapped, and electric wires fell into the street. People were killed by electric shock. Some were killed by the falling poles. And nearly a thousand died in the fires that broke out.
>
> The mayor saw that he must do something to make his city a safe place to live. He asked electricians to put electric wires safely underground. Then the mayor sent men out to take down the wooden poles.
>
> These electric wires were the beginning of America's amazing underground city in New York. Today the narrow streets and the sidewalks hide more than four million miles of wire. In some places there are so many wires and pipes that two fingers cannot be pushed between them. . . .*

1. A terrible snowstorm
2. How some people were killed
3. Putting wires underground
4. How an amazing underground city began

Since the first three ideas all lead up to the fourth one, perhaps you would agree that #4 is the best title. This type of exercise is one way of providing children with specific practice in determining main ideas. Other types of experiences would include the following:

1. After they have read a selection ask them such questions as these: "What do you think the author was trying to tell you?" "What was this story really about?" "Was there one big idea that the author was talking about?" "If you were the author, what is the one thing you'd want the readers to remember from this article more than anything else?"
2. Have children read a selection and then create a title for it
3. After they've read a story or an article, have them "capture the big idea" with a two-line or four-line verse. You'll need to do this together a few times before they can do it on their own. Here's an example for "Goldilocks and the Three Bears":

> Goldilocks bothered the bears.
> She even broke one of their chairs.
> But she'll never do that again.
> Not even now and then.

---

*From page 250 of "Air Pudding and Wind Sauce," *Keys to Reading* (Oklahoma City, OK: Economy Company, 1972), adapted from "Amazing Underground City," by Edward Hymoff (*Boys' Life*, August 1963).

Inferential thinking can be encouraged even with children at a very young age.

4. After older children have read a story, let them decide on the "basic theme": (a) people against nature, (b) people against people, or (c) people against themselves
5. After they have read a selection, have them decide whether the title "tells what the story was really about." Or you might ask them if it "tells what the author was really trying to say." Then have them create a "better" title

Recognizing Details that Support Main Ideas

This thought process can't really be separated from that of determining main ideas. When authors emphasize certain ideas or themes, they normally try to convince the reader by presenting numerous hints, illustrations, examples, or observations. Naturally they hope that the reader will pay attention to these details and see how they fortify the "big idea."

For an example of this, let's look again at the article on New York City's amazing underground city. Mr. Hymoff, the author of this article, didn't simply tell the reader, "Now I'm going to tell how an amazing underground city began." Instead he chose to present as many details as he thought necessary to illustrate and lead up to this idea. To help children realize what the author has done, the teacher will often need to have children "reconstruct" the author's purpose and procedures. This can be done by asking questions like these:

1. Why do you think this article is called "Amazing Underground City?"
2. What can you find in this article that seems to be "amazing?"
3. Was the author, Mr. Hymoff, trying to just tell you about the underground city or was he trying to tell you how this underground city began? Or was he doing both? What can you find in the article that will prove your point?
4. Mr. Hymoff tells us that in 1888 a terrible snowstorm hit New York City. Can you find anything in the first paragraph that would explain why he used the word "terrible?"
5. How did the amazing underground city begin?

Making Predictions

Research shows us that "good readers" tend to differ from "poor readers" in the amount of predicting they do (16). Good readers tend to spend much more time predicting what the author is going to say next. It stands to reason that people who anticipate "what's going to come next" are likely to be more involved in what they're reading and to understand it better. For example, what's going to happen next in the following story?*

> "Today I'll do it in six!" Barney said.
> Barney chose a log that seemed to be the right size. He raised the ax, gripped the handle tightly, and braced his knees.
> Whap! Whap! Splinters of wood shot out. Whap! He had cut more than halfway into the log.
> "If only Dad could see me now!" Barney thought.
> His final strokes must be clean in order to finish the log. Barney braced the log with his foot. Then he raised the ax. . . .

---

*From page 192 of "Air Pudding and Wind Sauce," *Keys to Reading* (Oklahoma City, OK: Economy Company, 1972), adapted from "The Magnificent Descent," by Dick Murdock (*Boys' Life,* August 1962).

"I shudder to think what will happen next," you may be saying. And that's good, for it shows you were involved in the story and predicting the next event. Your comprehension was high. Note, moreover, that your ability to predict was dependent on the two abilities already discussed—1) developing associations and images and 2) following a sequence of events or ideas.

The following are some types of experiences you may wish to use with children to help them to learn to anticipate what's coming next:

1. After they have read part of a story, have them guess what is going to happen next
2. Let them draw or pantomime what's coming next, after they have read a certain portion of a story
3. Have them continue the story in writing; then read the rest of the story and discuss how their endings differed
4. Have older children read a dittoed portion of a newspaper editorial or other passage presenting an argument; then have them discuss what they think the author would have said next. Then read the rest of the editorial to them so they can see how well they predicted. (The same thing can be done with an informative passage rather than an argumentative one.)

Understanding Cause-and-Effect Relationships

Cause-and-effect relationships are the nuclei of many stories and articles. Event B happens because of Event A; Event F occurs because of the personality of Character D; and so on. Unless children recognize such relationships, their understanding of an article or story will have little depth. In "The Amazing Underground City," for example, they would not really understand why the "mayor saw that he must do something to make his city a safe place to live" unless they connect this with the electric wires falling into the street.

The teacher's role is again one of asking thoughtful questions—this time ones that encourage children to notice the cause-and-effect relationships. Questions such as these:

1. Why did the mayor see that he must do something to make his city a safe place to live?
2. What caused the electric wires to fall into the street in the first place?
3. Why did so many people die in the snowstorm of 1888?
4. Why did the mayor have the electricians put the wires under the ground?
5. What kind of person do you think the mayor was? Do you think this had anything to do with what he decided to do after the storm of 1888?

The Nature of Critical Thinking

Critical thinking is not necessarily a more difficult form of thinking than inferential thinking. Nor is it always a clearly different form. Yet it does require a slightly different purpose on the part of the reader. When the reader uses inferential thinking, she is trying to gain a deeper understanding of what the author is saying or imply- ing. When she uses critical thinking, on the other hand, she is trying to apply judgments to what the author is saying. She is trying to determine whether the information she's reading is factual or non- factual, whether it is biased, whether it's a form of propaganda, whether it fits certain criteria, or whether it's logical. With inferential thinking, the reader is asking the question, "What's the author really saying?" With critical thinking the reader is asking, "What's my opin- ion of what the author is saying?" Inferential thinking requires intel- ligent guessing. Critical thinking requires intelligent judging. Such judging can take many forms, such as deciding whether information is factual or nonfactual, evaluating an author's ideas or a story char- acter's behavior according to particular criteria, or evaluating the logic of an author's statements.

Distinguishing between Factual and Nonfactual Information

This form of critical thinking can be broken down into at least eight smaller subskills:

1. Distinguishing between literal and figurative expressions
2. Distinguishing between real-life stories and fantasies
3. Distinguishing between real-life stories and satire
4. Distinguishing between factual statements and opinions
5. Recognizing differences between observations an author is mak- ing and inferences she is making
6. Recognizing differences between observations an author is mak- ing and judgments he is making
7. Detecting an author's bias and how this influences her statements
8. Deciding on the author's competence and how this may influence the accuracy of his statements

Here are the types of learning activities the teacher can use in order for her students to make improvements in these eight sub- skills. (The activities correspond in number to the subskills previously listed.)

1. Discuss the meaning of such figurative phrases as "shout- ing my head off" or "pulling my leg." Have the children think of

others they have heard. Have them picture in their heads or on paper "what the words seem to mean and what they really mean." The same type of thing can be done with metaphors that you and the children discover in descriptive passages. For example, in the sentence "John flew down the hallway to his classroom," what does *flew* seem to mean and really mean? (Other examples: Bill didn't get the *point* of my poem. That book is hard to *swallow*. I *plowed* right through my homework.)

2.   After they've read a fanciful story in their basal readers or library books, ask them whether it was a "real-life" story or a "make-believe" one. Have them explain their answers.

3.   Read aloud to the children the book called *The Enormous Egg* by Oliver Butterworth. This is a book which includes satire that most children in third through sixth grade will enjoy and understand. Ask them to discover how the author satirizes ("makes fun of" or "pokes fun at") advertisers, politicians, and others. Another book useful for this type of experience is Merrill's *The Pushcart War*. Discuss with them how Jean Merrill creates imaginary characters and situations that are very like real people and real situations. Help them understand that authors sometimes do this in order to avoid critizing people directly.

4.   Show them how to tell the difference between factual-type statements and opinions. Use the following nonsense statements as illustrations:
 a. A snurtzle has two eyes and three fleb pads. (factual)
 b. Snurtzles are very good at swinking. (opinion)
 c. A snurtzle can swink 50 gallons a day. (factual)
 d. It is clear that snurtzles are always flumptuous. (opinion)
Ask them what makes them sure that statements b and d are opinions. Then present them with a list of actual statements and have them decide which statements seem factual and which seem to be opinions. Have them justify their answers. (Note: for this type of exercise, a "factual" statement is not necessarily a "truthful" statement.) Then have them look for factual statements and opinions in their basal readers, library books, or social-studies textbooks.

5.   Have them learn to distinguish between observations and inferences by discussing two-part statements such as the following:

> Noticing: Jimmy Smith took the milk out of Mrs. Jones's refrigerator. (Observation)

> Guessing: Jimmy *stole* the milk. (Inference)

> Noticing: Jimmy Smith took the milk out of Mrs. Jones's refrigerator. (Observation)

Guessing: Mrs. Jones asked Jimmy to keep her milk while she was on vacation. (Inference)

6. Have them learn to distinguish between observations and judgments by discussing three-part statements such as the following:

Noticing: Jimmy Smith took the milk out of Mrs. Jones's refrigerator. (Observation)

Guessing: Jimmy *stole* the milk. (Inference)

Judging: Jimmy is a *thief*. (Judgment)

Noticing: Jimmy Smith took the milk out of Mrs. Jones's refrigerator.

Guessing: Mrs. Jones asked Jimmy to keep her milk while she was on vacation.

Judging: Jimmy is a nice kid.

After they've completed exercises such as these, have them look for examples in their basal readers, library books, or social-studies books of when the author is "noticing, guessing, or judging."

7. Have the children study magazine ads with the intention of detecting these three propaganda tricks:
   a. *Expert Appeal:* "Four out of five doctors recommend No-Ache Aspirin."
   b. *Winner Appeal:* "More people buy Shuvvy than any other car."
   c. *Star Appeal:* "Hefty Breakneck, star tackle for the Podunk Tigers, uses Left Tackle Deodorant. Shouldn't you?"

Ask them why the advertisers use these tricks. Have them talk about the times they have used these tricks in their own lives. For instance: *Expert Appeal*—"If you don't believe me, just ask my mother." *Winner Appeal*—"But Mom, all the kids are wearing Squishtight Jeans." *Star Appeal*—"Frankie Hacksaw is in sixth grade and he wears 'em." Ask them whether authors may sometimes use tricks like these in order to get them to believe something or do something. If possible, demonstrate this through the use of a basal reader, library book, or social-studies text. For many more ideas on propaganda analysis see May, *To Help Children Communicate* (11).

8. Have the children compare information in two science books or encyclopedias, one published recently and one published several decades ago; have them see how many disagreements they can find about topics such as Mars or atoms. Show them where to find the copyright date in books. Discuss the importance of currency for some information.

Evaluating According to Criteria

Even in the earliest grades, children can learn to evaluate according to definite criteria. At the end of a story that Mrs. Bracing had read to her second graders, for instance, she asked them the following questions:

1. Do you think it was fair for Mark to go in the boat before Jim? Why do you feel the way you do?
2. Which boy had the smarter plan? Why do you think so?
3. Do you feel that Mark was more honest than Jim? What makes you think the way you do?
4. Which boat was the most beautiful? Why?

Such questions encourage children to evaluate according to particular criteria, such as fairness, intelligence, honesty, and beauty.

Children in the upper grades in the elementary school can learn to develop their own criteria and to make judgments according to those criteria. At the end of a brainstorming session on ways of redecorating their classroom, for example, Mr. Frederiksen's fifth graders came up with these criteria, which they later applied to their list of ideas:

1. Cost (Will it cost too much money?)
2. Time (Will it take too much time?)
3. Space (Will it take too much space?)
4. Skills (Do we have the skills to do it?)
5. Agreement (Will other teachers, the janitors, the principal, other children, and parents probably agree that it's a good idea?)
6. Equipment and supplies (Can we get what we need to do it?)

These same criteria were later used on several occasions during their discussion periods on stories and articles they had been reading. In an article about space travel, for instance, their teacher asked them whether the building of a space platform might cost the country too much money? Or was it worth it anyway? Will it take us so much time that the people who are now paying for it will not be getting any benefits? Or is it important to create benefits for the next generation? Do we have enough of the skills required to do a good job? Or should we wait until we've learned more skills before we begin the project? And so on.

In both Mrs. Bracing's class and Mr. Frederiksen's class the children were learning to think critically about what they were reading. They were asked not just to understand the author or what the characters were doing in the author's story, but also to make judgments about the author's ideas or the character's behavior—judgments about fairness, intelligence, honesty, beauty, cost, efficiency, and other criteria that are important to children in their normal course of living and learning.

Evaluating According to Logic

Although some teachers have found that certain logical operations of critical thinking can be taught even at the first-level (15), it is likely that intensive training of evaluating-according-to-logic will be more fruitful in the upper grades. Evaluating according to logical reasoning usually involves a subtlety of thinking that older children can handle much more easily.

By *logical reasoning* I'm referring not to one particular skill, but to a set of subskills. These subskills would include such thinking operations as deducing conclusions from premises, recognizing assumptions, evaluating the validity of inferences, and deciding on the strength and validity of arguments. These operations may be taught as isolated exercises, but should then be applied to selections from basal readers, library books, social-studies texts, science texts, and even mathematics texts. The following are merely examples of the types of exercises that could be used.

Exercises Requiring Deductions

1. Study the following syllogism. Are the two premises true? Does the conclusion logically follow?

    Premise A: All people eat food.
    Premise B: All dogs eat food.
    Conclusion: People are dogs.

2. Study this syllogism.

    Premise A: People like to buy from a company they can trust.
    Premise B: Our company is one that people can trust.
    Conclusion: You should buy from our company.

Exercises Requiring Recognition of Assumptions

1. What assumptions are probably behind this statement? "We will arrive at the airport at 5:00 P.M. Saturday." Explain your answers.
    a. We expect to eat dinner at your house.
    b. No accident will occur on our way.

    c. Airplanes are usually on time.

    d. Saturday is a better time to arrive than Sunday.

  2. What assumptions are probably behind this statement? "This rancher's wife knows that Drab is better than any other detergent."

    a. A rancher's wife has to wash very dirty clothes.

    b. A rancher's wife should know what detergent is best.

    c. Drab gets clothes cleaner than any other detergent.

    d. Drab works better than old-fashioned soap.

Exercises Requiring Evaluation of Inferences

After reading each of the following passages, decide which of the inferences are probably true and which are probably false. Are any of them definitely true or false? Explain your answers.

  1. In Edwardson School, a poll of the students was recently made. It was found that most of the students like chocolate ice cream better than any other flavor. Over half of the students buy ice cream at the corner drug store at least twice a week. The main ingredients in ice cream are sugar and milk.

    a. Most of the students in Edwardson School would like sweetened chocolate milk if they had a chance to drink it.

    b. Edwardson students like strawberry milk shakes better than chocolate milk shakes.

    c. Most of the students at Edwardson School have a job or receive an allowance from their parents.

    d. The people who made the poll talked to more than half of the students.

    e. No one at Edwardson School likes chocolate candy.

  2. Now with new Scotch Boy Walplex, you can roll on new beauty in a single coat. It covers so well, one coat looks like two. New Walplex is especially made for rollers. That way there's practically no roller marks or splatter. No unpleasant paint odor, either. When you're finished painting, it's a snap to clean up. Soap and water takes all the paint off the rollers and brushes.

    a. This paint has a built-in second coat.

    b. A roller would work better than a brush with this paint.

    c. If you apply this paint with a roller, you'll get no roller marks or splatter.

    d. This paint has no odor.

    e. The paint can be washed off the walls with soap and water.

    f. Even if it takes a week to complete your painting job, you don't have to clean your roller until you're finished painting.

Exercises Requiring Evaluation of Arguments

Which of the arguments for the following statements are good ones and which are poor ones? Why?

1. People should drink milk.
   a. Yes, because we have a lot of cows in the world.
   b. No, because some people used to die from a disease carried in unpasteurized milk.
   c. Yes, because milk contains calcium, which is needed for strong bones.
   d. No, because cream is harmful to some people with heart ailments.
   e. Yes, because milk contains many vitamins.
2. Vote for Pinkston for President.
   a. Yes, he has been a soldier and fought for our country.
   b. No, he has never held any office before.
   c. Yes, he believes in democracy and freedom.
   d. No, he is short, fat, and bald.
   e. Yes, he has been a general and has been a leader of men for twenty years.
   f. No, he disobeyed a former President.

Exercises Requiring Logical Separation between Words and Things

1. Give several objects in the classroom a new name, e.g., call the chalkboard *wumpa* (or, if this is too hard for the children to remember, *scribble-slate*). Let the children make up names for a few other objects. Have everyone use the new names for a few days. Then discuss the principle of "a word is not the thing." Ask them questions such as these: Can a piece of chalk be used for writing whether we call it *chalk* or *friglew?* Can a chalkboard be used the same way whether we call it a *chalkboard* or a *wumpa?* If Nancy calls it *wumpa* and Larry calls it *chalkboard,* will they have any trouble talking about it? Is it really something to write on, or is it really a chalkboard, or is it really a *wumpa?* Is this really a pencil or something I call a *pencil?* Could it be called something else and still do what I want it to do?
2. After a week of using the new names given to classroom objects, make up different names for the same objects used in Exercise 1; use these names for a few days and discuss the principle again.
3. Same as Exercise 1: use a foreign language for purposes of naming objects.
4. Have the children look up multiple-meaning words such as *run* in a large, unabridged dictionary. How many meanings does it have? (*Run* has over 200 in the *Random House Dictionary.*) Why does it have more than one meaning? If I say just the word *run,* will you know what I mean? How will you know what I mean? If two people talk to each other and one person uses the word *run,* will the other person automatically know what the first person has in mind? Start a "30-Meaning Chart" having the students find words with thirty or more meanings and write them on a

chart. What does this show us about words and the things they represent? Are they really the same?

5. Discuss the common activity of name-calling. Why does calling some people a skunk or a rat or a dog hurt their feelings? How can a person whose feelings get hurt easily be helped to think about this? Is there something you can tell yourself if someone calls you a rat? What is the difference between a word and a thing?

The Nature of Creative Thinking

Creative thinking, when applied to reading, may involve the reader in a somewhat formal response to what he's been reading. Or it may simply involve him in a bit of constructive daydreaming. On the one hand, Sharon may be inspired (or required) to use the medium of drama, writing, or drawing in order to express the way she feels about a story she's just finished. On the other hand, Richard may be inspired simply to daydream about how he would have done it differently if he'd been the main character in the story. And perhaps on the basis of such a daydream, he may apply his idea in a situation related to his own life.

Creative thinking, because of its fluid and flexible nature, cannot be easily boxed into a definition; perhaps it would be safe to say that it includes many subskills related to the personality characteristics of flexibility, originality, inventiveness, and autonomy. The three that follow may serve as examples:

1. Inventing flexible alternatives
2. Applying ideas to a new situation
3. Translating ideas to another medium.

It is clearly somewhat different from literal, inferential, and critical thinking. Yet, as we shall see, it can't always be separated from them. For instance, Mr. Brown asked Rebecca to think of a way of solving a problem that was better than the way used by a story character. In doing so, he was encouraging Rebecca to think creatively. However, before she could think creatively about solving the problem, she had to first think critically about the way the character had solved it.

While critical thinking will require the reader to make judgments, creative thinking will often require her to come up with a better or different way. This is not always easy for children to do—particularly those who have had very limited experiences in their lives so far (or those who seldom get asked at home or school for their own ideas). While inferential thinking requires the reader to understand the author by reading between the lines, or anticipating the lines to come, creative thinking demands not so much that she understand the author but that she use the author as a springboard for her own ideas.

Perhaps the zenith of thoughtful response to something read is the creative response. For it is in the creative response that behavioral change seems to reside. It is one thing to search for main ideas and details, to visualize what is being said, and to think critically about it, but is quite another thing to take that extra step and respond personally, inventively, and constructively. Many of us have been inspired while reading to do something: to solve a problem, to share our emotions, to translate our feelings into a poem or a painting or some other medium, or to do something better than we've ever done it before. But this creative desire is often stymied by a seeming lack of time or energy or talent—or perhaps, more than anything else, by the habit of not responding. Could it be that too often we've been asked to "turn to the next page" or "go on to the next assignment," rather than to "take time to be yourself?" The following are some of the ways in which you can help children develop the habit of responding creatively:

1. Ask the children, before or during the reading of a story, to imagine how they might solve the problem that the main character has. Then, when they have finished the story, have them discuss or write about how they might have solved the problem in a different way.
2. Have them discuss how the main character's problem was similar to one they have right now. Encourage them to tell how they might solve those personal problems. On a later date, encourage them to tell how they actually did solve them.
3. Encourage them to share their feelings about stories or books they have read through drama, poetry, painting, and other media. For instance, a child can pretend that she's one of the characters in the story; she can describe herself and tell about one or two things she did in the story. Two children who have read the same book may enjoy dramatizing a scene from the book. Another child may decide to make a diorama (a small stage) describing a scene in his book. (For seventy more ideas on this see Appendix F.)
4. Give them time to construct things (castles, dragons, rockets, etc.) that they read about.
5. Let them share their favorite passages from stories by reading out loud to each other. (Give them practice time and assistance so that the experience is a positive one for both the audience and the readers.)

Using the Thinking Skills Holistically

The isolated exercises we've been discussing in this chapter and the previous chapter are useful in their own right in developing children's thinking skills. However, if we want children to use such skills for the purpose of communicating with authors and getting their messages, we will need to provide them with opportunities to practice them in an orchestrated way. An orchestra achieves its beautiful music in a holistic fashion. That is, the conductor does not add up the music from the woodwinds, strings, percussion, and brass to get a sum total called a "musical performance." The conductor helps the musicians interact in such a way that the musical performance becomes much more than the combination of individual solos. (That's right: the whole is greater than the sum of the parts.)

In the same way, the teacher needs to help children's subskills of thinking interact in such a way that "reading performance" is an "orchestrated" production, rather than a set of isolated tasks. Furthermore, she needs to help her students develop individual purposes, so that reading becomes an active experience. Let me illustrate this by showing you how Mrs. Fishbach worked with a small group of third graders. They were about to read a new story in their basal reader called "The School that Floated Away." (Please read this story before continuing.)

*"The School that Floated Away"**

Page 1
Wherever Hattie went there was trouble. One day a big pipe broke in the ground floor of the school. A teacher, named Miss Reacher, ran into the street to call a plumber.

Page 2
But before Miss Reacher could get a plumber, she ran into Hattie. "Hello, Miss Reacher," said Hattie. "How do you feel?"
"I feel fine," said Miss Reacher.
And then without thinking, Miss Reacher asked, "And how do you feel, Hattie?"

Page 3
Hattie-How-Do-You-Feel took a deep, deep breath and began to talk-talk-talk—
about the bump on her head,
why her finger was red,
the black-and-blue spot on her arm,
how she caught a bad cold at a farm. . . .

---

*Bank Street College of Education, *City Sidewalks* (New York: Macmillan Co., 1966). Reprinted by permission of the publisher. (Story divided into four parts by Frank B. May.)

Page 4

   Miss Reacher forgot all about the broken pipe, and by the time Hattie had stopped talking, the whole street was flooded and the school had floated away!

MRS. F: Suppose you were walking in the hall and you saw that a big pipe had broken and water was squirting all over the hall. What would you do about this problem? *(creative thinking, making predictions)*

JERRY: I'd run and tell the janitor.

MARIE: So would I.

MRS. F: What would you do, George?

GEORGE: I'd wrap something around the leak. Then I'd go tell the janitor.

MRS. F: Well, that's a good idea to tell the janitor. What do you think the janitor would do?

JOAN: He'd fix it.

MRS. F: Suppose he didn't know how to fix broken pipes. Then what do you think he would do?

GRETCHEN: I'll bet he'd call a plumber.

MRS. F: All right. Read the first page of this story to yourselves and see what happened when there was a leak in another school. . . . See whether people did what you thought they should do. *(Helping them make predictions)*

MRS. F: Brad, what happened in the school? *(literal thinking)*

BRAD: A pipe broke.

MRS. F: Yes, and what did Miss Reacher do about it? *(literal thinking)*

BRAD: She—she called a plumber.

MRS. F: Brad, would you try to find the sentence on page one that made you think Miss Reacher called a plumber? *(literal thinking)*

BRAD: "A teacher, named Miss Reacher, ran into the street to call a plumber."

MRS. F: Fine. But has she already called the plumber or is she going to?" *(inferential thinking)*

BRAD: (nodding vigorously) She already called one.

JERRY: Uh, uh. It says she ran into the street to call a plumber. It doesn't say she already called one.

BRAD: Oh yeah. She's going to call one.

MRS. F: That's very good detective work, you two. She's going to call one. Now then, do you think she did the right thing by running into the street to call a plumber? *(critical thinking)*

CHORUS: No . . . Yes . . . No.

MRS. F: Some say no and some say yes. Why do you say "no," Marie? *(critical thinking)*

MARIE: Because . . . she should have just used the phone in the office.

MRS. F: Why do you say "yes," Gretchen? *(critical thinking)*

GRETCHEN: (Thinking about it for the first time.) Because . . . because the water might be all over the place and she needed to get out of the building so she wouldn't get her feet all wet.

MRS. F: I see. Well, both of you have a good point. Before we find out what happens next, let's look back at the first sentence on page one. It says, "Wherever Hattie went there was trouble." It sounds to me as though the author is trying to give you a hint or a clue about this story. Do you know what the clue is? *(inferential thinking)*

GEORGE: That there's going to be big trouble in this story.

MRS. F: Yes, I think you're right. What do you think the trouble is going to be? (Listens to several ideas, then says): Read only the next page and see if you're right. Also see if Hattie will have anything to do with the trouble.

MRS. F: What do you think, George? Do you think Hattie is going to have something to do with the big trouble? *(inferential thinking)*

GEORGE: Yep.

MRS. F: Why do you think so? *(inferential or critical thinking)*

GEORGE: Because Hattie stopped her from calling the plumber.

MRS. F: Yes. You noticed that. Well, who can tell me this: what did Hattie say to Miss Reacher that stopped her from calling a plumber? *(literal thinking)* . . . Joan?

JOAN: Hattie said, "Hello, Miss Reacher. How do you feel?"

MRS. F: Was that a bad thing for Hattie to say . . . Marie? *(critical thinking)*

MARIE: No.

MRS. F: (smiling) Why not? *(critical thinking)*

MARIE: Because . . . it's what friendly people say to each other.

MRS. F: That's true. And what would you have done, Marie, if you were rushing out of the building to call a plumber and someone stopped you to ask you how you feel? *(creative thinking)*

MARIE: (thinking) I'd . . . I'd say, "I'm fine, thank you, but I have to run now."

MRS. F: (laughing) That sounds like a good idea. . . . But Jerry, what did Miss Reacher do? *(literal thinking)*

JERRY: She asked Hattie how she felt.

MRS. F: Yes. Do you think that was a good idea, Jerry? *(critical thinking)*

JERRY: No . . . because she should have just run out and got a plumber.

MRS. F: What do you think, Gretchen? *(critical thinking)*

GRETCHEN: I think she should have kept on running but she should have said something nice to Hattie.

MRS. F: That sounds like a good compromise. . . . Joan, the first part of the last sentence on page two says: "And then without thinking, . . ." What do you think that means? *(inferential thinking)*

JOAN: I don't know.

MRS. F: Would you look at the last sentence on the page and tell us who was not thinking. . . . *(literal thinking)*

JOAN: Miss Reacher?

MRS. F: Joan is probably right. But can anyone prove she's right? How do I know the author is talking about Miss Reacher not thinking and not about Hattie not thinking? *(literal thinking, sentence alteration and expansion, expression signals)*

GEORGE: Ooh . . . I know. . . .

MRS. F: Can you prove Joan is right, George?

GEORGE: Yeah, It says right there: "And then without thinking, Miss Reacher asked. . . .

MRS. F: Yes. That's right. So far, then, if there is going to be big trouble, do you think the author will say it's Hattie's fault or Miss Reacher's fault? *(inferential and critical thinking)*

GEORGE: He'll say it's Miss Reacher's fault . . . because she wasn't thinking enough.

MRS. F: Well, let's see if there really IS big trouble and whether it's Hattie's fault or Miss Reacher's fault. You can read page three now. . . .

MRS. F: Well, do you think there's really going to be big trouble? *(inferential thinking)*

BRAD: Naw. They're just talkin'.

MARIE: Oh yes there is. They're talkin' and talkin' and that water's going to go all over the place!

GEORGE: It sure is!

MRS. F: All right. Why don't you read page four to find out if you're right.

MRS. F: Well, what happened, Joan? Was there big trouble, just as George said there was going to be? *(literal thinking and critical thinking)*

JOAN: There sure was! The whole school floated away!

MRS. F: Yes. That's pretty big trouble, all right. Do you think Hattie or Miss Reacher is going to get into trouble now? What's going to happen next? *(creative thinking)*

GRETCHEN: We can't tell, Mrs. Fishbach. The story's all over.

MRS. F: (smiling) That's true, Gretchen, but if you were the author and you wanted to make this story longer, what could you say happened next? Does anyone have an idea? *(creative thinking)*

GEORGE: Ooh. I know . . . Miss Reacher and Hattie run after the school and tie some ropes around it so it won't get away.

MRS. F: That's a good idea. Does anyone else have an idea?

MARIE: I think they put Hattie in jail for talking so much . . . but they let her get out after she promises not to talk to Miss Reacher again when she's trying to get a plumber.

MRS. F: (smiling) Another good idea. Well, I've got a special story that I'm going to let you read now, but first I need to ask you one more question. Do you think this story about Hattie was a make-believe story or a real-life story? Jerry, what do you think? *(critical thinking)*

JERRY: I'd say . . . well, it's probably a make-believe story.

MRS. F: Why do you think so?

JERRY: Because . . . well, I don't think buildings float away like that just because a pipe breaks.

GRETCHEN: I've seen houses floating away on television.

JERRY: Yeah, but a school is heavier than a house . . . and besides houses only float away when there's a flood or something like that. Not just because a pipe breaks.

MRS. F: Well, I'll have to admit that it seems like a make-believe story to me. But I suppose if the pipe is big enough and it leaks for a long time, it might cause a flood. But it would sure have to be a big pipe, wouldn't it, Jerry?

JERRY: (holding out his arms) This big!

MRS. F: When you go back to your seats now, I'd like you to read another story that's probably a make-believe one. I'd like you to read it just for fun. It's about a cowboy who could throw a rope lasso around a tornado and keep it from destroying a town. Do you think a cowboy could do that?

CHORUS: No . . . Yes . . . No.

MRS. F: Well, you read it, and the next time we get together you can tell me what you think.*

Summary

When children read, they can communicate with an author on a much deeper level if they make use of higher-level thinking skills while reading. The higher-level comprehension requires inferential thinking, critical thinking, and creative thinking. The purpose of inferential thinking is to gain a greater understanding of just what the author means; the purpose of critical thinking is to apply judgments to what the author is saying or what the author's characters are doing; the purpose of creative thinking is to use the author as a springboard for our own ideas and feelings. For children to develop skill in using these modes of thinking, they need to be assisted by a teacher who knows how to both teach the thinking subskills in an isolated fashion and encourage them through orchestrated practice. Orchestrated, holistic practice requires skillful and imaginative questioning by the teacher—questioning that encourages children to make predictions, read reflectively, and prove the validity of their own ideas.

References and Suggested Reading

1. Ammon, Richard. "Generating Expectancies to Enhance Comprehension." *Reading Teacher* 29 (1975): 245–9.
2. Austin, Mary, and Morrison, Coleman. *The First R: the Harvard Report on Reading in the Elementary Schools.* New York: Macmillan Co., 1963.

---

*Note how the teacher provides additional time for children to practice holistic reading without questions to answer.

See particularly pages 35–43 on "Comprehension and Interpretive Skills."

3. Barrett, Thomas C. "Taxonomy of Reading Comprehension." *Reading 360 Monograph*. Lexington, MA: Ginn and Co., 1972.

4. Carin, A., and Sund, R. *Developing Questioning Techniques*. Columbus, OH: Charles E. Merrill, 1971.

5. Carroll, J. "The Nature of the Reading Process." In *Theoretical Models and Processes of Reading*, edited by H. Singer and R. Ruddell. Newark, DE: International Reading Association, 1976.

6. Comprehension Games Corporation, 63-10 Woodhaven Blvd., Rego Park, NY 11374. A source for the following comprehension games kits: Context Clues, Main Idea Travel Game, Main Idea Travel Game—Primary Edition, Drawing Conclusions, Fact or Opinion, Reading for Detail.

7. Davidson, Roscoe. "Teacher Influence and Children's Levels of Thinking." *Reading Teacher* 22 (May 1969): 702–4.

8. Davis, Frederick B. "Research in Comprehension in Reading." *Reading Research Quarterly* 3 (Summer 1968): 499–545.

9. Davis, Frederick B. "Psychometric Research on Comprehension in Reading." *Reading Research Quarterly* 7 (1972) 628–78.

10. Guzak, Frank J. "Teacher Questioning and Reading." *Reading Teacher* 21 (December 1967): 227–34.

11. May, Frank B. *To Help Children Communicate*. Columbus, OH: Charles E. Merrill, 1980.

12. Pavlak, Stephen A. "Reading Comprehension—A Critical Analysis of Selected Factors Affecting Comprehension, Ph.D. Dissertation, University of Pittsburgh, 1973.

13. Pearson, P. David, and Johnson, Dale D. *Teaching Reading Comprehension*. New York: Holt, Rinehart, and Winston, 1978.

14. Sanders, N. *Classroom Questions: What Kinds?* New York: Harper and Row, 1966.

15. Shotka, Josephine. "Critical Thinking in the First Grade." *Childhood Education* 36. (May 1960): 405–9.

16. Sims, Rudine. "Miscue Analysis: Emphasis on Comprehension." In *Applied Linguistics and Reading*, edited by Robert E. Shafer. Newark, DE: International Reading Association, 1979.

17. Singer, H. "Active Comprehension: From Answering to Asking Questions." *Reading Teacher* 31 (1978): 901–8.

18. Smith, Nila B. "The Many Faces of Reading Comprehension." *Reading Teacher* 23 (1969): 249–59.

19. Smith, Richard J. "Questions for Teachers—Creative Reading." *Reading Teacher* 22 (1969): 430–4.

20. Stauffer, Russell G. *Teaching Critical Reading at the Primary Level*. Newark, DE: International Reading Association, 1968.

21. Swenson, I., and Kulhavey, R. "Adjunct Questions and Comprehension of Prose by Children." *Journal of Educational Psychology* 66 (1974): 212–5.

22. Taylor, Frank D., et al. *Individualized Reading Instruction: Games and Activities*. Denver: Love Publishing Co., 1972. See pages 105–24 for games and activities on comprehension skills.

23. Thorndyke, P. "Cognitive Structures in Comprehension and Memory of Narrative Discourse." *Cognitive Psychology* 9 (1977): 77–110.

24. Tovey, Duane. "Improving Children's Comprehension Abilities." *Reading Teacher* 30 (1976): 288–92.

25. Weaver, Phyllis. *Research within Reach, a Research-Guided Response to Concerns of Reading Educators.* Newark, DE: International Reading Association, 1978.

Application Experiences for the Teacher-Education Class

1. With a small group of students in your class discuss why you agree or disagree with the following statements. Then compare your decisions with other groups.

Statements about Chapter 6

LITERAL LEVEL: Did the author say these things?

a. By teaching children each separate subskill of higher-level thinking, the teacher assures that they will automatically be able to use these subskills when they read independently.

b. When a child predicts what the author is going to say next, she is employing inferential thinking.

c. Inferential thinking skills cannot be taught, as they are based on the degree of intelligence a child possesses.

d. According to research, good readers seldom waste their time predicting what the author is going to say next.

e. Critical thinking requires a slightly different purpose from inferential thinking on the part of the reader.

f. Critical thinking requires intelligent guessing, whereas inferential thinking requires intelligent judging.

INFERENTIAL LEVEL: Did the author imply these things?

a. Teaching children to evaluate according to criteria (such as fairness, cost, and honesty) is not very practical.

b. It may be too difficult for children in grades one through four to learn to "evaluate according to logic."

c. Having children think creatively about what they read is probably less important than having them think critically.

d. It is better for a teacher to ask children the questions listed in a Teacher's Guide (and in the same order as listed in the Guide) than to create his own questions and order of questions.

2. Discuss how Mrs. Fishbach's lesson on "The School that Floated Away" might have been different had she relied entirely on the questions and

order of questions listed in a Teacher's Guide. Which questions did she probably think of (or get from the Teacher's Guide) before the lesson? Which ones did she probably create during the lesson?

3. To help you think a little more about asking questions that stimulate four types of thinking, try your hand at labeling the questions below. Write *a* if the question asks mainly for literal thinking; *b,* if mainly inferential thinking; *c,* if mainly critical thinking; and *d,* if it requires mainly creative thinking. In order to have a selection that you remember, we'll suppose you have been reading "Goldilocks and the Three Bears" with a group of children:

    a. Do you think it was a good idea for Goldilocks to go in the bears' house without knocking? Why or why not?
    b. What happened to the little bear's chair when Goldilocks sat on it?
    c. If you had been Goldilocks, what would you have done when the three bears came home?
    d. What happened right after the bears came home?
    e. How do you suppose Goldilocks felt after she broke the little bear's chair? What did she say that makes you think so?
    f. What would be another good title for this story?
    g. Is this story a real-life one or a make-believe one?
    h. Now that Goldilocks has gone to sleep in the little bear's bed, what do you think will happen next?
    i. What picture did you have in your mind when you read that sentence?

Here are some more just for fun (not for children):

    j. The author claims that Goldilocks was a gorgeous blonde. Is that a factual statement or an opinion?
    k. Which bear always got "done in" by Goldilocks?
    l. When the author reported that two out of the three bears like Sweet-Tooth Honey better than any other brand, which of these three propaganda devices was he using: expert appeal, winner appeal, or star appeal?

4. Go back over the twelve questions asked in #3 and see if you can label them first according to whether they would require literal, inferential, critical, or creative thinking, then according to the precise subskill discussed in either Chapter 5 or Chapter 6. For instance, Question #a could be labeled "Critical Thinking: Evaluating According to Criteria."

5. With a partner or small group develop a set of questions that might be used to stimulate various thinking skills. Use "The Three Little Pigs" as your story. Label each question in two ways: a) whether it asks for literal, inferential, critical, or creative thinking, b) what specific thinking subskill it requires, and c) whether it encourages children to develop individual purposes for reading. Then ask another small group to evaluate your questions according to criteria they establish.

Field Experiences in the Elementary-School Classroom

1. Plan a "higher-level thinking" lesson related to an assigned story or article. Teach the lesson to two or more children. Prepare prereading and postreading questions for each page in the story or article. The prereading questions should stimulate the children to read for their own purposes and for the purpose of understanding and appreciating the author's message. The postreading questions should encourage the interaction of four types of thinking skills: literal, inferential, critical, and creative. (See pages 145–147 and 174–178 for illustrations of these.) After you've completed the lesson, write a brief report on how you changed the questions and the order of the questions, what questions you added, and what questions you eliminated as a result of interacting with the children.

2. With a young child in any grade K through 2 try out the questions about "The Three Little Pigs" that you invented for Application Experience #5 on page 181. Discuss or write your results. How would you now change some of your questions? Which ones would you eliminate? Which new ones would you invent? (This experience can be carried out with an older child, providing you explain to him that you're trying to learn how to write better questions.)

CHAPTER 7

Reading readiness programs needn't be limited to workbooks.

Getting Children at any Grade Level Ready to Read

Chapter Preview

Reading readiness is a concept that should be of concern to teachers of all grades and subjects in which reading is a learning medium. In order for students to communicate with any author—or just to decipher the alphabetic code that the author is using—they will need a background of specific skills, vocabulary, and experiences. In this sense, the concept of readiness cannot be separated from the concept of difficulty; for without sufficient readiness a reading experience becomes too difficult, and both frustration and lowered self-concept occur rather than learning.

"Reading readiness" has sometimes been partitioned off into its own little sideshow, usually reserved for five- and six-year-olds and often consisting of colorful workbooks which they may mark in as directed by the teacher. Such exclusiveness is no worse, however, than the view, occasionally expressed by teachers of older children, that reading readiness is something those teachers of five- and six-year-olds "didn't do a very good job on." As one teacher of nine-year-olds put it, "I really can't understand what some of these kids did in the lower grades. They obviously are not ready for fourth-grade work!" To avoid belaboring this point, let's just remind ourselves that reading readiness is everybody's territory. The teacher who refuses to take Johnny where he is—at this particular moment—is not sufficiently concerned about a basic concept of teaching that applies to all levels and all subjects: readiness.

Those of us who write about reading readiness have sometimes confused the issue by making it seem as though reading and reading readiness were two distinct subjects with which teachers need to concern themselves. In reality a child's "readiness for learning to read" and his actual "learning to read" are part of the same operation. This is true whether we're talking about six-year-olds or twelve-year-olds. In either case the teacher, in order to teach successfully, must be concerned with what the learner has already learned. Whether the teacher wishes to teach a six-year-old how to decode the letter *t*, or a twelve-year-old to differentiate between facts and opinions, the same principle applies.

> We can't get humans ready until we know what we want them ready for.

Factors of Readiness for Which Teachers Are Responsible

But what about those children, whether they're six or twelve, who don't seem ready to learn any more than they already know about reading? Is the lack of readiness some sort of disease with causes that are wondrously complex? One might think so from the vast number of articles and books that have been written on this subject. In Table 7.1, for example, you can see some of the factors that classroom teachers and other professional educators have proposed as "causes" for insufficient reading readiness. A glance at the table should make it clear why a sensitive teacher may crumble under the weight of such obstacles. To make sure a child is really ready, it might appear as though you need to turn yourself into a physician, an ophthalmologist, an audiologist, a speech therapist, a clinical psychologist, a linguist, and a nutritionist—not to mention a skillful reading teacher.

Table 7.1 Factors Sometimes Associated with the Lack of Reading Readiness

underdeveloped intelligence	poor speech models in the home
subnormal metabolic rate	low cultural expectations for boys
inadequate diet	emotional instability
insufficient sleep	physical immaturity
poor articulation	inability to listen
insufficient oral vocabulary	inability to follow directions
vision defect	negative attitude toward school
hearing defect	negative attitude toward a teacher
disadvantaged background	directional confusion
low level of socialization	dyslexia (specific language
underdeveloped curiosity drive	disability)
little knowledge of letters	unfamiliarity with standard English
inadequate visual discrimination	nonEnglish mother tongue
inadequate auditory discrimination	no prior experiences with books
weak visual memory	inadequate self-concept
weak auditory memory	low sense of security
low socioeconomic level	low sense of belonging or esteem
low aspiration level of parents	no positive reinforcement from
low aspiration level of child	teacher
low level of teacher expectations	ill health

But very few would place such impossible expectations on classroom teachers. Those classroom teachers who do actually teach reading, however, should be expected to know three things: 1) how to teach certain readiness skills, 2) what special teaching techniques to use for those children who are weak in one or more readiness skills, and 3) the best way to have children's vision and hearing tested. The readiness skills for reading generally considered important are these:

1. Readiness skills required for sheer decoding of printed material
   a. Skills requiring mainly vision
      1. *good vision* (the ability to refocus as often as every one-half word, to cause the muscles from each eye to coordinate bifocally, and to perceive distinct letters in a book comfortably and clearly from a distance of approximately six to twelve inches) Testing children for these will be discussed near the end of the chapter.
      2. *visual discrimination* (the ability to notice differences between graphemes, e.g., *e* is a different letter from *c*)
      3. *letter recognition* (the ability to communicate with a teacher about the names of the letters in the alphabet, e.g., saying a letter's name when the teacher points to it)
      4. *visual memory* (the ability to recognize, recall, and produce graphemes and grapheme sequences, e.g., learn-

ing an irregular "sight word" by closing your eyes and spelling it in your mind)

5. *left-to-right orientation* (the ability to perceive graphemes and separate words in the proper sequence from left to right, e.g., teacher has child point to the fifth word in the line)

b. Skills requiring mainly listening

1. *good hearing* (the ability to detect easily and comfortably minor changes in the volume and pitch of speech sounds uttered in a soft voice). Testing hearing will be discussed near the end of the chapter.

2. *auditory discrimination* (the ability to notice differences between phonemes, e.g., short *a* has a different sound from short *e*

3. *auditory memory* (the ability to recognize and recall phonemes and phoneme sequences, e.g., thinking of words that rhyme or words that begin with the same sound)

4. *letter-sound association* (the ability to communicate with a teacher about the most common sounds associated with letters in the alphabet, e.g., saying the sound /t/ when a teacher points to *t*)

5. *auditory blending* (the ability to place phonemes in a sequence and to recognize the word this produces, e.g., child says /a/ + /n/ + /d/ and recognizes the word *and*)

6. *following oral directions* (the ability to attend to and follow a teacher's oral instructions, e.g., teacher asks child to circle the letter that is different from all the rest in the row)

7. *syllable sense* (the ability to hear the different syllables in a word, e.g., child can hear the four syllables in (un/sports/man/ship)

2. Readiness skills required for both decoding and comprehension of print

a. *oral vocabulary* (the ability to recall the meaning or function of words and morphemes that will be later seen in print, e.g., *to, the, this, Mrs., dog, boy, girl, done, undone, refixing*)

b. *syntax recognition* (the ability to understand common sentence patterns, alterations, and expansions when presented orally, e.g., child knows that "The apple was eaten by the boy" has the same meaning as "The boy ate the apple")

c. *context sense* (the ability to determine the meaning of a word by noticing syntactic and semantic clues in a sentence that has been presented orally, e.g., in the sentence "The princess dove into the swift flowing flistrow", the last word must mean something like a river)

d. *experiential association* (the ability to relate one's own background of experiences to information that is being presented orally, e.g., realizing what the speaker means by *rodeo* because of having been to one)

e. *predictive listening* (the ability to make an intelligent guess about what a speaker is going to say next, e.g., "I've just come back from Chicago. Have you ever been in _____ ?" Child predicts that the person will say "Chicago")
f. *thinking* (the ability to use literal, inferential, critical, and creative thinking while listening to ideas and questions presented orally, e.g., child can create a visual image in his mind of what a speaker is describing and can decide whether the image is a "scarey" one or not)

Such a list of readiness skills could be extended almost indefinitely by subdividing each of those already mentioned. But the skills previously described should serve as an illustration of the types of prerequisites that teachers have to think about before teaching a reading lesson. To take one example: if Susan is asked to think inferentially about something she has just read, she'll be at a disadvantage if she has seldom, if ever, been asked to think inferentially about something she has just heard. By providing such thinking experiences as part of listening lessons first, the teacher can increase the possibility of success when this is followed by reading lessons. If a teacher tries to teach a skill the first time through reading rather than listening, the child is burdened with a triple task: she has to translate the ideas from print to speech; she has to understand the message at the literal level; she has to think at the inferential level about what she has translated and understood.

Let's take another example of the need to pay attention to prerequisites. Ben is a six-year-old who is about to be taught a lesson on decoding *ch* and *sh* in words like *much* and *mush*. Halfway through the lesson, you realize that Ben is not really sure of what you're talking about when you say the letters, *c, s,* and *h.* You also discover that he really doesn't hear the difference between the /ch/ phoneme and the /sh/ phoneme. Obviously, Ben is not ready for the lesson you had in mind and needs a different lesson instead.

When Readiness Skills Are Taught

Most reading educators seem to agree that in teaching reading-readiness skills we should follow the psychological principle of "massed practice followed by distributed practice." What this generally means is that kindergarten and first-grade teachers provide the massed practice and teachers in the later grades provide the distributed practice. In theory, this probably should work. But in practice, the distributed practice often gets neglected. Teachers in the later grades will sometimes assume that "readiness has already been taken care of." Yet, as we've already seen, readiness is an all-pervasive need.

Rather than get ourselves in the trap of discussing "Kindergarten Readiness Programs," "First-Grade Readiness Programs," and so on, let's look instead at what we need to do to get children ready for the various subskills of reading that we've been talking about in the previous chapters. Let's assume as we do this that whereas kindergarten and first-grade teachers will have the greatest responsibility for readiness skills, teachers of later grades will have important responsibilities as well. Remember, even something "simple" like auditory discrimination can be a stumbling block for a small minority of older children. Every lesson you teach has prerequisites, and if ten-year-old Johnny can't meet those prerequisites, you're going to have to change your lesson plan or teach him the prerequisite skills before you can proceed.

Readiness for Phonic Analysis

When are children ready for instruction in phonics? Which of the following sets of answers is more valid when considering a particular child—the first set or the second?

First Set
When the child is emotionally mature.
When the child has a mental age of six and one-half.
When the child has completed his or her readiness workbook.
When the child has finished kindergarten.

Second Set
When the child can discriminate auditorily between phonemes.
When the child can discriminate visually between graphemes.
When the child can communicate with the teacher about the names of the letters that will be part of forthcoming phonics lessons.

At one time, the first set of answers was given more credence than the second set. Research and educators' experiences over the past several decades, however, have shown that the first set of answers is far too simple for such a complex situation (4, 7, 8, 12, 20, 23, 27, 31, 37, 38, 43). Today we realize that the first set includes variables that are much too vague and much too subject to individual variation to provide the teacher with any useful information about the readiness of his particular students. Some children learn to read in spite of their so-called emotional immaturity. Many can profit from reading instruction before they reach that magic "mental age" of six and one-half. For many children, a readiness workbook is a waste of time. And there are some children who want to read and should probably be given instruction in reading while still at the tender age of five. Examination of research reports (7, 12) and observation in American and British classrooms would illustrate the fallacies underlying the answers presented in the first set.

Most British children receive reading instruction at the age of five. However, just because children can learn to read at age five, this is not saying that children should learn to read at age five. Some children would be better off receiving formal instruction at age seven. In other words, there is no magic age for beginning reading instruction. Unfortunately, though, most parents want their children to learn to read when they're six. This expectation will occasionally present a teacher with one of those "unsolvable dilemmas." (Allen doesn't seem to be motivated to concentrate on the hard task of learning to read, but his parents want him to read.) Most teachers faced with this dilemma try to teach the child as much as he can comfortably learn, while at the same time attempting to delay the parents' expectations. ("Allen is beginning to show more interest in reading, Mrs. Smith. Your reading to him before he goes to bed must be helping. If we just keep working on his interest in reading, I'm sure he'll become more and more motivated to learn the skills that I'm introducing to him.")

The second set of answers assumes that phonic-analysis skills are dependent upon prerequisite skills. In other words, if you wish to teach a child to translate certain graphemes into phonemes, you must first be sure the child can tell the difference between one grapheme and another *(visual discrimination)*. You must also be sure she can tell the difference between one phoneme and another *(auditory discrimination)*. And, since letter names are handy labels for communicating about the translation of graphemes into phonemes, it is also wise to make sure the child can recognize those letters you'll be talking about to her.

These three readiness skills—auditory discrimination of phonemes, visual discrimination of graphemes, and letter recognition—have been shown to correlate significantly with early reading achievement (3, 6, 8, 14, 15, and 45). Furthermore, some of the reading programs that have emphasized these readiness skills appear to have been more successful than those that have not (16, 21, 23, 41). Other researchers, though (11), cite studies demonstrating that no advantage (on reading-achievement scores) was gained by children given formal instruction in letter recognition. Although the presently available research on this matter is conflicting, it seems likely that most children will benefit from the inclusion of these three skills in a readiness program.

It is possible that we may eventually determine through experimental research that formal, isolated, readiness programs have little to do with later success in reading. But even so, it is likely that we will continue to find many children who benefit from specific readiness instruction in conjunction with specific reading instruction. For instance, many students whose progress in phonic-analysis skills seems to be blocked by a lack of visual discrimination, letter recognition, or auditory discrimination will probably benefit from auxiliary instruction in one or more of those skills.

But how can those skills be taught—assuming that a child has not already picked them up with your tutelage? First of all, of course, they should not be taught to a child who already has acquired them, even if the parents have paid a book fee and the child is "entitled" to a readiness workbook. (How to find out whether a child has already acquired the skills will be discussed a little later.) But if the child is lacking these skills, and if the readiness workbook or other commercial materials seem inappropriate or insufficient, the types of exercises that follow might be used. Note first, though, that even children beyond the age of six or seven may lack these skills. The readiness exercises that follow are appropriate for them as well as for children in kindergarten or first grade.

Sample Readiness Exercises Used
to Prepare Children for Phonic Analysis

Visual Discrimination

Visual discrimination is the ability to notice differences between graphemes. This is a rather fundamental ability, of course, for without it a child can't learn to decode at all. Fortunately, studies show (9, 26, 27) that the vast majority of children can discriminate visually by the time they enter kindergarten. The teacher's job, then, becomes one of providing them practice in the right type of discrimination.

For many years it was thought that visual discrimination between letters and words should be preceded by having children notice differences in pictures and geometric shapes. Research (36, 45) demonstrates, however, that such exercises do not significantly influence reading readiness. Only exercises in which the children make discriminations between letters and words actually make a difference in how well children are prepared for phonic analysis. The following are the types of exercises which might be used:

1. "On the chalkboard are two pairs of words: *happy–happy* and *lazy–sleepy*. Will one of you put a circle around the pair that is the same? All right. Now here are some more pairs (on the chalkboard or on a worksheet) for you to look at. Circle only the pairs that are the same." (For the pairs that are different, use words that have gross differences, e.g., *hope–run*,

elephant–turtle.) Note: For children who have trouble with this exercise, be sure to point out the differences in words: the different lengths of the words, the different number of letters, even the names of the different letters if they've learned them. If you don't do this, you are merely testing the children, rather than teaching them.

2. Same as #1, but for the pairs that are different use words that differ only in the initial grapheme or cluster, e.g., *hope–rope, beer–deer, there–where.*

3. Same as #1, but for the unlike pairs use words that differ only in the final grapheme or cluster, e.g., *hop–hot, bang–bank, mold–mole.*

4. Same as #1, but for the unlike pairs use words that differ only in a medial grapheme or cluster, e.g., *hat–hot, rubber–rudder, master–masher.*

5. Same as #1, but use pairs of letters instead of words, starting first with unlike pairs that are grossly different such as *m–p* and moving to unlike pairs that require finer discrimination, such as *m–n,* or *d–b.*

6. Same as #5, but use cutouts of letters, so that children having trouble making discriminations can try fitting one letter on top of another.

7. Same as #6, but use dotted letters and have the children trace over each pair before deciding whether to circle it.

8. "On the chalkboard is a list of words. I'd like you to circle those that begin (or end) in the same way as the first word."

9. Same as #8, but emphasize medial graphemes instead of initial or final ones.

10. Same as #8, but use letters instead of words. "Circle those letters that are the same as the first one."

11. Same as #8, #9, and #10, but have them find the word or letter that is different from all the rest.

Letter Recognition

Letter recognition is the ability to communicate about the names of letters. There is no clear-cut evidence that children must know the letters of the alphabet before they can learn to read. In fact it would be quite possible to learn to read without ever knowing the names of the letters as long as one knew what sounds to associate with the letters. However, letter names are handy tools for teachers and children to use while reading instruction is being given. Most teachers will tell you that it's easier to teach reading when children know the letter names.

What this means in practice is that we would like children to know the letters in a very practical or operational sense. When a teacher points to a letter, the children will be able to say its name. Vice versa: when she says its name, they will be able to point to it.

When the teacher asks, "What letter do you see that is the same in all three of these words?" the children will be able to recognize the common letter and to say its name. While some teachers work on letter recognition alone, many teachers combine lessons on letter recognition with lessons on visual memory. With this approach, the children are taught to write the letters as they are learning to recognize them. There is probably considerable justification for this, as writing tends to reinforce one's memory of letter shapes. The following exercises, however, are for letter recognition only:

1. Play matching games in which the children match their letter cards to a letter card that the teacher or leader holds. Be sure to have them say the letter name as they match them.
2. Use the letter names as a "password." Hold up a letter card and have the children name the letter before they can pass from one activity to the next.
3. Put a new letter on the board each day, both in lowercase and uppercase. Several times during the day, ask someone to tell what the letter is. Review with flashcards those letters that have been on the board on previous days.
4. Encourage children and parents to watch "Sesame Street" together and to play games that require the use of the alphabet.
5. Write the names of several children on the chalkboard. Have each child in the group compare and contrast his name with one or two other names: length of names, number of letters, number of different letters, the names of the exact letters that are different, and so on. (This gives them practice on both letter recognition and visual discrimination.)

Visual Memory

Visual memory, when applied to reading readiness, is the ability to recognize, recall, and produce graphemes and grapheme sequences. This ability is more complicated than either visual discrimination or letter recognition and is based on the acquisition of these two simpler skills. With visual memory the child not only must be able to tell the differences between letters and know their names, she must also be able to write the letters—from memory—both in isolation and in sequence. Furthermore, she must be able to remember sequences that are actual words.

In Chapter 2, we discussed ways of using visual memory to teach children irregular words that we would like them to have as part of their sight vocabulary. As you will recall, this procedure required the children to look at the letters of the word and say them; close their eyes and imagine the letters while they say them silently; look at the letters again to see if their visual memory was correct; write the letters of the word in sequence without looking at them;

and check once more to see if they have written the word correctly. Readiness experiences that can be used in preparation for this type of procedure include the following:

1. Help each child to spell his own name orally and in writing.
2. Teach children to write each letter by introducing two or three letters at a time in the context of a word. For example, to teach the letters *s* and *e,* introduce them in the context of the word *see (SEE).* After they learn to write the *s* and *e,* both in uppercase and lowercase form, have them write the word in both forms: *see* and *SEE.*
3. Use visual-memory techniques to prepare the children for eventually learning irregular sight words. After children have developed good letter recognition, present any three letters visually to them. Use three-letter sequences that don't form a word, such as *f–m–b.* Have them follow these steps:
   a. Look at the letters and say them
   b. Close their eyes and imagine the letters while they say them silently
   c. Look at the letters again
   d. Write the letters in sequence without looking at them
   e. Look at the letters to see if they remembered them correctly
   Note: Treat this exercise as a game preceding exercise #4.
4. Teach them to spell, write, and recognize the words shown earlier in Table 2.2, page 43, "Basic Sight Vocabulary—Irregular Words Only." Learning these words will increase their skill in using visual memory to learn more difficult words. See the steps described on pages 44–47.

Auditory Discrimination

Auditory discrimination is the ability to notice differences between phonemes. Whereas studies show that most children have sufficient ability to discriminate visually by the time they enter school, many children, particularly those who rely on nonstandard dialects for most of their communication, need considerable help in improving their auditory-discrimination abilities (9, 26, 27). Some of the children who are weak in auditory discrimination can be helped through specific exercises. Others, however, do not seem to gain significantly from specific instruction and may need to be taught phonic analysis partially through the linguistic approaches discussed on pages 78–81 in Chapter 3. Generally speaking though, most children, whether they speak a standard or nonstandard dialect, seem to gain from a multisensory approach in which visual, auditory, and writing approaches are used. Thus, it is necessary to provide assistance in both auditory and visual discrimination, especially in conjunction with actual reading instruction. The following are exercises that may be used in developing improved auditory discrimination:

1. "Close your eyes and listen to these words: *hair, dare.* Keep your eyes closed and raise one finger if you think the words are the same. . . . Now listen to some more pairs of words. Each time you hear a pair of words that are the same, raise your finger." (Use pairs whose initial consonant phoneme is either the same or different, e.g., *far–car, head–head, that–bat.* Discuss immediately any pairs that cause trouble.)

2. Same as #1, but use pairs whose final consonant phoneme is either the same or different, e.g., *bag–back, man–map, run–run.*

3. Same as #1, but use pairs whose medial vowel phoneme is either the same or different, e.g., *here–hair, flip–flip, clip–clap.*

4. "Listen to these three words: *tiger, table,* and *top.* Can you think of some words that begin in the same way?" (Give positive reinforcement for any word that begins with the /t/ phoneme. Do other initial phonemes in the same way.)

5. Same as #4, but use words whose final phonograms are the same ("words that end in the same way"), e.g., *map, trip, tulip, flop.*

6. Same as #4, but use words whose final phonograms are the same ("words that rhyme"), e.g., *hall, ball, stall.* (Do the same thing for the various vowel sounds; see Chapter 14 for illustrations of the vowel phonemes.)

Auditory Memory

Auditory memory is the ability to recognize or recall phonemes and phoneme sequences. Whereas auditory discrimination requires only the ability to notice that one phoneme has a different sound from another, auditory memory requires that the child be able to concentrate on one phoneme at a time and to reproduce that phoneme in his own speech. At times he may be required to reproduce only one phoneme; at other times he may be required to reproduce a sequence of phonemes. For instance, a teacher may ask Ricardo to repeat the /a/ sound; or she may ask him to think of another word that starts with the /a/ sound; or she may have him think of a word that ends in the same way as *bat* and *cat,* thus requiring him to remember the sequence of the /a/ and /t/ sounds.

Children with a high level of auditory memory seem to be able to learn well through the analytic phonics method described on pages 76–78. Children with a low level of auditory memory will either need to have their "phonics" lessons reinforced through the substitution and phonogram methods described on pages 78–81 or they may need to be taught through the synthetic method described on pages 81–83. They may also gain from readiness exercises such as these:

1. "I'm thinking of something in this room that begins in the same way as the word *church.* What is it? That's right: *chalkboard.*" (Do the same for other initial phonemes.) After the children under-

stand the game, let them take turns being a leader. (Or whoever gets it correct gets to be leader.)

2. Same as #1, but use blends instead of single phonemes.

3. "I'm thinking of something in this room that rhymes with *hall.* That's right: *ball.*" (Do the same with other phonograms such as *ill, at, ape, ap,* and so on.) After the children understand the game, let them take turns being a leader.

4. "Who can make exactly the same sound I'm making: /a/? Now who can make this sound: /e/? Who can make this sound: /p/? Who can make this sound /m/?"

5. "Who can say these letters in exactly the same order as I say them: *p–b–a*?" (Do the same with other three-letter or four-letter sequences that do not spell an actual word.) The child who gets it correct can be the next leader.

Letter-Sound Association

Letter-sound association is the ability to communicate about the most common sounds associated with letters in the alphabet. This ability requires the combination of several visual and auditory abilities. When the teacher points to the letter *t,* and asks Wanda "What sound does this letter stand for?" Wanda has to be able to do several things. She has to use her visual abilities to recognize that this letter differs from other letters like *l, i,* or *f.* She has to use her auditory abilities to recall that this letter stands for the sound /t/ and to be able to reproduce that sound. Her ability to do all these things will make it easier for her to be taught either through the analytic phonics method described on pages 76–78 or the synthetic phonics method described previously on pages 81–83. Children who have trouble with this ability may be assisted through the linguistic approaches (substitution and phonogram) described earlier on pages 78–81. They may also be assisted through the following readiness exercises:

1. As children learn to recognize and say the letters of the alphabet, they are often taught the sound of the letters at the same time.

2. As children learn to write the letters of the alphabet, they are often taught the sound of the letters at the same time.

3. Children are sometimes taught "key words" to associate with each letter as they learn how to say and write them. For instance, when they learn the letter *p,* they are taught to associate it with a picture of a pig. This "key word" then reminds them that *p* usually stands for the sound heard at the beginning of *pig.*

4. "I'm going to point to a letter and then I'm going to call on someone to tell me what sound the letter usually stands for."

Auditory Blending

Auditory blending is the ability to place phonemes in a sequence and to recognize the word thus produced. If Michael decodes *a* as /a/, *n* as /n/, and *d* as /d/, he should recognize that he has produced the word *and*. As strange as it may seem, many children cannot do this without a considerable amount of assistance. They may be able to make the /a/ sound all right, the /n/ sound and the /d/ sound, but for some reason these three phonemes remain in the child's mind as separate distinct sounds. They do not become blended together into a recognizable word.

It is for this reason that synthetic phonics programs such as DISTAR have sometimes been recommended. These programs actually teach children how to blend phonemes together in order to make words. They are taught, for example, to say a word like *sun* very slowly, like this: /sssss–uuuuu–nnnnn/; then to say it faster: /sss–uuu–nnn/; and finally to say it "the right way": /sun/. For a more complete reminder of how this method works, see pages 81–83.

On the other hand, synthetic phonics programs may sometimes cause the very trouble they were designed to cure. By having children learn letter-sound correspondences first and then put them together to produce words, this type of program may actually be teaching children to perceive a word as a set of distinct phonemes. To exaggerate my point a bit, the word *bat* may be misperceived by some children as /buh/ + /a/ + /tuh/ and actually thought of as "buhatuh." You can see then why it is so important, when using a program such as DISTAR, that the exercises on blending are not neglected.

In order to help children learn auditory blending, it would probably be advisable to use a synthetic phonics method only for those children who do not seem to respond well to the more popular analytic phonics method. In addition, you may wish to reinforce the analytic phonics method with the linguistic approaches (substitution and phonogram) described earlier in Chapter 3. By using linguistic approaches alongside of the analytic method, you will be teaching children to see the spelling patterns that make up many words and to see the minimal contrasts between one letter-sound correspondence and another. Thus you will reduce the amount of auditory blending that needs to be done by the child in order to decode unknown words. Readiness experiences such as the following may also help:

1. Teach letters and letter sounds in the context of whole words as much as possible. For example, teach the letter *p* and the letter sound /p/ in association with pictures and words such as *pig, pie,* and *puppy*. Avoid an overemphasis on letters and letter sounds in isolation.
2. If you do have children pronounce isolated consonants, have them place their hand under their chin and press upward. This

will minimize the added vowel sound. This can also be accomplished by having them clench their teeth. Avoid having them add the short *u* sound /u/ to consonants.

3. If possible, avoid the notion of "sounding out" words. This procedure for decoding words should only be taught as a last resort to those who have trouble learning common spelling patterns (such as phonograms, VCE, VC, and so on). It is far better, for instance, to teach *cap* as /k/ + /ap/ than as /kuh/ + /a/ + /puh/.

4. If you do plan to use the synthetic phonics method, be sure to prepare the children for this type of instruction by teaching them how to blend phonemes to make a word. Start with words they already have in their oral vocabulary and have them say them slowly, faster, and fast. The word *much*, for instance, would be said: /mmmmm–uuuuu–chchchch/, then mmm–uuu–chchch, then /much/. Use words with fricatives such as /s/, /z/, /ch/, /sh/, /j/, /θ/, and /th/, or nasal sounds such as /m/, /ng/, or /n/: *sing, zing, chin, shush, judge, thin, them.* In this way, you can exaggerate the phonemes without adding a vowel sound to the consonants.

Left-to-Right Orientation

Occasionally a child will demonstrate difficulty in adopting our habit of reading from left to right and from top to bottom. Most children, though, seem to have little trouble picking up the habit of reading from left to right and from top to bottom. This is probably because parents and teachers have conditioned them into expecting words and sentences to be decoded that way. After all, it would be quite possible to read from right to left and from bottom to top.

One of the easiest ways for a teacher to condition children to our left-to-right convention is to develop experience charts with them. These are simply sentences dictated by the children and written in manuscript by the teacher on a large piece of paper. The children watch the teacher write the "story" from left to right and from top to bottom. After writing each sentence, the teacher reads it and has the children say it with her, passing her hand under the words in a left-to-right direction. Since the sentences are usually based on children's personal experiences, an experience chart seems to be a meaningful way to develop not only the concept of left-to-right, but also the useful concept that "reading is something like changing written words back into spoken words."

Some activities that are used to encourage a left-to-right and a top-to-bottom orientation are these:

1. While reading stories to children, occasionally turn the book around so that children can see it; point to the words as you read.

2. As you read to the children, ask them occasionally after you've turned a page where you should start reading.

3. Create language-experience stories with them.
4. Provide children with a sheet of paper (or space on the chalk-board) that has three rows of four rectangles. Write two sentences on the board containing a total of twelve words. Write these twelve words from left to right in three rows. Have the children copy the words in the same sequence, using the rectangles as their guide.
5. Read two or three of the Sunday "funnies" with a small group of children. Place the comic strip up on the board and point to the pictures as you read the words in the "balloons."
6. The same as #5, but block out the words in the "balloons" and have them make up their own words.
7. Have a primary-level typewriter available in the classroom for their use.

Following Oral Directions

Before children can learn skills in phonic analysis (or any other skill, for that matter) they need to learn how to follow the oral directions that teachers give them. Many times we may think that a child has reading problems, when in reality he simply doesn't understand the directions (or pay enough attention to them). One of the reasons Carl may not have paid attention is that he may not have been taught how to follow oral directions. Another reason is that his teacher may talk too much. Let's look at these two reasons one at a time.

Following directions for some children is easy because they have such good auditory memory. As they hear a set of directions, they store it in memory and then re-hear it as they prepare to follow what they're supposed to do. Those children with poor auditory memory, however, need to compensate by using visual memory, as well. Therefore, a teacher needs to teach children how to create "pictures in your mind" while listening to directions.

Suppose, for instance, the teacher wants the children to find all of the pictures with objects that start with the /s/ sound, to circle those pictures, and to draw a line from each circled picture to the large *S* at the top of the page. Some children could do this with only oral instructions. Many, though, will need to develop a picture in their mind of what they are to do. One way of helping them develop that picture, of course, is to illustrate the directions graphically on the board or on the page of a workbook. But that is often not enough for some children. In addition to illustrating it graphically, it would be a good idea to have them close their eyes and imagine themselves doing each of the three things in sequence: finding a picture, circling it, drawing a line from the picture to the large *S*. In this way, you will not only help them follow these particular directions, you will be teaching them a valuable scheme for following directions in general.

The second reason Carl may not have paid attention to the directions is that the teacher talks too much. No one likes to listen to the same voice all day long. No matter how good a voice you may have, children will tire of it. Studies have shown (10) that teachers often speak 50 to 80 percent of the words heard by the entire group in a classroom. Is it any wonder that kids sometimes tune out?

Here are some experiences that may increase children's ability to follow directions given orally:

1. Let children take your place as teacher as often as possible. For instance, let an older child sometimes read a story; have a child in the class lead the Pledge of Allegiance; have another child take lunch count, and so on.
2. Make your instructions a game as often as you can. Challenge them to follow the instructions "after I've told you only once." Praise those who succeed. Those who don't get your instructions should come to your desk—or to another student—for another quiet explanation. Don't force the entire class to listen to your instructions again in a loud, irritated voice.
3. Sometimes when you give instructions, you can ask children to complete the last word of each sentence. This provides novelty and keeps them on their toes.
4. Pantomime some of your instructions so that the children actually end up verbalizing them.
5. Give them a sequence of three numbers and have them repeat them in the exact order. Very gradually work up to five or more numbers. The child who repeats the sequence successfully gets to be the next leader.
6. Same as #5, but use "action words" instead, such as *jump, eat,* and *swim.* The use of action words will help them use their visual memory, as well as their auditory memory.
7. Same as #6, but have them pantomime the action words after you've given them all three at once.
8. Occasionally play "follow-the-directions games" such as "Simon Says" or others that you make up: "The first one to do all three things and in the right order gets to be the next leader. . . . You can't start until I tell you all three things and say 'go'. . . . Turn all the way around three times. . . . Bend at the waist and touch your toes. . . . Say your last name twice."

Oral Vocabulary

The decoding of printed words into spoken words is partly dependent upon sufficient experience with spoken words and with those things or concepts that the words represent. Most children could decode simple regular words like *cat* or *run* without prior experience in speaking or listening to them. That is, they could pronounce the correct phonemes in response to the graphemes, even though comprehension would not follow. This would not be "reading," however, as defined in this book. And they certainly would have difficulty decoding more complex words or irregular words without acquiring them first as part of their oral vocabulary. A two-syllable word such as *robin,* for instance, could just as easily be decoded as (rō′bən) rather than (rob′ən), unless the word were already in the decoders' reservoir of speaking and listening words. And an irregular word such as *one* would readily be decoded as (ōwn), were it not for the check provided by their oral vocabulary. So once again we see the interaction between decoding and comprehension and the interplay among the various communication skills. For children unhampered by major speech and hearing defects, the development of skill in decoding appears to be partially dependent upon the development of oral vocabulary. The following are some types of experiences that may assist in this development:

1.   A major means of fostering oral-vocabulary growth, as well as growth in other reading skills, is to provide children with a solid science program, particularly in the kindergarten through grade three years. Such science programs as Science—A Process Approach II (SAPA-II), Science Curriculum Improvement Study—Beginnings (SCIS), Elementary Science Study (ESS), and the Biological Sciences Curriculum Study—Elementary School Sciences Program (BSCS-ESSP) provide children with first-hand experiences in problem solving, producing knowledge, locating information, remembering, inferring, predicting, classifying, and in developing such concepts as *far/near, to/from, top/bottom, first/last,* and so on. Several studies (2, 5, 22, 36) have shown that children's participation in such systematic science programs has contributed to the growth of their oral language and their readiness for reading.

2.   Provide abundant verbal and nonverbal experiences so that concepts can be developed and associated with words:

. . . When a child has the chance to hear one good story after another, day after day, he is being taught to read. When his . . . year is a series of mind-stretching eye-filling trips, helping him know more solidly his world, he is being taught to read. When a child hears good adult language, he is being taught to read. When he creates with blocks, when he communicates with paint, when he uses his body freely as a means of expression, he is being taught to read. When a child stares, fascinated, at a picture—when he looks ever so carefully at the scale in his store or at the life in his aquarium, he is being taught to read. When he hammers ever so carefully at the workbench, fashioning his battleship, this too teaches him to read. When he uses his whole body—two eyes, two hands, two arms, two legs and knees and feet—to pull himself up a scary slanted climbing board, he is being taught to read. (20, p. 156).

*One way of fostering growth in reading readiness skills is to
provide children with a solid science program at an early age.*

3. Provide some type of show-and-tell experience for each
child at least once a week. Encourage each child to participate, even
if it means calling parents to get their help.

4. See Chapter 3 for many more suggestions on developing
vocabulary.

Diagnosing Readiness for Phonic Analysis through Tests

In some school districts, children are administered a reading-readiness test during their kindergarten year. The usefulness of such a test depends largely on the precautions that teachers take in interpretation. For one thing, the time between administration and interpretation is highly significant. Unless teachers interpret and act within a month or two after the test is administered, they are likely to make serious errors in their instructional strategy for a particular child. What often happens is that children are tested in April or May of their kindergarten year, and the test is interpreted in September or October by the first-grade teacher. For many children, a lot of learning and forgetting has gone on in the meantime.

For another thing, what the teacher chooses to interpret is also highly significant. Often only the total score is noticed, and the child is put into group A, B, or C accordingly. The assumption seems to be that the total score is a good predictor of an individual's capacity to learn to read. This may be wishful thinking. Since most of the correlations between total scores and subsequent reading achievement range between .50 and .60 (19), it can only be concluded that total scores on readiness tests are not very good for predicting an individual's achievement. They are pretty good for helping researchers compare the average score of one group with the average score of another group; and they are pretty good for separating the few extremely ready from the few extremely unready. On the other hand, for helping a teacher decide what specific skills to teach Bobby Smith, total scores are nearly useless.

If teachers are to get much use out of standardized tests, they must use them as diagnostic tools, studying the subtests or the items themselves and making notations on the specific skills a student lacks. Most readiness tests, for example, provide a measurement of children's visual- and auditory-discrimination skills, and some provide information on their letter knowledge. By looking at the subtest scores and by noting the types of mistakes made on the subtests, teachers can then plan specific lessons for specific children.

Some of the commonly administered reading-readiness tests are as follows:

1. Clymer-Barrett Prereading Battery, Personnel Press
2. Gates-MacGinitie Readiness Skills Test, Teachers College Press
3. Gesell Institute Readiness Tests, Harper and Row
4. Harrison-Stroud Reading Readiness Test, Houghton Mifflin
5. Lee-Clark Reading Readiness Test, California Test Bureau
6. Metropolitan Readiness Test, Harcourt Brace Jovanovich

7. Murphy-Durrell Diagnostic Reading Readiness Test, Harcourt Brace Jovanovich
8. Reading Aptitude Tests, Houghton Mifflin

If you do not have standardized test results available (or if you want to check their validity with your own individual assessment), you may wish to develop informal tests such as the following:

For letter knowledge.   Test each child individually by having him or her tell you the names of the letters that you have on a dittoed sheet. The letters should not be in alphabetical order, as it is possible for a child to "know" the alphabet by rote but be unable to recognize specific letters. Both capital and small letters should be listed. Simply circle the letters the child cannot name.

For visual discrimination.   Use as your model for test items the visual-discrimination exercises described previously in this chapter on pages 193–194. This test can be made a group test by asking the children to circle their answers on a dittoed sheet.

For auditory discrimination.   Use as your model for test items the auditory-discrimination exercises described previously in this chapter on pages 196–197. This also can be made a group test.

For left-to-right orientation.   Whether you need to test for this before phonics instruction begins is debatable. However, if you are curious about the left-to-right orientation of some children, a simple test is to hand them individually a cartoon from the Sunday "funnies." This cartoon should be one with several pictures in three or more rows and one that can be interpreted without reading the captions. Ask the child to tell you "what is happening in each picture" and observe the direction in which the child tries to "read" the pictures.

For oral vocabulary.   Some children's deficiencies or strengths in oral vocabulary can be observed during a show-and-tell period, while they are playing on the playground, when they are listening to the teacher read a story, and so on. But if you wish to be more certain about particular children, you can set up a situation like the following on an individual basis.

For each of three or four pictures that you present to them, ask them to tell you 1) what is happening, 2) what they think happened just before this, and 3) what they think will happen next. Their responses will give you a fair idea of how much extra time you should spend with them on developing their oral vocabularies. All children, of course, need continued assistance in developing their speaking and listening vocabularies. Some children, though, may be disadvantaged in this respect and need extra stimulation.

Readiness for Other Word-Recognition Skills

Now let's see how well you can predict the type of readiness activity that may help prepare a child for learning a particular reading skill that you learned in previous chapters.

Try matching the following readiness exercises with the set of word recognition skills:

Readiness Exercises	Word-Recognition Skills
_____ 1. The teacher says a sentence but omits a word. Children decide what words may fit in the sentence.	a. morphemic analysis
_____ 2. The teacher says a sentence, omits a word, and holds up a letter card to indicate how the word begins. Children decide what the word probably is.	b. syllabic analysis c. contextual analysis d. sight vocabulary
_____ 3. The teacher says something like, "I splash in the water." A child replies, "Yesterday I splashed in the water. Today I am splashing in the water."	e. dictionary use f. contextual-plus-phonic analysis
_____ 4. The teacher provides visual-memory experiences, such as writing two or three symbols on the board, covering them up, and asking the children to reproduce the symbols on their papers.	
_____ 5. The teacher has the children clap the syllables in words as they pronounce them.	
_____ 6. The teacher provides experiences that help the children learn alphabetical order.	

Answers:
1—c   2—f   3—a   4—d   5—b   6—e

If you got all the answers correct, you probably have guessed the secret: in predicting what type of readiness activity will be needed as preparation for learning a particular skill, it's necessary to understand what behavior that reading skill involves. If you understand, for example, that morphemic analysis involves the recognition in print of common roots, affixes, compound words, and contractions, you can help children get ready for this by providing preparatory oral-language experiences. As mentioned earlier, a teacher can help prepare children for decoding words in print by promoting the acquisition of those words in their oral vocabulary. In the same way, one can prepare them for recognition of morphemes by providing them with opportunities to speak and listen to a variety of morphemes. Many children have already had sufficient practice in this respect, but children who have come from homes in which verbal fluency is not highly valued may receive benefit from joining their classmates in exercises similar to the following.

Readiness Exercises for Contextual Analysis

To find out if readiness skills could be developed in the kindergarten year, a study of 4,000 children was conducted in the city of Denver. In this study they discovered that the experimental group, which received special instruction, not only learned the readiness skills, but also showed the greatest initial and long-range gains in both reading comprehension and reading vocabulary (7). What special instruction did these children receive while in kindergarten? In addition to instruction aimed toward improved auditory discrimination and improved letter recognition (which necessarily involves visual discrimination), they received four types of readiness exercises related to contextual analysis. These four exercises, which will now be described, should be of benefit to the kindergarten or first-grade teacher who is seeking exercises for a developmental readiness program—and to the teacher of older children who is seeking exercises for children having trouble with contextual analysis.

1. *Spoken context:* From sentences or short paragraphs read or spoken by the teacher, the pupils practiced using context to figure out several words that would make sense where the teacher had omitted a word. (Johnny drank his _____ . milk, juice, water)
2. *Context and initial consonant sounds:* The pupils practiced using the context of a sentence or paragraph read or spoken by the teacher and a beginning consonant sound supplied by her to think of the correct missing word. (Tom wants to cut a board in half. He needs a tool that begins with the same sound as *sit* and *sat.* He needs a _____ . saw)
3. *Context and displayed initial letter:* The children practiced using context and a viewed letter to figure out the missing word in a sentence or paragraph read or spoken by the teacher.
4. *Context and displayed word:* The teacher read or spoke a sentence or paragraph in which the word omitted was the only one that would make sense. At the same time, she displayed the entire printed word on a card and asked the pupils to name the word (7).

Readiness Exercises for Syllabic Analysis

1. Have the children clap or stamp as they pronounce words presented orally by the teacher.
2. Play a modified game of "Three Steps Off the Mudguard." Usually the leader calls the number of steps which the line of children may take toward him or her. If anyone takes more than the prescribed number of steps, that person may be tagged—unless she beats the leader to the opposite side. For the modified version, the leader calls a word rather than a number. The children must figure out the number of syllables in that word and take only that many steps.

3. For an exercise that also involves auditory memory—an ability that may be significantly related to reading achievement (25)—the teacher presents the children orally with three words in rapid succession. The children must remember the words, count the number of syllables in all three words combined, and say the correct number when called upon by the teacher. The first one correct gets to be the leader.

4. To help them gain the concept of syllabic stress or accent, have the children pronounce words that you present to them orally. As they pronounce them, they should clap their hands on the syllable that receives the greatest stress.

Readiness Activities for Dictionary Use

1. Teach them an alphabet song or verse to help them remember alphabetical order. While singing or saying it, the teacher or a child should point to the letters on a chart. One of the common alphabet songs is as follows:

"Lyrics"	*Tune*
A–B–C–D–E–F–G	c–c–g–g–a–a–g
H–I–J–K–L–M–N–O–P	f–f–e–e–d–d–d–d–c
Q–R–S–T–U and V	g–g–f–f–e–e–d
W–X and Y and Z	g–g–f–f–e–e–d
Now I know my ABC's	c–c–g–g–a–a–g
What do you really think of me?	f–f–f–e–e–d–d–c

2. Help children make their own picture dictionaries. Have one page in the dictionary for each letter of the alphabet—in alphabetical order. On each page is a picture the children have cut out to represent an object whose name starts with a particular letter. Usually the name of the object is written under it. Also on each page is the letter—both in lowercase and uppercase format—isolated in one corner.

3. Have a relay race against the clock. The first person dashes up to the chalkboard, writes *A* or *a* (depending on whether you specify small or capital letters), shouts /ā/, runs back, and hands the chalk to the next person. The next person runs up, writes *B* or *b*, shouts /bē/, and so on. Work toward a "world's record."

4. Make an alphabet board by pounding two sets of twenty-six small nails into a piece of plyboard. Purchase fifty-two circular tags with a hole punched near the edge. Write the capital letters on half of them and the small letters on the other half. Hang them on the two sets of nails. Turn some of them around so that the letters cannot be seen, and have the children tell you what letters are missing. After a child has said a letter that is missing, she can come up and turn the tag around to see if she was right.

Readiness for Comprehension

As you will remember, the raw materials of comprehension, excluding for the moment the higher-thinking skills, are made up of vocabulary (words), expression (pitch, stress, pause), and sentences (patterns, alterations, expansions). Since we have discussed on other occasions the importance of oral-vocabulary development to the subsequent development of reading vocabulary, we need not go into its role as a readiness skill again. Perhaps only two brief reminders need to be made: 1) helping children expand their reservoirs of words in their speaking and listening vocabularies enhances both their decoding skills and their abilities to comprehend words in print; 2) children's speaking and listening vocabularies are developed by providing them with experiences—both direct and vicarious—and with opportunities to talk about their experiences.

Readiness for reading with expression and for comprehending various sentence patterns, alterations, and expansions may be developed through the types of experiences that follow.

Readiness Experiences for Reading with Expression

1. The teacher should read often to the children, using expression that is moderately dramatic without becoming artificial and overly exaggerated. Be sure that a good proportion of your reading selections contain dialogue. Reading aloud to children can promote not only an awareness of pitch variations, stress signals, and pauses, but also an appreciation for good literature and a social bonding that occurs as a result of a mutually satisfying experience.

2. Play records made by famous storytellers. Such recordings as Caedmon's *Mother Goose,* narrated by Celeste Holm, Cyril Ritchard, and Boris Karloff, and Folkways' *Folk Tales from West Africa,* told by Harold Courlander, provide excellent examples of reading with expression, as well as fine entertainment.

3. Present a sentence to the children in a monotone, such as "That is my coat." Challenge them to say it in such a way that it means:

   a. The coat belongs to me, not to someone else. (That is <u>my</u> coat.)

   b. The one I'm pointing to, and not the other one, is mine. (<u>That</u> is my coat.)

   c. I'm talking about something I wear, not a young horse. (That is my <u>coat</u>.)

   d. The coat belongs to me now; it isn't just one that I used to own. (That <u>is</u> my coat.)

e. I'm wondering if it really is mine. (That is <u>my</u> coat?)

f. I'm wondering if it is really a coat. (That is my <u>coat</u>?)

g. I'm surprised that you think <u>I</u> would wear such a rag. (That is <u>my</u> coat!)

4. The reverse of #3. This time the teacher or leader says a sentence in various ways and the children try to guess what is meant.

5. Present a sentence to the children without any pauses, such as: Look Toby the clown is eating the peanut butter cookie and the ginger bread boy. Have them see how many different meanings they can get by pausing at different points in the sentence. There are at least a dozen different meanings that can be produced in this way, if you count the possible pause between *bread* and *boy* (. . . bread. Boy!)

Readiness Experiences for Sentence Comprehension

The exercises and teaching steps discussed in Chapter 5 on sentence alteration are also appropriate for readiness experiences, as long as the teacher doesn't expect the children actually to read the sentences. Such exercises can be done orally without any reading or writing taking place. As the children become more adept at reading and writing, of course, these skills should be combined with the oral-language skills to strengthen the quantity and quality of the learning. As a reminder of the teaching steps involved, these will now be repeated:

1. Introduce the children to a set of model sentences, all illustrating the pattern you wish them to understand.

2. Have them create sentences like the model ones (orally at first; later in writing).

3. Have them create alterations and expansions of the model sentences (as well as some of the other sentences they have created in Step 2).

Readiness for Thinking about What Is Read

You have seen that many reading-readiness exercises are quite similar to activities used for regular reading instruction. The essential difference is that readiness exercises often involve oral language with little or no print to decode, whereas reading exercises require first the translation of print into "speech." With this basic principle at your command then, it shouldn't be too difficult for you to match the following set of readiness activities with the set of thinking-reading skills. Answers will be found at the end of the matching exercise.

Readiness Activities

_____ 1. Having the children react to a book the teacher has read to them through drama, reading parts aloud to other children, imagining how they would have done things differently, construction, oral or written compositions, etc.

_____ 2. Having them dramatize homemade TV commercials and discuss selling techniques used

_____ 3. Having the children react to a book the teacher has been reading to them by discussing "pictures in their heads" or similar experiences they have had

_____ 4. Having children create titles for a story that the teacher has read to them

_____ 5. Having them listen to a tape recording of a factual description or narration: before listening to it, they are to decide what two facts they are most interested in learning about through their listening experience.

_____ 6. Having the children listen to two differing reports of an event and decide which one is closer to the truth

_____ 7. While reading a story aloud to the children, occasionally having them guess what is going to happen next

_____ 8. Having them follow a set of instructions that are presented orally

_____ 9. Reading a satire to the children and discussing the comparisons that the author wants the reader to make

Thinking-Reading Skills

a. Developing associations or images
b. Following a sequence of events, ideas, or directions
c. Recognizing and recollecting significant details
d. Determining main ideas
e. Predicting what should follow from what one has read
f. Distinguishing between literal and non-literal passages
g. Detecting propaganda and author bias
h. Determining accuracy of information
i. Responding creatively to what is read

Answers:

1—i   2—g   3—a   4—d   5—c   6—h   7—e   8—b   9—f

Reading Readiness as a Function of Vision

It may appear obvious that children are not ready to learn to read or to improve their reading abilities without good vision. And yet just how obvious is this? The word _vision_ represents much more than most people realize. The average person thinks of vision simply as "eyesight" and that 20-20 vision is "good vision." But good vision involves a host of skills.

Patrick had good vision, according to the Snellen test—the simple test most often used in schools. He could read all of the Snellen Chart with either eye, indicating that he had at least 20-20 eyesight and probably better. Patrick even learned how to read without too much trouble. But by the time he was in fourth grade, it was obvious to everyone that Patrick was in trouble. He read too slowly and he sometimes complained of blurred vision and headaches. He seldom understood what he read very well. His attitude toward reading and toward school was becoming more and more negative.

In desperation, Patrick's parents took him to an optometrist on the off chance that his headaches had something to do with his eyes. The optometrist used far more sophisticated tests than the Snellen Chart and found that Patrick's problem had to do with the type of vision most of us take for granted. Because of muscular imbalance and other defects, Patrick's eyes were not working together. One eye was shutting down and letting the other eye do all the work. This resulted in his missing words, phrases, and whole lines. Furthermore, his eyes were not focusing and refocusing as they're supposed to when one reads, thus causing him to lose his place and his train of thought.

After four months of intensive training, Patrick was taught how to use his eyes in a coordinated way. His reading comprehension and his attitude toward school both climbed rapidly. He began to enjoy reading and to search for books to read "just for pleasure."

The happy ending to Patrick's story is uncommon, because for many children such vision problems are never detected. Instead, parents and teachers too often assume that the child is "emotionally disturbed," "dyslexic," and, well—you name it. It is quite unfortunate—as well as unnecessary—that schools still are relying on the Snellen Chart, designed around the time of the Civil War—to test children's ability to see the chalkboard from the back of a normal-sized classroom. The usual Snellen Chart is useful for detecting myopia (nearsightedness) and amblyopia (dimness of vision), but it is practically useless for detecting astigmatism (poor focusing), hyperopia (farsightedness), or problems of control and coordination (similar to Patrick's problems).

Fortunately, for children of the future there is now a technique of testing children's eyes that will detect all of these problems. Furthermore, it's a test that can be administered by either a trained nurse or trained teacher. It's called the "Modified Telebinocular Technique" or the MTT. As yet, very few schools are using this new technique, but it is hoped that in the future it will become the standard procedure. If you would like more information on the MTT write:

Dr. Howard N. Walton
Southern California College of Optometry
2001 Associated Road
Fullerton, California 92631

Or you may wish to read a brief article on the MTT by Schubert and Walton in the November 1980 edition of *The Reading Teacher* (40).

Reading Readiness as a Function of Hearing

Like vision problems, hearing problems often go undetected, although probably not as often. When they go undetected, the child will usually suffer from feelings of being "dumb." She is simply not aware that other people hear better than she does; as a result she assumes that she's not as smart as other children. This assumption often leads to a negative attitude toward learning to read and learning in general.

Some school districts hire an audiologist who periodically tests the children's hearing. If your district does not provide such a service, it would be advisable for you to test your students' hearing informally. Studies (24) show that teachers who test their students' hearing can often detect hearing problems. One of the simplest procedures is to ask a parent or aide to take each child to a quiet room for a two-minute test. The parent has the child sit down and close his eyes. Then she puts a loud ticking watch (or a small clock) next to the child's ear and moves it slowly away until he raises a finger to indicate that he can no longer hear it. The actual distance away from the ear that will indicate hearing loss varies, of course, with the loudness of the tick and the quietness of the room. In general, though, if a child raises his finger much sooner than others in the class, the tester should recommend the child to the parents and principal for professional testing. Note: Such a procedure provides only a rough estimate of the child's ability to detect volume change. It does not detect his ability to detect pitch changes or phoneme differences (auditory discrimination). These can be detected only by the audiologist and teacher, respectively.

Once you have identified children with hearing problems, try not to embarrass them by making an issue of it. Talk in your normal voice but directly at their face without anything obstructing their view of your face. It's also a good idea to talk to them privately about any problems they're having because of their hearing difficulty.

Summary

As a summary for this chapter, let's distill it into a few generalizations about reading-readiness instruction:

1. Reading-readiness instruction needs to be carried on for all ages at all grade levels. It is not the exclusive preserve of kindergarten and first grade.
2. Readiness instruction should be both developmental and remedial. That is, it should be carried on as a regular part of the

curriculum—usually as that part of the language-arts program in which oral language is stressed. And it should be provided as specific background for those who are having particular problems in reading.

3. Readiness instruction should also be considered from the very broad standpoint of providing experiential background. In this sense, most of the things a teacher does with children can be considered as readiness for something else. That is, each experience has potential "readiness power." An effective teacher enriches ongoing experiences in order to increase their readiness power and capitalizes on previous experiences in order to help children learn something new.

4. Reading readiness may be a function of vision and hearing. Therefore, it is important for teachers to know the proper procedures for making sure that the various types of hearing and vision abilities are tested.

References and Suggested Reading

1. Anderson, Verna Dieckman. *Reading and Young Children.* New York: Macmillan Co., 1968. See Chapter 5 on "Getting Ready to Read" and also Appendix A on "Speech Sound Check," Appendix C on "Kindergarten Inventory," Appendix D on "Developing Readiness for the Context Clues," Appendix H on "Vocabulary Development," and Appendix L on "Suggestions for Teaching the Alphabet and for Alphabetizing."

2. Ayers, Jerry B., and Mason, George E. "Differential Effects of Science—A Process Approach upon Change in Metropolitan Readiness Test Scores among Kindergarten Children." *Reading Teacher* 22 (April 1969): 435–9.

3. Barrett, Thomas C. "The Relationship between Measures of Prereading Visual Discrimination and First-Grade Reading Achievement: a Review of the Literature." *Reading Research Quarterly* 2 (Fall 1965): 51–76.

4. Beller, E. Kuno. "The Concept Readiness and Several Applications." *Reading Teacher* 23 (1970): 727–37, 747, 765.

5. Bethel, Lowell J. *Science Inquiry and the Development of Classification and Oral Communication Skills in Innercity Children.* Unpublished Ph.D. dissertation, University of Pennsylvania, 1974.

6. Bond, Guy L., and Dykstra, Robert. "The Cooperative Research Program in First-Grade Reading Instruction." *Reading Research Quarterly* 2 (Summer 1967): 5–142.

7. Brzeinski, Joseph E., Harrison, M. Lucille, and McKee, Paul. "Should Johnny Read in Kindergarten?" *National Education Association Journal* 56 (March 1967): 23–5. Reprinted in *Reading and the Elementary School Child,* edited by Virgil M. Howes and Helen Fisher Darrow. New York: Macmillan Co., 1968, 157–60.

8. deHirsch, Katrina, Jansky, Jeanette J., and Langford, William S. *Predicting Reading Failure: A Preliminary Study.* New York: Harper and Row, 1966.

9. Deutsch, Cynthia P. "Auditory Discrimination and Learning: Social Factors." *Merrill-Palmer Quarterly of Behavior and Development* 10 (1964): 277–96.

10. Devine, Thomas G. "Listening: What do We Know after Fifty Years of Research and Theorizing." *Journal of Reading* 21 (January 1978): 296–304.

11. Downing, John, and Thackray, Derek. *Reading Readiness.* London: University of London Press, 1971.

12. Durkin, Dolores, "Early Readers—Reflections after Six Years of Research." *Reading Teacher* 18 (1964): 3–7.

13. Durkin, Dolores. "Reading Readiness." *Reading Teacher* 23 (1970): 528–34, 564.

14. Durrell, Donald, and Murphy, Helen. "Reading in Grade One." *Journal of Education* 146 (December 1962): 14–18.

15. Durrell, Donald D., and Murphy, Helen A. "Reading in Grade One." *Journal of Education* 146 (December 1963): 3–53.

16. Dykstra, Robert. "Auditory Discrimination Abilities and Beginning Reading Achievement." *Reading Research Quarterly* 1 (Spring 1966): 5–34.

17. Dykstra, Robert. "Summary of the Second-Grade Phase of the Cooperative Research Program in Primary Reading Instruction." *Reading Research Quarterly* 2 (Fall 1968): 49–70.

18. Golden, N. E., and Steiner, S. "Auditory and Visual Functions in Good and Poor Readers." *Journal of Learning Disabilities* 9 (1969): 476–81.

19. Harris, Albert J., and Sipay, Edward R. *How to Increase Reading Ability.* New York: David McKay, 1980.

20. Hymes, James L. "Early Reading Is Very Risky Business." *Grade Teacher* 82 (March 1965): 88 +. Reprinted in *Reading and the Elementary School Child,* edited by Virgil M. Howes and Helen Fisher Darrow. New York: Macmillan Co., 1968, 153–7.

21. Karnes, Merle B., et al., "An Evaluation of Two Pre-School Programs for Disadvantaged Children." *Exceptional Children* 34 (May 1968): 667–76.

22. Kellogg, Donald H. *An Investigation of the Effect of the Science Curriculum Improvement Study's First Year Unit, Material Objects, on Gains in Reading Readiness.* Unpublished Ph.D. dissertation, University of Oklahoma, 1971.

23. King, Ethel M. "Effects of Different Kinds of Visual Discrimination Training on Learning to Read Words." *Journal of Educational Psychology* 55 (December 1964): 325–33.

24. La Conte, Christine. "Reading in Kindergarten." *Reading Teacher* 23 (1969): 116–20.

25. Lieberman, Janet E. "The Effect of Direct Instruction in Vocabulary Concepts on Reading Achievement." Ph.D. dissertation, New York University, 1966.

26. Loban, Walter. *The Language of Elementary School Children.* Research Report No. 1. Urbana, IL: National Council of Teachers of English, 1963.

27. Lyon, Reid. "Auditory-Perceptual Training: The State of the Art." *Journal of Learning Disabilities* 10 (November 1977): 564–72.

28. Marchbanks, Gabrielle, and Levin, Harry. "Cues by Which Children Recognize Words." *Journal of Educational Psychology* 56 (1965): 57–61.
29. Mitchell, Ronald W. "Kindergarten Children's Responses to Selected Visual Discrimination Exercises in Reading Readiness Materials." Unpublished colloquium paper, University of Minnesota, 1965.
30. Nevius, John R. "Teaching for Logical Thinking is a Prereading Activity." *Reading Teacher* 30 (1977): 641–3.
31. Paradis, Edward, and Peterson, Joseph. "Readiness Training Implications from Research." *Reading Teacher* 28 (1975): 445–8.
32. Pavlak, Stephan A. "Reading Comprehension—A Critical Analysis of Selected Factors Affecting Comprehension." Ph.D. dissertation, University of Pittsburgh, 1973.
33. Petty, Walter T., Herold, Curtis P., and Stoll, Earline. *The State of Knowledge about the Teaching of Vocabulary*. Cooperative Research Project No. 3128. Urbana, IL: National Council of Teachers of English, 1968.
34. Reid, J. "Sentence Structure in Reading." *Research in Education* (May 1970): 23–7.
35. Rhodes, Lynn K. "I Can Read! Predictable Books as Resources for Reading and Writing Instruction. *Reading Teacher* 34 (February 1981): 511–8.
36. Ritz, William C. *The Effect of Two Instructional Programs (Science—a Process Approach and the Frostig Program for the Development of Visual Perception) on the Attainment of Reading Readiness, Visual Perception, and Science Process Skills in Kindergarten Children*. Ph.D. dissertation, State University of New York, Buffalo, 1969.
37. Rosen, Carl. "An Experimental Study of Visual Perceptual Training and Reading Achievement in First Grade." *Perceptual and Motor Skills* 22 (1966): 979–86.
38. Rosner, Jerome. "Auditory Analysis Training with Prereaders." *Reading Teacher* 27 (1974): 379–84.
39. Ruddell, Robert B. "The Effect of Oral and Written Patterns of Language Structure on Reading Comprehension. *Reading Teacher* 18 (January 1965): 270–5.
40. Schubart, Delwyn G., and Walton, Howard N. "Visual Screening—A New Breakthrough." *Reading Teacher* 34 (November 1980): 175–7.
41. Silvaroli, N. J., and Wheelock, W. H. "An Investigation of Auditory Discrimination Training for Beginning Readers." *Reading Teacher* 20 (December 1966): 247–51.
42. Strickland, Ruth G. "The Language of Elementary School Children: Its Relationship to the Language of Reading Textbooks and the Quality of Reading of Selected Materials." *Bulletin of the School of Education, Indiana University* 38 (July 1962).
43. Thompson, Bertha Boyd. "A Longitudinal Study of Auditory Discrimination." *Journal of Educational Research* 56 (March 1963): 376–8. Reports a high correlation between auditory discrimination and reading achievement.
44. Weintraub, Samuel. "Research: Oral Language and Reading." *Reading Teacher* 21 (1968): 769–73.
45. Wingert, Robert C. "Evaluation of a Readiness Training Program." *Reading Teacher* 22 (January 1969): 325–8.

Application Experiences for the Teacher-Education Class

1. With a small group of students in your class discuss why you agree or disagree with the following statements. Then compare your decisions with other groups.

Statements about Chapter 7

Literal Level: Did the author say these things?
   a.   Reading readiness should be completed in kindergarten and first grade.
   b.   A child's readiness for learning to read and his actual learning to read are part of the same operation.
   c.   Teachers of reading should not have to be responsible for knowing the best way to have children's vision and hearing tested.
   d.   Auditory blending is the ability to place graphemes in a sequence and to recognize the word thus produced.
   e.   A child is ready for instruction in phonics when he has a mental age of six and one-half and has completed his readiness workbook.

Inferential Level: Did the author imply these things?
   f.   The ambitions of parents may be a factor in determining when you begin reading instruction.
   g.   Teaching a child the names of the letters causes her to learn to read much better.
   h.   Readiness exercises in auditory and visual discrimination may be appropriate for children at any age.
   i.   A child who is weak in auditory skills should be taught to read strictly through visual means.
   j.   The Snellen Chart should not be used in the schools.
   k.   Standardized reading-readiness tests are not useful.

2. With a partner or a small group see if you can diagnose each child's "readiness" problem and decide what remedies to provide. Use the list of readiness skills on pages 188–190 for your diagnosis. Use the exercises on pages 193–212 for your remedies.
   a.   Randy has trouble thinking of rhyming words. When he does come up with a word, it frequently doesn't rhyme with the ones the other children have mentioned.
   b.   Marjorie can decode words like *stump, forest,* and *undergrowth* but can't comprehend them.
   c.   Arnold can't decode words that start with *br.* He decodes them as if they started with *bi.*
   d.   Karen can answer literal-level questions about what she reads, but she can't answer inferential-level questions.
   e.   Fred is always the last one to find a word in the dictionary.
   f.   Henrietta reads *tick* as *tack, run* as *ran,* and *pin* as *pen.*

3. With a partner examine a reading-readiness workbook and the accompanying teacher's guide. Which of the readiness skills described on pages 188–190 of *Reading as Communication* are introduced in the workbook? Which ones are highly emphasized? Do you think they are the ones which should be emphasized in a readiness workbook?

Field Experiences in the Elementary-School Classroom

1. Develop a brief reading-readiness test and administer it to one or more children. You may wish to use some of the ideas on page 206.

2. Teach a readiness skill to one or more children. You may wish to use ideas from Chapter 7 for your lesson.

3. Study a child's responses, item by item, to a reading-readiness test. Outline a program of reading readiness that you would suggest on the basis of your study.

4. Analyze how another teacher determines whether children are ready for a reading experience she is planning to give them. Also observe how she provides necessary readiness experiences. Does she sometimes provide oral-language experiences before similar reading ones? How? What changes in her "readiness" procedures would you make?

CHAPTER 8

If you teach a child how to read, but in the process, he learns to hate reading, what have you gained?

Increasing Positive Attitudes, Motivation, and Retention

Chapter Preview

Which of these goals go you think is the more important one for a teacher of reading to have?

1. To teach children how to read
2. To teach children to want to read

Not a very easy question to answer, is it? But you may want to think of it this way: if you teach Roger how to read, but in the process, he learns to hate reading, what have you gained? Will he go to books on his own for information and pleasure? If not, then what have we lost? We've lost one important avenue toward Roger's success in life—toward his emotional maturity, toward his social awareness, toward his intellectual vigor, and maybe even toward his economic self-sufficiency.

But does reading instruction have anything to do with such broad concerns as emotional maturity, social awareness, intellectual vigor, and economic self-sufficiency? It can have, providing a teacher thinks of growth through reading as well as growth in reading as the ultimate goals of reading instruction. But growth through reading is only possible if children want to read about their social and natural environment and if they want to enjoy literature. If reading instruction is limited to workbook exercises and skill lessons, though, it's quite unlikely that such desires will flower in the classroom. Furthermore, it's quite unlikely that children will perceive of reading as a holistic process that involves pleasure as well as work.

Let's talk in this chapter, then, about ways of making sure that Roger's attitude toward reading is positive, that Marjorie's desire to learn to read better is strong, and that most of Pat's days of learning to read provide a sense of achievement and success and "growing up." The three approaches we'll concentrate on are 1) providing a model, 2) providing motivation to learn, and 3) providing success through better retention. Later, in Chapter 13, we'll talk about the use of children's literature and book projects to make reading a pleasurable experience.

One of the things I've observed about human children is this: You can *teach* a child to read, but you can't *make* him read.

Providing a Model

Observations and research on children's desire to learn to read (or to improve their reading abilities) consistently point to one factor that stands out over all others: children who want to learn to read (or read better) usually have adult models in their lives who like to read; children who feel the opposite about reading generally do not. And yet it is not unusual to find parents who want their children to be good readers but who never crack a book in front of them. Nor is it unusual to find teachers who want their students to be good readers but who never read for pleasure in front of them or talk about what they've read. (They're often so busy teaching reading they don't take time to read.)

At the risk of going off the deep end, let me throw out a hypothesis for you to consider: those teachers who spend as much time on the "modeling approach" toward teaching reading as they do on subskill instruction will have greater success than those who spend all of their time on subskill instruction. Why I make such a statement is this: we humans are emotional as well as rational creatures. Most of us long to be inspired as well as instructed. Most of us, particularly as we grow up, want to imitate others who we admire. Let me hasten to comment, though, that I'm not advocating that teachers use only themselves as models. There are other people who will also serve for inspiration, including children's own classmates. Let's talk, then, about how teachers can promote themselves, parents, other adults, and children's peers as models.

First, the teacher herself. Mrs. Weaver obviously believes in the "modeling approach." For one thing, she reads to her class every day, even though they're in the fourth grade. She selects her "read-aloud books" very carefully—some with male heroes and some with female heroines, but all of them with literary quality and "an exciting plot." She reads a chapter every day just before they go home. "That way," she says, "I can end each day on a very positive note and they're eager to return to school the next morning." Mrs. Weaver doesn't have a "Hollywood voice" but she reads with enjoyment and with just enough expression to display her excitement without trying to make "a big dramatic production of it."

For another thing, Mrs. Weaver shares her own personal reading experiences with her class. Once or twice a week, during her students' daily morning "Newstime" she talks about something she has read—in a newspaper, a magazine, or a book. Often she brings that newspaper, magazine, or book to hold up while she talks to them: "not necessarily to show them a picture, but just to show them that here's something I like to read when I'm home." Furthermore, when the children are given their usual thirty minutes on Monday, Wednesday, and Friday for library books, she usually sits right up in the front of the class and reads a book of her own. "It's tempting," Mrs. Weaver says, "to use the time for planning and so on, but most of the time I can resist the temptation, because I know how important it is for children to watch me enjoy the process that I so fervently teach every day. Actually I feel hypocritical if I don't read in front of them."

Miss Weingardt uses herself as a model for her second graders in much the same way. But she also tries to involve the parents in the modeling approach. In October, for her second "Teacher-to-Parent Newsletter" of the year, this is what she said:

Dear Parents,

I do know how busy you are, so let me assure you that what I'm going to suggest will take no more than an average of five minutes a day. And it's for a very worthy cause: your child. (I know that some of you are already doing the things I'm going to suggest, and to you let me just say thank you!)

From what we know about children, it appears that the good readers usually have parents who read themselves. These parents enjoy reading and like to share what they read with others. Their children evidently like to imitate them. Therefore, what I'm going to ask you to do (unless you already do it) is this:

1. Would you read something pleasurable to yourself and in front of your child—at least once a week?
2. Would you read something pleasurable to your child at least twice a week? (It doesn't have to be at bedtime; anytime will do: before the bus comes, right after supper, anytime)
3. Would you make sure all television sets, radios, tape recorders, and stereos are turned off for at least thirty minutes each evening, so

Children who want to read usually have adult models in their lives who like to read.

that your child will be tempted to fill in the time with pleasurable reading or creative play?

If you will do these three things (or continue doing them), I feel confident you will be helping me to help your child.

Sincerely,
Marianne Weingardt

P.S. If you would like me to send you a list of good books to read aloud to your child, please sign below and return the bottom portion of this sheet through your child.

Yes, I would like you to send me a list of good "read-aloud books."

———————————————————

Mrs. Weingardt decided that this letter was so important, she sent it to each home by mail. "It cost me a few dollars' postage," she said, "but my principal liked the idea so much, he's going to try to get some funds just for this purpose."

In some schools the classroom teachers have the assistance of "special teachers" such as the physical education teacher, the music teacher, and the art teacher. These teachers are asked to mention occasionally some information that they got from their own reading and to casually discuss the kinds of books and magazines that they like . They are also asked to recommend specific children's books or magazines on sports, musicians, and artists. Even the principals get in on the act in some schools by visiting classrooms, talking about things they like to read, and recommending specific books for children. Schools fortunate enough to have librarians often set aside time for them to present "book chats" on new books that have just arrived. In a few schools, the entire "community" gets involved, with the cook, janitor, nurse, secretary, principal, teachers, aides, and children all taking a twenty-minute "reading break" each day. In other schools, local celebrities are brought in to talk about topics of interest to children and to mention—without too much fanfare—the kinds of things they enjoy reading.

Mr. Peterson is a fifth-grade teacher who likes to use "peer modeling" as well as adult modeling. Once a week the children in his class meet for forty minutes in "Book Clubs" consisting of five or six children each. These clubs are not developed according to subject interest or already established friendships. Instead, membership is carefully planned by Mr. Peterson. "Each club," he says, "has two good readers, one or two average readers, and one or two poor readers. For the first twenty minutes they sit around the same table and just read whatever interests them. For the last twenty minutes, they tell each other a little bit about what they've been reading. It's quite simple really, but it seems to motivate all of them to do more reading—especially the average and poor readers, who are inspired by the good readers."

Many other teachers, at all grade levels, use Mr. Peterson's approach. Some teachers also encourage book sharing and peer modeling by incorporating "book projects" into their reading programs. Two or three times a week, children get to sign up to share their book project, such as a dramatic skit, a brief reading, a television advertisement on the book, an advertising poster, and so on. When they complete their project, they tell where the book can be obtained, and receive some type of "book certificate" or other symbol of accomplishment. (Book projects are discussed thoroughly on pages 367–372 and in Appendix F.)

Providing Motivation

Children's attitudes toward reading can be greatly influenced by how well teachers of reading employ basic psychological principles of motivation. These principles seem to be appropriate whether a person is teaching reading, mathematics, swimming, cooking, fire-fighting, janitoring, or even pickpocketing (judging from Fagin's success with Oliver and his other boys.) Let's look at four of these principles.

Principle One: Help Them Satisfy Their Basic Needs

According to Maslow's well-known "theory of motivation" (1954), human beings have basic types of needs: physiological comfort, physical and psychological safety, belonging and love, esteem from self and others, self-actualization, and knowledge and appreciation. The physiological needs for food, warmth, and sleep are generally dominant until they become at least partially satisfied. Once satisfied, however, they give way to the need for safety (security, stability, and structure). Having satisfied the physiological needs and the safety needs, human beings are then usually dominated by the need for belonging (love, companionship, friendship, affection).

As each set of needs is satisfied, the next set in the hierarchy takes over—after love, the need for esteem (importance, success, self-respect, recognition); after esteem, the need for self-actualization (self-fulfillment, satisfying one's potential, meeting one's self-ideal, doing what one is fitted for); and finally, after self-actualization, the needs that relate most to schooling (knowledge, understanding, and appreciation). This hierarchy of needs is shown graphically in Figure 8.1.

Generally speaking then, the "lower" needs must be at least partially met before the "higher" needs of self-actualization and intellectual understanding will emerge. In a practical sense, this means that the teacher who ignores Bobby's lower needs will find it rather difficult to motivate him to learn something just to satisfy his intellectual curiosity or to satisfy his desire to become a more skilled person. These so-called lower needs must be dealt with during the entire school day, of course, but even during a brief lesson a teacher who is conscious of them can be more successful than one who is ignorant of them.

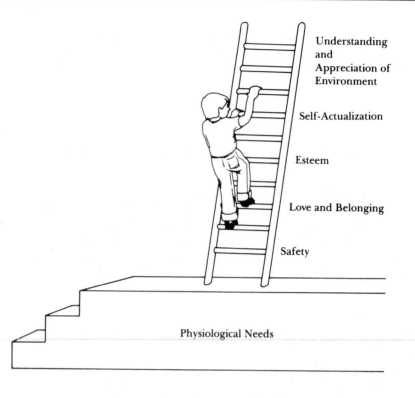

Figure 8.1. *The Ladder of Human Needs*

Let's take, for example, the physiological needs of oxygen and exercise. Teachers may easily fall short of motivating children simply because they have failed to make sure that everyone has enough oxygen. Without a sufficient supply of oxygen, the brain becomes sluggish, curiosity dies, and boredom is the response to your frantic efforts to "teach them something." Making sure there is plenty of fresh air in your classroom is a help, of course, but it's often not enough. What some teachers have discovered is that some type of invigorating activity at periodic intervals is essential to most children throughout the day. Such activity, rather than interfering with learning, actually seems to enhance it.

This doesn't mean that your classroom must be conducted like a three-ring circus, of course. It does mean, though, that large-muscle movement should be encouraged frequently. Even if you do no more than ask them to touch their toes before they sit down for a reading lesson, you will stand a better chance of getting their intellectual attention. And during the lesson you can get them up to the board occasionally or have them pantomime a word or sentence. (A few teachers behave as though their students were bodiless minds: lavatory use is strictly scheduled, getting out of seats without permission is forbidden, and one intellectual activity follows another without any break for a physical activity.)

Which of these times would be best for having a session of dancing, rhythms, or dramatic play?

1. Just before recess so they can take their noise and excitement outside afterwards
2. Between two quiet intellectual sessions so they get the exercise they need
3. Right after recess because they'll be calmer then

It might be a good idea to use the dancing, rhythms, or dramatic play as an opportunity for plenty of movement—a chance for a physical break between two intellectual activities.

We've talked about a physiological need and how it can be met prior to and during your reading instruction. Now let's talk about the need for safety or security. This need can be met during your reading instruction in a number of ways—by providing each child with success, by accepting mistakes as natural allies of learning, and by assuring that the instruction is carried on under reasonably orderly conditions. Obviously children are not going to feel secure if a lesson confronts them with a series of failures. To be motivated to engage in an intellectual exercise, they must experience success during that exercise. (More about success in a moment.) Nor are children going to feel secure if they perceive an intolerant attitude toward their mistakes. Nor will they feel secure if other children are continually "misbehaving" and things seem "out of control" to them.

Suppose you ask Jimmy to circle a VCE word and he circles a VC word. Which of these would be your best response?

1. Boys and girls, did Jimmy circle the right kind of word?
2. No, Jimmy, you weren't listening. You'd better sit down.
3. Not quite, Jimmy. You've circled a VC word. See if you can circle a VCE word.

You may argue that Response 1 would be the best response because "it would keep the rest of the kids alert." That's true, it would. They'd be all ready to pounce as soon as one of their "friends" went up to the board. But think of the harmful side effects that may be incurred—a loss of security, a loss of a sense of belonging, and a loss of esteem, all in one blow. Response 2 would certainly not give the child a feeling of success; it would more than likely have a negative effect on his sense of security. Only in the case where the teacher feels the need to use negative reinforcement with a "nonlistener" would this type of response be a useful one.

Response 3 does provide the child with an opportunity for success without destroying his sense of security. Thus it would probably motivate him to continue learning.

Sarah is a second grader with a minor articulation problem. Her teacher feels that Sarah is a "needy child." Sarah's need for love (affection, warmth, friendliness, and sense of belonging), like the need for security and the physiological needs, has to be considered throughout the school day. But even during a single lesson it can be partially met by letting her know that her teacher and her peers are on her side in her efforts to learn to read. In order to meet both the need for security and the need for a sense of belonging, the teacher should vigorously discourage children from making fun of those who make mistakes. This effort is made considerably easier, of course, when the teacher refrains from careless smiles and sarcastic remarks.

Instead of reading "I see three cookies on the table," Sarah reads it, "I see free cookies on the table." What would be the best response for the teacher to make?

1. Sarah, let me help you make the *th* sound in the word *three*. Watch my mouth.
2. Sarah, I've told you many times—the *th* digraph is not pronounced /f/.
3. Free! I didn't know the cookies were free. Did you, boys and girls?*

The need for esteem can be met during a lesson by making children feel important to you and their peers. A child who is rarely called upon, for example, is not going to feel very important. And yet this can easily happen when the teacher hurries to "cover the material" or calls on only the brightest students in order to save himself or herself the effort of teaching the slower ones. (This may happen especially when the teacher is tired.)

Ms. Ronalds has decided to use a bit of team competition on a phonics game at the end of a lesson. Which would be the best way to select the teams?

1. Let two captains "choose up" the sides. This is the way they're used to doing it on the playground.
2. Ms. Ronalds should choose the teams, carefully balancing them with "strong" and "weak" players.
3. Let each child draw "blindly" from a set of cards labeled "Team A" and "Team B" because this is fairest.

If Ms. Ronalds lets captains choose the teams, how important will the last people chosen feel? Perhaps the playground approach should be reserved for the playground; Ms. Ronalds should be more concerned with human needs than with the "proper form." If Ms. Ronalds is skillful enough, she may be able to choose the teams herself without harming anyone's sense of importance. Sometimes, though, the chance approach works best, especially if you firmly discourage the children from cheering the "good guys" that get on their team and moaning about the "bad guys." (Some teachers feel that team competition on academic games is not worth the side effects and use individual or cooperative-type games instead.)

---

*Such responses are not fantasies of the author. They are based on comments heard in actual classrooms.

When teachers are aware of a child's physiological needs and her needs for security, belonging, and importance, the child is much more likely to be motivated toward self-actualization and intellectual understanding. The need for self-actualization, for most children, includes the desire to communicate better. Most children seem to perceive communication, including the act of reading, as "adult" and something they would like to be able to do as skillfully as adults do. Children who seem not to want to learn how to communicate better ("disadvantaged" children from all ethnic groups and economic strata) are frequently those who have been unable to meet their "lower" needs. Attempts to motivate such children without taking their needs into account will often be unsuccessful.

In addition to being aware of basic needs, there are other principles that you will find useful for motivating children to learn from reading instruction.

Principle Two: Teach Them at the Appropriate Level of Difficulty

Perhaps Principle Two is violated more than any other principle of motivation. Most teachers learn quickly from experience that a learning task that is too easy for children will be boring, and one that is too hard will cause them to withdraw. This is easy enough to see, but what can be done about it? How can you select a learning task that will be just the right level of difficulty for each child?

Probably you can't. But to motivate children successfully, you have to make the attempt to come as close as possible to a task that will challenge them but not overly frustrate them. As an illustration of this point, let's take Coach Cassidy, the track coach for Emerson High, working with a high jumper named Phil Peterson. Coach Cassidy puts the cross bar down fairly low the first time, so that Phil can clear it "with no sweat." Then he raises it slightly so that a little more effort has to be expended by Phil the next time. Then the coach raises it again—not so high that Phil misses and becomes frustrated, but just high enough to make him put a little more effort into the jump than he did the time before. This same gradual increase is continued, making the task hard enough to be challenging but easy enough to be positively reinforcing: high enough to spur on the jumper to greater achievement, low enough to assure success. Success and difficulty go hand in hand to motivate the learner.

For the reading teacher, the task of finding the right level of difficulty is not as easy. A major step in the right direction is to teach diagnostically rather than use a shotgun approach. This means you must find out, through informal testing procedures, approximately what level each child is reading on and specifically what reading deficiencies he has. Having assessed the levels and problems of each pupil, you will be able to teach them individually and to form small groups of pupils who are experiencing the same difficulties, or are on approximately the same developmental level.

But suppose the lesson you're teaching is obviously not at the right level: for some children it's too easy, and for some it's too hard. In this case, it's best to abbreviate your planned lesson and to spend the extra time working with the children who are having trouble, while the rest move on to a follow-up activity or to reading in library books.

In no case is it advisable to ignore the difficulties that some children may be having, thinking "they'll get it when they're older." There is nothing more dampening to motivation than to have one concept after another go by you and to fall farther behind. Nor is it advisable in your planning for the lesson to overlook the prerequisites for the lesson. By carefully listing in your mind (or on paper) the concepts which the children need before they can understand the lesson, and by teaching those prerequisite concepts first, you can avoid a serious motivation problem.

Halfway through a lesson on finding the root in words having an *ed* suffix, you notice that Ronny understands it well and is looking quite bored. Which of these may be best to do?

1. Challenge him to find the root in some nonsense words like *ruckled* or some hard words like *investigated*.
2. Do nothing special for him, as extra practice never hurt anyone.
3. Tell him that since he knows so much perhaps he'd like to take over the lesson.

Principle Three: Provide Them with Frequent and Specific Feedback

In brief, the procedure for following Principle Three is to present a small amount of information and to follow this information with a request for some type of response from the student—answering a question, circling something on the board, completing a worksheet, taking a test. Feedback is then provided to the students in the form of a nod of approval, the correct answer to compare with their own answer, a score, a token, or whatever will inform them about the adequacy of their understanding.

If you have been skillful in presenting information, the feedback you give them will usually be positive reinforcement, and they will want to continue learning. With elementary-school children, it is generally best to expose them to information for only a very brief period of time (often only a few seconds) before having them respond in some way and giving them feedback related to their responses.

Which type of oral feedback for a worksheet would probably be the most motivating?

1. Your grade on this was C−, John. You must try harder on the next one.

2. You missed five out of twenty on this, John. Not bad . . . not bad . . . could be better, but not bad.
3. You have a good understanding of the VCE pattern, John. You missed only one of the questions on that. Since you missed four of the words with a VV pattern, perhaps I should help you a bit more on that. Now, do you see this word here? It has. . . .

Principle Four: Add Novelty to Their Learning Experiences

This principle is perhaps so simple it needn't be discussed. But what about the children in some classrooms who daily suffer the tedium of teaching procedures and workbook formats that never vary? The novelty principle may be simple and obvious, but how often we teachers ignore it—although it's easy to understand why an overworked elementary-school teacher may prefer the comfort of familiarity.

Following the novelty principle needn't be as time- and energy-consuming for the teacher as it sounds. Something as simple as having the children occasionally write on butcher paper with a felt pen instead of the usual chalkboard routine often is enough to cause a sharp rise in motivation. Or sitting on the floor instead of on chairs. Or teaching a reading lesson in the afternoon instead of the morning. Or using sign language for part of the lesson. Or using a game for part of the lesson. Or giving a different piece of colored chalk to each child to use at the board: little things that take a bit of imagination but not much extra energy on the teacher's part.

If you'd like to remember these four principles of motivation you may want to make up some type of mnemonic (memory) device. Here's one that I like to use:

NOVELTY NEEDS LEVEL FEEDBACK.

By remembering that sentence I can remember to think about novelty, concern myself with children's basic needs—especially for belonging and importance, teach at a level that is moderately challenging but not frustrating, and provide immediate and specific feedback whenever possible.

Providing Success through Better Retention

The old adage that nothing succeeds like success applies to the learning of reading skills as much as any other endeavor in life. The child who feels successful during the process of learning to read will generally have a positive attitude toward reading itself. The child who feels unsuccessful will often take out his frustration by misbehaving, by refusing to read, and by sabotaging the teacher's efforts to provide remedial instruction. (The child-saboteur may even go to such lengths as purposely doing poorly on tests in order to prove that he's "too dumb to learn to read anyway, so why try.")

In order for success to occur as she is learning to read, a child must retain what she's learning long enough to practice it thoroughly in normal reading situations. If Millie learns several sight words during a reading lesson but then forgets them before she reads a story in a basal reader containing those words, her sense of success will not be enhanced by the lesson.

It may be tempting for teachers to perceive success for a child in terms of how much praise or how many points he gets for performing nonholistic tasks, such as circling all the words that start with the /sh/ sound. Praise and worksheet points for isolated tasks may be necessary ingredients of success, but they're really only the peripheral measures. The real measure of success is whether the child, on his own, reading by himself, can holistically apply what he's learned in reading lessons, can enjoy the process of reading, and can communicate effectively with an author; thus, the absolute necessity for him to retain those skills and concepts he learns during reading lessons.

Let's assume that by concerning yourself with their basic needs and by using the principles related to novelty, feedback, and difficulty, you have now sufficiently motivated your students—they are ready to learn certain concepts necessary to skilled reading. How should these be taught? Is there a way for children to experience them so that they understand them quickly and well—so well that they don't forget them in a few days? To answer this question, we must consider four additional principles of learning.

Principle Five: Teach for Mastery

In a nutshell, this principle means to teach with thoroughness and meaningfulness. It means to avoid covering material for the sake of covering. It sometimes means to teach toward the accomplishment of specific performance objectives. And, it always means that what is taught should be clear and make sense to the learner.

Two of the following practices would be helpful in encouraging "learning for mastery." Which practice would not encourage learning for mastery?

1. Dividing the reading text by the number of school days and assigning that many pages each day
2. Basing the content of a lesson on the children's previous experiences
3. Comparing and contrasting the concept you're teaching with other concepts

Method 1, believe it or not, is approximately the procedure used by some teachers—and understandably, too, if their goal is "coverage" rather than "mastery." Procedure 2 is one that adds meaning to the lesson, uses positive transfer from previous learning to new learning , and therefore aids in the goal of mastery. Procedure 3 is one of the best means of adding depth of meaning to a concept, thus making it easier to master.

But why teach for mastery? Who cares whether children master what you teach them? Isn't it enough simply to introduce them to something and let them master it later if they wish? These are very appealing questions, ones that often arise when the teacher is getting discouraged and ready to give up on Betty and Tommy. And, undoubtedly there are some things which should only be introduced rather than mastered—things that lie in the realm of appreciation such as listening to symphonic music or having an enjoyable craft experience. But what about a basic skill, such as reading—one that a person is expected to have and to use throughout life; one that, if not acquired, will often cause a person to think of herself as a failure? Here it seems that we're talking about something that should be learned very well indeed.

What happens to Christina when she doesn't master what is taught in one lesson, and another, and still another? That's right, her accumulated failures begin to interfere with future learning. Furthermore, she gradually develops a habit of not learning and forms a picture of herself as a person who is incapable of learning.

In brief, mastery is best obtained by not covering too much new information at once. And this leads us to the next principle.

Principle Six: Provide Massed Practice Followed by Distributed Practice

One may think that this principle means simply to "give them lots of practice and review often." But as usual it's not as simple as that. If Glenda has learned a word with quite a bit of meaning, such as *mother* or her own name, she'll remember it with little or no practice. But for less meaningful words like *the, there, here,* and *come,* it is likely that she'll need massed practice at first, followed by distributed practice later. Frequent, closely-spaced practice of only a few new words is provided at first, making sure that the child is decoding the words correctly. This is followed by practice that is distributed over several days or weeks, with the space between practice periods getting longer and longer.

There is no magic formula for this distribution. It will depend on how meaningful the material is, how motivated the child is, and what problems the child is having in learning the material. The main things to remember in developing a practice schedule are: 1) the student may need considerable guidance in the introductory session; 2) the practice sessions that immediately follow the introductory session should be brief, frequent, and closely spaced; and 3) the remaining practice sessions should be farther and farther apart.

Which of these do you think is the best schedule of practice for learning to decode long *a* with the VV spelling pattern?

1. During a twenty-minute lesson, with a ten-minute worksheet right after the lesson, for three minutes before going home, three minutes twice the next day, three minutes once the following day, three minutes once during the following week, and just occasionally for the rest of the year.
2. During a forty-minute lesson, a twenty-minute worksheet, and a fifteen-minute review a month later
3. During a ten-minute lesson, a ten-minute worksheet, and a five-minute review once a week for the rest of the year

If you decided that the first schedule would provide the children with massed practice at first and distributed practice thereafter, you were right. Schedule 2 is not as uncommon as it may seem, although frequently the review period is omitted.

Mr. Rogers, for example, often uses this schedule, not because he is striving for mastery, but rather because he is striving for greater coverage. That is, he wants to cover as many concepts as possible in a single lesson. For instance, Mr. Rogers may try to teach a single lesson on decoding words with a VV pattern, such as *boat, bait,* and *beat,* without first having three separate lessons—long /o/ in a VV pattern, long /a/ in a VV pattern, and long /e/ in a VV pattern. Except for a review lesson, this would generally be too much to cover in one lesson, not only because of the overload of information but because of the fatigue factor.

Schedule 3 has the virtue of brevity, but probably doesn't allow for enough guided practice at first.

Principle Seven: Get Everyone Involved Each Step Along the Way

If you want maximum learning to take place, try to get each child involved in each problem you pose and each question you ask, each step along the way.

Which of these approaches in Mr. Sanchez's class would get the greatest number of students involved?

1. John, would you please go to the board and circle a word with the VCE pattern? (Mr. Sanchez watches John.)
2. Now I'd like someone to go to the board and circle a word with the VCE pattern. (Mr. Sanchez looks from one child to the next.)
3. Whose turn is it to go to the board? Mary? OK, you go to the

board and circle a word with the VCE pattern. (Mr. Sanchez watches Mary.)

4. Now, boys and girls, please watch while I circle the words that have a VCE pattern.

Approach 4, as you probably noticed, requires the responsibility of no one but the teacher, although he may hope that all the children will actually watch—and think about what they're watching. Unfortunately, this is often a vain hope. Very little tension or challenge has been developed; all that the children have to do is tilt their heads in the direction of the board, thus fooling Mr. Sanchez into thinking that learning is taking place. Approach 1 and approach 3 require the responsibility of one child, but the others are free to dream and scheme. The only approach that is likely to get them all involved is 2 since none of them is sure who's going to be called upon next. (Naturally this approach can't be used all the time or novelty would suffer.)

Now let's try another situation. Which of these would encourage the most involvement?

1. Present a little bit of information, give them a problem or question, present a little more information, give them a problem or question, present a little more information.
2. Present all your information at once and then ask if there are any questions. Then say, "Well, if there are no questions, I assume you understand it perfectly."
3. Present a problem or question, give them a little bit of information, present another problem or question, give them a little more information, present another problem or question.

Did you recognize method 2 as a familiar approach? It has been rumored that an occasional college professor will use such an approach.

Either method 1 or 3 would work much better, with method 3 usually having the slight edge. For example, children would probably get more involved in the learning process if you began a lesson with a problem—e.g., "Who can tell me a word that has the same beginning sound as the word 'pet'?"—rather than beginning the lesson with information, e.g., "The three words on the board all begin with the /p/ sound."

Why does active involvement seem to increase learning and retention? For one thing, by getting a student personally involved, you've increased the amount of emotional impact that the instruction has; and learning that takes place "with feeling" generally is retained longer. For another thing, the personal involvement results in the student's receiving a greater amount of feedback and reinforcement—usually of a positive nature if you've done a good job of teaching. Positive reinforcement strengthens the desire to learn; feedback provides the learners with a check on how well they are doing.

Principle Eight: Help Positive Transfer Occur

Positive transfer is the effect that previous learning has in helping a person learn something new. Teachers and researchers have discovered, however, that positive transfer often does not take place automatically. Rather, it takes place only when the learner perceives the similarity between one learning situation and a subsequent one. And frequently the similarity has to be drawn to the learner's attention by the teacher.

In which of the following situations would positive transfer most likely take place?

1. Learning to decode *cat,* followed soon by learning to decode *mouse*
2. A lesson on decoding the letter *b,* followed soon by a lesson on decoding the letter *d*
3. Learning to decode *cat,* followed soon by learning to decode *cats*
4. A lesson on decoding long *a* in a VCE pattern (e.g., *bake*), followed soon by a lesson in decoding long *i* in a VCE pattern (e.g., *bike*)

Very little positive transfer can take place in alternative 1, since it would be difficult for the learner to perceive any similarity between the decoding of *cat* and *mouse*. In alternative 2, the learner may perceive the similarity between the two learning situations, all right; but that's just the problem. Rather than having positive transfer take place, you are more likely to have negative transfer. In fact, children often get the *b* and the *d* confused, especially if one is introduced before the other one is learned quite well. (Once the two have become confused, however, about all you can do is to bring them together in the same lesson and show the learner how the two of them differ.)

In alternative 3, the learning of the word *cat* will probably help the child learn the word *cats,* particularly if she learns the word *cat* quite well before the word *cats* is introduced—and particularly if the teacher helps the child to see what it is that makes the two words similar and different. Alternative 4 is also conducive to positive transfer, providing again that the long *a* in a VCE pattern is first mastered and providing the teacher helps the child to see the essential similarity between the two situations (that the VCE pattern generally makes both the *i* and the *a* represent long sounds.)

Of course, there's one type of transfer which the reading teacher wants more than any other: to have the children decode words they meet in books and on cereal boxes just the way they learned to decode them in a reading lesson. This is why most teachers try to provide practice in context during the course of a lesson. In fact, you may remember two of the steps recommended for a phonics lesson in Chapter 3: Step 1 provides meaningful context for introducing words that contain the phonic signal you wish the children to learn; and Step 10 provides practice in context. By thus making the practice during instruction very similar to the long-range skill that you're trying to develop, positive transfer is more likely to take place.

If you'd like to remember these four principles of "success through retention," you may want to make up another mnemonic device. One that works well for me is this:

INVOLVED MASTERS PRACTICE TRANSFER.

This sentence reminds me to get every learner involved in every step of the lesson; to teach for mastery rather than coverage; to use massed practice during the lesson and follow this with distributed practice over the next few days and weeks; and to teach in such a way that positive rather than negative transfer occurs.

Summary

In this chapter, we've talked about three major ways of developing positive attitudes toward reading: by providing various adult and peer models; by following the motivational principles of novelty, needs, level, and feedback; and by establishing better retention and success through the principles of involvement, mastery, practice, and transfer. Teachers need to think of the ultimate goals of reading being growth through reading, as well as growth in reading. This means that helping children want to read is as important as helping them learn how to read.

References and Suggested Reading

1. Cronbach, Lee L. *Educational Psychology.* New York: Harcourt, Brace, and World, 1977.
2. Glaser, Robert. "Learning." *Encyclopedia of Educational Research*, 4th ed. New York: Macmillan Co., 1969, 706–33.
3. Honig, Werner K. ed. *Operant Behavior: Areas of Research and Application.* New York: Appleton-Century-Crofts, 1966.
4. Hunter, Madeline. *Motivation Theory for Teachers.* (programmed booklet) El Segundo, CA: TIP Publications, 1967.
5. Hunter, Madeline. *Reinforcement Theory for Teachers.* (programmed booklet) El Segundo, CA: TIP Publications, 1967.
6. Hunter, Madeline. *Retention Theory for Teachers.* (programmed booklet) El Segundo, CA: TIP Publications, 1967.
7. Hunter, Madeline. *Teach More—Faster!* (programmed booklet) El Segundo, CA: TIP Publications, 1969.
8. Hunter, Madeline. *Teach for Transfer.* (programmed booklet) El Segundo, CA: TIP Publications, 1971.

9. Klausmeier, Herbert J., and Davis, J. Kent. "Transfer of Learning." In *Encyclopedia of Educational Research,* edited by Robert L. Ebel, 4th ed. New York: Macmillan Co., 1969, 1483–93.

10. Klausmeier, Herbert J., and Goodwin, William. *Learning and Human Abilities, Educational Psychology.* New York: Harper & Row, 1975.

11. Maslow, Abraham H. *Motivation and Personality.* New York: Harper & Row, 1970.

12. May, Frank B. "An Improved Taxonomical Instrument for Attitude Measurement." *College Student Survey* 2 (Fall 1969): 31–35.

13. White, William F. *Psychosocial Principles Applied to Classroom Teaching.* New York: McGraw-Hill, 1969.

Application Experiences for the Teacher-Education Class

1. Each person in the class can be given one of the following statements to defend or deny. After a few minutes of preparation, all those who have statement #1 should first explain in their own words why it is either true or false and then read one or two sentences from the book that will demonstrate the author's position on the statement. (The same procedure can be followed for the rest of the statements.)

Statements about Chapter 8

a. To teach children to want to read is even more important than to teach children how to read.

b. Growth in reading is the ultimate goal of reading instruction.

c. Adults can often be hypocritical with children about the importance of reading.

d. Those teachers who spend as much time on the "modeling approach" as they do on subskill instruction will have greater success than those who spend all of their time on subskill instruction.

e. The most important models are parents.

f. Reading out loud to children may interfere with the vital practice time in reading to themselves that children need.

g. Teachers who read just for their own pleasure while on the job are wasting taxpayers' money.

h. Children's attitudes toward reading are partially the result of how concerned their teachers are with novelty and basic needs.

i. Whether a child enjoys reading or not has very little to do with retention.

j. The concepts of difficulty and success, when it comes to learning to read, are inseparable ideas.

2. With a small group examine the following "case studies" and decide what to do in each case. Be prepared to tell the other small groups what learning principle or principles you used in making your decision.

Case Study One: During a lesson on the VCE pattern you discover that all but two of the children have not yet mastered the long and short sounds of the vowel letters. What should you do?

a. Postpone your lesson on the VCE pattern and teach all of the long and short sounds of the vowel letters.

b. Have the two children do something else while you teach the rest of the group the long and short sounds of the vowel letters.

c. Continue the lesson the best you can; otherwise you may never cover what you're expected to cover in a year's time.

Case Study Two: You are planning to show a film to your fourth-grade class, in order to prepare them for some social studies reading they will be doing. Which of these procedures would be best?

a. Show the film without stopping and give a test at the end of it.

b. Stop the film every few minutes, ask a question, have them write a brief answer, discuss the answer briefly before proceeding.

c. Show the film without stopping, ask the children if they enjoyed it, tell them that maybe you'll show another film next week.

Case Study Three: Which of these presentations of a follow-up assignment may be the most motivating?

a. All right, boys and girls, please get out your workbooks and turn to page 186.

b. Well, as usual, boys and girls, the person who gets his worksheet all right will get a gold star on his paper.

c. Here's your airplane—I mean, your worksheet. Just unfold it, and we'll look at the directions together. I'll let you fly your airplanes as soon as you get everything correct on your worksheet.

Case Study Four: Suppose that you have decided that Janice, a seven-year-old, needs to learn sixteen irregular words by sight. You provide her with a set of flash cards with the words printed on them and ask her to practice the words with a knowledgeable friend. How should she practice them for five or ten minutes a day so that mastery is obtained?

a. Eight words the first day, eight more the second day, and all sixteen on the third day

b. Four words the first day, the same four plus four more the second day, the same eight plus four more the third day, the same twelve plus four more the fourth day, all sixteen the fifth day, all sixteen three or four days later, only those she's still having trouble with the next day, all sixteen the next day, all sixteen two weeks later

c. All sixteen every day until she gets them all right

Case Study Five: Which of these will probably produce the greatest amount of learning? One of them is not so good, but it's a toss-up between the other two.

a. All of you close your eyes and put your finger on your chin whenever you hear a word with the sound of long *a* in it.

b. Jackie, will you help the girls and boys by putting up your hand whenever you hear a word with the sound of long *a* in it.

c. All right, see if you can catch me. I'm going to say ten words after you close your eyes. The words that have a long *a* sound in them I'll say louder than the rest—but I may make a mistake. You put your finger on your chin when you think I've made a mistake.

3. According to one theory of attitude formation (12), the development of an attitude toward reading (or anything else) goes through four stages: experimenting, agreeing, sharing, and proselytizing. For example, Dennis first experiments by selecting a library book and reading it on his own. If experiences like this are successful, he then is willing to agree verbally that reading is fun. Such agreement may then lead him to share reading experiences with others (by reading books that others recommend and so on). And finally he gets so enthusiastic about reading he tries to convince others to read something. With one or two others, see if you can make up a "reading attitude inventory" by creating a list of statements for children to agree or disagree with that will give you an idea of how good they feel about reading. Include at least one for each of the four stages. The list of statements has been started for you:

　　1) "It's fun to get someone else to read a book that you like." (proselytizing)

　　2) "I'd be willing to read a type of book I've never tried before." (experimenting).

After you have thought of five or six more statements, compare yours with those that others have created.

Field Experiences in the Elementary-School Classroom

1. With one or more children, try out the "reading-attitude inventory" that you and others created in class. If possible, do this in an interview rather than passing it out as a checklist. In this way you will get more insights into why children feel the way they do about reading; use the interview questions just as a foundation for a "frank discussion."

2. Find out the different ways the teacher you're working with uses the modeling approach toward improving children's attitudes toward reading. What are some other ways that you can think of using the modeling approach?

3. What principles of learning does the teacher you're working with use to motivate the children and increase their retention? Precisely how does she do this? Are there some principles to which you would give greater attention?

4. Select three children and try to find out through observation and interview how much time they spend in one week reading just for their own pleasure or information. If possible, try to find out why the three children differ in the amount of personal reading that they do at home and school.

PART TWO

Individualizing and Managing Your Reading Instruction

Chapters

CHAPTER 9

Expecting each child to read at grade level or higher is like expecting each child to be at the average weight or more for his class.

Determining Each Student's Instructional Level

Chapter Preview

In this chapter we'll be talking about a concept that is vital to the success of those who are attempting to teach children to read—the concept of "reading level." A teacher can apply the ideas of communication and holism to his teaching of reading but fail to teach a child to read by ignoring the concept of "reading level."

This concept, although it appears on the surface to be a common-sense notion, evidentally is more subtle than we'd like to think. The unfortunate fact is that many children are faced daily with materials and ideas that are too difficult. If you were to ask them how they feel about this, some would express anger and frustration, but many would express self-contempt. Their comments may include these: "I'm a dummy," or "I just can't get it," "I'm not a very good reader," or "I'm not very smart."

Such a self-concept can be quite detrimental to a child's further progress. And it can be quite damaging to her motivation for communicating with an author. Once Ginger feels she's too "dumb" to learn, the teacher may have ten times the problem of teaching her. Mrs. Randolph may want Ginger to learn to communicate with an author, but if Ginger feels too much pain and too little self-esteem, she may not want to make the potentially dangerous effort.

> Humans can get strangely upset if a child is not at the proper grade level in his reading class.

The Concept of Reading Level

Let's look, then, at the concept of *level* as it applies to the teaching of reading. Suppose you were assigned to teach a group of thirty randomly selected fifth graders. What range in reading levels (or abilities) would you expect to find? Would they all score at the fifth-grade level (between 5.0 and 5.9) on a reading-achievement test? Obviously not, but how many in the class would you expect to score above or below the fifth-grade level: one or two? one fourth of them? one half? If you picked the last answer, you would probably come closest to being correct. Furthermore, the range of overall ability in reading may encompass the second-grade through the eighth-grade level.

What if you were assigned to a first-grade class instead? The range may not seem as great, but it would be just as important as the range among fifth graders. A typical group of first graders would contain children who are already reading at the first- or even second-grade levels, some who are just beginning to read, and some who need considerable help in developing reading-readiness skills.

It's probably obvious, then, that a reading teacher shouldn't use the same instructional material for every child in the room. One book would be all right for some of the children, boring and unchallenging to others, and terribly frustrating to still others. Yet this is exactly the way reading was taught by many teachers not too many decades ago. And this is the way social studies, science, and other subjects are often taught today. (See Chapter 15 on teaching reading and study skills in the content areas).

So how are you going to decide just what basal reader or other instructional material to use for each child? The following are some of the sources of information that teachers use for this purpose:

1. Recommendations from the previous teacher
2. Standardized test scores
3. Group-administered tests developed by the basal-reader publisher
4. Informal reading inventories
5. The cloze technique

Let's look at each of these sources to determine their strengths and weaknesses.

Recommendations from the Previous Teacher

Many teachers place their students in instructional materials according to the recommendation of the previous teacher. If Mrs. Fisher, who taught Nancy in the second grade, recommends on Nancy's cumulative folder that she be placed in the 3_2 reader at the beginning of third grade, Miss Green, the third-grade teacher, often does just that. And, on the surface, this seems like the logical thing to do in many cases. Since Mrs. Fisher knows that Nancy has completed the 3_1 reader by the end of second grade, it seems only rational to recommend the 3_2 reader for third grade and for Miss Green to follow such a recommendation.

There are several flaws, though, in this logical rationale. First of all, Mrs. Fisher may have done what many teachers have done in the past. She may have decided on Nancy's instructional level at the beginning of second grade and then never tested Nancy in the middle of the school year or at the end of the year to see what level of

Research shows that some teachers judge a child's actual reading ability on the basis of a child's cooperativeness and other such traits rather than on decoding and comprehending abilities.

achievement she had reached then. Thus, all she essentially had Nancy do during the year was to follow along with the group in which she was placed. Since Nancy's group finished the 3_1 reader, Mrs. Fisher recommended that she begin third grade at the 3_2 level. In other words, she ignored Nancy's individual progress and simply treated her as a group member—exactly like all the other children in Nancy's group.

A second flaw in this simplistic transition from Mrs. Fisher to Miss Green is that of ignoring the three summer months—as if no reading growth or decline could possibly take place during that time. To take just one example of how fallacious this is, Aasen (1) used various devices to encourage children to read during the summer months, thus improving their reading grade by 0.7 years, as contrasted to no improvement for a control group.

A third flaw in the Fisher-to-Green transfer is the assumption that a recommendation by a former teacher is based on some hard objective data about a child's actual reading performance. A study by Brown and Sherbenou (4) demonstrates that this may often not be the case. Their study showed that a teacher's perception of a child's reading abilities may be highly related to how much he likes the child's nonacademic behavior in the classroom. In contrast, the relationship to the child's actual performance on reading tests may be quite low. To put it another way, it seems quite possible that many teachers judge a child's actual reading ability more on the basis of a child's cooperativeness and other such traits than on decoding and comprehension abilities.

What this means, in a practical sense, is that one should use the recommendation from the previous teacher as only one bit of information and only after determining the answer to three questions: 1) What actual procedures did the teacher use to arrive at her recommendation? 2) Do those procedures justify putting a great deal of faith in the recommendation? 3) What did the child do during the summer that would possibly make a difference in her reading development?

Standardized Tests

Before we can talk about the use of standardized reading tests, perhaps we should first review the meaning of "standardized." Standardized tests have several things in common. For one thing, they are designed to be administered in the same way to each child or group of children taking the test. Directions are read from a manual, the exact time for each subtest is supposedly kept the same from group to group, and the same sequence of subtests is followed.

For another thing, standardized tests are *norm referenced.* What this means is that the test publishers first administer the tests to groups of children called *norm groups,* who supposedly represent the rest of the population. The average scores for children at different grade levels become the norms. As an example of this, if the norm group of fourth graders gets an average score of 43 out of 60, the score of 43 then becomes a norm for all other fourth graders who later take the test.

Another common feature of standardized tests is the manner in which raw scores are translated into standardized scores. Such standardized scores usually take the form of percentiles, stanines, or grade-equivalent scores. The type most often used by teachers is the grade-equivalent score. The grade equivalent score for a raw score of 43 out of 60, mentioned in the last paragraph, may be anywhere from 4.0 to 4.9 depending upon when the norm group took the test. If the norm group took the test during the first week of school, the grade-equivalent score for 43 would be 4.0, indicating the very beginning of fourth grade. If the norm group took the test after five months of school had elapsed, the grade-equivalent score for 43 would be 4.5.

Misinterpretation of the Term "Grade Level"

Frank Roberts, a fourth grader, was administered a standardized reading test, along with his classmates, during the first week of school. He scored a total of 35 and received a grade-equivalent score of 3.6. His teacher, Mr. Jackson, was very concerned because Frank was "reading below grade level." Such a concern is often expressed by teachers and administrators. There seems to be an assumption that every child should be reading at his grade level or higher. However, this assumption is based on the lack of realization of how the grade-level norm was originally obtained. It was obtained, as mentioned, by getting the average score of the norm group at a particular time during the school year. Since an *average score* means, roughly, "the score in the middle," 50 percent of the norm group had to score at-or-below the average score; 50 percent of the norm group had to score at-or-above the average score. Thus, if the norm group is representative of the total population, a teacher should theoretically expect half of the children to score at-or-below "grade level" and half to score at-or-above grade level. Of course, it never works out this neatly, because a norm group can never come that close to representing every other group in the population. But the point should be clear, nevertheless: it is expecting much too much to have every child at-or-above grade level.

Types of Standardized Reading Tests

There are basically four types of standardized reading tests. These are as follows:

1. Group survey tests that are part of a battery of school achievement tests
    Examples: the *Stanford Achievement Test*, the *California Achievement Test*, the *Metropolitan Achievement Test*, the *Iowa Test of Basic Skills*, and the *Sequential Tests of Educational Progress* (STEP)
2. Group survey tests that measure only reading abilities
    Examples: the *Nelson Reading Test, Revised*, the *New Developmental Reading Tests*, the *Gates-MacGinitie Reading Tests*, and the *Iowa Silent Reading Test*
3. Group diagnostic tests
    Examples: *Silent Reading Diagnostic Tests*, the *Stanford Diagnostic Reading Test*, and the *Doren Diagnostic Reading Test*
4. Individual diagnostic tests
    Examples: the *Durrell Analysis of Reading Difficulty*, the *Gates-McKillop Reading Diagnostic Tests*, the *Diagnostic Reading Scales*, the *Gray Oral Reading Test*, and the *Woodcock Reading Mastery Test*

The major difference between the survey and diagnostic tests is in the degree to which the information gained about a child is specific. Whereas the survey tests usually provide only general scores on vocabulary, comprehension, and sometimes rate, the diagnostic tests provide scores related to more specific skills such as phonic analysis, morphemic analysis, auditory discrimination, literal comprehension, inferential comprehension, and so on.

Selecting Appropriate Standardized Reading Tests

Any test, standardized or not, should have *validity:* that is, it should actually measure what you want it to measure. A test calling for spelling, an encoding process, is not a valid test of decoding. A test calling for the child to select the best from four synonyms for a word is not necessarily a valid test of his ability to understand that word in context. A test that calls for a child to read passages and answer questions related to the passages may be a valid test of reading comprehension, but it is not necessarily a valid test of decoding. A test written in the fifties or sixties may not be a valid test for children living in the eighties.

Any test, standardized or not, should have *reliability,* that is, it should give you very consistent results from one testing time to the next and from one form to another. If Johnny ranks near the top of the group with Form A of the test, he should rank near the top with Form B. The *correlation coefficient* between the two forms should be high; acceptable coefficients usually are considered to be .80 or above, although some experts on testing prefer them to be .90 or above.

To determine the validity and reliability of a standardized test, one should examine the test manual that accompanies the test. For greater certainty, it is advisable to consult one of the following sources of test reviews:

1. Buros, Oscar K., ed. *Mental Measurements Yearbook.* Mt. Ranier, MD: Gryphon House, Inc., 1965, 1972, 1978 and any later revisions.
2. Grommon, Alfred H., ed. *Reviews of Selected Tests in English.* Urbana, IL: National Council of Teachers of English, 1976.
3. Tuinman, J. Jaap, ed. *Review of Diagnostic Reading Tests.* Newark, DE: International Reading Association, 1976.

Teachers and administrators need to be clear in their minds as to the purpose of administering a particular type of test. A standardized survey test, for instance, does some things well and other things poorly. It can tell you how well different groups or programs in a school are doing (on the average), but it is far less effective in telling you how well each individual is doing. (See the next section for further discussion of this.) A standardized diagnostic test, of the individually administered type, can yield a great deal of information about a particular child. However, these tests are usually much more difficult and time-consuming to administer and are therefore generally administered to only a small proportion of the children and by trained reading specialists. A standardized diagnostic test, of the group-administered type, takes far less time to administer and provides several scores, rather than the few scores provided by a survey test. Nevertheless, if one's purpose is to get very specific information about each child's reading deficiencies, it is important to keep the test booklets, as well as the test scores. By looking at the way a child responded to each item on the test you can get many specific insights into that child's strengths and weaknesses. Your purpose, then, should determine the type of standardized test you use, if any; it should also determine how you use the test scores and the test booklets.

Some Limitations of Standardized Tests

Standardized tests usually have greater reliability because of their length than more informal tests created by teachers, basal-reader publishers, and others. However, they often have less validity; that is, they less often measure exactly what the teacher wants to measure. Some other limitations are as follows:

1. They are usually so long (in order to increase their reliability) that they are administered to groups instead of individuals. Thus the teacher is deprived of being able to observe each child "in action."
2. They are usually timed, thus penalizing those who read well but slowly.
3. They often present conditions that are not typical of the reading act. For example, they ask children to respond to multiple-choice questions, which require recognition of the correct answer; reading, on the other hand, requires skills and their interrelationships that are far more complex.
4. They frequently overrate a child's reading level, thus encouraging some teachers to place a child in a reader that is too difficult and frustrating to her.
5. Some children are good readers but poor test takers. This is particularly true with standardized tests. Special forms are passed out, the right kind of pencil must be used, everyone in the room is sighing and moaning, the tension rises to fever pitch as the teacher looks at the clock and says, "Ready, begin." For some children, this kind of atmosphere is not very conducive to good thinking and careful reading.
6. The reading passages in standardized tests are usually quite short. A child who does well on short passages requiring little retention may not do as well on longer selections in basal readers and other materials.
7. The norm group quite likely will not truly represent the particular group of children you are instructing.

8. Standardized reading tests, especially group-administered ones, are not well suited to determining whether a child can read longer in a holistic manner—integrating the various subskills, searching for the author's message, and appreciating the reading act as a communication one.

Group-Administered Tests Developed by the Basal-Reader Publisher

Some publishers of basal readers have developed norm-referenced tests similar to standardized reading tests. Because of this similarity they suffer from some of the same validity problems. On the other hand, they tend to be somewhat more valid than a regular standardized test. This is because the passages and words are similar to or the same as those used in the basal readers produced by the same publisher.

Other publishers develop criterion-referenced tests that are used for placement of children in the readers. Rather than use a norm group, the publishing team has developed short tests that sample the various skills taught through the basal-reader program. On each short test, the child is expected to score at a minimum level in order to demonstrate his reading competence. This minimum level, often 80 percent, is called a *criterion*. By administering these short skill tests in the same order as the skills are presented in the basal-reader program, and by adding up the scores on these tests, the teacher can arrive at a score that can then be converted into an estimate of the child's instructional reading level. Because these tests are group administered, however, they sometimes lack the validity that can be gained through individual administration. Also because the tests are so short they may lack reliability. Furthermore, the nature of the objective-type tests, as well as their brevity, makes the testing situation quite different from the actual reading act.

Informal Reading Inventories

An informal reading inventory (IRI) is a testing technique that allows a teacher to assess a child's reading levels individually by listening to him read several selections (usually from various levels of basal readers). General decoding skill is determined by counting miscues*

---

*A miscue is simply the manner in which a child reads a word or sentence differently from the way the author wrote it. The author writes: I love my big dog, Pat. The child reads: I love the dog, Pat. Thus we have two miscues.

noticed during the oral reading. General reading comprehension is determined by asking questions of the child, either after the oral reading or after he reads another selection silently.

The main purpose of an informal reading inventory (IRI) is to determine what book to place a child in for reading instruction. The informal reading inventory is not a standardized achievement test. It is a technique that experienced teachers have found to be useful in determining three levels of a pupil's reading: the *independent level* (the level at which the pupil can read easily with no help from others), the *instructional level* (the level at which the pupil can read with some fluency but with enough difficulty to make instruction necessary), and the *frustration level* (the level at which the pupil understands little of what is read and makes many miscues.

The informal reading inventory can help you determine, for example, that Alice can probably handle third-grade reading material independently, that fourth-grade material is about right for using during reading instruction, and that most fifth-grade material, unless she's extremely interested in it, will be too frustrating for her.

In this chapter, we'll concentrate on a very simple form of informal reading inventory—one that requires no coding of the miscues. Instead you'll only have to recognize them and count them. My purpose in this chapter is to give you an easy and quick way of determining the instructional level of your students. In Chapter 14, you'll learn how to use a coding system to record the precise forms of miscues that each child makes as she reads out loud to you. You'll also learn in that chapter how to carry on "miscue analysis" during the same time that you administer an informal reading inventory.

Miscues that are Counted During an IRI

Before we get into the procedures for administering a simple form of the informal reading inventory, you'll need to know what types of miscues to look for as a child is reading to you. Here are the miscues that are often counted when administering the IRI:

Omission of words	Then he saw his mother coming. . . . He saw his mother coming.
Insertion of words	The forest was a big park. In the forest was a big park.
Child doesn't try word	Teacher has to pronounce the word for the child after a five-second pause.
Repetition of word or phrase	The boy went to school. The boy went to—went to—school.

*Self-correction of word or phrase	He saw his teacher. He was—he saw—his teacher.
Word substitution	She worked with him. She worked with them.
Wrong word order	Over he went. He went over.
Nonsense substitution ("Mispronunciation")	He flew in a helicopter. He flew in a hillycopy.

Preparing an Informal Reading Inventory

Many textbook publishers now provide teachers with an IRI that contains portions of stories and articles that are the same or similar to those in the publisher's basal-reading series. A basal reader, as you may recall, is a book of fictional stories, plays, poems, and nonfictional articles designed to match the instructional levels of a particular grade. Each reader is part of a series that usually includes pre-primers, a primer, a first reader, and one or two books per grade up through eighth grade. They are frequently sold with workbooks, a teacher's guide, and other supplementary materials.

It an informal reading inventory is not available to you from a basal-reader publisher, you may wish to use one of those developed independently of a basal-reader company. The *Ekwall Reading Inventory* (7) is an example of one of these; the *Classroom Reading Inventory* by Silvaroli (18) is another. Johns (11) has prepared an annotated bibliography on informal reading inventories that will be useful to anyone wanting more detail on the IRI.

Some teachers prepare their own informal reading inventories by finding *portions* of stories and articles (from 75 words at the pre-primer level up to 200 words for fifth grade and up). These stories and articles are usually selected from the basal readers or other graded material which they are using for reading instruction. While some teachers simply choose their story portions from the middle third of the book, others try to check the accuracy of their selections by using a "readability formula" on them. You will find one of these formulas and the procedures for using it on pages 375–377 in Chapter 13.

---

*There is considerable debate among reading educators as to whether one should count "self-corrections." For an explanation of why some people count them, please see the later section called "Whether to Count Self-Corrections."

Administering an Informal Reading Inventory

1. Before having the pupil read the selections, try to develop a relaxed atmosphere. Make the test an informal one. (More specific ideas on this will be suggested under "Developing Good Testing Conditions.")

2. Unless you have a very good idea already of the child's reading level, have her begin reading at the preprimer level. It is better to start the testing too low than too high. That way she'll develop a feeling of self-confidence. (Even when you're fairly certain of a child's level, it's best to drop down one or two levels.)

3. As the child reads, count her miscues without making a big issue of it. Use tally marks on a pad in your lap or simply use your fingers, writing down the number of miscues at the end of each selection. (Don't count proper nouns, titles, punctuation, or nonstandard dialect.)

4. Now that you've obtained the miscues on a particular passage, you may now wish to check her comprehension. This can be done in a number of ways: a) simply ask her to tell what the story was about in her own words, then rate her comprehension as good, fair, or poor; b) ask her five to ten questions that you have already developed about the story; c) have her read another story or article (at the same level) silently and ask her questions about that; d) use the form of miscue analysis described in Chapter 14. If you're going to choose the first alternative of simply asking her what the story was about, you may wish to stimulate her thinking a bit more with questions like these:

   1. Can you tell me about something in this story that makes the title a good one?
   2. Is this story a real-life story or a make-believe story? How can you tell?
   3. What do you think was the most important thing that happened in this story? Why do you think so?

   If you're going to choose the second or third alternative, a score of 90 percent on comprehension questions is usually considered the independent level; 70 percent, instructional; 60 percent questionable; 50 percent frustration.

   Some educators question the value of having a child read both orally and silently for an IRI, especially since this adds to the length of the test and the child's fatigue. Research has demonstrated a rather high relationship between silent-reading comprehension and accuracy of word recognition in oral reading. Bond and Dykstra (3, pp. 41–2), for example, found correlations of .78 to .85. This high relationship seems to exist also between silent-reading comprehension and accuracy of word recognition in silent reading, as well. Dykstra (6, p. 59), for instance, found correlations ranging between .75 and .81.

5. Stop the testing when the child has finished a selection that has been obviously frustrating. This usually occurs by the time she

has an average of one miscue for every ten words in the selection. (If the selection is 100 words long and the child has 10 miscues, she has most likely reached her frustration level.)

Developing Good Testing Conditions

There are several things you can do when administering an IRI to encourage a relaxed atmosphere and to increase the accuracy of the test. Some of these are as follows:

1. Make sure the child is seated in such a way that he is not distracted by your keeping track of his miscues.
2. Take a few moments to develop rapport, e.g., talk about one of his interests or a recent event in his life.
3. Explain the reason and nature of the examination. Something like this: "Billy, I'd like to hear you read for a while so I can decide what book you should be reading. Do the best you can, but don't worry if you make mistakes, because your mistakes will help me see how I can help you this year. If you have trouble reading a word, try figuring it out all by yourself first. Then if you can't get it, I'll tell you what the word is. After each story, I'll ask you to tell me what it was about. All right, Billy, let's start this story called 'Boys and Girls.' "
4. Don't give the IRI during recess or any other time the student can't devote full attention to it. (If the test is viewed as a punishment, your results will not be valid.)
5. Administer the IRI where the child can't see his peers without turning around.
6. Make sure he is near enough to you to enable you to hear miscues clearly.
7. Allow for a minimum of distractions and interruptions. Tell the rest of the class that you shouldn't be disturbed while you're working with "Johnny." If necessary, allow time between each examination for working with other children.
8. Make sure the lighting on the reading passages is excellent. This may have a significant effect on the level of the book in which you place the child.
9. Allow a full five seconds for the child to decode a word before pronouncing it for him. (Try not to "jump the gun.")
10. Keep the testing situation "light and breezy." A formal, over-serious approach may reduce the validity of an IRI.

Scoring the Noncoded Informal Reading Inventory

Scoring this form of the IRI, which we'll call the "noncoded form," is quite easy. But the secret to making it easy is to compute the number of miscues for each reading passage ahead of time. The independent level is generally considered to be about 98 percent; in other words, the child is "allowed" no more than two miscues out of a hundred words. The frustration level is generally considered to be about 90 percent: the child miscues on at least ten out of a hundred words.

Let's take an example of how this would work in practice. Suppose you ask Alice to read a preprimer selection of 100 words. Ahead of time you would have "computed" that 98 percent of 100 words would be 98 words. This means she can miss up to two words and be at the independent level.

Ahead of time you would have also computed that 90 percent of 100 words would be 90 words. This means that if she has miscued on 10 words, she is at the frustration level. It also means that if she misses between three and nine words, she may be at the instructional level.

However, the instructional level is often divided into two categories: if a child gets between 97 and 94 percent of the words correct (no more than 6 percent incorrect), and her comprehension is good for the selection, you can be fairly certain that the selection represents her instructional level. If she gets between 93 and 91 percent correct and her comprehension is still good, the selection may represent her instructional level; with only fair or poor comprehension, however, you can be fairly certain that the selection is at a level that is too difficult for her.

Let's now imagine that you are a second-grade teacher and have obtained your selections from preprimer to grade six. For each selection you would then carry on the following calculations:

1. Multiply the number of words in the selection by .02 (2%). This will give you the number of miscues allowable for the independent level. (Example: 100 × .02 = 2 miscues)
2. Multiply the number of words in the selection by .10 (10%). This will give you the number of miscues indicative of the frustration level. (Example: 100 × .10 = 10 miscues)
3. Multiply the number of words in the selection by .06 (6%). This will give you the *lower* limit of miscues indicative of the *probable* instructional level. (Example: 100 × .06 = 6 miscues)

Now you are ready to construct a record sheet similar to the one in Table 9.1 and to ditto off enough for each child in the class. You will notice that once you have computed the miscues at the .02, .10, and .06 levels, you won't need to do any further computations. You can merely fill in the rest. For instance, for the preprimer level (with 100 words), we know that the .02 level is simply two miscues, the .10 level is ten, and the .06 level is six. Therefore, the independent level is two miscues, the frustration level is ten miscues, and the instructional level would have to range between three and six miscues. And this means that the "questionable level" would have to range between seven and nine miscues. (Please check with Table 9.1 to see how this works when you have more than 100 words.)

Table 9.1 Record Sheet for Administering a Noncoded Informal Reading Inventory

Name _____ Grade _____ Date _____

	Total Words	Total Miscues	Independent Level (about 98%)	Frustration Level (about 90%)	Instructional Level (about 97–94%)	Questionable Level	Compre-hension
Preprimer	100		2	10	3–6	7–9	
Primer	150		3	15	4–9	10–14	
First							
Reader	189		4	19	5–11	12–18	
2_1	200		4	20	5–12	13–19	
2_2	181		4	18	5–11	12–17	
3_1	150		3	15	4–9	10–14	
3_2	175		4	18	5–11	12–17	
4	200		4	20	5–12	13–19	
5	192		4	19	5–12	13–18	
6	165		3	17	4–10	11–16	

Table 9.2 Record Sheet for a Particular Child Given an IRI

Name _____ Grade _____ Date _____

	Total Words	Total Miscues	Independent Level (about 98%)	Frustration Level (about 90%)	Instructional Level (about 97–94%)	Questionable Level	Compre-hension
Preprimer	100	1	2	10	3–6	7–9	
Primer	150	3	3	15	4–9	10–14	
First							
Reader	189	8	4	19	5–11	12–18	
2_1	200	15	4	20	5–12	13–19	
2_2	181	19	4	18	5–11	12–17	

. . .

Let's now imagine that Alice reads several selections. (The selections will be the same for every child in your classroom if they are all going to use the same basal reading *series*.) Let's also imagine that Table 9.2 (page 262) represents the way you have recorded her performance.

As you can see from looking at Table 9.2, Alice can read the preprimer and primer selections at the independent level. She would need no instruction at either level. However, she miscues eight times during her reading of the "first reader," indicating that this may be a good book to have her start in for the year.

Since Alice has not reached the frustration level yet, you decide to have her continue reading. When she reads the 2_1 selection, she miscues a total of fifteen times. This puts her at the questionable level for this selection. If her comprehension of this selection had been quite good, you might have decided to begin the year reading in the 2_1 book. However, her comprehension was only fair. Therefore, you speculate that it may be better for Alice to start her year reading in the first reader. If she does well in that book, you will soon move her up into the 2_1 book.

Just to be certain, though—and because she has not yet reached the frustration level—you have her continue reading. This time, in the 2_2 book, she reaches the frustration level. Since her comprehension* is quite poor, you feel comfortable with your decision to place her in the "first reader."

Some Political and Emotional Matters Related to Reading Levels

You've just made a professional decision to place Alice De Boer in the first reader for the first part of the year. Now let's make the problem more difficult for you. It so happens that Alice is in the second grade. Her first-grade teacher recommended on her report card and in her cumulative folder that Alice be started in the 2_2 book at the beginning of second grade. Furthermore, her standardized test score for reading at the end of first grade was translated into a grade-equivalent score of 2.6. Unfortunately many people interpret this to mean that the child is ready to read what the "normal" child in the sixth month of second grade is ready to read. (More about this erroneous interpretation later.) And to make matters even worse for you, both Alice and her parents are upset because you're putting her "back" in the first reader.

You decide to talk to Miss McCloskey, her first-grade teacher. She says: "Alice is one of those children who have been pushed a lot by her parents. According to her kindergarten teacher, she was even

*Note: See number four on page 259 for ways of estimating comprehension.

reading a bit before she got into kindergarten. As a result she was given reading instruction in kindergarten."

"That sounds okay to me," you say.

"Right," Miss McCloskey says. "But the trouble is, when Alice got her report card at the end of kindergarten, her teacher had recommended—in big bold letters—that she start first grade in the 2_1 book!"

"I begin to get the picture," you say.

"Yes. It turned out that Alice was good at memorizing words, but she couldn't really read them. She had no concept of phonics, for instance, or any other decoding skill. She was relying entirely on memory."

"So what did you do?" you ask her.

"I started her in the 2_1 book, but I had to move her quickly back to the first reader."

"How did she do in the first reader?"

"Quite well, but she knew the words from memory. I decided to pull her out of the basal series entirely for a while and had her work on a special phonics program."

"How did that work?"

"Fine, until the parents started complaining that I'd pulled her out of the 'top' reading group."

"Did you put her back in the 2_1 book?"

Miss McCloskey sighs. "Eventually, I did, after a running battle with the parents for months."

"And is that why you recommended her for the 2_2 book at the end of first grade?"

She shrugs her shoulders. "What else could I do? If I'd recommended her for anything lower, her parents would have been in the principal's office. And besides, I looked bad enough moving her up only one-half year. To most people looking at the report cards at the end of kindergarten and first grade, it would be obvious that I simply hadn't done my job—right?"

You pat her on the shoulder and nod your head with sympathy. Then you walk out of her room and wonder what in the world you're going to do. (Do you see now why this section is called "Some Political and Emotional Matters Related to Reading Levels?")

Naturally I'd like to be able to give you a definite solution for this problem. But the solution will vary with each teacher and with each child. On the other hand, you can arrive at a solution (even though it isn't a perfect one) by finding answers to these questions:

1. How sure are you of your IRI results? Try using another set of selections from the same series and see if you get similar results.

2. How fair is the informal reading inventory? This question is often asked and is caused by a confusion as to the major purpose

of the inventory. The main purpose of the IRI is to help you instruct each child at a level that is not too easy or too difficult. Probably the single most unfortunate mistake that teachers make in teaching reading is to use instructional material that is too difficult for the child, thus causing frustration, anxiety, and a lowering of the child's self-concept.

Ekwall (8) carried on a study of the anxiety level of children who reached the frustration level in reading. His conclusions were somewhat alarming:

> We are certainly doing students no favor by easing the criteria and thus placing them at a level in which they are physiologically frustrated. For example, students in the Ekwall polygraph study, when they became frustrated, exhibited the same signs as someone afraid of a crowd, or of someone about to get up to give a speech before a large audience, or of someone shaken by an automobile accident. Is it any wonder that students do not choose to read difficult material unless forced to? Can you imagine a situation in which every time you were forced to read you experienced the feelings of a person after an automobile accident? (9, p. 665)

You can see then how important it is for you to determine the child's instructional level and not to teach that child at a level of frustration. The IRI can help you find that level that would be best for instruction. It is not being "unfair to count so many miscues against a child." On the contrary, it is unfair to the child to count too few of the miscues.

3. Why bother with an IRI? Why not just use the grade-equivalent score of the standardized reading test? We talked about this quite a bit in a previous section. To emphasize the point made earlier, though, let's look at another opinion. Schwartz, a reading and test-construction expert, has this to say about the use of standardized tests:

> One of the most blatant misuses of test results is the not infrequent practice of equating a grade level score with a graded reading text. So, for example, a child whose raw score on a survey test of reading converts to a grade level of 3.5, is given a 3_2 reader, the teacher erroneously assuming a connection between the grade level equivalent on the test and the level of difficulty of the reading text. No such connection exists! . . . a grade level equivalent for a given score is simply the average score achieved by all children at that grade level in the standardization sample, and has nothing whatsoever to do with graded texts. As a matter of fact, the level of difficulty represented in a 3_2 reader is usually higher than material that receives a third grade designation on a reading test. The poor youngster who is given a 3_2 reader on the basis of achieving such a score is surely in for trouble . . . (17, p. 367).

To put it another way: The grade equivalent scores for the particular standardized test used in your school district were not designed to match the grade levels of the particular basal reading series you are using. Such an assumption is made probably because we are sometimes fooled by numbers.

4.   How much support do you have from your principal for the decision you would like to make? Have you explained your reasons for your desired decision? Will the principal support your decision and help explain it to the parents?

5.   Are there any ways you can work with the parents to arrive at a decision that will be best for the child?

Whether to Count Self-Corrections

As teachers learn to use the informal reading inventory they often ask this question: "Why should we count self-corrections? Don't these simply show that the child is good enough at reading to recognize her own mistakes?" This is an excellent question because it shows an insight into the nature of reading—that reading is a process of making sense out of an author's message.

Some reading experts feel that a self-correction should not be counted as a miscue since self-correction is a positive indicator that the reader is comprehending. Furthermore, self-correction tends to be more highly developed as children get older and better at reading. Thus, they argue that teachers should not be too hasty about correcting mistakes for children when they read, as they will learn to correct their own as they discover that what they read doesn't make sense the way they're reading it.

This argument is a good one to remember when we're in the process of instructing children. Too often we stop children after every miscue, thus not giving them a chance to learn self-correction strategies.

However, when administering an IRI some of us (perhaps a minority of reading educators) feel it is important to count all of the types of miscues previously listed, including self-corrections. This is to avoid the possibility of placing a child too high and frustrating him. The IRI is one of those testing devices that has been created through trial-and-error processes. Various reading experts through the years have experimented with different ways of scoring the IRI and have come up with a few that work. The one being recommended here is just one approach. However, it does seem to provide a valid, "classroom-workable" estimate of what book to place a child in for "instruction without frustration." Furthermore, it is a reasonably reliable method; several teachers listening to the same tape recording of the same child will tend to agree on the placement of the child when using the methods prescribed in this chapter.

It's true that the IRI scoring procedure advocated here does not match the procedures one would recommend for actual instruction. But such a matching of procedures is hardly that crucial. What does matter is that various forms of the IRI provide a nonthreatening means of estimating a child's reading levels.

Remember that the worst mistake is overestimating the child's instructional level, thus making instruction time a frustrating, anxiety-ridden time for him. On the other hand, if most of the child's miscues for a passage are self-corrections or repetitions, it is probably advisable to raise your estimate of his instructional level one notch. For example, if your computation of the instructional level is 2_1 and most of his miscues are self-corrections or repetitions, it is generally safe to raise your estimate to 2_2.

Practice in Using the Informal Reading Inventory

The best way for you to understand an informal reading inventory is to administer one to a child. Until you have that opportunity, though, here's a passage from "Lunch on a Boat"* that you can use for practice in counting miscues and in computing levels. If you see the letter *P* over a word, it simply means that the teacher had to pronounce it for the child.

Author	*Tommy*
One hot day, Roy went on a boat ride.	One hot day, Roy went on a boat ride
He went with his teacher and his school friends.	and he went with his teacher and his school friends.
It was cool on the water.	It was cool on the water.
And it was fun.	And it was fun.
The boat went by big city houses.	The boat went by big city houses.
Slow boats and fast boats	Shops boats—slow boats and fast boats
went by in the water.	went by in the water.
Roy saw a little boat	Roy was a little boat
pull a big boat	pulled by a big boat.
Then it was time for lunch.	Then—then it was time for lunch.
Some children had lunch with them.	Soon—some children had lunch with them.

*Bank Street College of Education, *Around the City* (New York: Macmillan Co., 1965). Reprinted by permission of the publisher.

Author	*Tommy*
Some children had money for hot dogs.	Some children had money for hot dogs.
All the children had milk.	All the children had milk.
Roy had a hot dog.	Roy had a hot dog.
His friend Máx said,	His friend Max said,
"Look at the house boat, Roy."	"Look at the house boat, Roy."
Roy turned around fast.	Roy turned around fast.
His hot dog fell	His—his hot dog fell
in the water.	in the water.
"It fell!" said Roy.	"It fell!" said Roy.
"My hot dog fell.	"My hot dog fell.
Now I have no hot dog.	Now I have no hot dog.
And I have no money."	And I have no money."
"Here, Roy," said Max,	"There—here, Roy," said Mac.
He gave some money to Roy.	"I have some money," said Roy—to Roy.

Miscues that should be counted (M): _____

Percent of words decoded correctly: _____
    (out of 133 words) $(133 - M) \div 133 = \%$

Reading level this selection represents (independent, instructional, questionable, or frustration): _____

Comments: _____

Using the Cloze Technique for Determining Reading Levels

In Chapter 2 we talked about the use of the cloze technique to assist in the development of a child's semantic vocabulary. Other authors (10, 12, 13, 14, 15, 16) suggest many additional instructional uses for this technique. Frequently, however, the cloze technique has been used as a substitute for the informal reading inventory or some type of standardized test. Rather than have the child read a normal selection from a basal reader or other material, as one does with the informal reading inventory, the teacher has him read a selection that has every tenth word omitted. (Some recommend every fifth word.) The child then reads the selection silently and guesses the words that are missing, writing them down as he guesses them. If he guesses at least 40 percent of the exact words missing (2), or 80 percent of the appropriate synonyms (19), the selection is considered to be representative of the instructional level for the child. Zintz (20) recommends a more refined set of percentages:

> Over 50 percent exact guesses = independent reading level
> 40 to 50 percent = instructional reading level
> Fewer than 40 percent = frustration level

This procedure has distinct advantages and disadvantages when compared with an informal reading inventory or with a combined IRI and miscue analysis. Perhaps its major advantage is that it can be administered to a group, rather than to one individual at a time. The child merely writes the missing words, and the teacher, in scoring, ignores misspellings. Its main disadvantage is its lack of diagnostic precision. You can get a rough idea of a child's general comprehension of selections this way, and a rough idea of his frustration, instruction, and independent levels. However, you can't carry on any type of miscue analysis that would allow you to ascertain his reading strategies and specific reading problems. Moreover, in order for this approach to be reliable, the selections must be quite long—about 400 to 600 words (2). However, when a very quick procedure needs to be employed for grouping children, this technique can be used first and then followed up with an IRI, or an IRI combined with miscue analysis.

Summary

In this chapter we've discussed the concept of reading level, and how failure to pay attention to this concept can cause teachers to provide reading instruction that is highly frustrating to children. We also talked about the importance of having a child read in a book that is at the right level for him. We discussed a method of finding that level through the use of a simple, noncoded informal reading inventory. And, we discussed the uses and weaknesses of standardized reading tests, teacher's recommendations, and the cloze technique.

References and Suggested Reading

1. Aasen, Helen B. "A Summer's Growth in Reading." *Elementary School Journal* 60 (1959): 70–4.
2. Austin, Mary C., and Huebner, Mildred H. "Evaluating Progress in Reading through Informal Procedures." *Reading Teacher* 15 (March 1962): 338–43.
3. Bond, Guy L., and Dykstra, Robert. "The Cooperative Research Program in First-Grade Reading Instruction." *Reading Research Quarterly* 2 (Summer 1967): 5–142.
4. Brown, Linda L., and Sherbenou, Rita J. "A Comparison of Teacher Perceptions of Student Reading Ability, Reading Performance, and Classroom Behavior." *Reading Teacher* 34 (February 1981): 557–60.
5. Crowell, Doris C., and Klein, Thomas W. "Preventing Summer Loss of Reading Skills among Primary Children." *Reading Teacher* 34 (February 1981): 561–4.

6. Dykstra, Robert. "Summary of the Second-Grade Phase of the Cooperative Research Program in Primary Reading Instruction." *Reading Research Quarterly* 1 (Fall 1968): 49–70.

7. Ekwall, Eldon E. *Ekwall Reading Inventory.* Boston: Allyn and Bacon, 1979.

8. Ekwall, Eldon E. "Should Repetitions be Counted as Errors?" *Reading Teacher* 27 (January 1974): 365–7.

9. Ekwall, Eldon E., and English, Judy. "Use of the Polygraph to Determine Elementary School Students' Frustration Level." Final Report, U.S. Dept. of HEW, Project #0G078, 1971.

10. Gove, Mary K. "Using the Cloze Procedure in a First-Grade Classroom." *Reading Teacher* 29 (October 1975): 36.

11. Johns, Jerry L., et al., eds. *Assessing Reading Behavior: Informal Reading Inventories, an Annotated Bibliography.* Newark, DE: International Reading Association, 1977.

12. Jongsma, Eugene. *The Cloze Procedure as a Teaching Technique.* Newark, DE: International Reading Association, 1971.

13. Lopardo, Genevieve S. "LEA-Cloze Reading Material for the Disabled Reader." *Reading Teacher* 29 (October 1975): 42.

14. McCracken, Robert A. "The Informal Reading Inventory as a Means of Improving Instruction." In *The Evaluation of Children's Reading Achievement,* edited by Thomas C. Banch. Newark, DE: International Reading Association, 1967.

15. Schneyer, Wesley J. "The Cloze Procedure for Improving Reading Comprehension." *Reading Teacher* 19 (December 1965): 174.

16. Schoenfeld, Florence. "Instructional Uses of the Cloze Procedure." *Reading Teacher* 34 (November 1980): 147–51.

17. Schwartz, Judy I. "Standardizing a Reading Test." *Reading Teacher* 30 (January 1977): 364–8.

18. Silvaroli, Nicholas J. *Classroom Reading Inventory.* Minneapolis, MN: William C. Brown Company, 1973.

19. Smith, Richard J., and Johnson, Dale. *Teaching Children to Read.* Reading, MA: Addisson-Wesley, 1980.

20. Zintz, Miles V. *Corrective Reading.* Minneapolis, MN: William C. Brown Company, 1972.

Application Experiences for the Teacher-Education Class

1. With a small group of students in your class discuss why you agree or disagree with the following statements. Then compare your results with other groups. Note: One or more statements may be purposely ambiguous in order to stimulate your thinking abilities.

Statements about Chapter 9
LITERAL LEVEL: Did the author say these things?
   a. The concept of "reading level" is a common-sense notion.

b. A reading teacher should never use the recommendation from the previous teacher.

c. The informal reading inventory is not a standardized achievement test.

d. When developing your own IRI, select portions from the beginning of each book.

e. You should multiply the number of words in a selection by .06 to get the number of miscues allowable for the independent level.

INFERENTIAL LEVEL: Did the author imply these things?

a. If a child reads a selection of 300 words with six miscues, that selection would represent her independent level.

b. If you were assigned to teach a fourth-grade class, you would be justified in expecting a reading range from grade one through grade seven.

c. It would be wise to assess each child's instructional level at the beginning, in the middle, and at the end of the school year.

d. The most important miscue levels are the 2-percent level, the 6-percent level, and the 10-percent level.

e. When administering an IRI, efficiency should be your major concern.

2. Discuss the case study of Alice De Boer described under the section "Some Political and Emotional Matters Related to Reading Levels." What reading book would you place her in for instruction? Why? What things would you do before you decided on her placement?

3. Mr. Lightbody feels that Heidi's self-corrections, repetitions and meaningful substitutions or omissions that do not change the author's message simply show that she is a good reader who cares about comprehension. He decides when administering an IRI not to count these. Compare his results and discuss the implications. (Assume that each selection is exactly 100 words in length.)

	Mr. Lightbody's Scores	*Actual Miscues*
Preprimer	1	2
Primer	2	5
First Reader	4	9
2_1	5	10
2_2	6	12
3_1	8	14
3_2	10	23

4. Under the section "Practice in Using the Informal Reading Inventory," you have a comparison between an author's message and Tommy's rendition. What level does this selection represent for Tommy—independent, instructional, questionable, or frustration? Compare your results with those of other people in the class. How many miscues should you

have counted? What types of miscues did Tommy make? *Why* did he make the miscues that he did? How successful was Tommy in getting the author's message?

5. With a partner or small group first complete the record sheet for Carl. Decide on the reading level that each selection represents for Carl. Then decide what book you will use for Carl's instruction during the first part of the school year. (See Table 9.1 for a model. See pages 260–261 for calculations that you need to make in order to complete the record sheet.)

Name *Carl Roberts* **Grade** 3 **Date** _____

	Total Words	Total Miscues	Independent Level (about 98%)	Frustration Level (about 90%)	Instructional Level (about 97–94%)	Questionable Level	Comprehension
Preprimer	119	3					*fair*
Primer	132	3					*good*
First							
Reader	151	3					*good*
2_1	163	4					*good*
2_2	159	6					*good*
3_1	179	10					*good*
3_2	183	8					*good*
4	195	18					*good*
5	186	17					*poor*
6	192	21					*poor*

The preprimer selection represents the _____ level for Carl.
primer _____
first reader _____
2_1 _____
2_2 _____
3_1 _____
3_2 _____
4 _____
5 _____
6 _____

Field Experiences in the Elementary-School Classroom

1. Develop your own informal reading inventory by using portions from each book in a basal series used in one school district. Remember to select portions between 75 and 200 words from the middle of each

book. Each selection should have a beginning, middle, and end. You may wish to use portions from informational articles as well as portions from fictional stories.

2. Administer an informal reading inventory to one child. Determine the book that you would recommend for the child's instructional level. Document your choice in a report of your calculations and observations. Include a record sheet similar to Table 9.1 in your report.

CHAPTER 10

The effectiveness of basal readers depends a great deal upon their skillful and flexible use by the teacher.

Teaching with Basal Readers

Chapter Outline

Chapter Preview

Over 90 percent of the primary-grade teachers (grades K–3) and over 80 percent of the intermediate-grade teachers (grades 4–6) use books called *basal readers* as their major instructional aid in teaching reading (6). A large percentage of the teachers of grades seven and eight also use them. In this chapter we'll talk about why basal readers are so popular, what a modern basal reading program looks like, its advantages and disadvantages, and some of the organizational plans that teachers employ while teaching with basal readers. In the next chapter we'll discuss organizational procedures more thoroughly and how some teachers combine a basal reader program with a performance based program called a "skills management system."

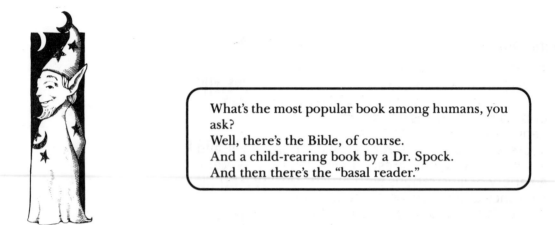

What's the most popular book among humans, you ask?
Well, there's the Bible, of course.
And a child-rearing book by a Dr. Spock.
And then there's the "basal reader."

The Popularity of Basal-Reading Programs

The basal reader became a popular teaching medium with the introduction of the *McGuffey Series* around 1840. Today basal-reader publishers still follow McGuffey's main plan: to present children with a series of ever-more-difficult stories, articles, poems, and plays by controlling the vocabulary of the books in which such reading selections are incorporated. McGuffey tried to control the vocabulary by controlling the length of the words, beginning with two- and three-letter words and leading up to longer and longer ones. Today publishers control the vocabulary in three ways: 1) by using high-frequency words at first and gradually introducing words of lower frequency, 2) by using mostly regular words at first and gradually introducing words whose spelling pattern is irregular, and 3) by using a great many high-interest words at first (*mom, dad, ball, eat*) and gradually introducing words that are more abstract and less relevant to children's immediate concerns.

This systematic approach toward helping children learn to read has great appeal to most educators. And for good reason, since it tends to work much better than presenting children with something too difficult such as the *Bible* or *Pilgrim's Progress*—two books favored by educators in our country before the advent of basal readers.

Basal-reading programs (also called *basal series*), consisting of readers, teacher's guides, workbooks, and other instructional materials, tend to be popular with both beginning teachers and experienced teachers. They can provide teachers, as well as the principal, the parents, and many children, with a sense of security and purpose. When used flexibly, they can be reasonably effective. When followed slavishly without regard for individuals, alternative procedures, or for input from the children in the class, they can lead to boredom, failure, and a hatred for reading. It depends, to a great extent, on the knowledge, skill, and sensitivity of the teacher. Later in the book we'll talk about ways of avoiding such "basal-reader traps." But for now, let's look at the nature of basal-reading programs and at some criteria for good basal readers.

Publishers of Basal Readers

There are many adequate basal-reading programs on the market today. Publishers of these programs will be happy to send you a brochure describing their series. The following companies, among others, might be considered:

- Addison-Wesley Publishing Company, Jacob Way, Reading, MA 01867
- Allyn and Bacon, 470 Atlantic Avenue, Boston, MA 02210
- American Book Company, 450 West 33rd Street, New York, NY 10001
- Economy Company, 1901 North Walnut, P.O. Box 25308, Oklahoma City, OK 73125
- Ginn and Company, 191 Spring Street, Lexington, MA 02173 (Use a hard *g* to pronounce this.)
- Harcourt Brace Jovanovich, Inc., 757 Third Avenue, New York, NY 10017
- Harper & Row, Publishers, Inc., 10 East 53rd Street, New York, NY 10022
- Holt, Rinehart, and Winston, 383 Madison Avenue, New York, NY 10017
- Houghton Mifflin Company, 2 Park Street, Boston, MA 02107 (Use a long *o* to pronounce this: Hō′tən)
- Laidlaw Brothers, Thatcher and Madison, River Forest, IL 60305
- J. B. Lippincott Company, East Washington Square, Philadelphia, PA 19105
- Macmillan Company, 866 Third Avenue, New York, NY 10022
- Charles E. Merrill Publishing Company, 1300 Alum Creek Drive, Columbus, OH 43216

- Open Court Publishing Company, P.O. Box 599, La Salle, IL 61301
- Scott, Foresman and Company, 1900 East Lake, Glenview, IL 60025

Because there is such a large number of companies that are publishing respected basal series today, it would be impossible to describe each of them to you. Instead, let me briefly describe the characteristics that are common to many of them. This description should not be interpreted as meaning that there are no major differences among the basal-reading programs that publishers have produced. Basal programs differ considerably in the decoding and comprehension skills that are emphasized; they also differ in whether they emphasize a phonics or linguistic approach—as well as in many other ways. The best way to notice such differences is to examine a teacher's guide at the same grade level from several reading programs.

A General Description of a Basal-Reading Program

Basal-reading programs today use a "continuous-progress" approach. Rather than developing one reader (textbook)* for each of the eight grades in the elementary school, the series authors prepare instructional materials for approximately seventeen *levels*, ranging from "readiness" materials for kindergarten and first grade all the way up to sophisticated anthologies for grades seven and eight. This large number of readers and materials encourages a teacher to instruct children at their own reading level, rather than instruct them according to their designated grade level.

In a first-grade classroom, for instance, some children who are weak in auditory discrimination, visual discrimination, or other prereading skills may be working at Level A with a set of prereading or readiness materials. This set of materials helps a teacher determine children's specific reading-readiness deficiencies and provides instructional plans and activities for remediation of those deficiencies. Other children in the same first-grade classroom may be working at level B with materials at a slightly higher level. The level B materials might assist the teacher in making sure that children develop such abilities as paying attention to spoken context clues, learning letter names and sounds, and reading a small set of high-frequency words. By the end of the first grade, some children may

---

*For purposes of discussion in this chapter, the term *reader* will refer to any paperback pre-primer or primer as well as any hardbound book in a basal series.

be working as high as level F, with a hardbound book and other materials. By this time, the children might be concentrating on such skills as decoding vowel letters, paying attention to commas, and getting the main idea. As you can see, then, today's basal-reading programs do permit a moderate degree of flexibility and individualization.

Types of Materials

The range of instructional materials available to the teacher using a modern basal series is quite extensive. The materials in most basal-reading programs, for instance, include the following:

1. Readers (softbound and hardbound books of stories, poems, plays, and articles)
2. Teacher's Guides (manuals that contain precise lesson plans, informational articles for teachers on the teaching of reading, review and enrichment activities, games, models for teaching reading, annotated lists of children's library books, scope and sequence charts for teaching skills, and other information)
3. Practice Books (workbooks for reinforcing skills and concepts that have already been taught through the use of the readers and the teacher's guides)
4. Testing materials (tests, inventories, and record-keeping devices that allow teachers to determine each child's reading levels, strengths, and weaknesses, and to assess his progress as he moves through the program; see Chapter 11 for more detail on this part of the program)
5. Ditto masters (for reproducing worksheets that help the teacher not only reinforce reading-skill development and provide extra practice for those who need it, but also provide enrichment experiences in spelling, writing, and other language skills)
6. Instructional aids such as charts, work cards, "Big Books" (large reproductions of readers at the lower levels), and game boxes (designed for the busy teacher who doesn't have time to make all of her own instructional devices)
7. Minibooks (supplementary paperback library books)
8. Dictionaries (perhaps one for levels D through H, a more advanced one for levels I through L, and an even more advanced one for levels M through Q)

Some companies also sell cassettes and sound-filmstrips for children to use in classroom listening stations or for teachers to use with small and large groups. These cassettes and filmstrips are designed to reinforce earlier lessons and to provide enrichment experiences (such as listening to an author read her own book while the child reads along.)

Criteria for Good Basal Readers

High-quality basal programs today must meet a number of standards. Before discussing a few of these standards, let's put them in the form of questions you can use in examining some of the basal series:

1. Do the illustrations and content represent both sexes fairly and without stereotyping?
2. Do the illustrations and content represent different ethnic, age, and racial groups fairly and without stereotyping?
3. Do the selections rate high in interest, clarity, and literary merit?
4. Do the illustrations represent a variety of styles and an artistic quality?
5. Is there a balance of emphases among the various decoding approaches?
6. Are higher-level thinking skills encouraged?
7. Do the oral- and silent-reading experiences emphasize communication and holism?

Now let me illustrate each of these criteria by showing you brief selections from various basal-reading programs. Although none of the publishers of basal series meets these criteria 100 percent of the time, they all seem to be working toward meeting them more often than in the past.

Representation of Both Sexes

Representing both sexes fairly and without stereotyping has been a serious challenge for publishers of modern basal series. In the past the majority of books—both basal readers and library books for children—have been biased against women and girls (16). Several studies have shown how men and boys have been far more frequently given story roles calling for courage, honesty, intelligence, and creativity—while women and girls, both in illustrations and content, have more often been portrayed as timid, unimportant, or nonexistent (17).

To give you just a notion of the extent of this bias, I have examined Walker's list (25) of 1000 words that have had the most frequent occurrence in both voluntary and assigned reading (including basal readers) in grades three through nine in the United States. By looking just at these high-frequency words, we can get a good idea of the degree to which our written language has been reinforcing the notion that males in our society are more important than females. The following words were found to be in Walker's list of high-frequency words and were selected as objective indicators of sex bias: *girl* vs. *boy; man + men* vs. *woman + women + lady; he* vs. *she; her* vs. *his; father* vs. *mother; daughter* vs. *son; sister* vs. *brother.* Table 10.1 shows the results of the comparisons between "male words" and "female words."

Table 10.1 shows that the word *girl* was found only 45 percent as often as the word *boy* in Walker's list of high-frequency words. The combination of the words *woman, lady,* and *women* occurred only 22 percent as frequently as the combination of *man* and *men.* (The words *gentleman, gentlemen,* and *ladies* did not occur as high-frequency words in Walker's list.) Further examination of Table 10.1 reveals that "female words" occurred much less frequently than "male words" in every comparison but the one between *mother* and *father,* in which case *mother* showed up 103 percent as often as *father.* Even when the *mother–father* comparison is included, however, male words were used almost three times as often as female words.

It may be tempting to overlook the comparison between male and female pronouns, since it is often assumed that male pronouns can be "generic" and refer to both males and females. It may also be tempting to omit the words *man* and *men,* since they are also considered "generic" at times. However, studies show that such so-called

Table 10.1   A Comparison of the Frequencies of Female Words and Male Words Found in Walker's List of 1000 High-Frequency Words Occurring in Both Voluntary and Assigned Reading in Grades Three through Nine in the United States.

Female Words (F)	Male Words (M)	Female Percent of Male Words
girl 2,357 (occurrences)	*boy* 5,222 (occurrences)	45
woman + lady + women 2,296	*man + men* 10,645	22
she 14,111	*he* 47,665	30
her 11,444	*his* 29,387	39
mother 3,806	*father* 3,691	103
daughter (less than 534)	*son* 965	55
sister 612	*brother* 1,205	51
total 35,159	total 98,780	36
total without *mother* 31,353	total without *father* 95,089	33
total without *she* and *her* 10,604	total without *he* and *his* 21,728	49

But these were British soldiers. How could she trust the enemy?

Before she could decide what to do, she felt a tug at her blue bundle. It was the man called Dow. "Smells like fresh bread there," he said. Quickly, Ellen snatched the bundle away. Then suddenly she felt herself grabbed around the waist by two big hands and whisked across the side of the boat. She was too surprised and frightened to make a sound.

The man with the red cheeks laughed as he set her down on the bench beside him. "No noise from you," he growled.

177

Figure 10.1. *A sample page from a nonsexist basal reader selection. (From Ester Wood Brady, "My Name Is Toliver, Sir," in Gateways, Boston: Houghton Mifflin, 1981, p. 177.)*

generic words as *he, him,* and *man* are not truly generic. Many people, contrary to popular opinion, will not think of women and girls when confronted with such words; they think specifically of men and boys. Ernst (7), for example, investigated masculine "generic" pronouns and nouns with 418 students ranging from preschool through college to determine whether masculine generic terms were interpreted as referring to females to the same extent as males. Results indicated that with both the nouns and the pronouns, the receiver of the language was more likely to interpret it as referring to males than to females. Harrison (10) found that junior-high students visualized predominantly more males when presented with masculine generic terms such as *man, mankind,* and *he* than they did when presented with terms that were inclusionary, such as *humans, people,* and *they.* Kidd (12) found similar results with college students when they were confronted with masculine generic pronouns.

It is likely that any aspect of society, including its language, that supports and maintains the negative stereotype of women as inferior to men is detrimental to society. It is detrimental toward the development of healthy self-concepts as girls mature into women. It is detrimental toward the development of positive relationships between the sexes. And it is thus detrimental toward the development of mentally healthy people in a mentally healthy community.

The direct referral to males more than females in basal readers and other children's books, and the use of so-called generic language that is not truly generic, are outdated customs that should be relegated to historical documents. The alternated use of *he* and *she* along with *her* and *him,* the substitution of plural nouns followed by *they* for singular nouns followed by *he,* and the conscious attempt by authors to place females in the center of the stage as often as males— these are minor but important changes that are gradually being made in basal readers and other books. They need to be made, not just to satisfy the child in all of us who demands fairness, but to help achieve our need for people to grow up with healthy self-images, the ability to view the opposite sex without stereotyping, and a desire to relate with compassion toward other all human beings, regardless of gender.

An illustration of a story that portrays a girl as courageous, intelligent, and creative is the one by Esther Wood Brady found in the Houghton Mifflin reader called *Gateways.* The story is entitled "My Name is Toliver, Sir," and tells of Ellen Toliver, who is given the responsibility of carrying an urgent message to General Washington during the Revolutionary War. Using her wits and her "whistle-a-happy-tune" sense of bravery, she manages to get aboard a redcoats' boat, stand up to a bullying soldier, and accomplish her mission. As Figure 10.1 shows, she even manages to get a lift into the redcoats' boat—but only because the bullying soldier wants to get her bag of bread. Little does he realize that the message to Washington is buried in the bread.

Representation of Different Ethnic Groups, Ages, and Races

Some stories found in basal readers and other children's books can encourage the very thing that an education is supposed to be discouraging, namely stereotyping of people. Rather than setting minds at liberty to think about individuals, some books and stories encourage the freezing of minds instead, causing children to view people of different cultures, races, or ages as homogeneous and inferior rather than as heterogeneous and equal. Let's look at some of the specific characteristics of books and stories that encourage such stereotyping:

1. Fake authenticity. This characteristic is often revealed when authors attempt to make their characters and setting more believable (without doing sufficient homework). Perhaps the most horrifying example of this can be found in the hardcover edition of *Mary Poppins.* In the chapter called "Bad Tuesday" the author, Pamela Travers, tried to add authenticity by putting these words in the mouth of a Black woman:

"Ah bin 'specting you a long time, Mary Poppins," she said, smiling. "You bring dem chillun dere into ma li'l house for a slice of watermelon right now. My, but dem's very white babies. You wan' use a li'l bit black boot polish on dem. Come 'long, now. You'se mighty welcome."

Puerto Ricans and Chicanos are still occasionally shown in children's stories as incapable of speaking English without breaking it into bits or changing every fish into "feesh" and chair into "share." Asian-American children used to be shown spending all their living moments celebrating the Lunar New Year. Thus, rather than authenticity, children often received stereotypes or caricatures.

2. Nonproportional representation. This characteristic used to show up especially in stories about children in a large city. Whereas you would expect some of the characters to be Black, some to be Asian American, some White, some Puerto Rican, and so on, you would find only White characters or perhaps a token Black shining shoes or a Chinese laundry worker. Such omission can imply that cultural groups other than the White majority group are not very important. And, of course, by relegating the token "Third Worlder" to a low-paying job, the story has further strengthened the image of "inferiority" that some children have about Third-World people.

3. Unchallenged racist acts. An example of this characteristic can be found by reading *The Slave Dancer,* which won the Newbery Award in 1974 for the preceding year's "most distinguished" children's book. Racist comments and acts are sometimes portrayed in this book without a single one of the characters showing concern, rebellion, or disgust. This can't help but leave some young readers with the impression that such a racist act is acceptable.

4. White acceptance. In two famous books, *The Cay* by Theodore Taylor and *Bright April* by Marguerite DeAngeli, the Black person is finally accepted by a White person as an equal. At first blush these stories look like truly anti-racist ones. And yet the authors both seem to be making the assumption that White is the norm to which a Black person must strive. In neither of these books does the author deal with the acceptance or nonacceptance of the White by the Black. Another assumption, furthermore, is that Third World people want to be the same as Whites. This is insulting to many Third Worlders who would just as soon be appreciated for their differences.

5. White paternalism. The most celebrated example of this characteristic can be found in the 1923 Newbery Award winner, *The Voyages of Doctor Dolittle,* by Hugh Lofting. In Isabelle Suhl's review of this book for the Council on Interracial Books she illustrates Lofting's white paternalism in this way:

> Doctor Dolittle . . . arrives on Spidermonkey Island off the coast of Brazil in search of the "Red Indian," Long Arrow, the world's greatest naturalist. On his first day on the Island, Doctor Dolittle rescues Long Arrow and a group of Indians entombed in a cave and brings fire to the heretofore fireless Indians of Popsipetel. This makes him so popular that he is constantly followed about by crowds of admirers. "After his fire-making feat, this childlike people expected him to be continually doing magic." He solves problem after problem for the Indians and eventually they ask the "Mighty One" to become "the King of the whole Spidermonkey Island." Dolittle, as the Great White Father, dutifully accepts his new role as king, but after a while he wants to go home. But, in the words of Dolittle, "these people have come to rely on me for a great number of things. We found them ignorant of much that white people enjoy. . . . I cannot close my eyes to what might happen if I should leave these people and run away. . . . They are, as it were, my children. . . . I've got to stay."

A later book called *Tecumseh,* published in 1965 and written by Luella Bruce Creighton, included this statement: (page 47) ". . . Exceptional intelligence glowed in his unusual eyes, hazel colored, deep set, and abnormally quick to observe. These were strange eyes in an Indian face. Could it be that somewhere in the background in the generations there had been a drop of white blood? . . ."

Such blatant white paternalism is difficult to find in children's stories today. But it's still there in more subtle form. In *Josie's Handful of Quietness,* for example, a White man attaches himself to a Chicano migrant family and causes their lives to change for the better. One can easily infer from this book that the Chicano family couldn't have improved their lives without the wisdom of this fatherly White man. Some stories with a central-city setting have a standard character—the great White father or mother, in the garb of a kindly social worker, who somehow manages to keep the Third-World child out of trouble.

6. *Whitewashing.* This type of racist characteristic occurs whenever authors attempt to make light of the injustices carried out by Whites against Non whites. In *The Slave Dancer,* for instance, one of the crew makes this comment about the captured Blacks:

> Do you think it was easier for my own people who sailed to Boston sixty years ago from Ireland, locked up in a hold for a whole voyage where they might have died of sickness and suffocation? . . .

The author never corrects this unrealistic and unjust comparison by having another character point out the differences between the Irish and African situations. Nor does she present a balanced perspective on who was mainly responsible for the African slave trade. A child could easily read this story and come away with the impression that the major culprits were the Africans who captured and sold other Africans—rather than the Whites back in America who used them as slaves.

In *Chinatown Sunday: The Story of Lillian Der,* by Carol Ann Bales, the author states that the "Chinese opened up more and more laundries and restaurants so that they did not have to compete with white workers." This type of statement has two implications: 1) it implies that the Chinese did not want to compete, whereas in reality they were not allowed to compete (thus, the author has performed a whitewash job); and 2) it tells the Chinese-American child that Chinese Americans are good citizens who accept their place in White society and never resist the will of the superior majority group. This is certainly an inaccurate and demoralizing self-concept for a minority child to attain.

7. *Classism.* In many children's books about Blacks, Mexican Americans, Puerto Ricans, Native Americans, or Asian Americans, the Third-World families are depicted as poor and living in a ghetto. While this may lend an aura of reality to some stories, racial stereotypes can be encouraged when all Third Worlders are shown to be members of the lower economic class.

As an example of a basal-reader story that is nonbiased toward different ethnic groups, ages, or races, let's look briefly at the Houghton Mifflin story called "Are Your Arms a Hundred Years Old?" This story is part of a Newbery Medal Honor Book written by Sharon Bell Mathin and portrays a loving relationship between a young boy named Michael and his great-great Aunt Dew, who happens to be

100 years old. And she can "prove it," too, since she has a box with a hundred pennies in it, one for each year of her life. As Michael slowly counts each penny, she tells him an important event in her personal life and in the life of the country for each year since her birth. Although Aunt Dew speaks in her own "Black dialect" and Michael speaks in his own "Standard dialect" there are no communication barriers between them. Michael, more than anyone else in his family understands Aunt Dew and her vital secret—that if you want to live to be one hundred, you first "have to have a hundred penny box. . . . Somebody special got to give it to you. . . . And soon as they give it to you, you got to be careful 'less it disappear."

As shown in Figure 10.2, Michael didn't want to take any chances on losing his good friend, Aunt Dew. From his way of thinking, the best way of keeping Aunt Dew around for a long time was to hide that penny box!

Selections of High-Interest, Clarity, and Literary Merit

Most basal-reading programs today include numerous selections by writers noted for their craftsmanship and creativity. Portions of the following books, for example, have been incorporated in the Houghton Mifflin readers; these books have been recognized by the Association for Library Service to Children for their "originality, excellence of literary style, respect for the personality of the reader, and acceptance by children":

> . . .and now Miguel by Joseph Krumgold
> And Then What Happened, Paul Revere? by Jean Fritz
> Annie and the Old One by Miska Miles
> Beyond the High Hills by Knud Rasmussen
> Dragonwings by Laurence Yep
> The Endless Steppe by Esther Hautzig
> Flashlight and Other Poems by Judith Thurman
> Flower Moon Snow by Kazue Mizumura
> Founding Mothers by Linda Grant DePauw
> The Foundling by Lloyd Alexander
> Frog and Toad Together by Arnold Lobel

As another example, selections by the following well-known writers are among those chosen for the Economy Company's *Keys to Reading* basal-reading program:

Mary Austin	Frank Baum
Betty Baker	Nathaniel Benchley

He'd tell Aunt Dew right now that they had a good place to hide the hundred penny box. The best place of all.

Michael got down from the huge bed and walked quietly back down the hall to his door and knocked on it very lightly — too lightly for his mother to hear.

Aunt Dew didn't answer.

"Aunt Dew," he whispered after he'd opened the door and tiptoed up to the bed. "It's me. Michael."

Aunt Dew was crying.

Figure 10.2. *A sample page from a nonracist basal reader selection. (From Sharon Bell Mathin, "Are Your Arms a Hundred Years Old," in* Gateways, *Boston: Houghton Mifflin, 1981, p. 366.)*

Michael Berenstain	Lilian Moore
Harold Berson	Ogden Nash
Barbara Brenner	Mary Peacock
James Buechler	Miriam Clark Potter
Marchette Chute	Christina G. Rossetti
Crescent Dragonwagon	Allen Say
Benjamin Elkin	Miriam Schlein
Eleanor Farjeon	James E. Seidelman and
Rose Fyleman	Grace Mintonye
Wilson Gage	Marjorie Weinman Sharmat
Joan Hanson	Shel Silverstein
Homer	Liesel Moak Skorpen
Rachel Isadora	Robert Louis Stevenson
Bil Keane	Jane Thayer
Joe Lasker	J.R.R. Tolkien
Helen Louise Miller	Janice May Udry
A. A. Milne	

Illustration 10.3 provides an example of the criterion of high interest, clarity, and literary merit. This illustration is from a story in the Economy Company reader, called *A Hundred Circling Camps*. In this story, "The Treasure of Sumiko's Bay," the author, Barbara Chamberlain, portrays an exciting scene with imagery, naturalness of thought and language, and with insight into human nature.

A Variety of Illustrations with Artistic Quality

The illustrations in most basal series today often include those that many of us would call "works of art." Part of this is the result of more sophisticated printing techniques, which allow artists to use nearly any technique and medium. Part of it is the result of better selection of artists by publishers. In many series, for instance, illustrations by winners of the Caldecott Medal have been included. Furthermore, to provide novelty from one story to the next, most publishers of basal-reading programs use hundreds of different illustrators, with their own particular style and choice of media.

Figures 10.4 and 10.5 are samples of the variety and quality of illustrations included in most basal series today. These were selected from the Harcourt, Brace Jovanovich basal reader called *People and Places*.

Before we continue, let me explain that from this point on only one basal series will be used for illustrations of points that are being made. This will make it easier for you to see how a particular publisher's point of view about the reading process influences the teaching techniques advocated in the publisher's "teacher's guides." A publisher who feels that reading is primarily a phonic process, for

174281

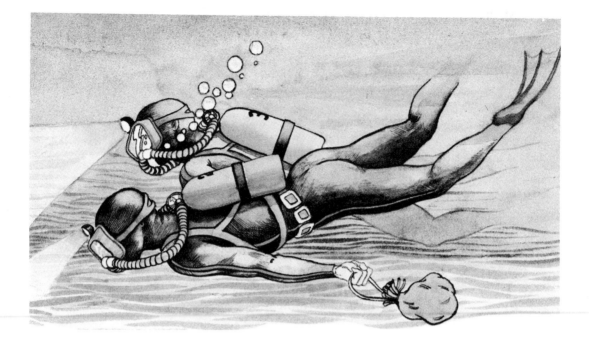

There was a chance to do something! She raced home to tell her plan to Grandmother.

After their plans were finished, Sumiko and her grandmother spent five nights on the beach, sleeping when they could. During the day Sumiko tried ways of slipping quietly through the water, not making a splash or sound. Knowing that she could swim better than anyone in the village lessened her fears of being caught when the robbers *did* come.

"I may have to give up tomorrow, Sumiko. My old bones like to sleep in our home," her grandmother said. "And now that the moon has left, we can't see very well."

Sumiko had been sleeping for only a short time when a sound from the bay woke her. She heard splashing from the direction of the oyster rafts. "Of course! They waited for a dark night!" She whispered to her grandmother to awaken the people of the village. Then Sumiko slipped silently into the water.

87

Figure 10.3. *A sample page from a basal reader selection of high interest, clarity, and literary merit. Adapted from "The Treasure of Sumiko's Bay" by Barbara Chamberlain, Jack and Jill magazine,* copyright © 1975 by the Saturday Evening Post Company.

"Found what?" asked his brother.

"The answer," Joseph said. "Hot air is lighter than cold air. So it can float up, the way smoke floats up. It's as easy as that. I think we're going to fly at last."

Figure 10.4. *A sample illustration from a basal reader. (From Dino Anastasio, "The First Hot Air Balloon," From PEOPLE AND PLACES by Margaret Early et al., copyright 1979 by Harcourt Brace Jovanovich, Inc. Reproduced by permission of the publisher.*

Figure 10.5. *A sample illustration from a basal reader. (From "The Elves and the Shoemakers," From PEOPLE AND PLACES by Margaret Early et al., copyright 1979 by Harcourt Brace Jovanovich, Inc. Reproduced by permission of the publisher.*

instance, will advocate techniques that are quite different from those advocated by a publisher who feels that reading is a process of communicating with an author. The series that will be used from here-on-in will be the Houghton Mifflin Reading Program. This program was selected not because it is the "best" series. It was selected as a representative of programs that attempt to emphasize meaning more than decoding. Since most programs use such an emphasis today, it is my personal belief that many basal-reading programs are as good as the Houghton Mifflin program. Use of the Houghton Mifflin program for most of the illustrations should be seen in the light of my attempt to add clarity to your reading rather than as an endorsement of one particular program.

A Balance among Decoding Approaches

There have been periods of time in the history of basal readers when one decoding skill has been emphasized over all the others. Visual memory was glorified during the "look-say" era. Sentences were more important than words in another era. Phonics was king during another. Today there is more of a tendency toward a balance among the various means of decoding, although basal-series publishers still vary in the amount of emphasis given to "phonics vs. meaning." The Houghton Mifflin Program, as indicated earlier, will be used as an illustration of a "meaning emphasis" type of program. In the teacher's guide, the teacher will find contextual analysis emphasized somewhat more than phonic analysis from Level A on through Level O. This is because of the series authors' stated belief that through such an emphasis on context "students are conditioned to expect and look for meaning as they read."

In Level A, for instance, children are first taught to anticipate words that will make sense in sentences that the teacher reads to them (a type of oral "fill-in-the-appropriate-word" exercise). The teacher, for example, reads "Ivan poured a glass of _____ for the baby." The children select appropriate answers from pictures of a hook, water, milk, and comb. As children go through the Level A reader, they learn the phonic-analysis skill of associating sounds with letters, but this is always tempered with the need to pay attention to context clues. As an example of this, see Figure 10.6, a page from the Teacher's Guide to *Getting Ready to Read*. Notice how the guide suggests that the letter *d* be decoded in the context of a meaningful sentence: "I helped Mom put the _____ into the dishwasher." Notice also how the guide suggests that the teacher ask the children why they wouldn't choose the word *dentist* instead, thus making sure that the children think about what word makes sense rather than what word starts with *d*.

Decoding Printed Words in Spoken Context   h d

OBJECTIVE   To have children use spoken context and letter-sound associations to decode printed words beginning with *d* and *h*.

MATERIALS FOR THE LESSON

Getting Ready to Read: page 78
Getting Ready to Read, Big Book: page 78
Pencils or Crayons

PREPARING FOR THE LESSON

Model activities are provided in the Reference Handbook for your use with those children who, in your judgment, still need preparatory exercises. See Reference Handbook, page 413.

TEACHING THE LESSON

Distribute copies of *Getting Ready to Read.* **Help children find page 78.**

Say: Look at this page. What do you see? … *(Answers will vary.)* **Allow time for children to respond. If necessary, help children discover that there are words on the page. Let's find out what the words are on this page.**

ROW 1   Point to number 1. Say: Find Row 1. … Now look at the word at the beginning of this row. **Put your finger under d.** Put your finger under the letter at the beginning of this word. What is this letter? … *(d)* This word begins with the letter *d,* so you know that this word begins with the sound for *d.*

   This word names one of the pictures in this row. **Point to the pictures.** Look at these pictures. Who will name these pictures? … *(cups, dentist, forks, dishes)* **Point to the pictures in left-to-right order and have them named.**

   Point to the word *dishes.* I'll read a sentence and leave out this word. Think of a word that makes sense and begins with the sound for *d.*

   Listen: I helped Mom put the **(make a hand gesture or pause)** into the dishwasher.

Who'll read this word? … *(dishes)* This word is *dishes.* *Dishes* makes sense with what I read and begins with the sound for *d.* Listen: I helped Mom put the *dishes* into the dishwasher. How did you know the word wasn't *dentist?* … *(Dentist doesn't make sense.)* *Dentist* begins with the sound for *d,* but it doesn't make sense. Listen: I helped Mom put the *dentist* into the dishwasher. How did you know the word wasn't *cups?* … (*Cups doesn't begin with the sound for* d.) *Cups* makes sense but it doesn't begin with the sound for *d.* How did you know the word wasn't *forks?* … (*Forks doesn't begin with the sound for* d.) *Forks* makes sense, but it doesn't begin with the sound for *d.*

   Continue using the same procedure for the remaining three rows:

ROW 2
      WORD: *hat*
      PICTURES: *vest, hat, hippopotamus, coat*
      CONTEXT: Mom made me a blue _____ to wear to school.
      CHECKING WORDS: *vest, hippopotamus, coat*

ROW 3
      WORD: *duck*
      PICTURES: *duck, boy, girl, desk*
      CONTEXT: We watched the _____ swimming in the pond.
      CHECKING WORDS: *boy, girl, desk*

ROW 4
      WORD: *horse*
      PICTURES: *helicopter, goat, horse, cow*
      CONTEXT: "I gave the _____ some food and water," said Gael.
      CHECKING WORDS: *helicopter, goat, cow*

PRACTICE

Distribute pencils or crayons.

ROW 1   Say: Look at the word in Row 1 again. **Put your finger under d.** Put your finger under the letter at the beginning of this word. … What is this letter? … *(d)* Put a line under *d.* … This word begins with the sound for *d* and names one of the pictures in this row.

   I'll read a sentence and leave out this word. Think of a word that makes sense and begins with the sound for *d.* Put a

Figure 10.6. A sample page from a basal reader teacher's guide.
(From William K. Durr and Robert L. Hillerich, Teacher's Guide:
Getting Ready to Read, *Boston: Houghton Mifflin, 1981, p. 275.*

Encouragement of Higher-Level Thinking Skills

There was a period of time in the history of basal readers when publishers actually encouraged teachers to carry on a discussion only at the literal level of understanding. Questions in the Teacher's Guides were mainly of the "who did what" variety. Today basal-series authors have incorporated sample questions in the Teacher's Guides, which, if not followed slavishly, can encourage thinking at many levels—literal, inferential, critical, and creative.

In the Houghton Mifflin Program children are encouraged through the Teacher's Guides to think at these different levels—literal, interpretive, and evaluative/creative—from the earliest readiness level all the way through the eighth-grade reader. To see how this is done at one of the earliest levels, notice Figures 10.7 and 10.8. In Figure 10.7, we have four pages from a story selected from the Level B reader called *Bears*. In this story three birds are trying to find a new home. The teacher, following the Teacher's Guide, motivates the children before each page, then checks and develops their comprehension after each page. After the entire story has been read, she then carries on a discussion at various levels of thinking. (See Figure 10.8 for a demonstration of this.)

Oral and Silent Reading with an Emphasis on Communication and Holism

Many of today's basal-reading series are designed to encourage teachers and children to put more emphasis on the communication aspects of reading. There is less of a tendency today than in the past to treat reading as a set of isolated subskills and more of a tendency to show reading as more than the sum of its separate parts. There is more emphasis, for example, on silent reading than on oral reading. This in itself communicates to the child that reading is a thinking, communicating process, rather than a mechanical, sounding-it-out-process.

But even oral reading, in many of today's programs, is treated differently (11). No longer are teachers encouraged to stop a child every time he makes a reading error. Instead teachers are encouraged in most Teacher's Guides to use oral-reading practice for various purposes. If children are going to read to each other in an actor-audience situation, then they are given time to practice what they will read; those who are not reading look at the "actor," rather than at their books. In this way reading is used as a communication process—one that can entertain and inform others. If children are going to read orally so that the teacher can check on their decoding and comprehension skills, the teacher will first have them read the story silently and then have them reread the story out loud, either as a play or as a challenge to them to prove the hypotheses and

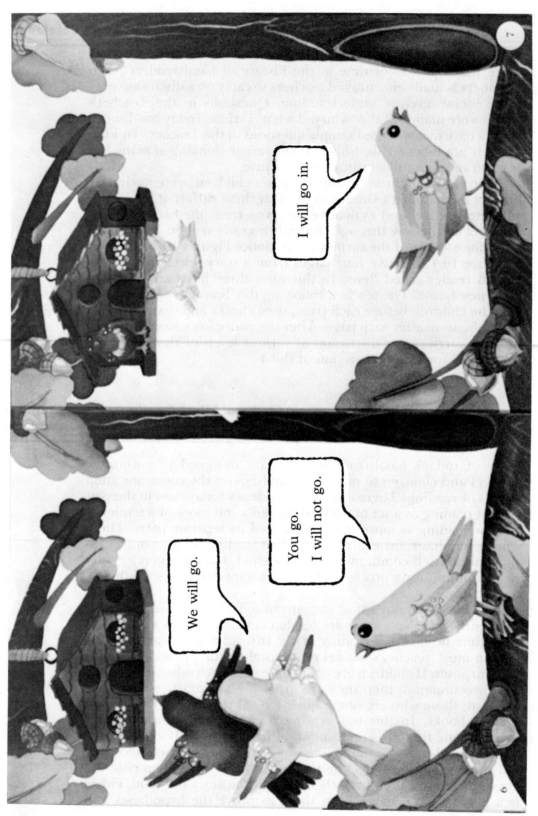

Figure 10.7. Sample pages from a basal reader. (From Tim Johnson, "I Will Go," in Bears, Boston: Houghton Mifflin, 1981, pp. 6–9.)

Extending Comprehension

TEACHER'S NOTE   The boldfaced letters **L, I,** or **E** appear before each question in the Extending Comprehension section. These letters designate each question as literal, interpretive, or evaluative and creative Literal questions **(L)** require only that children understand and remember what is directly stated in the selection. Answers are provided for all of these questions. Interpretive thinking questions **(I)** require that children go beyond the literal understanding of the selection to derive implicit, or not directly stated, meanings from the selection. Although answers to these questions sometimes may vary, examples are given as guidelines. Evaluative and creative questions **(E)** require children to use their higher mental processes to make evaluations and judgments based on the selection and the story characters. Children are also asked to offer opinions and are encouraged to think creatively. An important characteristic of evaluative and creative questions is that they do not necessitate single, specific answers that are the same for all children. Therefore, answers are not provided for these questions, although children are expected to justify their responses.

When the children have finished the story, have them close their books. Then conduct a short discussion, using some of the following questions as stimuli:

I   1.   What were the birds deciding about in this story?   *(whether or not to move to a birdhouse)*

E   2.   Which bird did not want to leave the tree?   *(Yellow Bird)* Why do you think Yellow Bird did not want to leave the tree?

I   3.   Why do you think Yellow Bird decided to move to the birdhouse after all? *(probably because Yellow Bird saw that some squirrels were moving into the hole in the tree)*

E   4.   Do you think Yellow Bird will be happy in the birdhouse?   Why or why not?

L   5.   At the end of the story, which animals were going to live in the hole in the tree?   *(the squirrels)*

E   6.   Do you think Yellow Bird would have stayed at the tree if the squirrels had not moved in?   Why or why not?

E   7.   Do you think Red Bird and Blue Bird wanted Yellow Bird to move to the birdhouse with them?   Why or why not?

I   8.   In what ways were the three birds alike or the same?   *(The birds looked the same except for their color; they all lived in the tree and all moved to the birdhouse.)*   In what ways were they different?   *(They each were a different color; Red Bird and Blue Bird wanted to live in the new birdhouse, Yellow Bird wanted to stay at the familiar tree.)*

E   9.   Where do you think the birdhouse came from?   **Encourage divergent thinking.**

Figure 10.8.   *Sample from a page of a basal reader teacher's guide.* (*From William K. Durr et al.*, Teacher's Guide: Bears, *Boston: Houghton Mifflin, 1981, p. 29.*)

Oral Reading

If during *oral reading,* a child has difficulty with a word, *do not hesitate to tell the child what that word is.* At the same time, you will want to make a mental note that the child needs further practice in recognizing that word and in using letter-sound associations and context clues.

Interrupting the reading at this time in order to help a child decode the word would tend to divert the child's attention away from reading with proper expression and would defeat the major purpose of the oral reading. That type of guidance can be conducted more effectively during the silent reading period or in conjunction with the exercises in the *Teaching Reading Skills* section of each unit.

The major emphasis during the oral reading period should be placed on reading the text with the voice intonations — emphases, pauses, and inflections — called for by the situation in the story.

At this level, oral reading is one of the best indicators of the child's grasp of the mechanics of reading and of the child's understanding of what is being read. If children can convert the printed form of the language that is seen on the page of a book into its familiar spoken form and can read the lines with the natural expression that they would use if they were saying them, you can usually be sure that children understand what they are reading and that they are aware of the purpose of reading.

Figure 10.9. *Sample from a page of a basal reader teacher's guide. (From William K. Durr et al.,* Teacher's Guide: Bears, *Boston: Houghton Mifflin, 1981, p. 29.)*

predictions they have made. In any case, the emphasis is on understanding or appreciating what the author has said. (Only if the teacher were trying to test a child on decoding skills would she have him read out loud to her without first having him read a selection silently.)

Let's look at some examples of how communication and holism are encouraged in the Houghton Mifflin Program. In Figure 10.9, we have a teaching suggestion from the Teacher's Guide to *Bears,* a preprimer for first-grade children. Note particularly the third paragraph of the teaching suggestion: "The major emphasis during the oral reading period should be placed on reading the text with the voice intonations—emphases, pauses, and inflections—called for by the situation in the story."

As another example of Houghton Mifflin's emphasis on communication, examine Figure 10.10. In this teaching suggestion on oral reading, this time from the Teacher's Guide to the intermediate-grade-level reader called *Gateways,* we again see an emphasis on such holistic considerations as "the author's message," grasping "the meaning the author intended," and "ability to communicate." Since Figure 10.10 provides several specific ideas on oral reading, you may wish to read all of it.

Lesson Procedures Often Used

Most basal-reading lessons follow a fairly similar format. A few new words are introduced before the children read a selection so that these words don't become stumbling blocks during the reading of the selection. (Less and less of this is done, however, as children get older. Such a decrease is designed to encourage older children to rely more and more on context clues and other decoding skills they've learned to use in deciphering new words.) After new words are introduced, the teacher motivates the children to read one or more pages silently. Then she checks and develops their comprehension for those pages. This sequence of motivation, reading, and checking is then continued until the selection has been read in its entirety. Some teachers then have the children reread the selection orally for various purposes. This experience is often followed by a lesson on a decoding or comprehension skill, a workbook assignment, and either some review exercises or some enrichment experience in which children read related material or engage in another type of language-arts experience related to the selection.

As an example of this sequence, let's look at the Houghton Mifflin plan in the Teacher's Guide to *Moonbeams* for the story called "Winifred." Before you examine the plan, though, please keep in mind that this is just one approach. Teachers should definitely vary their approaches according to individual children and materials. See Chapter 11 for other approaches.

1. Summary of the story (written for the teacher only)
2. Introducing New Words: idea, people, either (teacher shows and discusses words and their meanings. See pages 44 to 47 and 54–58 of *Reading as Communication*
3. Setting the scene (". . . The girl in the picture is Winifred. What do you think she is doing? . . . Winifred likes to make things. As you read the story, you will find out what happens when she makes things.")
4. Motivation and Silent Reading ("Look at the picture on page 125. The woman in the picture lives next door to Winifred. Read pages 124, 125, 126, and 127 to yourself to find out about Winifred's problem and what she plans to do about it.")

Oral Reading

Oral reading is a useful and valuable activity that should not be neglected at the intermediate level. Although it is a useful diagnostic tool for the teacher, it is of particular value to students. It can help to develop students' speaking vocabulary, diction, and ability to communicate by making them sensitive to such elements of voice control as stress, pitch, and juncture. Oral reading helps students better understand the relationships between written and oral language and, therefore, helps them become better silent readers; comprehension of material read silently improves when students have internalized the elements of voice control. Students may also discover that reading difficult material aloud to themselves improves their understanding of it. In addition, when students are accustomed to reading orally in a relaxed atmosphere, they respond with confidence when asked to read aloud later in more formal settings. Finally, oral reading gives students a way to share with others the information and pleasure they have received from what they have read silently.

The HOUGHTON MIFFLIN READING PROGRAM provides a variety of oral reading experiences. In some of these experiences, students are concerned with specific techniques. In all the oral reading experiences, however, students are primarily concerned with the most important component of good oral reading: a thorough understanding of the material to be read aloud. Through these experiences students learn that a reader must first have grasped the meaning the author intended and the mood and feeling the author meant to evoke; only then can that reader convey those elements to an audience. Therefore, students must always first read silently any material they will later read aloud to an audience. In directing these various oral reading experiences, the teacher may sometimes engage students in discussions, demonstrations, and practice of specific techniques; chiefly, however, the teacher should focus attention on how a reader can most clearly present the author's message.

In this Teacher's Guide, the simplest and most direct use of oral reading is required as part of the section headed Extending Comprehension. In most units students are asked to find and be prepared to read aloud a passage that supports the answer to a question about the particular selection under discussion. Those students who are not called upon to read should listen to determine if the passage actually does support the answer.

Under the heading Oral Reading, more formal instruction is provided in specific techniques of reading aloud. The teacher leads students in developing standards for oral reading and in applying those standards to passages chosen from selections they have read. Some of the standards deal with the mechanics of oral reading, such as holding a book correctly. Other standards deal with interpretation — how to read specific material. Discussion of the standards should always focus on how they help a reader express to listeners what the author means.

Students listening should not follow the text in their readers but should pay close attention to the person reading and should be prepared to offer helpful comments or alternative interpretations.

Individual experience in oral reading in a true audience situation is provided in three or four units per magazine within the section headed Motivation and Silent Reading. In these units, the reader has prepared for an oral presentation and presents material that is new to the listeners, thereby learning the importance of conveying accurately the ideas, thoughts, and feelings of the author. The listeners have a true purpose for paying attention, since the material is unfamiliar and is related to what they will read silently; they should concentrate on the content rather than on the reader's delivery.

The effectiveness of these individual oral reading experiences depends upon advance preparation by the reader and teacher. In some units, the reader introduces a selection in the students' text by reading the first part of it aloud. In other units, the reader finds and reads aloud material relevant to the text selection, either organizing the material and writing a report or reading directly from a source book. In both cases, the reader must be familiar with the material to be read and must be aware that his or her presentation is meant to motivate the listeners to read the selection. Thorough preparation for the oral reading includes practice in which the teacher hears the student read the material ahead of time to insure that he or she understands it and can pronounce all the words correctly.

When material prepared in advance is to be read aloud by a student during the motivating discussion for a selection, notice is given to the teacher in the Oral Reading section of the preceding unit.

The suggestions for Reading and Language Enrichment found at the end of each unit may also include ideas for reports and projects that require oral reading. These, too, create a situation in which the reader's role is to convey new information to the audience.

The opportunities for oral reading provided in the HOUGHTON MIFFLIN READING PROGRAM by no means exhaust the possibilities. To provide a model for students, the teacher should occasionally read aloud or play recordings of oral reading. In addition, students should be asked, when appropriate, to read aloud such materials as school bulletins, class correspondence, and poems and sections of stories or content area material that they have read independently.

Providing ample and varied experiences in oral reading is an important element of the HOUGHTON MIFFLIN READING PROGRAM. Such experiences help to produce students who read with interest, pleasure, confidence, and the vital understanding that the printed page contains an author's voice.

Figure 10.10. *Sample from a basal reader teacher's guide. William K. Durr et al., Teacher's Guide BEARS. Copyright © 1981 by Houghton Mifflin Company. Reprinted by permission.*

5.   Checking and Developing Comprehension ("What was Winifred's problem? . . . What did the woman next door suggest to Winifred?" etc.)

6.   More Motivation and Silent Reading Followed by Checking and Developing Comprehension
     a. Pages 128–130
     b. Pages 131–134
     c. Pages 135–137

7.   Extending Comprehension (a discussion based on questions at the literal, interpretive, and evaluative/creative levels) after the story has been completed.

8.   Oral Rereading of the Selection (For this story the children are invited to choose parts they liked and to read them aloud. For other stories the children are often asked to scan for information and to read it aloud; or to prove a statement; and so on. Teachers often postpone the oral rereading until a later time or day.

9.   Basic Reading Skill Instruction (Introduction of a decoding or comprehension subskill; this part is usually postponed until a later time in the day or week.)

10. Practice Book (workbook) assignment explained (This usually follows the basic reading skill instruction and provides opportunities both for the children to apply what they've learned and for the teachers to determine which children need more help.)

11. Assessment Test (This is for those teachers using a Skills Management System; see Chapter 11 for further details.)

12. Application and Maintenance Exercises (A review of decoding and comprehension skills previously introduced in the program; often followed by Practice Book assignments. This part is nearly always a separate lesson at a later time.)

13. Reteaching and Enrichment (The reteaching exercises are for those who seem to need additional skill instruction; the enrichment activities provide independent and group experiences designed to enhance children's interest in reading or to develop other language arts skills in listening, writing, and speaking.)

Organizational Plans for Using a Basal-Reading Program

There are numerous ways that teachers and administrators have developed to allow for the variations among children, teachers, space, time, and materials, when using basal readers as the basic medium of reading instruction. It would be difficult to recommend one of these ways over any of the others, since their utility depends so much on the particular conditions of learning in a particular school. Let me simply describe them for you so that you can contribute toward making an intelligent choice of plans in whatever school situation you find yourself.

The Self-Contained Plan

With the self-contained plan, each teacher divides her group of approximately thirty children into two to four (and most often three) reading-instruction groups. This is done after administering informal reading inventories or looking at other information on each child's general reading ability. In a self-contained classroom, the same teacher teaches all of the groups—usually representing the "above-average," the "average," and the "below-average" students in the class. The reading groups meet with the teacher at different times of the day (or week). While one group meets with the teacher, the other groups are working on workbook assignments, reading-enrichment activities (such as library-book reading), or even completing work in another subject such as mathematics. (See Chapter 11 for more information on actual grouping, teaching, and evaluating of students.)

The main advantage of this approach is that one teacher can usually obtain a good understanding, during the entire year, of each child's reading strengths and weaknesses. This is particularly true since she instructs him in most of the other subjects as well. The main disadvantage is that children may be placed in a reading group that is too far above or below their abilities simply to make it more possible for a teacher to manage an instructional program for everyone. For instance, if the general reading range in the class is all the way from Level F to L, and the teacher feels he can only handle three groups, the children in Level L may have to work in materials below their abilities and the children at Level F may have to work in materials above their abilities. (The teacher may decide, for instance, to use the Level K reader for the top group and to have all those children who tested at Levels J, K, and L be included in this group.)

The Joplin Plan

The "Joplin Plan" is sometimes referred to as the "Cross-Grades Plan." Basically the plan goes like this. Instead of one teacher trying to handle three groups of children who are at very different levels, the teachers in a school building all teach reading at the exact same time; each works (during that time only) with children who are reading at about the same level. At nine o'clock, let's say, a bell is rung and all the children go to their reading teacher. For a few children this may mean staying in their homeroom; but for most children, it will mean going to another teacher for forty-five minutes or more. Mrs. Jones may teach only Levels A and B; Miss Franklin may teach only Levels C and D; Mrs. Char may teach only Level E (since so many children are reading at that level); Mr. Webster may teach Level F, G, and H (because there are so few children reading at those levels), and so on, down the halls of the school building. There are many versions of the Joplin plan, but this will give you a rough idea of how it works.

The main advantage of the Joplin Plan is that the range of reading abilities that a single teacher has to face is drastically reduced. The main disadvantage is the potential lack of transfer from reading instruction to actual reading of library books, social-studies texts, and other texts in other subjects. Johnny's reading teacher seldom gets the opportunity to see to it that he practices, in actual reading situations, those skills that she has taught him. Johnny's homeroom teacher, unless she communicates extremely well with his reading teacher, is often not fully aware of Johnny's reading strengths and weaknesses during the time she is having him read materials related to other subjects.

The Track Plan

The "track plan" can be used alongside either the Joplin plan or the self-contained plan. With this approach, the school district makes available to the teacher not just one basal series, but two or three (or in some cases an "advanced form" and an "easy form" of the same series). This is done to increase the flexibility of grouping children. Let's take the extreme situation, for example, in which the teacher wishes to move a child back one or two levels from the one he was in at another school in another city that used the same basal series. In other words, she feels he has been pushed too fast and needs to gain more skills that he's missed along the way. Rather than have the child read exactly the same reader he already read while in the other city, she'll put him, along with a few other children, in another series that he hasn't seen before. As you can well imagine, there are numerous variations of the track system, depending upon the needs of the teachers and children.

The main advantage of the track system, as already mentioned, is the flexibility of grouping that such a system provides. The main disadvantage is that the teacher now has to become familiar with two or three series rather than one. This can be quite a burden, particularly to the beginning teacher; but wherever a particular school population is highly mobile, it may be one of the most reasonable solutions.

The Staggered-Day Plan

Instead of the usual three groups found in most self-contained classrooms, with the staggered-day plan we have the pupils divided into four groups of about six to nine pupils each. Two of these four groups come to school one hour earlier than the other two groups. These twelve to eighteen "early birds" receive instruction in reading until the "late birds" arrive. In the afternoon the early birds leave school one hour before the late birds do. The late birds, who are also divided into two groups, stay behind to receive their instruction in reading.

The main advantage of the staggered-day plan is that the teacher has more time to give individual attention to children in a subject that is so vital. The main disadvantage is that this plan works well only in schools to which children can walk rather than taking a school bus. In "consolidated" schools that ship children in from all over the city, the extra cost of transportation that the staggered-day plan requires can be quite prohibitive.

There are numerous other plans for organizing reading instruction, such as the variety of plans created through team-teaching situations. However, all of them attempt to provide greater individualization of instruction—some through more homogeneous grouping, some by providing greater choice of basal readers, and some by working with fewer children at one time.

Limitations of Basal Reading Programs

Basal-reading programs have two types of defects—one that is inherent in the very idea of a basal reader, and the other in the way that basal readers are sometimes used (or abused). The inherent weakness in basal readers is the idea that children can be best motivated and instructed through a highly systematic, adult-structured set of procedures and materials. There seems to be little doubt among educators that a basal-reading approach can motivate and instruct moderately well, but there are many of us who have nagging doubts about its being the best approach for all children. These doubts are often expressed in the form of questions.

1. Aren't many human beings motivated by the opportunities for making choices? If so, how many choices are we really giving children when we use a basal-reading program? If they had more choices, wouldn't they want to read more—and isn't that what we desire more than anything else?
2. Is there really a definite sequence that children should follow in learning reading skills? The research so far (3, 5) seems to tell us that there is no magic sequence. Programs such as "language experience" and "library-book-individualized," which have no definite sequence, seem to allow children to achieve as well as basal reading programs do.
3. In controlling vocabulary, skill sequence, and content so tightly are we sometimes damaging the very essence of reading—the desire between two individuals, the reader and author, to communicate? If the next thing the reader will communicate about with an author is determined by what comes next in the reader, does that type of conditioning result in students who truly want to read? (It gives one pause.)

The other defect in basal-reading programs is that of their abuse by the teachers who rely on them. Such abuse is not the fault of a program, of course, but it can often lead to a limited degree of success, both for the teacher and his students. Here are two of the ways in which teachers may sometimes find themselves abusing a basal-reading program:

1. By placing a child in a reader that is far too difficult or easy for him. (In defense of the teacher, this is usually done because most teachers find it difficult to handle more than three groups. And thus the dilemma: we can't drive teachers out of their minds in order to place every child in the right reader; yet if we don't place every child in the right reader, we may end up discouraging a large number of children.)
2. By assuming that basal readers teach, when in reality, the teachers have to do most of the teaching (and the children have to do all of the learning). Many teachers, in order to cover so many pages a day will skip a good portion of the skill-building exercises and reviews, as well as the enrichment experiences and the library-book reading that are so important for application and motivation. When "coverage" rather than "mastery" becomes the goal, the basal-reading program becomes both the horse and driver rather than the cart.

Summary

Basal series are the most popular type of instructional material used in our country for teaching reading. They seem to provide teachers, principals, parents, and many children with a sense of purpose and security and are particularly appreciated by those inexperienced teachers who have had little training in how to teach reading. Today's basal-reading programs come close to meeting some very high standards, such as the inclusion of illustrations and content that represent the various ethnic groups, sexes, age groups, and races fairly and without stereotyping. Basal-reading programs have been used with at least a moderate degree of effectiveness by most teachers using them. However, they probably have inherent weaknesses and are also used improperly by those teachers who aim for coverage rather than mastery. In many cases, it would be advisable for teachers to supplement a basal-reader program with a language-experience approach (Chapter 12) and a "library-book-individualized program" (Chapter 13).

References and Suggested Readings

1. Aukerman, Robert C. *The Basal Reader Approach to Reading.* New York: John Wiley and Sons, 1981.

2. Barnard, Douglas P., and DeGracie, James. "Vocabulary Analysis of New Primary Reading Series." *Reading Teacher* 30 (1976): 177–80.

3. Baxter, Katerine B. "Combatting the Influence of Black Stereotypes in Children's Books." *Reading Teacher* 27 (March 1974): 540–4.

4. Bond, Guy L., and Dykstra, Robert. "The Cooperative Research Program in First Grade Reading Instruction." *Reading Research Quarterly* 2 (Summer 1967): 5–142.

5. Britten, Gwyneth E. "Danger: State Adopted Texts may be Hazardous to Our Future." *Reading Teacher* 29 (October 1975): 52–8.

6. Dykstra, Robert. "Summary of the Second-Grade Phase of the Cooperative Research Program in Primary Reading Instruction." *Reading Research Quarterly* 1 (Fall 1968): 49–70.

7. Ernst, S. B. *An Investigation of Students' Interpretations of Inclusionary and Exclusionary Gender Generic Language.* Ph.D. dissertation, Washington State University, 1977.

8. Frasher, Romona, and Walker, Annabelle. "Sex Roles in Early Reading Textbooks." *Reading Teacher* 25 (May 1972): 741–9.

9. Graebner, Dianne Bennett. "A Decade of Sexism in Readers." *Reading Teacher* 26 (October 1972): 52–8.

10. Harrison, L. "Crow-Magnon Woman—in Eclipse." *Science Teacher* 42 (April 1975): 8–11.

11. Heinrich, June S. "Elementary Oral Reading: Methods and Materials." *Reading Teacher* 30 (1976): 10–15.

12. Kidd, V. "A Study of the Images Produced through the Use of the Male Pronoun as the Generic." *Moments in Contemporary Rhetoric and Communication* 1 (Fall 1971): 25–9.

13. Litcher, J. H., and Johnson, D. W. "Changes in Attitudes towards Negroes of White Elementary Students after use of Multiethnic Readers." *Journal of Educational Psychology* 60 (1969): 148–52.

14. Meisel, Stephen, and Glass, Gerald G. "Voluntary Reading Interests and the Interest Content of Basal Readers." *Reading Teacher* 23 (April 1970): 655–9.

15. Miller, Harry B., and Hering, Steve. "Teacher's Ratings—Which Reading Group Is Number One?" *Reading Teacher* 28 (January 1974): 389–91.

16. National Council for Teachers of English. *Classroom Practices in Teaching English, 1976–1977: Responses to Sexism.* Urbana, IL: National CTE, 1977.

17. National Education Association. *Sex Role Stereotyping in the Schools.* Washington, DC: National Education Association, 1977.

18. O'Donnel, Holly. "Cultural Bias: a Many Headed Monster." *Elementary English* 51 (February 1974): 181–9.

19. Parker, Lenore D., and Campbell, Ellen K. "A Look at Illustrations in Multi-Racial First Grade Readers." *Elementary English* 48 (January 1971): 67–74.

20. Rose, Cynthia, et al. "Content Counts: Children have Preferences in Reading Textbook Stories." *Elementary English* 49 (January 1972): 14–19.

21. Rowell, E. H. "Do Elementary Students Read Better Orally or Silently?" *Reading Teacher* 29 (1976): 367–70.

22. Rubin, Rosalyn A. "Reading Ability and Assigned Materials: Accommodation for the Slow but not the Accelerated." *Elementary School Journal* 75 (1975): 373–7.

23. Schreiner, Robert, and Tanner, Linda R. "What History Says about Teaching Reading." *Reading Teacher* 29 (1976): 468–73.

24. Stauffer, Russell G. "Slave, Puppet or Teacher?" *Reading Teacher* 25 (1971): 24–9.

25. Walker, Charles Monroe. "High Frequency Word List for Grades 3–9." *Reading Teacher* 32 (April 1979): 803–12.

Application Experiences for the Teacher-Education Class

1. Each person in the class can be given one of the following statements to defend or deny. After a few minutes of preparation, all those who have statement a. should first explain in their own words why it is either true or false and then read one or two sentences from the book that will demonstrate the author's position on the statements. (The same procedure can be followed for the rest of the statements.)

Statements about Chapter 10

   a. Publishers today control the vocabulary in basal readers by using high-frequency words at first and then gradually switching to irregular words.
   b. Children in grade one usually work with a Level A reader; in grade two, Level B; and so on.
   c. A basal-reading program usually consists of a set of readers and a set of workbooks.
   d. The illustrations and content of a basal reader should represent different ethnic, age, and racial groups fairly and without stereotyping.
   e. Sexual stereotyping in basal readers has very little to do with mental health.
   f. The image of "woman as mother" has been the dominant image in children's books.
   g. An author should never try to be authentic in describing characters and settings.
   h. The book entitled *Charlotte's Web* by E. B. White is one that illustrates the criterion of nonracism.
   i. Whereas basal-series authors used to place a primary emphasis on visual memory as a decoding device, today's authors tend to place an emphasis on contextual analysis and phonics.
   j. Most basal series today emphasize literal thinking at the primary grades and higher-level thinking at the intermediate and junior-high grades.

k.   During oral-reading experiences, teachers should interrupt a child whenever she misses a word and help her sound it out.

l.   Having children read orally with an emphasis on stress, pitch, juncture (pauses), and diction can do very little toward helping them read silently.

m.   When children read orally they should not read silently first.

n.   With the Joplin plan, the same teacher teaches all of the groups, usually representing the above-average, average, and below-average students in the class.

o.   With the "track" plan, two of four groups come to school one hour earlier than the other two groups.

p.   The only limitations of a basal-reader program are those which the teacher places on it.

2.   With a small group examine an up-to-date basal-reading program. Discuss the series in your small group in terms of the seven criteria listed on page 280. Then report on your findings to the rest of the class. Read or show examples to them.

3.   With a small group compare a few Teacher's Guides from a modern basal series with a few from an old basal series. What differences do you notice in terms of the seven criteria on page 280? Report on these differences to the rest of the class.

4.   With a small group compare the "male" vs. "female" words (see page 281) between two or more basal series. To do this, select two or three pages from each reader for your count; limit your count to *he* vs. *she*, *her* vs. *him*, and male nouns vs. female nouns (such as *father, mother, Jane, John, uncle, aunt, boy, girl, woman, man* combined). Be sure to count the total words on each page as well, so you can compare percentages rather than frequencies, e.g., 40 male nouns divided by 1000 total words equals 4 percent; 20 female nouns divided by 1000 equals 2 percent. Report on your findings to the rest of the class.

Field Experiences in the Elementary-School Classroom

1.   Teach a lesson by using the Teacher's Guide to a basal reader. In what ways did the guide limit you or your students? In what ways would you modify the lesson next time? In what ways did the guide help you?

2.   Try planning and teaching your own lesson related to a selection in a basal reader. Do not look at the Teacher's Guide until after you have taught the lesson. How was your lesson similar and different? What did you lose by creating your own? What did you gain?

CHAPTER 11

A skills management system can't measure how well a child integrates the various subskills, appreciates the author's manner of speaking, or enjoys thinking creatively about what the author has said.

Using a Performance-Based Approach

Chapter Preview

A "performance-based approach" is not exactly a teaching method. It's a way of determining how well your students are learning the skills and concepts you are teaching them. It's also a way of thinking about the effectiveness of your teaching. By using a performance-based approach, you will be concentrating on three things. 1) What specific type of behavior or performance of the child should you observe in order to determine how effective your teaching was and how well each child has learned from that teaching? 2) What type of evaluation conditions will help you observe the child perform? 3) How well does the child have to perform in order for you to be satisfied that she has learned what you taught?

Since human beings can't read minds as well as we can, they sometimes rely on a special type of observation called "the performance based approach."

Nature and Limitations of Performance-Based Approaches

In essence all performance-based approaches consist of procedures for testing and feedback. The feedback, when the procedures are working well, is immediate and specific, and is provided both to the teachers and to the students. Such feedback tells the students how well they have learned and tells the teachers how well they have taught.

Such a testing-feedback system, often referred to as a "skills-management system" or an "SMS," can be quite helpful when the learning consists of single isolated subskills, such as "decoding the cluster *qu*" or "finding the main idea through key sentences." This is because tests that will objectively measure such simple abilities can easily be devised. An SMS (skills-management system), however, won't be as useful in measuring more holistic concerns such as "showing genuine interest in reading for information and pleasure" or "integrating various subskills in order to communicate with the author." This is because tests can't be easily devised to measure such complex abilities and attitudes objectively.

The fact that the usefulness of a performance-based approach is limited should not keep us from taking advantage of what utility it does have. As teachers of reading, we have little choice but to spend at least part of our instructional time teaching specific subskills (as well as subconcepts such as *consonant, word,* and *sentence*). In this sense we are slightly similar to bowling instructors who must show their students how to perform the specific subskills of "taking your steps," "gripping the ball," "swinging the ball," and "placing the ball," before helping students learn how to integrate the subskills. A bowling instructor could teach by simply saying, "Here's how you do it," and then demonstrating the procedures as one integrated skill. But many of his students would have trouble learning this way. Imagine how difficult it would be for children to learn to read this way! The number of variables for them to observe and imitate would be beyond most of them. Because of the great amount of time that we must spend on the teaching of specific subskills and subconcepts, we need an efficient means of evaluating and recording children's progress in learning them.

Components of a Skills-Management System

Most skills-management systems have these components: 1) a set of ten to fifty performance objectives per reading level, 2) a checklist for recording each child's performance on each objective, 3) one or more assessment tests on each objective, 4) survey retention tests, and 5) placement tests. To illustrate these five components, let's look at the same basal-reading program we examined in Chapter 10: the Houghton Mifflin Reading Program. As suggested in the last chapter, you probably should examine other programs to notice the similarities and differences.

In the Houghton Mifflin Program the performance objectives are placed, in a highly abbreviated form, on a checklist called a "Cumulative Individual Reading Record Folder." For example, on the checklist is the objective "following directions"; followed by a *criterion score* (minimum acceptable score) of 4. By looking at the actual test (Figure 11.1) we can tell what this abbreviated performance objective really represents. The child is given a sheet of paper with a park scene depicted on it. Included in the picture are some fish, a dog wearing a hat, a duck in a chair, a frog wearing a hat, a bear wearing a hat, and a duck in a pond. The teacher simply asks the children to read the directions to themselves and then checks to see that they understand. The directions include putting an *R* on the hat of the frog, an *M* on the duck by the bear, and so on. Since the child has five different directions to follow, and the criterion score is 4, we can assume that the performance standard is four out of five, or 80 percent. Here's what this would look like, then, as a nonabbreviated performance objective:

★ Put an **X** on one of the fish.

1. Put an **R** on the hat of the frog.
2. Put an **O** on the hat of the dog.
3. Put an **A** on the hat of the bear.
4. Put an **X** on the duck in the chair.
5. Put an **M** on the duck by the bear.

UNIT 2   SKILL CA1·2

Number Correct _____

STOP

5

Figure 11.1.   Sample test. (From Joseph Brzeinski and Hugh Schoe-phoerster, Test Manual: Moonbeams, Boston: Houghton Mifflin, 1981, p. 5.)

Given a picture of several objects and written directions to follow, the child can write a specified letter on each of five objects with 80 percent accuracy.

Some reading programs include both a list of nonabbreviated performance objectives and the abbreviated ones on a checklist. Many school districts create their own list of nonabbreviated performance objectives when the basal series they are using does not provide one. The main advantage of such a list is that the teacher and other interested adults can determine precisely what ability has been tested. There is a tendency otherwise to fool oneself into thinking that children can do more than what a test actually measures. If the checklist only says "following directions," for instance, one may be fooled into thinking that Jacob has demonstrated that he can follow any directions. In reality, Jacob has only demonstrated that he can follow one very simple and specific form of direction. Such a skill as "following directions" needs to be applied, retaught, and applied again in a great variety of situations before you can conclude that Jacob has learned it.

For the Houghton Mifflin Level F reader called *Moonbeams,* the checklist includes twenty abbreviated performance objectives. By examining these, you can see the types of performance objectives that a teacher is expected to help children meet at one reading level. (The criterion scores have been omitted.)

1. Categorizing
2. Following directions
3. Short *o* sound
4. Long *o* sound
5. Predicting outcomes
6. Ending *en,* (n)
7. Commas in a series
8. Apostrophe: possessive
9. Word referents
10. Sound association
11. Changing *y* to *i* before endings
12. Sound association for *z*
13. Multi-meaning words
14. Short and long *u* sounds
15. Cause-effect relationships
16. Sound associations for *qu, squ*
17. Main idea
18. The vowels *o* and *u*
19. Reviewing the alphabet
20. Noting important details

To give you an idea of the type of tests used to measure children's progress in meeting these objectives, look at Figure 11.2, which shows a Houghton Mifflin test on "Categorizing" (performance objective #1).

B TEST ONE
Categorizing

★ Put an X by the ones that can sleep.

X dog   X boy   ______ paint   X girl

1. Put an X by the ones that have feet.

X bear   X tiger   ______ rock   X dog

2. Put an X by the things you can find in a school.

______ home   X book   X door   X floor

3. Put an X by the things you can do.

X follow   ______ chair   X help   X think

4. Put an X by the things you can eat.

______ door   X cake   X bread   X fish

5. Put an X by the things you can put on.

X coat   ______ feet   X hat   X shorts

STOP

UNIT 1   SKILL CA10•2   Number Correct ______

4

Figure 11.2. ***Sample test. (From Joseph Brzeinski and Hugh Schoephoerster,*** **Test Manual: Moonbeams,** ***Boston: Houghton Mifflin, 1981, p. 4.)***

Types of Tests Used in a Skills-Management System

The normal testing sequence for the Houghton Mifflin Program is similar to that of most (but not all) other basal programs. At the beginning of the school year, the teacher administers one or more placement tests to all those children whose reading level has not yet been determined. Houghton Mifflin provides both a group test and an individual test for this purpose. The group test is called the *Vocabulary and Skills Inventory* (VSI) and the individual test is called the *Informal Reading Inventory* (IRI). The VSI attempts to place children by providing test items on specific reading subskills and vocabulary. The IRI attempts to place children by having them read selections at a variety of levels. Some teachers rely on VSI at the beginning of the year and use the IRI only for children coming into the classroom later in the year. Some teachers use only the IRI. Others use both.

Once children are placed, teaching the basal-reading units can begin. A unit usually consists of one lesson involving the guided silent and oral reading of a selection in the reader, one lesson on a reading subskill, and one lesson of reteaching or enrichment. After each unit, an "Assessment Test" (in worksheet format) may be given. Those children who don't do well enough on this test are then given extra instruction. Then a parallel form of the Assessment Test can be administered.

After several units have been completed, a retention test called the *Tests of Basic Reading Skills* can be administered. This is a much longer test than an "Assessment Test" and covers all of the subskills covered in the previous several units. Weaknesses discovered through the use of this test are remedied before moving on to the next unit.

At three separate times during the completion of Levels D through J, children may be administered one of the forms of the *Phonic Inventory*. This inventory is designed to assess each student's mastery of grapheme-phoneme associations. A special set of *Survey and Diagnostic Tests* may also be used following the completion of Level A, *Getting Reading to Read*. The Survey Test assesses what children have learned from the Level A materials and instruction. The Diagnostic Test is given only to those children who do not score at a specified level on the Survey Test.

With some basal-reading programs, such as the HBJ Bookmark Reading Program published by Harcourt Brace Jovanovich, a test may be administered to survey the major skills taught during an entire level. Figure 11.3, for instance, shows one of the eight parts of the "Cumulative Test" for Level Nine. As you can see, this part—Part 3—relates to decoding skills. Figure 11.4 shows Part 4, which relates to comprehension skills.

Read each sentence. Draw a line under the word that makes sense in each sentence. The word must have the sound you hear at the beginning of <u>girl</u> or the sound you hear at the beginning of <u>faint</u>.

Do you like to read about _____?	whales	<u>ghosts</u>	give
A scream is a _____ sound.	terrible	gold	<u>ghastly</u>
The monkey rode in on an _____.	<u>elephant</u>	ox	atmosphere
Do you have _____ milk?	laugh	<u>enough</u>	more
That was a very _____ job.	<u>tough</u>	cough	easy

Draw a line under the two words in each box that have the same vowel sound.

<u>suit</u>	<u>hook</u>	floor	<u>good</u>
<u>blew</u>	<u>should</u>	<u>fool</u>	shout
show	shot	<u>true</u>	<u>would</u>

Read each sentence. Draw a line under the word that makes sense in each sentence. The word must have the same vowel sound as <u>now</u> or the same vowel sound as <u>voice</u>.

The child played with a new _____.	voyage	<u>toy</u>	ball
She got lost in the _____.	<u>crowd</u>	woods	cloud
I will _____ the show.	<u>enjoy</u>	watch	coin
They left the city, heading _____.	sound	<u>south</u>	west

Draw a line under the two words in each row that rhyme with the dark word at the beginning.

go	<u>though</u>	cow	<u>know</u>	through
lie	away	<u>sigh</u>	see	<u>buy</u>
late	heat	feet	<u>freight</u>	<u>wait</u>
care	deer	<u>air</u>	<u>wear</u>	fear

Copyright © 1979 by Harcourt Brace Jovanovich, Inc.
All rights reserved

Figure 11.3. *Sample Test. (From Maurine A. Fry and Jerry D. Harris,* Teacher's Edition: Cumulative Tests, Levels 8 and 9, *New York: Harcourt Brace Jovanovich, 1979, p. 19.)*

Read each selection below. Then draw a line under the reason why each was written.

Turtles belong to the same family as snakes and lizards. Like snakes and lizards, turtles are cold-blooded. This means that they have no way to heat their own blood. Rather, turtles become hot or cold like their surroundings.

But a turtle's shell makes it different from snakes and lizards. Some turtles' shells are like big rocks, and some look like worn leather.

to help us picture a scene
<u>to tell us something true</u>
to tell us a make-believe story
to make us think about a
serious problem

When Tommy opened his eyes after sneezing, he saw a big, gray elephant. "You call that a sneeze?" asked the elephant. "With my long trunk, I can show you a real sneeze. Ah . . . chooo!" Suddenly Tommy felt himself flying through the air. He landed in the next town. "You call that flying?" asked a bird. "Watch this!"

to help us picture a scene
<u>to tell us something true</u>
to tell us a make-believe story
to make us think about a
serious problem

Number the sentences in each box from 1 through 3 to show the order in which they took place.

_2_ When summer came, Maria took a long trip on the bus to get there.

_3_ Her uncle met her at the bus station.

_1_ Maria's uncle wrote to her and invited her to visit his farm.

_3_ Now Ben was ready to listen to his teacher and to work hard at his lessons.

_2_ Ben walked into the building for the first day of school.

_1_ Before he left for school, Ben ate an egg and a roll.

Copyright © 1979 by Harcourt Brace Jovanovich, Inc.
All rights reserved

20 Part score — Comprehension: _____ out of 8   4

Figure 11.4. *Sample test. (From Maurine A. Fry and Jerry D. Harris,* **Teacher's Edition: Cumulative Tests, Levels 8 and 9, New York: Harcourt Brace Jovanovich, 1979, p. 20.)**

Other Skills-Management Systems

Most of the basal-reading programs now include some type of skills-management system. However, there are also systems that a school district may purchase that are not directly connected to a basal-reading program. One of these systems is the "Wisconsin Design for Reading-Skill Development" published by National Computer Systems (6). There are approximately 300 subskills included in the "Wisconsin Design" with performance objectives written for each skill. Assessment is carried on both by teacher observation and by worksheet-type tests of twelve to twenty-five items. "Pupil Profile Cards" that may be punched by the teacher are used for purposes of keeping a record of each child's progress. As described by one of the authors, these punch cards are highly useful in forming groups for specific instruction:

> . . . As students demonstrate mastery of the respective skills, a special notcher is used to open the hole next to the identified skills. Thus when teachers are ready to group their students for skill instruction, they simply set the cards on their edge, pick the skill they want to teach, run a skewer through the appropriate hole, and lift the cards. Cards having the hole notched open, fall from the skewer; those that are not notched (representing students needing skill instruction) remain on the skewer . . . (5, p. 63).

A "Teacher's Resource File" provides ideas to the teacher on how to teach the various subskills.

Another SMS that is independent of a specific basal-reading program is the "Fountain Valley Teacher Support System in Reading" published by Richard L. Zweig Associates (2). There are over 350 specific subskills in this system. With this system, testing directions are provided on cassette so that the students may administer and even score their own tests. A checklist called the "Continuous Pupil Progress Profile in Reading Folder" is used to keep track of each student's progress in developing specific skills. A list of commercial teaching materials, cross-referenced to the subskills is also provided to the teacher, thus assisting him in finding ideas for teaching each skill.

A third SMS that is independent of a particular basal-reading program is the "Prescriptive Reading Inventory (PRI)," published by McGraw-Hill (7). A set of ninety subskills and corresponding performance objectives is provided to the teacher. In order to group students with this system, the teacher administers several tests that are sent off to the publisher for machine scoring and the results stored in computer banks. Computer-printed profiles on each student are then sent back to the teacher in order to help her make decisions on grouping. These profiles take the place of the usual checklist and look very much like the usual checklist used in basal-reading programs. If the child has mastered a particular skill, the computer prints a +; if review is recommended, the computer prints an R; for nonmastery, the computer prints a −. Another printout tells the teacher which children may be grouped for work on the various skills. For assistance in instruction, a list of commercially available teaching materials is provided to the teacher.

A Skills-Management System in Operation

Mrs. Randolph teaches second grade in a self-contained classroom. Her school district has purchased the Houghton Mifflin Reading Program, and she and her students will be using it for the first time. During the first week of school, she uses the two types of placement tests provided by Houghton Mifflin. First she administers the group test called the *Vocabulary and Skills Inventory* (VSI). Although many teachers use only the VSI for placement purposes, Mrs. Randolph decides to administer the individual test called the *Informal Reading Inventory* (IRI), as well. "This way," she says, "I can be much more sure of placing each child in the right book." (She plans to rely exclusively on the IRI for children coming into her class later in the year after the group test has already been administered.) This is what Mrs. Randolph finds:

- Level A. . . .2 children
- Level B. . . .4
- Level C. . . .3
- Level D. . . .3
- Level E. . . .2
- Level F 5
- Level G. . . .4
- Level H. . . .2
- Level I 2

Mrs. Randolph is distressed at such a wide range but finds that there's nothing she can do about it. The other two second-grade teachers, as well as the principal, like the self-contained approach toward teaching reading and prefer not to use some kind of Joplin plan. Her principal tells her that next year, after they've been in the program for a year, he'll assign children to teachers on the basis of Houghton Mifflin Reading levels and "narrow the range" for each teacher. But for this year, she'll have to do the best she can. Here's what she decides to do:

1. Administer the *Survey and Diagnostic Tests for Getting Reading to Read* to the six children in Levels A and B. The Survey Test, you

may remember, is designed to assess the main skills that children are to learn at Level A of the Houghton Mifflin program. The Diagnostic Test is given to those children who score too low on the survey test. Mrs. Randolph finds that three of the children need to take the Diagnostic Test.

2.   Place all six children in the Level B reader but give additional help to those children who had to take the Diagnostic Test, using the information from the Diagnostic Test to determine the special help they need.

3.   Administer the *Tests of Basic Reading Skills* for Level C to the eight children at Levels C, D, and E. (This test would normally be given upon completion of the Level C reader.) Mrs. Randolph finds that three of the eight children are lacking some skills normally taught at Level C.

4.   Place all eight of the children in the Level D reader but give additional help to those three children who had difficulty with *The Tests of Basic Reading Skills* for Level C.

5.   Place the five children at Level F and the four children at Level G in the Level F reader.

6.   Place the two children at Level H and the two children at Level I in the Level H reader.

By skillfully using the various tests provided in a skills-management system, Mrs. Randolph has brought order out of chaos. Although her placement tests showed that she had children reading at nine different levels, she now has only four reading groups, a far more manageable number. She also knows the specific deficiencies that several individuals need to have remedied.

Mrs. Randolph's situation was discussed only as an illustration. No two teachers will have the same management situation. And even Mrs. Randolph's situation will change as the year passes. A new child or two may join her class later in the year. Some of the children may need to be reassigned to a different group because of very rapid or very slow progress. Others may need to be challenged through more library-book reading.

Other Ways of Individualizing through a Performance-Based Approach

Some teachers use a language-experience approach to reading instruction, in which children write or dictate most of their own reading material. Some use an individualized reading program, in which the major reading material for children is comprised of library books. Both of these approaches lend themselves to a moderate use of a skills-management system. By using the SMS provided by either a basal-reader publisher or another publisher, the teacher can utilize the tests for determining children's strengths and weaknesses and for practice exercises as well. The use of an SMS with these two approaches is discussed in more detail in Chapters 12 and 13.

When using a basal series, however, there are also a variety of ways of using an SMS. We have already described one approach illustrated by Mrs. Randolph's situation. Another approach is that of having two types of groups: basal reader groups and skill groups. The basal-reader groups are based on placement tests and remain fairly stable all year long. The skill groups, on the other hand, are based on specific deficiencies ascertained through diagnostic tests and change approximately every two weeks, depending on who needs what kind of help.

With this type of skills-group approach, the teacher might meet with the basal-reader groups twice a week, let's say, twice a week with the skills groups, and once a week with individuals who are having very special problems. While working with the basal-reading groups, she would concentrate on helping them communicate with the authors, emphasizing the integration of comprehension and decoding skills in order to understand and appreciate what each author has to say. While working with the skills groups, she would concentrate on those isolated decoding and comprehension skills that diagnostic tests indicate need more development. (See Table 11.1).

Table 11.1   Schedules for Combining Basal Reader Groups and Skill Groups*

A. Sample Schedule

Time	Monday	Tuesday	Wednesday	Thursday	Friday
8:50 to 9:00	Teacher explains what groups will be doing; also explains specific assignments.				
9:00 to 9:20	Level G basal	Skill Group 1	Level G basal	Skill Group 1	Special-help group
9:20 to 9:40	Level H basal	Skill Group 2	Level H basal	Skill Group 2	Library-book sharing
9:40 to 10:00	Level I basal	Skill Group 3	Level I basal	Skill Group 3	Library-book sharing

B. Detailed Schedule

Monday
  9:00 to 9:20   Level G basal group has guided silent and oral reading with teacher
                  Level H basal group reads their basal-reader selection independently
                  Level I basal group reads library books
  9:20 to 9:40   Level G . . . library books
                  Level H . . . discusses with teacher the basal selection just read
                  Level I . . . reads their basal-reader selection independently
  9:40 to 10:00   Level G . . . enrichment worksheets or activities (suggested by teacher's guide)
                  Level H . . . library books
                  Level I . . . discusses with teacher the basal selection just read

Tuesday
  9:00 to 9:20   Skill Group #1 meets with teacher for new skills lesson
                  Skill Group #2 works on review-type worksheets or activities
                  Skill Group #3 goes to learning centers in the room with games and activities
                  centered around skills previously taught by the teacher

continued

Table 11.1— continued

B. Detailed Schedule

9:20 to 9:40	Skill Group #1 works on "follow-up" worksheets, tests, or activities
	Skill Group #2 meets with teacher for new skills lesson
	Skill Group #3 works on review-type worksheets or activities
9:40 to 10:00	Skill Group #1 goes to learning centers
	Skill Group #2 works on follow-up worksheets, tests, or activities
	Skill Group #3 meets with teacher for new skills lesson

Wednesday

9:00 to 9:20	Level G reads basal selection independently
	Level H has guided reading with teacher
	Level I reads library books or works on book projects
9:20 to 9:40	Level G discusses with teacher the basal selection just read
	Level H reads library books or works on book projects
	Level I works on enrichment worksheets or activities
9:40 to 10:00	Level G reads library books or works on book projects
	Level H works on enrichment worksheets or activities
	Level I has guided reading with teacher

Thursday

9:00 to 9:20	Skill Group #1 . . . review-type worksheets or activities
	Skill Group #2 . . . checks worksheets and other previous work with teacher
	Skill Group #3 . . . follow-up worksheets, tests, or activities related to Tuesday
9:20 to 9:40	Skill Group #1 . . . library books or book projects
	Skill Group #2 . . . learning centers
	Skill Group #3 . . . checks previous work with teacher
9:40 to 10:00	Skill Group #1 . . . checks previous work with teacher
	Skill Group #2 . . . library books or book projects
	Skill Group #3 . . . library books or book projects

Friday

9:00 to 9:20	Teacher meets with "special-help group" (which changes from week to week)
9:20 to 10:00	Children share their books and book projects

*Note: A skill group may include children from different basal-reader levels.

The diagnostic tests used for this approach may include long-range tests, such as the *Vocabulary and Skills Inventory (VSI),* the *Survey and Diagnostic Tests,* and the *Phonics Inventory* provided by the Houghton Mifflin Company. Diagnostic tests may also include the retention tests that are normally used at the end of several units, such as Houghton Mifflin's *Tests of Basic Reading Skills.* And it may include other tests purchased from other companies. In any case, a progress checklist is usually used in conjunction with the diagnostic tests. See Figure 11.5 for an example of this.

Lesson plans for skills groups are developed through the use of teacher's guides for basal readers, through the teacher's own creative planning, and through the use of basal series short-range assessment tests as worksheets and instructional guides.

One skill group for two weeks, for example, may include Janice, Donald, Fred, Marge, Susan, and Billy, all of whom are having difficulty decoding the long vowel graphemes *ea, oa,* and *ai.* Ten children are having trouble detecting main ideas and are placed in

B: BEARS

Date

Word Recognition	Form A CS	Form B	TBRS CS
Word Recognition			12
1. Digraph *th* D1·7b	4		4
2. Following Directions CA1·1	4		4
* 3. Comma of Address C4·2a			
4. End Sounds *l, t* D1·7c	4		4
5. End Sounds *n, p* D1·7c	4		4
6. Letter Sounds & Context D1·7	3		4
7. Digraph *sh* D1·7b	4		4
8. Word Referents C3·1a	3		4
* 9. Exclamation Mark C4·1c			
10. Cluster *fr* D1·7d	3		4
11. Drawing Conclusions CA5·2	3		4
* 12. Clusters *lp, mp* D1·7e			
* 13. Intonation			
14. Predicting Outcomes CA6·2	2		4
15. Cluster *st* D1·7d, e	3		4
16. Noting Details CA2·1	2		4
17. Categorizing CA10·2	3		4
18. End Sounds *m, d, g* D1·7c	4		4

C: BALLOONS

Date

Word Recognition	Form A CS	Form B	TBRS CS
Word Recognition			12
1. Noting Correct Sequence CA3·3	2		4
* 2. Contractions with *'s* D1·7f			
* 3. Sound Association for *x* D1·7c			
4. Plurals D1·7h	4		4
* 5. Verbs Ending with *s* D1·7g			
6. Clusters *sw, fl* D1·7d	2		4
7. Letter Sounds & Context D1·7	3		4
8. Cause-Effect Relationships CA7·2	2		4
9. Word Referents C3·1a	3		4
10. Main Idea CA4·2	2		4
11. Digraph *ch* D1·7b	4		4

D: BOATS

Date

Word Recognition	Form A CS	Form B	TBRS CS
Word Recognition			12
1. Following Directions CA1·1	3		4
* 2. End Sounds *nt, nk* D1·7e			
* 3. Ending *ing* D1·7g			
4. Digraphs *th, sh, ch* D1·7b	4		4
5. Predicting Outcomes CA6·2	2		4
6. Sound Associations *c/s/* D1·7n	3		4
* 7. Ending *ed* D1·7g			
8. Noting Important Details CA2·1	3		4
9. Clusters *fl, sw, fr, pl* D1·7d	2		4
10. Multi-meaning Words C1·1c	2		4
11. Categorizing CA10·2	2		4
* 12. Reviewing Endings *s, ed, ing* D1·7g			
13. Word Referents C3·1a	3		4
14. Drawing Conclusions CA5·2	3		4

E: SUNSHINE

Magazine 1   Date

Recognizing High-Frequency Words	Form A CS	Form B	TBRS CS
Recognizing High-Frequency Words			12
1. Cause-Effect Relationships CA7·1, 2	2		4
2. Short *a* Sound D1·7l	4		4
3. Long *a* Sound D1·7l	4		4
* 4. Quotation Marks, Comma CA4·8a			
5. Correct Sequence CA3·3	2		4
6. Doubling Consonants Before Endings D1·7j	4		4
7. Sound Associations for *y* D1·7l	2		4
8. Dropping Final *e* Before Endings D1·7j	4		4

Magazine 2   Date

Recognizing High-Frequency Words	Form A CS	Form B	TBRS CS
Recognizing High-Frequency Words			12
* 9. Contractions with *'s, n't, 'll* D1·7f			
10. Sound Associations for *oo* D1·7m	2		4
11. Compound Words D1·7o	2		4
12. Ending *er* D1·7g	2		4
13. Predicting Outcomes CA6·2	2		4
14. Short *e* Sound D1·7l	3		4
15. Long *e* Sound D1·7l	3		4
* 16. Intonation			
17. Sound Associations for *ai, ay* D1·7m	3		4
18. Drawing Conclusions CA5·2	2		4

Magazine 3   Date

Recognizing High-Frequency Words	Form A CS	Form B	TBRS CS
Recognizing High-Frequency Words			12
19. Short *i* Sound D1·7l	3		4
20. Long *i* Sound D1·7l	3		4
* 21. Sound Association for *kn/n* D1·7b			
22. Multi-meaning Words C1·1c	3		4
23. Main Idea CA4·2	2		4
24. Short and Long *a, e,* and *i* D1·7l	4		4

KEY

1. Digraph *th*   D1·7b

↑ Skill Description   ↑ Skill Reference Number

Basic Reading Skill Lesson

**Figure 11.5.   *Sample progress checklist. (From* Cumulative Individual Reading Record Folder, *Boston: Houghton Mifflin, 1981, p. 2.)*

a different skill group for the same two weeks. Two other groups have different problems to work on during the two-week period. At the end of the two-week period, an assessment test is administered to see if any of the children needs special assistance.

As an option to the skills approach just suggested, you may wish to use skills groups only for those who have not reached a criterion score on an assessment or retention test (the assessment test having been given at the end of one unit, the retention test having been given at the end of several units). With this procedure, you would teach the basic skills lesson for a basal-reader unit, give children an assessment test, and then form a small skills group for remedial instruction. The same procedure would be used after administering a retention test. Children in the basal-reader group who do not need remedial-skills instruction are given options of library-book reading or special language-enrichment projects provided by basal-reader publishers.

Developing Your Own Performance-Based Approach

Unfortunately, some teachers and administrators perceive a performance-based approach as a "mere testing program." A more beneficial way of looking at a performance-based approach is to perceive it as a way of thinking about teaching. As teachers we play three distinct but interrelated roles—the planning role, the interacting role, and the evaluating role. We plan what we're going to teach; we interact with children in such a way that they can learn through our teaching procedures; we evaluate our effectiveness as teachers and their progress as students.

The three roles of teaching are cyclical. Suppose, for example, we discover through our evaluator's role that Sarah needs more help on decoding the *oa, ea,* and *ai* digraphs. We would then put on our planning-role hat and plan learning experiences for Sarah that would promise to remedy her deficiency. Next we would play the role of interactor and provide a learning experience for her. While interacting with Sarah we would no doubt be evaluating the effectiveness of the learning experience. Such evaluation often leads to some on-the-spot planning, which would in turn lead to modifications in the way we are interacting with her. At the conclusion of the interaction we would again do some evaluation to see whether we succeeded in teaching her what we wanted to teach. This would lead to further plans—to give her more help on the same problem, or to move her on to another learning situation.

Performance objectives can play a vital part in helping us play the role of evaluator, which in turn will help us improve our planning and interacting roles. By *thinking* in terms of performance objectives, we can remember to ask ourselves: 1) What behavior should we observe in order to find out how effective our planning and interaction have been so far? 2) What would be the best conditions for observing and evaluating this behavior? 3) How well does each child have to perform in order to demonstrate to us that sufficient learning has taken place?

To illustrate the value of performance objectives in teaching reading subskills or subconcepts, let's look at one teacher who thinks in terms of performance objectives and one teacher who doesn't. First, the one who doesn't:

Mr. Garland writes the following words on the board: *hat, hate, fat, fate, hop, hope, rid, ride.* He asks Penny to circle the words that include a long-vowel sound. He then asks Penny how she knew which ones to circle. She replies "I circled the ones that had an *e* at the end." Mr. Garland says, "Right!" Then he asks the entire group of four

There are many ways of individualizing through a perform-ance-based approach.

children whether they understand. They all nod their heads and he sends them back to their seats.

Mrs. Morehouse writes the same eight words on the board but in a more random order: *hat, fat, hate, hop, ride, hope, rid, fate*. She then asks Penny to circle just one of the words that have a long vowel sound and to pronounce the word. Next she asks the other three children to do the same thing one at a time. Then she says: "Look at the words you have circled and make up a rule that will help us remember which words like this usually have a long vowel sound in them." She waits until everyone has his hand up before calling on Janet. Janet gives her rule and receives praise for it. Mrs. Morehouse calls on each of the other children to state their rules. Tommy's is incorrect and she helps him change it by looking again at the words they have circled. Next she gives them a brief worksheet requiring them to match words like *hat* and *ride* with the correct pictures. One child gets less than eight out of ten correct and receives further instruction on an individual basis. Finally, Mrs. Morehouse has them turn to a page in their basal readers and "find all of the one-syllable words with a long vowel." Each child finds one and pronounces it.

Mr. Garland had no performance objectives. He played his role as interactor but neglected to play his role as evaluator. This caused his planning role to be played very poorly. Mr. Garland neglected to ask himself what behavior of each child he should observe in order to find out what the learners understood. He was satisfied with the success of one child—Penny—and the nodding of heads by the others.

Mrs. Morehouse, on the other hand, knew that she wanted each child to do something that would demonstrate her understanding. Therefore, she made sure she had enough words on the board so that each of the four children could circle at least one. She gave each child enough time to think of his own rules. Furthermore, she asked each of them to verbalize a rule. Finally, she gave them all a chance to practice what they had learned by presenting them with a brief worksheet; this worksheet also provided her with an additional opportunity to evaluate the effectiveness of the lesson.

Mrs. Morehouse hadn't written out her performance objectives. She had only thought about them. If she had written them out—a practice that becomes less necessary with experience—here's what they might have looked like:

1. Each child will be able to come to the board and circle a word that probably has a long vowel sound becaue of its VCE pattern.
2. Each child will be able to verbalize, in his own words, a rule for remembering the usual vowel sound in a one-syllable VCE word.
3. Each child will match five VCE words and five VC words to the appropriate picture on a worksheet. At least 8 out of 10 of the matchings will be correct.
4. Each child will find and decode one VCE word on page 78 of their basal reader.

How to Create Performance Objectives

A well-conceived performance objective meets the following four criteria.

1. It is a thought about the behavior of the learner, rather than the teacher.
2. It is a thought about observable behavior, rather than vague and unseen improvement.
3. It includes the precise conditions under which the learner's behavior will be demonstrated and evaluated.
4. It includes the standards for the specific behavior expected (or hoped for) by the teacher.

Practice Exercise 1

Which of the following thoughts meet the first criterion? Check those that are thoughts about the behavior of the learner rather than the teacher.

_____ 1. To teach the children to recognize words containing vowel letters representing a long sound
_____ 2. To be able to circle all of the words containing vowel letters representing a long sound
_____ 3. To write the letters of the alphabet in the correct order
_____ 4. To explain the origin of our alphabet through the use of film
_____ 5. To involve the students in creative drama

Answers for Practice Exercise 1
Numbers 1, 4, and 5 may be noble "aims" but they do not meet the first criterion of a performance objective. They are thoughts about the teacher, rather than the learner. Statements 2 and 3 are not complete performance objectives, but they come closer to being performance objectives than the other three, since they are thoughts about the learner, rather than the teacher.

Practice Exercise 2

Which of the following thoughts meet the second criterion? Check those that are about observable behavior.

_____ 1. To understand the phonic principles involving the long-vowel sound
_____ 2. To circle those words in a list that contain vowel letters representing a long sound
_____ 3. To know the alphabet
_____ 4. To appreciate the value of correct enunciation
_____ 5. To read out loud from a list of words only those that contain short vowel sounds

Answers for Practice Exercise 2
Numbers 1, 3, and 4 do not meet the second criterion. Although numbers 2 and 5 are not complete performance objectives, they come closer to being performance objectives than the other three, because they indicate the actual behavior that the teacher can observe. The problem with the first one is that the teacher hasn't yet thought of what behavior to look for that will show him that the children do "understand the phonic principles involving the long vowel sound." In the third one, the teacher hasn't yet decided what performance by the children will indicate that they do "know the alphabet." What is the problem with the fourth one?

Practice Exercise 3

Which of the following meet the third criterion? Check those that include the precise conditions under which the learner's behavior will be evaluated.

_____ 1. When given a list of words, each child will be able to circle those on the list that contain vowel letters representing the long sound without first hearing someone pronounce the words.
_____ 2. To be able to circle those words that begin with the letter _b_
_____ 3. Given three weeks of practice, the student will be able to circle words containing vowel letters representing a short sound
_____ 4. To demonstrate his knowledge of the alphabet by numbering a list of words according to alphabetical order
_____ 5. Presented with a list of words and a list of generalizations about the decoding of vowel letters, the student will match the generalizations with the correct words.

Answers for Practice Exercise 3
Numbers 2 and 3 do not meet the third criterion, whereas the other three do. It is true that in the second one the expected behavior is clear: to be able to circle those words that begin with the letter _b_. However, the conditions under which the behavior is to be demonstrated are not clear. Will the words be in list form or embedded in sentences? Will the words be pronounced by the teacher or will the student have to pronounce them for himself? In the third one it is true that a prior condition is stated: Given three weeks of practice. However, the conditions under which the behavior is now to be demonstrated are not clear. What conditions may have to be established in order to evaluate the behavior?

Practice Exercise 4

Which of the following meet the fourth criterion? Check those that include the standards expected or desired.

_____ 1. To recite the alphabet in correct order within thirty seconds
_____ 2. To read a set of directions to a partner with sufficient clarity to enable him to follow the directions accurately without referring to them again
_____ 3. To review a library book orally with sufficient enthusiasm and clarity that at least one person in the class raises his hand when asked immediately after the review, "Who would like to read the book?"
_____ 4. To read the story in the basal reader starting on page 23 and to do the accompanying worksheet
_____ 5. Given a list of fifteen words, the student will number them in alphabetical order.

Answers for Practice Exercise 4
Numbers 4 and 5 do not meet the fourth criterion, whereas the other three do. Number 4 gives a rough idea of the behavior expected—read the story and do the worksheet—but does not indicate the standards of performance desired. The teacher has not thought about how well she wants students to read the story and how well she expects them to perform on the worksheet. In statement 5 it might be assumed that the student should be able to number the words in alphabetical order with 100-percent accuracy. Generally speaking, though, this is not a realistic goal—for two reasons: 1) because a teacher can usually tell that a child understands an idea even though he does not achieve 100-percent accuracy and 2) it is often impossible to avoid some ambiguity in a "test" situation.

Setting Standards Ahead of Instruction

Whatever degree of accuracy seems reasonable, whether it be 90 percent or only 70 percent, it is probably best to decide upon the minimum acceptable standard ahead of instruction. In this way you will have some way of determining (albeit in an arbitrary way) which children should receive additional instruction after the initial instruction has taken place. Those teachers who have ignored this step often find themselves making statements such as this at the end of a none-too-successful lesson: "Well, some of them didn't understand that too well, but most of them got it." Or they excuse themselves by saying, "They'll get it next year." Of course, next year those children are even further behind.

Recognizing Performance Objectives

Now that you have become familiar with the four criteria of performance objectives, it is time to see if you can differentiate those statements that meet all four criteria from those that do not. Check each of the following statements that you consider to be complete performance objectives; that is, check only those that meet all four criteria. (They need not be "perfectly" written or ones with which you agree.) Some suggested answers can be found at the end of the exercise.

Practice Exercise 5

_____ 1. Given a worksheet with five brief reading selections, each of them followed by four choices, each student will read the selections silently and choose the correct main idea for at least four of five selections. The choice of the main idea will be shown by a check mark.

_____ 2. Given a set of directions, the student will be able to follow them with 100-percent accuracy.

_____ 3. Using a classroom dictionary, the student will, for each word presented orally by the teacher, find the word and write down the correct page number within fifteen seconds.

_____ 4. Each student will pantomime in front of the class something the main character did as described in a library book the student read recently.

_____ 5. Given a written list of statements, some of which are facts and some of which are opinions, the student will be able to recognize all of the statements that are opinions.

_____ 6. After finishing the story in the basal reader, each student will be asked to write another ending—one that fits the rest of the story, the nature of the characters, and the nature of the setting.

_____ 7. Given ten questions on the history of the alphabet, the student will get at least seven of them right.

_____ 8. Given a good night's sleep and a hearty breakfast, each student will do well on the standardized vocabulary test tomorrow.

_____ 9. Okay, now I'd like you, Bill, to pronounce this list of words on the tape recorder; first say the number and then the word. Then I'd like you, Jim, to go back when he's finished and listen to the words. Just number your paper from one to twenty and circle the number of any word you think he didn't pronounce clearly or correctly. Then you two get together and talk about those words that are difficult for Bill. Keep working on them until you think Bill can pronounce all of them correctly.

_____ 10. Given plenty of practice, the student will know the 220 Basic Sight Words with 100-percent accuracy by the end of the year.

Answers for Practice Exercise 5

1. *Check*

2. *No check.* The conditions are not clearly stated. How are the directions to be given—orally or in writing?

3. *Check.* (Note that the standards are stated in terms of both speed and accuracy: 100-percent accuracy is implied by the word "correct" and the phrase "for each word.")

4. *No check.* The performance standards are not stated. To what extent should the pantomime be successfully executed? (For example: "Over half the class indicates an understanding of what event was being pantomimed by raising their hands.")

5. *No check.* What does it mean "to be able to recognize"? What does the student have to do to demonstrate this recognition?

6. *Check.* (Were you fooled on this one? Notice that standards do not have to be thought of just in terms of accuracy or speed. Some performance by students can only be assessed in a qualitative manner.)

7. *No check.* The behavior is not stated; nor are the conditions clear. We know the student should "get" seven out of ten, but what does he do? Are the questions a multiple-choice type or an essay type or what?

8. *No check.* What does it mean to "do well"? The performance standards are not clear. (Incidentally, the conditions under which the behavior is to be performed have been simply stated as "standardized vocabulary test." The extraneous information about sleep and breakfast refers only to prior conditions.)

9. *Check.* (Actually, a complete performance objective—in this case clearly communicated to the learner.)

10. *No check.* What behavior should the student demonstrate to show that he or she knows the words? What are the conditions under which the behavior will be evaluated?

Some Words of Caution about Performance-Based Teaching

The following are suggestions for avoiding some common pitfalls of performance-based approaches:

1. While a performance-based approach is useful for teaching the small, isolated subskills of reading, it cannot help you teach children to read holistically. This can only be done by having them actually use the subskills in harmony. (See pages 145–147 and 174–178 for examples of this.)

2. A teacher should think in terms of both "enabling objectives" and "terminal objectives." If you will look back at page 328, you will notice that Mrs. Morehouse has two enabling objectives: each child has to circle a word with a VCE pattern, and each child has to verbalize a rule for remembering the usual vowel sound in a one-syllable VCE pattern. Also on page 328 you will see that Mrs. Morehouse has two terminal objects: each child has to get

8 out of 10 correct on a worksheet, and each child has to apply what he has learned by finding a VCE word in his basal reader and pronouncing it correctly. (At least one of your terminal objectives should be an application-type objective.)

Summary

The performance-based approach is a means of evaluating the effectiveness of teaching and learning. It is also a way of thinking about the teaching process, consisting of the integration of planning, interaction, and evaluation roles. The SMS or skills-management system is the most popular form of the performance-based approach today and is usually used in connection with a basal-reading program. However, it can be used for other types of programs as well. All performance-based approaches include procedures for testing and feedback. These procedures are highly useful for the teaching of the isolated subskills of reading but are not very appropriate for the holistic concerns related to reading instruction.

References and Suggested Reading

1. Bloom, Benjamin S. et al. *Handbook on Formative and Summative Evaluation of Student Learning.* New York: McGraw-Hill, 1971.
2. *Fountain Valley Teacher Support System in Reading,* Richard L. Zweig Associates, 1971.
3. Johnson, Dale D., and Pearson, P. David. "Skills Management Systems: a Critique." *Reading Teacher* 28 (1975): 757–64.
4. Mager, Robert F. *Preparing Instructional Objectives.* Belmont, CA: Fearon, 1962.
5. Otto, Wayne et al. *How to Teach Reading.* Reading, MA: Addison-Wesley, 1979.
6. Otto, Wayne, and Chester, Robert D. *Objective Based Reading.* Reading, MA: Addison-Wesley, 1976.
7. *Prescriptive Reading Inventory.* New York: CTB/McGraw-Hill, 1972.
8. Proger, Barton B., and Mann, Lester. "Criterion-Referenced Measurement: the World of Grey versus Black and White." *Journal of Learning Disabilities* 6 (1973): 72–84.
9. Rude, Robert T. "Objective-Based Reading Systems: an Evaluation." *Reading Teacher* 28 (1974): 169–75.
10. Thompson, Richard A., and Dziuban, Charles D. "Criterion-Referenced Reading Tests in Perspective." *Reading Teacher* 27 (1973): 292–4.

Application Experiences for the Teacher-Education Classroom

1. Working with a partner, modify the following statements in order to make them agree with what the author said or implied. Change the words in any way you wish.

   Statements about Chapter 11

   a. A performance-based approach has nothing to do with teaching.
   b. When you use a performance-based approach, you must concentrate on what a child knows.
   c. In a performance-based approach, the feedback is given to the teacher, rather than the student.
   d. A skills-management system is used in measuring children's desire to read for information and pleasure and, also, how well they can integrate the subskills of reading in order to communicate with an author.
   e. An SMS includes performance objectives, checklists, and tests.
   f. When a teacher checks "following directions" on Brenda's checklist, this means that Brenda is capable of following directions in most situations.
   g. A unit in a basal-reading program usually includes one lesson involving the selection in the reader, one lesson of reteaching or enrichment, and one period of library-book reading.
   h. A skills-management system is not really useful for individualizing a reading program.
   i. Teachers play three interacting roles—planning, evaluating, and babysitting.
   j. The evaluating role is carried on at the conclusion of a lesson; thus performance objectives are used only then.

2. With a partner or small group, plan a way of using an SMS in connection with the following lesson. Develop specific performance objectives to use for the lesson. Mr. Heideman wishes to teach four children how to decode words whose roots end in y and whose suffixes are *er, est,* and *ed.* For example.

steady	steadier
study	studied
funny	funniest

   Develop a lesson plan that incorporates what you know about skills-management systems and performance objectives. Write out your lesson procedures and any other procedures that you think you should use. Refer to pages 326 to 328 for illustrations. When you have finished, compare yours with those produced by others in the class.

3. With a partner examine the following objectives to see whether they fulfill all the requirements for a complete performance objective. For

each one of the objectives, indicate whether it fulfills all the requirements or indicate what is missing. Circle the letter of the best answer.

a. "Whatever else I do today, I've got to get David to realize how important it is for him to learn to read. If he doesn't learn to read, he'll have trouble all through school."
    1) fulfills all requirements
    2) no clearly observable behavior
    3) no conditions of evaluation
    4) no evaluation standards
    5) 2 and 3
    6) 2 and 4
    7) 3 and 4
    8) 2, 3, and 4

b. Given plenty of practice on phonic analysis, each student will know how to do it with 90-percent accuracy at the end of the year.
    1) fulfills all requirements
    2) no clearly observable behavior
    3) no conditions of evaluation
    4) no evaluation standards
    5) 2 and 3
    6) 2 and 4
    7) 3 and 4
    8) 2, 3, and 4

c. "Look, my objective is just to get those kids to enjoy reading. It's as simple as that. Don't give me that stuff about performance objectives and long-range outcomes. Anyone with half a brain can tell whether or not kids enjoy reading."
    1) fulfills all requirements
    2) no clearly observable behavior
    3) no conditions of evaluation
    4) no evaluation standards
    5) 2 and 3
    6) 2 and 4
    7) 3 and 4
    8) 2, 3, and 4

d. Given a magazine advertisement, the student will be able to state in writing at least two fallacies in the advertiser's argument and justify in writing, to my satisfaction, that the fallacies are indeed fallacies.
    1) fulfills all requirements
    2) no clearly observable behavior
    3) no conditions of evaluation
    4) no evaluation standards
    5) 2 and 3
    6) 2 and 4
    7) 3 and 4
    8) 2, 3, and 4

4. Work with a partner to examine an assessment test or retention test used in connection with a particular basal reader. By examining a spe-

cific subtest carefully (usually consisting of one or two pages) you should be able to decide what performance objective this test actually represents. For example, does the test measure "following directions" in general or does it really measure something much more limited? See pages 313 to 314 for an illustration of this. When you've actually written the performance objective, discuss your objective and test with others in the class.

5. With a partner, develop an assessment test to go along with Application Experience #2.

Field Experiences in the Elementary-School Classroom

1. Examine an SMS checklist for a "good reader" in the classroom. If you were in charge of this child's reading education, on what subskills would you provide special instruction? What special enrichment experiences might you provide this child? Now examine an SMS checklist for a "poor reader." Ask yourself the same two questions. How do you answers differ for the two children? Compare your results with others in your teacher-education class.

2. Administer a brief assessment test on a unit in a basal reader, or a longer retention test on several units. What problems did you or the students have during the administration of the test that may influence the results? If possible, administer a different form of the same test on a later day to the same children. What differences in the results did you find? Why do you think they occurred?

CHAPTER 12

The children keep their own personal word bank at their desks in order to carry on teacher directed activities.

Using Language-Experience Approaches

Chapter Preview

While most elementary-school teachers use one of the basal-reader approaches to teach reading, a growing number are using one of the language-experience approaches either as a substitute or a supplement. Rather than rely upon basal readers as the medium of instruction, they rely as well (or instead) upon the language of their students. Children dictate or write their own reading selections and thereby learn in a practical way that reading is a form of communication and that authors and readers are truly communicators. Teachers use the selections created by their students as instructional material for teaching readiness, decoding, and comprehension subskills. They keep track of children's progress by using a skills-management system or some other form of careful observation.

Human children are sometimes their own best teachers.

Students Who Can Learn from a Language-Experience Approach

There are a variety of types and ages of students who are being taught successfully through a language-experience approach. Many kindergarten teachers use a language-experience approach to get children ready for more formal instruction in first grade. Children in small or large groups dictate their ideas to the teacher, who prints them, exactly as dictated, immediately on the chalkboard or on tagboard charts. The teacher reads the ideas back to the children and then encourages them to "read" (say) the ideas with her, thus getting the kindergarten children used to the idea that printed words can represent spoken words. A left-to-right reading orientation is developed; letter names are taught or reviewed; visual and auditory discrimination are reinforced—all through the use of such "experience charts."

In first grade, such an approach is taken several steps further. Children not only dictate stories, they begin to write their own as well. In addition, they concentrate on learning specific words, phoneme-grapheme relationships, morphemes, and all the decoding and comprehension subskills normally taught in first grade. As the year progresses they read not only their own stories and the stories of their peers, but the stories of adult authors as well. Library books and basal readers become opportunities to apply the communication skills they have gained through creating and reading their own stories and books.

In second grade and later grades, language-experience approaches are used to enrich children's understanding gained through more formal reading instruction, and through the social studies, science, and other areas of the school curriculum. Charts, stories, magazines, newspapers, and books are created by the children as records of what they are learning, experiencing, and feeling. These materials then provide enrichment-reading experiences for the children.

Children who need remedial instruction, at any grade level, can be helped through a language-experience approach. This is especially true of those youngsters in grades three through twelve who have been "turned off" by too many previous experiences with completing worksheets and drilling on subskills. For many remedial readers, a language-experience approach can provide a first glimpse into the real meaning of reading. Tyrone, for example, was a leader of a small "gang" of third-grade boys who hated "readin' and goin' to school." Their teacher decided in desperation to try a language-experience approach. Her husband came to school one morning and gave Tyrone's gang an exhilarating ride around the playground in

There are a variety of types and ages of students who are being taught successfully through a language-experience approach.

his sportscar. When they got back, the teacher took dictation while they excitedly took turns telling her about their adventure. When their story was finished, they read it with the teacher and then proudly to the entire class. For the first time, reading made sense!

Tyrone's teacher duplicated their story so they could take it home to read to their parents. She then formed a special reading group, called appropriately "Tyrone's Gang." This reading group created numerous experience stories, learned many reading skills through the use of the stories, and gradually joined the world of book readers.

Children who do not speak Standard English can be taught at first through a language-experience approach. In this way their own language is not denigrated, but used as the first building block toward learning to read. Since early reading is primarily a matter of translating print into speech, it is highly important that such print represent the way children normally speak. (The use of a language-experience approach in teaching reading to speakers of nonstandard English is discussed in further detail in Chapter 16.)

Rationale and Research Related to Language-Experience Approaches

By now you can probably write your own rationale for the use of a language-experience approach. A language-experience approach utilizes the present language of the child. It does not rely on language created by adults. Thus, the translation of print back into speech (or subvocal thought) is usually natural and meaningful. Furthermore, children quickly learn the most important concept about the reading process: 1) that it involves communication with a person who wrote down his thoughts; 2) that it is not a subject in school, a torturous process of "sounding out" words, or an endless conveyer belt of worksheets and workbook pages. In addition, a language-experience approach does not separate the language arts into separate skill areas of reading, writing, speaking, and listening. All four avenues of language are used in combination in order to take advantage of children's natural desire to communicate. (Some limitations of language-experience approaches will be discussed in a later section.)

A vast majority of the research studies on language-experience approaches have demonstrated that they are as effective as basal-reader approaches and may even have special advantages (8). Perhaps the greatest fear that educators and parents have about the use of a language-experience approach is that children will not gain as much in vocabulary as children being taught through other approaches. Hall summarizes the research on vocabulary this way:

A persistent criticism of language experience instruction is that students may not develop a satisfactory reading vocabulary, since the lack of vocabulary control and the lack of systematic repetition may be detrimental to learning. The research refutes this criticism. Language experience instruction presents learners with meaningful vocabulary, and a reading vocabulary *is* acquired by learners through the use of LEA (8, pp. 27–28).

Others have been afraid that a language experience approach would not expose children to the graphophonic regularities in our language (such as the change in meaning and pronunciation between *can* and *cane* and the consistency in pronunciation of phonograms such as *ill, at,* and *ap*). In a study by Dzama (6), however, it was discovered that the words used by first graders in language-experience programs provided ample examples for learning such regularities. Other studies (2, 5) have shown that LEA students tend to learn graphophonic decoding skills about as well as those students in basal programs. Furthermore, studies (3) have shown, not surprisingly, that LEA students usually become better spellers than students taught by a basal approach.

A Word of Caution

If a language-experience approach works so well, why aren't the majority of elementary-school teachers using it for teaching reading? Probably for three reasons: 1) because it has only recently been seriously advocated in textbooks and courses on the teaching of reading (10); 2) because of the fear that some teachers and principals have of public criticism for not using a more "systematic" basal approach; and 3) because it takes a lot more skill and work to teach reading this way than it does with basal-reading programs. With a language-experience approach, the teacher must do one-hundred percent of the daily planning. With a basal-reader approach, the teacher is given a big assist by the Teacher's Guide.

Because it is such an important approach, however, an increasing number of teachers and principals are accepting the idea of using it, at least as a supplementary procedure (14). Techniques of using a language-experience approach in this way will be discussed in a later section. Right now, let's look at some actual procedures for working with children.

Procedures for Creating Group-Experience Charts

Group-experience charts (or stories) may be created with the entire class on some occasions, such as a field trip to a farm or zoo. But to get every student involved, it is best to develop most experience stories in smaller groups of less than ten children. What this often means in actual practice is that teachers divide the class into about four language-ability groups, based on observations of the children, test results, and comments from other adults who have known the children.

Experience stories are generally created and used in this order:

1. Developing interest in writing a story
2. Discussing the story topic
3. Dictating and writing the story
4. Reading the story created
5. Using the story to teach and learn reading subskills

Steps one through four are completed during the first sitting (of fifteen to thirty minutes). Step five is completed at one or more later sittings.

Developing Interest

This approach, like any other, can become dull and lifeless if the teacher does not concern herself enough with the motivational principles discussed in Chapter 8. The experiences and topics selected by the teacher, and the procedures she uses in communicating about them, should be planned in terms of providing novelty, meeting basic needs, fitting the level of difficulty appropriate for the children, and providing specific and immediate feedback. To be successful in using a language-experience approach, it is extremely important that the teacher plan stimulating experiences and topics for children to "write" about.

The following is a list of sample experiences and topics:

1. The hamster in our classroom
2. What things are blue?
3. Our biggest wishes
4. What we like to do after school
5. The movie we saw about stars
6. The experiment we did about air
7. How it would feel to be a balloon
8. Halloween is coming!
9. What we think of ghosts
10. What teachers do
11. What parents do
12. Our favorite foods
13. Our trip to the supermarket
14. What makes us mad
15. How yesterday is different from tomorrow
16. How here is different from there

17. What we do on the playground
18. What it might be like to be deaf
19. *Mike Mulligan and His Steam Shovel*
20. A daydream we just had

This is just a tiny sample of the possibilities for experience stories. You may wish to examine the *Peabody Language Development Kits* by Dunn and Smith (4), as well as Van Allen's *Language Experiences in Reading* (16), and Hall's *Teaching Reading as a Language Experience* (7). All contain numerous ideas for language-experience activities.

Discussing the Story Topic

Some teachers get in a hurry when using an LEA and have children start dictating or writing too soon. In most cases it works much better to have a general discussion of the topic or experience before writing about it. Such a discussion usually gets the ideas flowing, as one thought stimulates another. Research on creativity (15) shows that this type of verbal stimulation before compositions are expected can actually produce more creative and longer compositions than you would get by simply having the children write or dictate without discussion. Teachers often worry that a discussion will lead to everyone's saying or writing the same thing when it comes time to producing the actual story. Some of this "copycat" behavior will occur, it's true, but this is far better than having several children not communicate at all. Remember, the purpose in developing experience stories is to teach the communication skills of speaking, listening, writing, and reading rather than to produce "original" compositions. As usual, process counts much more than product.

It would be difficult to emphasize this point too much: the oral-language experiences that children engage in are just as important for the development of reading skills as the actual reading experiences. Oral-language growth at any grade level is a major factor in producing greater growth in both reading and writing. In the case of experience stories, a good oral discussion usually leads to easy and natural dictation or writing, followed by easy and natural reading of the composition.

The two stages of developing interest in a story and carrying on a discussion preceding story production are inseparable stages. The teacher can develop interest and start the discussion, for instance, by asking an open-ended question about a caged animal that she has brought in:

TEACHER: What do you think this hamster feels about your looking at him?
JERRY: I think he's happy.
TEACHER: Why, Jerry?
JERRY: Because he has someone to play with.

TEACHER: (nodding appreciatively) He doesn't seem very frightened, does he?

MONA: He's got long whiskers.

TEACHER: Yes, they're quite long. How long would you say they are? Are they as long as this pencil?

FRANK: (laughing) They're not that long. They're as long as . . . as long as my little finger.

TEACHER: Yes, I think you're right, Frank. What else do you notice about this little hamster . . . Stephen?

STEPHEN: He's got sharp teeth.

TEACHER: How can you tell?

STEPHEN: Because . . . because they're pointed and because he can chew up those little round things real fast.

TEACHER: Yes, he can, can't he? Those little round things are sometimes called *pellets* and they're what he likes to eat. Do you know what they're made of?

STEPHEN: I don't know. Nuts maybe.

TEACHER: Well, in a way, you're right! They're made from the seeds of wheat and barley and other grains like that. Since nuts are a kind of seed, Stephen, you were almost right!

STEPHEN: (smiling) Yeah.

Dictating and Writing the Story

After the discussion has continued awhile, the teacher begins the dictation period by moving to the chalkboard and asking something like this: "Who would like to begin our story today? We need a sentence at the top that will remind us what we've been doing just now . . . Julie?"

JULIE: "We've been lookin' at a funny little hamster."

TEACHER: All right, let's write that down. I'll start way at the top and way over on the left side. I'll start with a capital letter. (She writes: We've been looking at a funny little hamster.) That's what Julie said: "We've been looking at a funny little hamster." Who would like to have the next turn . . . Stephen?

STEPHEN: He has real sharp pointed teeth.

The dictation continues until everyone has had a turn or until the group feels that the story is complete. Here's an example of what a finished story may look like:

A Funny Little Hamster

We've been looking at a funny little hamster.
He has real sharp pointed teeth.
He has whiskers as long as my little finger.
He lives in a wire cage, and he keeps looking at us.

The funny little hamster runs races with himself.
The funny little hamster ain't got a friend to live with.
But we can be his friends.
We'll feed him and give him water and play with him.

When taking dictation the teacher avoids the temptation to edit the children's language. In other words, if a child says "ain't," the teacher writes "ain't." She does not attempt to control the vocabulary or sentence structure or grammar in any way. The only modification she would make is in spelling: When a child mispronounces a word, she doesn't spell it according to the mispronunciation. The teacher spells it correctly and lets him read it in any way he wishes later.

One reason the teacher avoids editing grammar, vocabulary, and sentence structure, of course, is to make sure the child perceives reading as a true communication process, rather than a process of pleasing adults. Teachers who edit more than spelling will find that children are less willing to volunteer their ideas. Since the teacher's use of standard spelling does not seem to inhibit children's communication, it is probably wise to avoid nonstandard spelling. Some children will take offense if they discover you've been misspelling words to allow for their peculiar way of pronouncing them.

Another reason the teacher avoids editing grammar, vocabulary, and sentence structure is that children tend to read their sentence as they have dictated it, rather than as the teacher has edited it. Thus, the important link between print and speech has been broken, causing children to have more difficulty developing a sight vocabulary and a feeling for the importance of reading for comprehension.

Reading the Story Created

The story that children create is read many, many times, both by the teacher and by the students—but each time in a slightly different way. Some teachers read the story as they write it, word by word. Some wait until an entire sentence has been written and then read it back to the children. Some do both and then read the entire story to the children after it has been completed. In any case, a successful teacher reads the story to the children before asking them to read it with her or to read it by themselves.

After reading the story to the children, the teacher then asks the children to read it with her. Next she calls on children to read one or more sentences by themselves, helping them as soon as they run into trouble. The important thing is that the reading experience is an enjoyable, successful one. (One way of assuring this success is to have children read by themselves only the sentence that they dictated. Later, after the story has become more familiar, they are asked to try other sentences.)

Using the Story to Teach and Learn Reading Subskills

The day following the creation of a story the children are usually shown a lined, tagboard version of the same story and presented with a dittoed personal copy as well. The teacher has also prepared a word card for each word in the story. These materials, along with others, are used for the purpose of teaching vocabulary, decoding skills, comprehension skills, or possibly, readiness skills. Each of these types of skills will be discussed separately in later sections.

Procedures for Creating Personal-Experience Stories

After children have become familiar with the process of developing group-experience stories, they are usually given opportunities to develop their own personal stories. At first these stories are dictated to the teacher or another person (hired teaching aide, parent, volunteer, teacher trainee, child from another room). Gradually, as children develop writing skills, they are written entirely by the children themselves.

Motivation for developing such personal stories arises from many sources. Often a small-group or total-class experience story can lead to additional stories created by each child (or by several children) in the classroom. Following the group-experience story on the hamster, for example, the teacher could have inspired children in small groups each to write a brief, separate story—one each on what the hamster eats, how it plays, how it sleeps, what its mouth and nose are like, what its eyes and ears are like, and so on. Or she might have inspired each child to write a brief adventure of "the funny little hamster."

Other motivations for writing personal stories could include the following:

1. A picture that the child has drawn or painted while working in the "art corner"
2. A class discussion on a peculiar object that the teacher has brought to school
3. A follow-up on having a turn during a show-and-tell period
4. A special trip taken over the weekend or holiday
5. An illustration that the child has made of a group-experience story
6. A show seen on television
7. A response to seeing a photograph of himself
8. A picture book read either by the teacher or by the child
9. A "big plan" for making something
10. A chance to contribute a page to a group-produced book

Essentially the same procedures used for developing group-experience stories are used for personal stories. Interest is developed in creating the story; the topic is discussed with the teacher or another person; the story is dictated or written; the child experiences himself and other people reading his story; the story is used by the teacher to provide practice in learning reading skills.

Teaching Vocabulary

Vocabulary development is a very personal process. The words that relate to a child's own experience, particularly when those experiences have been highlighted by either positive or negative emotions, are those that are learned and retained most easily (11, 17). Sylvia Ashton-Warner (1), in her successful attempt to teach Maori children of New Zealand, found that one child who had great difficulty learning words such as *come* and *look,* could quite easily learn words like *kill, knife,* and *gaol (jail).*

Because of the personal nature of vocabulary building, teachers who use a language-experience approach usually try to personalize the acquisition of vocabulary. To do this, the teacher asks each child to develop a personal "word bank." A word bank usually takes the form of small (1½ by 2½) cards kept by the child in a small box or other container. A word is written for the child on a card whenever she demonstrates that she can read it. After the teacher passes out a dittoed copy of a group-experience chart, for instance, children are asked to underline those words that they know. If Barbara successfully reads her underlined words to the teacher, the teacher makes out a card for each word and gives them to her for her word bank. The same procedure of underlining and presenting word cards is used for personal experience stories as well. Other words that children learn, such as those gained from noticing the labels for things that the teacher has taped-up in the room, can also be added to their individual word banks.

The individual word banks have several major functions:

1. To serve as a record of the reading vocabulary of individual children
2. To serve as references for creative writing and spelling
3. To provide reinforcement through repeated exposure to words
4. To serve as stimulus words for examples during skill instruction
5. To provide independent activities with word games, matching activities, and sentence building
6. To provide examples for group language study (7, p. 61)

The children keep the word banks at their desks to practice with each other, to match with the words in their dittoed stories, and to play games suggested by the teacher. They bring them to the small-group meetings to use as their own suggested examples of a graphophonic pattern (such as words with a VC spelling pattern) and to help the group create "group word banks."

Group word banks are created by both the small groups and the entire class. This type of word bank is designed to help children become more aware of word categories and sentence patterns. Examples of group word banks would be Color Words, Action Words, Sound Words, Names of Animals, Homophones, and Feeling Words. This type of "bank" is often printed on large tagboard charts so that children can refer to them when they are producing stories. Sometimes the words are also printed on cards and placed in boxes so that children can use them for independent activities suggested by the teacher.

The words in the group word banks are accumulated gradually throughout the year. One way of starting them is to ask children in a small group to look through their personal word banks and find all of the color words they can find (or action words or whatever category the teacher wishes to emphasize). Once the group word banks are printed on tagboard, they become a quick reference for various activities such as producing group stories or creating sentences. In creating sentences, a child can select, for example, an animal word and an action word (Dogs dig . . .). The rest of the group then tries to alter and expand this basic sentence (The frisky young dogs dug deep holes all over the garden).

Teaching Decoding and Comprehension Subskills

In addition to teaching vocabulary through children's stories and word banks, the teacher can also instruct children in phonic analysis, morphemic analysis, contextual analysis, and a few of the comprehension skills. Most of the comprehension skills are best taught when children have reached the stage of reading library books or basal readers. This is particularly true of skills related to inferential, critical, or creative thinking. This is because children's earliest stories often do not have enough thought-provoking content. On the other hand, the language-experience approach provides a firm foundation for developing comprehension skills, because of its total emphasis on meaning and communication.

Phonic analysis is taught by having the children notice how letters represent sounds and how spelling patterns determine sounds. For instance, the teacher may indicate three words in a story that all start with the letter *p*, then pronounce the three words with the children, and next ask the children what sound they hear at the beginning of each word. He may also find two words with the same final phonogram, such as *night* and *fight*. This could lead to a short lesson on the *ight* phonogram. He may point out the difference between the words *hat* and *hate* in a story, and how the VC pattern and VCE pattern predict different sounds. Having introduced a particular graphophonic concept through a story, the teacher would later review this concept, both by using later stories and by follow-up skill lessons.

Morphemic analysis is taught by having children notice compounds, contractions, roots, suffixes, and prefixes in their stories and word banks. Contrasts are made, for instance, between such words as *happy* and *unhappy, happy* and *happiness, fast* and *faster.* Context analysis is taught by blocking out words in a story and asking children to predict the word or words that would fit in the blank. This is usually followed by a brief discussion of the clues that enabled them to make such good predictions.

Although, as I mentioned earlier, it's difficult to teach the more complex comprehension skills through experience stories, it is possible and desirable to teach some of the more simple ones. After a story has been completed, for example, the teacher can have the children think of a title that "really shows what your story is about," thus engaging them in thinking of main ideas. She can ask them about specific details ("Who can show us what Frank said about how long the hamster's whiskers are?"). She can have them alter and expand some of the sentences in the story. And she can have them read with the proper intonation.

Teaching Readiness Skills

A language-experience approach provides numerous opportunities for getting children ready for the world of print. By emphasizing meaning and communication from the very beginning, it prepares children for reading in the true sense of the word. By emphasizing oral-language skills, it prepares children for natural and meaningful translation from print into speech. And by placing an emphasis on communication, it also avoids such readiness blocks as the perception of reading as "sounding out words" or reading for words rather than ideas.

Specific readiness skills can be taught in the same way that decoding skills can be taught. The experience stories provide the examples; the teacher helps the children notice the appropriate clues. Children can be asked, for example, to match word cards to words in the story, thereby emphasizing visual discrimination. "Letter cards" can be used in the same way. Visual memory, to take another example, can be developed by holding up a word card, covering up the word card, and then asking a child to find the word in the story. Finer discrimination can be taught by using a group word bank of children's names. Names that look alike, such as *Timmy* and *Tammy*, can be compared. While teaching visual discrimination and memory, the teacher can also help them learn (or review) the names of letters. Auditory discrimination and memory can be reinforced by having children think of words that "start in the same way" or words that rhyme. The left-to-right orientation is taught through the natural development and "reading" of an experience story.

Keeping Track of Children's Progress

Evaluation of children's progress in learning to read can be done in somewhat the same way used with a basal approach. A full-fledged skills-management system can be used, such as the "Wisconsin Design" (12), the "Prescriptive Reading Inventory" (13), or one from a basal series. Appropriate assessment and retention tests are administered throughout the year and records are kept on each child. For those teachers who wish to use a more informal approach, a skills-management checklist is kept on each child, and a checklist is completed on the basis of both tests and classroom observations. Tests are used only for those skills on which teachers observe children having trouble. Following the tests or observations, the children are given special lessons on those subskills that have not been learned well through the normal language-experience program.

Combining Language Experiences with Other Approaches

Many teachers use a language-experience approach as a supplement to their regular reading program. Some first-grade teachers, for instance, use language-experience approaches during the first semester and then switch the children gradually into a basal program. At the end of the first semester, children are administered informal reading inventories and other placement tests provided by the basal-series publisher. Because of the progress of most children, though, very few of them will have to start at the earliest level of the basal program.

Other first-grade teachers use a language-experience approach right along with a basal-reading program from the very first. The two programs can be quite compatible if the teacher uses the basal program primarily for skill development and the language-experience approach primarily for the development of the concept of reading as communication.

Many teachers rely upon language-experience stories to augment the stories provided by basal readers. Word banks are derived from both basal and experience stories. In this way, the teacher can combine both the element of structure provided by a basal approach and the elements of communication and creativity provided by a language-experience approach.

Teachers of the upper grades often use experience stories as a method of personalizing what children learn through the social studies, science, and other areas. In one class, for example, Mr. Walters encouraged his fifth graders to develop personal and group-written books on their imagined life in the Middle Ages. In another, Mrs. Fredekind had one group of fourth graders make an experience chart listing the steps for a science experiment they had "invented." This chart was used by the rest of the class in order to "replicate the study."

Handling the Limitations Related to Language-Experience Approaches

Perhaps the greatest limitation to a language-experience approach is not inherent in the approach itself but in the transition to another approach. Some children who have started out learning to read "à la-LEA" become frustrated after moving into a basal program. Such frustration is quite understandable and usually occurs when the teacher using a basal program does not provide ample time for writing creatively and expressing oneself in group discussions. (It's a little like giving an adult a job, respecting her ideas and opinions for a year, giving her many choices for her own way of handling things, and then suddenly presenting her with a very autocratic boss who wants things done exactly his way.) As I've implied, this limitation is not as strong when the teacher using a more structured approach provides numerous opportunities for the children to express themselves in discussions and through writing.

A second major limitation is that of the resistance sometimes offered by parents. Some parents become confused by a language-experience approach and get the idea that children are "not really learning how to read—they're just memorizing little stories that they're making up. Why, my Johnny can't even sound out words yet." Such criticism is bound to be discouraging to teachers. Most teachers, though, avoid such criticism by carefully explaining their instructional approach at the beginning of the school year—either in a letter to the parents or in a general meeting with them. This is followed up by newsletters that explain the language-experience approaches in more detail. Children are also asked to take home certain experience stories to read to their parents. The first ones selected for this honor are usually ones that contain mostly words that a child already has in his personal word bank. Furthermore, they are stories that do not contain nonstandard grammar. As the year progresses, however, and the parents seem to understand the program more thoroughly, the stories are selected with less scrutiny. Conferences are usually scheduled with parents of each child so that the teacher can show them the stories that their child can now read, the word bank he has developed, the assessment and retention test results, and the checklist of mastered skills.

Summary

Language-experience approaches utilize a child's own language in order to teach him how to read. Research shows that language-experience approaches are effective in teaching readiness skills to kindergarten children and reading skills to children in the early grades, as well as remedial students in later grades. Group-experience charts and personal-experience stories, along with individual and group "word banks," provide the major media of instruction. The usual order for developing charts and stories is 1) developing interest in writing a story, 2) discussing the story topic, 3) dictating and writing the story, 4) reading the story created, and 5) using the story to teach and learn reading subskills, such as phonic analysis, morphemic analysis, and context analysis. Some type of skills checklist or a full-fledged skills-management system is used for evaluating children's progress in learning the subskills of reading. Many of the teachers who use a language-experience approach use it as a supplement to a more highly structured approach such as a basal-reading program. Those who use only a language-experience approach usually find it advisable to explain their program thoroughly to parents.

References and Suggested Reading

1. Ashton-Warner, Sylvia. *Teacher.* New York: Simon and Schuster, 1963.
2. Bond, Guy L., and Dykstra, Robert. "The Cooperative Program in First Grade Reading Instruction." *Reading Research Quarterly* 2 (1967): 5–142.
3. Cramer, Ronald L. "An Investigation of First-Grade Spelling Achievement." *Elementary English* 47 (1970): 230–7.
4. Dunn, Lloyd M., and Smith, James O. *Peabody Language Development Kits,* Levels I, II, III. Circle Pines, MN: American Guidance Service, 1965, 1966, 1967.
5. Dykstra, Robert. "Summary of the Second-Grade Phase of the Cooperative Research Program in Primary Reading Instruction." *Reading Research Quarterly* 4 (1968); 49–70.

6. Dzama, Mary Ann. "Comparing Use of Generalizations of Phonics in LEA, Basal Vocabulary." *Reading Teacher* 28 (1975): 466–72.

7. Hall, Mary Anne. *Teaching Reading as a Language Experience.* Columbus, OH: Charles E. Merrill Co., 1976.

8. Hall, Mary Anne. *The Language Experience Approach for Teaching Reading, a Research Perspective.* Newark, DE: International Reading Association, 1978.

9. Henderson, Edmund H., et al. "An Exploratory Study of Word Acquisition among First-Graders at Midyear in a Language Experience Approach." *Journal of Reading Behavior* 4 (1972): 21–31.

10. Hoover, Irene. "Historical and Theoretical Development of a Language Experience Approach to Teaching Reading in Selected Teacher Education Institutions." Ph.D. dissertation, University of Arizona, 1971.

11. Olson, David R., and Pau, A. S. "Emotionally Loaded Words and the Acquisition of a Sight Vocabulary." *Journal of Educational Psychology* 57 (June 1966): 174–8.

12. Otto, Wayne, and Askov, Eunice. *Rationale and Guidelines.* The Wisconsin Design for Reading Skill Development, National Computer Systems, 1973.

13. *Prescriptive Reading Inventory.* New York: CTB/McGraw-Hill, 1972.

14. Staton, Janette. "Initial Reading Practices in Open Education Environments in the Midprairie States." Ph.D. dissertation, Oklahoma State University, 1974.

15. Torrance, E. Paul. "Creative Thinking of Children." *Journal of Teacher Education* 13 (December 1962): 448–60.

16. Van Allen, Roach. *Language Experiences in Reading.* Chicago, IL: Encyclopaedia Britannica Press, 1974.

17. Veatch, Jeanette, et al. *Key Words to Reading,* 2d ed. Columbus, OH: Charles E. Merrill Co., 1979.

Application Experiences for the Teacher-Education Class

1. With a small group of students in your class discuss why you agree or disagree with the following statements. Then compare your decisions with other groups.

Statements about Chapter 12

a. Language-experience approaches are useful for young children who are progressing at the normal rate but not very useful for older children who need remedial instruction.

b. By using the actual language of the child, we can make reading a more natural experience.

c. Vocabulary control with an LEA is determined by the teacher rather than a teacher's guide.

d. A language-experience approach often develops better spellers than a basal approach.

e. Most teachers use a basal approach rather than an LEA because a basal approach requires less planning.

f. With an LEA, children do not need to be placed into reading groups.

g. The most important step in producing experience stories is to develop children's interest.

h. It is important to have children write or dictate without discussion, as this prevents children from copying each other's ideas.

i. It is very difficult to teach decoding skills via an LEA.

j. It would be difficult to teach vocabulary with a language-experience approach without the use of individual and group word banks.

k. A skills-management system would be totally inappropriate with an LEA.

l. Parents are usually the greatest supporters of a language-experience program.

2. With a partner or a small group examine the experience story called "A Funny Little Hamster" on page 346. Make a list of as many specific phonic-analysis, morphemic-analysis, and context-analysis skills as you can that you may be able to teach through the use of this story. For example, could you teach a lesson on contractions? Which ones? Compare your list with lists made by others in the class.

3. Divide up the class into several groups and assign a topic to each group for the development of a group-experience chart. Each group should appoint one person as their teacher-recorder. Go through the five stages of development suggested on pages 344–348. Then share your stories with other groups. Here are some topics you may like to use:

a. Here's how you make muddy gravel soup. . . .

b. Here's why applesauce can be dangerous to your health. . . .

c. Here's how to scratch your back, eat chocolate pudding, and read a textbook assignment at the same time. . . .

d. The monster who ate important belongings of college students. . . .

e. What students know about teachers. . . .

f. What teachers know about students. . . .

Field Experiences in the Elementary-School Classroom

1. Help a few children develop a group-experience story. Use only the first four steps described on pages 344–347. (What highly interesting, but brief, experience can you help them have first?)

2. Using a group-experience story or a personal-experience story, teach one or more reading subskills.

3. Help a small group of children bind a book that they have created. Simple means of binding books are described in the books by Van Allen, Hall, and Dunn and Smith, and also in the free booklet called *Cover to Cover* published by the Encyclopaedia Britannica Press, 425 North Michigan Avenue, Chicago, IL 60611. Most libraries have other books on this subject as well.

CHAPTER 13

*Through individual conferences a teacher can get to know
each child quite well.*

Individualizing Reading Instruction through Children's Literature

Chapter Outline

The Reality of Individual Differences
Children's Literature to the Rescue
Types of Trade Books Available
Ways of Fostering Children's Use of Trade Books
More Ways to Foster Children's Use of Trade Books
Using Children's Literature in an "Individualized-Reading"
    Program
Teaching Skills through a Trade-Book-Individualized Reading
    Program
Managing Individual Conferences
Questions to Ask During a Conference
Teaching Vocabulary
Record Keeping
Easing into an Individualized Program
Summary
Application Experiences for the Teacher-Education Class
Field Experiences in the Elementary-School Classroom

Chapter Preview

In the '50s and early '60s, an instructional approach called "Individualized Reading" became popular. With this approach, library books, rather than basal readers, were the chief instructional materials. Instead of meeting daily with reading groups, the teacher spent most of her instructional time in individual conferences. Skills were taught through both individual conferences and instruction given to temporary groups. Because this approach often deteriorated into little more than recreational reading, its popularity waned for over a decade. But now, because of the availability of skills-management systems for supplementing an individualized reading program, and because of the strong appeal of its philosophy, it seems to be making a good comeback. We'll be looking at this type of reading program in this chapter. But before we look at it in detail, we'll first examine the important role of children's literature (often referred to as "library books" or as "trade books") in any reading program.

> Some humans called teachers keep children so busy learning how to read, the children seldom have time to read.

The Reality of Individual Differences

There was a time in educational writing when the term "individual differences" could be found in just about every paragraph. The term implies something teachers have always known—even back in the days of teaching children to "catch fish with their bare hands and scare woolly haired bears with fire." People learn at different speeds and in different ways. How easy that is to say! And yet how very difficult to do anything about it. Most basal-reading programs, for example, allow for different speeds of learning, but none of them allows adequately for different ways of learning. Most teachers, moreover, become adept at pacing the learning differently for different individuals. But few become adept at the far more difficult process of varying the learning style.

The pedagogical problem of individual differences can be quite severe when it comes to reading. We know, for instance, that teachers working in self-contained classrooms usually have students whose general reading abilities vary by several grade levels. A fifth-grade teacher may have to work with children whose reading-achievement grade-level scores range from 2.0 to 8.0. At the same time, each child's specific reading abilities may also vary by several grade levels. Let's compare Sally's scores with Virginia's scores as an example of this. Sally and Virginia both had a general-ability total score of 5.0. But here's how they scored on the specific-skill subtests:

	Sally	*Virginia*
Vocabulary (isolated)	5.7	3.4
Vocabulary (in context)	4.1	5.1
Paragraph understanding (literal)	5.2	4.5
Paragraph understanding (interpretive)	2.7	5.9
Phonics knowledge	6.3	4.5
Phonics application	5.8	2.6
Morphemic analysis	3.5	7.8
Total score	5.0	5.0

In spite of such differences between Sally and Virginia, however, they would most likely be placed in the same reading group and be assigned the same basal reader. To make matters worse, Sally is crazy about animal stories—horse stories and dog stories in particular—and almost any stories dealing with the great outdoors. Virginia, on the other hand, does not care for this kind of story at all. Virginia likes stories of teenage romance, as well as realistic stories about racial strife and other social phenomena.

Children's Literature to the Rescue

What can a teacher of reading do about such differences? One way is to ignore the differences and assume that "what's good for one is good for all." But, of course, this approach only leads to frustration. Another way is to individualize your skill instruction; and we've talked about that in previous chapters. A third way is to put more planning time and energy into your "children's-literature program." For some teachers, this may mean going all the way to an "individualized-reading" program. For others, it may mean decreasing the amount of time on basal readers and workbooks and increasing the amount of time spent with what children often refer to as "real books."

High quality "trade books" (library books) have much to offer children and their teachers. They offer 1) opportunities for individualized personal growth, 2) motivated individualized practice of reading subskills and their integration, 3) enrichment of the social studies, science, and other areas of the curriculum, 4) models and inspiration for creative writing, and 5) aesthetic experiences. Let's look briefly at each of these potential virtues.

Psychologists tell us that one of the chief ways in which people develop values, ambitions, and a self-concept is through emotional identification with another person—by imagining ourselves to be that person or by becoming like that person. Trade books, particularly biographies and fiction, offer infinite opportunities for such identification. A single book, of course, is not likely to provide as powerful a model as, say, a likable teacher or an admired parent. Yet thinking about your own experience with books would probably cause you to remember the times that books made a difference in how you felt—about yourself, about human behavior, about animals, perhaps, or about beliefs you once held. Even if we're unwilling to accept the possibility that a book could cause any permanent change in behavior, it is hard not to believe that a book can at least reinforce one's developing values or make one question these values.

From a very practical, skill-oriented standpoint, trade books also provide motivated practice for those comprehension and decoding skills that the teacher wants the children to acquire. The practice is "motivated" by the fact that children are reading books of their own choice, and, if the books are the right choice, they are giving them pleasure. Even in the first grade, children can experience such practice today; several series of books are now available for children of this age.

One of these series is the *Beginner Books* series, including the first one in the series entitled *The Cat in the Hat* by Dr. Seuss. And for the true neophyte, there's the series called the *Beginning Beginner Books*. One of the books in this series—*Bears on Wheels* by Stan and Jan Berenstein—has only fourteen different words, and surprisingly enough, is usually fun for both children and adults to read. Another series is the *I Can Read* books, including *Frog and Toad Are Friends* and *Frog and Toad Together*—the first of which was a 1971 Caldecott Honor Book and the second of which was a 1973 Newbery Honor Book. There is also an *Early I Can Read* series, including the book on a favorite children's topic: *Dinosaur Time*. In addition, there are several good series available from basal-reader publishers (see pages 277–278).

Without the use of trade books ("children's literature"), it would be nearly impossible to achieve some of the objectives of the newer social-studies and science programs. In the social-studies area, for example, the teacher is usually trying to help children identify with the problems, values, and life styles of different people. Simply reading about these people in a textbook will not accomplish this aim. Social-studies textbooks, because of their wide coverage, tend to be somewhat shallow, expository, and intellectual. It is very difficult for children to identify with the people talked about in the textbook, and it is also very difficult for them to find enough meaningful associations and examples. More learning in depth, more emotion is needed. Films and other audiovisual media help a great deal, but trade books—fictional, informational, biographical—offer vital opportunities for emotional involvement and intensive study.

As a model and inspiration for children's own creative writing, it is hard to beat children's literature. Your author has never had such interesting, highly motivated writing occur in his classroom as that which follows the conclusion of books he has read aloud. Numerous teachers have had the same experience. If the teacher has helped the children become aware of an author's use of words, the characters' personalities, and the subtleties of the plot, many children will be bursting with ideas for extending the story, changing its ending, or even writing a sequel. A similar type of enthusiasm—although not always as strong—often follows the conclusion of a book they have read by themselves. Whether this same type of enthusiasm for expressing themselves in an interesting way carries over into speech is difficult to measure. My own experience tells me that a "touch of grandeur" lingers on for a while at least, as children try out new phrases, new words, and new ways of arranging them. (This same phenomenon often occurs with adults after they've watched a Shakespearean drama or listened to poetry read aloud.)

And this leads us to another virtue of high-quality trade books—that of the aesthetic experience provided by the book itself. Some of the best writing and graphic art today can be found between the covers of a children's book. (And probably some of the worst as well, it should be admitted.) Marguerite Henry's *King of the Wind,* to take just one example, is rich in beautiful prose, sensitive characterization, and subtlety of plot development. To read a book such as this is to achieve that intangible something called an *aesthetic experience.* One feels better for having experienced it, and perhaps that is enough justification for reading any book. Then, too, there is the aesthetic experience provided by the superb illustrations found in many picture books and other children's books today. Offset printing has made it possible for artists to use freely and creatively any graphic media they wish. A look at some of the books illustrated by Ezra Jack Keats, Symeon Shimin, Leo Lionni, and Marcia Brown will offer the reader the opportunity to test this assertion.

Two coveted awards have been associated with, and perhaps partly responsible for, the aesthetic quality of children's books. One of these is the John Newbery Medal, presented each year to "the author of the most distinguished contribution to American literature for children." The book whose author will receive the award is selected by a committee of the Children's Services Division of the American Library Association. This committee selects the book that it considers to be the best one published the previous year, and also a number of runner-up books for that same year. A list of the winners since 1922 may be found in Appendix H. It should be emphasized that not all of the award-winning books are enjoyed by children, and many of them are better read aloud by the teacher because of their difficulty.

The other highly coveted award is the Caldecott Medal, presented each year to "the artist of the most distinguished American picture book for children." The winning book and illustrator, along with several runners-up, are selected by the same committee that selects the winner for the Newbery award. A list of the winners since 1938 may be found in Appendix J.

To limit one's selection of books, however, to the winners and runners-up for the Caldecott or Newbery awards, is to make the error of attributing some godlike power to the committee of human beings who make such awesome decisions each year. On the other hand, it is probably wise to read several of them to sharpen one's own awareness of those qualities that make certain books seem great and others mediocre.

Types of Trade Books Available

In many libraries across the United States the "juvenile" circulation accounts for at least one-half the total circulation. This is a distinct rise from 1939, when the juvenile circulation accounted for only one-third of the total circulation (6). Part of this increase probably comes about as the result of the vast growth in the publication of juveniles—from 852 new titles in 1940 to over 3000 in recent years. Along with this quantitative growth has come an increase in the variety of children's books available. The ever-popular mysteries and fantasies now must compete for shelf space with fictional stories of ever-increasing realism, with informational books on nearly every conceivable subject, and with a host of other types.

Teachers who wish to foster children's growth through reading should be aware of these various types of trade books, so that they may participate in the process of getting the "right" book to the "right" child at the "right" time. But perhaps you're already aware of the various types. To test your awareness, try the matching exercise that follows: see if you can "find" the type of books that "a child needs." (Feedback and immediate reinforcement can be obtained by checking the answers at the end of the matching exercise.)

If you got twelve or more correct, you should probably celebrate this event in some way, for these sixteen categories and their descriptions are slightly ambiguous and rely upon subtle distinctions. Some teenage romance stories, for instance, could be classified as realistic-fiction books. Some science-fiction books could be classified as fantasies, to take another example. Precisely how one decides to classify a particular book, of course, is not very important. What is important is that you become familiar, if you're not already, with the various types of books that are available to children at various age levels.

Naturally, if you're teaching second graders, you can forget about the teenage romance stories, but all of the other types have been published for children of this age. The teacher of children in the intermediate grades will want to become familiar with all sixteen types—even the picture books, many of which have been published for children beyond the primary grades.

The best way to become truly familiar with children's books is not to read anthologies or reviews, but to read and enjoy the books themselves. (It's probably a good idea to keep a card file on the books

The Type You Will Look for When . . .

_____ 1. A fiction book that portrays people coping with the universal problems of life as these problems exist in modern times

_____ 2. A fiction story that concentrates on finding clues and discovering why and how an incident took place

_____ 3. A book of short selections, most of which describe the essence of something—sometimes in colorful language, sometimes in rhyming or rhythmic patterns of words

_____ 4. A book in which the story is told or information given in two ways—both at the same time: One way is through words and the other way is through numerous illustrations.

_____ 5. A fiction story of an adolescent coping with the universal problems of love

_____ 6. A book of legends, fables, tall tales, epics, myths, old fairy tales, or any other traditional stories formerly handed down by word of mouth

_____ 7. A fiction story in which situations or characteristics—usually of a realistic nature— are exaggerated to the point of amusement

_____ 8. A fiction book in which an animal, such as a dog or horse, becomes a heroic figure in a realistic way

_____ 9. A fiction book based on principles or possibilities of nature and often involving future times, space travel, and other worlds

_____ 10. A nonfiction book about a noteworthy person

_____ 11. A fiction story in which success in an athletic game is an important element of the conflict and is generally related to the "game of living"

_____ 12. A book of fiction stories written in drama format—nearly all dialogue

_____ 13. A nonfiction book that explains natural and social phenomena or suggests experiments, activities, or procedures

_____ 14. A fiction book that emphasizes historical settings and usually historical characters or events

_____ 14. A fiction story involving considerable danger, courage, and a struggle with the natural elements

_____ 16. A fiction story (created in writing rather than handed down orally) in which the events are not only improbable but seem to be impossible, e.g., talking animals, magic wands, tiny people, events conflicting with present scientific knowledge

A Child Needs or Wants a

a. picture book
b. book or folk tales
c. sports story
d. biography
e. historical-fiction book
f. science-fiction book
g. realistic-fiction book
h. mystery story
i. animal story
j. fantasy
k. informational book
l. outdoor-adventure story
m. teenage romance story
n. book of poetry
o. humorous story
p. book of plays

Answers:

1—g 2—h 3—n 4—a 5—m 6—b 7—o 8—i 9—f 10—d
11—c 12—p 13—k 14—e 15—l 16—j

you read—to jog your memory later.) In your reading of children's books, it is hoped that you will keep four things in mind.

1. *Read books for a wide range of age levels:* Remember that children at any grade level vary tremendously in their reading abilities and interests. Carolyn Haywood's books, for instance (e.g., *B is for Betsy, Eddie and his big deals*) are excellent for the average reader in grades two and three. But some children at this grade level will be reading fourth- and fifth-grade books, such as *Henry Huggins* by Beverly Cleary or *Little House on the Prairie* by Laura Ingalls Wilder, while others will be reading simple picture books like *Where the Wild Things Are* by Maurice Sendak or *Millions of Cats* by Wanda Gag.
2. *Read a variety of book types:* In this way you can be more helpful to the child who is looking for "a real scary mystery," or "something really true to life," or even "a real good sports story."
3. *Read them with a sense of involvement from cover to cover:* Skimmed books are as bad as poorly digested meals. Only by reading books thoroughly can you prepare yourself to share them honestly with children.
4. *Start by reading several that are considered by many to be of "good" quality:* Then when you come across poor-quality books, you will recognize them almost instantly; thus you will avoid wasting your own time and be able to recommend high-quality books to children. In the suggested references at the end of this chapter, you will find sources listed (1, 6, 17, 18) that will help you decide on which books are likely to be worthy of your time. In Appendix I you will find "A Starter List of Good Books for Children," which may be of use to you in your selection.

Ways of Fostering Children's Use of Trade Books

There are several ways of encouraging children to make use of trade books. One of these is simply to allow plenty of time for them to read. In spite of the hustle and bustle of a modern classroom, it is often a better place in which to read than the home. At home, remember, reading must frequently compete with the omnipresent "big eye," with its tempting tidbits of instant culture and instant action.*

Many teachers sincerely believe that they do offer their students enough time to read trade books during the school day. When pressed to define what they mean by "enough time," though, some

---

*Numerous studies have shown that the average elementary-school child watches television more than thirty hours per week.

of them answer like this: "I let them read all during the day. Whenever they get their assignments done, they're supposed to get out a library book and read quietly." What this generally means in practice is that the same three or four students who always get their assignments done early are doing about 90 percent of the reading. Most of the others either spend all their time on the textbook-workbook assignment or, if they do finish early, they have so little time to read before the next assignment befalls them, they usually decide not to bother.

A first-year teacher wanted to know why his fifth-grade students didn't seem to want to read. When he was asked how much time they had for "free reading," he said, "Well, whenever they finish their other assignments—and sometimes I give them a ten-minute free-reading period before lunch." It was suggested to him that he try something for two weeks—giving them two thirty-minute periods a week for free reading. In two weeks' time he had changed his mind about most of his students: "It takes some of them five to six minutes to get started, but once they get going, I can't tear them away from their books."

In many libraries across the U.S., the "juvenile" circulation accounts for at least one-half the total circulation.

Fader and McNeil (4) recommend a timed approach in which, during the first week, only five minutes a day is set aside for intensive reading. This time is gradually increased until the children are reading intensively for thirty to forty minutes per day. In their book, they explain how this "Uninterrupted Sustained Silent Reading" (USSR) program may be encouraged. Their success with this approach leads them to advocate it for those children who are reluctant to read.

Some may wonder where to find all that time. But if "the reading child" is the ultimate outcome we desire, it seems imperative that the time be found and that time spent on less important outcomes be whittled down. Perhaps it will be conceded that an hour a week is not too much time to allow for the major objective of reading instruction. (It should be pointed out, of course, that a thirty-minute block of free-reading time is too long for many children below the third grade. But unless one allows at least fifteen minutes, some children won't make the effort to get started.)

A second way to encourage children's use of trade books is to provide them with a wide choice. This can usually be done in various ways, depending on the school and municipal facilities. Many schools today have their own libraries. Some teachers take their children to nearby municipal libraries to check out a collection which they then take to the classroom. A vast number of teachers encourage their students to purchase their own paperback books at a reasonable price from one of the Scholastic Book Clubs. These books, and other paperbacks available from bookstores, are usually printed from the same plates as the original hardbound copies, and the quality of selections is generally high. A few publishers have come out with fairly large classroom collections of paperbacks designed for an "individualized reading program." One example of this is the *Reading Spectrum* published by Scholastic* and the *Pal Paperback Kits* published by Xerox. School libraries, municipal libraries, county libraries, state libraries, book clubs, book stores, publishers—some way can be found by a resourceful teacher to provide students with a variety of trade books.

Another way of encouraging trade-book reading is to help children find books that are not too difficult. Children can easily become discouraged if one book after another offers them little more than frustration. Teachers who make it a habit to read children's books themselves have little trouble offering children guidance in this respect. There are also numerous lists of easy-reading books for those children whose interests are beyond their reading skills. One of the most complete lists is given in the book by Spache entitled *Good Reading for Poor Readers* (16), which has been frequently revised to keep it up to date.

---

*For a list of Scholastic book collections write to: Scholastic's Readers' Choice, 904 Sylvan Avenue, Englewood Cliffs, NJ 07632.

More Ways to Foster Children's Use of Trade Books

A fourth way to foster the habit of reading trade books is to suggest books to children that may seem to relate to their needs and interests. Gradually during a school year a teacher can get to know his pupils' interests, hobbies, and personal problems—through informal conversations and observations, and sometimes through a formal interview or questionnaire. The teacher who also becomes familiar with children's books is in the enviable position of being able to suggest specific books to specific children for particular interests or problems that they may have. Perusal of book reviews is also helpful to the teacher in this respect. Excellent reviews can be found in books by Arbuthnot (1), Sutherland (18), and Huck (6), and in *Hornbook Magazine.* Some of the basal-reader publishers now have incorporated book reviews in their teacher's guides. *Reading Teacher,* the monthly journal of the International Reading Association, publishes an annotated list each year of "Classroom Choices: Children's Trade Books." This list is comprised of books that are selected primarily by children and includes annotations that tell how each book fits into the school curriculum.

Still another way to promote trade-book reading is to establish means for sharing books or reacting creatively to them. The old-fashioned book report, it goes without saying, doesn't generally meet this need. A better approach—one that many teachers have found to be much more successful—is to encourage various types of sharing and creative projects following the completion of a book. In Appendix F you will find about seventy "Book Projects for Children and Teachers," which you can modify to fit the age level and interests of your particular students. All of these have been tested in classrooms and appear to be interesting and worthwhile to children.

Of course, the guidance the teacher offers is often the key factor in making them interesting and worthwhile. Simply passing out a list of projects is not very motivating. Probably the most effective form of guidance is that of reading children's books and carrying on some of the projects yourself. For instance, one of the oral projects suggested is to "put on a puppet play about one part of the book." You can imagine what an inspiration your sharing a book in this way could be for children to read "your" book or to share theirs in a similar fashion. Don't make your presentation so awe inspiring, though, that they'll be afraid to emulate you. Use a simple scene and puppets that the children could easily make themselves. Along with the more creative approaches, just chatting a bit about a book you have read will usually encourage many in the class to read the same one. In addition to guiding by showing, however, the teacher can occasionally meet with individuals for a few minutes to talk about books they have recently read and ways they may share them with others. (Incidentally, sometimes a child would prefer simply to share his book with you alone.) Or, you can have children get together in small groups once a week or so to talk about books they have been reading. (See page 226.)

Although the oral projects, the arts-and-crafts projects, and the drama projects listed in Appendix F are usually carried on by the children with great enthusiasm, teachers report that the written projects are often greeted at first with something less than spontaneous joy. Here again the teacher's leading the way will sometimes help immensely. A special bulletin board or "class book" for written projects is generally a must. Here the teacher's and children's written projects that have been donated may be seen by others. (Again, however, don't overawe them with your writing powers, or yours will be the only one there.) For children below the fifth grade, special praise in front of the class may also work in inspiring the "writing road to fame."

A final way of instigating the trade-book habit is to use extrinsic forms of positive reinforcement. We've already talked about intrinsic forms, such as finding books that are easy enough, making a wide choice available, and providing avenues for sharing and reacting creatively. All of these are directly involved with the act of reading itself. But sometimes this isn't enough, and some type of symbolic or even tangible reward may have to be used. This is a bit dangerous, of course, because if you're not careful, the extrinsic reward may become more important to some children than the intrinsic reward of pleasurable reading. For reluctant readers, however, it is probably worth the risk.

One form of extrinsic reward is simply that of having the children keep a personal record of the books they read. By checking these records with the children every few weeks and by praising them for the quality or variety, or, in some cases, the quantity of reading they have done, you can often spur children on to further reading. Some teachers like to add a bit of spice to the record keeping by providing small rectangles (about one-half inch by four inches) of colored paper that represent book spines. On each slip of paper the child writes the title and author of the book she has just finished; then the slip of paper is pasted on a dittoed "shelf," and the ditto sheet is placed in her folder or notebook.

Along with an individual-record scheme such as the one just described, you may wish to keep a class record of "Books We Have Read." However, note that this does not refer to a competitive form of record, such as a chart of names with so many stars after each name. Such a record may easily do more harm than good, since the slowest readers have no chance to "win the race," and because many children will falsely claim to have read certain books just to win it. What is being referred to is a cooperative record similar to the thermometer graph so often used for community-chest or blood-bank drives. Or you may wish to construct a "class book shelf," using different-colored paper for different types of books. For this type of project you can have the children put the title and author on the front of the piece of paper and their name on the back; these "books" can then be "taken off the shelf" and returned in an envelope to each child at the end of the year.

Some teachers give symbolic tokens for books that children say they have read; some prefer to give them only for books shared through projects. Whatever tactic teachers use, though, they shouldn't defeat the purpose by becoming too serious or demanding about it. Encourage rather than nag, inspire rather than require, help them cooperate rather than compete—these should be the mottoes of a teacher who desires to foster the reading of trade books for information and pleasure.

Using Children's Literature in an "Individualized-Reading" Program

Some teachers choose to go all the way with trade books and to use them as the major form of instructional material for teaching reading skills. With this approach, the children do the actual selection of materials to read. To differentiate this approach from other ways of individualizing reading instruction, let's call it the "trade-book-individualized reading program" or the TBIR program. The TBIR program is based on three principles espoused several decades ago by the child-development specialist, Willard C. Olson. The three principles are called *seeking, self-selection,* and *self-pacing.* In essence, what Olson was saying was that children by nature, are seeking organisms who are curious about their environment and want to learn about it. Such learning is best motivated and maintained when children are given many opportunities to make their own selection of stimuli and experiences and to explore at their own individual pace. Olson felt that these principles applied to the processes of learning to read, and thus he supported the TBIR movement. Similar views of learning were advocated before Olson by Dewey, Froebel, Rousseau, and other educational philosophers.

Research done on TBIR programs (10, 12, 15, 21) has had inconclusive results. In general it appears that the success of such a program depends upon the skill and enthusiasm of the teacher. It is likely that those who are successful in using a TBIR program are knowledgeable about the nature of reading, the various ways of teaching it, the means of managing such a flexible program, and the ways of finding books that fit children's needs and interests. It is definitely not a program to enter lightly without adequate preparation.

**Teaching Skills through a
Trade-Book-Individualized Reading Program**

Many people think of a TBIR program as one in which children are taught reading skills in a one-on-one manner during individual reading conferences. This is not the case. Although it may be a romantic notion to have the teacher on one end of the log and the attentive student on the other, this type of teaching has only limited possibilities in a classroom full of thirty active and ego-oriented children.

Most teachers who use a TBIR program employ a great many group-teaching techniques. Although they may teach some skills during an individual conference, most of the skill instruction is carried on with small groups of children with similar skill deficiencies. Mrs. Spiegal, for instance, may determine during an individual conference that Sandra needs help on decoding vowel-letter patterns. Although she may spend a moment teaching one of those patterns, she will also make a record of Sandra's problems and make sure she later receives instruction along with other children who are having similar problems. (Occasionally, the teacher may decide the entire class needs instruction on the same skill.)

Because of the availability of skills-management systems (discussed in Chapter 11), it is now somewhat easier to manage the skill-development component of a TBIR program than it used to be in the '50s and early '60s. An SMS provides the teacher with assessment tools, instructional materials, and record-keeping devices—all of which had to be invented or "scrounged up" by the pioneers of the TBIR program. With an SMS, a teacher can test her children to see what skill lessons they need. She can then divide children into temporary groups in order to teach those skill lessons. And she can keep reasonably accurate records of children's progress by using post tests and skill checklists.

The skills-management system, as you may recall from Chapter 11, can be purchased by the school district from systems publishers; or an SMS sold with a basal-reader program can be used. McGraw-Hill, for example, publishes a system, independent of basal readers, called *PRI Reading Systems* (14). Other examples of independent systems are the *Wisconsin Design* (13) and the *Fountain Valley Teacher Support System in Reading* (5). As you discovered in Chapters 10 and 11, however, a skills-management system attached to a basal-reader program can also be used as an independent system. The teacher simply uses the skill lessons in the teacher's guides and the various forms of tests provided by the publisher. The basal readers themselves then serve primarily as anthologies of good stories that children may or may not read depending on their own desires (although they are also sometimes used for teaching comprehension skills and for application of decoding skills.)

There are, of course, all sorts of ways of scheduling the instruction of skills. One teacher, for example, schedules seventy-five minutes of individual conferences with her students three days a week and seventy-five minutes of small-group instruction two days a week. (On these two days she meets with three groups for about twenty-five minutes each.) Another teacher does it this way:

- Monday: Individual conferences—50 minutes; skill group A—25 minutes
- Tuesday: Individual conferences—50 minutes; skill group B—25 minutes
- Wednesday: Individual conferences—30 minutes; skill group C—20 minutes—skill group D—20 minutes
- Thursday: Individual conferences—30 minutes; skill group C—20 minutes—skill group D—20 minutes
- Friday: Individual conferences—50 minutes; book sharing—25 minutes

In addition to this type of scheduled instruction, the teacher using a TBIR program usually carries on spontaneous instruction during some of the conferences. Frequently after a conference in which a particular skill has been discussed, he will assign a brief skill worksheet to the child to take back to her desk.

Managing Individual Conferences

The most common questions asked about individual conferences seem to be these: 1) how long should they be? 2) how often should they be? and 3) what should happen during a conference? Unfortunately, there are no easy answers to these questions; they depend on your purpose for a particular conference with a particular child. You may decide to give Jerry two conferences a week of about fifteen minutes each; Patricia, one conference a week of about ten minutes; and Randy, one conference every two weeks for five to ten minutes. Jerry, you see, is so far behind the rest of the class in skill development that you decide he needs a lot of individual help. Patricia is doing reasonably well in skill development and responds well to the small-group instruction she has been receiving from you. Randy is so advanced in his skill development that your major purpose in meeting with him is to provide praise and show interest in what he has been learning about through his reading.

Some teachers, on the other hand, feel it's important to give each child the same number of conferences and about the same amount of time. Consequently they schedule each child for one conference a week for about ten minutes each. With thirty students, this adds up to 300 minutes per week or one hour per day.

As to what happens during a conference, this, of course, varies widely with the different needs of the children, whether it's early in the school year or later, and with what the teacher has planned to emphasize during a particular week. Early in the school year, the first few conferences are often used for administering informal reading inventories and diagnostic tests. This enables the teacher to determine the instructional, independent, and frustration levels for each child and to assess his decoding and comprehension deficiencies.

Once the testing has been completed, the individual conferences can be used for a while to help children develop skill in selecting their own library books. This is usually done by listening to a child read out loud in order to see how difficult the book she has already selected seems to be for her, and by providing praise and encouragement. During these early conferences, the teacher often tries to determine some of the child's reading interests, which he then records in a notebook or folder for further reference. This will enable him to help each child find appropriate books when they go into the library or look for books elsewhere.

Checking Books for Readability

Some teachers teach their students to use a rule of thumb that a book will be too difficult if there are more than three or four "hard words" per page. (I can recall teaching that rule myself the first time I used a TBIR program. Fortunately the children ignored my rule and selected their books on the basis of interest, print size, book thickness, and the myriad of standards that children use for selecting books.) This rule would only make sense if every page of every book had the same number of words on it. A better way of helping children select books of the right difficulty is to put some type of mark inside the front cover of a book to indicate its approximate level. This can be done (with the help of the school librarian) to the books in the school library by marking an A for books of grades one to two reading level, a B for books of grades three to four reading level, and so on. The levels can be determined by referring to *Good Reading for Poor Readers* by Spache, the *Elementary School Library Collection,* or similar sources.

Another way of determining reading levels of books is to use a "readability formula." Many such formulas have been invented but none has proved to be better than estimates made by teachers who are knowledgeable of children and children's books. One of the best ways of determining, for instance, whether a book is suitable for an "average" second grader is to ask an experienced second-grade teacher. Most of the formulas, moreover, take far more time than it's worth in order to estimate the grade level of a book. One "formula," though, that is relatively easy and quick to use is the graph developed by Edward Fry and shown in Figure 13.1.

Directions for Using the Readability Graph

1. Select three one-hundred-word passages near the beginning, middle, and end. Skip all proper nouns in your count.

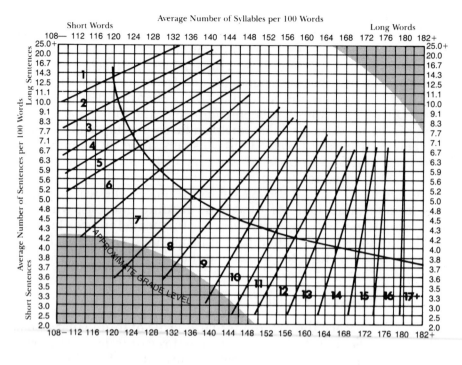

Figure 13.1. *Fry's graph for estimating readability. (From Edward Fry, "A Readability Formula that Saves Time,"* **Journal of Reading** *11 [April 1968]:513.)*

2. Count the total number of sentences in each hundred-word passage (estimating to nearest tenth of a sentence). Average these three numbers.

3. Count the total number of syllables in each hundred-word sample. There is a syllable for each vowel sound; for example: cat (1), blackbird (2), continental (4). Don't be fooled by word size; for example: polio (3), through (1). Endings such as *-y, -ed, -el,* or *-le* usually make a syllable, for example: ready (2), bottle (2). It may be convenient to count every syllable over one in each word and add 100. Average the total number of syllables for the three samples.

4. Plot on the graph the average number of sentences per hundred words and the average number of syllables per hundred words. Most plot points fall near the heavy curved line. Diagonal lines mark off approximate grade-level areas.

   Plotting these averages on the graph we find they fall in the fifth-grade area; hence the book is about fifth-grade difficulty level. If great variability is encountered either in sentence length or in the syllable count for the three selections, then randomly select several more passages and average them in before plotting.

For example,

		Sentences per 100 words	Syllables per 100 words
100-word sample	Page 5	9.1	122
100-word sample	Page 89	8.5	140
100-word sample	Page 160	7.0	129
		3)24.6	3)391
	Average	8.2	130

Having labeled the library books by level, you can advise each child on the approximate level for him. In giving such advice, however, be sure to give it rather loosely rather than firmly. There are many times that children can read books that would normally be too difficult except for the fact that the subject is so interesting. For those books that have not been labeled by level, the child is probably best left to guessing the level himself. Most children become quite adept at selecting books at the appropriate level, partly by their own experience, and partly by finding out in sharing periods what other children have been reading successfully.

Other Uses for Conferences

Another thing that is often done during a conference with a child is to encourage her to vary her reading interests. If Debbie has been reading nothing but horse stories, you may try to interest her in another type. Sometimes this is done by suggesting a specific title of a book, such as one that includes horses in the setting of the story but emphasizes a theme which is different from the usual theme of a horse and child helping each other survive. Other times it is done by using some type of extrinsic reward for reading several types of books. A "story train" is one example of this type of reward: each child has her own story train (made during an art lesson) consisting of construction-paper cars, engine, and caboose, each of a different color. Each color represents a different type of book—fantasy, sports, information, and so on. Whenever the child completes a particular type of book she gets to place a star on the appropriate train car. The goal is to have at least one star on each car by the end of the year. (The story train is usually kept in the child's folder rather than placing it on a group chart; a group chart usually encourages negative competition and negative self-images.)

Conferences are often used as a time to reinforce a skill or a word that was taught to the child during a recent small-group lesson. This can be done spontaneously or by asking the children in a small group to "look for an example in your library books of what you've learned today; write down the page number, and show me the example during your next conference with me." Conferences are also used for the very important process of building enthusiasm for school, for learning, and for reading. It is one of the few times that the child has the chance to relate to the teacher all by himself. As one teacher put it: "Through individual conferences I've come to know each child quite well!"

Questions to Ask During a Conference

Conferences are also used for developing thinking skills. In this regard, a teacher's questioning strategies are just as important with the TBIR program as they are with a basal-reading program. In either type of program, your purpose is to enhance children's communication with an author and to develop their thinking skills. Asking questions that only tap literal thinking is equally poor for both types of programs. If you always ask a child "Who is the main character of this story?" or "What is this story about?" you are merely encouraging him to read for shallow details. If you want him to read with greater depth, try varying the questions each time and try using plenty of questions at the inferential, evaluative, and creative levels. Here are a few examples of open-ended questions at these levels that can be used for any book:

Inferential

1. You say this story is about Jeff Roberts? Is Jeff struggling against another person, against himself, or against nature? Why do you think so? (main ideas)
2. Can you tell me about something in this book that makes the title of the book a good one? (recognizing details that support main ideas)
3. You've read about half of the book now. What do you think is going to happen next? (making predictions)

Critical

1. Is the story you're reading a real-life story or a make-believe story? What makes you think so? (real-life vs. fantasy)
2. Would you say this book (nonfiction) is full of facts or opinions? Can you give me an example of a fact that the author gives? Can you give me an example of an opinion? (fact vs. opinion)
3. Do you think this author is biased in any way? (Or, for younger children): How do you think the author feels about _____ ? Do you think she likes them? (detecting author's bias)
4. Do you think Jeff Roberts (the main character) did anything that showed he was strong, or fair, or kind? (evaluating according to criteria)

Creative

1. Jeff Roberts had a problem in this story. What was it? (inferential level) If you were Jeff Roberts, how would you solve that problem? (inventing flexible alternatives)
2. Do you have any problem in your life that is like the one Jeff Roberts had? How do you think you might solve that problem? (applying ideas to a new situation)
3. Now that you've finished this book, what kind of book project would you like to do about it? Is there a project that you've never tried before? (translating ideas to another medium)

Teaching Vocabulary

Teachers using a TBIR program often have children keep track of unfamiliar words that they run across during their reading of library books. One teacher, for example, has children make a bookmark for each new book. On the bookmark the children write down each word that causes them trouble. Then when they have an individual conference with her they talk about those words that are difficult to decode or understand.

Another teacher, who is concerned that children always learn words in context, has the children keep track of "hard words" by writing down on a sheet of paper the page number, the entire sentence, and the underlined word. One other teacher uses the bookmark idea but has them write both the word and the page number. That way the child doesn't have to write the entire sentence, but the teacher can have him find the word again during the conference and help him use context clues to discover the meaning.

Record Keeping

Record keeping is a vital component of a TBIR program. Without adequate records, teachers won't know what skills to emphasize for each child, what reading interests each one has, how much a child has read during the year, how deeply she is comprehending and thinking about what she reads, and what to tell parents during parent conferences. (Some parents may be worried, anyway, once they find out that basal readers and workbooks are not being used as they once were. Thus it is highly important to communicate with parents about the program and about their child's progress.)

A folder is usually kept for each child, in which is placed his SMS checklist of skills, his test results, samples of his responses on worksheets, notes on his reading interests, a list of new words he is mastering, and a record of his actual reading. This last record is often kept by the child. Each time, for example, that Janet reads a new book she fills in information on her Book Record sheet. The following is a sample of such a sheet:

	Reading Record				
Name: Janet Fromkin				Year: 1982–83	
Author	Title	Pages Read	Rating 0–5	Project	
Buck	*The Big Wave*	All	4	*Oral #3*	
O'Dell	*Islands of the Blue Dolphins*	All	5	*Drama #6*	
Jones	*All about Tar*	6	0	*None*	
Baker	*Walk the World's Rim*	All	4	*(My own idea)*	

Easing into an Individualized Program

As you can see by now, a TBIR program can be a highly exciting and worthwhile form of reading instruction. At the same time, it requires a considerable amount of knowledge and management capability on the part of the teacher. For most first-year teachers it is probably not the approach to take. By the second year, however, you may wish to ease into this type of individualized program. Some teachers try it for the first time by having only the "top group" engaged in the

TBIR program while the other groups continue in the basal-reading program. Then, as the teachers gain experience, they have other groups gradually join the top group.

Another way to break into the TBIR program is to use it only on one day per week at first, but with the entire class. As you develop skill in handling the program on a once-a-week basis, you can then increase the program to two days per week, and so on. This type of approach is more satisfying to those teachers who don't wish to single out the children in the top group as "privileged." In either case, whether you break in with one group or with one day per week, some type of gradual adjustment to individualized program is probably advisable.

Summary

An individualized program in which children read library books rather than basal readers can be an exciting and worthwhile way of teaching reading. However, it requires considerable skill, knowledge, and management capability on the part of the teacher. Whether a teacher uses this type of approach or a more traditional approach, the encouragement of library-book reading is essential to a successful reading program. It's easy for teachers to get so wrapped up in the teaching of reading skills that they forget to let their students read. It's easy to get overzealous about bringing every child "up to snuff" in one year's time and to forget the real purpose behind all that skill development. And it's easy to come to the conclusion that "if I just teach them the skills now," they'll have plenty of time "outside of school" or "later in life" to read for their own purposes and pleasure. But the long-range outcome which a teacher has to keep in mind is the person who learns to enjoy reading and who wants to turn to authors as an important means of gaining information and pleasure. Providing children with decoding and comprehension skills, of course, is essential for helping them reach that outcome. Yet it is not the only provision that must be made. Other provisions are equally essential. One of these is that of time: time during a busy school day to develop the habit of turning to books—for satisfying curiosity, for solving problems, and for having vicarious adventures. Time provided by a teacher who knows how to organize the days and weeks and months so that both growth through reading and growth in reading can take place.

References and Suggested Reading

1. Arbuthnot, May H. *Children's Books Too Good to Miss.* Ashtabula, OH: Western Reserve Press, 1971.

2. Barbe, W., and Abbott, J. *Personalized Reading Instruction.* New York: Parker, 1975.
3. Criscuolo, Nicholas P. "Mag Bags, Peg Sheds, Crafty Crannies and Reading." *Reading Teacher* 29 (January 1976): 376–8.
4. Fader, Daniel N., and McNeil, Elton B. *Hooked on Books: Program and Proof.* New York: G. P. Putnam's Sons, 1968.
5. *Fountain Valley Teacher Support System in Reading.* Richard L. Zweig Associates, 1971.
6. Huck, Charlotte S. *Children's Literature in the Elementary School.* New York: Holt, Rinehart, and Winston, 1976.
7. Hunt, Lyman. "The Effect of Self-Selection, Interest, and Motivation upon Independent, Instructional, and Frustration Levels." *Reading Teacher* 24 (1970): 146–51, 158.
8. *Individualized Reading from Scholastic.* Englewood Cliffs, NJ: Scholastic Book Services.
9. Johns, Jerry L., and Hunt, Linda. "Motivating Reading: Professional Ideas." *Reading Teacher* 28 (April 1975): 617–9.
10. Johnson, R. H. "Individualized and Basal Primary Reading Programs." *Elementary English* 42 (December 1965): 902–4.
11. Lapp, Diane, ed. *Making Reading Possible through Effective Classroom Management.* Newark, DE: International Reading Association, 1980.
12. Macdonald, James B., et al. "Individual versus Group Instruction in First Grade Reading." *Reading Teacher* 19 (May 1966): 643–7.
13. Otto, Wayne, and Chester, Robert D. *Objective Based Reading,* Reading, MA: Addison-Wesley, 1976.
14. *Prescriptive Reading Inventory.* New York: CTB/McGraw-Hill, 1972.
15. Safford, Alton L. "Evaluation of an Individualized Reading Program." *Reading Teacher* 13 (April 1960): 266–70.
16. Spache, Evelyn. *Reading Activities for Child Involvement.* Boston: Allyn and Bacon, 1976.
17. Spache, George D. *Good Reading for Poor Readers.* Champaign, IL: Garrard, 1974.
18. Sutherland, Zena. *Children and Books.* Chicago: Scott, Foresman, 1977.
19. Taylor, Frank D., et al. *Individualized Reading Instruction, Games and Activities.* Denver: Love Publishing Company, 1972.
20. Veatch, Jeanette. *Reading in the Elementary School.* New York: Ronald Press, 1966.
21. Vite, Irene W. "Individualized Reading—the Scoreboard on Control Studies." *Education* 81 (January 1961): 285–90.

Application Experiences for the Teacher-Education Class

1. Each person in the class can be given one of the following statements to defend or deny. After a few minutes of preparation, all those who have statement a. should first explain in their own words why it is

either true or false and then read one or two sentences from the book that will demonstrate the author's position on the statement. (The same procedures can be followed for the rest of the statements.)

Statements about Chapter 13

a.   An "individualized reading" program is not really individualized.

b.   The major justification for a TBIR program is the wide range of individual differences found in any elementary-school classroom.

c.   If two children both score at the 5.0 grade level on a reading test, this means they have the same reading abilities.

d.   Children's literature offers children opportunities for personal growth.

e.   The major practical use for children's literature is to provide reading for enjoyment.

f.   The Caldecott Medal is presented each year to the author of the most distinguished contribution to American literature for children and is awarded by the American Tradebook Association.

g.   There are really only two important classifications of children's books: fiction and nonfiction.

h.   It is a good idea to read those books considered by experts to be of good quality before reading widely in children's books.

i.   It is often true that the same three or four children in a classroom do most of the library-book reading.

j.   There is really no good way for a teacher to help a child select a library book.

k.   The purpose of "book projects" is to make sure the child has read the book.

l.   Skill instruction with a TBIR program is a catch-as-catch-can operation and need not be systematic.

m.   The Wisconsin Design program is a program for combining art and reading.

n.   With the TBIR program the individual conferences take about five minutes per day.

o.   The main activity during an individual conference is having a child read out loud to the teacher.

2.   With a partner make up three open-ended questions that could be used in an individual conference for any book a child has read. The questions should include one that helps a child to develop images or associations about what she has read (or is now reading), one that helps her follow a sequence of events or ideas, and one that helps her think about specific and important details. See pages 378–379 for an illustration of this.

3.   Carry on an individual conference with a partner about a book (preferably a children's book she has just read or is in the process of reading). If your partner has not read one recently, she can use a movie or television show as a substitute. (Again, a children's book would be best, however.) Ask your partner a few of the questions listed on pages 378 to 379 to encourage inferential, critical, and creative thinking. Also

discuss an unusual word that she came across in her reading (or view-ing). Check her comprehension of one or two paragraphs after she has read them silently. In addition, check her decoding skills by having her read two or three paragraphs out loud. Keep notes on the conference.

Field Experiences in the Elementary-School Classroom

1. Conduct an individual conference with one child related to a library book he has been reading. Ask him some questions you made up in your teacher-education class for Experience #2. Also ask a few ques-tions from the list on pages 378–379. Check his comprehension of one or two paragraphs after he has read them silently. In addition check his decoding skills by having him read two or three paragraphs out loud. Keep notes on the conference. If possible, share these notes with another teacher who has been working with the same child.

2. Examine the school library to see whether any system has been devel-oped there for helping children find books at the right level of difficulty. If no system has been developed, think about a system that can be used. If there is no school library, find out other ways that teachers in the building help children get access to a variety of library books.

PART THREE

Special Concerns Related to Reading Instruction

CHAPTER 14

A child's perception of what reading is will determine to a large extent how he learns to read.

Evaluating through Miscue Analysis and Other Diagnostic Tools

Chapter Preview

The evaluation role is one of the most important roles that a teacher plays. Unless this role is played well, the quality of the planning and interacting roles suffers. When it comes to something as complex as reading instruction, careful and continual evaluation are crucial to a teacher's success. In this book so far, we've talked about a variety of evaluation principles and techniques, which we'll review briefly before going on to new ideas. After the review we'll discuss three diagnostic evaluation tools in greater detail. First we'll talk about miscue analysis and how it can be used as a diagnostic teaching technique. Then we'll look at how miscue analysis can be used as a diagnostic testing technique when combined with an informal reading inventory. Finally we'll discuss the use of an informal word-recognition inventory as a diagnostic instrument.

Sometimes humans are much smarter than they think they are. I've noticed that even their errors often demonstrate their use of intelligence.

A Review of Evaluation Principles in this Book

Evaluation principles have been emphasized in each of the chapters of this book so far. Rather than discuss each of them again, let me refer you to Table 14.1. In this table you can see at a glance that the evaluation role of a reading teacher is a busy one.

Table 14.1   Evaluation Principles Emphasized in Each Chapter

Chapter	Evaluation Principle
1	The most important growth that a child makes in reading is in learning to communicate with an author. (He can learn all of the subskills and still not be a good reader.) It is important to assess this growth and not just his growth in subskill development.
2	Whether a word is part of a child's sight vocabulary is illustrated by her instant recognition of the word in print. Whether a word is part of her semantic vocabulary is illustrated by her grasp of an author's message, and not simply by her selection of the correct synonym on a test.
3	A pupil's phonic-analysis abilities should not be assessed by his ability to "sound out" words one letter at a time. (Try to "sound out" *knight,* for example.) It should be assessed by determining whether he recognizes common spelling pat-

continued

Table 14.1—continued

Chapter	Evaluation Principle
	terns, pays particular attention to initial graphemes, and combines phonic analysis with context analysis.
4	A child's skill in syllabication should not be measured by asking her to draw lines between syllables. It should be measured by asking her to show the effects on pronunciation of dividing a word in different ways.
5	A student's literal comprehension of a reading selection is not a yes-and-no type of thing. It involves a highly complex interaction of recognition of context signals, sentence structures, intonation clues, visual images, sequence, and significant details. The effectiveness of this interaction can best be assessed through an in-depth discussion of the selection with the teacher.
6	Higher-level thinking skills are sometimes ignored in our assessment of children's reading abilities. Children who truly communicate with an author use inferential, critical, and creative thinking as well as literal thinking. A skillful questioning strategy needs to be employed by the teacher in order to assess children's higher-level thinking abilities.
7	The concept of readiness for reading can't be separated from the concept of evaluation. To make sure children are ready for a particular reading experience, the teacher has to assess what they already know first. The concept of readiness should be important at every grade level and to every learning experience.
8	It is just as important to evaluate a child's desire to read as it is to evaluate his ability to read. If his desire to read is weak, it may have something to do with the teacher's failure to follow principles of motivation and retention or with the lack of a "modeling approach."
9	Perhaps the most crucial evaluation decision that a reading teacher makes is what book to place a student in for instructional purposes. Using an informal reading inventory and other sources helps the teacher make this decision.
10	The teacher's role includes the evaluation of instructional materials as well as children. Basal readers and other materials should meet definite criteria of excellence.
11	A performance-based approach, such as a skills-management system, can be highly useful in determining how well children are learning isolated subskills of the reading process. It is far less useful in determining how well a child can integrate the subskills and communicate with an author.

continued

Table 14.1—continued

Chapter	Evaluation Principle
12	A language-experience approach, if it is to be effective in actually teaching reading skills, needs to have a strong evaluation component. Since the teacher is faced with a program that has no built-in assessment devices, it is important that she supplement the program with skill checklists, think in terms of performance objectives whenever appropriate, and possibly employ a full-fledged skills-management system.
13	A trade-book-individualized-reading program needs to have a strong evaluation component similar to the one required with language-experience approaches.

The Nature of Miscue Analysis

The purpose of "miscue analysis" is to help the teacher discover answers to questions like these: What strategies is Jane using to decode unfamiliar words? Is she guessing wildly or is she using context clues? Is she relying too much on phonics? Is she ignoring phonic clues? Are some of her miscues a result of inadequate decoding skills or simply a result of a nonstandard dialect? Questions such as these are answered through analyzing the miscues made by a child during the time she is reading orally.

Do you remember from Chapter 1 the miscues that Tommy made:

Author: Roy saw a little boat pull a big boat.
Tommy: Roy was a little boat pulled by a big boat.

What you're doing when you carry on miscue analysis is simply asking yourself why. Why did he make his first miscue? Why did he make the next one? And so on. By answering these questions you'll often be able to learn about a child's reading strategies and his notion of what reading is. Once you've discovered his strategies for reading and his perception of reading, you may have come much farther toward helping him become a better reader.

If we take Tommy's miscues as an example, we can speculate that Tommy's perception of reading is probably that "reading is a meaningful process." Imagine Tommy defining it this way: "Reading is retelling a story in a way that makes sense." Since Tommy doesn't think it makes sense for a little boat to pull a big boat, he doesn't even see the way the author wrote the story. Therefore, he reads the sentence in a way that makes sense to him!

Now that we have a rough hypothesis for what Tommy's perception of reading is, let's see if we can find out what his strategies for reading are. Well, what's Tommy's first miscue? He sees the word *saw* as *was*, isn't that right? That tells us a little bit about his strategies. He predicts what words are coming next, for one thing. And that's a good strategy to have. But in this case he predicts *was* instead of *saw*.

Does he have a strategy for checking on his predictions? Does he glance at the first letter of the word he predicts, for instance, to see if it starts with the appropriate letter? Evidently not, for he goes right on reading. As a result, Tommy ends up with the idea that "Roy *was* a little boat. . . ." But this doesn't bother him, for after all, most people give their boat a name. So far, so good, as far as Tommy is concerned.

Now we come to the fifth word in the sentence. The author is saying, "Roy saw a little boat pull a big boat." But Tommy, you remember, is talking about a little boat named *Roy*. Naturally, then,

Your concern when listening to a child read should be for the process rather than the product.

he wouldn't say, "Roy was a little boat pull a big boat." That simply doesn't make good grammatical sense. To make good sense one would have to say, "Roy was a little boat pulled by a big boat." We now know a little bit more about Tommy's reading strategies. As far as he's concerned, a sentence should make sense both semantically and syntactically.

So what do we *know* from listening to Tommy read just one sentence? Well, actually we know very little, but we can begin to make some hypotheses that we can check as he continues to read. We can hypothesize that Tommy perceives reading as a form of communication and not just a process of "sounding out" words. We can also hypothesize that his strategies for reading include the strategy of go for broke. That is, he goes for the big message and doesn't concern himself very much with the little clues. He ignores the little clue of the second word in the sentence starting with *s* instead of *w*. He ignores the little clue that there is no suffix *ed* at the end of *pull*. (And, as you'll see later, he ignores little clues like periods, question marks, and capital letters as well.)

As we continue listening to Tommy read, we discover that our hypotheses are probably correct. He consistently goes for the big message and ignores the little clues. We now have a better idea of how to help him improve his reading. We don't want to spoil his perception that reading is a form of communication. But we do want to increase the accuracy of his reading by encouraging him to pay attention to at least the first letter in a word (*s* instead of *w*), to pay attention to suffixes (*pull* instead of *pulled*), and to develop a better visual memory of important sight words like *saw* and *was*.

Using Miscue Analysis as a Diagnostic Teaching Tool

Now that you've seen a sample of miscue analysis in action, you can probably see how useful a device it can sometimes be to the teacher— whether she's using a basal-reader program, a language-experience approach, a trade-book individualized program, or some combination of these approaches. Whenever you have the opportunity to listen to a child read to you, you can listen to a child's miscues and ask yourself why he's making them. In this way, as we did with Tommy, we can find out more about his perception of reading, his reading strategies, and what type of special instruction he needs.

What this means, of course, is that your concern when listening to a child read should be for the process rather than the product. Be concerned not so much for a perfect performance that you create by correcting every mistake Lisa makes, but rather for the processes she is using in order to perform for you. Does her performance signify to you that she perceives of reading as a process of sounding out each word correctly for you? Does her performance signify that she perceives of reading as a task to rush through as fast as possible in spite of mistakes?

It's true that you may wish to stop a child sometimes when her rendition doesn't make any sense. ("That sentence didn't make sense to me, Lisa; would you try it again, please?") Many times, however, the child will gain more if you just listen to her read, and carry on miscue analysis while you're listening. In order to do this, you may have to take a few notes, such as the following: Lisa: *was* for *saw* or *pulled by* for *pull*. This will help you remember her miscues and allow you to think more about them later.

Suppose, for example, that Mrs. Franklin sees this: "The dog ran over to Sammy and barked and barked at him." But Kevin reads this: "Da dog went over to Sammy and bock and bock at him." Mrs. Franklin knows that Kevin's mother tongue is Black English rather than Standard English. Therefore, she realizes that Kevin has performed a double translation—from print to Standard English to Black English—on the printed words *The* and *barked*. She also realizes that in substituting *went* for *ran* he has done little damage to his comprehension of the passage and simply used *went* because he had predicted that *went* would occur in that sentence slot. Mrs. Franklin decides not to stop Kevin but merely records "*went* for *ran*—Kevin—initial letter." Later she will work with Kevin and a few other children on paying more attention to first-letter clues.

On the other hand, suppose that Susan reads the same sentence like this: "Then Doug ran *other* to Sammy and *backed* and *backed* at her." Mrs. Franklin sees immediately that Susan is relying almost exclusively on minor phonic clues and is paying no attention to syntactic clues (*other* does not fit grammatically where *over* should be); or to semantic clues (*Sammy* and *her* don't match and people seldom *back* at others). Mrs. Franklin knows she has her work cut out for her. Susan needs to be taught to read for meaning rather than empty words. Mrs. Franklin knows this because she has carried on miscue analysis while Susan was reading. She does not stop to correct her after each word that she reads wrong.

Using Miscue Analysis as a Diagnostic Testing Tool

In addition to using miscue analysis as a diagnostic teaching tool, you may also wish to combine it with an informal reading inventory. This will allow you to determine a child's reading levels and specific reading problems at the same time. As a child reads out loud to you, you will count miscues, as usual, in order to determine whether the selection she's reading is at her instructional level or some other level. But you can also record the specific miscues she makes, so that you can later determine her reading strategies and the specific type of instruction she needs. To carry on this type of combined evaluation, you will need to learn some type of "marking code" and how to transfer your coded information onto a "miscue-analysis checklist."

**A Marking Code for Combining
Miscue Analysis with an Informal Reading Inventory**

The teacher may wish to make up his own marking code or use the following:

How Child Reads	*How to Mark*
1. *Omission* (of words, morpheme, phrase, or line) *Child:* . . . he saw his mother coming.	*Author:* ⟨Then⟩ he saw his mother coming.
2. *Insertion* (of word, morpheme, or phrase) *Child:* In the forest was a big park.	*Author:* ‸ᴵⁿ The forest was a big park.
3. *Teacher's decoding* (after five seconds) of a word or phrase. *Child:* The . . . was very big.	*Author:* The dinosaur *t** was very big.
4. *Repetition of word or phrase* *Child:* The boy went to—went to—school.	*Author:* The boy went to ̶R̶ school.
5. *Self-correction of word or phrase* *Child:* He was—he saw—his teacher.	*Author:* He was He saw his teacher.
6. *Word substitution* *Child:* She worked with them.	*Author:* She worked with *them* him.
7. *Wrong order* *Child:* He went over.	*Author:* ⟨Over⟩he went.↙
8. *Nonsense substitution* *Child:* He flew in a hillycopy.	*Author:* He flew in a *hillycopy* helicopter.
9. *Long hesitation* (but less than five seconds) *Child:* I . . . wish I could go.	*Author:* I ✓ wish I could go.
10. *Incorrect phrasing* (usually indicated by pauses for breath) *Child:* She ran down the street and into her house.	*Author:* She ran down the|street and into|her house.
11. *Punctuation definitely ignored* *Child:* "Help mother," she said.	*Author:* "Help ⌐ Mother⌐" she said.

---

*Some teachers use a *P* to indicate that they have pronounced it for the child.

Scoring and Recording the Combined Miscue Analysis and IRI

Many scoring schemes have been devised for a combined miscue analysis and informal reading inventory. Some of them, however, require too many agonizing judgments and take too long to learn and to use. A simple and reasonably reliable scoring and recording procedure follows:

1. Mark (with your coding system) every miscue, as this record will be helpful later when you complete the "miscue-analysis checklist."
2. When computing reading levels, however, record but don't count miscues on proper nouns or titles. Record but don't count miscues due to a nonstandard dialect, as these are not really reading miscues. Record but don't count punctuation, hesitations or poor phrasing. Count all other miscues, one point for each miscue, except for phrases that are corrected, repeated, or transposed.
3. For corrections and repetitions count only one point for the total part repeated or self-corrected, whether it is one word or two or more connected words.
4. For two or more words that are transposed, count only one point.
5. If the same word is missed more than once, count it each time.

A Coded Sample of a Reading Selection

The following is a selection read by Tommy into a tape recorder and later marked by his teacher.

"Lunch on a Boat"**

One hot day, | Roy went on a boat ride

and He went with his teacher | and |

his school friends.

It | was cool on the water.

And it was fun.|

*Bank Street College of Education, "Lunch on a Boat," in *Around the City* (New York: Macmillan Co., 1965.)

The boat went | by big city | houses. |

(shops) *
Slow boats and fast boats | went by

in the water. |

Roy saw *~ a little | boat pull *ed |

(by)*
a big boat.

R *
Then | it was time for lunch. |

(soon) *
Some children had lunch | with them. |

Some children had money

for hot dogs. |

All the children | had milk. |

Roy | had a hot dog. |

P
His friend Max said, |

"Look at | the house boat, Roy." |

Roy turned around fast.

(He) *
His hot dog fell in the water. |

"It fell[!]" said Roy. |

"My hot dog fell. |

Now I have no hot dog. |

And I have no money." |

(There) *   Mac
Here, Roy," said | Max.

*I have *   (said)*
He gave some money to Roy. |

First let's see whether this selection represents Tommy's instructional, frustration, or independent level. Then we'll examine the miscues carefully to see what they tell us about his reading strategies and specific problems. Here are the miscues that we will count in estimating reading level:

1. insertion of *and*
2. corrected substitution of *shops . . .* for *slow . . .*
3. "transposal" of *saw* (substitution of *was* for *saw*)
4. insertion of *ed* suffix
5. insertion of *by*
6. repetition of *then*
7. corrected substitution of *soon* for *some*
8. repetition of *his*
9. corrected substitution of *there* for *here*
10. substitution of *I* for *he*
11. substitution of *have* for *gave*
12. corrected substitution of *said Roy* for *to Roy*

You will notice that, for the purpose of computing reading levels, we do not ocunt the teacher's decoding of *Max* or Tommy's substitution of *Mac* for *Max*, since *Max* is a proper noun.

The total number of countable miscues is twelve. Since there are 133 words in the total selection, this means that his word recognition score is 91 percent (133 − 12 = 121 . . . 121 divided by 133 equals .91). This places this particular selection in the questionable range. As you may recall from Chapter 9, the estimates for reading levels are often based on the following percentages:

Independent	98%
Instructional	94–97%
Questionable	91–93%
Frustration	90% or less

An Application of Miscue Analysis

Now let's use the miscue-analysis technique with the same selection. First you may notice that his phrasing is somewhat poor, even on this primer selection. In the sentence "It was cool on the water," for instance, he takes a deep breath after the word *It* rather than taking it at the period *before* the word "It," or taking it after the word *cool* or *water.* This tells us that he needs help in learning to pause (and breathe if necessary) at the end of sentences or phrases. It also tells us that he has never really learned the importance of punctuation and intonation and how they aid in both comprehension and communication. As another example of this, notice the sentence "Look at the house boat, Roy." Rather than pause at the comma, he pauses (and even takes a breath) right after the word *Look*.

Next, let's look at all of the words he hesitated on before pronouncing them. Normally a long hesitation indicates either that the child wasn't expecting that word, or he's unsure of the word he's hesitating on, or he's not sure of the next word coming up. Here's a list of the words he hesitated on and the words that follow:

One hot day, Roy went . . .

He went with his teacher . . .

and his school . . .

It was cool on . . .

The boat went by big . . .

Roy turned around . . .

His friend Max said . . .

What clues do we get from this? If his strategy is to go for the big message and ignore little clues, he may be "overpredicting." When he reads "One hot day," for instance, he predicts that the next word is going to be *the*. When the word *the* doesn't show up, he hesitates, until he realizes that the word is *Roy:* "One hot day, Roy went on a boat ride." Look at the rest of the hesitations and see whether this hypothesis may explain his hesitations.

So you see that in each case he may have been predicting a word other than the one that appeared? What's another possibility? Maybe he's just unsure of the actual words he's hesitating on: *Roy, his, his, cool, by, turned,* and *Max*. If so, is there something that these words have in common? Do they all have an irregular spelling pattern, for instance? Do they show that he doesn't understand vowel-letter patterns like VC and VCE? This doesn't seem to be the case, does it? There's nothing very consistent about the actual words on which he hesitates.

Well, then, perhaps it's the words that follow that worry him. By hesitating on *his*, for example, he has more time to decode the following word *teacher*. Here are the words that follow the actual hesitations: *went, teacher, school, on, big, around, said*. These do seem to be more difficult words than the actual hesitation words. So now we have three hypotheses that may explain his hesitation: 1) he's overpredicting without first glancing at the first letter of the word, 2) he's stalling for time so he can figure out the following word, 3) his sight word vocabulary is weak.

Let's go back and look at the type of actual miscues that he made. What type was most predominant? If you'll look back at our list on page 400, you'll see that the most common type of miscue was substitution. Seven out of twelve of the miscues involved a substitution, although one was also classified as a transposal and four of the substitutions were self-corrections. Why does he make so many substitutions? Is it because he doesn't pay attention to first-letter clues? Are his substitutions meaningful, or do they lack good grammatical or semantic sense? Let's look.

His first substitution (which he corrected) is "Shops boats and fast . . ." for "Slow boats and fast. . . ." Is this grammatically sensible? No, and probably this is why Tommy corrects it. Is it semantically sensible for him to start out with the word *Shops?* Yes, probably, since he's just been reading about the boats going by "big city houses." Perhaps he anticipated that the boat would also go by shops as well. But notice again how Tommy ignores the "little clues." The word *slow* starts with *s-l-o,* whereas the substitution word *shops* starts with *s-h-o.* Does Tommy need to become more observant about initial-letter *clusters* as well as initial letters?

As we look at the rest of his substitutions, we realize that they all make good grammatical and semantic sense. Obviously Tommy is trying to read for meaning, even though his accuracy of reading leaves much to be desired.

Using a Miscue-Analysis Checklist

In Figure 14.1 you have a sample checklist that may be used for recording a child's miscues. By having each child read several selections, you can get a more reliable idea of his instructional reading level and his reading strategies and problems as well. By tape recording the child as he reads, you can later record the miscues on the Miscue-Analysis Checklist (MAC) and then look for definite patterns. On Tommy's checklist, for example, you can see that he has a large number of self-corrections (observation 1) and an enormous number of substitutions (observations 14, 15, and 16). His phrasing is quite poor (observation 9), so poor in fact, that the teacher stopped counting after the primer selection. Observations 3 and 4 show that he hesitates over words a great deal, so much in fact, that his teacher has to pronounce many of the words for him as the material gets more and more difficult. (Rather than try to apply phonic analysis, his pattern is either to come up with a substitution or to wait for the teacher to decode the word.)

Tommy's comprehension (observation 11) is rather amazing, considering all of the miscues he makes. But this is because so many of his miscues are sensible substitutions; thus he doesn't lose the big

Level of Reading Passage

Observations°	Pre	Pr	1	2¹	2²	3¹	3²	4	5	6
1. Self-corrections		4	1	3	6					
2. Repetitions		2	5	1	3					
3. Words pronounced by teacher		1	6	7	11					
4. Long hesitations		6	4	6	8					
5. Transpositions		1		1						
6. Mispronunciations					1					
7. Morpheme omissions	2		2		3					
8. Morpheme insertions	1	1	3							
9. Incorrect phrasing	6	10	X	X	X					
10. Punctuation ignored		2	4	2	7					
11. Answers incorrect				1½	1					
12. Whole-word omissions			1							
13. Whole-word insertions		1	1		1					
14. Acceptable substitutions		1	4	5	15					
15. Nonsemantic substitutions		2	2	6	7					
16. Nongrammatical substitutions			1	1	6					

Inferences	Pre	Pr	1	2¹	2²	3¹	3²	4	5	6
①. Basic irregular sight words not known (See Table 4.2.)			?	X	X					
②. Weak in phonic analysis skills		X	X	X	X					
3. Weak in structural analysis skills		?								
4. Nonstandard dialect										
5. Weak in contextual analysis: semantic clues					?					
6. Weak in contextual analysis: grammatical clues					?					
7. Comprehension poor										
⑧. Punctuation not understood		?	X	X	X					
⑨. Needs help on phrasing	?	X	X	X	X					

° Observations 1–5 most often (*but not always*) related to weak word recognition skills.
  Observations 6–8 most often (*but not always*) related to dialect differences.
  Observations 9–16 most often (*but not always*) related to weak comprehension skills.

Figure 14.1. *Miscue Analysis Checklist for Tommy. (From Frank B. May,* To Help Children Read, *Columbus, OH: Charles E. Merrill, 1978, p. 176.)*

meaning that the author intends him to get. Besides, by having the teacher decode several of the words for him, he can hang on to the thread of the author's message.

So if you were Tommy's teacher, what inferences might you make about his reading problems? We already know his strategies: to go for the big meaning, to wait for help from the teacher, to guess whenever possible, rather than use phonic analysis, to ignore little clues like punctuation, initial letters, clusters, and phonic patterns. If you'll look at the bottom half of the miscue-analysis checklist, you'll see that the teacher came up with four major inferences: that he needs help on some basic irregular sight words, on phonic analysis, on punctuation, and on phrasing. Without a doubt, she's learned a great deal about Tommy's reading abilities from using miscue analysis and some type of miscue-analysis checklist. (Transcript 1 in the Instructor's Manual shows a complete analysis of the five selections that Tommy read into a tape recorder.)

Follow-Up Instruction after a Miscue Analysis

Tommy's teacher now knows that he needs help on irregular sight words, phonic analysis, punctuation, and phrasing. What should she do about it? The first thing she may want to do is to administer some type of diagnostic word-recognition test so that she can determine exactly what irregular sight words he doesn't know and what specific weaknesses in phonics he has. In a moment we'll talk about this type of test.

Another thing Tommy's teacher may wish to do is to work with him individually in a conference setting. Here are the kinds of steps she could use in such a setting.

1. Identification of behavior to be changed: Have Tommy listen to the tape recording while he reads the same passages silently. See if he can "discover the differences between the author's words and his own words." If he doesn't notice them, gently point them out to him. For example, show him the actual phonic clues he is ignoring. (If one is a phonic clue he doesn't already know, of course, then he'll need a special lesson on it, preferably in a small skill group of children needing the same lesson.)
2. Analysis and correction of miscues: Go back to each substitution (and to some of the self-corrections as well) and ask him why the word he substituted did not fit the phonic clues.
3. Positive reinforcement of desired behavior: Praise him each time he recognizes a phonic clue that he ignored.
4. Practicing desired behavior: Have him read more passages to you with the idea that for the time being all clues should be

noticed, not just context clues. This will slow him down considerably at first, but you can gradually help him speed up again. Remember, your goal is not to make Tommy a word-by-word phonics reader. That would do more harm than good. Your goal is to make him a more efficient reader—one who uses just enough clues to decode the word correctly 95 percent of the time. If he ends up using self-corrections or acceptable substitutions about 5 percent of the time (one word out of twenty), this would be no cause for alarm but would indicate instead a mature reader.

5. Schedule reinforcement to strengthen desired behavior: Schedule several brief conferences—frequently at first and then more and more infrequently—during which time Tommy will read to you.

6. Extinction of undesired behavior: During the series of brief conferences, use praise often at first, but gradually diminish it; point out his miscues at first, but gradually shift to ignoring Tommy's miscues and using only occasional praise for "noticing all the clues."

Using the Word-Recognition Inventory

It is often wise not to stop the assessment of reading skills with the IRI and MAC. These procedures are not systematic enough for determining highly specific weaknesses. Although they are quite suitable for assessing reading levels and for providing insights into reading strategies and major problems, they can seldom delineate specific word-recognition problems. They cannot tell you, for instance, on which particular phonic elements Tommy needs help.

This raises a serious problem. To be very precise about the nature of a child's word-recognition problems would require a huge battery of tests and the assistance of a remedial-reading specialist. Obviously this type of analysis cannot be done for each child—given the present facilities of the public schools. But you can, as a classroom teacher, make an intelligent estimate of each child's specific deficiencies by administering a word-recognition inventory of an informal nature. One inventory of this type is presented in full in Appendix H. (The directions for administration are included there.) A small portion of this inventory follows so that you can get an idea of its contents.

The greater portion of the "Word Recognition Inventory" in Appendix H will be satisfactory for most children who are seven and above. For younger children, however, the inventory may be too difficult—because they are not far enough advanced in a developmental reading program and because of the use of nonsense words in parts

The Baf Test

Part I: Consonant letters, digraphs, and clusters

(For those whose instructional level is at least "Primer")

This part of the inventory should be administered individually. You will need to reproduce a copy of this page for each child. The children should be encouraged to try decoding each nonsense word without your help. If they miss one, simply circle it and have them continue. Be sure to pronounce the first two for them (*băf* and *căf*) with a short /a/ and have them pronounce those two correctly before they continue.

Name of Student _____

Directions to be Read or Told to the Student

These words are nonsense words. They are not real words. I'd like you to think about what sounds the letters have; then read each word out loud without my help. Don't try to go fast; read the list slowly. If you have any trouble with a word, I'll just circle it and you can go on to the next one. The first word is *băf*. Now you say it. The second is *căf*. Now you say it . . . . All right, now go on to the rest of the words in row 1."

A	B	C	D	E	F	G	H
			Consonant Letters				
1. baf	caf	daf	faf	gaf	haf	jaf	
2. kaf	laf	maf	naf	paf	raf	saf	
3. taf	vaf	waf	yaf	zaf	baf	bax	caf
			Consonant Digraphs				
4. chaf	phaf	shaf	thaf	whaf	fack	fang	fank
			Consonant Clusters				
5. blaf	braf	claf	craf	draf	dwaf	flaf	fraf
6. glaf	fraf	fand	plaf	praf	quaf	scaf	scraf
7. skaf	slaf	smaf	smaf	spaf	splaf	spraf	squaf
8. staf	straf	swaf	thraf	traf	twaf		

Part II: Vowel letters, vowel digraphs, and clusters

(For those whose instructional level is at least "Primer")

This part of the inventory should also be administered individually. You will need to reproduce a copy of this test for each child. The children should be encouraged to try decoding each nonsense word without your help. If they miss one, simply circle it and have them continue. Be sure to pronounce the first one for them (*băf*) and have them pronounce it correctly before they continue. Note that for 3G (*boof*), the children should be asked to pronounce it two ways; circle it if they cannot. The same is true of 5B (*bufe*).*

Name of Student _____

Directions to be Read or Told to the Student

"These words are nonsense words. They are not real words. I'd like you to think about what sounds the letters have; then read each word out loud without any help. Don't try to go fast; read the list slowly. If you have any trouble with a word, I'll just circle it and you can go on to the next one. The first word is *baf*. Now you say it . . . . All right, now go on to the rest of the words in row 1."

A	B	C	D	E	F	G
1. baf	bafe	barf	baif	bawf		
2. bef	befe	berf	beaf			
3. bof	bofe	borf	boaf	bouf	boif	boof*
4. bif	bife	birf				
5. buf	bufe*	burf				

of the inventory. (In case you are curious as to why nonsense words were used, the nonsense words avoid the problem of Tommy's pronouncing a word correctly simply because it is already part of his sight vocabulary, when you may be testing for phonic knowledge or skill in morphemic analysis. For example, if he pronounces a regular word like *cape* correctly, is this because the word is already quite familiar to him or because he uses phonic knowledge to decode it?)

You will notice that the inventory gets progressively more difficult and that each part is recommended only for those whose instructional level is at a certain point. Part VII, for example, on decoding syllables, is recommended only for those whose instructional level is at least 2^1. If a child's instructional level is not at least 2^1, it is doubtful that very much remedial attention should be given to syllabication and accent at this time. Emphasis should be placed instead on phonic analysis and the development of sight vocabulary, introducing syllabication later as part of a developmental program. In other words, testing the child for something that is probably beyond his level of normal skill development is likely to be a waste of time for you and the child.

Correcting Assessed Difficulties

If children have a perfect or near-perfect score on each part of the word-recognition inventory, yet make several errors during the combined informal reading inventory and miscue-analysis session, it is likely that they have developed the habit of simply ignoring phonic, structural, or contextual clues. If this is the case, then merely pointing out the habit to them during a private conference will sometimes be the only remedy needed—particularly if their reading is tape recorded so they can hear the errors they are making, and particularly if you handle the conferences in a way similar to the way suggested for Tommy. (See pages 404 to 405.)

Using a Group-Assessment Chart

What about the child who doesn't have a perfect score on each part of the word-recognition inventory? As you may expect, this may apply to most of the children in your class. Even your very best readers will usually have a few deficiencies in their decoding skills that need work.

In Chapters 2, 3, and 4 are suggestions for helping children learn to recognize phonic, morphemic, and context clues and to build up their sight vocabularies. A teacher could apply these suggestions on a one-to-one basis with each child, but it's far more efficient to develop skill groups instead. To determine which children will be in each group, teachers often use a checklist from an available skills-management system (such as the portion of one shown in Chapter 11 on page 325. Another way is to use a group-assessment chart, similar to the one shown in Figure 14.2. You will notice in this chart that the names of the children in your class can be listed across the top of the chart and the specific word-recognition problems listed on the left-hand side. Then for each child you can check the problem she seems to have, according to the results of your word-recognition inventory. When you're finished, you will have a record of how many children, and which ones, seem to need help with each particular word-recognition skill. For instance, you may discover that seven chil-

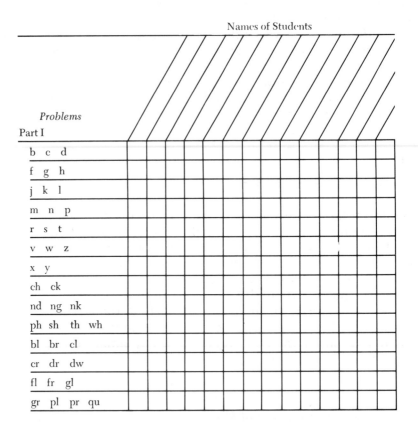

Figure 14.2. *Group-Assessment Chart for Recording Deficiencies in Word-Recognition Skills. Instructions: Each problem listed may be considered as one remedial or review lesson (or set of lessons, depending on how many follow-up lessons are required). Check the deficiencies each child has, according to the results of the Word-Recognition Inventory shown in Appendix H in the back of the book. Then decide which children should be grouped together temporarily for a remedial or review lesson. For example, if three children missed the b, two missed the c, two missed the b and c, and one missed the b, c, and d, you may decide to treat these eight children as an instructional group and provide them with one or more lessons on b, c, and d combined.*

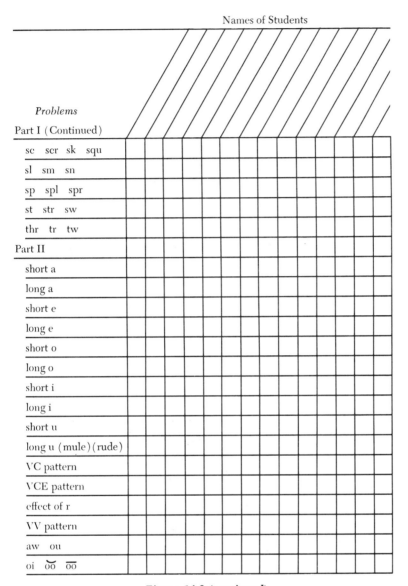

Names of Students

Problems
Part I (Continued)

sc scr sk squ											
sl sm sn											
sp spl spr											
st str sw											
thr tr tw											

Part II

short a											
long a											
short e											
long e											
short o											
long o											
short i											
long i											
short u											
long u (mule)(rude)											
VC pattern											
VCE pattern											
effect of r											
VV pattern											
aw ou											
oi ŏŏ ōō											

Figure 14.2 (continued)

dren need help with the VCE pattern. On one or more (usually more) occasions, then, you would meet with those children in a group and provide them with instruction concerning that pattern. For some children one or two meetings are all that will be necessary. For others, several meetings may be required. The Group Assessment Chart may now be used again, this time to indicate those children who no longer have the deficiency.

	Names of Students										
Problems											
Part III											
Basic Sight Words: Irregular only.											
Part IV											
Context: semantic											
Context: grammatical											
Part V											
it's don't you've											
won't she'll he'd											
they're who's they'd											
Part VI											
Roots: Simple Suffixes											
Roots: Root Changes											
Roots: Prefixes											
Generalization 1											
Generalization 2											
Generalization 3											
Part VIII											
Syllabication											
Accent											
Phonic Analysis											

Figure 14.2 (continued)

Using Miscue Analysis with Children Speaking Nonstandard Dialects

As mentioned earlier, many children whose mother tongue is not Standard English make numerous miscues that do not really reflect reading errors as such. A child whose mother tongue is Black English rather than Standard English may read: *He look at the picture* rather than *He looks at the picture.* This usually does not reflect a reading problem. What the child is doing is simply translating Standard into Black English in order to make the most sense out of the sentence.

In order to carry on miscue analysis (and to use an informal reading inventory accurately) with a child whose mother tongue is not Standard English, it is necessary to understand his dialect and how it differs from the standard dialect. In Chapter 16, some differences between so-called Standard and Black English, as well as some differences between Standard English and "Spanish dialects" are explained. (Transcripts 2 and 3 in the Instructor's Manual show miscue analysis completed on a child speaking a Black dialect and a child speaking a Spanish dialect. By examining these analyses, you can see how the teacher must adjust her scoring and diagnostic procedures.)

Summary

Of all the evaluation techniques discussed in this book so far, miscue analysis comes the closest to helping the teacher determine how well a child perceives reading as a process of communicating with an author. By applying miscue analysis while a child reads aloud, the teacher may be able to determine not only the child's perception of the reading act, but his strategies and specific problems as well. By combining miscue analysis with an informal reading inventory, she can estimate his reading levels besides. Since a miscue analysis does not always provide the teacher with sufficient precision of diagnosis, she may also wish to administer some type of informal word recognition inventory as well. Devices such as the miscue-analysis checklist and the group-assessment chart enable the teacher to record children's specific problems and to group children for skill lessons.

References and Suggested Reading

1. Barrett, Thomas C., ed. *The Evaluation of Children's Reading Achievement.* Newark, DE: International Reading Association, 1967.
2. Bormuth, John R. "The Cloze Procedure: Literacy in the Classroom." In *Help for the Reading Teacher: New Directions in Research,* edited by William D. Page. National Conference on Research in Reading, 1975, 60–90.
3. Davis, F. "Psychometric Research on Comprehension in Reading." *Reading Research Quarterly* 7 (1972): 228–78.
4. Ekwall, Eldon E. *Locating and Correcting Reading Difficulties.* Columbus, OH: Charles E. Merrill, 1977.
5. Farr, Roger. *Measurement and Evaluation of Reading.* New York: Harcourt Brace Jovanovich, 1970.

6. Goodman, Kenneth S. "A Linguistic Study of Cues and Miscues in Reading." *Elementary English* (October 1965): 639–43.

7. Goodman, Kenneth S. *The Psycholinguistic Nature of the Reading Process.* Detroit: Wayne State University Press, 1968.

8. Goodman, Kenneth S. "Analysis of Oral Reading Miscues: Applied Psycholinguistics." *Reading Research Quarterly* 5 (1969): 9–30.

9. Goodman, Kenneth S. "Reading: a Psycholinguistic Guessing Game." In *Theoretical Models of the Reading Process,* edited by Harry Singer and Robert B. Ruddell. Newark, DE: International Reading Association, 1976, 497–508.

10. Pikulski, John. "A Critical Review: Informal Reading Inventories." *Reading Teacher* 28 (November 1974): 141–51.

11. Smith, Richard J., and Johnson, Dale D. *Teaching Children to Read.* Reading, MA: Addison-Wesley, 1980.

12. Stufflebeam, Daniel L., et al. *Educational Evaluation and Decision-Making in Education.* New York: Peacock, 1972.

13. Worthen, B. R., and Sanders, J. R. *Educational Evaluation: Theory and Practice.* Charles A. Jones, 1973.

Application Experiences for the Teacher-Education Class

1. With a partner or small group modify the following statements in any way you can to make them agree with the statements or implications of the author.

Statements about Chapter 14

a. A pupil's phonic-analysis abilities should be assessed by his ability to sound out words one letter at a time. (See Table 14.1.)

b. Miscue analysis is a technique of determining children's reading levels.

c. A good reader pays attention to semantic and syntactic clues but skips over little clues like phonic signals and punctuation.

d. When you listen to a child read aloud be sure to stop her whenever she makes a mistake.

e. When using miscue analysis and preparing to use a miscue-analysis checklist, do not record miscues related to dialect, proper nouns, hesitations, or poor phrasing.

f. A long hesitation indicates that the child is unsure of the word on which he's hesitating.

g. Miscue-analysis checklists provide the teacher with a record of the exact phonic-analysis problems and other word-recognition problems that a child has.

h. The "Baf Test" provides a measure of the degree a child is baffled by the meaning of a paragraph.

i. Some children understand phonics but seldom employ phonic analysis skills.

    j.   A group-assessment chart tells a teacher what remedies to apply for specific word-recognition deficiencies.

    k.   When a child translates a Standard-English reading selection into nonstandard English, this is truly a reading problem.

2. With a partner or small group carry on miscue analysis by examining Transcript 1 in the Instructor's Manual, the selections read by Tommy. Use a copy of the blank miscue analysis checklist at the end of Transcript 4 in the Instructor's Manual to record the miscues, then compare your results with the Miscue Analysis Checklist for Tommy at the end of Transcript 1 in the Instructor's Manual. If the two checklists disagree, decide why they do.

3. With a partner or small group carry on miscue analysis by examining Transcript 2 in the Instructor's Manual, the selections read by Pamela, a speaker of both Black English and Standard English. Use a copy of the blank miscue analysis checklist at the end of Transcript 4 in the Instructor's Manual to record the miscues; then compare your results with the miscue analysis checklist for Pamela at the end of Transcript 2 in the Instructor's Manual. If the two checklists disagree, decide why they do.

4. With a partner or small group carry on miscue analysis by examining Transcript 3 in the Instructor's Manual, the selections read by Eulogio, a speaker of both Spanish dialect and Standard English. Use a copy of the blank miscue analysis checklist at the end of Transcript 4 in the Instructor's Manual to record the miscues; then compare your results with the miscue analysis checklist for Eulogio in the Instructor's Manual. If the two checklists disagree, decide why they do.

Field Experiences in the Elementary-School Classroom

1. Listen to a child read to you without the use of a tape recorder. See if you can carry on miscue analysis as you listen. Jot down your notes after you listen to him read. (Be sure to have him read at least one selection that is close to his frustration level—after having him read one or two easy selections.) What do you think is his perception of reading? What do his reading strategies seem to be? What specific reading problems do you think he has?

2. Administer to one child the "Baf Test" and any other part of the Word-Recognition Test in Appendix H for which you feel you have time. What specific reading difficulties do you think she has? What specific ideas do you have for helping her overcome those difficulties?

3. With one child combine the use of miscue analysis with an informal reading inventory. Use any IRI you wish along with a miscue analysis checklist. Be sure to use a tape recorder so you can record very specific miscues as shown on pages 397-399. When you have determined the child's reading perceptions, strategies, levels, and problems, decide what specific remedies you would like to employ.

If your instructor or supervising teacher would like you to hand in a report, you may wish to use this format:

A. *Miscue Analysis Checklist*

B. *Perceptions:* Reading to this child seems to be a process of....It is also a process of....

C. *Strategies:* This child gets through a reading selection by paying attention to these clues: .... She ignores these clues: .... She relies mainly on....

D. *Levels:* Her instructional level is probably...because....Her frustration level is probably...because....Her independent level is probably...because....

E. *Specific Problems:*
  1. Irregular sight words ⸻
  2. Phonic elements ⸻
  3. Morphemes ⸻
  4. Dialect ⸻
  5. Semantic context clues ⸻
  6. Syntactic context clues ⸻
  7. Comprehension skills ⸻
  8. Punctuation ⸻
  9. Phrasing ⸻

F. *Specific Remediation Activities* (for 1-9 above)

G. *Coded Selections from an IRI* (appendix to your report)

H. *Results of a Word Recognition Inventory* (appendix to your report)

CHAPTER 15

When we read with comprehension we have to create images in our minds.

Teaching Reading and Study Skills in the Content Areas

Chapter Preview

Reading instruction may begin with basal readers, language-experience stories, or self-selected library books. But the bulk of what a school-age person learns about reading and through reading takes place during the reading of "content-area" materials. From third grade through twelfth, the student is expected to read at least 50,000 pages from science textbooks, social-studies textbooks, literary anthologies, laboratory manuals, and so on. This number of pages, if spread end to end would stretch approximately nine miles. That's a lot of reading! Yet, it's just a fifty-yard dash compared to what has to be read by those marathoners who continue on through college, graduate school, and a lifetime profession that requires daily reading in order to keep up to date. Becoming a better, more efficient, more flexible, and more reflective reader is a learning process that may end at one's funeral, but certainly not at one's primary-school graduation. This is why nearly every teacher becomes a reading teacher (whether he wants to be or not). Nearly every subject that children and adults study today in our society must be partially learned through the process of reading.

It is sometimes assumed by parents and teachers alike that once you teach a child the basic skills of reading, she should be able to read anything—a science text, a math text, you name it. Not so, of course. To take a simple illustration: even something as easy to use as a telephone book requires special skills that need to be learned. Tammie may be able to read a sixth-grade basal reader, a library book on dinosaurs, and a long report on flying saucers that she wrote by herself, but still fail miserably in finding the telephone number of a good eye doctor whose office is not too far away.

Every type of reading material—as well as every content area—has its own peculiarities that have to be learned. Each content area has its own special vocabulary (and jargon), its own style of structuring sentences, its own logical organization, its own required reading speed, and its own assumptions about what experiences the reader has already had. Reading as a "psycholinguistic guessing game" can be played much more effectively if the teacher helps students get used to those peculiarities and develop the reading skills and strategies necessary to cope with them. Most adults would think it unwise to send a child on a long, difficult journey with only a map and no instructions on how to use a map. In the same way, it is unwise to send the child through the communication maze he is expected to get through during his life, without first explaining to him some of the keys to the communication map.

Humans have to teach their children nearly every-thing—even how to use a telephone book. I've never figured out how to read one of these myself. They have a yellow one and a white one, and the yellow one looks quite different inside from the white one. I think the yellow one has something to do with money, but I'm not sure.

Why Content-Area Material Is So Hard to Read

There are several readability factors that make content-area mate-rials, such as textbooks in social studies, mathematics, and science, difficult for children to read. Four factors of major importance are: 1) vocabulary—the degree to which new and unfamiliar words are introduced, 2) sentence structure—the extent to which unusual sen-tence alterations and sentence expansions are used by the author, 3) paragraph structure—the degree to which topic sentences are used and all sentences within a paragraph relate to each other, and 4) imagery—the extent to which the reader must struggle to create images in her mind of what the author is describing. Each of these factors can effect dramatically the level of intelligent psycholinguistic guessing a reader can carry on as she reads.

Vocabulary

All of the content areas have their own specialized vocabulary, sometimes referred to as "jargon." It's difficult to talk about the social studies, for instance, without referring to the word *culture,* or to talk about the natural sciences without using the word *energy.* In mathematics we talk about *sets* and *operations.* In order to comprehend what they read in the content areas, children must rather quickly face these specialized words and be able to pronounce and understand them. (For ideas on teaching specialized vocabulary, see the next section—"Developing Children's Content-Area Reading Strategies.")

Sentence Structure

As children are given more and more content-area materials to read, the number of dependent clauses (subordinate clauses) that they must face increases as well. Notice the dependent clauses (in italics) in the following sentences:

> Social Studies: The Zambezi is a river in Southern Africa, *flowing about 1,650 miles southeast through Rhodesia and Mozambique to the Indian Ocean.*
> Science: Moisture and heat are two agents of chemical change *that can create compounds from two or more elements.*
> Mathematics: *Because of the commutative principle,* the order in which certain operations are performed will not change the result.

This increase in subordinate clauses is just one of many types of alterations and expansions of sentence patterns that make content-area reading more difficult than many basal-reader stories or library books. (For a list of other types of alterations and expansions, as well as ideas for helping children learn them, see page 136 and pages 137 to 138.)

Paragraph Structure

Guthrie (5), after reviewing results of experimental studies, concluded that a highly readable paragraph contains two features: 1) a topic sentence at the beginning of the paragraph and 2) coherence among the sentences in a paragraph. Unfortunately, many authors do not always write paragraphs with these two features. (Furthermore, such writing may become rather dull to mature readers.) The following are examples of paragraphs that are easy to read and more difficult to read:

> *Easy:* The skate is a strange looking fish. It's a flat fish with both eyes on top rather than one eye on each side of its head.

As you look down on it, it appears a little like a diamond-shaped kite with a tail. The skate's tail looks as if it belongs to a snake rather than a fish.

More Difficult: As you look down on it, it appears a little like a diamond-shaped kite with a tail. Its tail looks as if it belongs to a snake rather than a fish. But it's a fish, all right. It's a flat fish with both eyes on top rather than one eye on each side of its head. And with those eyes it searches constantly for food. The skate is a strange looking fish.

The second paragraph is more difficult to read for two reasons: 1) you have to wait until the end of the paragraph to find out the main idea that the author wishes to express and 2) the fifth sentence does not relate directly to the topic sentence or to the rest of the sentences. Research (5) shows that with this type of paragraph children find it more difficult to recall significant details.

Children need to be taught how to determine the topic sentence in a paragraph and which sentences support the topic sentence. This is often done through workbook exercises related to basal-reader stories. However, once this skill has been introduced in this way, it should be applied to content-area materials. The following directions are those that may be used for an activity designed to provide practice on this skill: "Underline the topic sentence in each paragraph. (A topic sentence gives the main idea of the paragraph. It's the sentence that ties all the other sentences together.) Cross out any sentence that does not have anything to do with the topic sentence in the paragraph. The first paragraph has been done for you."

Imagery

When we read with comprehension, we have to create images in our minds: sights, sounds, smells, tactile sensations, muscular sensations, tastes. Reading in the content areas requires an enormous amount of heavy-duty "image-ing" (image making). With lightweight stories from basal readers or library books, such image making can become almost automatic, particularly when the child has been assisted in finding books and stories of the right difficulty. With content-area material, however, children are often expected to slow down and "figure out" just what picture or sensation in the mind the author wants the reader to make. Let's look at the same three sentences again to see the extent of image making that is required:

Social Studies: The Zambezi is a river in Southern Africa, flowing about 1,650 miles southeast through Rhodesia and Mozambique to the Indian Ocean.

Science: Moisture and heat are two agents of chemical change that can create compounds from two or more elements.

Mathematics: Because of the commutative principle, the order in which certain operations are performed will not change the result.

Images, of course, are based on our own personal experiences. In the sentence about the Zambezi River, for example, we need to have had experiences similar to the following in order for understanding to take place:

1. Seeing rivers in reality or in pictures
2. Seeing Africa on a map or globe or journey
3. Using directions (N, S, E, W, SE) on a map
4. Hearing the word *flowing* when referring to liquid
5. Traveling for many miles and noticing how long it takes
6. Seeing oceans in reality or in pictures

What this means in an instructional sense is that teachers need to help children learn strategies for increasing their own image-making power. Such power will in turn enable children to do a better job of psycholinguistic guessing as they read: for as images are created in their minds, they become more capable of predicting the words and sentences that should follow.

Developing Children's Content-Area Reading Strategies

Before children's image-making power can be used effectively in making intelligent psycholinguistic guesses, several related subskills need to be developed. These subskills, usually emphasized in the middle and upper grades, are as follows:

1. Using a flexible reading rate ✓
2. Using an appropriate speed set
3. Skimming and scanning
4. Developing a visual memory for sequential events
5. Finding reading materials at the right level of difficulty
6. Developing specialized vocabularies
7. Reading graphic materials
8. Locating information ✓
9. Recording information
10. Using the PQ3R method
11. Reading content-area materials for a purpose

Developing a Flexible Reading Rate

Research (11) has shown that many people read various materials inflexibly—at the same speed—even though the content of the materials or their purposes for reading them vary considerably. Research (14) also shows, however, that students can be taught to vary their speed to match the materials. Many children who read a great many light, fictional books find themselves trying to read textbooks with the same rapid speed, even though they can't understand them at this speed. On the other hand, that smaller number of children who usually limit their reading to informational materials may attempt to read fiction at the same careful pace.

The task of helping some children read more flexibly, however, can't be successfully tackled until you've first helped them overcome their tendency to read everything too slowly. Obviously children can't be truly flexible until they are actually capable of reading at various speeds. So let's tackle this problem first. The following is a list of some of the factors that usually account for those habitually slow readers.

1. Materials too difficult.   This is an obvious cause of some cases of slow reading, although one that is frequently ignored. In the past, science, social-studies, and math textbooks have usually required children to read well beyond their own personal reading level. This situation is getting better (8) as publishers attempt to "tone down" the vocabulary and sentence-structure load. However, school districts still tend to buy content-area textbooks with the idea that every child in the same grade will be reading the same one. Since we know that children's reading levels within a single grade level vary tremendously, you can see what a burden this puts on some children. In a later section we'll address ourselves to the procedures teachers can use to ease this burden.

2. Reading word-by-word.   Such behavior is usually brought about by well-meaning primary-grade teachers who concentrate on having children "sound out" words rather than communicating with an author. Unless the child learns to read for meaning and to look for context clues rather than just phonic clues, the word-by-word habit can continue right into the upper grades. Suggestions for eliminating this habit can be found on pages 69 to 70 and pages 88 to 89.

3. Inadequate word-recognition skills.   Children who cannot easily decode words through visual memory, phonic analysis, morphemic analysis, or contextual analysis will either read very slowly or guess very wildly. See Chapters 2, 3, and 4 for specific suggestions on helping these children.

4. Insufficient comprehension. This weakness can be quite complex. Most often it appears to be related to poor habits of creating images while one reads and of predicting what the author is going to say next. Suggestions for developing these skills may be found in Chapter 5 and in a later section of this chapter.

5. Vocal or subvocal reading. Vocal reading is simply reading out loud (usually by whispering) when silent reading is called for. This habit is fairly common with beginning readers, but with practice in silent reading, it usually disappears—although it may be more persistent with those children who have not had opportunities for both vocal and silent reading from the very beginning of reading instruction. Subvocal reading is also quite common among beginners—and even among some adults. The most primitive form of subvocal reading is moving the lips. Although this habit may be easily overcome, many people then progress to moving the muscles related to the tongue, throat, and vocal chords.

The disadvantage of these habits, of course, is that they limit one's reading speed to one's talking speed—which is much lower than one can potentially read. Whereas a fast speaking rate is about 200 words per minute, fast readers can read up to 900 words per minute, providing they read every word (9), and even faster than that if one defines reading as "just getting the gist of what is written."

It is doubtful that teachers of primary-grade children should be overly concerned with subvocal reading, although most competent readers by the end of this period of schooling can readily overcome the habits of whispering and lip moving. Generally all that is needed is to draw their attention to the habits. Some competent readers, however, may find it easier to overcome them by putting their fingers on their lips or by holding something between their teeth while they are engaged in silent reading. Research (3) shows, however, that subvocalization may actually assist less able readers and should not be discouraged until comprehension has considerably improved.

Children in the intermediate grades can be shown how to detect the more subtle muscular movements by having them feel these movements while they are reading. For detecting tongue movements, have them place a finger on the middle of the tongue and read a passage silently. If Aaron, a competent reader, finds it difficult to read at all or feels his tongue tensing, he should be told something like this: "Keep feeling your tongue while you read, but see if you can get your tongue very soft and relaxed. Don't try to hear the words in your head. Try just to see them instead."

Sometimes movements of the tongue, throat, and vocal chords can be detected by having children place their thumbs and forefingers against their "Adam's apples" while they read something silently. In this case, subvocal reading will be indicated by small muscular spasms or vibrations. Some children will not be successful in detecting muscular movements but will report that they hear themselves talking when they read silently. In any case the "cure" for subvocal reading seems to require a combination of relaxing the tongue and throat muscles and consciously trying not to hear oneself read. This procedure is not easy for many children, and should be practiced only with very simple material. Even then, the teacher should not expect very many children to catch on quickly. Too many variables are involved for this to be a one-shot cure. Probably one of the best long-range treatments is a steady diet of fairly easy trade books, particularly fictional accounts that sweep the reader along, causing him to devour books in large gulps. This type of opportunity, along with occasional reminders, is all that many children need.

Subvocal reading, as mentioned earlier, should not be viewed as some sort of disease to be stamped out once and for all. Many of us—if not all of us—who have overcome the habit of subvocal reading, revert to it when material is hard to comprehend. In fact, sometimes a passage may be so difficult that we'll find ourselves whispering in an attempt to understand it. Perhaps this is only one more illustration of what the linguists call the "primacy of speech."

6. *Lack of purpose for reading.* Many slow readers read slowly simply because they are not driven by any urge to find out something. For years Jimmy Miller, a slow reader, has been reading merely to please the teacher or to "get it done." He has little concept of what it means to communicate with an author because he's never learned that authors have much to say to him personally. His perception of reading is similar to that of Jack Jacob's perception of his painting job. Jack is a painter's apprentice and it's his job to scrape off the excess paint from the windows of the buildings his boss paints. He likes to start at the top and scrape off each window from left to right in the first row. Then he moves down to the second row and again scrapes off each window from left to right, and so on. In the same way Jimmy Miller scrapes each word off the page and lets the letters fall to the floor.

If Jimmy had experienced some language-experience approaches during his earlier years in school, and if he had been given numerous "directed-reading-thinking-activities" throughout his school years (as described in Chapters 5 and 6), perhaps he would not now be such a slow learner. He would understand that reading is a form of communicating (rather than getting a job done) and that one needs to read for specific purposes. Yet it is never too late for Jimmy to learn these two things. Language-experience approaches may be used at any level of education, such as having him dictate stories about something important in his personal life or involving him in meaningful experiences that he and others can then describe to the teacher on a group chart. Other ideas for helping Jimmy will be found in the later section entitled "Reading Content-Area Materials for a Purpose."

Children CAN learn to read at a fast, slow, or medium pace depending upon their purposes and the difficulty of the materials. But before such training is attempted, the six factors just discussed should be considered and appropriate remedies for each child applied. It does little good, for instance, and may even do harm, to put a child through rate-building exercises until their reasons for reading everything too slowly are alleviated.

Various mechanical devices such as tachistoscopes and pacers have been used for years with the intent of increasing students' reading speed. Results of such practices have been too inconsistent, however, to be very encouraging (although these devices do provide incentive for some children). A simpler approach, and one that seems to work as well, is a three-component program similar to one advocated and treated by Harris and Sipay (6). The first component is that of diagnosing and treating the more basic reading problems such as inadequate word-recognition skills, insufficient comprehension, and so on. The second component is that of encouraging a good deal of voluntary reading of easy trade books in order to develop fluency. The third component is a series of rapid-reading exercises, for which the children's words-per-minute and questions-answered-correctly are recorded.

Motivation related to these exercises is enhanced by having the children keep a graphic record of both their reading rates and comprehension scores. (Or you may wish to have them keep only a rate graph, "fining" themselves thirty words per minute for each comprehension error.) There are numerous commercial materials available for such exercises, including the *Standard Test Lessons in Reading* (Teachers College Press) for children above grade 3, *Developing Reading Efficiency* (Burgess) for children above grade 5, and the units called "Rate Builders" in the upper levels of the *SRA Reading Laboratories* (Science Research Associates).

Helping Children Develop the Appropriate Speed Set

Every child who enjoys backseat driving in the family car is aware of the need for different speeds. One speed is fine for freeway and turnpike driving but highly hazardous for mountain roads with snakelike curves. Once the teacher has helped children develop the capacity to read at different speeds, it then becomes a matter of explaining to them the virtue of reading different materials at different speeds and of helping them establish a *speed set* for each type of material they are about to read.

For example, the teacher can compare the importance of reading flexibly to the importance of eating different types of food at different rates. Whereas butterscotch pudding (light fiction) can be gobbled with gusto, one needs to chew raw carrots (informational material) in a thoughtful manner. Otherwise, digestion (understanding) is seriously hindered. A person doesn't need to chew butterscotch pudding, and ought not to gobble raw carrots. Such explanations should be supplemented with occasional reminders that help the children establish the proper set before they begin to read. If they are about to read informational material, for instance, they could be reminded that they will now be dealing with "raw carrots" rather than "butterscotch pudding."

A more specific set can be established, however, by discussing with them their purposes for reading a particular selection. If Donald's purpose, for example, is simply to find out what an authority has to say about a very specific topic, it is often a waste of his time to read an entire chapter or even entire pages. By using an index and by scanning until he finds a key word related to the topic, he not only saves himself a lot of time, he reads actively rather than passively— varying his rate of reading according to his purposes. This manner of reading is the type of mature behavior a teacher should be encouraging.

Skimming and Scanning

Another way of encouraging children to develop a flexible reading rate is to teach them how to engage in the processes of skimming and scanning. There are many instances when people do not need to read every word in a selection in order to get the information they need. The most obvious example of this is the telephone book again. One would hardly read the entire telephone book or even an entire page in order to find the name of someone you wish to call. This ability to find quickly one tiny bit of information is called *scanning* and is one that many children pick up quickly. Others (usually those, it seems, who have developed the perception of reading as a word-by-word, sounding-out process) find this to be a difficult skill to acquire.

Basically, the technique for teaching the scanning skill is that of giving children a limited time to find a specific bit of information in a fairly simple selection that they are all asked to read. Three types of scanning are usually taught this way. Thomas and Robinson (16, p. 216) refer to these three types as levels:

Level 1: Scanning for a bit of information that stands out easily—the date of a historic discovery in science, or the university with which a noted author was affiliated

Level 2: Scanning for an answer that is worded like the question

Level 3: Scanning for an answer that is worded differently from the question

174281

An example of a level 1 scanning assignment might be this: "How long is the great white shark in the story you're about to read?" An example of a level-2 scanning assignment might be as follows: "Does the great white shark circle its prey when it hunts or does it go straight in for the kill?" An example of a level-3 scanning assignment might be like this: "Do you think a great white shark is a cautious hunter or a fearless one. . . . Find something on this page that will support your opinion."

While the scanning skill is highly useful for finding specific facts, the skimming skill has another function. With skimming, one is trying to get the gist of a story or article, rather than find a very specific answer to a very specific question. Skimming is often used when one is trying to decide whether or not a library book is going to be a good one to check out (either for pleasure, for carrying out a school assignment, et cetera.)

Skimming is very much like the first step in the PQ3R method. By reading the first paragraph, the subheadings, and the last paragraph, you are engaged in skimming. If the purpose, though, is to make sure a book has the kind of information or story that one wants, however, many people extend their skimming by reading the first (and sometimes the last) sentence in each paragraph for several pages. In other words, they look for topic sentences that will give them a rough idea of what the author is going to say. Sometimes they extend their skimming further by glancing through the index and table of contents. Some people skim this way simply to "pick up ideas" without having to read an entire book. (Bookstore proprietors will tell you that many people go into bookstores just for this purpose and never buy a single book.)

As with the process of teaching scanning, to teach skimming the teacher needs to provide questions and tests that encourage rapid, selective reading rather than slow, compulsive reading. Questions that encourage skimming would include some like these: "What is this book going to be about?" "What information do you think there will be in this article that will be useful or interesting to you?" "Is this book fiction or nonfiction?" "Will this book give you the information you need for your report on modern-day Eskimos?"

Developing a Visual Memory for Sequential Events

Much of what a child encounters in content-area materials requires a good visual memory for sequential events in order for comprehension to occur. Let's take a "story problem" in mathematics as an illustration of this:

Jim leaves his house with a pocketful of money. He buys a present for his mother for $8.95. When he gets home he has

$6.35 left. How much money did he have in his pocket before he bought the present for his mother?

This is the kind of problem that often gives children (and some adults) "fits." Many children will see the word *left* in the problem and assume that to "get the answer" you must subtract $6.35 from $8.95. By doing this, they're showing that they're not reading with comprehension. They're not creating in their minds a visual image of what sequence is occurring.

What they should be picturing in their minds is Jim leaving his house with a large wad of money in his pocket. Then they should see him giving some of that money to a storekeeper. Then they should picture this:

Wad of money in Jim's pocket . . . take away money for present . . . equals money left. Finally they should picture themselves adding the money left in Jim's pocket to the money he spent on the present in order to get right back to the money he had in his pocket in the first place: $6.35 plus $8.95 equals $15.30. In other words they should be forming a visual sequence of a subtraction situation but one that requires addition to solve it. (Alas, what they should be picturing and what they actually see are often entirely different. What they often see is simply the word *left.*)

The cure for this is sometimes quite simple. Rather than explaining the problem verbally over and over to the children, the teacher can realize that the difficulty lies with faulty visual imageing. By engaging in a bit of spontaneous drama—Jim leaving home with a wad of money in his pocket and so on—the children can learn to see what's really happening in a story problem.

This same need for good visual memory for sequential events occurs when children are reading science and social-studies texts. Fortunately, in some of these texts, the publishers have included pictures of the sequence that is being described. It's important, then, for the teacher to help the children examine the pictures before they are asked to read. In this way they will have the pictured sequence in their minds as they read. Of course, this form of directing the children should not be continued indefinitely. Eventually all you should have to say is "Study the pictures first and then read the words." (As most students who have not been trained this way will tell you: "I like a book with pictures because I don't have to read as much." In other words, they perceive the pictures as decorations rather than as aids to visual memory.)

A great deal of science can come alive for children if you have them draw their own pictures of what they read in science texts. By having them compare pictures that they've drawn with pictures they later find in encyclopedias and other books, you can not only motivate careful reading, but also teach them to read for images and not for words. A great deal of social studies can come alive if you have them recreate historical events, geographical customs, and economic transactions through spontaneous creative drama.

Ideas that are presented to children through reading of social-studies texts can often be made more visual and meaningful through creative dramatizations. The following is a description of one teacher's approach toward the use of creative drama in his fifth-grade social-studies program: Mr. Novick and his pupils were studying European exploration of the Americas. The class was divided into five groups, one that chose to study Coronado, one to study Columbus, and so on. Each group was given help in finding information from library sources and the textbook. Each group then planned a skit that would present the major ideas about the explorer. The plans were presented by each small group to Mr. Novick. Mr. Novick praised them for their work but asked questions to show them where they still needed to do more research. After further research, the groups modified their plans for their skits and again presented their ideas to Mr. Novick. If Mr. Novick approved their plans, they were free to rehearse their skits in earnest.

Once all five groups had their skits ready, they presented them in a theater-in-the-round fashion (skit in the middle of the room—audience in a circle). After each skit was over, the audience provided praise and specific suggestions for improvement. Further rehearsals prepared the groups for their presentation of the skits to another class.

Mr. Novick's approach was very well structured and certainly made the social-studies reading more visual and real to the children. However, not all drama experiences related to the content areas need to be this elaborate. Once the children have become used to giving spontaneous skits, they can be invited at any time to dramatize something they've been reading. After one small group has tried it, another group can be asked to give an interpretation. Inviting another class into the room (or another group in a team-teaching situation) can be reserved for very special occasions when the children have decided with you to polish a skit for a larger audience.

Finding Reading Materials at the Right Level of Difficulty

Another strategy that a student needs to learn in order to increase her retention and image-making power is to find reading materials that are challenging enough without being too difficult. Children who have been engaged in a trade-book-individualized-reading program (TBIR program) seem to have less difficulty with this than children who have been taught to read primarily through basal-reading programs. They are used to looking for books that match their reading abilities.

Naturally, such a strategy can't be taught if the teacher insists on having every child "doing social studies" in the same textbook. Of course, there's nothing wrong in having every child using the same textbook for studying pictures, maps, and indexes, and for developing scanning and skimming skills (see the later section on scanning and skimming). What may be wrong is to expect every child to be able to read the same book. A more successful approach is to have a variety of textbooks and tradebooks available (in the room or in the library) that offer similar information at different levels of reading.

What this means in actual practice is that teachers need to be willing to have children read for specific purposes rather than for the covering of specific pages. Rather than assignments of definite pages to read in a definite textbook, their assignments look more like this:

> "Where did Columbus get the idea that it would be safe to sail westward in order to reach the East Indies? What made him so sure of himself? Why did he want to make the journey? Was he trying to get rich, or do you think he had other plans? If you had been a sailor at that time, do you think you would have gone with him?"

With open-ended assignments like this, children are encouraged to read in a variety of sources and to look for sources that are within their reading capabilities.

Children's Literature Once More to the Rescue

Today libraries are chock-full of trade books that can be used to supplement textbooks in the social, biological, and natural sciences. Books by Alvin and Virginia Silverstein, for example, can help children in grades three through six to a better understanding of humans and animals. Their series, *All About Them* and *Systems of the Body,* provide several books that are highly readable and informative. Another science author, Seymour Simon, has written over fifty books designed to help young children understand in everyday language the interesting facts and principles concerning the earth, space, and animals. His *Meet the Giant Snakes* and *Danger from Below: Earthquakes, Past, Present, and Future* are just two examples of the solid but easily digested "food" in this author's larder.

It would take several hundred pages to describe the thousands of trade books that are now available to teachers and students of the content areas in the elementary school. A good source for becoming familiar with these types of books is *Children and Books* by Sutherland, Monson, and Arbuthnot. To give you just the flavor of what is available, the following is a list of a few authors and books concerned with the social studies and the sciences.

The Biological Sciences

1. Aliki, *The Long-Lost Coelacanth and Other Living Fossils,* 1973.
2. Amon, *Reading, Writing, Chattering Chimps,* 1975.
3. Bendick, *The Mystery of the Loch Ness Monster,* 1976.
4. Cole, *A Frog's Body,* 1980
5. Dowden, *The Blossom on the Bough: A Book of Trees,* 1975
6. Halmi, *Zoos of the World,* 1975
7. Levine, *Lisa and her Soundless World,* 1974
8. McClung, *How Animals Hide,* 1973
9. Silverstein, *Exploring the Brain,* 1975

The Physical Sciences

1. Adler, *Magic House of Numbers,* 1974
2. Branley, *Color: From Rainbows to Lasers,* 1978
3. Freeman, *Gravity and the Astronauts,* 1971
4. Maestro, *Oil: The Buried Treasure,* 1975
5. James and Barkin, *The Simple Facts of Simple Machines,* 1975
6. Lauber, *Tapping Earth's Heat,* 1978
7. Navarra, *Earthquake,* 1980
8. Nixon, *Glaciers: Nature's Frozen Rivers,* 1980
9. Watson, *Binary Numbers,* 1977

The Social Sciences

1. Aliki, *Mummies Made in Egypt,* 1979
2. Baker, *Settlers and Strangers: Native Americans of the Desert Southwest and History as They Saw It,* 1977
3. Bales, *Chinatown Sunday: The Story of Lillian Der,* 1973
4. Bernheim, *In Africa,* 1973
5. Cartwright, *What's in a Map?* 1976
6. Clarke, *The American Revolution 1775–83: A British View,* 1967
7. Erdoes, *The Native Americans,* 1979
8. Fisher, *The Factories,* 1979
9. Foster, *The World of William Penn,* 1973
10. Kurelek, *Lumberjack,* 1974
11. Macaulay, *Underground,* 1976
12. Meyer, *Eskimos: Growing Up in a Changing Culture,* 1977
13. Rau, *The People of New China,* 1978
14. Steele, *Westward Adventure: The True Stories of Six Pioneers,* 1962
15. Singer, *We All Come from Puerto Rico, Too,* 1977
16. Warren, *Pictorial History of Women in America,* 1975
17. Wolf, *In this Proud Land: The Story of a Mexican American Family,* 1978

Using Peer-Written and Teacher-Written Material

There may be a few children in your class whose reading skills are so poor they have trouble with both textbooks and trade books. In this case you may wish to provide them with peer-written or teacher-written material. Peer-written material is obtained by asking certain children to contribute their written reports to the classroom or school library. Teacher-written material is obtained by paraphrasing textbook material in very simple language. In either case, it's a good idea to use some type of attractive binding (and even illustrations if possible). It's also advisable to type these "homemade" materials with large type and to include no more than one paragraph on each page.

In Chapter 2 we discussed the importance of verbal and nonverbal experiences to the acquisition of a semantic vocabulary. As you may recall, in that chapter we examined the hypothetical case of a child learning the phrase *rozaga hunt*. Using Dale's Cone of Experience as our model, we had David going on an actual rozaga hunt in order to get the deepest understanding of the phrase. Unfortunately teachers have neither the time nor money to explain most content-area terms that well. Consequently, they have to resort to contrived experiences, creative dramatics, motion pictures, still pictures, verbal analogies, and other aids. All of the ideas described in Chapter 2 for developing sight and semantic vocabularies through basal readers and library books apply equally well to content-area textbooks. (For a quick review, you may wish to refer to pages 50–58.)

The basic strategy the child must learn for dealing with specialized words in content areas is not to ignore them. This tends to be a strong habit for some children by the time they reach the intermediate grades—a habit that carries right on into adulthood. Their thinking, when you talk to them about it, seems to be something like this: "Oh, it's just a word that we use a lot in science." If they can pronounce it, they are often content with that much success. Because of this attitude, it's often important for teachers to prepare children for reading a content-area selection by discussing key words ahead of time. The word *energy*, for instance, may be placed on the chalkboard in sentences incorporating many context clues:

The horse had enough *energy* to pull a heavy wagon.

The chemical *energy* in a car battery is enough to run a starting motor.

By turning on the toaster you can change electrical *energy* into heat *energy* and toast your bread.

A door knob changes muscle *energy* into mechanical *energy*.

Then, after they've read the sentences, have them carry on a discussion of what they think energy is. After a brief discussion, have each child write down her own definition in one simple sentence. Then she can look up the word in a dictionary or in a glossary or a science book to see how close she came. (This technique of getting children involved is sometimes referred to as "placing your bets before the race begins.")

Reading Graphic Materials

Harris's and Sipay's comment on the interpretation of graphs and tables is probably accurate: "Entirely too many students today have the habit of skipping past anything of this sort with the briefest glance" (6). It is likely, moreover, that such behavior was as common in the recent past as it is today. Your author remembers his own reluctance to give such visual aids anything more than "the briefest glance" until he suddenly realized they were more fun than the dull text that frequently accompanied them. A graph or table offers a student something that exposition seldom provides—the chance to get actively involved in "creating" your own information. Take the graph shown in Figure 15.1, for example. See how much information you can "create" without the need of any accompanying text. (Please look at Figure 15.1 before continuing.)

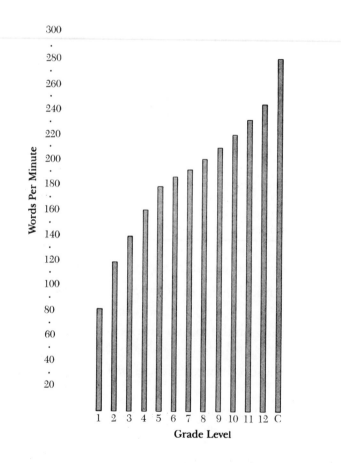

Figure 15.1. *An Estimate of Student's Average Reading Rates of Informational Material Grades 1 through College. Based on information reported by Taylor, Frackenpohl, and Pettee (16, p. 12).*

Having "invented" your own facts and generalizations based on the graph in Figure 15.1, perhaps you would agree that graph reading is more fun than exposition like this: "Average reading rates seem to vary almost directly with grade level. In a study by Taylor, Frackenpohl, and Pettee (16) they found that the average reading rate for first grade was eighty words per minute. For second grade, however, they found that the rate was one hundred fifteen words per minute. For third grade the rate was one hundred thirty-eight words per minute, while for fourth grade, the rate was one hundred fifty-eight words per minute. For fifth grade. . . ." Pretty dull and hard to assimilate this way, isn't it?

Now look at Table 15.1 and see what information you can generate on your own. Here, too, it can be seen that reading information presented in this manner would probably be more interesting than reading the same information in a long, fact-studded paragraph.

Table 15.1   Sex Differences between Boys and Girls in Reading Retardation Measuring One Year or More Retardation*

Grade	Percent Boys Retarded	Percent Girls Retarded
2	9.7	4.2
3	14.7	7.1
4	23.6	12.0
5	25.5	11.6
6	13.7	9.9

*Arthur W. Heilman, *Principles and Practices of Teaching Reading,* 4th ed. (Columbus, OH: Charles E. Merrill, 1977), p. 74. Reproduced with permission of the author and publisher.

Maps can also be a fascinating way for children to gain information—witness the enthusiasm of children reading the map related to the journey of Bilbo Baggins in Tolkien's *Hobbit.* And so can diagrams and pictures, as shown by the eagerness displayed by children following diagrams for building model airplanes or studying pictures of dinosaurs.

If graphs, tables, maps, diagrams, and pictures can be so interesting, why are they often passed over with only the briefest glance? There are probably numerous reasons for this, including the possibility that they take more energy to read than simple exposition. But perhaps the biggest reason is that children have had too few opportunities to discover that reading them can be fairly easy and enjoyable. One way of bringing about such a discovery is through having the children create graphs, maps, tables, diagrams, and informational pictures of their own. As a start you may wish to have them use simple information that you provide them—such as average winter temperatures in various parts of the world, or other such statis-

A globe can be a fascinating way for children to gain information.

tical data found in almanacs. But as rapidly as possible it is advisable to get them involved in gathering their own information and then translating that information into graphic or tabular form. There are almost limitless possibilities for such projects—a graph comparing the number of children in fifth grade who prefer vanilla, chocolate, and strawberry ice cream; a map of the classroom, the school, or the neighborhood; a diagram of "my dream house" or of "how to make a simple glider"; a table showing school enrollment during the past ten years; a mural giving a reasonably accurate interpretation of village life in the Middle Ages.

All of these projects can be displayed for other children to read and discuss. In this way, some of the guided practice necessary for learning to appreciate and understand "visuals" can be provided—just as through the construction of these visuals they will be able to discover for themselves the need for some type of scale on maps, graphs, diagrams, and informal pictures; the need for symbols such as color or special lines, and the need for accurate titles and labels.

Locating Information

In order for children to become adept in using content-area materials, they need to learn how to locate precisely what information they want. The skill of locating information can be broken down into subskills such as these:

1. Examining titles to determine appropriateness of books
2. Using a table of contents
3. Using an index
4. Using the glossary available in some books
5. Gaining information from appendixes
6. Finding appropriate visuals—maps, tables, graphs, pictures, and diagrams
7. Using the library card catalog
8. Using encyclopedias and other library reference books

Whereas most basal-reader programs include useful exercises on many of the locational skills, these skills are usually mastered best through actual "research projects" in which children seek information in trade books, textbooks, encyclopedias, and other library references. Textbooks, though, such as those used for social studies or science, are often handy to use as raw material when the teacher desires to introduce or review locational skills with several students at the same time. Since several copies of a textbook are usually available, each child receiving instruction can look at the same example at the same time. Guided practice should not be limited to textbooks, however, as positive transfer is much more likely to take place when children also employ the locational skills with trade books and reference books they have found for themselves in the library.

As soon as children begin to use textbooks in science and social studies, they can begin to receive guided practice in "finding the secret treasures hidden within a book." Questions similar to the following are generally useful in helping children discover for themselves the usefulness of indexes, glossaries, illustrations, and so on. (To increase your own involvement and to gain a better understanding of the utility of such questions in aiding discovery, you can try answering these questions as they relate to the book you are reading right now. Feedback can be found at the end of the list of questions.)

1. On what page can you find the beginning of an alphabetical list (called an *index*) of most of the things talked about in this book? _____

2. If you wanted to find out something in this book about how to increase children's reading speed, what topic would you look for in the index: children's reading speed? rate of reading? how to increase children's reading speed? reading rate? reading speed? Try those that you think may work and see which one is in the index.

3. On exactly what pages would you find information about children's reading speed? _____

4. On what page near the front of this book can you find a list of chapter titles? _____

5. On what page is there a table that might give you information about graphemes? _____

6. Between what pages is the chapter on phonics? _____

7. On what pages can you find suggestions for other books and articles to read on teaching phonics? _____

8. Looking only at the titles of articles suggested for additional reading on phonics, which one looks as if it may lead you to information on the so-called First Grade Studies. (Just indicate the number of the reference.) _____

9. If you were trying to find the library number of this book, which drawers would you look for in the card catalog? (Use letters.)
   a. The _____ drawer if I knew the first author's name.
   b. The _____ drawer if I knew the title.
   c. The _____ drawer if I only knew the subject of the book.

10. On what page in this book is the word *phonogram* defined? _____

11. Between what pages is there an appendix describing numerous "book projects?" _____

12. If you wanted to find out something about "how to teach deaf children to read," which two encyclopedia volumes would be most likely to contain the information you want? H T D C R
_____

Answers:
1. 551   2. rate of reading   3. 423–6   4. 3   5. 73   6. 63, 94   7. 89–90   8. 2
9. M or Ma (May)   R or Re (Reading)   10. 76   11. 524, 531
12. D (Deafness) or R (Reading) or H (Hearing Impaired)

In addition to the use of discovery questions similar to those just described, a teacher can also get children actively involved as "library detectives." A "detective's badge" or similar token can be given to those children who "find all the clues" or "solve the mystery." In this type of activity, children are usually given clue cards or a list of clues and sent to the library ("the place in which the crime took place") singly, in pairs, or in supervised groups. The following "clues," though facetious in this instance, are the types of clues that could be used:

1. The kind of weapon used in the crime was a revolver used by the Barsimians in the War of Tulips. What was the name of the weapon?

2. The main suspect in this case was last seen in the city of Atlantis. In what country is this?

3. The main suspect has the same name (or alias) as the man who wrote *Call of the Tame*. What is the suspect's name?

4. The motive for the crime probably had something to do with narcotics. From what you can find out about narcotics, why do you think the money was stolen, and who else besides the main suspect do you think was responsible for this crime?

A simpler form of this type of activity involves "clues" that are more direct, though less imaginative. With this form no "crime" has been committed, and the clues are simply research problems geared to specific locational skills. The following "clues" will serve as examples:

1. Find in the card catalog the author of *Call of the Tame.*
2. What book in this library tells about the War of Tulips? You'll find it in the subject catalog under one of these topics: War of Tulips, Wars, Battles, or Tulips.
3. Use an encyclopedia to find out the name of the revolver used by the Barsimians in the War of Tulips.

Some teachers also create the necessity for practicing locational skills by requiring children to prepare an oral or written report. Providing certain precautions are taken (see *They All Want to Write* by Burrows, Ferebee, Jackson, and Saunders), this is probably a worthwhile learning experience for most children. However, requiring such a report without first providing specific training in locating, comprehending, and recording information, and without providing specific guidance during the preparation of the reports, will generally lead to frustration for the teacher and negative reinforcement for the children.

Recording Information

When children read content-area selections, they sometimes may wish to go no further than locating the appropriate material and comprehending it. On certain occasions, though, such as preparation for a report or gathering data for a hobby, children will need to record some of the information. This process seems to be a burdensome and cumbersome one to many students. Perhaps this is largely the result of numerous unguided attempts, leading to a negative attitude and to practicing of clumsy techniques. Many teachers, it appears, ask children to "take notes" on what they read without first giving them the necessary training. As a result, the children usually end up copying information verbatim rather than jotting down its essence. It is not a rare phenomenon to see high school and college students continuing this habit.

There are at least two useful approaches to the training needed in this respect. One of them is the traditional outlining approach, which calls for two steps: 1) teaching children the procedure by actually outlining portions of textbooks with them and 2) having them apply the outlining procedure to the taking of notes.

For instance, take the previous portion of this chapter. The student who had received training in outlining will record the main ideas and important details in a manner similar to the following:

I. Locating Information
   A. Specific skills related to use of
      1. Book titles
      2. Table of Contents
      3. Index
      4. Glossary
      5. Appendixes
      6. Visuals—maps, tables, graphs, pictures, diagrams
      7. Card catalog
      8. Encyclopedias and other references
   B. Teaching techniques
      1. Basal-reader exercises
      2. Social-studies or science textbooks
         a. "Secret treasure" for children to discover
         b. Discovery questions leading to use of A.1–A.8
      3. Library detectives
         a. Detective's badge or other token
         b. Clues requiring use of A.1–A.8
      4. Preparation for reports
II. Recording information
   A. . . .
   B. . . .

The outline approach is appropriate when students have a rather general assignment to learn all they can about a topic, or to read certain pages in a text, or when they are preparing for a report on a general topic. However, it is probably more common in out-of-school situations to read informational sources for a specific purpose—to find the answer to a burning question, to learn how to do a particular thing related to a hobby, and so on. When this is the case, note taking may be simply a matter of jotting down answers, rather than outlining a topic in logical arrangement.

Let's suppose, for instance, that you wished to read for the specific purpose of answering this question: How fast do high school students read? Using the graph in Figure 15.1, your note taking may look like this:

1. 9th grade—about 214 w.p.m.—average for informational material
2. 10th grade—about 224 w.p.m.—"
3. 11th grade—about 237 w.p.m.—"
4. 12th grade—about 250 w.p.m.—"

To take another example, suppose your purpose in reading is to review for a test that requires you to list ways of helping children learn the skills involved in locating information. In this case, rather than outlining or writing down verbatim all that pertains to this objective, one may take notes as follows:

1. Use discovery-type questions to guide them through the use of these skills with social-studies or science textbooks.
2. Use exercises provided in basal-reader program.
3. Have children become library detectives; give them clues requiring the use of locational skills.
4. Have them use locational skills in preparing reports.

These two approaches to note taking—the outlining technique and the specific-purpose technique—can both be taught to children as soon as they have demonstrated their ability to decode and comprehend informational materials and to write well enough to read their own writing. For some children this will be during the third grade or even earlier; for others, it will be much later. It is very doubtful, however, that the teaching of note-taking skills should be reserved for high school, for by this time too many bad habits will have developed.

Using the PQ3R Method

In the beginning of this book you were urged to try the PQ3R method if you had not already done so. To refresh your memory, this approach can be summarized as follows:

1. *Preview* the first paragraph, the subheadings, and the last paragraph.
2. Change each subheading into a *question* before reading a section.
3. *Read* the section to answer the question.
4. *Recite* to yourself the answer to the question.
5. *Review* the entire selection by repeating steps two and four (question and recite) for each section.

The PQ3R method has had a good track record and seems to help many people comprehend and retain content-area reading material better than when they use no system whatever (17). In fact, some of the newer basal-reader series are now introducing this method in middle-grade readers with selected informational articles. (It is not an appropriate method for fiction.)

Perhaps the most effective means of introducing this approach is to have every child using the same book temporarily. This can be done by giving every child in the classroom a lower-grade social-studies or science textbook for a few days. Rather than present the entire approach to the students in one session, it's best to introduce and practice one step at a time. Take two or three days to teach the preview step, for instance, before moving on to the question step. Before assigning them a few pages to read, have them use the preview step (first paragraph, subheadings, last paragraph). Then ask them such questions as these:

"What do you think this selection is going to be about? What else is it going to be about? What do you think the author will talk about first? What next? What we've just done is called a *preview*. Have you ever noticed how they use a preview on television—just before a movie or a show is going to start? Why do you think they do that? Why do you think it would be a good idea to preview something before you read it? Do you think it would get your mind ready for what the author is going to say to you?"

After they have learned the preview step well, introduce the question step. Go through an entire selection and show them how to change the subheadings into questions. Then go back and ask them again how they would change the first subheading into a question. As soon as they agree on an appropriate question (or questions) for that section, have them read in order to answer the question. Once they have agreed on the best answer to the question, move on to the next subheading and try the method again. Be sure when you're practicing the PQ3R method that you work on it only ten or fifteen minutes per day, so that they get the idea that it's a snappy method that works rather than an additional burden that they're now going to have to put up with in school.

Once they've learned the preview and question steps well, you're ready to "prove" to them how well the entire PQ3R method works. Give them a very short assignment; ask them this time not only to preview, question, and read, but to recite to themselves after each section, and then go back and review each section. Promise them that they will do very well on a short test that you will give them when they are finished. (Be sure that the questions that you write for the test are directly related to the most obvious questions into which they will most likely change the subheadings.

The PQ3R method will quickly fall into disuse unless you give them opportunities to practice it frequently. Whenever there is an informational article in a basal reader that a small group is using, for example, you can use this as an opportunity to reinforce their skill in using the method.

Reading Content-Area Materials for a Purpose

Perhaps the most important strategy of all for children to develop toward the reading of content-area materials is that of acquiring a purpose for reading the material. There is nothing more wasteful of a student's time and natural curiosity than to attack a reading assignment with no motivation to learn anything in particular. As you may have guessed, this type of nonmotivation can reach epidemic proportions by the time children reach the sixth or seventh grade.

There are many reasons for this nonmotivation, of course, depending on the particular child that we're discussing. But two of the most likely causes for such a poor attitude toward reading content-area materials are these: 1) assigning too many pages for one assignment (13) and 2) assigning pages to read without helping children develop any sense of excitement about what they will gain from reading them.

As for the number of pages in one assignment, it is far better to assign too few pages than too many. Remember, you are developing habits and not just covering material. The best way of developing children's habit of not completing a reading assignment is to assign so many pages that they experience fatigue and give up. Ask any high-school teacher and she will tell you of the numerous students who have learned that the best way of handling a long reading assignment is simply not to read it.

As for assigning pages without developing a sense of purpose and excitement, probably no one is more guilty of this than college professors—the very people who serve as the "last-stop" models for those who become elementary and high-school teachers. But, alas, this gives us no excuse to get even and do the same to children. Instead, we can use a variety of "interest getters" to make sure that most of our students will WANT to read the assignment in content-area materials.

Using the D-T-R-A Approach

Let's go back to the directed-teaching-reading activity" described in Chapter 5 as an example of what I'm talking about. The teacher wanted the children to read about the "Amazing Underground City" in New York; how the space under streets was filled with pipes and wires and other things; and how this underground city got started. She didn't say to the children "For your social-studies reading, I want you to read pages 257 to 265." Instead, she sparked their interest with an intriguing question: "Do you know what kinds of things you can find underneath the streets here in New York City?" This led to some intelligent hypothesizing (pipes?) as well as to some imaginative guessing (monsters?) By the time they were through with their pre-reading discussion, the children were eager to read and find out two things: 1) What *is* under there? and 2) Was my guess right or not? In other words, the teacher used two types of "interest getters": first, sparking their curiosity about the unknown, and second, having them place their bets before the race begins (more mundanely known as "making predictions.")

Using Interest Getters

There are many other forms of "interest getters" that you may wish to try before children are asked to read in content-area materials. Here are just a few of them:

1. *Believe it or not:* (before having them read an article about automobile manufacturing) "Would you like to own your own car someday? . . . Do you think you could make your own car? . . . If you were going to make your own car, how many different kinds of parts do you think you'd have to put into it? . . . Did you know that to make a car today it takes 300 different kinds of parts . . . and not only that, those parts come from 56 countries! . . . As you read this article, see if you can find out what some of those different parts are and where they are made."

2. *Battle of the ages:* (before reading about one or both of the paired topics)
   a. "Who do you think was braver—the crew of astronauts who went to the moon, or the crews of the Nina, Pinta, and Santa Maria?"
   b. "Whose discovery was more important to people: Pasteur's or Einstein's?"

3. *Puzzle appeal:* (before reading an article that attempts to solve the puzzle)
   a. "How can the richest nation on earth have so many poor people?"
   b. "What do you think you would find if you looked under the streets of New York City?"

4. *Picture appeal:* (have them look at a picture related to an article they're going to read) "What do you think is happening in this picture? . . . What else? . . . Why do you think this is happening? . . . Does it happen anywhere else, do you think? . . . Read this article and see if your ideas are correct."

5. *Prove me wrong:* (present a stereotype or another type of false statement, then have them read in order to prove you wrong)
   a. The commutative property works for addition, subtraction, multiplication, and division.
   b. Solar energy won't be useful to us for another thousand years!
   c. All monkeys are alike!
   d. Our sun is the biggest star in the whole universe!

6. *Best prediction:* (don't let children know which article or section they're going to read, just give them the title) "From hearing the title, I'd like you to write down three things you think the author will say. Put your name on this sheet, fold it up, and place it in this prediction box. After you're finished reading, we'll see whose predictions came closest."

Summary

Reading in the content-areas such as science, mathematics, and social studies requires specialized vocabulary and reading skills. Since children and adults spend so much time in the reading of informational, nonfictional material, it's important that teachers prepare them for this type of reading. Content-area materials are difficult to read because of the abstractness of the writing and the reader's need for constant production of sensory images and associations related to previous experiences. Teachers can assist children in the development of strategies which will enable them to do a better job of producing these images and associations and thus retaining better the material they have read. Such strategies include the development of a flexible reading rate, the development of visual memory for sequential events, the ability to understand graphic materials such as maps and diagrams, the ability to scan and skim, and several others. Above all, however, the student must learn to read with purpose. The teacher can assist a great deal in encouraging purposeful reading by using a variety of "interest getters."

References and Suggested Reading

1. Askov, Eunice N., and Kamm, Karyln. "Map Skills in the Elementary School." *Elementary School Journal* 75 (1974): 112–21.
2. Braam, Leonard. "Developing and Measuring Flexibility in Reading." *Reading Teacher* 16 (1963): 247–54.
3. Bruinsma, Robert. "Should Lip Movements and Subvocalization during Silent Reading Be Directly Remediated?" *Reading Teacher* 34 (December 1980): 293–96.
4. Chambers, Dewey W. *Children's Literature in the Curriculum.* Chicago: Rand McNally, 1971.
5. Guthrie, John T. "Paragraph Structure." *Reading Teacher* 32 (April 1979): 880–1.
6. Harris, Albert J., and Sipay, Edward R. *How to Increase Reading Ability.* New York: David McKay, 1979.
7. Herber, Harold L. *Teaching Reading in Content Areas.* Englewood Cliffs, NJ: Prentice-Hall, 1970.
8. Johnson, Roger E. "The Reading Level of Elementary Social Studies Textbooks is Going Down." *Reading Teacher* 30 (May 1977): 901–5.

9. Karlin, Robert. *Teaching Elementary Reading, Principles and Strategies.* New York: Harcourt Brace Jovanovich, 1979.

10. Luffey, James L., ed. *Reading in the Content Areas.* Newark, DE: International Reading Association, 1972.

11. McDonald, Arthur S. "Research for the Classroom: Rate and Flexibility." *Journal of Reading* 8 (January 1965): 187–91.

12. Robinson, H. Allan. *Teaching Reading and Study Strategies: the Content Areas.* Boston: Allyn and Bacon, 1975.

13. Smith, Richard J., and Johnson, Dale D. *Teaching Children to Read.* Reading, MA: Addison-Wesley, 1980.

14. Spache, George D., and Spache, Evelyn B. *Reading in the Elementary School.* Boston: Allyn and Bacon, 1979.

15. Sutherland, Zena, et al. *Children and Books.* Chicago: Scott Foresman and Co., 1981.

16. Taylor, Sanford E., et al. *Grade Level Norms for the Components of the Fundamental Reading Skill.* Research Information Bulletin No. 3, Educational Development Laboratories, 1960.

17. Thomas, Ellen Lamar, and Robinson, H. Alan. *Improving Reading in Every Class.* Boston: Allyn and Bacon, 1977.

Application Experiences for the Teacher-Education Class

1. With a small group of students in your class discuss why you agree or disagree with the following statements. Find a page number in the text to support your opinion. Then compare your decisions with other groups.

Statements about Chapter 15

a. The bulk of what a school-age person learns about reading and through reading takes place during the reading of self-selected library books.

b. Once you teach a child the basic skills of reading, she should be able to read anything—a science text, a math text, you name it.

c. Reading in the content areas requires an extraordinary degree of the literal-thinking skill called "developing images and associations."

d. Habitually slow readers must first be cured of this problem before you can help them become "flexible" readers.

e. Helping children develop a "visual memory for sequential events" is important for math reading and can be strengthened through creative dramatics.

f. Children should learn to read standard content-area textbooks, rather than relying upon children's literature.

g. Sometimes peer-written or teacher-written booklets are the best solution to textbooks that are too difficult for some children.

h. The basic strategy that the child must learn for dealing with specialized words in content areas is not to ignore them.

i. The reader of graphs, tables, and maps has the opportunity of creating her own information.

j. Children often hate taking notes on what they read because they have not been taught easy and efficient ways of doing it.

k. The five steps of the PQ3R method should be taught in the same lesson rather than separately.

l. Scanning and skimming are really the same thing.

m. "Interest getters" should really not be necessary by the time children are in the fourth grade.

2. Use the PQ3R method for a week with one of your college courses. Report to your teacher-education class on effects you think this method had on your retention of the material you were supposed to have learned through your reading for that course. Did it increase your ability to concentrate? Do you think you are better prepared for a test on the material you read while using this method? Why or why not?

3. Divide the class into four groups: a math group, a natural-science group, a physical-science group, and a social-studies group. Find two or three paragraphs from a textbook pertaining to your content-area. Then decide on the following:

a. What "interest getter" would you use to get students to want to read them? (See pages 444–445 for examples.)

b. For what two key words will you help students develop stronger images and associations? Precisely how will you do this? Plan the exact procedures you will use. (See pages 428 to 430 for examples.)

c. In what way can you use creative dramatics with students to help them understand the paragraphs?

d. Try out your ideas with one of the other groups.

Field Experiences in the Elementary-School Classroom

1. With one or more children, teach the level-1 and level-2 scanning skills described on pages 427–428. What different strategies did you have to use in order to help the children with the two different levels? (In other words, what clues did you teach them to look for with level-2 scanning that were different from the clues you taught them to look for with level-1 scanning?)

2. Plan and carry out a lesson based on Experience #3 under "Application Experiences for the Teacher-Education Class." Try out your lesson with two or more children. Choose one of the children's textbooks and two or three pages rather than two or three paragraphs.

3. With one or more children create an "elevation map" of the classroom. Help them decide on an appropriate scale, such as "one inch is equal to one foot," or whatever is appropriate for the size of paper you will be using. Help them decide on an appropriate key to show the height of different objects in the room (for example: green could be used for objects less than 12 inches tall). What concepts about maps were you able to teach through this experience? How could you have them apply these concepts to reading other elevation maps?

CHAPTER 16

Many dedicated teachers have been doing something to make their curriculum more multicultural.

Teaching Children Who Differ in Language and Culture

Chapter Preview

A great many dedicated teachers have been doing something to make their curriculum more multicultural and to provide special reading instruction to those children who speak a dialect or language that differs from standard English. However, much more needs to be done by classroom teachers to help these children learn to read well without denying their cultural heritage and their particular form of language.

In this chapter we will look at five special ways in which classroom teachers can relate better to these children. These are 1) appreciate other cultures and vernaculars, 2) use vernacular as a temporary teaching medium, 3) provide abundant readiness experiences, 4) help improve self-concepts, and 5) use a multimedia approach.

It's a miracle that human beings ever understand each other at all.

The National Survey on Compensatory Education

A great many dedicated teachers have been doing something to make their curriculum more multicultural and to provide special reading instruction to those children who speak a dialect or language that differs from Standard English. The average picture across the country, however, has not been looking too good. Allington (2) reports on a study of compensatory education carried on by the Educational Testing Services, funded by the U.S. Office of Education, and reanalyzed and interpreted by a committee of the International Reading Association. This is what they found:

1. Children whose mother tongue was not Standard English were "overrepresented in compensatory programs."
2. Compensatory reading instruction was pervasive in the 70s. Over 14,000 school districts received federal money, with many more receiving funds from state and local governments.
3. Only one-third of the compensatory teachers (sometimes referred to as "Title I teachers") had frequent help from reading specialists.
4. Only 60 percent of the compensatory teachers received special training in diagnosing and remediating reading problems.
5. Children receiving compensatory reading instruction received an average of only thirty minutes of instruction per day from compensatory teachers. In two out of three cases this was all the reading instruction they received. In other words, the compensatory instruction, which was supposed to be extra reading instruction, designed to supplement the regular classroom teacher's instruction, usually took the place of regular instruction. (Thirty minutes per day is substantially less than the amount usually recommended for regular instruction.)

6. Compensatory teachers on the whole tended to use the same teaching strategies with compensatory readers that are often used with regular readers. The basal reader, for example, was the dominant medium of instruction. Worksheets were "pervasive." Oral reading consumed a great amount of time.

7. Compensatory readers, on the average, got very little time to read just for enjoyment.

Although Allington's report does provide evidence representing only the average compensatory program, the picture is not very encouraging. There are no easy solutions to the problem, either. What we'll be talking about in this chapter is not some type of "three-step panacea" to the problem, but some of the variables that teachers and administrators need to keep in mind. The most important variable, perhaps, is the attitude of the teachers and principals who work on a daily basis with children who do not speak Standard English in the home. The second major variable is the instructional approach toward these children. A multifaceted approached, rather than a "business-as-usual . . . more of the same . . . give 'em lots of extra drill" approach will be recommended. Let's begin with a discussion of attitude and then move on to the kind of multifaceted approach that I'm talking about.

Attitudes of Teachers

As mentioned earlier, a large number of people in the United States do not speak Standard English in the home. Instead they speak a Spanish dialect, a Black dialect, a Chinese dialect, a Vietnamese dialect, a Native American dialect, and so on. The instructional techniques used in teaching reading to children whose home language is not Standard English are often quite similar to those used with other children. The major differences in instruction are usually in emphasis rather than in actual technique. We will get to this later in the chapter. First, though, we should discuss a more important factor in the successful instruction of children who do not use Standard English in the home. This factor is the teacher's attitude. Several studies (6, 16, 36) have shown that it may be this factor more than anything else that determines how well children of minority subcultures learn to read.

Appreciate Their Culture and Vernacular

'Twas the night before Christmas, and
   all through the house,
Not a creature was stirring, not even a
   mouse.

The stockings were hung by the chimney
  with care,
In hopes that St. Nicholas soon
  would be there.
              Clement C. Moore

Era la noche antes la Navidad y
  en todo la casa,
No creatura mova, ni siquiera un
  ratôn.
Las medias estuvieren colgaron cerca de la chiminea
  con cuidado.
En esperanza que Papá Navidad
  viniere pronto.
              Susan B. Eliot

Both renditions of this classical narrative poem seem equally charming. I hope you'll agree with me that all languages and dialects can be equally beautiful and useful. If you do have this attitude, I think it will make it much easier for you to work with children who differ from you in culture, language, or dialect. Teachers who feel that their language, dialect, or culture is superior to those of their students are likely to have considerable difficulty teaching them to read.

> You will become a more successful teacher if you become a student too. If you try to learn as much as you can of the language and the customs of the person you will be teaching, both you and your student will have more success in learning a new language and new customs (28, p. 140).

Suppose we have two adults, one named Eulogio and the other named Sally. Sally offers to teach Eulogio more English than he already knows and to teach him some of the customs of people living in the city of Seattle. Eulogio says, "I would like to learn your language better and your customs better. For your kindness I will teach you some Spanish and tell you about some of our customs in Mexico."

"Well, thanks," Sally says, "but I have a hard enough time just speaking my own language without cluttering up my mind with foreign phrases."

She laughs heartily, while Eulogio looks hurt and confused and laughs very uneasily.

"As for Mexico," Sally adds, "I'd love to learn about your quaint customs."

The effects of Sally's remarks on Eulogio's feelings are obvious, of course. The effects of her attitude on their friendship and on their ability to learn together should also be obvious. That this attitude can be equally damaging when adults work with children does not seem to be as obvious, judging from the behavior of some

One out of every six people in the United States does not use
English as his or her first language.

adults. Perhaps they forget that children are as sensitive and proud
as adults (if not more so).

The point I'm trying to make, of course, is that teachers
should not so much "help" children learn Standard English as they
should share on an equal basis their different languages or dialects.

We will discuss this issue much more thoroughly in the next section, but for now we are talking about an essential attitude that teachers must have to be effective with minority children.

This problem of attitude occurs all over the world. Children on the border between Brazil and Uruguay, for example, speak a dialect that is quite dissimilar from the dialect used in the schools. Eloisa (21) says that these border children are typically way behind the other children in the schools. The problem, she says, is the teachers. Many of them refuse to treat the border dialect as a valid language with long roots in history and one through which its users "can express their full personalities."

Dialect Defined

What is a dialect? Most people know what is meant by a *language.* But what is a dialect? To the person who speaks it, it's the "mother tongue." To the person who speaks the same language but a different dialect, it's "sloppy speech," or "jibberish," or "lower-class speech," or "hoity-toity talk." Referring facetiously, for a moment, to the "newspaper report" in Chapter 1, a dialect is what causes "frothing of the mouth by upper-class and lower-class dogs alike." Like Dr. Feline, who discovered about 3000 different "fanguages" in the world, human linguists have discovered about 3000 different *languages* in the world. And, like Dr. Feline, who discovered that most fanguages had several dogalects, they have found that most languages have several dialects. And they generally have found that people make fun of the linguistic noises that other people make. Perhaps it's just one of the many ways we have of trying to make ourselves feel good about ourselves. After all, everyone knows that saying "Grrr rowlf *urr* yelp" is much superior to saying "Grrr rowlf *orr* yelp."

To get serious again, a dialect is a variation of a language that differs from other variations in three ways. First, it differs *phonologically;* that is, it differs in the way people produce phonemes or in the particular phonemes that are used. For example, in some parts of the deep South native speakers say /fee-ish/ for *fish,* adding a long *e* sound before the short *i* sound. People in the North, who use the short *i* sound, find that addition quite amusing (although some linguists say that the southern dialect comes closer to the English of the British Isles in colonial days).

Second, it differs *grammatically.* That is, it may differ in the way verb tense, negation, number, and other structural changes are signaled. For instance, someone speaking Black English may say, "From now on, I don't be playing," whereas someone speaking Standard English (or Anglo English) will say, "From now on, I'm not going to play."

Third, it differs *lexically.* That is, the actual words or vocabulary used may differ. Someone speaking Black English may say, "Please carry me home," while someone speaking Anglo English will say, "Please take me home." Someone in certain parts of New England will call a toilet a "flush." Others will call it a "water closet" or a "toilet."

Dialect differences are not indications of sloppy speech, as some people are prone to claim. They are systematic variations of a common language. If you listen to two people speaking Black English, for instance, the differences between black and white dialects are consistent. If a person whose mother tongue is Black English is speaking to a person whose mother tongue is Standard English, there may be a tendency for the person speaking Black English (particularly a child) to switch back and forth between Black English and Standard English. This is especially true in a situation where speakers of Black English are made to feel that their dialect is inferior—which is sometimes the case in a school setting.

Let us look now at some fairly systematic differences between Black English and Standard English:

Table 16.1   *Some of the Differences between Standard English and Black English*

1. Omission of the /s/ phoneme at the end of the third person singular, present tense verb, e.g., He *look* at the picture.
2. Omission of /s/ on plural nouns preceded by quantitative modifier, e.g., I got thirteen *pencil.* I got several *pencil.* I got many *pencil.*
3. Omission of /s/ in possessive case, e.g., Give me *Bill* pencil.
4. Addition of /s/ to first person or third person plural forms of verbs, e.g., I *sees* it. They *lets* us do it.
5. Omission of the /d/ phoneme at the end of words, e.g., *tole* for *told, ba* for *bad.*
6. Substitution of the /d/ phoneme for voiced /th/ at the beginning of words, e.g., *deh* for *the, dat* for *that.*
7. Use of present-tense form for past-tense verbs, e.g., He *ring* the bell yesterday. Yesterday I *jump* rope.
8. Variations on forms of *to be,* e.g., They *is readin'.* They *be readin'.* They *readin'.*
9. Double negative for emphasis, e.g., I *ain't* got *no* candy.
10. Omission of /r/ at the end of words and syllables, e.g., *foe* for *four, Pass* for *Paris, cat* for *carrot.*
11. Omission of /l/ at the end of words or near the end of words, e.g., *foo* for *fool, fought* for *fault, hep* for *help.*

Now let's look at some differences between Spanish and English that cause both teachers and children confusion:

What do these dialect differences mean in practice? In general, they mean that speakers of Black English and of Spanish would probably benefit from a language-experience approach combined with systematic instruction in the decoding processes. It further indicates that whereas a phonics approach may be quite appropriate

Table 16.2   Some Differences between Standard English and Some of the Spanish* Dialects

1. The /th/ heard in *thanks* may be pronounced as /t/, making *thanks* sound like *tanks*. In some dialects the voiced /th/ may be pronounced /d/, making *those* sound like *doze*.
2. The /ch/ sound and the /sh/ sound may be interchanged, e.g., *chin* may be pronounced *shin* after the child has learned the /sh/ sound.
3. The short /i/ sound may be pronounced like long /ē/, e.g., *tin* becomes *teen*.
4. The voiced /s/ heard in *rise* and the unvoiced /s/ heard in *rice* may be interchanged, e.g., *rise* becomes *rice* or *police* becomes *please*.
5. The /v/ sound heard in *very* may be pronounced more like /b/, making *very* sound like *berry*. Also the /b/ may become /v/ in medial positions, e.g., *havit* for *habit*.
6. In words that have a *voiced* consonant sound at the end (the sound made by vibrating the vocal chords while the mouth is in a consonant position), the voiced sound may be omitted, e.g., *robe* becomes *rope*, *five* becomes *fife*, *dead* becomes *debt*, and *tug* becomes *tuck*.
7. The /s/ sound at the beginning of a word may be preceded by a vowel sound if the /s/ sound is blended with a consonant, e.g., *stop* becomes *es-top*.
8. Noun determiners are sometimes omitted, e.g., She is *doctor*.

*For more detail on dialect differences, See Ching (10).

with children whose mother tongue is Black English, this approach may not work well with some Spanish-speaking children (42). In Spanish there is no sound of *h*, no final *nk*, and no initial-*s* consonant blend. "The pronunciations of many letters—the *j*, the *d*, the *v*, and the *r*—in many positions within words in English are significantly different even though the visual appearances are the same" (43, p. 26). A linguistic approach, one that emphasizes visual differences rather than auditory differences, will probably be more appropriate for many Spanish-speaking children.

But before we look more thoroughly at instructional techniques, let us look at cultural differences that sometimes exist between minority children and majority children.

Cultural Differences

Majority-culture children in our society are often taught to look to the future, to set goals for the future, and to set smaller subgoals that will help one reach the larger goals. "Some day you'll be a successful businessman like your father. But that means you're going to have to do well in high school so you can get into college. And that means you'll have to learn to read well and write and spell. So you had better get that homework done!" Although many minority children are taught exactly the same thing, there are some who are not.

Some minority children, as well as their parents, have had little experience with the type of success in which most school teachers believe. Instead they have experienced considerable failure, as far as school-related tasks are concerned. Therefore, they are not used to the "goal-setting" approach that many teachers advocate.

This in no way means that the children are "lazy," which is the label that some teachers attach to them. It does mean that other means of motivating them to learn will have to be tried. Some teachers have been successful with behavioral-management techniques that require the teacher and child to establish short-range goals and the exact reinforcement that will motivate the child to reach those goals one at a time. The reinforcement varies with the child; it may mean the use of a playground ball at recess, or tokens that can be later turned in for prizes, or special time with the teacher—it all depends on what the child considers to be a reward. But it does not mean such vague promises as going on a field trip someday, or moving on to the next grade, or getting a job when you grow up.

Another major cultural difference is the way children look at achievement. Many "majority" children are taught to achieve on an individual basis—to have the best batting average, to be the best speller, to win a gold medal for oneself. Some minority children are not motivated to achieve in such an individualistic way. In the Mexican-American culture, for instance, a child's identity is often closely related to the family's identity. Achievement for the family (or extended family group, including certain friends) is often more important than self-achievement. Siblings are considered to be important and often act as substitute parents. The "good of the whole" is generally a strong value.

In other words, some Mexican-American children are used to achieving for the benefit of a group, and the process of achieving is a group process. For them the learning process is better in a "human" setting, working either directly with the teacher or with other students, rather than working by themselves. For them, learning needs to be more of a social affair in which peers work together, or older students help younger students, or the teacher works directly with the students. Lawrence (30) describes the successful use of sixth graders to help first graders learn to read after she had first trained the sixth graders in the use of the language-experience approach. Himmelsteib (27) had ninth graders act as buddies to third graders in selecting library books and in playing reading games. Boraks and Allen (4) developed a more elaborate plan, in which college students taught fourth and fifth graders to tutor each other in an inner-city school. The children were taught tutoring behavior such as promoting positive response patterns, keeping others on task, explaining the objectives, giving praise, and helping others verify their own responses. Breiling (5) describes a program in which parents are trained by teachers to work with their own children—how to encourage their children, how to use reading games, and how to have the children read to them for ten minutes a day. Improvement in enthusiasm as well as sight vocabulary has been the reported result of this program.

As a contrast to these studies, however, Cohen and Rodriquez (13) have shown that with very young Mexican-American children (first graders), the most effective approach was not a group procedure, but a highly individualized one in which reading instruction was aimed toward precise behavioral objectives. In fact, the more self-directed (rather than teacher-assisted) the instruction was, the higher the children seemed to achieve.

To continue itemizing cultural differences between majority children and minority children is to run the risk of establishing more false expectations than already exist for minority children. Minority children differ among themselves as much as majority children do. To expect every minority child to want to work with a buddy is as unsuitable as expecting all majority children to work on their own. The point I'm trying to make is that cultural differences do exist that will definitely affect the type of motivation that each child brings to the learning task. When one motivational approach doesn't work with some children, the temptation for a few teachers is to consider those children lazy, or "deprived," or in some way inferior. What I'm urging instead is that the teacher examine the possibility that cultural differences are interfering with the teaching-learning relationship.

You may remember from Chapter 8 that one of the principles of motivation is to help children satisfy their basic needs, including needs for affection and security. By understanding children's cultural background, by letting them know that you appreciate their culture and want to learn from it, and by gearing your motivational approaches to their cultural upbringing, you can help to make children feel secure and loved—and ready to learn.

Different Ways of Dealing with Differences

We have learned that for a child to interact creatively and productively with education he must retain his personal integrity and be able to value what he and his family stand for. So one solution offered is that the Maori needs to feel proud of his heritage. . . . The child who enters school speaking Maori should be taught to read in Maori (12, p. 339).

The Melting-Pot Approach

At the present time, four different approaches to helping minority children learn to read are being used. The first one is the *melting-pot approach*. With this approach, you simply teach the child to read in Standard English, hoping that she will pick up enough understanding of Standard English through normal day-to-day communication in the classroom, on the playground, through television, and through other contacts with speakers of Standard English. That this approach has sometimes been a failure has been attested to by several reports (39, 43, 44).

The ESL Approach

A second approach is the *English-as-a-second-language-approach.* With this approach, children are first taught to speak in Standard English before they are expected to learn to read in Standard English. This approach has the theoretical virtue of building a child's language naturally from the oral skills of listening and speaking to the written skills of reading and writing. It also has the theoretical virtue of not labeling a child's language or dialect as "incorrect," seeking instead to teach Standard English as a second dialect or language—one that is necessary for all citizens to know in order to become "successful," both socially and financially.

However, there is a tendency for those who advocate and use this method to look at those who do not speak Standard English as "handicapped." They often propose that Standard English be taught as soon as possible so that the "handicapped students" can function properly in a regular classroom (18). With this approach, it is almost as though we were trying to drown out the children's earlier means of communicating by saturating them with Standard English. Instead of building upon the preschool language learning of these children, we tend to ignore that learning and proceed to start all over again. Children enter school and are encompassed by a strange new world of school language (22). Is it any wonder that children whose home language is not Standard English often do poorly on tests of language skills?

One can certainly forgive and even applaud such sincere attempts to help minority children cope with the problem of reading Standard English. The English-as-a-second-language (ESL) approach is surely a more humane one than the melting-pot approach. However, with respect to the Black children who have been put through an ESL program, the evidence is not very encouraging. Studies by Cagney (8), Hall and Turner (25), Rystrom (38), Weener (47), Peisach (33), and Eisenberg (20), for example, all seem to indicate that the problem that some Black students experience in learning to read is not in their inability to speak Standard English—or even to understand it. In Cagney's study (8), for instance, a group of first graders who were fluent speakers of Black English and whose home language was Black English were exposed to a set of language-experience stories written by other children. Half of the stories were written in Standard Dialect and half were written in a Black dialect. They were read to the children by a teacher who was fluent in both Standard and Black English. The children were then asked questions about the stories designed to test their comprehension. On the average, the children made significantly more correct responses to questions about the stories written in Standard English than to questions about the stories written in Black English.

In other words, it would appear that most children who speak Black English as their native language have been sufficiently exposed to Standard English (via television and other sources) to understand it, even though they may not be fluent speakers of Standard English. The assumption that they must learn to speak Standard English fluently before they can learn to read it is probably erroneous. Furthermore, it is likely that attitudinal and cognitive variables are more important than dialect differences.

With respect to Spanish-speaking children, there appears to be no evidence that they would benefit from learning to speak Standard English fluently any more than children who speak Black English. It is likely that they need abundant exposure to Standard English before they are expected to learn to read it, but fluent speech in Standard English is probably not necessary. What often happens, it appears, is that those of us who are attempting to provide assistance to minority children get our goals confused. If our goal is to have every child speaking fluent Standard English, then Kaplan's facetious suggestion (29) may be applicable: adopt "sufficient totalitarian methods to disseminate it within the population." But if our goal is the more realistic one of teaching every child we can to read, and if our main concern is that they comprehend what they read, rather than "read orally with elegance," then the English-as-a-second-language approach is probably not the solution.

The Common-Core Approach

A third approach being tried is the *common-core approach*. In this approach, reading materials that have been developed to minimize dialect and cultural differences are used. Shuy (41) suggests that only three grammatical forms are troublesome to developers of these materials: 1) negation *(doesn't have* vs. *ain't got no)* 2) past conditional *(Mother asked if I ate* vs. *Mother asked did I eat)* and 3) negative + be *(When I sing he isn't afraid* vs. *When I sing he don't be afraid).* In order to minimize cultural differences, the subject of science is often used.

This approach may work with children speaking Black English, though no research evidence of its effectiveness is presently available. Obviously, this approach in its totality will not work for Spanish-speaking children, since the differences between Spanish and English are often too great. However, the greater use of science as medium for discussion, for preparing language experience charts, and for resulting reading materials may help to bridge the gap between cultures.

The Native-Vernacular Approach

A fourth approach is the *native vernacular approach*. With this approach, minority children are first taught to read and write in their mother tongue, whether that be Puerto Rican Spanish, Cantonese Chinese, Sioux, Black English, or some other language or dialect. While they are learning to read and write in their native vernacular, they are exposed to Standard English through working with Standard-English-speaking children in such activities as art, music, and physical education. Sometime before the end of third grade, they are given instruction in English as a second language.

The native-vernacular approach has strong appeal to those of us who feel that a child's culture and vernacular should be respected and utilized in instructional programs. We can start where each child is with respect to language development, rather than start over; and we can have the child reading as soon as majority children are, thus avoiding the stigma and devastation of failure.

Unfortunately, this type of program has serious drawbacks. The most serious drawback, of course, is one of resources, since this program requires skilled teachers who can communicate in Spanish, Black English, Chinese, and so on. It also requires reading materials that are written in the various languages and dialects.

The problem of finding suitable reading materials can be handled partly through the use of the language-experience approach to reading instruction. According to Hall (24), this approach is particularly appropriate for use with minority children because it makes it possible to have reading materials that match both their experiences and their language patterns. As Ruddell (36) points out, reading comprehension is a function of the similarity between the patterns of language structure used by the person reading and those used in the reading materials. Since with the language-experience approach, children read what they have written or dictated, such similarity is assured.

In addition to the use of language-experience charts or stories, a supply of bilingual materials is gradually being developed, such as the Miami Linguistic Reader Series published by D. C. Heath. This series for English and Spanish languages is designed to teach Spanish-speaking children not only to read Standard English, but to pronounce it with precision. Several other publishers also have developed or are developing bilingual materials (43). It should be pointed out, however, that when Black English materials have been published, the reaction from both Whites and Blacks in the community has tended to be quite negative. Black parents have been particularly incensed, as they've felt that their children need to learn the Standard English that will allow their own youngsters to "get ahead" in our society.

The problem of finding suitable teachers may be diminishing, as more and more universities train people to work in bilingual settings. However, it should be admitted that the greatest demand for these teachers is in population centers where Spanish-speaking and Black English-speaking children are concentrated. It is a rare school district that hires bilingual teachers when only a few minority children are present in the schools (even though in 1970, in the Lau vs. Nichols decision (28), the U.S. Supreme Court declared that under Title VI of the 1964 Civil Rights Act, "all school districts are compelled to provide children who speak little or no English with special language programs which will give them an equal opportunity to an education").

To make this problem more graphic, suppose you are teaching in California, and in your classroom of first graders you have two children who speak Spanish, one who speaks with a Black dialect, and one who speaks with a Cantonese dialect. There are no other children in the school who speak these vernaculars. The principal tells you to "do what you can with them." Unfortunately, you speak only Standard English. You understand only half of what the Black child says and nothing of what the Chinese-speaking and Spanish-speaking children say. Although there are few teachers who have to face this difficult a situation, there are many teachers who have a few children whose language they cannot understand.

The language-experience approach may be called for in this type of situation, but there's no way for you to take dictation, since you can't understand what they're saying. What should you do? Ignore them until they have picked up enough English? Not a very humane or professional solution. What about finding special tutors for them? This is what some teachers have been able to do. By scouring the community they have found volunteers who were shown how to use the language-experience approach with the youngsters. (In a few cases they have been lucky enough to have federal funds for hiring tutors.)

The solution to the dilemma teachers face is not an easy or inexpensive one. In fact, there is presently insufficient evidence to show that the bilingual approach actually works. Ching (10) cites three studies in which the bilingual approach was compared with the traditional Standard-English approach. In only one of these studies did the researchers find that the bilingual approach was superior and in that one, both the schools and the teachers' training were superior at the start.

It is most likely that bilingual approach will require school settings in which teachers have extra training and motivation. So far, however, we have no assurances based on experimental research. Most of the arguments for the bilingual approach at the present time are based on logic, politics, subjective observations, and humanitarian concern. Yet a concerted effort to assist minority children must be made, and the bilingual approach seems to be the most promising one at this point. As Nila Banton Smith explains:

> There is a rapidly growing philosophy in regard to dialects and the teaching of reading which is widely advocated by many well-known

linguists. These linguists differ somewhat in regard to details, but fundamentally all of them agree to 1) accept the child's dialect as his native language; 2) provide him opportunities to read in his own dialect as a precedent to or along with reading in Standard English; and 3) combine teacher guidance, appropriate materials, teacher and peer associations to aid him in acquiring ability to speak and read with increasing fluency in Standard English as a second language while maintaining his native language (42, p. 139).

Provide Abundant Readiness Experiences

In Chapter 7, we discussed the concept of readiness as an all-pervasive concern of every teacher at every grade level—as well as the need for preparing children for new reading skills by first having them practice the skills with oral language. In addition, we talked about the importance of providing experiential background so that children could bring meaning to the printed page. This notion of readiness is even more urgently needed when you are working with those minority children who speak a different dialect or language.

Suppose, for instance, you're helping Brenda, a child who speaks Black English, to read this sentence: "Mother asked if I had opened the window." Brenda may be able to decode this sentence properly, but how do you know she understands it? If she were speaking her own dialect, rather than reading yours, she might say, "Mother asked did I crank the window." Sometimes when children who speak Black English are reading Standard English, they will translate as they go along. For example, instead of reading "Mother asked if I had opened the window," Brenda might read, "Mother asked did I crank the window," or she might just say, "Mother asked did I open the window." This type of instant translation should probably be encouraged rather than corrected, as it demonstrates that Brenda is comprehending what she reads. On the other hand, if she doesn't translate, it's a good idea sometimes to stop after every sentence or two and get her to tell you or show you what the words mean. If she doesn't know what they mean, then you need to demonstrate the meaning and help her make the translation.

Naturally it helps if you're bidialectal yourself, or bilingual if you are working with a child speaking another language. But even if you're not, you can still act as a mediator between one vernacular and another—by asking questions, demonstrating, and by encouraging translation.

This is just one example of how you can provide readiness experiences for those who are trying to learn to read Standard English. Chapter 2 suggested other ways to help children bring meaning to the printed page: through direct experiences, through vicarious experiences, and through talking about those experiences.

Help Them Improve Their Self-Concepts

Wattenburg and Clifford (46) found that measures of children's self-concepts were better at predicting their reading achievement than the usual intelligence and readiness tests. But perhaps we don't need research reports to prove the obvious. It is readily apparent that people's conceptions of themselves influence and direct their behavior. If Janice feels she's a lousy cook, she's not likely to try hard at being a good cook, for fear of having more dismal failures. In fact, her negative self-concept in this case will probably influence her cooking behavior in such a way that she does burn the roast and "lump-up" the gravy. In a similar manner, if Sammy develops a concept of himself as a lousy reader, his chances for success are greatly reduced.

> Research conducted in the areas of self-concept and the role of teacher expectations as they correspond to academic achievement shows them to be interrelated. Poor achievement leads to a lowered self-image which results in continued poor achievement (6, p. 361).

How does Sammy develop the concept of himself as a poor reader? There are several ways, but perhaps the most direct way is through daily failure to be able to read a word, or name a letter, or complete a worksheet, or answer the teacher's question, or perform the host of minor tasks that the teacher places before him. But then there's the indirect way of developing his negative self-concept and that is through perceiving the teacher's expectations of his failure.

There are a number of studies (16, 44) that demonstrate the possibility that many teachers working in inner-city schools with a preponderance of minority children have low expectations for the students' performance. Furthermore, self-concept measures for children in these school correlate quite highly with perceptions of teachers' feelings toward them. In other words, if Sammy feels he's an inferior student, it is likely that he also perceives that his teacher thinks he's an inferior student. On the other hand, in situations where teachers communicate to their students that they believe in them and believe they can learn, the performance of the students tends to improve. This is not an indisputable "law of human nature" or a principle that works with every individual, but in general it seems to be a demonstrable cause-and-effect relationship (36).

How can teachers help children improve their self-concepts? For one thing, they can respect their vernacular and culture, a principle we have discussed in an earlier section. Another way is through the use of the child's vernacular as a temporary teaching medium.

> A child's use of his native language when he is learning to read is a very important factor in his success, for success in reading in any language is determined to a great extent by the student's attitude

toward what he is trying to do. If he hears, speaks, and feels what is already known to him, he is more comfortable than if he is bombarded by strange sounds and sights. Once he feels at ease or successful, in reading his own language, he is more receptive to acquiring another language and the culture it represents (28, p. 236).

Another way is through providing models that children can emulate. One reason that some children perceive themselves as nonreaders is that the people they identify with do not read. In a study by Nichols (31), for instance, she found that none of the fathers of a group of "nonreading" black boys used reading in his daily activities to any appreciable extent. Furthermore, the fathers placed a low value on reading. In addition, she found census figures that showed that for the top five occupations engaged in by black men in this particular region not one required the use of reading or clerical skills. Nichols did discover, however, that many of the black men in this region were highly skilled story tellers and that the boys gained status through imitating these men. In fact, many of the boys were superb storytellers by the age of ten. She suggests that the language-experience approach be used with students in this type of situation so that their stories can be captured in print and then used to inspire reading.

In addition to the use of language-experience stories, Nichols suggests that men in the community who use reading in their work be brought in for short visits with the children. Others have suggested that various adults be brought in to read to children, that biographies of famous minority people be read, and that their pictures be hung up on the school walls for inspiration. In general, providing identification figures to children is probably an important way to assist children in improving their self-concepts.

One other way of helping children elevate their self-concepts should be mentioned. And this is done simply (but not really so simply) by improving the quality of your teaching. In Chapter 8, we discussed several ways of doing this, including the use of such learning principles as helping children satisfy their basic needs for love and esteem, teaching them at the appropriate level of difficulty, and providing them with frequent and specific feedback. These principles alone, if adhered to, will often assure greater success for your students, and thus provide them with positive ammunition for feeling that they really are "good students" and they really are going to learn to read.

Use a Multimedia Approach

The importance of quality teaching was just discussed. One way of improving the quality of teaching and thus the quality of learning is through the use of a variety of media. Using a multimedia approach is recommended especially for the satisfaction of two basic learning principles discussed in Chapter 8: providing motivation through novelty and encouraging retention through mastery. The following media are those that teachers have found especially useful in working with minority children.

Television

The average child watches television between 30 and 40 hours per week (1). This is as much time as most children spend in school. Rather than ignoring it or wishing it would go away, some teachers have used it as a stimulus for reading and writing lessons. For example, children can prepare experience charts based on television programs they have agreed to "all watch on the same night." They can describe details of an advertisement to each other and have the group guess the product. The teacher writes down the names of the products and later has the children read them. They can be assigned the task of finding VCE words, or -*at* words, or any other kind of words in the titles of shows they watch. They can find out how to spell the names of their favorite stars and help each other read them. The list of television-related activities is probably endless.

Language-Experience Charts

This medium is brought up again because of an important debate concerning its use. Should you edit children's dictation so that only Standard English is written on the charts? Some say yes: that it is necessary from the very beginning to show children the "correct" form and not let them develop habits of using "incorrect" English. Others say that you defeat the purpose by editing, since your purpose is to help the child see the relationship between orally expressed thoughts and the written form of those thoughts.

Some say you will insult the child if you change her language and destroy some of the intrinsic motivation derived from seeing her exact words portrayed in print. Others say you'll insult her more if you print it just the way you hear it. Rogers (35), for instance, says it would be highly insulting to a child who says "Thim thaings stank," to write it exactly that way. People tend to perceive that they speak the standard dialect spoken by television personalities, even though an objective observer would say that they definitely do not. Therefore, Rogers says that you should help the child realize that written language is Standard English and write it that way. Instead of writing "Thim thaings stank," the teacher should say, "Yes, those things stink," and write "Those things stink." If the child says "He be always there," the teacher should say, "Yes, he is always there," and write it that way.

Many educators do not agree. They feel that too much editing destroys the values of the language-experience approach. From a practical teaching standpoint, I side with those linguists (23, 39) who argue for building a reading program upon children's present language. I make one exception to the exact transcription of children's dictation, however, and that is the spelling of the words that the child gives you. I've found that it's embarrassing and confusing to the children to use anything other than standard orthography. In other words, write "Them things stink" and "He be always there." After you have written it and you and the children have read it, the child who dictated it may possibly decide on her own that it should be changed. This is the time to edit it. Editing it beforehand tends to be highly unmotivating, and the dictation becomes sparse.

Listening Experiences

You may want to consider two types of listening experiences. One type is the "listening-reading transfer lesson" described by Cunningham (14). In this type of lesson, students are taught that the things they can do after listening to a passage are the same kinds of things they can do after reading a passage. Two parallel lessons are planned. In the first one, let's say on finding main ideas, the children listen and respond in a specific way. Immediately following this lesson, they read a passage and respond in the same specific way. This approach is similar to the one described in Chapter 7 on readiness. The difference lies in the immediate transfer from a listening lesson to a reading lesson. This type of immediate transfer seems to be very useful to minority children who are experiencing some difficulty making the connection between listening to Standard English and reading Standard English.

Another type of listening experience is that of listening while reading. We are not referring to the old-fashioned and potentially damaging practice of "round-robin reading," in which each child takes a turn reading a page while the other children fidget or wait nervously for their turns. We're referring to the practice of occasionally having the teacher read a story while everyone else reads along with the teacher silently. This same procedure can be modified by using listening tapes in a listening center.

The potential advantage of this technique is that of getting minority children used to hearing Standard English while they are reading it. There is some evidence that this approach, when combined with other language experiences, such as creative dramatics, discussions, and creative writing, can lead to significant progress in reading (40).

A Structured Decoding Program

After the children have had what appears to be sufficient oral-language experiences with Standard English and you have decided that they are ready for more intensive reading of Standard English, what type of decoding program should be used? As mentioned earlier, the evidence so far indicates that a phonics program should be tried with children who speak Black English or some other dialect, whereas a linguistic program should be tried with children who speak Spanish or some other distinct language.

This is certainly no hard-and-fast rule. There are many children, Black and White, who have difficulty with a strictly phonics method because of their weak auditory abilities. Trying to strengthen those abilities doesn't seem to be the answer (26). It seems to be preferable simply to switch those children to a linguistic program that relies more on visual discrimination and memory.

Some type of structured decoding program, however, should probably be incorporated into the overall reading program. Having the children continue to rely on the sight words they have picked up through work with experience charts does not seem to be an effective approach (9, 19).

Pattern Books

Children who do not use Standard English as their first language can benefit from the use of "pattern books," also called "predictable books." With a pattern book, according to Rhodes (34, pp. 511–12) "children can quickly begin to predict what the author is going to say and how he is going to say it. By the time the teacher has read a few pages aloud, most children in the room can chant the text right along with the teacher."

The Bus Ride (Scott, Foresman Reading Systems, Level 2, Book A, 1971) is a good example of a pattern book. Part of the book goes like this:

> The girl got on the bus.
> Then the bus went fast.
>
> A boy got on the bus.
> Then the bus went fast.
>
> A fox got on the bus.
> Then the bus went fast . . .

Another example of a pattern book is *The Great Big Enormous Turnip* by Alexei Tolstoy (Franklin Watts, 1968). Part of this book goes like this:

> The mouse pulled the cat.
> The cat pulled the dog.
> The dog pulled the granddaughter.
> The granddaughter pulled the old woman.

The old woman pulled the old man.
The old man pulled the turnip . . .

In general, the procedure for using pattern books is first to read the story to the children while they listen (and begin to chant if they can). Then the teacher reads it with the children. And finally the children read it by themselves—either as a group or individually. Some teachers also encourage the children to add to the pattern—either orally or in writing, depending upon their abilities and enthusiasm.

Rhodes (34) provides a good bibliography of pattern books in her *Reading Teacher* article. To give you the flavor of this bibliography, here are a few of the books that she recommends:

Adams, Pam. *This Old Man,* Grossett and Dunlap, 1974.
Aliki. *Go Tell Aunt Rhody,* Macmillan, 1974.
Beckman, Kaj. *Lisa Cannot Sleep,* Franklin Watts, 1969.
Brown, Margaret Wise. *Goodnight Moon,* Harper and Row, 1947.
de Regniers, Beatrice Schenk. *May I Bring a Friend?* Atheneum, 1972.
Keats, Ezra Jack. *Over in the Meadow,* Scholastic, 1971.
Mack, Stan. *10 Bears in My Bed,* Pantheon, 1974.
Preston, Edna Mitchell. *Where Did My Mother Go?* Four Winds Press, 1978.
Wondriska, William. *All the Animals Were Angry.* Holt, Rinehart and Winston, 1970.

For another example of the use of patterning in reading, speaking, writing, and listening, you may wish to refer to Chapter 5, pages 135–138 on the subject of "Creative Grammar."

Multiple Texts and Trade Books

Children who do not speak Standard English at home need the opportunity for horizontal progress as well as vertical progress in reading. Since they are much less used to using Standard English, it is advisable to have on hand several different books at the same reading level. For example, rather than have Brenda read only the primer in one basal-reading series, let her read several primers from different series. In this way she can consolidate her progress and gain confidence in her ability to read fluently. Instead of rushing her on to the first reader, introduce her to several trade books that are on the primer level. To put this another way, don't rush and don't push. Let Brenda enjoy her victory before giving her another difficult challenge. Allow time for a language or dialect that is foreign to her to seem more natural and "gentle on the mind."

Summary

In working with children who do not speak Standard English in the home, teachers should be able to appreciate the children's culture and vernacular and to communicate this appreciation to them by learning about them and from them. It is advisable to use their own vernacular as a temporary teaching medium and to treat Standard English as another language rather than the only language. Readiness in the form of direct and vicarious experience, along with oral communication, is a continual necessity. Perhaps most important of all, there is a need to assist them in improving their self-concepts by providing them with numerous small successes, by providing them with models, and by expecting that they will improve their reading skills. And finally, it is suggested that a multimedia approach that includes television, language-experience charts, a structured phonics or linguistic program, multiple texts and trade books, and listening experiences be used. But perhaps the most important thing of all to remember is that all children must be treated as individuals, with individual needs, concerns, and learning styles.

Sources of Materials and Information on Bilingual and Bicultural Programs

1. International Reading Association
   Executive Secretary
   800 Barksdale Road
   Newark, DE 19711

2. English as a Second Language Program
   Center for Applied Linguistics
   1717 Massachusetts Ave. N.W.
   Washington, DC 20036

3. National Association for Bilingual Education
   University of Texas at San Antonio
   4242 Piedras Drive East
   San Antonio, TX 78285

4. Teachers of English to Speakers of Other Languages (TESOL)
   Executive Secretary
   School of Languages and Linguistics
   Georgetown University
   Washington, DC 20007

5. Executive Secretary
   National Council of Teachers of English
   1111 Kenyon Road
   Urbana, IL 61801

6. Bilingual-Bicultural Office
   State Department of Public Instruction
   Capital of your state, Your state

References and Suggested Readings

1. Adams, Anne H., and Harrison, Cathy B. "Using Television to Teach Reading Skills." *Reading Teacher* 30 (October 1975): 45–51.

2. Allington, Richard. "Teaching Reading in Compensatory Classes: a Descriptive Summary." *Reading Teacher* 34 (November 1980): 178–83.

3. Bethell, Thomas. "Becoming an American." *Newsweek* (May 26, 1975): 13.

4. Boraks, Nancy, and Allen, Amy Roseman. "A Program to Enhance Peer Tutoring." *Reading Teacher* 30 (February 1977): 479–84.

5. Breiling, Annette. "Using Parents as Teaching Partners." *Reading Teacher* 30 (November 1976): 187–92.

6. Burg, Leslie A. "Affective Teaching—Neglected Practice in Innercity Schools?" *Reading Teacher* 28 (January 1975): 360–3.

7. Burling, R. *English in Black and White*. New York: Holt, Rinehart, and Winston, 1973.

8. Cagney, Margaret A. "Children's Ability to Understand Standard English and Black Dialect." *Reading Teacher* 30 (March 1977): 607–10.

9. Chall, Jeanne S. *Learning to Read: the Great Debate*. New York: McGraw-Hill, 1967.

10. Ching, Doris C. *Reading and the Bilingual Child*. Newark, DE: International Reading Association, 1976.

11. Claerbaut, David. *Black Jargon in White America*. Grand Rapids, MI: Eerdmans, 1972.

12. Clay, Marie M. "Early Childhood and Cultural Diversity in New Zealand." *Reading Teacher* 29 (January 1976): 333–42.

13. Cohen, S. Alan, and Rodriquez, Samuel. "Experimental Results that Question the Ramirez-Castaneda Model for Teaching Reading to First Grade Mexican Americans." *Reading Teacher* 34 (October 1980): 12–18.

14. Cunningham, Patricia M. "Transferring Comprehension from Listening to Reading." *Reading Teacher* 29 (November 1975): 169–72.

15. Dallman, Martha, et al. *The Teaching of Reading*. New York: Holt, Rinehart, and Winston, 1978.

16. Davison, H. and Lang, G. "Children's Perceptions of their Teachers' Feelings toward them Related to Self-Perception, School Achievement, and Behavior." *Journal of Experimental Education* 29 (December 1960): 107–18.

17. Dixon, Carol N. "Teaching Strategies for the Mexican American Child." *Reading Teacher* 30 (November 1976): 141–5.

18. Donoghue, Mildred R. *The Child and the English Language Arts*. Minneapolis, MN: William C. Brown, 1971.

19. Dykstra, Robert. "Summary of the Second-Grade Phase of the Cooperative Research Program in Primary Reading Instruction." *Reading Research Quarterly* 1 (Fall 1968): 49–70.

20. Eisenberg, Leon, et al. "Class and Race Effects on the Intelligibility of Monosyllables." *Child Development* (1968): 1077–9.

21. Eloisa, Maria Garcia De Lorenzo. "Frontier Dialect: A Challenge to Education." *Reading Teacher* 28 (April 1975): 653–8.

22. Feeley, Joan. "Teaching Non-English Speaking First Graders to Read." *Elementary English* (February 1970): 199–208.

23. Goodman, Kenneth. "On Valuing Diversity in Language." *Childhood Education* 46 (November 1969): 123–4.

24. Hall, MaryAnne. *The Language Experience Approach for the Culturally Disadvantaged*. Newark, DE: International Reading Association, 1972.

25. Hall, Vernon C., and Turner, Ralph R. "The Validity of the 'Different Language Explanation' for Poor Scholastic Performance by Black Students." *Review of Educational Research* 44 (1974): 69–81.

26. Harris, Albert J. "Practical Applications of Reading Research." *Reading Teacher* 29 (March 1976): 559–65.

27. Himmelsteib, Carol. "Buddies Read in Library Program." *Reading Teacher* 30 (October 1975): 32–5.

28. Johnson, Laura. "Bilingual Bicultural Education: A Two-Way Street." *Reading Teacher* 29 (December 1975): 231–9.

29. Kaplan, Robert B. "On a Note of Protest (in a Minor Key)." *College English* 30 (January 1969): 386–9.

30. Lawrence, Dolores. "Sparta Revisited." *Reading Teacher* 28 (February 1975): 464–5.

31. May, Frank B. *To Help Children Communicate.* Columbus, OH: Charles E. Merrill, 1980.

32. Nichols, Patricia C. "A Sociolinguistic Perspective on Reading and Black Children." *Language Arts* 54 (February 1977): 150–7.

33. O'Brien, C. *Teaching the Language Different Child to Read.* Columbus, OH: Charles E. Merrill, 1973.

34. Peisach, E. Cherry. "Children's Comprehension of Teacher and Peer Speech." *Child Development* 36 (February 1965): 467–80.

35. Rhodes, Lynn K. "I Can Read! Predictable Books as Resources for Reading and Writing Instruction." *Reading Teacher* 34 (February 1981): 511–18.

36. Rogers, John R. "Should Experience Charts be Edited?" *Reading Teacher* 30 (November 1976): 134–6.

37. Rosenthal, R., and Jacobson, L. *Pygmalion in the Classroom.* New York: Holt, Rinehart, and Winston, 1968.

38. Ruddell, R. B. "The Effect of Oral and Written Patterns of Language Structure and Reading Comprehension." *Reading Teacher* 18 (January 1965): 273.

39. Rystrom, Richard. "Dialect Training and Reading: a Further Look." *Reading Research Quarterly* 5 (Summer 1970): 581–99.

40. Saville, Muriel R., and Troike, Rudolph C. *A Handbook of Bilingual Education.* Teaching English to Speakers of Other Languages. Newark, DE: International Reading Association, 1971.

41. Schneeberg, Helen. "Listening While Reading: a Four Year Study." *Reading Teacher* 30 (March 1977): 629–35.

42. Shuy, Roger W. "A Linguistic Background for Developing Beginning Reading Materials for Black Children." In *Teaching Black Children to Read,* edited by Joan Baratz and Roger Shuy. Washington, DC: Center for Applied Linguistics, 1969, 117–37.

43. Smith, Nila Banton. "Cultural Dialects: Current Problems and Solutions." *Reading Teacher* 29 (November 1975): 137–41.

44. Thonis, Eleanor Wall. *Literacy for America's Spanish Speaking Children.* Newark, DE: International Reading Association, 1976.

45. U.S. Commission on Civil Rights. *A Better Chance to Learn: Bilingual-Biculture Education,* Clearing House Publication #51, Washington, DC, May 1975.

46. Vacca, Joanne L. "Bidialectish-Choose Your Side." *Reading Teacher.* 28 (April 1975): 643–6.
47. Wattenburg, W. W., and Clifford, C. "Relation of Self-Concept to Beginning Achievement in Reading." *Child Development* 35 (June 1964): 461–7.
48. Weener, Paul D. "Social Dialect Differences and the Recall of Verbal Messages." *Journal of Educational Psychology* 60 (February 1969): 194–9.

Application Experiences for the Teacher-Education Class

1. With a partner or small group decide whether you personally agree with each statement, now that you've read Chapter 16. Discuss your reasons for agreement or disagreement with the rest of the class.

Statements about Chapter 16
   a. Compensatory classes provide extra help in learning to read for many children, including children whose first language is not Standard English.
   b. Compensatory teachers should be getting much more help from reading specialists.
   c. Skill development is perceived by most compensatory teachers as far more important than helping children learn to enjoy reading.
   d. A teacher's negative attitude toward those who don't speak Standard English can be a major stumbling block in teaching children to read.
   e. An intelligence test based primarily on vocabulary is always going to be biased toward one or more subcultures in our society.
   f. A teacher with a multicultural reading program must be a student as well as a teacher.
   g. A dialect is a mother tongue.
   h. When a child says, "From now on, I don't be playin' with you," this is an example of "sloppy English."
   i. A strong phonics approach is the best way to work with children whose mother tongue is Spanish.
   j. The ESL approach works the best with minority children of all types.
   k. Self-concept development is often as important as skill development in improving a child's reading.
   l. Language resides on the hub of the self-concept; a teacher who abuses a child's language abuses the personal integrity of the child.

2. With the entire class discuss "minority children" you have known or worked with. What differences in personalities, cultural expectations, and learning styles do you notice among the different individuals? Discuss the dangers in stereotyping children by using labels, canned programs, and group characterizations.

3. With two or three others, make the attempt to discuss your prejudices honestly with each other. If possible admit one prejudice that you have toward people who speak a different dialect or language. Help each other think of ways that you will be able to overcome this prejudice as you teach. In what ways can you become a student as well as the teacher?

4. If you haven't had a chance to do so yet, examine with a partner the combined informal reading inventory and miscue analysis done with Pamela, a fourth-grade central-city black child who speaks both Standard English and Black English. This is available in Transcript 2 of the Instructor's Manual. Which miscues does she make that are true reading errors; which are merely dialect translations? In what specific ways would you instruct her in reading?

5. If you haven't had a chance to do so yet, examine with a partner the combined informal reading inventory and miscue analysis done with Eulogio, a fifth grader from a Spanish-speaking home. This is available in Transcript 3 of the Instructor's Manual. Which miscues does he make that are true reading errors; which are merely dialect translations? In what specific ways would you instruct him in reading?

Field Experiences in the Elementary-School Classroom

1. Using the procedures learned in Chapter 14, carry on miscue analysis with a child whose mother tongue is not Standard English. Which of his miscues are truly reading errors; which are dialect translations? What recommendations would you make for providing reading instruction to this child?

2. In what specific ways are the self-concepts of minority children in the building being enhanced or damaged? What specific changes would you make if you had the authority? What specific educators would you want to work with in order to bring about these changes?

3. Be a "student" to one of the minority children in the school. Learn some of his dialect or language. Try to learn about some of his cultural behavior and values that differ from yours. Find ways to show your appreciation for his instruction.

CHAPTER 17

Labeling a child as hyperactive or as dyslexic serves no useful purpose.

Helping Slow and Disabled Learners

Chapter Foreword

Perhaps one of the most stimulating challenges to be met by
elementary-classroom teachers is teaching children who have had great
difficulty, for whatever reason, in learning to read. Though local school
districts have traditionally provided support services (e.g., Title I,
remedial reading, special education) for some of these children, there
has been an increasing tendency to ask classroom teachers to assume or
share instructional responsibility. This requires elementary teachers to
have basic knowledge of the reading disability areas as well as
corresponding teaching techniques for classroom use.

There is a great need, in this writer's opinion, to de-mystify the topic of reading disability for teachers and parents. For too long teachers and parents have been led to believe that many children will have difficulty in learning to read due to some innate, often intangible, deficit or malfunction. Such an orientation may inadvertently cause teachers to say, "No wonder I couldn't teach him!" Though continued research and investigation into the possible causes of reading disabilities may one day lead to prevention and treatment, it is best, from the vantage of the teacher and child with a reading problem, to avoid causal labels and to focus on how to teach the child.

A comprehensive discussion of the reading disability area is beyond the scope of any one book or chapter. However, this chapter does provide an introductory examination of the nature of reading disability, raises questions about critical issues such as the labeling of children (e.g., "dyslexic"), and suggests specific instructional procedures. The reader will readily discover that elementary classroom teachers can incorporate basic teaching techniques within the reading program. As is always the case, teachers must decide for themselves how much instructional time may be devoted to the suggested methodology.

Perhaps one of the underlying assumptions inherent in the discussion to follow is that all children can learn to read, even those who have encountered learning difficulties, when the teacher provides for curricular modifications within the regular reading program.

David H. Martinez
Portland State University

> In general, my friends, even though humans are strange and amusing creatures, most of them do seem to really care.

In the last chapter we talked about children who need special help in learning to read because of cultural, dialect, or language differences. In this chapter we'll look at other types of "minority" children who need special reading instruction. These children are in the minority because they are either slow learners in general or disabled learners when it comes to reading and other communication skills. To oversimplify this for a moment, the difference between a "slow learner" and a "disabled learner," when it comes to reading, is really one of definition more than teaching practices. Techniques that prove useful for particular "disabled learners" often prove useful for particular "slow learners," and vice-versa. By definition, though, a slow learner is one whose IQ is "well below average." A disabled learner's IQ is at least average but his ability to perform certain school tasks (such as reading and writing) is well below what would be expected of him.

The approximate proportion of so-called slow learners in the general school population is 16 percent (17). Out of this total of slow learners, about 87 percent are considered "borderline children," with IQs ranging roughly from 70 to 85 percent. The other 13 percent of the slow learners (about 2 percent of the general school population) are generally classified as "retarded" and are often placed in highly specialized learning environments. In this chapter we'll be talking only about those slow learners who are considered "borderline," since these children experience much of their total instruction from regular classroom teachers.

The approximate number of so-called disabled learners in the general school population is more difficult to discover. Some say 6 percent, some say 15 percent, some say higher. The problem is one of definition. If we were to agree, for instance, that over one-fourth of those children who do speak Standard English in the home have problems learning to read, how many of those children will we say have trouble because of a learning disability, and how many because of a low intelligence quotient? If we arbitrarily say that 85 is a low IQ, then we could say that all those children having difficulty learning to read whose IQs are above 85 will be classified as "disabled," rather than "slow." If, on the other hand, we arbitrarily say that 95 is a low IQ, then we will come up with a lower number of disabled readers and a higher number of slow readers. You can see then what an arbitrary and sometimes meaningless distinction is made between groups of children who are having trouble learning to read.

Perhaps the most accurate statement made on the number of disabled readers in the general population was made by a HEW committee on reading disorders:

> Where studies compute the extent of reading retardation beyond that which is attributable to lack of mental ability, the proportion of children who display reading disorders . . . appears to be in the 15 percent range . . . (37, p. 20).

What does all this mean to the elementary teacher working with thirty students randomly assigned to your classroom? It means that on the average you would expect to have four or five disabled readers and three or four who are having trouble learning to read because of a low IQ. The actual number, of course, will vary tremendously, depending on the school population.

The Need for Common Yet Differentiated Treatment of Slow and Disabled Readers

Although the causes and the characteristics of slow vs. disabled readers may differ, the methods of working with these two groups of children are often the same. Both groups, for example, must be taught more slowly and with more repetition than the so-called normal readers. But what is most important to realize is that each group—disabled and slow—differs a great deal within itself. The teacher, for instance, may need to use instructional procedures that differ more between two slow learners than between one slow learner and one disabled learner. To put it even more bluntly, all slow learners in one's class should not be treated alike; all disabled learners should not be treated alike; all gifted learners should not be treated alike; and so on. What follows in the rest of this chapter needs to be accepted in this spirit. What I'm trying to suggest is a range of possibilities for the teacher, rather than a fixed set of procedures.

Case Study of a Disabled Reader

Ralph is a nine-year-old boy wearing many invisible labels on his back. He's been called a "nonreader," a "dyslexic," a "disabled reader," and a host of other things. Ralph has straight blond hair, blue eyes, and a smile that would melt all but the sternest of teachers. His above-average intelligence is demonstrated daily by his witty remarks and his ingenious ways of getting into trouble. Until recently he was considered hopeless by his regular classroom teachers and by his former compensatory-program teacher.

Although he is almost ten, he is only in the third grade, since he was held back a year. Until Miss Burnette came along, he was the number-one troublemaker in the school. Miss Burnette is the new third-grade teacher at Jefferson Elementary School, and Ralph is in love with her—as much as a nine-year-old boy can be in love with a twenty-five-year-old woman.

"Ralph has been a hyperactive child since birth" according to his mother. "He's always been more interested in fiddling with things or getting into mischief than in looking at books or talking to people. Even when he's watching TV, which is quite a lot, he's got his hands fiddling with things or he's climbing on something, or he's pestering someone. He's not like his sister at all. She's much quieter and likes to read. She's been saying real words since she was one year old, but Ralph—Ralph didn't say his first word until he was two. And he's always talked so fast and mushylike I still have trouble understanding him at times."

Ralph is not a typical disabled reader, because there is no such thing as a typical disabled reader. Ralph's particular symptoms have caused him to be labeled by his teachers and parents as a "dyslexic," a label that doesn't help him much, since it simply refers to a child showing difficulty in learning to read (in spite of average or above-average intelligence and in spite of a variety of normal instructional strategies employed by his teachers). Ralph not only reads very poorly, he spells atrociously, writes illegibly, speaks haltingly with weak enunciation, and performs in physical-education class, according to his teacher, "like a calf dancing a polka." Some would say that Ralph is "discombobulated." Others would say he has "specific language disabilities," or "specific learning disabilities" (as if these longer labels somehow come closer to the truth.)

The Nature of Ralph's Learning Disabilities

To explain the disabled reader's situation a little better, we'll continue to use Ralph as an example. In October Ralph's grade-equivalent score on a standardized reading-achievement test was 2.1, although the norm was 4.2. On a standardized diagnostic inventory, his reading score was 1.5. Both standardized scores, as low as they were, estimated his reading performance at too high a level. On an informal reading inventory, for instance, he reached frustration level while reading a preprimer passage.

Figure 17.1 shows how he read the preprimer selection. He miscued thirteen times on sixty-five words, giving him a word recognition score of 80 percent. Miscue analysis (notice his meaningless substitutions for "Two girls run" and "Three boys run) demonstrates that his main strategy is to get through, rather than to comprehend. With considerable help from Miss Burnette, he answered two out of four comprehension questions correctly, for a score of 50 percent. On the Baf Test he showed that he didn't have a sure grasp of digraphs, consonant clusters, and vowel patterns. Furthermore, he knew only twelve out of ninety-six irregular sight words. (See Chapter 14.)

On weekly spelling tests Ralph was getting three or four out of fifteen correct, until Miss Burnette decided to give him only six words a week. Now he sometimes gets five or six correct. In mathe-

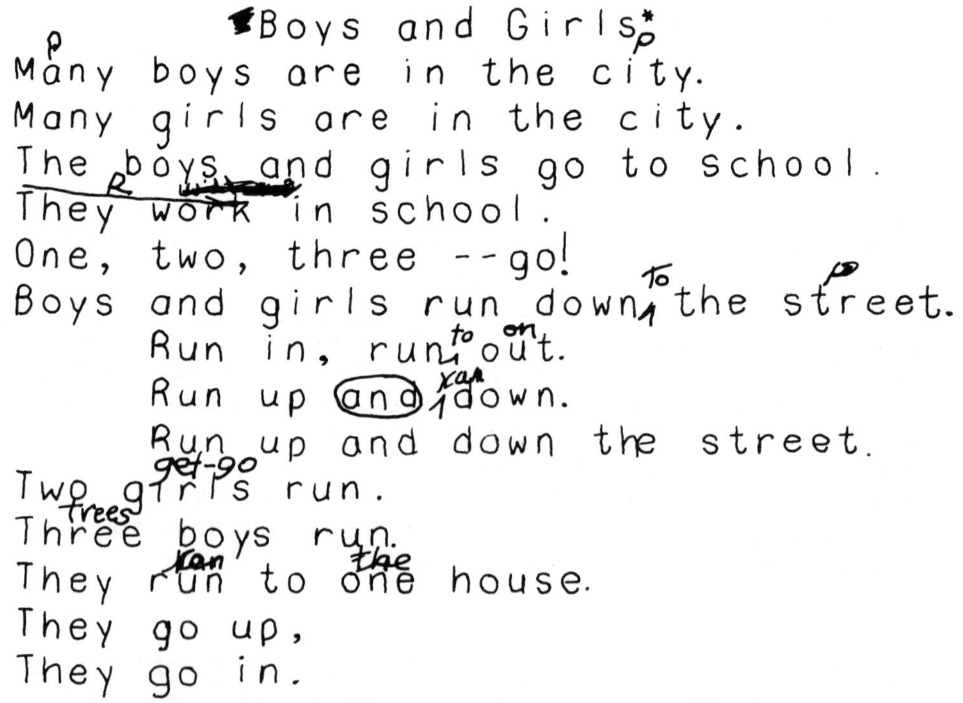

Boys and Girls

Many boys are in the city.
Many girls are in the city.
The boys and girls go to school.
They work in school.
One, two, three --go!
Boys and girls run down the street.
Run in, run out.
Run up and down.
Run up and down the street.
Two girls run.
Three boys run.
They run to one house.
They go up,
They go in.

Figure 17.1. ***Ralph's Response to the Preprimer Level of an Informal Reading Inventory. Bank Street College of Education,*** **In the City** ***(New York: Macmillan Co., 1965). Reprinted with permission of the publisher.***

matics he often surprises his teacher with his understanding of operations and with his reasoning ability, but he usually makes so many "silly" mistakes on his computations that he scores poorly on assignments and tests. "In science," Miss Burnette says, "Ralph is a whiz—as long as he can experiment with things instead of read about them." In creative writing he shows a mild degree of inventiveness, though he has to translate his illegible handwriting for his teacher.

Figure 17.2 shows a sample of Ralph's creative writing in response to a picture of an old woman wearing a fur coat and cra-

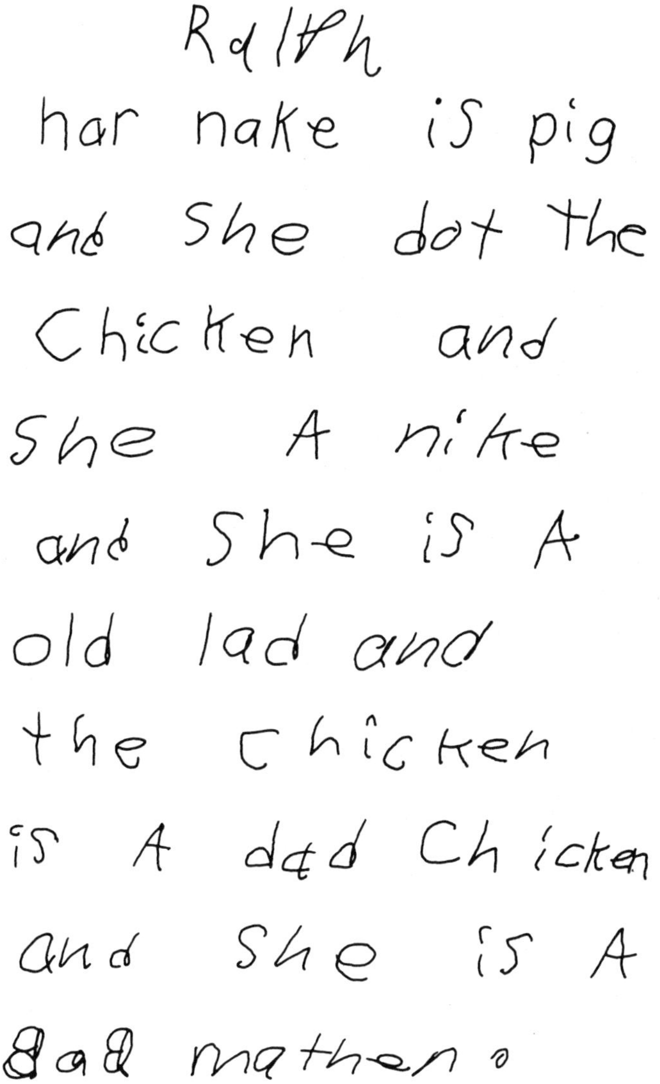

Ralph

har nake is pig and she dot the chicken and she A nike and she is A old lad and the chicken is A dad Chicken and she is A bad mathen.

Figure 17.2. *A Sample of Ralph's Creative Writing in Response to a Picture.*

dling a live chicken in her arms. The word *chicken* had been spelled for him on the chalkboard. His story should be translated, according to Ralph, as follows:

> *Ralph*
> His name is pig and she got the chicken and she is nice and she is an old lady and the chicken is a bad chicken and she is a bad mother.

Ralph worked very hard on this story for Miss Burnette and produced one of his best papers in his school career. In spite of his efforts, as you can see, he inverted the *g* in *got,* reversed the *b* in *bad,* made little distinction between capital and lowercase letters, and misspelled several words. For Ralph, the act of writing is agony.

Figure 17.3 shows another sample of Ralph's writing, this time in response to a field trip he took with several other children who work with Ms. Benjamin, the new compensatory-program teacher. These children went to Ms. Benjamin's basement darkroom to develop photographs she had taken of them. Her friend, Mr. Eliot, had built the darkroom for her with black plastic. Ralph's story should be translated as follows:

> We took four pans and we had fun and Mr. Eliot put plastic all over me and a boogie monster was in the black. The boogie monster he hit me and I kicked him and the boogie monster was right beside Terry. The four pans were full of junk and we had a machine and we had a piece of cardboard and there's a magic trick that put it on the cardboard. The end.

Here's how one group of children, all "compensatory readers," experienced the same field trip:

> *How We Made Our Pictures*
> *by*
> *Group 7*

Ms. Benjamin took our pictures. Then she opened the film can in the darkroom. She took the film out of the can and wound it on the reel. Then she put it in the tank. Then we put the developer in the tank. We put the cover on the tank and shook it for seven minutes. We took the cap off and poured it out. We then poured in the stop-bath. We shook it for three minutes. Then we poured it out. We took the reel out of the tank and washed all the chemicals out. We hung it up to dry.

Then we went over to Ms. Benjamin's house on Friday afternoon. We went downstairs in the cellar to the darkroom. First we took off our coats and put them on a table. Then we went into the darkroom and found all these chemicals. We took the pictures out of a bag and put them in the enlarger. Then Ms. Benjamin took out the paper and put it in the enlarger. Ms. Benjamin cleaned the pictures. We timed them in the enlarger for four seconds. Then we put the picture in Mike's developer. Then we put it in Sandy's stop-bath. Sandy put it in Betty's fixer.

We went upstairs and had milk, peanut butter, and crackers. We put the pictures in the dryer. When the pictures were dry, we went back to school.

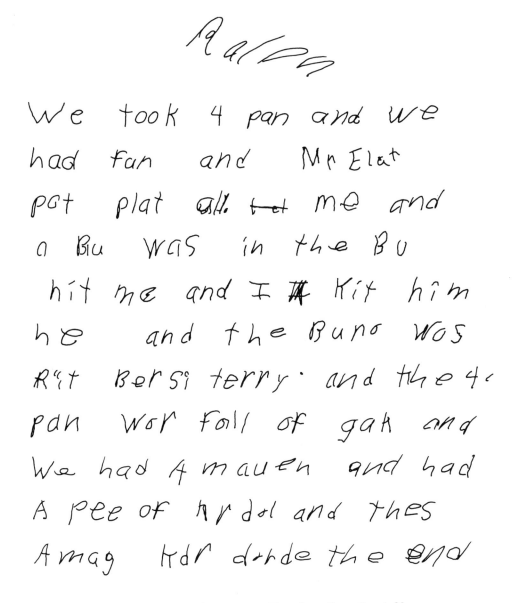

Figure 17.3. *A Sample of a Language-Experience Story Created by Ralph.*

As seen in Figure 17.2, Ralph not only has difficulty with the mechanics of writing but also has difficulty expressing himself. His teachers feel that most of this is his inability to concentrate—especially when he is asked to write. Concentrating on the details of developing photographs, for example, may have been an arduous task, though he carried out his part with a reasonable degree of seriousness. When it came time to record his experience in writing, moreover, the additional concentration that it required seemed to be too much for him, and he resorted to a tale of a "boogie monster." In addition to the problem of concentration, Ralph may also have had difficulty perceiving and understanding the operations involved in developing the photographs. This would have resulted in a foggy memory of the experience.

The difficulty that Ralph experiences appears to be one of intake. The messages coming in from the environment seem to be weak and distorted. It's as if his nerves are like garden hoses that someone is standing on, thus partially obstructing the flow to the brain. This analogy is merely illustrative, of course, and not to be taken seriously. Exactly what causes this intake problem is not known, though possible explanations will be considered later.

In November, Ms. Benjamin administered the *Slingerland Tests for Identifying Children with Specific Language Disabilities* (33). This battery of tests demonstrated to Ms. Benjamin that Ralph's visual memory and auditory memory were both quite poor. For instance, flash cards with words printed on them were presented to Ralph one at a time; after each one was flashed he was delayed for a short period and then asked to select from among four alternatives the word that had been flashed. For *along* he selected *alone*, for *happy* he selected *haqqy*, for *neighbor* he selected *neihgbor*, for *37* he selected *73*, and so on. Similar problems occurred when words were presented to him orally, rather than on flash cards.

His weaknesses in visual and auditory memory were particularly noticeable when he had to use his kinesthetic abilities and write the word rather than select from alternatives. When shown the word *thundering*, he wrote *t–h–u–e–n–d–r–o–n–b*. When presented with this phrase orally—"saw this first girl"—he wrote *scr ther gur feir*. It was clear to both Ms. Benjamin and Miss Burnette that Ralph was a child with severe reading disabilities.

Several studies cited by Klasen (18) show that Ralph is not alone. The signs of severe reading disability, on the surface at least, seem to be neurological ones, according to Klasen:

1. *Poor coordination:* Ralph, for example, can't jump a rope.
2. *Lack of fine-motor control:* He has great difficulty forming manuscript letters, although he does much better with cursive, since he can move from one letter to the next without removing his pencil from the paper.

3. *Directional confusion:* Ralph reverses, inverts, and transposes letters and words, e.g.,
   reversals: *b* for *d, d* for *b, q* for *p, p* for *q, saw* for *was, was* for *saw*
   inversions: *u* for *n, n* for *u, p* for *b, b* for *p*
   transpositions: *neihgbor* for *neighbor, s–p–r–t* for *s–t–p–r*
   When he draws a circle, he sometimes draws it in a clockwise direction and sometimes in a counterclockwise direction.

4. *Speech defects:* Ralph's stuttering is very mild, but he seems to be struggling to put his thoughts into words, resulting in words and syllables that seem jumbled; his enunciation is very weak, making it hard for others to understand him.

5. *Visual and auditory perceptual disorders:* Ralph often (though not always) shows these perceptual disorders when asked to rely on either his discrimination abilities or his memory abilities.

6. *Concentration problems:* Ralph is quite hyperactive, which in itself causes concentration problems. He often complains that words are confusing to him. In addition he shows an unwillingness to concentrate (perhaps because his past attempts at concentrating yielded little success in perceiving and understanding).

The Inaccuracy of the Dyslexia Label

The term *dyslexia,* although a short and once-popular term, is an inaccurate label for the condition we are discussing in this chapter. The original meaning of the word was simply "the inability to read." A dictionary definition of the word is "an impairment of the ability to read due to a brain defect" (36). However, this still does not capture the nature of the malady experienced by Ralph and other children like him.

From a practical standpoint, what teachers generally notice are inabilities in reading, spelling, handwriting, speaking, and certain activities related to physical education—roughly in that order. The title of Clarke's book *Can't Read, Can't Write, Can't Talk Too Good Either* (6) is perhaps the most sensible, down-to-earth definition that can be given.

Because of the confusion surrounding the word *dyslexia,* many researchers and teachers now refer to this condition as *learning disabled.* However, no label can come close to describing the difficulties which these youngsters experience. In fact, the use of labels probably does more harm than good in some cases. It would appear that educators are making the same mistake that psychiatrists used to make by attempting to categorize disturbed people as manic depressives, hebephrenic schizophrenics, paranoics, and so on. Once people were classified, the tendency was to treat all people in the same category the same way and ignore individual differences. There is considerable danger that we will fall into the same trap.

There is also considerable danger in overusing the labels *dyslexic* or *learning disabled* to apply to anyone who is having trouble learning to read. Unfortunately, once children are labeled this way they are sometimes forgotten or rushed off to a specialist without first examining one's own teaching methods and one's own way of relating to the particular children in question.

Allington (1) presents several cogent arguments against the use of labeling.

1. Most of the labels simply do not have a single commonly accepted definition. For example, what is a *hyperactive* child? Is it one who disrupts the classroom? Is it the "normal" restless active boy? Is a child *dyslexic* just because he reverses the *b* and the *d*? Many children do this for the first two grades.
2. Labels provide no useful information. Rather than label a child, it might be far better to determine the specific skills that are deficient and make plans for remediation.
3. Labels are often a feeble attempt to define the cause of the ailment (e.g., Poor Ralph can't spell "cuz" he's got dyslexia). Knowing the causes is really not that useful in applying treatment anyway, according to Allington.
4. Assigning labels is beyond the professional skill of most teachers.
5. Labeling children only shifts the burden of failure to them. Perhaps a better label under which academic underachievers might be placed is *teaching disabled*. This term more adequately describes the situation. We are not faced with children who *cannot* learn, but with children who need instruction somewhat different from that provided in regular classrooms. These children can learn; it is the teaching that needs modification (1, p. 367).

Classroom Diagnosis of the Reading or Language Disabled Child

It would appear that the earlier a person's disability is detected, the easier it is to treat (16, 34). But how does one determine whether a child is sufficiently disabled to require special instructional strategies in the classroom or perhaps special instruction by a compensatory teacher? By definition, a disabled child is one whose intelligence is average or above. But can a valid and reliable measure of intelligence be obtained? What about "reading-expectancy formulas"? Are they really helpful? Let's look at some possible answers to these questions.

The decision as to when a child is sufficiently disabled to require special instruction is truly an arbitrary one. There are presently no standardized tests of reading disability, and it is doubtful that such tests would be useful. Slingerland (33) and Jordan (16) have both developed diagnostic tests for reading and language disabilities, which may be used by specialized teachers. However, a simple observation checklist can be used by the classroom teacher to detect the most severe cases of disability. The following checklist is suggested as a means of structuring the observations that you make of your students. Please note that no one of these observations, by itself, is an indication of reading and language disabilities.

Table 17.1   Classroom Teacher's Observation Checklist for Reading and Language Disabilities

General Behavior

_____ 1. Shows average or above-average intelligence in some way, e.g., does well in science reasoning or mathematical reasoning, shows sense of humor, or has ingenious ways of getting into trouble

_____ 2. Often has trouble expressing himself/herself

_____ 3. Often shows poor eye-hand coordination

_____ 4. Appears nervous or anxious in many situations

_____ 5. Tends to get frustrated easily

_____ 6. Withdraws when things get too difficult

_____ 7. Has far too much energy (or sometimes far too little)

_____ 8. Has trouble concentrating

_____ 9. Has trouble remembering directions, names, or other details

_____ 10. Has trouble making lasting friendships

Reading Behavior

_____ 1. Standardized reading achievement score: at least one year below grade level in grades 2–3 and two years below in later grades

_____ 2. Standardized individual diagnostic score: at least one year below grade level in grades 2–3 and two years below in later grades

_____ 3. Informal reading inventory: at least one year below grade level in grades 2–3 and two years below in later grades

_____ 4. Baf Test: 30-percent error in grades three and above (see Chapter 14).

_____ 5. Irregular sight words: 50-percent error in grades three and above (see Chapter 14).

_____ 6. Has considerable trouble concentrating on reading task even when working directly with teacher

_____ 7. Frequently guesses wildly at words rather than using word-analysis skills

_____ 8. Forgets words shortly after learning to read them

_____ 9. Asks teacher to decode words rather than using word-analysis skills

_____ 10. Transposes letters or words or syllables while reading

_____ 11. Loses place in reading passage easily

_____ 12. Often does not seem to know the meaning of what he or she has read

_____ 13. Usually a word-by-word reader

_____ 14. Makes many errors on worksheets

continued

Table 17.1— (Continued)

Writing Behavior

_____ 1. Does very poorly on spelling tests, usually getting more words wrong than right

_____ 2. Creative writing has 30 percent or more of the words spelled wrong

_____ 3. Transposes words, letters, or syllables

_____ 4. Reverses letters such as *b* and *d, p* and *q*

_____ 5. Inverts letters such as *n* and *u* or *p* and *b*

_____ 6. Usually guesses at spelling rather than using phonics

_____ 7. Forgets how to spell a word shortly after learning it

_____ 8. Has considerable trouble concentrating on learning how to spell words

_____ 9. Does not remember how to spell common prefixes or suffixes

_____ 10. Substitutes one suffix for another

_____ 11. Draws circles inconsistently counterclockwise and clockwise

_____ 12. Has considerable difficulty drawing a circle that is round and connected

_____ 13. Usually makes letters with one stroke if possible; lifting pencil tends to cause confusion

_____ 14. Writes as little as possible

_____ 15. Writing that requires memory of sequence and details is quite difficult

_____ 16. Writing is very laborious

_____ 17. Uses personal abbreviations for long difficult words

_____ 18. Has particular trouble with letter size and shape but also shows inconsistent spacing, alignment, and slant

---

The intepretation of this observation checklist is again an arbitrary one. Certainly if you check half or more of the items within each of the three categories (and if the half you check includes the first one in each category), the chances that you are working with a child with a severe disability is highly probable.

In addition to the Observation Checklist, you may wish to use one or more individual tests with the child who you suspect is disabled. Slingerland (33) has devised an elaborate and highly specific set of diagnostic tests entitled *Slingerland Screening Tests for Identifying Children with Specific Language Disability.* There are three forms of the test battery: Form A for grades 1 and 2, Form B for grades 2 and 3, and Form C for grades 3 and 4. They include copying tests, tests of visual and auditory perception linked with memory, tests of visual and auditory perception linked with discrimination, memory, and kinesthetic response (writing). Most of the items pertain to letters, words, and numbers rather than shapes.

Another elaborate set of diagnostic tests for specific language disability has been developed by Jordan (16). Jordan's tests include an "oral-screening test" in which the child reads out loud to the examiner; a "written screening test for specific reading disability" in which the children write such things as the days of the week; and a "vision-screening test for binocular control for sustained reading and handwriting" by which a child's tendency to distort visual images or to become frustrated by them is determined.

Both the Slingerland and Jordan test batteries can be highly useful to a person trained in their administration and interpretation. However, they are quite time-consuming and generally administered by a resource teacher or a remedial-reading teacher, rather than the classroom teacher. If the classroom teacher wishes to obtain more information on a child suspected of having a reading-language disability (in addition to the information obtained from the "Observation Checklist") the RAD Test found in Appendix G may be useful. The RAD Test (Rapid Assessment of Disability) may verify one's suspicions aroused by the observation checklist.

Other Psychological Measurements Related to Reading Disabilities

During the late sixties and early seventies the emphasis among those educators concerned about disabled readers was "diagnosis and remediation of specific deficient-learning abilities." The assumption was that since reading seemed to require such specific abilities as visual perception, visual discrimination, visual memory, and the auditory counterparts, the solution to the problem of disabled readers was to diagnose their perceptually related weaknesses and then strengthen them. "If George is having trouble with auditory discrimination, so that he can't handle phonics too well, just work on auditory discrimination until he discriminates at a sufficient level."

Unfortunately, this hasn't worked out so well. Diagnostic tests such as the *Frostig Tests of Perception* and the *ITPA (Illinois Test of Psycholinguistic Abilities)* seem to have a very low relationship to reading achievement (14, 29, 5). Furthermore, training programs designed to correct perceptual deficiencies have generally worked no better than traditional reading instruction (15). Studies by Bateman (3), Hammill, et al. (13), Robinson (31), and Wiederholt and Hammill (38) support Harris's contention (15) that the limited time that is available for reading instruction would be better spent directly on reading skills than on attempting to make everyone strong in visual and auditory perception, discrimination, and memory first. Therefore, spending a lot of time diagnosing a disabled reader's specific visual and auditory perceptual deficiencies may not be practical.

A study by Hare (14) showed that a large group of second graders who had scored low on both the Frostig visual tests and the ITPA auditory tests still were reading at grade level, in spite of the fact that their intelligence scores were only average. It is evident that there's a lot more to reading than perception and the related discrimination and memory skills. Reading is too complex an act to think that we can "cure" disabled readers merely by strengthening their deficient perception skills. Reading also involves cognition, self-concept, attitudes toward learning, and a host of other mental and motivational factors.

One more thing should be discussed about psychological measurements before we move on to a discussion of remediation. Since "disabled readers," by definition, are those with average or above-average intelligence, how does one know whether the child has average or above-average intelligence? This is a somewhat ludicrous question, since one wonders what precise differences in instructional strategies there would be for those who have an IQ of 90 or above and are pronounced "disabled" and those who have an IQ of 85 or below and are pronounced "slow learners." Nevertheless, the question of intelligence is bound to come up and one needs some type of answer.

One could look at the IQ scores in the cumulative folder, of course, but these are often not valid since they are based on a group test that often requires the very skill on which the disabled learner is weak—namely, reading. And even if the child has been given an individual intelligence test, the IQ may still be an invalid measurement for four reasons: 1) the IQ may be a verbal measure rather than a performance measure; 2) the person giving the intelligence test may have had poor rapport with the child during the administration of the test; 3) the test may have been culturally biased; and 4) the child may have had an off day because of illness, emotional disturbance, or some other problem. Probably a better indication of intelligence level would be the judgment of two or more people who have worked with the child.

Many teachers and researchers have attempted to use something called the "reading-expectancy age" in order to determine whether children are potentially capable of reading better than they are. A common formula is one developed by Harris (15) and reads as follows:

$$[2(MA) + CA] \div 3 = REA$$

For example, if Ralph's mental age (MA), as determined by his score on an intelligence test, were 10 and his chronological age (CA) were 10, then his reading expectancy age would be $(20 + 10) \div 3$, or 10, also. If his MA were 7 and his CA were 10, then his REA would be 8 and one would not expect him to do as well in reading as an average ten-year-old. If his MA were 13 and his CA were 10, then his REA would be 12 and one would expect him to do much better than an average ten-year-old.

The reader has a right to be amused by such formulas, since the reading-expectancy age is highly dependent on the "mental age" that is derived from the score on an intelligence test. And, as just pointed out, the use of intelligence scores is not often valid. Dore-Boyce, Misner, and McGuire (12) used regression analysis to demonstrate that on four different REA formulas the mental age accounted for most of the variance. Thus, the value of reading-expectancy formulas, to aid in determining which children can be classified as disabled, is highly questionable.

Ways of Working with Slow or Disabled Children

Four principles need to be kept in mind when working with slow or disabled children:

1. Learning should be multisensory whenever possible.
2. Most of the instruction needs to be highly structured.
3. As much as possible, learning needs to be meaningful.
4. Personal contact must be abundant and consistent.

Both slow and disabled readers seem to have trouble receiving language. Spoken words and written words are sent toward their ears and eyes, but at least four obstacles stand in the way.

1. The impressions of language that they actually receive in the brain seem to be weak, muffled, and distorted, thus making both discrimination and memory very difficult. Therefore, there is a need for a multisensory approach that encourages stronger reception of language (Principle 1).
2. They have considerable difficulty concentrating on the reception and production of language, thus necessitating a highly structured program with small steps and minimal distractions (Principle 2).
3. They often find the experience of attempting to receive and produce language a meaningless one. It makes no sense to them. Thus, the teacher must attempt to provide meaning for them (Principle 3).
4. They often feel left out—abandoned. Consequently, only instruction that is highly personal and consistently affectionate can be very effective (Principle 4).

The Multisensory Approach

The words that Ralph receives through his ears and those he receives through his eyes seem to have only the vaguest impact on his brain. One way of attempting to overcome this problem is to teach him to bring three sensory modes into operation simultaneously during the act of reception. For example, when Miss Burnette wants Ralph to learn the letter *b*, she shows him the letter in print and says the letter to him. She then reminds him how to make the *b* on the chalkboard, using large movements, starting the letter at the top and producing it with one motion—without taking her chalk off the board. She then traces the letter and says it simultaneously. Next she has Ralph look at the letter and say it. Following this, he is expected to look at it, say it, and trace it with his hand simultaneously. Then he writes it on the board, using the full swing of his arm. He then traces it and says it simultaneously. Then he moves to his desk and writes it two or three times on his paper, saying it each time he writes it. And finally he circles any *b* he finds on a worksheet. A similar approach is used for learning sight words such as *the, there,* or *off.*

Chapter 8 emphasized the need for massed practice followed by distributed practice. If ever this principle were needed, it is in the teaching of slow or disabled readers. Furthermore, not only should the massed practice (such as the lesson on *b* just described) be multisensory, but the distributed practice as well. Before Ralph goes to see Ms. Benjamin, he is shown the letter *b* by Miss Burnette once more and asked to read it and trace it in the air. When he arrives at Ms. Benjamin's door he hands her a note from Miss Burnette explaining what he has recently learned. Ms. Benjamin asks him to read the letter *b*, trace it, and even shout it. Not only does he trace the letter in the air, he traces it on fine sandpaper or felt or wet paint. The same is true of words. The word *there* is written (for his two teachers) with chalk, with felt pen, with finger paint, with a wooden stylus on a "magic-erase" wax tablet. The correct sequence of letters in each word is accented again and again—visually, auditorily, kinesthetically, tactually.

Every conceivable device for keeping the multisensory approach from becoming drudgery must be used—novelty in writing tools, novelty in writing surfaces, novelty in praise, games used as rewards for good work. The multisensory approach is slow and painstaking, but it needn't be painful. Children—especially hyperactive ones—enjoy getting out of their seats to write words, trace them, circle them, find them, and manipulate them.

Spelling and reading need to go hand in hand during many of the learning experiences. Research demonstrates a strong interrelationship and interdependence between spelling and word-recognition skills (39). Ms. Benjamin often has Ralph not only shout the words, but the letters as well. Spelling races, however, are never used since precision rather than speed is what slow and disabled children need in order to sharpen the images of what they receive.

Using a Highly Structured Approach

Actual lessons on writing, spelling, word recognition, and comprehension need to have a high level of structure when working with slow and disabled children. This in no way rules out the use of the language-experience approach (which will be discussed shortly), but it does mean that most subskill practice needs to be tightly sequenced in short steps with abundant feedback. In most cases things need to be explained, rather than learned through discovery. The discovery approach with slow and disabled children has the disadvantage of allowing the children to learn something wrong the first time, thus adding to the confusion rather than eliminating it. Whenever possible, try to make the first impression a clear, precise, and unambiguous one.

Since writing and reading tend to reinforce each other (39) it is often advisable to include writing activities with your lessons on reading skills. However, special precautions need to be taken with disabled learners. Slingerland (34) suggests that when disabled learners are asked to write regular letters in manuscript form they be encouraged to make them in one stroke whenever possible. For example, instead of having them write the letter *a* with two strokes like this ɑ encourage them to write it with one stroke like this: *a*. Perhaps the best that a teacher can do is observe carefully what happens when disabled learners attempt to create manuscript letters. If they seem to get confused when they lift their pencil to make separate lines, try having them produce letters with one stroke whenever possible. In fact, with some children, it may be best to transfer from manuscript to cursive writing as soon as possible. Cursive writing, since it's connected and requires little removal of the pencil from the paper, appears to be easier for some disabled learners. Ralph, for example, writes his name in manuscript this way:

In cursive he writes it this way:

Another disabled learner named Doug simply could not produce manuscript letters in a legible fashion. His teachers had mistakenly kept him from transferring to cursive right up to fifth grade. In fifth grade he was finally allowed to try cursive and made dramatic improvement in the legibility of his writing. Even then Doug was in trouble with letters like *f, b, g,* and *y,* but by following numbered diagrams of the letters he finally mastered them. The *f* diagram, for instance, looked like this:

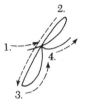

Structuring Spelling and Word-Recognition Experiences

In Chapter 2, several steps for helping children learn sight vocabulary were suggested. Since we're now talking about slow and disabled learners, those steps should be modified. The following procedures seem to work well for most slow and disabled learners when developing their reading and writing sight vocabularies:

Step 1:   *Introduce the words in context,* but no more than two or three.
    a. Write a sentence containing the words on the chalkboard, e.g., "Who put my ball there?" he said.
    b. Read the sentence to the children.
    c. Have them read (say) the sentence with you.
    d. Point to one of the underlined words, pronounce it, and ask a child to spell it out loud. Have her pronounce it after she has spelled it. Have a different child do the same with each underlined word.

Step 2:   Have the children enhance their visual, auditory, and kinesthetic memory of each word.
    a. Have each child write each word on the chalkboard, saying each letter out loud as he writes it.
    b. After writing a word, he should then trace it while spelling it out loud again.
    c. Have him close his eyes and trace it while spelling it out loud.
    d. Have them cover up the correct spelling and write it again on the chalkboard; then check to see if it is correct.

(Step 2, as you may have noticed, is different for slow and disabled learners from that described for normal learners in Chapter 2. To help you remember this difference you may think of Steps 2 a, b, c, and d as all to be completed at the chalkboard:

    a. Write and say letters
    b. Trace and say letters (eyes open)
    c. Trace and say letters (eyes closed)
    d. Cover . . . Write . . . Check

Step 3:   Have them be seated and write the words on paper.
    a. Have them look at a word again and spell it out loud to themselves.
    b. Cover the word and ask them to write the word on their papers.
    c. Uncover the word and have them check.
    d. Check each child's paper to make sure she has the word correct.

Steps 4 through 8: Same as those on pages 44 to 47 in Chapter 2.

Other word-recognition skills, including phonic analysis, contextual analysis, and structural analysis also need to be taught in a systematic structured way—again with small steps and frequent feedback. It is advisable to use some type of commercially prepared program for this purpose, since the sequential steps have already been developed for these programs, and the danger of going too fast will be minimized. Whether you should use a predominantly phonics (auditory) program or a predominantly linguistic (visual) program cannot be stated in advance since slow and disabled learners vary so much in the type that suits them best. Ralph, for instance, after trying various phonics and linguistic programs with both Miss Burnette and Ms. Benjamin, seemed to learn best through one of the linguistic programs, namely, the Sullivan Associates' *Programmed Reading Books* (with the teacher, an aide, or another child working with him). The tiny steps, frequent repetitions, and meaningful cartoons seemed to be just what he needed. Other slow or disabled learners working with both Ms. Benjamin and Miss Burnette were happy with different types of programs, working for a while with the Open Court phonics program and later with the Economy Company's basal series, *Keys to Reading*—a program that emphasizes both phonics and comprehension.

In other words, no one program can be recommended for slow or disabled children. It is advisable to try different programs to see which ones seem to fit each child best. In selecting programs to try, however, make sure they're the type that move slowly and systematically enough to fit the children's need for repetition and feedback. In any case, don't expect a slow or disabled learner to work too much on his own. Frequent guidance and support is needed. Even though Ralph, for example, was working in a programmed reading book designed for independent work, Miss Burnette, Ms. Benjamin, an aide, and an advanced reader worked through most of the pages with him.

Structuring Comprehension Exercises

Lopardo (21) suggests a cloze-type device for structuring some of your comprehension lessons with slow and disabled readers. This device encourages more holistic and communicative reading. First, the children dictate a story to the teacher, who transcribes it on an experience chart. Before the teacher meets with them again she rewrites the story on another experience chart, this time deleting every fifth word. The children then read the new version, putting in words that make sense in the blank spaces and explaining why they choose each word. Finally they check the two charts to see how well they match. This technique encourages the children to think about what they are reading, rather than just reading word by word from memory.

Another structuring device is to have one child read to other children who do not have a book. Before the first child can pass on the book to the next one, all of the children have to agree on what the first reader said. This device forces them not only to listen for understanding, but to read for understanding as well. If the message did not get across to the audience, then the child reads it again, this time attempting to communicate (and therefore read) more clearly.

A third technique for providing a high level of structure to the slow or disabled children's comprehension exercises is sometimes to ask the children a question after every sentence or two. Having them concentrate on only one or two sentences at a time enables them to develop the habit of searching for meaning in each sentence, rather than reading each word as a separate meaningless unit. Schwartz and Sheff (32) recommend that children be taken through specific steps as they read: posing a problem, reasoning while reading, and verifying. In the following dialogue, they provide us with an example of their approach. (In this dialogue, the children have been reading about dinosaur fossils.)

Posing a New Problem

> TEACHER: Who wants to give us a new idea of what you think they can find out from the skeleton?
>
> JOE: Their shapes, what they look like.

Reasoning while Reading and Verifying

> TEACHER: Those are good ideas. Let's read the next sentence to find out exactly.
>
> KEITH: (Reads) Sometimes the bones show signs that they were broken while the dinosaur was living.
>
> TEACHER: That's unusual. I found out something I didn't know. What did you find out? . . .

LANCE: The dinosaur's bones are broken! How can a dinosaur's bones get broken? . . .

All three techniques—deleting words on experience charts, getting agreement on meaning from listeners, and asking questions after every sentence to foster hypothesizing and verification—encourage slow or disabled learners to read for comprehension. And they help these children to realize, perhaps for the first time, that reading can be a meaningful experience.

Making Reading Experiences Meaningful

From the very first dictated story, the blind child realizes, if he did not already know from home experience, that oral language can be *saved* in the form of Braille. Braille immediately has a *use* for him and learning to read and write it is not a chore detached from any purpose, but rather a discovery of how to help order his world of experiences (11, p. 274).

This analogy between a blind child and a slow or disabled learner should not be taken literally. The point is that all children who are learning to read, whether they are blind, linguistically different, average, gifted, slow, or disabled, need to feel that the process is a meaningful one. And one of the best ways of bringing meaning into the learning-to-read process is to use a language-experience approach. In this way, the slow and disabled child can learn to view reading as a holistic process and also gain skill in making intelligent psycholinguistic guesses.

This may sound like advice contrary to advice just given: to use a highly structured approach. However, what I'm suggesting is that the language-experience approach be used in conjunction with a highly structured approach. Ralph, for example, spends an average of four hours per week working in a linguistic reader, working on the spelling and decoding of sight words, and working to improve his handwriting. An average of two hours per week is spent on dictating or writing experience stories and using those stories and simple library books as reading material.

Ralph is particularly fond of using the tape recorder to dictate his stories, having someone transcribe them, and then reading them the next day. (This technique is described in considerable detail (35) by Smith.) Like most children, Ralph seems to be genuinely thrilled to see his own creations "in print," and he invariably gets great pleasure out of reading them to others. If the same stories had been written by someone else and given to him to read, he would not have been able to read them. But because he has written them himself and because they are based on his own direct or imaginary experiences, he can read them with considerable skill (relative to his normal reading).

Of course, much of this reading is based on memory, rather than on precise decoding. Nevertheless, he is receiving excellent practice on the type of mature reading that we eventually want him to master—reading based primarily on comprehension. And, even more important for Ralph now, reading is a meaningful act—it makes sense to him.

All children need someone to care.

Making Reading a Personal Affair

As mentioned earlier, many slow or disabled children feel left out or even abandoned. Their sense of belonging is weak because of numerous failures to communicate with people, to achieve lasting friendships, and to achieve in the way that their peers are achieving. Perhaps even more than children who are achieving at normal levels, they need someone who cares for them and is concerned enough to give them the extra time it takes to help them learn in spite of their condition—someone who will help them stop feeling so inferior.

Their bad luck (in being a slow or disabled learner in the first place) often follows them to school, however. For, according to research (25), it appears that most teachers prefer teaching the better readers. Even without research studies, casual observation in classrooms will demonstrate that some teachers have far less patience with poor readers than with good ones. And because of this, the children who need the most help are often those who get the least.

In fact, this may be the most serious problem of all for children like Ralph—simply not getting enough help of the right kind when they need it. As a result, their self-concept deteriorates; they withdraw rather than risk further failure, and learning to read becomes a meaningless, multi-senseless, impersonal, and chaotic experience.

Yet teachers who care for people like Ralph can help. (See the books by Jordan (16), Kirk (17), and Slingerland (34) for additional ideas.) After his first successfully written experience story, Ralph read it with ease to his reading teacher, Ms. Benjamin. He was so thrilled by his success and the praise he received, he spruced up his courage and asked his regular classroom teacher Miss Burnette if he could read it to the class.

He read it beautifully. And the children—even those who had laughed at him before—were stunned. Spontaneously, without any signal from the teacher, they clapped loud and long. Some even slapped him on the back and told him what a good reader he was.

Ralph has never been the same since. He now considers himself a reader. And with the help of caring, affectionate teachers, some day he'll be just that.

Summary

An elementary-school teacher, working with thirty children randomly assigned to her classroom, is likely to have several children who are either slow or disabled learners. Although these two types of learners differ according to definition and causal factors, they differ even more from one individual to the next. The teacher needs to avoid thinking of them according to labels such as "dyslexics" or "slow learners" or "disabled learners" and think of them as specific individuals with specific problems and instructional needs. On the other hand, many of the methods of diagnosis and teaching used for normal readers can be used in modified form with slow or disabled learners. These learners are in particular need of multi-sensory and highly-structured reading lessons. But they also need, just as normal children do, to perceive reading as a meaningful, communicative experience. Furthermore, they need, even more than normal children, to experience reading instruction as a personal friendly interaction with an affectionate caring teacher.

References and Suggested Reading

1. Allington, Richard L. "Sticks and Stones . . . but will Names Never Hurt Them?" *Reading Teacher* 28 (January 1975): 364–9.
2. Bannatyne, Alexander. *Language, Reading and Learning Disabilities.* Springfield, IL: Charles C. Thomas, 1971.
3. Bateman, Barbara. "The Efficiency of an Auditory and a Visual Method on First-Grade Reading Instruction with Visual and Auditory Learning." In *Perception and Reading*, edited by Helen K. Smith. Newark, DE: International Reading Association, 1968, 105–12.
4. Blair, Timothy R. "ERIC/RCS Spelling, Word Attack Skills." *Reading Teacher* 28 (March 1975): 604–7.
5. Carroll, John B. "Review of the ITPA." *Seventh Mental Measurements Yearbook*, Vol. 1, edited by Oscar K. Buros. Mt. Rania, MD: Gryphon House, Inc., 1972, 819–23.
6. Clarke, Louise. *Can't Read, Can't Write, Can't Talk Too Good Either, How to Recognize and Overcome Dyslexia in Your Child.* Baltimore: Penguin, 1974.
7. Cohen, Alice Sheff, and Schwartz, Elaine. "Interpreting Errors in Word Recognition." *Reading Teacher* 28 (March 1975): 534–7.
8. Cohn, Marvin, and Stricker, George. "Inadequate Perception vs. Reversals." *Reading Teacher* 30 (November 1976): 162–7.
9. Cohn, Robert. "The Neurological Study of Children with Learning Disabilities." *Journal of Exceptional Children* 31 (December 1964): 179–85.
10. Cox, Mary B. "The Effect of Conservation Ability on Reading Competency." *Reading Teacher* 30 (December 1976): 251–8.
11. Curry, Rebecca Gavurin. "Using LEA to Teach Blind Children to Read." *Reading Teacher* 29 (December 1975): 272–9.
12. Dore-Boyce, Kathleen, et al. "Comparing Reading Expectancy Formulas." *Reading Teacher* 30 (October 1975): 8–14.
13. Hammill, Donald D., et al. "Visual-Motor Processes: Can We Train Them?" *Reading Teacher* 27 (February 1974): 469–78.
14. Hare, Betty. "Perceptual Deficits are Not a Cue to Reading Problems in Second Grade." *Reading Teacher* 30 (March 1977): 624–8.
15. Harris, Albert J. "Practical Applications of Reading Research." *Reading Teacher* 29 (March 1976): 559–65.

16. Jordan, Dale R. *Dyslexia in the Classroom*. Columbus, OH: Charles E. Merrill, 1977.

17. Kirk, Samuel A., et al. *Teaching Reading to Slow and Disabled Learners*. Boston: Houghton Mifflin Co., 1978.

18. Klasen, Edith. *The Syndrome of Specific Dyslexia*. Baltimore: University Park Press, 1972.

19. Koppitz, Elizabeth. *Children with Learning Disabilities*. New York: Grune and Stratton, 1971.

20. Lieberman, Isabelle, et al. "Letter Confusion and Reversals of Sequence in the Beginning Reader: Implication for Orton's Theory of Developmental Dyslexis." ERIC Reports ED 096 605. Reprinted from *Cortex* 7 (1971): 127–42.

21. Lopardo, Genevieve S. "LEA—Cloze Reading Material for the Disabled Reader." *Reading Teacher* 30 (October 1975): 42–4.

22. Martin, Paul. "Drugless Help for Learning Disabled Children." *Let's Live* 44 (October 1976): 24–31.

23. Martin, Paul. "Megavitamins, the Mind and Dr. Cott." *Let's Live* 45 (February 1977): 11–16.

24. Mavrogenes, Nancy A., et al. "A Guide to Tests of Factors that Inhibit Learning to Read." *Reading Teacher* 29 (January 1976): 342–58. An annotated list, including critical evaluation, of diagnostic tests for children with specific language disabilities.

25. Miller, Harry B., and Hering, Steve. "Teacher's Ratings—Which Reading Group is Number One?" *Reading Teacher* 28 (January 1975): 389–91.

26. Montgomery, Diane. "Teaching Prereading Skills through Training in Pattern Recognition." *Reading Teacher* 30 (March 1977): 616–23.

27. Mreschar, Renate I. "Influence of Upbringing on the Problems of Dyslexic Children." *Reading Teacher* 29 (May 1976): 838–41.

28. Naiden, Norma. "Ratio of Boys to Girls among Disabled Readers." *Reading Teacher* 29 (February 1976): 439–42.

29. Newcomer, Phyllis L., and Hammill, Donald D. "ITPA and Academic Achievement: A Survey." *Reading Teacher* 28 (May 1975): 731–41.

30. Orton Society, 8415 Bellona Lane, Towson, MD 21204. Numerous publications on dyslexia, most of them in inexpensive pamphlet form.

31. Robinson, Helen M. "Perceptual Training—Does it Result in Reading Improvement? In *Some Persistent Questions on Beginning Reading*, edited by Robert C. Aukerman. Newark, DE: International Reading Association, 1972, 135–50.

32. Schwartz, Elain, and Sheff, Alice. "Student Involvement in Questioning for Comprehension." *Reading Teacher* 29 (November 1975): 150–4.

33. Slingerland, Beth H. *Slingerland Screening Tests for Identifying Children with Specific Language Disability*, rev. ed. Cambridge, MA: Educators Publishing Service, 1970.

34. Slingerland, Beth H. *A Multi-Sensory Approach to Language Arts for Specific Language Disability Children, a Guide for Primary Teachers*. Cambridge, MA: Educators Publishing Service, 1971.

35. Smith, Lewis B. "They Found a Golden Ladder . . . Stories by Children." *Reading Teacher* 29 (March 1976): 541–5.

36. Stein, Jess, Editor-in-Chief. *The Random House Dicationary of the English Language.* New York: Random House, 1973.

37. Templeton, A. B., et al. *Reading Disorders in the United States.* Developmental Learning Materials, 1969.

38. Wiederholt, J. Lee, and Hammill, Donald D. "Use of the Frostig-Horne Visual Perception Program in the Urban School." *Psychology in the Schools* 8 (July 1971): 268–74.

39. Wilson, Marilyn. "A Review of Recent Research on the Integration of Reading and Writing." *Reading Teacher* 34 (May 1981): 896–901.

Application Experiences for the Teacher-Education Class

1. With a partner or small group change the following statements in any way you wish in order to make them agree with the statements or implications of the author.

Statements about Chapter 17

   a. Slow learners are mentally retarded.

   b. A disabled learner is essentially the same as a slow learner when it comes to reading.

   c. One out of every three children in the U.S. is either a disabled or slow learner when it comes to reading.

   d. Children who are disabled readers tend to be easy-going, as if they didn't really care that much about their learning problems.

   e. The best label for a child like Ralph is "dyslexic."

   f. The problem of the disabled reader is certainly not an environmental one.

   g. The best tests for diagnosing specific language disabilities are the Frostig Tests of Perception and the ITPA.

   h. When working with slow learners or disabled learners it is important to limit the informational input to one sense at a time.

   i. When teaching slow and disabled learners to spell and decode sight words, it is best to have them work at their desks and to use manuscript rather than cursive.

   j. The cloze-type exercise is far too difficult for slow or disabled learners.

   k. The language-experience approach is not structured enough for slow or disabled learners.

2. With a partner or small group study the information about Ralph in Transcript 5 in the Instructor's Manual. If you were Ralph's teacher, what specific reading deficiencies would you work on first? What instructional strategies would you use? Share your ideas with others in the class.

3. Invite a teacher who works daily with slow and disabled learners to discuss some of the children she is working with and some of her specific instructional procedures.

Field Experiences in the Elementary-School Classroom

1. Using the "Observation Checklist" on pages 491–492, observe over a period of several days a child who has been classified as a disabled learner. If possible, do the same with a child who has been classified as a slow learner. What similarities and differences do you notice? Are these differences due to different types of children or simply to different individuals? What evidence do you have for your conclusions?

2. Using the methods for teaching spelling and decoding of sight words described on pages 44–47 and 498–499, teach two or three sight words to one or more children who are slow or disabled learners.

3. Observe a "compensatory" teacher teaching reading and a regular classroom teacher teaching reading (preferably to children of the same grade level). What differences in teaching techniques and materials do you notice? What other differences would you recommend?

Appendixes

Chapter Outline

Appendix A

More Games and Activities for Developing Children's Vocabularies

1: Word Chase.   Materials: Game board (see below), place markers such as plastic cars or buttons, one die. Home spaces should be four different colors (same four colors as markers).

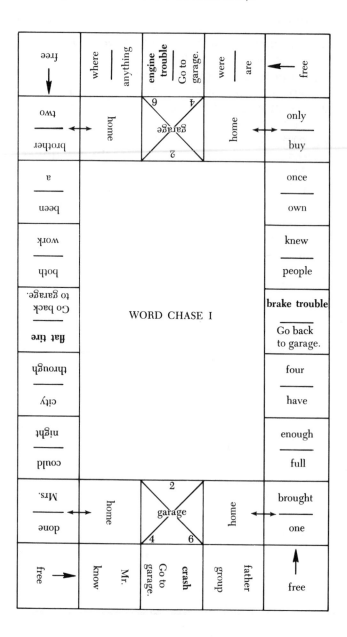

Object of game: First person to get from his home space all around the board and back to home space wins.

Procedures: (two to four may play)

1. Players roll die to see who goes first. Highest number goes first.
2. Each person rolls die and moves number of spaces indicated.
3. When person lands on a space, he must read both words out loud.
4. If a player doesn't read words correctly (as decided by other players), he must move back to where he was.
5. Second person on same space bumps first person's marker all the way back to his home space.
6. After going all the way around, player must roll the exact number on the die to get back into home space and win.
7. A 2, 4, or 6 must be rolled to get out of the garages.

Values of game:

1. Practice in decoding high-frequency irregular words
2. Strengthening of visual memory of high-frequency irregular words

Adaptations of game: Make Word Chase I, Word Chase II, and Word Chase III, using 32 out of the 96 words in Table 2.2 each time. May also be used for high-frequency regular words or for words with phonic elements that you wish to emphasize.

2: Word Toss. Materials: four boards that are about one-inch by six-inches by 30 inches, 12 two to three inch nails, three rubber or plastic rings.

WORD TOSS

One point for throwing ring in here

Procedures: (best for two to four players)

1. Each person tosses three rings. Person with highest score goes first.
2. Leader shows a word with flash card (about three seconds).
3. If player reads word correctly, gets to throw three rings.
4. Leader keeps score with tally marks.
5. Whoever has most points at end of ten minutes (or some other designated time) is the winner.

   Values of game:

1. Practice in decoding high-frequency irregular words
2. Strengthening of visual memory of high-frequency irregular words

   Adaptations of game: May also be used for high-frequency regular words or for words with phonic elements that you wish to emphasize.

3: Steal the Words.   Materials: 64 (three by five) cards with 16 different high-frequency irregular words printed on them; each word is printed twice on four different cards (once right-side up and once upside down).

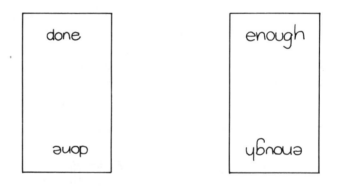

   Object of game: Person with biggest pile of cards at end of game wins.
   Procedures: (two to four may play)

1. Draw a card to see who goes first. Person with word with most letters deals cards.
2. Dealer gives four cards face down to each person after shuffling cards.
3. Dealer then places row of four cards face up in middle of playing area.
4. Person to left of dealer goes first.

5. If player has card that is the same as a card in the middle of playing area, she picks it up and places both cards face up in a pile close to her. (This forms the pile of words that others may later steal.) Before picking it up, however, she must read word to satisfaction of other players.

6. If player does not have a card that is the same as one in the middle, she must place one of her cards in the middle, thus adding to the selection in the middle.

7. If a player has a card that is the same as the top card of another player's pile, she must first read the word on the card out loud and then say STEAL THE WORDS as she takes the other player's pile and places it on top of her own.

8. *A pile of words may be stolen only at the time of a person's regular turn!*

9. After the players have each used up their four cards, the dealer deals out four more cards to each one; this time, however, the dealer does *not* place any more in the middle of the playing area.

10. Dealer places extra cards in center during her final deal.

11. When the final cards have been dealt and played, the game is over.

12. Last person to take a card with her card gets all the rest of the cards in the middle.

Values of game:

1. Practice in decoding high-frequency irregular words
2. Strengthening of visual memory of high-frequency irregular words

Adaptations of game: Make six decks: Steal the Words I, II, III, IV, V, and VI to provide practice on all 96 words in Table 2.2. Can also be used for high-frequency regular words or for words with phonic elements that you wish to emphasize.

4. Word checkers. Materials: Inexpensive or homemade checkerboard; set of checkers; paper labels slightly smaller than the squares on the checkerboard; print a different word on each label—twice so that each player can see the word right-side-up.

Object of game: First person to get all of other person's checkers wins; or the person who has the most checkers at the end of a designated time such as ten minutes.

Procedures: Two people may play. Follow same procedures as with regular checkers with these exceptions:

1. Before person can move his checker, he must say the word or words that are on his path, including the word he finally lands on.

2. When a person cannot decode (pronounce) a word correctly, he loses his turn.

Values of game:

1. Practice in decoding high-frequency irregular words
2. Strengthening of visual memory of high-frequency irregular words

Adaptations of game: May also be used for high-frequency regular words, words with phonic elements you wish to emphasize, or words you wish them to be able to define as well as pronounce

*5. **Boggle**.*   A game that combines spelling and decoding; 16 lettered cubes. Purchase from Warren's Educational Supplies, 7715 Garvey Avenue, Rosemead, CA 91770.

*6. **Context Clues Game**.*   A game that develops vocabularies through the use of context clues. Purchase from Lakeshore Curriculum Materials, 2695 E. Dominguez Street, P.O. Box 6261, Carson, CA 90749.

*7. **Crossword Puzzles**.*   Laminated colorful puzzles at different levels of difficulty. Purchase from Ideal School Supply, 11000 South Lavergne, Oak Lawn, IL 60453.

*8. **Educational Password Game**.*   A game based on popular television show. Purchase from Milton Bradley, 74 Park Street, Springfield, MA 01101.

*9. **Picture Words for Beginners**.*   An activity of matching words and pictures. Purchase from Milton Bradley; see #A8 for address.

*10. **Rummy-Nyms**.*   A game similar to rummy; one deck for synonyms, one for antonyms. Purchase from Little Brown Bear Associates, Box 561167, Miami, FL 33156.

*11. **Synonym Puzzles**.*   A set of "jigsaw puzzles" allowing children to match synonyms. Purchase from Incentives for Learning, 600 West Van Buren Street, Chicago, IL 60607.

*12. **Word Cover**.*   A game similar to Bingo for learning high-frequency words. Purchase from Houghton Mifflin, One Beacon Street, Boston, MA 02107.

*13. **Distar Language I and II**.*   A set of materials for developing vocabulary and language skills. Purchase from Science Research Associates, 259 East Erie Street, Chicago, IL 60611.

14. The Language and Thinking Program. Readiness materials for developing vocabulary and language skills. Purchase from Follett Educational Corporation, 1010 West Washington Blvd., Chicago, IL 60607.

15. Peabody Language Development Kits. Pictures, puppets, and lessons for development of oral vocabulary and language skills. Purchase from American Guidance Service, Publishers' Building, Circle Pines, MN 55014.

Appendix B

More Games and Activities for Developing Phonic Analysis and Other Decoding Skills

1. e-Boat Adventure. Materials: Game board (see below), place markers such as buttons or cardboard boats, one die

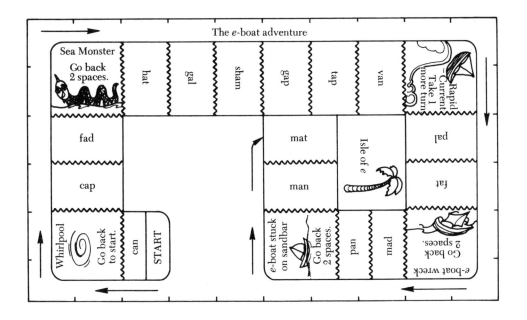

The *e*-boat adventure

Object of game: First one to get onto the Isle of *e* wins the game.

Procedures: (best for two to four players)

1. Roll die to see who goes first. Highest number goes first.
2. Each person rolls die and moves number of spaces indicated.

3. When player lands on a word, she must read the word out loud as it is first and then as it would be with a final *e*.
4. If player doesn't read word correctly both ways (and in the correct order) player must move back to where she was. (Other players decide.)
5. It is all right to have more than one *e*-boat on a space.
6. To land on the Isle of *e* player must roll the exact number on the die.

Values of game:

1. Practice in decoding VC words
2. Practice in discriminating between VC and VCE patterns
3. Development of positive feelings about "reading" as a school subject
4. Indirect practice in spelling VC and VCE words
5. Practice in reading common phonograms such as *ad, an, at*

Adaptations of game: Use other VC-VCE contrasts such as *pin-pine, bit-bite,* and *rip-ripe.*

2. Wild Things. Materials: A deck of 52 (3 × 5) cards with words having *r*-controlled vowels written on them (except for eight "wild cards"). There should be five "suits": *ar, er, ir, or,* and *ur.*

Object of game: first one to get rid of all cards in hand wins.

Procedures:

1. Deal five cards to each player face down.
2. Place rest of deck face down in center of the table.
3. Turn top card face up on the side of the deck to form discard pile.
4. Person to left of dealer begins play.
5. Each player plays (discards) only one card; then it's the next person's turn.

6. In order to play, each player must be able to discard one card from hand by following suit *(ar, er, ir, or, ur)*. Player must read word out loud to the approval of other players or lose turn. Example: If *hurt* is top card on discard pile, player must discard a *ur* word.

7. If player does not have a word following suit, he may play a card having a word beginning with the same first letter as the top card on discard pile. This now changes the suit. Example: If *hurt* was down and next player discarded *harm,* next player must play an *ar* word or another *h* word.

8. A player may change suit anytime by playing a wild thing and calling out the suit he wishes to change to. Example: Plays wild card and says, "I want to change it to *e-r* words."

9. If player does not have a playable card, he must draw one card from deck and lose turn.

Values of game:

1. Practice in decoding words with *r*-controlled vowels
2. Practice in discriminating among words with *r*-controlled vowels

Adaptations of game: Use the four basic vowel patterns as suits: VC, VCE, VV, and CV. The player not only reads the word but calls out the pattern as well.

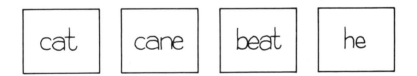

Another adaptation is the use of phonograms as suits, such as *at, ack, am, an,* and *ap.*

3. Animal Race. With this game board the child matches pictures and beginning sounds after choosing his track for racing with one to three other children. Purchase from Houghton Mifflin; see address under #A12.

4. Build It. A game that teaches the decoding of consonant letters and short-vowel letters. Purchase from Remedial Education Press,

Kingsbury Center, 2138 Bancroft Place, N.W., Washington, DC 20008.

5. Phonetic Quizmo. A lotto-type game designed to teach the decoding of consonant letters and clusters. Purchase from Milton Bradley; see address under #A8.

6. Split Words. An activity for building words from wooden blocks with consonant letters, consonant clusters, and phonograms printed on them. Purchase from American Teaching Aids, Box 1652, Covina, CA 91722.

7. Blend Dominoes. A game designed to have children build words containing consonant digraphs and consonant clusters. Purchase from Lakeshore Curriculum Materials; see #A6 for address.

8. Ugly Oogly. A card game requiring the blending of consonant letters or clusters with phonograms. Purchase from Little Brown Bear Associate; see #A10 for address.

9. Autophonics. Games similar to bingo involving "vehicles" to drive. Teach the decoding of vowel letters, vowel digraphs, and diphthong clusters. Purchase from Warren's Educational Supplies; see #A5 for address.

10. Sea of Vowels. Children travel by "submarine" in search of treasure; teaches "long and short vowels." Purchase from Ideal School Supply; see #A7 for address.

11. Quiet Pal Game. Children build words with "silent letters" in them. Purchase from Warren's Educational Supply; see #A5 for address.

12. Tick-Tack-Go. Board games on decoding vowel letters and patterns. Purchase from Little Brown Bear Associates; see #A10 for address.

13. Vowel Wheels. Five activities in which children move discs to produce words. Purchase from Milton Bradley; see #A8 for address.

14. Advanced Prefix and Suffix Puzzles. Three piece "jigsaw" puzzles requiring children to match prefix and suffix with root. Order from Developmental Learning Materials, 7440 Natchez Avenue, Niles, IL 60648.

15. Compound Word Game. Children use cards to form compound words. Purchase from Developmental Learning Materials; see #B14 for address.

16. Mousetrap. A card game in which compound words are analyzed and synthesized. Order from Little Brown Bear Associates; see #A10 for address.

17. Syllable Scoreboard. Children use a basketball gameboard and move across the board according to the number of syllables in words drawn from a "ball bin." Purchase from Developmental Learning Materials; see #B14 for address.

18. Durrell-Murphy Phonics Practice Program. Picture cards which can be used by the child without adult supervision. Purchase from Harcourt Brace Jovanovich, 757 Third Avenue, New York, NY 10017.

19. Get Set Games. Various games on decoding skills. Purchase from Houghton Mifflin; see #A12 for address.

20. Intersensory Reading Method. Books, cards, and other materials on beginning phonics. Purchase from Book-Lab, 1449 37th Street, Brooklyn, NY 11218.

21. The Phonovisual Method. Charts, books, manuals, and cards for teaching phonics. Purchase from Phonovisual Products, 12216 Parklawn Drive, Rockville, MD 20852.

22. Speech-to-Print Phonics. Cards with manual on teaching phonic skills. Purchase from Harcourt Brace Jovanovich; see #B18 for address.

23. Sullivan Remedial Reading Program. A set of programmed workbooks with cartoons. Purchase from Behavioral Research Laboratories, P.O. Box 577, Palo Alto, CA 94302.

Appendix C

More Games and Activities for Developing Comprehension Skills

1. Main Idea Travel Game. Both the primary and the intermediate edition of this game use a playing board, one die, six colored markers, 110 story cards, and other materials to help children learn how to detect main ideas in reading selections. Purchase from Comprehension Games Corporation, 63-110 Woodhaven Blvd., Rego Park, NY 11374.

2. Drawing Conclusions.   A game containing five bingo cards, one spinner, 80 plastic markers, 110 story cards and other materials designed to help children learn how to draw conclusions. Purchase from Comprehension Games Corporation; see #C1 for address.

3. Fact or Opinion.   A game containing a playing board, one die, six markers, 110 story cards, and other materials related to learning this comprehension skill. Purchase from Comprehension Games Corporation; see #C1 for address.

4. Reading for Detail.   A game that contains two spinners, a playing board, six plastic horses, 72 story cards, and other materials. Purchase from Comprehension Games Corporation; see #C1 for address.

5. Reading Rx.   This is a box of activity cards with hundreds of games and activities for reinforcing decoding, comprehension, and reference skills. Purchase from Tarmack/Tac, 8 Baird Mountain Road, Asheville, NC 28804.

6. Reading Skills Builders.   Short reading selections in magazine format designed to help teach specific comprehension skills at all grade levels. Purchase from Reader's Digest Services, Educational Division, Pleasantville, NY 10570.

7. SRA Reading Laboratory.   Multilevel and color coded cards with short selections and related questions for all grades. Purchase from Science Research Associates, 259 East Erie Street, Chicago, IL 60611.

Appendix D

More Ideas for Language-Experience Stories

1. Have the children see how long they can make this sentence: "The bear chased the girl." They may change the sentence or the words in any way they wish. After they have made the sentence as long as they wish, they may also add more sentences.
2. Ask them to think of ideas for making the classroom more attractive.
3. Ask pupils to choose one picture (from a large set of pictures) to tell or write a story about. Give them a day or two to think about their idea. Then have them come to a quiet corner one at a time to tell you the story (or to tell it into a tape recorder). Let the child hold the picture while telling the story.

4. Find pictures that tell a story, e.g., a child crying who is obviously lost. Have children tell or write (or both) what is happening now, what happened just before the picture, and what is going to happen after the picture.

5. Make a "touch book" with a different texture on each page: sand paper, wax paper, silky material, etc. Number each page and pass around the book. When a child has a turn with the book, she is to write down the page number and also at least five words that describe how the material feels. The child then hands in the paper to the teacher and passes on the book. (This is an excellent activity for a learning center.) Some children may need help by having a large chart of "touch words" from which to select words for their own lists.

6. Ask pupils to make up one or two sentences that describe you, the teacher. Have fun reading them aloud, while at the same time discussing the kinds of words and phrases that can be used to describe a person's appearance and personality. Have them use suggestions from your discussion to develop a paragraph about themselves.

7. Have the children make up a story or just tell about their own drawings or paintings. Take dictation during the telling or use a tape recorder. Or have them write up their story after telling it.

8. Develop a class story based on an event that occurs during the school day, such as an unusual fire drill or an animal that gets into the room. The teacher takes dictation from the class.

9. Read two or three Dr. Seuss books to the children and discuss the imaginary animals that he created. Have them create their own imaginary animals on paper and tell or write about them.

10. Have the children close their eyes and imagine an imaginary character, such as a strange animal or funny person. Have them describe their characters one at a time and help weave them together into a story as they describe them. You may either stop here or write the characters on the board and have the children make up a story about them. They may use part of the story already created if they wish.

11. Have some of the children bring in toys to explain to the others. Have them pretend they are toy manufacturers and think of ways together of improving the toys. Accept even their wildest impossible ideas; in fact, encourage such ideas. If you wish, you can then have them write a story about a toy maker and how he tried to make the "best toy in the world."

12. Have children read each other's palms. Encourage them to tell exactly what adventures their partners will have, exactly how they will make their fortune, etc.

13. Each person writes a detailed description of a character from a familiar story—one they've all read in class, favorite bedtime stories, etc. Then each person reads her description and the rest of the class guesses who was described.

14. Make up "balloon adventures" about a helium-filled balloon and its travels around the world. An effective "starter" is bringing such a balloon to school and releasing it.

15. Have the children get in groups of four or five. Put several words on the chalkboard that might suggest a story, such as *sailboat, waves, rocks,* and *beach.* Each person in a group starts a story and then passes it on to another person in his group until the teacher says time. When each person has added something to each of the stories, have the children read the stories to see how similar and different they are.

16. Pass a newspaper funny with the words cut out to each child. Have them write their own dialogue.

17. Have a class puppet, one that talks to the children every day, telling about an adventure he had (the teacher had) about something he saw one of them doing that he didn't think was such a good idea, about how proud he is of them, etc. Let the children make up adventures for him.

18. After practicing with some What-if questions (such as What if all the trees in the world were cut down?) have them write their own What-if story.

19. After a period of spontaneous drama, have them write up the story they created.

20. Write a title on the board, such as "The Danger Zone," or "Flying Is for the Birds." Have each person write three sentences as a beginning of a story. Then have them put their names on their papers, fold the papers in half twice, and put them in a large box. They will then blindly pick one from the box and finish the story. Finally they will hand the story to the person who began the story, so that all may see how their story turned out.

21. Give each child five 3 × 5 index cards or other small pieces of paper. Have them write WHO, WHEN, WHAT, WHERE, and WHY on the five cards. After WHO they are to write the name and description of a character they have created. After WHAT they should tell something the character did. After WHEN and WHERE they should tell the time and place of the action. After WHY they should explain why the character did what he or she did (the motive).

    For example, WHO: Bill Robertson, a jeweler, age 40, tired looking, graying hair, nail biter. WHAT: stole some of his own jewelry. WHEN: during a summer day when no customers were in the store. WHERE: in his own jewelry store in Chicago in a run-down shopping area. WHY: he wanted to claim he was robbed and collect the insurance money so he could send his daughter to college.

Have the children put the cards in separate boxes: a WHO box, a WHAT box, a WHEN box, a WHY box, and a WHERE box. Mix the contents in the boxes and let the children each select five new cards—one from each box. They are to use their new cards, but only the ones that help them think of a story.

22. Have them create a story from a single Where Sentence. Give each child a sentence on a piece of paper, e.g., I went to the circus, or I went to a farm, or I went to a grocery store. It is all right if several children have the same sentence, but they should all begin with I went to. . . ."

    Show them how to create a "story" from a sentence. Put this sentence on the board: I went to the new shopping mall. Under the sentence write the words: *when, who, what, why.* Then show them how to ask questions that will help them describe their trip. For instance: When did you go? Whom did you see or go with? What did you do there? Why did you do these things?

23. Have them create a story from a single Who Sentence. This is similar to 22. Work with Who Sentences such as I saw Mrs. Twilliger, that lady who sells strange things. Ask questions about where, when, what, and why. For example, where did you see Mrs. Twilliger? When did you see her? What was she doing when you saw her? Why was she doing it?

24. Have them create a story from a single What Sentence, e.g., He was dropping cotton balls from an airplane. Ask who, when, where, and why questions.

25. Have them create a story from a single When Sentence, e.g., It was on a dark, foggy night at the beginning of summer vacation. Ask where, who, what, and why questions.

26. Have them create a story from a single Why Sentence, e.g., She was tired of having those kids tramp across her lawn and pick her flowers. Ask who, where, what, and when questions.

27. Have them create new adventures for their favorite cartoon characters such as Snoopy and Charlie Brown. This is especially good shortly after they have seen a Charlie Brown TV special.

28. Have them create new adventures for their favorite TV character.

29. Have them create a newspaper story about a game they just played on the playground. Be sure to have them include the who, what, when, and where in their story, and the why if it's appropriate.

30. Have the children make up Crazy Titles and put them in a grab box for other children to pick from blindly. An example of a Crazy Title would be: "The Lion Who Ran the People Zoo" or "The Girl Who Walked Backwards."

Appendix E

Sources of High-Interest Low-Vocabulary Books for Children

Publisher and Address	Title	Reading Grade Level	Interest Grade Level
Benefic Press	Animal Adventure Series	pre–1	1–4
10300 W. Roosevelt Rd.	Butternut Bill Series	pre–1	1–6
Westchester, IL 60153	Cowboys of Many Races	pre–5	1–6
	Cowboy Sam Series	pre–3	1–6
	Dan Frontier Series	pre–4	1–7
	Moonbeam Series	pre–3	1–6
	Racine Wheels Series	2–4	4–9
	Sailor Jack Series	pre–3	1–6
	Space-Age Books	1–3	3–6
	Sports Mystery Stories	2–4	4–9
	What Is It Series	1–4	1–8
Book-Lab	The Hip Reader	pre–3	4–9
1449 37th St.			
Brooklyn, NY 11218			
Children's Press	About Books	1–4	2–8
1224 West Van Buren St.	The Frontiers of America	3	3–8
Chicago, IL 60607	I Want to Be Series	2–4	4–6
	True Book Series	2–3	3–6
Field Educational Publications	Checkered Flag Series	2–4	6–12
2400 Hanover St.	Jim Forest Readers	1–3	1–7
Palo Alto, CA 94002	The Morgan Bay Mysteries	2–4	4–11
Fearon Publishers	Pacemaker True Adventures	2	5–12
6 Davis Drive			
Belmont, CA 94002			
Frank Richards Publishers	Getting Along Series	3–5	4–8
330 First St., Box 370			
Liverpool, NY 13088			
Garrard Publishing	American Folktales	3–4	2–6
1607 N. Market St.	Discovery Books	2–3	2–5
Champaign, IL 61820	First Reading Books	1–2	1–4
Mafex Associates	Magpie Series	1–3	4–8
111 Barron Ave.	Target Series	2–4	4–9
Johnstown, PA 16906	Citizens All	1–3	4–8

Publisher and Address	Title	Reading Grade Level	Interest Grade Level
Random House 201 E. 50th St. New York, NY 10022	Gateway Books Step-up Books	2–3 2–3	3–8 3–9
Reader's Digest Services Educational Division Pleasantville, NY 10570	Reading Skill Builders	1–4	2–5
Scholastic Magazine and Book Services 50 W. 44th St. New York, NY 10036	Action Libraries	2–3	4–7
Franklin Watts, Inc. 730 Fifth Avenue New York, NY 10019	Let's Find Out Series	2–4	5–6
Xerox Educational Publications Education Center Columbus, OH 43216	Know Your World	3–5	4–8

Appendix F

Book Projects for Children and Teachers

Section A: Oral Projects

1. Try to interest others in a book you have read by reading an interesting part to the class. Practice before you read to them.
2. Read an exciting part to the class. Stop reading right in the middle of the action. Practice before you read to them.
3. Tell about one character in the book. Tell why he is such an interesting person. Make the others in the class want to know more about him.
4. Show on a globe or map how you would get from your home to where the story took place. Tell how you would travel there. Then tell something about this place. Tell a little bit about why it was important in the story. Make the others in the class wish they could go there.

5. Pretend you are one of the characters in the book. Describe yourself and tell one or two things you do in the story. If others have already read the book, ask them to guess who you are.

6. Find an object which is important in the book you just read. Show it to the class and have them guess what it is and why it might be important in the story. Give them a few hints but don't tell them too much.

7. Play "Twenty Questions" with the class. Have them think of the object or person you have in mind that was important in the story. First tell them whether it is "animal, vegetable, or mineral." After the game give them some hints as to why the object or person was important, but don't tell them too much.

8. Tell the class some interesting facts that you learned about a country you read about. Then ask them three or four questions to see what facts they can remember.

9. Tell how you would have done something differently than the way a person in the story did it.

10. Prepare and present a TV commercial of your book. Try to interest others in "buying" your book.

11. Read to the class two or three poems from a book of poems you have read. Be sure to practice several times before you do this. You may wish to use the tape recorder for practicing.

12. Find someone else who has read the same book of poetry. Read to the class two or three poems together. You might try different arrangements as with a song. For example, one person could read the first verse, the other person read the second verse, and then read the third verse together.

13. See if you can recite from memory a favorite poem from a poetry book you have just read.

14. Dress up as a character in the book and tell about yourself—or about one of the adventures you had.

15. After reading a book of folk tales, see if you can learn one of the stories well enough to tell to the class.

16. Look up the author in *The Junior Book of Authors* or *More Junior Authors* (in the reference section of the library). Tell the class a few interesting things about him.

17. Make up another adventure for one of the characters. Tell the adventure to us.

18. Make up a new ending for the book. Tell your ending to the class after you first tell a little bit about the beginning and the middle. Don't tell them the real ending, though.

19. Have a panel discussion about a book that three or four of you have read. Tell how you agree and disagree about some of the characters or about part of the story.

20. Tell about an adventure you had that was similar to one a character in the book had.

21. Meet in small groups to chat about books you have read.

Section B: Drama Projects

1. Pantomime a scene from your book. Have the class guess what you were doing. Tell them only enough to get them interested in the book.
2. Plan so that you and a friend read the same book. Then prepare and present a skit on a part of the book. You may have to make up some of your own dialogue, or you can say what the characters said in the book.
3. Tape record a skit based on the book. You may have to make up some of your own dialogue and make your voice sound like several different people. Play the tape recording to the class.
4. Put on a puppet play about one part of the book.
5. Play "Meet the Author." Find someone who has read the same book. One person pretends to be the author and the other interviews him. The interviewer asks questions about the book, about the author's life (if you can find information about his life), etc.
6. Pretend you are the author of the book and you are trying to get someone to publish it. Tell the "publishing staff" (your class) why it would be a good book to publish. Let them ask you questions.
7. Play charades with the class. Act out each word of the title. See how long it takes for the class to guess the title.
8. If several others have read this book, pantomime a scene from the book—*by yourself*. Then ask the class to guess the *title* of the book. See if they can also guess the author.
9. Pretend you are a character in the book you have read. Find someone who will pretend he is a character in a different book he has read. Carry on in front of the class a conversation between the two characters. You might tell each other about some of your adventures or about some of the people you know (those who were described in the books).
10. Put on a play by yourself in which you play two or three parts. Make name cards for each character. Each time you switch parts hold up one of the cards.
11. Find some dolls that can be used to represent characters in your book. Put on a doll play about one part of your book.
12. Put on a play with one or two others. Have the class guess the title and author of the book.

Section C: Written Projects

1. Write an advertisement for the book you have read. Put the ad on the bulletin board. Be sure to tell where the book may be found and a few things about why it's a "marvelous" book.
2. Write a letter to a friend and try to persuade her to read the book you just read.

3. Make up a new table of contents for your book. Use your imagination to invent chapter titles which would interest someone else in reading the book.

4. Read two or three chapters of the book. Then write down what you think will happen in the next chapter. Draw a line under what you have written and read the next chapter. Then write briefly about how close you were with your guess.

5. Make a brief outline of your book. Use Roman Numerals for the chapters, and so on. See example below:

Tom Sawyer

  I. Tom plays, fights, and hides
   A. Tom tricks Aunt Polly
   B. Siddy gets Tom in trouble
   C. Tom fights with a new boy
   D. Tom returns home late at night
 II. The glorious whitewasher

6. Write about something that happened in the book in the same way a newspaper reporter would describe it. A reporter tries to answer these questions: Who? What? When? Where? Why? Don't forget to make up a snappy headline for your newspaper article.

7. Write a pretend letter to a character in the book. Tell the character how his or her life is the same or different from yours.

8. Write a real letter to the author of the book. Send the letter in care of the publisher.

9. Make a short diary for one of the characters in the book. Describe three or four days as if you were the person in the book.

10. Pretend you are one of the characters in the book. Write a letter to another character in the book.

11. Add another chapter to the book. Tell what happened next, or what adventure was left out.

12. Write an ending to the book which is quite different from the one the author wrote.

13. Write about *two* books you have read that are on the same topic. Tell how the books are similar and different.

14. See how good your memory is. Describe the important details in one chapter. Draw a line under your description. Then reread that chapter. Write down any important details you left out.

15. Write about an adventure you had that was like an adventure a character in the book had. Tell how the two adventures were alike and different.

16. Read in an encyclopedia or in another factual book about a person, place, or thing described in your book. Write down some of the things you learned this way that you did *not* learn from the book itself.

17. Try to make a list of all the characters in the book from memory. List both their first and last names. Draw a line under your list. Now skim through the book to see if you remembered all of them. Write down any you didn't remember. How good was your memory for names?

18. Write about the character in the story that you would most like to have for a friend. Tell why he or she would be a good friend. Also write about the character that you would *not* like to have for a friend. Tell why.

19. Write about how you would have solved a problem a different way from the way a character in the book did.

20. Pick two characters from the story. Write about how they were alike and how they were different.

21. Make a list of words or phrases in the story that helped you almost to see or hear or smell or feel or taste something described in the story.

22. Write a poem that tells about one adventure in the book.

Section D: Arts and Crafts Projects

1. Make clothes for a doll to match a character in the book. Display it for the rest of the class to see. Make sure you have a card by it with the name of the book, the author and your name.

2. Make an object which is important in the book you just read. Have the class guess what it is and why it might be important in the story. Give them a few hints but don't tell them for sure.

3. Make a flannel board or bulletin board display about your book.

4. Make a comic strip about one of the scenes in your book. Put it on the bulletin board.

5. Make a diorama (a small stage) that describes a scene in the book. Use a cardboard box for the stage. Make the objects and people in your scene out of clay, cardboard, pipe cleaners, papier mache, or any other material.

6. Make a mobile representing five or six of the characters in the book.

7. If the book doesn't have a book jacket, make one for it. Be sure to put a picture on it and all the necessary information. A used manila folder might be good to use.

8. Make a "movie" of one scene in your book. Use a long piece of butcher paper. After you draw a sequence of several pictures, roll the butcher paper. Then ask two people to unroll it as you describe the scene to the class.

9. Make a picture of one scene in the book. Put it on the bulletin board. Underneath it put the title and author and two or three questions about the scene. Try using crayon, chalk, or charcoal.

10. Same as 9. Use tempera or water color.

11. Same as 9. Use collage materials: bits of paper, cloth, or other materials.

12. Study the illustrations in the book. What kinds of techniques did the artist use? See if you can make an illustration of a part

in the book that was not illustrated. Try to use some of the same techniques as the artist did. Put your illustration on the bulletin board. Be sure to name the illustrator that you imitated.

13. Make a time line of the story. Use main events rather than dates. Draw pictures to illustrate the main events.

14. Read half or more of the book. Then draw three pictures to show three different ways the book might end. Put them on the bulletin board, along with a card giving the title, author, your name, and "Three Ideas on How this Book Might End."

15. Make a scrap book of things related to the book. Be sure to label what you put in your scrap book.

16. Make a map to show where the characters went in the story.

Section E: Demonstration Projects

1. Demonstrate a science principle you learned from your book by performing an experiment in front of the class.

2. Show the class how to make something you learned how to make from reading your book.

3. Show the class how to do something you learned how to do from reading your book.

Appendix G

The RAD Test—Rapid Assessment of a Disabled Reader

Directions for Administration. Note to teacher: This test is not a diagnostic test. Its purpose is to provide you with a means of quickly determining which children in a group may have "specific language disability."

Part A: Visual-Kinesthetic Memory

Directions to teacher: Print the following words or letters at least 1½ inches high with heavy black felt pen on white cardboard about three inches by eight inches:

1. bad	6. hobby
2. your	7. eighty
3. top	8. minnow
4. nuts	9. whenever
5. JKBF	10. stumbles

Show each card one at a time in the order given. (Do not have the number printed on the card. Just say the number as you show it.) Expose the card for about ten seconds while the students hold their pencils high over their heads.

When you have turned the card over, count five more seconds and say "Write word number one." The children are then to write the word next to the number one on their sheet of paper. Give them about fifteen seconds to write the word; then ask them to raise their pencils above their heads again.

Repeat this procedure for each of the ten words. Do not show a word again once you have turned over the card.

Part B: Auditory Memory and Visual Discrimination

Directions to teacher: Have the following words and letters ready to read to the students:

11. quick	16. mommy
12. fyqt	17. thought
13. saw	18. surround
14. bedc	19. running
15. bubbles	20. everyone

Say each word (or series of letters). Say each one twice. While you are saying each one, the students should have their paper turned over. After you have finished saying a word (or series of letters) twice, count five seconds and say, "Turn over your paper and find the words or letters in row one. Draw a circle around the word or letters I just said."

Allow about ten seconds for them to circle a word (or a series of letters.) Then say "Put your pencil down and turn over your paper. Listen for the next word or letters."

Repeat this procedure for each of the ten words (or series of letters). Do not say a word (or series of letters) more than twice.

RAD Test

Student's Name _____ Grade _____
Teacher's Name _____ Date _____

Part A:

1. _____	6. _____
2. _____	7. _____
3. _____	8. _____
4. _____	9. _____
5. _____	10. _____

Part B:

11. puick	qnick	quick	pnick	kciuq
12. fypt	tqyf	ftyq	fyqt	tyqf
13. was	saw	sam	mas	zaw
14. dceb	dbce	bedc	peqc	becd

15. buddles	dubbles	selbbub	bubbles	bnbbles
16. mommy	wowwy	ymmom	mymmo	mowwy
17. thouhgt	tghuoht	thought	thuoght	thuohgt
18. snrronud	surround	dnuorrus	sunnourd	surruond
19. nurring	runners	running	gninnur	rurring
20. evyerone	oneevery	evenyoue	everyone	evenyone

Directions for Scoring RAD Test. To derive a score from this test, simply add up the number of items in the twenty-item test that were correct. Now compare the papers in the bottom third of the group with those in the top third. Those children who are disabled learners will usually stand out. This is not a very precise assessment but it gives you a way of quickly determining which children need to be observed more closely.

To be somewhat more precise about your assessment, you can use the Diagnostic Grid for the RAD Test shown on the next page. For each incorrect item, place a check mark to designate the type of error or errors exhibited. Then derive a total for each type of error. Do you find several reversals, transpositions, inversions, substitutions, insertions, omissions? Do the test results coincide with your observations on the Observation Checklist (pages 491–492)? If so, you have candidates for special instruction.

Appendix H

An Informal Word Recognition Inventory (Including the BAF Test)

The purpose of the following inventory is to enable a teacher to achieve a greater degree of individualization in her reading instruction. By determining the specific word-recognition problems which each student has, the teacher should be able to use temporary grouping and individual instruction to help students overcome their difficulties.

Although the first three parts of the inventory must be administered individually, all of the other parts may be administered as group tests. After half or more of the school year has passed, it would be advisable to administer the inventory again to determine the type of instruction that is still necessary.

Part I:* Consonant Letters, Digraphs, and Clusters

(For those whose instructional level is at least "Primer")

This part of the inventory should be administered individually. You will need to reproduce a copy of this page for each child.

---

*This part and Part II, in combination, have been dubbed by the author as "The BAF Test."

	1	2	3	4	5	6	7	8	9	10	11	12	13	14	15	16	17	18	19	20	Total
transposition																					
letter reversal																					
inversion																					
substitution																					
omission																					
insertion																					
word reversal																					
letter form																					
letter size°																					
spacing																					
alignment																					
slant																					
mix°°																					

Formation of circles in Part B: _____connected _____disconnected _____circular _____noncircular

_____counterclockwise _____clockwise_____inconsistent direction

Comments:

Recommendations:

° Disregard whether child has mixed capital and lowercase letters or cursive and manuscript.

°° Check here with LC when child mixes lowercase and capital letters. Check with MC when child mixes manuscript print and cursive.

Figure H.1. *Diagnostic grid for RAD Test.*

The children should be encouraged to try decoding each nonsense word without your help. If they miss one, simply circle it and have them continue. Be sure to pronounce the first one for them /băf/ and have them pronounce it correctly before they continue. It is also a good idea to correct the second one if they miss it (*caf* is pronounced /kăf/).

Name of Student _____

Directions to be Read or Told to the Student

"These words are nonsense words. They are not real words. I'd like you to think about what sounds the letters have; then read each word out loud without my help. Don't try to go fast; read the list slowly. If you have any trouble with a word, I'll just circle it and you can go on to the next one. The first word is /băf/. Now you say it. . . . All right, now go on to the rest of the words in row 1."

	A	B	C	D	E	F	G
				Consonant Letters			
1.	baf	caf	daf	faf	gaf	haf	jaf
2.	kaf	laf	maf	naf	paf	raf	saf
3.	taf	vaf	waf	yaf	zaf	baf	bax

	A	B	C	D	E	F	G	H
				Consonant Digraphs				
4.	chaf	phaf	shaf	thaf	whaf	fack	fang	fank
				Consonant Clusters				
5.	blaf	braf	claf	craf	draf	dwaf	flaf	fraf
6.	glaf	graf	fand	plaf	praf	quaf	scaf	scraf
7.	skaf	slaf	sma	snaf	spaf	splaf	spraf	squaf
8.	staf	straf	swaf	thraf	traf	twaf		

Part II: Vowel Letters, Vowel Digraphs, and Vowel Clusters

(For those whose instructional level is at least "Primer")

This part of the inventory should also be administered individually. You will need to reproduce a copy of this test for each child. The children should be encouraged to try decoding each nonsense word without your help. If they miss one, simply circle it and have them continue. Be sure to pronounce the first one for them /băf/ and have them pronounce it correctly before they continue. Note that for 3G (boof), the children should be asked to pronounce it two ways; circle it if they can't. The same is true of 5B (bufe).

Name of Student _____

Directions to be Read or Told to the Student

"These words are nonsense words. They are not real words. I'd like you to think about what sounds the letters have; then read each word out loud without any help. Don't try to go fast; read the list slowly. If you have any trouble with a word, I'll just circle it and you can go on to the next one. The first word is /băf/. Now you say it. . . . All right, now go on to the rest of the words in row 1."

	A	B	C	D	E	F	G
1.	baf	bafe	barf	baif	bawf		
2.	bef	befe	berf	beaf			
3.	bof	bofe	borf	boaf	bouf	boif	boof
4.	bif	bife	birf				
5.	buf	bufe	burf				

Part III: Basic Sight Vocabulary—Irregular Words Only

(For those whose instructional level is at least "Primer.")
This part of the inventory should also be administered individually. You will need to reproduce a copy of this page for each child. Start the student randomly at any one of the 16 rows. Circle any word which the children do not recognize instantly. Even a self-correction should be considered an error. If they can complete three rows with no more than one error, you probably need not continue. If they make more than one error, you may wish to check them on all ninety-six of the words. If they miss more than ten of the words, they probably should be given special assistance on those words that they missed.

Name of Student _____

Directions to be Read or Told to the Student

"I would like you to read each of these words without my help. Many of these words are hard to read. If you don't know a word right away, I'll just circle the word and you can go on to the next one. All right, I'll point to the row where you should start."

A	B	C	D	E	F
anything	give	great	Mrs.	says	very
a	could	group	night	should	want
because	do	have	nothing	some	water
again	does	head	of	something	was
almost	done	knew	brother	the	were
another	door	heard	on	sometimes	wanted
always	buy	know	off	their	what
any	enough	light	one	they	where
are	four	only	long	who	thought
been	from	dog	other	there	father
both	friend	many	own	through	goes
brought	full	might	people	to	work
house	don't	money	put	together	you
city	live	mother	right	today	would
come	gone	Mr.	said	two	your
year	they're	school	our	there's	once

Part IV: Context Analysis

(For those whose instructional level is at least "First Reader.")

This part of the inventory can be administered as a group test. Simply reproduce a copy of the ten sentences for each child whose instructional level is at least First Reader.

The child who misses any of the last four probably needs help in recognizing grammatical clues. The child who misses any of the first six probably needs help in recognizing semantic clues.

Directions to be Read or Told to the Student

"Write your name and the date at the top of the sheet. For each sentence below circle the letter of the word or nonsense word that best fits in the blank. *I will read each sentence and word to you.*

In the first one, for instance, circle *a* if you think Sally tried to catch *his* horse. Circle *b* if you think it should be *their* horse. Circle *c* if you think it should be *her* horse. Circle *d* if you think it should be *our* horse.

1. Sally's horse ran out of the barn. Sally tried to catch ____horse.
    a. his b. their c. her d. our
2. Bill ran as fast as he could and jumped _____ the rope.
    a. off b. over c. onto d. out
3. The _____ yelled when they saw that their ship was sinking.
    a. salesmen b. savages c. servants d. sailors
4. Jim pulled on the rope until his hands were _____ .
    a. ripe b. rough c. ready d. round
5. As Tom fell from the roof he _____ for help.
    a. scrubbed b. scraped c. screamed d. scratched
6. The tired farmer leaned _____ on his plow.
    a. heavenly b. hastily c. heavily d. heartily
7. Jerry _____ his brother.
    a. bappy b. boodily c. baffed d. binny
8. The _____ is here.
    a. flammered b. flump c. fleppily d. flunted
9. This was a very _____ yard.
    a. pelly b. pollingly c. pills d. peppily
10. Mary ran very _____ to the store.
    a. chobby b. chebs c. chibbily d. chupping

Answers to Part IV

| Semantic Clues: | 1c | 2b | 3d | 4b | 5c | 6c |
| Grammatical Clues: | 7c | 8b | 9a | 10c |

Part V: Meaning of Contractions

(For those whose instructional level is at least First Reader)

This part of the inventory can be administered as a group test. Reproduce a copy of the nine sentences for each child whose instructional level is at least First Reader.

Directions to be Read or Told to the Students

Write the meaning of each underlined word. Notice the example. The underlined word is a contraction, meaning I am. Therefore I am was written in the blank. Do the others in the same way. Be sure to read each sentence to yourself before you decide what the contraction means."

Example: I am I'm coming, Mother.

1. _____ I think it's time to go.
2. _____ Please don't eat the flowers.
3. _____ You've done it again.
4. _____ Why won't you go?
5. _____ She said she'll be there.
6. _____ He'd just finished when his father arrived.
7. _____ I know they're here some place.
8. _____ Who's taken my pencil?
9. _____ I know they'd do it if they could.

Answers to Part V

1. it is
2. do not
3. you have
4. will not
5. she will
6. He had
7. they are
8. Who has
9. they would

Part VI: Recognition of Roots and Affixes

(For those whose instructional level is at least 2^1.)

This part of the inventory can be administered as a group test. Reproduce a copy of the nineteen words for each child whose instructional level is at least 2^1.

Directions to be Read or Told to the Students

"Write the *root* of each word that you see below. Before you start, look at the example. What is the root of *tells*? What is the root of *cherries*? What is the root of *unhurt*? Now do the rest of them on your own."

Examples: (a) tells *tell*
           (b) cherries *cherry*
           (c) unhurt *hurt*

Part A	*Part B*	*Part C*
1. roads _____	8. pennies _____	14. unzips _____
2. washed _____	9. sleepily _____	15. refills _____
3. blacker _____	10. rubbing _____	16. becomes _____
4. eating _____	11. cupped _____	17. amounts _____
5. sticky _____	12. maker _____	18. derails _____
6. newly _____	13. pasting _____	19. preheats _____
7. greenest _____		

Answers to Part VI

1. When the suffixes *es, ed, er, est,* or *ly* follow the letter *i*, the root word can be recognized by dropping the suffix and changing the *i* to *y*, e.g., #8 and 9. ·
2. When the suffixes *ed, er,* or *ing* follow a doubled consonant letter, the root word can be recognized by dropping both the suffix and one of the consonant letters, e.g., #10 and 11.
3. When the suffixes *ed, er,* or *ing* follow a single consonant letter, a consonant digraph, or a consonant blend, sometimes the root word can be recognized by dropping the suffix and adding a final *e*, e.g., #12 and 13.

Part VII: Decoding Syllables

(For those whose instructional level is at least 2¹.)

This part of the inventory can be administered as a group test. You will need to reproduce a copy of the twelve words for each child whose instructional level is at least 2¹.

Directions to be Read or Told to the Students

"On your paper you have a list of twelve nonsense words. I'd like you to do three things with them. First, draw a line between each syllable. Then underline the syllable that you think has the strongest sound. And then decide whether the vowel in the syllable you have underlined has a long sound or a short sound. Put S for short or L for long in the blank. Let's go through the examples together. Then you can do the rest on your own."

Examples: run/ning __S__   re/play/ing ___L___

1. b o t t o n_____   7. v i s k e t_____
2. p a s h e r_____   8. c h o c k e r_____
3. m a m b l e_____   9. t i f l e_____
4. c o b i n_____   10. n i v e r_____
5. u n l i n n i n g____ 11. r e b a n n i n g____
6. f o a t i n g_____   12. d e a n i n g_____

Answers for Part VII

1. b o t/t o n _S_   7. v i s/k e t _S_
2. p a s h/e r _S_   8. c h o c k/e r _S_
3. m a m/b l e _S_   9. t i/f l e _L_
4. c o/b i n _L_ *or* c o b/in _S_   10. n i/v e r _L_ *or* n i v/e r _S_
5. u n/l i n/n i n g _S_ 11. r e/b a n/n i n g _S_
6. f o a t/i n g _L_   12. d e a n/i n g _L_

Generalizations Tested in Part VII

Syllabication

1. Each syllable contains a vowel phoneme. (All twelve words are illustrations of this principle.)
2. The letters *le,* along with the preceding consonant letter, form a separate syllable, e.g., numbers 3 and 9.
3. A word may be divided between two vowel letters if they are not a digraph or if they do not represent a diphthong, e.g., numbers 6 and 12.
4. A word may be divided between two consonant letters if they are not a digraph, e.g., numbers 1, 2, 7, and 8.
5. A consonant letter may belong to the syllable of either the preceding or following vowel letter, e.g., numbers 4 and 10.
6. A consonant digraph usually belongs to the syllable of the preceding vowel letter, e.g., numbers 2 and 8.
7. A prefix normally forms a separate syllable, e.g., numbers 5 and 11.

Accent

8. For a word having a prefix, usually the first or second syllable after the prefix is accented, e.g., numbers 5 and 11.
9. For a two-syllable word without a prefix, usually the first syllable gets the accent, e.g., all those except numbers 5 and 11.

Phonic Analysis

10. The phonic analysis techniques used on one-syllable words generally apply to an accented syllable in a multi-syllabic word, except for a root which has lost its final *e.* All the accented syllables in numbers 1–12 are illustrations of this principle.

Group-Assessment Chart for Recording Deficiencies in Word-Recognition Skills

Instructions: Each problem listed below may be considered as one remedial or review lesson (or set of lessons, depending on how many follow-up lessons are required). Check the deficiencies each child has, according to the results of the Informal Word-Recognition Inventory. Then decide which children should be grouped together temporarily for a remedial or review lesson. For example, if three children missed the *b,* two missed the *c,* two missed the *b* and *c,* and one missed the *b, c,* and *d,* you can treat these eight children as an instructional group and provide them with one or more lessons on *b, c,* and *d* combined.

Names of Students

Problems

Part I

b c d															
f g h															
j k l															
m n p															
r s t															
v w z															
x y															
ch ck															
nd ng nk															
ph sh th wh															
bl br cl															
cr dr dw															
fl fr gl															
gr pl pr qu															
sc scr sk squ															
sl sm sn															
sp spl spr															
st str sw															
thr tr tw															

Part II

short a															
long a															
short e															
long e															
short o															

continued

Names of Students

Problems											
Part II (Continued)											
long o											
short i											
long i											
short u											
long u (mule)(rude)											
VC pattern											
VCE pattern											
effect of r											
VV pattern											
aw ou											
oi o͝o o͞o											
Part III											
Basic Sight Words: Irregular only.											
Part IV											
Context: semantic											
Context: grammatical											
Part V											
it's don't you've											
won't she'll he'd											
they're who's they'd											
Part VI											
Roots: Simple Suffixes											
Roots: Root Changes											
Roots: Prefixes											
Generalization 1											

continued

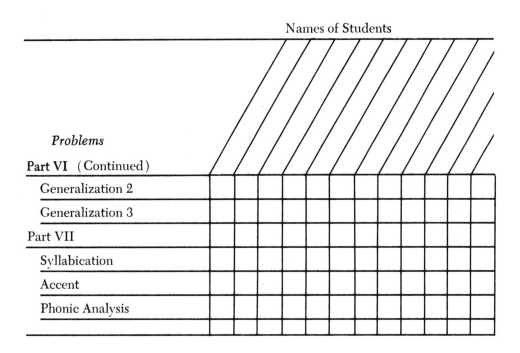

Names of Students

Problems

Part VI (Continued)

Generalization 2										
Generalization 3										
Part VII										
Syllabication										
Accent										
Phonic Analysis										

Appendix I

A Starter List of Good Books for Children

by Eric A. Kimmel and Frank B. May

Picture Books:
Stone Soup, Marcia Brown
Mike Mulligan and His Steam Shovel, Virginia Lee Burton
The Snowy Day, Ezra Jack Keats
Make Way for Ducklings, Robert McCloskey
Where the Wild Things Are, Maurice Sendak
Millions of Cats, Wanda Gag
Horton Hatches the Egg, Dr. Seuss
Thirteen, Remy Charlip and Jerry Joyner (wordless)
John Henry, An American Legend, Ezra Jack Keats

Folk Tales and Myths:
Grimm's Fairy Tales, Jakob and Wilhelm Grimm
East of the Sun and West of the Moon, Peter Christian Asbjornsen and
    Jorgen E. Moe
English Fairy Tales, Joseph Jacobs
Tall Tale America, Adrien Stoutenberg

Tales for the Third Ear, Verna Aardema
Zlateh the Goat, Isaac Bashevis Singer
The Book of Greek Myths, Edgar and Ingri Parin D'Aulaire
Norse Gods and Giants, Edgar and Ingri Parin D'Aulaire
And It Is Still That Way, Byrd Baylor
The Sound of Flutes, Richard Erdoes

Realism:
Durango Street, Frank Bonham
The House of Sixty Fathers, Meindert DeJong
Dragonwings, Laurence Yep
The Noonday Friends, Mary Stolz
Are You There, God? It's Me, Margaret, Judy Blume
The Pigman, Paul Zindel
Bridge to Terabithia, Katharine Paterson
It's Like This, Cat, Emily Neville
The Big Wave, Pearl Buck

Outdoor Adventure:
Swiss Family Robinson, Johann Wyss
Island of the Blue Dolphins, Scott O'Dell
Julie of the Wolves, Jean C. George
My Side of the Mountain, Jean C. George
Call It Courage, Armstrong Sperry

Biography:
Amos Fortune, Free Man, Elizabeth Yates
Daniel Boone, James Daugherty
Carry On, Mr. Bowditch, Jean Lee Latham
The Endless Steppe, Esther Hautzig
America's Paul Revere, Esther Forbes
Will You Sign Here, John Hancock?, Jean Fritz
Freedom Train, The Story of Harriet Tubman, Dorothy Sterling

Historical Fiction:
The Witch of Blackbird Pond, Elizabeth Speare
The Courage of Sarah Noble, Alice Dalgliesh
Men of Iron, Howard Pyle
Johnny Tremain, Esther Forbes
The Little House In The Big Woods, Laura Ingalls Wilder
Treasure Island, Robert Louis Stevenson
Little Women, Louisa May Alcott
Warrior Scarlet, Rosemary Sutcliff
The King's Fifth, Scott O'Dell
Walk the World's Rim, Betty Baker

Fantasy:
The Enormous Egg, Oliver Butterworth
Rabbit Hill, Robert Lawson

Mary Poppins, P. L. Travers
The Borrowers, Mary Norton
The Wind In The Willows, Kenneth Grahame
Alice in Wonderland, Lewis Carroll
Pinocchio, Carlo Collodi
The Wizard of Oz, L. Frank Baum
Mrs. Frisby and the Rats of NIMH, Robert C. O'Brien
The Hobbit, J. R. R. Tolkien
The Lion, The Witch and the Wardrobe, C. S. Lewis
Lizard Music, D. Manus Pinkwater
House of Stairs, William Sleator
Charlie and the Chocolate Factory, Roald Dahl
Tuck Everlasting, Natalie Babbit

Science Fiction:
A Wrinkle in Time, Madeleine L'Engle
The Wonderful Flight to the Mushroom Planet, Eleanor Cameron
A Wizard of Earthsea, Ursula K. Le Guin
The White Mountains, John Christopher
Dragonsong, Anne McCaffrey
Tunnel in the Sky, Robert Heinlein
Dandelion Wine, Ray Bradbury

Humor:
How to Eat Fried Worms, Thomas Rockwell
Henry Huggins, Beverly Cleary
"B" Is For Betsy, Carolyn Haywood
Mrs. Piggle-Wiggle, Betty MacDonald
The Great Brain, John D. Fitzgerald
Henry Reed, Inc., Keith Robertson
Homer Price, Robert McClaskey

Poetry:
In a Spring Garden, Richard Lewis
Beastly Boys and Ghastly Girls, William Cole
Nightmares, Jack Prelutsky
Tirra Lirra, Laura Richards
Songs of Childhood, Eugene Field
It Doesn't Always Have to Rhyme, Eve Merriam
The First Book of Poetry, Isabel J. Peterson
The Monster Den, John Ciardi
The Peaceable Kingdom, Elizabeth Coatsworth
Peacock Pie, Walter De la Mare
Like Nothing at All, Aileen Fisher
Wind Song, Carl Sandburg
Ashanti to Zulu: African Traditions, Margaret Musgrove
A Child's Garden of Verses, Robert Louis Stevenson
The World of Christopher Robin, A. A. Milne

Information:
Pagoo, H. C. Holling
Frontier Living, Edwin Tunis
The Birth of Sunset's Kittens, Carla Stevenson
Dinosaurs, Herbert Zim
The Art of Ancient Greece, Shirley Glubok
How Far Is Far? Alvin Tresselt
A Tree Is a Plant, Clyde Robert Bulla
The Story of Ants, Dorothy Shuttlesworth
101 Science Experiments, Illa Podendorf
The Game of Baseball, Sam and Beryl Epstein
The Courtship of Animals, Millicent E. Selsam
Knights, Castles and Feudal Life, Walter Buehr

Animal:
The Incredible Journey, Sheila Burnford
Bambi, Felix Salten
Along Came a Dog, Meindert DeJong
Gentle Ben, Walt Morey
The Yearling, Marjorie Rawlings
Misty of Chincoteague, Marguerite Henry
Old Yeller, Frederick B. Gipson
Black Beauty, Anna Sewell
Where the Red Fern Grows,
Big Red, Jim Kjelgaard
King of the Wind, Marguerite Henry

Mystery:
The Egypt Game, Zilpha Keatley Snyder
The House With the Clock in Its Walls, John Bellairs
Encyclopedia Brown, Donald Sobol
Secret of the Emerald Star, Phyllis Whitney
The Alley, Eleanor Estes
The Witch's Daughter, Nina Bawden
The Mystery of the Hidden Hand, Phyllis Whitney
The Mysterious Christmas Shell, Eleanor Cameron
The Case of the Cat's Meow, Crosby Bonsall

Sports:
All American, John R. Tunis
The Trouble with Francis, Beman Lord
Rookie First Baseman, Cary Paul Jackson
First Serve, Mary Towne
Matt Gargan's Boy, Alfred Slote

Plays:
100 Plays for Children, edited by A. S. Burack
Short Plays for Children, Helen Louise Miller

Thirty Plays for Classroom Reading, Donald D. Durrell and B. Alice
    Crossley
Children's Plays from Favorite Stories, Sylvia E. Kamerman
Dramatized Folk Tales of the World, Sylvia E. Kamerman

Appendix J

Newbery and Caldecott Award Books

Newbery Award Books and Year of Award
Story of Mankind (van Loon)—Liveright '22
Voyages of Dr. Dolittle (Lofting)—Lippincott '23
Dark Frigate (Hawes)—Little '24
Tales from Silver Lands (Finger)—Doubleday '25
Shen of the Sea (Christmas)—Dutton '26
Smoky the Cowhorse (James)—Scribner's '27
Gay Neck (Mukerji)—Dutton '28
Trumpeter of Krakow (Kelly)—Macmillan '29
Hitty, Her First 100 Years (Field)—Macmillan '30
Cat Who Went to Heaven (Coatsworth)—Macmillan '31
Waterless Mountain (Armer)—McKay '32
Young Fu of the Upper Yangtze (Lewis)—Holt '33
Invincible Louisa: Anniversary Edition (Meigs)—Little '34
Dobry (Shannon)—Viking '35
Caddie Woodlawn (Brink)—Macmillan '36
Roller Skates (Sawyer)—Viking '37
White Stag (Seredy)—Viking '38
Thimble Summer (Enright)—Holt '39
Daniel Boone (Daugherty)—Viking '40
Call It Courage (Sperry)—Macmillan '41
Matchlock Gun (Edmonds)—Dodd '42
Adam of the Road (Gray)—Viking '43
Johnny Tremain (Forbes)—Houghton '44
Rabbitt Hill (Lawson)—Viking '45
Strawberry Girl (Lenski)—Lippincott '46
Miss Hickory (Bailey)—Viking '47
Twenty-One Balloons (du Bois)—Viking '48
King of the Wind (Henry)—Rand McNally '49
Door in the Wall (de Angeli)—Doubleday '50
Amos Fortune, Free Man (Yates)—Dutton '51
Ginger Pye (Estes)—Harcourt '52
Secret of the Andes (Clark)—Viking '53
And Now Miguel (Krumgold)—Crowell '54
Wheel on the School (de Jong)—Harper '55
Carry On, Mr. Bowditch (Latham)—Houghton '56

Miracles on Maple Hill (Sorensen)—Harcourt '57
Rifles for Waitie (Keith)—Crowell '58
Witch of Blackbird Pond (Speare)—Houghton '59
Onion John (Krumgold)—Crowell '60
Island of the Blue Dolphins (O'Dell)—Houghton '61
Bronze Bow (Speare)—Houghton '62
Wrinkle in Time (L'Engle)—Farrar '63
It's Like This, Cat (Neville)—Harper '64
Shadow of a Bull (Wojciechowska)—Atheneum '65
I, Juan de Pareja (de Trevino)—Farrar '66
Up a Road Slowly (Hunt)—Follett '67
From the Mixed-up Files of Mrs. Basil E. Franweiler (Konigsburg)—
    Atheneum '68
High King (Alexander)—Holt '69
Sounder (Armstrong)—Harper '70
Summer of the Swans (Byars)—Viking '71
Mrs. Frisby and the Rats of NIMH (O'Brien)—Atheneum '72
Julie of the Wolves (George)—Harper '73
Slave Dancer (Paula Fox)—Bradbury '74
M. C. Higgins, The Great (Hamilton)—Macmillan '75
Grey King (Cooper)—Atheneum '76
Roll of Thunder, Hear My Cry (Taylor)—Dial '77
Bridge to Terabithia (Paterson)—Crowell '78
The Westing Game (Raskin)—Dutton '79
A Gathering of Days: A New England Girl's Journal, 1830–1832 (Blos)—
    Scribner '80
Jacob Have I Loved (Paterson)—Crowell '81

Caldecott Award Books and Year of Award
Animals of the Bible (Lathrop)—Lippincott '38
Mei Li (Handforth)—Doubleday '39
Abraham Lincoln (d'Aulaire)—Doubleday '40
They Were Strong and Good (Lawson)—Viking '41
Make Way for Ducklings (McCloskey)—Viking '42
Little House (Burton)—Houghton '43
Many Moons (Thurber & Slobodkin)—Harcourt '44
Prayer for a Child (Field & Jones)—Macmillan '45
Rooster Crows (Petersham)—Macmillan '46
Little Island (MacDonald & Weisgard)—Doubleday '47
White Snow, Bright Snow (Tresselt & Duvoisin)—Lothrop '48
Big Snow (Hader)—Macmillan '49
Song of the Swallows (Politi)—Scribner '50
Egg Tree (Milhous)—Scribner '51
Finders Keepers (Nicolas)—Harcourt '52
Biggest Bear (Ward)—Houghton '53
Madeline's Rescue (Bremelmans)—Viking '54
Cinderella (Brown)—Scribner '55
Frog Went A-Courtin' (Langstaff & Rojankovsky)—Harcourt '56
A Tree is Nice (Udry & Simont)—Harper '57

Time of Wonder (McCloskey)—Viking '58
Chanticleer and the Fox (Cooney)—Crowell '59
Nine Days to Christmas (Ets & Labastida)—Viking '60
Baboushka and the Three Kings (Robbins)—Parnassus '61
Once a Mouse (Brown)—Scribner '62
Snowy Day (Keats)—Viking '63
Where the Wild Things Are (Sendak)—Harper '64
May I Bring a Friend (de Regniers)—Atheneum '65
Always Room for One More (Leadhas & Hogrogian)—Holt '66
Sam Bangs & Moonshine (News)—Holt '67
Drummer Hoff (Emberley)—Prentice '68
Fool of the World and the Flying Ship (Ransome)—Farrar '69
Sylvester and the Magic Pebble (Steig)—Simon '70
Story, a Story (Haley)—Atheneum '71
One Fine Day (Hogrogian)—Macmillan '72
Funny Little Woman (Mosel)—Dutton '73
Duffy and the Devil (Zemach)—Farrar '74
Arrow to the Sun (McDermott)—Viking '75
Why Mosquitoes Buzz in Peoples Ears (Aardema)—Dial '76
Ashanti to Zulu: African Traditions (Musgrove)—Dial '77
Noah's Ark (Spier)—Doubleday '78
The Girl Who Loves Wild Horses (Goble)—Bradbury '79
Ox-Cart Man (Hall and Cooney)—Viking '80
Sables (Lobel)—Harper '81

Index

About the Author

Dr. May is the author of four text-books for preservice and inservice teachers: *Teaching Language as Communication, To Help Children Read, To Help Children Communicate,* and *Reading as Communication.* He has been a Professor of Education at the University of Wisconsin, Washington State University, the University of Puget Sound, the University of North Carolina, and is now a Professor of Education at Portland State University in Portland, Oregon. His teaching experience also includes all of the grades from one through twelve and in a variety of locations from East to West: Pelham, New Hampshire; New York, New York; Greensboro, North Carolina; Dayton, Ohio; Chicago, Illinois; and Pullman, Washington. Dr. May's informal but insightful style has made him a much-sought-after speaker and consultant across the country—particularly in the areas of creativity, communication skills, and learning processes.